Phil Edmonston

LEMON-AID

2011|2012

USED CARS and TRUCKS

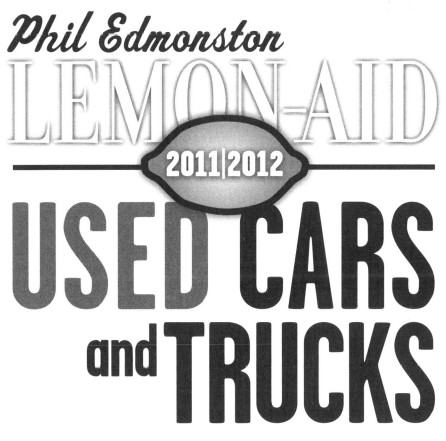

DUNDURN

TORONTO

Editing: Jade Colbert, Andrea Douglas, Greg Ioannou
Design: Jack Steiner
Printer: Webcom

1   2   3   4   5   15   14   13   12   11

We acknowledge the support of the Canada Council for the Arts and the Ontario Arts Council for our publishing program. We also acknowledge the financial support of the Government of Canada through the Canada Book Fund and Livres Canada Books, and the Government of Ontario through the Ontario Book Publishers Tax Credit program, and the Ontario Media Development Corporation.

Care has been taken to trace the ownership of copyright material used in this book. The author and the publisher welcome any information enabling them to rectify any references or credits in subsequent editions.
J. Kirk Howard, President

Printed and bound in Canada.
www.dundurn.com

Dundurn Press
3 Church Street, Suite 500
Toronto, Ontario, Canada
M5E 1M2

Gazelle Book Services Limited
White Cross Mills
High Town, Lancaster, England
LA1 4XS

Dundurn Press
2250 Military Road
Tonawanda, NY
U.S.A. 14150

CONTENTS

KEY DOCUMENTS

Lemon-Aid is a feisty owner's manual that has no equal anywhere. We don't want you stuck with a lemon, or to wind up paying for repairs that are the automaker's fault and are covered by secret "goodwill" warranties. That's why we're the only book that includes many hard-to-find, confidential, and little-known documents that automakers don't want you to see.

The following charts, documents, and service bulletins are included in this index so that you can stand your ground and be treated fairly. Photocopy and circulate whichever document will prove helpful in your dealings with automakers, dealers, service managers, insurance companies, or government agencies. Remember, most of the hundreds of summarized service bulletins outline repairs or replacements that should be done for free.

Introduction
A YEAR OF LIVING DANGEROUSLY

The year was the auto industry's *annus horribilis*: 2009 brought us Toyota's "creeping" carpets and "sticky" throttles, Indian-built Nano minicar spontaneous combustion, lower car prices, and higher-priced fuel.

Safety-related recalls in the States were up 55 percent to 16.4 million vehicles, the highest number since 2005, and Transport Canada reported recalls jumped by 70 percent to their highest level since 2004. Even with the sales improvement late in the year, 2009 industry sales fell 21.2 percent from the year before to 10.4 million, according to *Autodata*. And as the recession took its toll, Chrysler and GM were forced into bankruptcy by Washington bureaucrats in April and June.

Both companies subsequently burned through billions of dollars in government bailouts and quickly emerged from bankruptcy. Much to the surprise of most auto analysts, GM began making huge profits, selling fewer vehicles after it ditched Hummer, Pontiac, Saab, and Saturn, while Chrysler stiffed its creditors and hitched its wagon to Fiat, that renowned maker of quality vehicles—*not*.

Ford, though, was the biggest sales winner after spurning government bailouts (although it did share one $25 million pot earmarked for "clean" technology) and having sold several years earlier many of its assets not essential to its core business.

The Asian and European automakers posted mixed results, with Volkswagen, Mercedes-Benz, and BMW leading the sales surge, as the South Korean automakers posted substantial gains in market share. Meanwhile, Japanese auto brand Suzuki turned in horrendously low sales figures due to its small dealer network and lack of new products. Toyota learned to eat humble pie and poured on the dealer sales incentives and customer rebates following dramatically lower sales in North America due mainly to the company's ongoing safety and quality problems.

Tata Motors, the Indian-based automaker that recently bought Jaguar and Land Rover, has found itself stuck with thousands of super-cheap Nano minicars that nobody wants. Apparently, buyers became wary of the $2,500 little cars after a handful of fires were reported by the local media. Plus, consumers in the developing world opted for small cars that offer more interior space, horsepower, and convenience features found in competing South Korean and Japanese makes.

It's not surprising that car buyers have become suspicious of the safety of new cars and the solvency of automobile manufacturers. As new car prices fell this year, more lower-priced used vehicles entered the North American market as a result of lease returns from the halcyon days of 2007 and cancelled dealers liquidating their stock. Now as we go into 2011, good-quality used cars and trucks are still relatively cheap and plentiful.

For example, recently built large trucks and SUVs now cost almost half their original list price because fuel costs are nudging upward. Still, this is the time to buy because what you save on the purchase cost and a lower depreciation rate will more than compensate for the extra fuel.

Imagine: A 2009 Buick Enclave AWD that sold originally for $44,595 can now be bought for only $27,000. Its sister trucks, the 2009 Chevrolet Traverse and GMC Acadia, sell for only $23,000.

A used GM Enclave (*left*), Traverse (*right*), or Acadia are excellent large SUV buys. Gas-guzzlers for sure, but cheap and reliable.

Even an all-equipped 2008 Yukon Denali (a *Lemon-Aid* Above Average buy) that sold for $66,295 can now be bought for only $29,000. At the other end of the choices available, a fuel-frugal 2008 Honda Civic LX that listed new for $21,000 can now be picked up for $12,500. Incidentally, post-2006 models incorporated many new safety and quality improvements.

But there are also a lot of unsafe and unreliable used vehicles for sale to the unwary. "Orphan" cars, Toyotas, and Ford Windstars are the worst of a bad lot.

Toyota's Travails

Toyota's reputation for manufacturing safe and reliable vehicles took a huge hit at the beginning of 2010 when the automaker's president, Akio Toyoda, apologized to U.S. Congress, claiming he did not know his cars would suddenly accelerate or lose their brakes. Congress did not believe him and slapped the company with a $16.4 million fine for delaying the recall of these vehicles. Akio dried his tears and paid the fine.

"Oh! What a feeling!"...Whoosh..."Help!"

In the meantime, *Lemon-Aid* learned that Toyota knew all along that some sudden, unintended acceleration incidents were caused by faulty computer modules, and the company took steps to replace, free of charge, the defective parts.

During government hearings held in Washington and Ottawa in February and March 2010, Toyota promised that, henceforth, the automaker would treat consumer safety complaints with greater seriousness and attention.

Unfortunately, just the opposite has occurred in Canada. Even after Toyota promised to clean up its act, *Lemon-Aid* has received complaints relating to the inadvertent deployment of airbags and hood latch failures.

Toyota inadvertent airbag deployments

Imagine you are cruising down the highway with your family and suddenly your Toyota's front and side airbags explode. If you manage to avoid running off the road, you will quickly find that the car is undriveable and may set you back almost $6,500 to fix.

One owner of a 2005 Toyota 4Runner asked Toyota to stand behind its product and replace the airbags. Toyota refused. Forget the tears; forget the promises; and don't count on Mr. Toyoda's help. In Canada, Toyota CEO Stephen Beatty reigns supreme. His office essentially told the driver to fuddle duddle, to use Pierre Trudeau's expression.

Lemon-Aid has printed the Plaintiff's Statement of Claim in Part Two (pages 69–70) as a guide for others who have experienced safety failures on any make of vehicle. Toyota's response is also included as an example of that company's hypocrisy in rejecting legitimate Canadian claims on serious factory-related safety defects.

Ford Windstar Axle Failures

The ubiquitous Ford Windstar minivan returns this year with a recall campaign that really isn't one.

Keep in mind that the Windstar (1995–2003) was one of the worst minivans Ford ever built, rivalling the Taurus/Sable and front-drive Lincoln Continental, which, not surprisingly, were built on the same platform with similar components.

Well, Ford has known for years that the Windstar's axles can suddenly collapse due to excessive corrosion. So in November 2010 the automaker fessed up to the defect and asked owners to bring their Windstars in for a free axle replacement. Oops, one problem: Ford won't have any replacement axles before spring 2011 (see Ford Windstar review in Part Three).

More Recalls Coming

Auto recalls in Canada spiked 70 percent to 1,858,904 vehicles in 2009, the highest level since the industry hit a record 3.6 million in 2004. Early signs point to even more safety-related recalls in 2010, mainly because of recent reports of faulty throttle controls, delayed hybrid braking, and sudden brake loss and steering failures.

Transport Canada generally plays second fiddle to Washington when it comes to auto safety investigations and recalls. Fewer recall campaigns carried out in Washington means less recall action in Ottawa.

For the past two years, the U.S. Department of Transportation through its National Highway Traffic and Safety Administration (*www.safercar.gov*) has been playing catch-up by recalling vehicles given a pass under the Bush administration. That's why so many cars have been recalled in both countries during the past year. Among these recalls, airbag and brake failures as well as sudden, unintended acceleration are predominant. Now, steering loss has joined the pantheon of major safety failures affecting recently minted new cars and trucks.

Many post-1995 steering assemblies are electric and don't require a hydraulic pump and engine power to function. This saves drivers 0.1 percent on their fuel consumption. However, owners report the new steering feature feels "loose," gives little steering feedback, fails without warning, and is costly to repair.

It is obvious that companies like BMW, GM, and Mazda know this problem exists, but they are hesitant to admit to these deficiencies because of their legal liability.

Mazda is in deep trouble for having prior knowledge of its steering failures and not acting quickly to correct the problem. The automaker knew several years ago that the steering was defective on Mazda3 and Mazda5 models, but the company waited over a year to notify dealers through a "Product Improvement Program" bulletin that they could repair the vehicles under warranty.

Steering recalls and investigations

The practice of using common parts and platforms among many models increases the extent of a recall when something goes wrong. Plus, the increased reliance upon computer technology and cheaper, more fuel-efficient components in autos is making them vulnerable to more recalls such as these:

- BMW MINI Cooper (2004–05)
- BMW Z4 (2003–05)
- GM Cobalt (2005–10)
- GM G5 (2007–10)
- Mazda3 (2007–09)
- Mazda5 (2007–08)
- Toyota Corolla (2009–10)

Replacing proven designs with rushed-to-production, lighter-weight but relatively untested components is asking for trouble.

Lethal luxury

Recalls and internal service bulletins tell us luxury cars aren't necessarily safer than small, entry-level models. For example: Last September, Italian automaker Ferrari recalled its 458 Italia sports cars after four of them caught fire; and General Motors is recalling about 1.5 million vehicles worldwide for a problem with a heated windshield wiper fluid system that could lead to a fire. The recall affects 2006–09 model year pickups, SUVs, and cars sold under the Buick, Cadillac, Chevrolet, GMC, Hummer, and Saturn brands. GM conducted a similar recall in 2008 but has had new reports of fires in vehicles that were supposedly fixed. In other words, GM is recalling its recall. GM plans to disable the washer fluid heating module and will pay owners/lessees $100 for losing the feature. GM says it is aware of five fires, but no injuries or crashes. V8- and V12-powered BMW 5 Series, 6 Series, 7 Series built between 2002 and 2008, and Rolls-Royce Phantom models built between 2003 and 2010 have just been recalled for braking problems. And do we really have to mention the exploding Rolls-Royce engines that grounded Qantas Airbus 380 planes?

Risky Orphans

Used-car buyers should steer clear of vehicles that have been "orphaned" after being sold to foreign interests.

Volvo, for example, was bought from Ford earlier this year for $1.5 billion (U.S.) by Geely, a Chinese truck manufacturer with no experience in North America and limited experience in automobile manufacturing and marketing. The 13-year-old company is barely known abroad, and will face the formidable task of integrating the two corporate cultures. It also has to make a profit with what has been a perennial money-loser for Ford, which originally paid $6.45 billion for Volvo in 1999. Having lost its quality edge after being purchased by Ford a decade ago, the quality of Volvo models' content, parts, and servicing support will be further diluted, spelling trouble for buyers of used Volvos, who will get little sympathy from dealers.

The primary problem with buying many orphaned brands and models is the high cost of servicing. Parts become rarer and rarer, driving up the cost. It becomes difficult to find mechanics who can spot the likely causes of some common failures because fewer mechanics work on those vehicles all the time and have current service bulletins to guide them. The automaker will drop warranty extensions along with the models. These factors result in plummeting resale value for a car that nobody wants.

Volvo: Is it Swedish, American, or Chinese? Stay away until things get sorted out.

Purchasing orphaned vehicles is risky not only with Volvo models. In the past few years Jaguar and Rover have been sold to Indian manufacturer Tata Motors, and Saab has been acquired by a luxury automaker in the Netherlands. Don't expect these brands to have much of a future. Auto shoppers should be careful to avoid buying a car that can be neither serviced nor sold.

Bargain Orphans

Some cars that are no longer manufactured can be classified as "good" orphans if they were made in large numbers with generic, non-complicated drivetrains and simple fuel delivery and computer systems. Some Saturn and most Pontiac and Oldsmobile SUVs fit into this category. With these vehicles, you get a bargain price for the car itself, easy-to-find, competent repairs, and good parts availability. Some bargain Asian orphans include the Acura Integra, Honda Prelude, Hyundai Tiburon, and Toyota Echo or Solara.

What's New in *Lemon-Aid* This Year?

This year's *Lemon-Aid Used Cars and Trucks*

- Rates more vehicles and adds a roof crashworthiness rating
- Augments its jurisprudence section with Nova Scotia's new "Lemon Law"
- Lists more unreported judgments
- Provides more online resources not commonly known to buyers
- Takes a fresh look at so-called "green" vehicles that are more hype than help

I have written more than 150 editions of *Lemon-Aid*. Yes, I still get angry when I look at the lies, hypocrisy, and deceit rampant in Canada's auto industry.

That's why I am still around.

Phil Edmonston

April 2011

Part One
DEALS AND STEALS

"Friendly" Arrogance

Chrysler was poorly run during its alignment with Daimler AG, and larded up with debt, hollowed out by years of mismanagement, Chrysler under [private equity firm] Cerberus never had a chance .... GM's board of directors was utterly docile in the face of mounting evidence of a looming disaster; and former GM chairman and chief executive Rick Wagoner set a tone of "friendly arrogance" that permeated the company.

STEVE RATTNER
FORMER HEAD OF THE PRESIDENTIAL TASK FORCE ON THE AUTO INDUSTRY
ASSOCIATED PRESS
OCTOBER 21, 2009

Why Buy Used?

Buying a used vehicle is easier than buying new, and you can end up with reliable wheels for less than half what the car originally cost. Plus, there is less of a showroom shakedown—confusing figures, payment plans, and costly "extras"—awaiting you. You get a car that has already been scratched, dented, and corroded, but this saves you from that sickening feeling when new-car imperfections first appear.

About 30 percent of the car fleet in Canada—about 6 million of the 20 million cars on the road—are 10 years old or older. The transformation from new to used occurs as soon as the sales contract is signed, creating a huge pool of less-expensive used vehicles for buyers to choose from and making it much easier to get a discount through smart haggling.

Both private sellers and dealers find used-car sales profitable. In fact, most private owners discover they can get about 20 percent more for their trade-in than what most dealers would offer. Dealers also make more money selling used vehicles

The 2008 Ford Escape 4×4 SUV (*left*) and the 2008 Hyundai Tucson (*right*) are small SUVs recommended by *Lemon-Aid*. Both vehicles sold new for about $28,000. The Escape, though, took a bigger depreciation hit and is now worth only about $13,000, or $2,000 less than the Hyundai. Why? Because buyers are willing to pay a premium for what they consider better-made, Asian vehicles.

than they make selling new cars and trucks, and they aren't burdened by such things as the manufacturer's suggested retail price, freight charges, options loading, high floor plan interest rates, reduced commissions, and warranty charge-backs. The savings generated by these simpler transactions often go straight into the dealer's and buyer's pockets.

This was the main attraction for hundreds of Chrysler and GM dealers who wanted to stay in the car business after their new-car franchises were cancelled last year. Many have opened used-car lots that specialize in the same models the dumped dealers once sold and serviced as new vehicles.

Car dealers get their vehicles from fleets, lessees, wholesalers, trade-ins, and private sales. Some of the less reputable dealers will buy from auctions vehicles that other dealers unloaded because they weren't good enough to sell to their own customers.

Chrysler, GM, and Ford dealers generally have an abundance of "young" used vehicles (many just coming off lease) for sale, while dealers selling import brands are chronically short of product because owners keep these vehicles three to four years longer. The majority of private sales are comprised of vehicles six years or older, while independent used-car dealers get most of their profit from selling anything that can be driven away.

The Honda Civic is Canada's favourite small car. In the States, it's the Toyota Corolla that rules the small-car roost. Downsized SUVs—such as the Subaru Forester, the Honda CR-V, and the Toyota RAV4—make up almost half of our small-car market but account for only one-quarter of the sales south of the border. As far as minivans go, we believe that less is more and, therefore, favour small imports over Detroit's unreliable front-drives and rear-drive gas hogs. The exceptions are trucks and sports cars (yes, the 2011 Mustang beats the pants off the Chevy Camaro).

VEHICLES THAT WILL LAST 15 YEARS OR MORE

Ford Crown Victoria, Escape, Grand Marquis,
  Mustang, and Ranger
GM Chevy Van, Express, Savana, and Vandura
Honda Accord, Civic, CR-V, Odyssey, and Ridgeline
Jeep Wrangler and YJ

Mazda 323 and 626, B-Series trucks,
  Miata, and Protegé
Nissan Frontier and Sentra
Toyota Camry, Corolla, Echo, Solara,
  and Tercel

Despite higher fuel costs that average $1.09 a litre as of November 2010, Canadians are still in love with their cars. Back in the '70s, the average car racked up 160,000 km before it was dropped off at the junkyard. In the '90s, the average car reached 240,000 km before it was recycled. Nowadays, new models are expected to see 300,000 km before they're discarded.

JAPANESE CAR SALES IN CANADA 2009–2010

Rank	Car	Status	October 2010	% Change
#1	Honda Civic	↔	4,203	+6.8
#2	Toyota Corolla	↔	2,801	−25.9
#3	Mazda3	↔	2,654	−26.6
#4	Honda Fit	↑	1,557	+249.1
#5	Toyota Matrix	↓	1,555	−18.1
#6	Honda Accord	↓	1,162	+22.8
#7	Nissan Altima	↓	1,095	+9.8
#8	Toyota Venza	↔	902	−40.3
#9	Nissan Sentra	↓	792	−1.1
#10	Subaru Impreza	↑	742	−3.8

Source: *Automakers* and The Automotive News Data Center

Clearly the models with the softest prices are Toyota's Corolla, Matrix, and Venza, the Mazda3; Subaru's Impreza; Nissan's Sentra; and Suzuki's SX4, which didn't even make it on the sales chart. Look for sweeter new-car sales incentives in the early spring of 2011 to flatten used-car values. Prices for Hyundai and Kia will be harder to bargain down.

A Good Time to Buy

There are lots of reasons why 2011 is a good year to buy a used car or truck—as long as you stay away from some of the rotten products. Fortunately, there's not as much late-'70s and early-'80s junk out there as there once was, and 2006 and later models are safer and come loaded with extra convenience and performance features, like standard electronic stability control, increased roof crashworthiness, and safer front and side full-torso airbags. Additionally, there are a lot of cheap vehicles to choose from as sellers compete with lower new-car prices, and a growing off-lease inventory.

But dealers aren't giving anything away. For example, they are selling fuel-efficient small cars for more than last year as gas prices creep higher. This has forced smart shoppers to buy slightly older, downsized vehicles, or shop the South Koreans, to keep costs manageable.

But lower fuel consumption and cheaper prices aren't the only factors to consider. Vehicle quality and dependability are equally important. Sure, you can prance around telling your friends how you "stole" that five-year-old Chrysler Caravan, GM Venture/Montana, or Ford Windstar/Freestar—until you have to spend $3,500 for engine or transmission work (or both, in GM's case). Granted, some of the junk is fairly well known, and vehicles are safer now; however, many Detroit models are loaded with nonessential convenience and performance features that fail around the fifth year of ownership. Chief among these are navigation systems, adaptive cruise control, tire pressure sensors, ABS, automatic sliding side doors, and sunroofs.

HARD TO MANUALLY OPEN/CLOSE SIDE SLIDING DOORS	
BULLETIN NO.: 23-007-10	DATE: JUNE 9, 2010

OVERVIEW: This bulletin provides diagnostic steps to determine if the sliding door motor is adding resistance to the mechanical operation of the sliding door.
MODELS: 2001–07 Town & Country/Caravan/Voyager

Chrysler's sliding door fix will require an hour's labour, plus $200 for the door motor. No "goodwill," just a goodbye.

POWER SLIDING DOOR FUNCTION INOPERATIVE	
BULLETIN NO.: T-SB-0085-09	DATE: MARCH 13, 2009

APPLICABILITY: Customers with 2004 through 2007 Sienna vehicles may experience a condition where the power function of the sliding door is inoperative. A new service part has been developed so that the replacement of the entire motor/cable assembly is not required.

Toyota has also had frequent sliding door failures. Its sliding door fix takes over four hours and is covered only under the original warranty for 3 years/60,000 km. A secret "goodwill" warranty applies to those customers who rant and rave the most after their warranty has expired.

Luxury Lemons

But let's not pick just on Ford, GM, and Chrysler. European automakers make their share of lemons as well. For example, J.D. Power and Associates has consistently ranked Mercedes' quality as worse than average. If, however, you have been a steady reader of *Lemon-Aid* since 1991, you've been wary of Mercedes' poor quality for almost two decades and probably saved money buying a Lincoln Town Car or Toyota Avalon instead. BMW owners have proven to be some of the most satisfied with their cars' overall dependability when compared with most other European makes, including Audi, Jaguar, Porsche, Saab, Volkswagen, and Volvo.

Lincoln's front-drive Continental (a failure-prone Taurus in disguise) and Mercedes' unreliable luxury cars and SUVs are proof positive that there's absolutely no correlation between safe, dependable transportation and the amount of money a vehicle costs. In fact, almost the opposite conclusion could be reached with most front-drive Lincoln and Cadillac luxury cars. Rear-drive Lincolns and Cadillacs, however, have always performed well after many years of use.

Chrysler "luxury" means beautiful styling and lousy quality control. Its luxury rear-drives, like the 300 and Magnum, that once sold at a 10 percent premium are now piling up on dealers' lots due to their reputation as gas-guzzlers with serious automatic transmission, fuel, and suspension system problems, as well as body deficiencies. It's hard to believe, but a used 2009 Chrysler 300 Touring that originally sold for $32,095 is now worth barely $16,000. Depreciation also takes a pretty big bite out of Asian luxury car values: a 2008 Lexus IS 250 that once cost $32,000 now sells for $19,000.

Four Decades of Hits and Misses

Hits

Acura—CL Series and Integra

BMW—135i, 3 Series, and 5 Series

Chrysler—Colt, 2000 and later Neons, Stealth, and Tradesman vans (invest in an extended warranty for the automatic transmission)

Ford—Crown Victoria, Econoline vans, Escape, 1991 and later Escorts, Freestyle/ Taurus X, Grand Marquis, Mustang V6, and Ranger

GM—Enclave, Escalade, Express, Firebird, Rainier, Savana, Tahoe, Terrain, Traverse, Vandura, and Yukon

Honda—Accord, Civic, CR-V, Element, Fit, Odyssey, and Pilot

For the best Mustang fuel economy, you must get a new 2011 V6-equipped version. It dumps the lethargic, archaic (four-decades-old), 9.8 L/100 km 210 hp 4.0L V6 in favour of a sizzling 305 hp 3.7L V6 that increases fuel economy to 7.6 L/100 km. GM's Camaro doesn't have a prayer.

Hyundai—Accent, Elantra, Santa Fe, Tiburon, Tucson, and Veracruz

Kia—Rondo

Lexus—All models

Lincoln—Mark series and Town Car

Mazda—323, 626, Mazda3, Mazda5, Mazda6, Miata, Protegé, and Tribute

Nissan—Sentra and Versa

Saturn—Outlook

Suzuki—Aerio, Esteem, and Swift

Toyota—Avalon, Camry, Corolla, Cressida, Echo, Highlander, Matrix, Sienna, Sequoia, and Tercel

VW—Beetle Convertible and Jetta TDI

Misses

Audi—A3, A4, A6, A8, and Q7

BMW—7 Series, Mini Cooper, and X5

Chrysler—300, Avenger, Caravan, Charger, Dakota, Durango, Grand Caravan, Intrepid, LHS, Magnum, Neon, New Yorker, Pacifica, PT Cruiser, Sebring, Sprinter, and Town & Country

Daewoo—All models

Ford—Aerostar, Contour, Explorer, F-150, 2003 and later Focus, Mystique, Sable, Taurus, Tempo, Topaz, and Windstar/Freestar

GM—Avalanche, Aveo, Canyon, Catera, Cimarron, Cobalt, Colorado, CTS, Envoy, Fiero, G6, Grand Prix, HHR, Impala, the Lumina/ Montana/Relay/Silhouette/Terraza/ Trans Sport/Venture/Uplander group of minivans, Malibu, SRX, STS, and TrailBlazer.

Hyundai—Excel, Pony, pre-2006 4-cylinder Sonatas, and Stellar

Infiniti—G20

The GM Lumina, Montana, Relay, Silhouette, Terraza, Trans Sport, Venture, and Uplander are likely the worst minivans ever built. The Truth About Cars (*www.thetruthaboutcars.com*) said this in August 2006, almost three years before GM's bankruptcy: "In short, the Uplander's performance doesn't even deserve the noun…. If bankruptcy is the only way to stop GM from inflicting crap vehicles like the Uplander on unsuspecting rental car drivers and (God forbid) buyers, then I can't help but wish the world's largest automaker a speedy Chapter 11."

Jaguar—All models

Jeep—Cherokee, Grand Cherokee, Commander, Compass, and Patriot

Kia—Rio, Sedona, Sephia, Sorento, Spectra, and 2006 and earlier Sportages

Lada—All models

Land Rover—All models

Lincoln—Continental front-drive

Mercedes-Benz—190, C-Class, CLK, GL-Class (V8), M series, R-Class, S-Class, and SLK

Merkur—All models

Nissan—240Z, 250Z, 260Z, pre-2005 Altimas, Armada, B210, Quest, and Titan

Porsche—All models

Saab—All models

Saturn—L-Series, ION, Relay, S-Series, and VUE

Suzuki—Forenza, Samurai, Verona, and X-90

Toyota—Previa and RAV4

VW—EuroVan, Passat, Rabbit, and Touareg

Note in the list above how many so-called premium luxury brands have fallen out of favour and have been orphaned by shoppers and then abandoned by the automakers themselves. Their hapless owners are left with practically worthless, unreliable cars that can't be serviced properly.

Also, keep in mind that some Japanese makes from Honda, Lexus, Mazda, Nissan, and Toyota have had a resurgence of engine and transmission problems, in addition to an apparent overall decline in reliability and safety.

For example, Nissan engineers have worked overtime during the past six years to correct Altima, Maxima, Quest, and Titan glitches, and Toyota's Tacoma and Tundra pickups have had such serious corrosion, sudden acceleration, drivetrain, and suspension problems that the automaker has continually recalled the vehicles and even bought back at 150 percent of their resale value those trucks too rust-cankered to repair.

Evidently, as they capture more of the market share, most Japanese automakers are coasting on their earlier reputations and cutting back on quality, thereby committing the same mistake Detroit did 40 years ago when it switched to front-drives and let quality be damned. That said, the Asian automakers are still ahead of American manufacturers in terms of quality control.

Top 10 Safety and Reliability Problems

In spite of the hand wringing over the Chrysler and GM bankruptcies last year and the probability that Ford's Volvo division and General Motors' Hummer, Pontiac, Saab, and Saturn will soon shut their doors, I have little sympathy for these automakers. They were warned repeatedly over the past four decades, by *Lemon-Aid* and by independent journalists, that the dangerous junk they were selling and their cheapskate warranty handouts would lead to their downfall.

Over the past decade, many quality issues have afflicted major auto manufacturers, but these are the top 10:

1. Minivan sliding door failures
2. Chrysler's biodegradable automatic transmissions
3. Ford's cruise-control fires
4. Ford leaking tire valve stems
5. Ford Explorer rollovers
6. Ford and GM diesel engine failures
7. General Motors airbag defects
8. Toyota sudden acceleration
9. Toyota "lurch and lag"
10. Toyota truck corrosion

I've spent 41 years battling automakers and dealers who lie through their teeth as they try to convince customers, financial analysts, and journalists that their vehicles are well made and that the "few" defects reported (like those shown above) are caused mainly by the proverbial nut behind the wheel, poor maintenance, or abusive driving. That's why the auto industry gets little support from consumers—a lie is one thing Canadian consumers won't buy.

Chrysler Automatic Transmissions

Since the early '90s, practically all models in Chrysler's front-drive lineup have had disposable automatic transmissions. What adds insult to injury, though, is that Chrysler regularly stiffs its customers with transmission repair bills that average about $3,000—about half the average vehicle's worth after five years—when the warranty expires. Since this is far less than what a new car or minivan would cost, most owners pay the bill and then hop onto the transmission merry-go-round, replacing the same transmission at regular intervals. Go ahead, ask any transmission shop.

Ford Cruise-Control Fires

Imagine sleeping soundly while your car, truck, minivan, or SUV catches fire in the garage below your bedroom.

Earlier this month Ford Motor Co. expanded its largest recall ever, adding 4.5 million vehicles equipped with faulty cruise-control switches. It's the eighth recall for this problem over a 10-year period, for a total of 16 million Ford vehicles with defective cruise-control switches manufactured by Texas Instruments.

The switches can short-circuit and cause under-hood fires—even when the vehicle is turned off and parked. The switches have been linked to at least 550 vehicle fires nationwide, as well as damaged homes and property.

The new recall includes the following vehicles:

- 1995–2003 Ford Windstar
- 2000–2003 Ford Excursion diesels
- 1993–1997 and 1999–2003 Ford F-Series Super Duty diesels;
- 1992–2003 Ford Econoline
- 1995–2002 Ford Explorer and Mercury Mountaineer
- 1995–1997 and 2001–2003 Ford Ranger
- 1994 Ford F53 motorhomes

Ford stopped installing the switches in 2003 model year vehicles, and admits that its lawyers have settled out of court "a number" (estimated to be in the hundreds) of fire claims linked to the cruise-control switch. But the company still faces dozens of lawsuits, including several claiming serious injuries and deaths of car owners and family members that allegedly occurred when their Ford vehicles burst into flames.

Ford is voluntarily recalling the vehicles listed in the table that follows due to another factory screw-up that can lead to vehicle fires. Its engineers found that if brake fluid leaks through the speed-control deactivation system into the speed-control system's electrical components, those components may corrode, which can lead to overheating and may start a fire at the switch. This condition may occur at any time, even if the speed control is not in use or if the vehicle is parked. (For more information, call 1-888-222-2751 toll-free or visit *www.ford.com*.)

Parts for the speed-control system recall are now available for passenger cars and trucks only. For affected cars and trucks, Ford will install a fused jumper harness between the speed-control deactivation switch and the speed-control mechanism. This jumper harness acts as a circuit breaker, eliminating the electrical current at the switch if the switch becomes shorted. Because the electric circuit to the speed control deactivation switch is always alive, refraining from using the speed-control system will have no effect on the overheating switch. However, Ford *does* suggest

---

SPEED-CONTROL SYSTEM RECALL

TRUCKS CARS

1997–2002 Expedition 1992–98 Town Car

1998–2002 Navigator 1992–98 Crown Victoria

2002–03 Blackwood 1992–98 Grand Marquis

1993–96 Bronco 1993–98 Mark VIII

2000–03 Excursion 1993–95 Taurus SHO automatic

1992–2003 Econoline E-150, E-250, E-350 1994 Capri

1996–2003 Econoline E-450

2002–03 Econoline E-550

1998–2002 Ranger

1998–2001 Explorer/Mountaineer

2001–02 Explorer Sport, Sport Trac

2003–04 F-150 Lightning

1993–2003 F-Series

1995–2002 F-53 Motorhome

Note: Diesel-engine-equipped vehicles are excluded.

---

that owners *not* park an affected vehicle in a garage until the entire repair has been completed.

Sleep tight!

Ford Explorer Rollovers

Ford Explorer rollovers weren't an aberration; they were a microcosm of the denial of responsibility and the high-powered lobbying that goes on throughout the auto industry when auto manufacturers are found to be both irresponsible and dishonest. When tires started shredding in South America and the Middle East, and injuries and deaths from Ford Explorer rollovers started to mount, Ford used a secret warranty program to pay off Explorer owners because it knew both the Explorer and its tires were at fault. When the media discovered the cover-up, Ford lied to both customers and officials, saying either that the company wasn't aware of the tire failures or that it was all Firestone's fault. Both excuses were shot down in subsequent probes carried out in Saudi Arabia and Venezuela.

The Venezuelan federal Institute for the Defense and Education of the Consumer and the User recommended in September 2000 that both Firestone and Ford face criminal charges for their roles in creating and using defective tires that had led to at least 47 deaths in that country since 1998.

The Venezuela recommendation didn't go very far; however, shortly thereafter, the U.S. Supreme Court did uphold a $55 million punitive-damage class action lawsuit against Ford (see Part Two). *Lemon-Aid* advises readers against buying

Firestone or Bridgestone tires due to driver complaints of poor highway performance and premature failures related to the poor quality of these tires.

Leaking Tire Stems from China

Here's one example, among many, of why *Lemon-Aid* is so distrustful of auto parts imported from China.

Just when you thought Ford had learned its lesson from the hundreds of millions of dollars it paid out for faulty Firestone tires causing Ford Explorer rollovers over a decade ago, the automaker repeats its error. This time, it's cracked, leaking tire valve stems imported from China. Made by Topseal, a subsidiary of the Shanghai Baolong Automotive Corporation, these stems were used on many of Ford's 2007 model vehicles—including the Ford Explorer. NHTSA has recorded dozens of complaints from car owners, like the following from the owner of a 2007 Ford Explorer with factory tires:

> Approximately May or early June 2008 my vehicle Low Tire Pressure light came on. I discovered a cracked valve stem causing [a] leak. Dealer repaired and attempted to file [a] road hazard claim.... Approximately Aug. 08, 2008 [the] Low Pressure indicator again came on. Discovered another cracked stem leaking air on a different tire. Vehicle mileage was approximately 34,700 [55,840 km]. Repaired at dealer on Aug. 09, 2008 for a fee.... On Sept. 30, 2008 I read [a] news report about Dill valve stem issue (NHTSA action number: PE08036). Inspected tires–and discovered [the] same splitting of valve stems as depicted in news article and Dill Air Controls web site on the other two remaining original equipment tires. Dealer replaced both valve stems...for a fee. Removed valve stems with no additional damage and returned to me.... Spare tire visually inspected and found no visible defects on stem. Spare is mounted under vehicle with valve facing up against underbody protecting stem from elements. Ford statement to news media indicates that Ford's position is that their original equipment is not subject to [the] same issue.... I find that all 4 original equipment valve stems exhibited [the] same cracking defect as [the] Dill recall. Stems replaced on Oct. 01, 2008 show "07 tr414 030" and "08 tr414 018" and both have a triangular logo. As all 4 stems were replaced, the only original valve cap I have came from the spare tire and displays "Topseal," the numbers "317" and "630" and what appears to be the same triangular logo as is on the valve stems.

Although Ford lies through its corporate teeth and says leaking tire stems is not a safety issue, Explorer rollover hearings almost a decade ago proved that any variation in tire pressure could easily cause an SUV rollover.

Faced with this danger, owners of Fords and other vehicles manufactured from late 2005 through 2008 should get their tire stems inspected and replaced if they were made by Topseal. Also, if you have bought a replacement tire or valve stem, you should check up on its country of origin.

The cost of the replacement should be borne jointly by the selling dealer and Ford of Canada after they are notified by registered letter that a refusal of the claim will mean a quick trip to small claims court. Lawsuits have already been filed against several tire retailers and Dill Air Controls Products LLC, the North Carolina—based distributor of Topseal valves to retail tire stores and other distributors. These lawsuits should be airtight winners (pun intended), inasmuch as Dill admitted liability on its website at *www.dillaircontrols.com/tovalvesteminstallers.html*:

> We are diligently investigating concerns raised regarding how certain snap-in valve stems produced overseas in the second half of 2006 withstand exposure to high ozone levels. If you replace one valve stem for being cracked, we recommend replacing all four valve stems on the vehicle.

Airbag Failures

Airbags often fail to deploy when they should, deploy too late, or deploy when they shouldn't, leaving accident victims seriously—and sometimes fatally—injured. And, consumer advocates say, studies show automakers and the federal government could care less.

An investigation conducted by the *Kansas City Star* found that the National Highway Traffic Safety Administration (NHTSA) is doing very little to protect consumers from the threat of airbag failure, and that even when it does take action, the process for issuing airbag recalls is painfully slow.

The *Star's* analysis of NHTSA's accident database between 2001 and 2006 showed at least 1,400 people died in front-impact car accidents after airbags failed to deploy. And this number is on the conservative side, as the newspaper did not count accidents that involved side-impact crashes where the airbag did not work, nor did it count fatal crashes that involved principal impacts to the left or right fender, accidents where victims died after being ejected, or when a crash involved a vehicle rollover. The *Kansas City Star* investigators also did not count airbag failure if a vehicle caught fire or was submerged in water. Had the *Star* included such accidents in its investigation, the death toll would have risen by more than 4,000 fatalities.

The newspaper's investigation also found that the number of accident fatalities that occurred when an airbag did not inflate has risen dramatically over the past several years. Since 2001, the number of deaths in accidents where airbags failed has gone up about 50 percent. And in 2006, there was a 14 percent increase in such fatalities. Still, NHTSA does not see the failure of so many airbags as a problem. According to the *Star*, when told about the 1,400 fatalities, a NHTSA spokesperson told the newspaper, "It's not a surprise to us."

GM Engine Gaskets

Afflicting most of GM's lineup since 1994, intake manifold gasket failures cause engine oil or coolant leaks and can cost from $1,000 to $5,000 to repair if the engine is overheated. Following *Lemon-Aid*'s prodding, GM began paying off owners' claims in 1999 under a 7-year/160,000 km secret warranty extension.

GM's stubborn refusal to accept blame and pay all owners' claims led to one of the largest class actions ever brought against an automaker in Canada. Seeking $1.2 billion in damages, the lawsuit was filed in Toronto on June 20, 2006, by Stevensons LLP on behalf of an estimated 400,000 owners of 1995 through 2004 model year vehicles equipped with 3.1L, 3.4L, 3.8L, or 4.3L engines. (Stevensons LLP: Colin Stevenson, 416-599-7900; and Harvin Pitch, Counsel, 416-865-5310. *Kenneth David Stewart v. General Motors of Canada Limited and General Motors Corporation*; Ontario Superior Court of Justice; Court File No. 06-CV-310082PDI; June 20, 2006; Amended Statement of Claim.) By August 2008, these lawsuits were settled for up to $800 per claimant.

Toyota "Lag and Lurch"

Toyota Motor Corp. says the gas pedal design in more than 4 million Toyota and Lexus vehicles makes them vulnerable to being trapped open by floor mats, thus explaining why the vehicles hesitate and then surge when accelerating from a stop, But anecdotal reports from Toyota owners, interviews with auto safety experts, and a *Los Angeles Times* review of thousands of federal traffic safety incident reports point to another, more plausible culprit: the electronic throttles that replaced mechanical systems eight years ago. A survey of safety incidents recorded by NHTSA confirms this theory:

> Traffic slowed as it approached an entrance ramp. I applied pressure to the brakes to disengage the cruise control and slow vehicle, nothing happened. Did this several times and also tried to turn cruise off from steering column lever. Cruise did not disengage, car did not slow, my 2009 Lexus RX350 ran into the rear end of the rock hauler truck in front of me.

•

> The contact owns a 2008 Toyota Camry. While driving 65 mph [105 km/h], the vehicle hesitated. The vehicle would then surge forward and became difficult to control. The contact stated that there was an occasional three second hesitation before the vehicle would begin to move when the accelerator pedal was depressed. Toyota stated that they were unaware of such failure. The current and failure mileages were 650. The consumer stated the cruise control was unreliable even on a slight slope with downshifting. The vehicle would also hesitate to move from a stop.

•

> As I arrived at my home and drove up into my driveway I experienced an unexplained acceleration on my 2008 Toyota Tundra that made me react to slam on the brakes and cause the truck to slide on an unpaved (dirt) surface in my yard and slide into the trunk of a pine tree and damaging the front bumper to my truck. I heard on the news

that there was a recall for the floor mats on this vehicle to be removed if it did not have clips to hold the mat in place. My truck does have the clips to hold the mat in place and prevents the acceleration pedal from getting lodged with the mat. I do believe the acceleration problem was caused by an unknown defect and not the floor mat.

The *Times* found that reports of sudden acceleration in many Toyota and Lexus vehicles shot up almost immediately after the automaker adopted the so-called drive-by-wire system. Total complaints of sudden acceleration for the Lexus and Camry in the 2002–04 model years averaged 132 a year. That's up from an average of 26 annually for the 1999–2001 models, the *Times* review found.

The average number of sudden acceleration complaints involving the Tacoma jumped more than 20 times, on average, in the three years after Toyota's introduced drive-by-wire in these trucks in 2005. Increases were also found on the hybrid Prius, among other models.

"These incidents are coming in left and right where you can't blame the floor mats," says Sean Kane, president of the consulting company Safety Research and Strategies. "So they are chipping away at a problem that is widespread and complicated without having to unravel a root cause that could be very expensive."

Toyota Frame Corrosion

Toyota has two serious corrosion problems that affect the safety of their pickups. 1995–2000 Tacomas with rust-damaged frames and 2000–2003 Tundras with corroded crossmember supports could cause the spare tire to fall off the truck. The excessive rusting is caused by inadequate anti-corrosion undercoating applied at the factory. According to the April 14, 2008, edition of *Automotive News*, Toyota will repair or buy back the affected pickups. Dealers will first inspect all affected Tacomas and Tundras, free of charge, and apply an extended 15-year frame-rust warranty. Trucks with minor frame pitting will be repaired for free; Tacomas with more serious damage will be bought back at 150 percent of the "excellent" value listed in the U.S.-published *Kelley Blue Book* guide, regardless of the truck's condition. Tundras that have damaged crossmembers will be repaired for free, and those Tundras that cannot be repaired will be "handled on a case-by-case basis." Toyota hasn't said how much it will pay to buy back the Tundras.

Diesel Defects

All three Detroit manufacturers have had serious injector problems with their newest diesel engines. Ford is covering repair costs through a variety of "goodwill" programs, while GM and Chrysler argue that their recent bankruptcy absolves them from any liability.

Nevertheless, J.D. Power's 2004 Vehicle Dependability Study found that Ford and Chevrolet diesel pickups were worse performers than similar gas models, while Dodge and GMC trucks were better overall. Owners of Volkswagen diesels reported up to twice as many engine problems as did owners of VWs that burn gas.

Chrysler

Although Chrysler's Cummins engine has been the most reliable diesel sold by American automakers, it also has had some serious manufacturing flaws, involving lift-pump failures that compromise injector-pump performance. Here's how independent mechanic Chuck Arnold (*chuck@thepowershop.com*) describes the problem:

> Low fuel pressure is very dangerous because it is possible for the engine to run very well right up to the moment of failure. There may be no symptom of a problem at all before you are walking. If you notice extended cranking before startup of your Cummins 24-Valve engine you should get your lift pump checked out fast. Addition of fuel lubricant enhancing additives to every tank of fuel may minimize pump damage and extend pump life. Finally, Cummins and Bosch should re-engineer their injector pump to make it less sensitive to low-fuel-pressure-induced failure. Existing safety systems designed to limit performance or signal engine trouble need to be redesigned to work when fuel pressure is inadequate so that very expensive injector pumps are not destroyed without warning.

Incidentally, Chrysler's "Customer Satisfaction Notification No. 878" authorized the free replacement of lift pumps in some 2000 and 2001 Dodge pickups.

Tell the judge: They did it then, they should do it again.

Ford

F-Series 2003 and 2004 model year trucks equipped with the 6.0L Power Stroke diesel engine were so badly flawed that they couldn't be fixed, forcing Ford to buy back over 500 units. Wary customers are snapping up Ford's earlier 7.3L diesels, which are apparently more reliable, though less powerful (275 hp versus 325 hp). Power Strokes have a history of fuel injectors that leak into the crankcase, and, on the 7.3L diesel, water can leak into the fuel tank, causing the engine to seize. Other glitches affect the turbocharger, the fuel injection control pressure sensor, and the engine control software.

> The 6-liter Power Stroke diesel V8, built by a unit of Navistar for Ford, commands nearly half the U.S. market for diesel pickups. But a raft of problems and repeat trips to dealerships for repairs has left some owners upset, threatening Ford's efforts to rebuild a reputation for quality vehicles.
>
> Soon after the new engines went on sale in November in heavy-duty Ford pickups and the Ford Excursion sport-utility vehicle, owners started reporting problems. Among the costliest is fuel seeping into the engine's oil supply in amounts large enough to ruin the engine. Other complaints included engines that ran roughly or stalled, lack of power at low speeds and harsh shifts.

JUSTIN HYDE
REUTERS, AUGUST 20, 2003

One Ford dealer mechanic has seen it all:

> You name it, we've seen it. Oil "blowing" into the cooling system (fortunately, not the other way around), numerous running problems, tubes blowing off the turbos, and oil leaks. We had one truck with 8 miles [13 km] on it that we had to pull the engine on. It was a truck going to Hertz, so it wasn't a big deal to the customer, Ford owned [it] anyway, but still, it was a new truck coming off the autohauler sounding like it had a 5 hp air compressor running under the hood and a dead skip.
>
> We're pulling heads off of a 6.0 now with 4,000 miles [6,400 km] on it. All these problems I've mentioned are on trucks with less than 20,000 miles [32,000 km]. My diesel tech constantly wishes that since they had worked all the kinks out of the 7.3, Ford would have kept it. So far, we've had six buybacks. The one we're pulling the heads off of now will be the next. Before this, I only had one buyback, in four years.

After years of stonewalling and rejecting *Lemon-Aid*'s criticism and owners' refund claims for faulty 6.0L diesel truck engines, Ford now agrees that its engines were crap and has demanded that the supplier of these engines, International Engine Group, pay the automaker compensation for the defective diesels. Ironic, isn't it? Ford is now doing to International what many angry owners of Power Stroke 6.0L-diesel-equipped trucks threatened to do to Ford. And, as in the Ford Explorer/Firestone tire debacle, neither company will admit guilt, or even apologize to owners, for their shoddy product.

Ford's 2008–09 6.4L diesels are continuing to use faulty fuel injectors that may leak fuel into the engine crankcase, causing the oil level to rise and possibly

---

ENGINE–LACK OF POWER

BULLETIN NO.: 10-2-2   DATE: FEBRUARY 15, 2010

FORD: 2008–10 F-Super Duty
ISSUE: Some 2008–10 6.4L F-Super Duty vehicles may experience a lack of power during acceleration and perhaps the illumination of the check air filter message in instrument cluster message center. The lack of power condition may occur when the air filter element becomes packed with snow, thereby restricting required air flow to the engine. This service bulletin allows for the free installation of a protective grill under the base warranty.
NOTE: THE WINTER GRILL COVER MUST BE REMOVED WHEN TEMPERATURES ARE GREATER THAN 50°F (10°C) (32°F (0°C) WHEN TOWING) OR ENGINE DAMAGE CAN RESULT. THE SNOW DEFLECTOR GASKET CAN REMAIN INSTALLED IN THE VEHICLE YEAR-ROUND.

ENGINE–REDUCED POWER

BULLETIN NO.: 08-06-04-054A   DATE: JANUARY '7, 2010

2007–10 Silverado and Sierra 2500/3500 Series Equipped with Duramax Diesel Engine (RPO LMM)
SUBJECT: Snow or Ice Ingestion into Air Cleaner Element, Malfunction Indicator Lamp (MIL) Illuminated, Engine Power is Reduced Message Displayed, DTC P0101 Set (Perform Repair as Outlined).

damage the engine. Ford set up a "goodwill" warranty extension (Campaign 09B08) to replace these leaking injectors for free, but that program expired in September 2010. Nevertheless, Ford is now paying for replacements under a "goodwill" warranty on a case-by-case basis. What does all this mean? Don't take no for an answer.

Also, both Ford and General Motors have had problems with snow accumulation in the air filter element, restricting air passage to the engine and possibly causing severe engine damage. Both companies are liable for the free repair of any damage called by this poor design. Or did they imagine Canada was a snow-free zone?

General Motors

GM's diesel engine failures primarily affect the 6.5L and 6.6L Duramax engine. The 6.5L powerplants are noted for cracked blocks, broken cranks, cracks in the main webbing, cracked cylinder heads, coolant in the oil, loss of power, hard starting, low oil pressure, and oil contamination. Duramax 6.6L engines have been plagued by persistent oil leaks and excessive oil burning, and by defective turbochargers, fuel-injection pumps, and injectors, causing seized engines, chronic stalling, loss of power, hard starts, and excessive gas consumption. To its credit, GM has a Special Policy program that extends the warranty to 11 years on injection pumps installed in 1994–2002 models. GM also extended the fuel injector's warranty coverage for owners of 2001 and 2002 Duramax 6600—equipped pickup trucks. Another program, Special Policy #04039, was set up in June 2004 to give additional warranty protection for seven years from the date the vehicle was placed into service, or for 330,000 km (200,000 miles)—whichever comes first. Finally, anecdotal reports from diesel owners tell *Lemon-Aid* that engine head gasket repairs or replacements are covered by a "goodwill" policy for up to 7 years/160,000 km.

ENGINE—OIL LEAKS FROM CHARGE AIR COOLER/TURBOCHARGER

BULLETIN NO.: 09-06-93-001A   DATE: FEBRUARY 12, 2010

2007–09 Chevrolet Kodiak; 2007–10 Chevrolet/Sierra and GMC Light and Medium Duty Trucks; 2007–10 Chevrolet Silverado; 2007–09 GMC TopKick.

SUBJECT: Engine Oil Leaks from Charge Air Cooler and Turbocharger Air Inlet Adapter (Replace Clamp and/or Turbo Inlet Duct/Pipe)

CONDITION: Some customers may comment on an engine oil leak from the rear of the engine near the flywheel housing. Upon further investigation, a technician may find oil in the charge air cooler or turbocharger air inlet adapter.

A detailed list of all the many parts covered by GM's emissions warranty is available at *ww2.justanswer.com/uploads/mcvgreg/2008-04-20_165903_2004-Trailblazer-Emission-Control-Warranty.pdf.*

Four Decades of Lies and Litigation

Ralph Nader didn't poison Corvair sales; GM's stonewalling and sleuthing of Nader's private life (is he gay, crazy, corrupt?) sealed the car's fate.

Think of the bad cars of the '60s, and the Ralph Nader—targeted Chevrolet Corvair comes to mind. Yet by the time Nader's bestselling book *Unsafe at Any Speed* came out in 1965, the car's handling had been substantially improved. No, Nader didn't "kill" the Corvair. What torpedoed the Corvair were GM's lies and cover-ups, and their stalking of Nader, who was a scheduled witness at upcoming Senate hearings on auto safety in February 1967.

"The requirement of a just social order," Nader told the senators, "is that responsibility shall lie where the power of decision rests. But the law has never caught up with the development of the large corporate unit. Deliberate acts emanate from the sprawling and indeterminable shelter of the corporate organization. Too often responsibility for an act is not imputable to those whose decision enables it to be set in motion."

Following Nader's testimony, GM President James M. Roche reluctantly admitted, after many denials, that his company—without his knowledge—had hired a private eye to peer into Nader's personal life by questioning over 50 of his friends and colleagues. Roche apologized twice to the Senate Committee and Nader, and gave this assurance: "It will not be our policy in the future to undertake investigation of those who speak or write critically of our products."

GM then agreed to a $425,000 out-of-court settlement of Nader's lawsuit against the company for invasion of privacy. That money was subsequently used to finance many of Nader's non-profit public-interest groups, including the Center for Auto Safety, an organization that effectively forces automakers to correct safety defects and cease fraudulent activities.

Dishonest practices, poor quality control, and a reckless disregard for public safety have always been a part of the automobile industry. When I founded the Automobile Protection Association in Montreal in the fall of 1969, American Motors was giving out free television sets with its new cars, and the TVs lasted longer than the Eagle. (Ford gave free Dell computers to 2005 Focus buyers.) Volkswagen had a monopoly on hazardous and poorly heated Beetles and, later, self-starting Rabbits. Ford was churning out disintegrating cars and trucks, and was denying that it had a secret "J-67" warranty to cover rust repairs. Chrysler's entire product line was rain-challenged—stalling and leaking in wet weather because of misaligned body panels and faulty ballast resistors, distributor caps, and rotors. Later on, the company's automatic transmissions would laughingly be called "biodegradable" by some independent car journalists.

Japanese and European cars imported into Canada during the '70s were unreliable rustbuckets, yet they got a toehold in the North American car market because the Big Three's products were worse—and they still are. Seizing the opportunity, foreign automakers smartened up within a remarkably short period of time. They quickly began building reliable and durable cars and trucks, and offering them fully loaded and reasonably priced.

Meanwhile, American automakers continued pumping out dangerous and unreliable junk throughout the '90s, including GM's Chevy Vega, Firenza, and Fiero, as well as most Saturns, Cavaliers, Sunbirds, and the Lumina/Trans Sport minivan; Chrysler's Omni, Horizon, Dynasty, Imperial, Concorde, Neon, and post-1990 minivans; and Ford's Pinto, Bobcat, Tempo, Topaz, Taurus, Sable, Contour, Mystique (Mistake?), Merkur, Bronco, Explorer, and Windstar. Not surprisingly, sales continued to nosedive.

Then, in the early '90s, Detroit got a second chance to prove itself. The minivan carved out a popular new marketing niche, and American SUVs such as the Ford Explorer were piling up profits. But, as Micheline Maynard makes crystal clear in *The End of Detroit* (Doubleday, 2004), the American auto industry's arrogance disconnected its products from reality, and by focusing mainly on high-profit trucks and SUVs, Detroit abandoned the average car buyer.

American automakers lost the knack for making quality machines three decades ago, when they became more interested in the deal than in the product. Suppliers of high-quality components were often rewarded with increased demands for price cuts and with sudden changes in specifications. Quality dropped and owner loyalty shifted to Asian automakers that used identical suppliers but treated them better.

Today, the Detroit automakers' quality control is still below average when compared with Japanese and South Korean automakers. Where the gap is particularly noticeable is in engine, automatic transmission, airbag, and anti-lock brake reliability, as well as fit and finish. And, according to *Consumer Reports* and J. D. Power and Associates, Chrysler is the worst of a bad lot.

You can reduce your risk of buying a lemon by getting a used vehicle rated as Recommended in this guide—one that has some of its original warranty still in effect. This protects you from some of the costly defects that are bound to show symptoms shortly after your purchase. The warranty allows you to make one final inspection before it expires, and requires both the dealer and the automaker to compensate you for all warrantable defects found at that time, even though they may not be fixed until after the warranty expires.

Why Smart Canadians Buy Used

According to the Royal Bank of Canada, the average Canadian's take home income hasn't kept pace with the rising costs of purchasing and owning a new vehicle. Read on to learn five more reasons why Canadians increasingly prefer to buy used vehicles rather than new ones.

Less Initial Cash Outlay, Slower Vehicle Depreciation, "Secret" Warranty Repair Refunds, and Better and Cheaper Parts Availability

It simply costs too much to own a new car or SUV. New-vehicle prices average around $30,000 and insurance can cost almost $2,000 a year for young drivers. CAA calculated that once you add financing costs, maintenance, taxes, and a host of other expenses, the yearly outlay in 2010 for a small-sized car like a Chevrolet Cobalt driven 18,000 km a year is $6,257, or $7.14 a day; a Dodge Grand Caravan may cost about $8,568 a year, or $23.47 per day; and, surprisingly, a Toyota Prius hybrid, touted for its fuel frugality, hovers in the middle with a yearly outlay of $7,333, or $20.09 a day.

For a comprehensive though depressing comparative analysis of all the costs involved in owning a vehicle over one- to 10-year periods, access Alberta's consumer information website at *www.agric.gov.ab.ca/app24/costcalculators/vehicle/getvechimpls.jsp*.

Remember also that used vehicles aren't sold with $1,600–$2,000 transport fees or $495 "administration" charges, either. And you can legally avoid paying some sales tax when you buy privately. That's right: You'll pay at least 10 percent less than the dealer's price, and you may avoid the federal Goods and Services Tax that applies in some provinces to dealer sales only.

Depreciation savings

If someone were to ask you to invest in stocks or bonds guaranteed to be worth less than half their initial purchase value after three to four years, you'd probably head for the door. But this is exactly the trap you're falling into when you buy a new vehicle that will likely lose up to 60 percent of its value after three years of use.

When you buy used, the situation is altogether different. That same vehicle can be purchased three years later, in good condition and with much of the manufacturer's warranty remaining, for less than half its original cost.

Secret warranty refunds

Almost all automakers use secret "goodwill" warranties to cover factory-related defects long after a vehicle's original warranty has expired. This creates a huge fleet of used vehicles that are eligible for free repairs.

We're not talking about merely a few months' extension on small items. In fact, some free repairs—like those related to Mercedes engine sludge and GM diesel engines—are authorized up to 11 years or more as part of "goodwill" programs. Still, most secret warranty extensions hover around the five- to seven-year mark and seldom cover vehicles exceeding 160,000 km. Yet there are exceptions, like this secret catalytic converter (an emissions component that's part of the exhaust system) warranty that will pay for the converter's replacement up to 10 years, or 120,000 miles (193,000 km), on all Chevrolet Malibu and Pontiac G6 models.

Incidentally, automakers and dealers claim that there are no "secret" warranties, since they are all published in service bulletins. Although this is technically correct, have you ever tried to get a copy of a service bulletin? Or—if you did manage to get a copy—did the dealer or automaker say the benefits are applicable only in the States? Pure weasel speak!

Parts

Used parts can have a surprisingly long lifespan. Generally, a new gasoline-powered car or minivan can be expected to run with few problems for at least 200,000–300,000 km (125,000–200,000 miles) in its lifetime and a diesel-powered vehicle can easily double those figures. Some repairs will crop up at regular intervals along with preventive maintenance, and your yearly running costs should average about $1,000. Buttressing the argument that vehicles get cheaper to operate the longer you keep them, the U.S. Department of Transportation points out that the average vehicle requires one or more major repairs after every five years of use. Once these repairs are done, however, the vehicle can then be run relatively trouble-free for another five years or more, as long as the environment isn't too hostile. In fact, the farther west you go in Canada, the longer owners keep their vehicles—an average of 10 years or more in some provinces.

Time is on your side in other ways, too. Three years after a model's launch, the replacement parts market usually catches up to consumer demand. Dealers stock larger inventories, and parts wholesalers and independent parts manufacturers expand their output.

Used replacement parts are unquestionably easier to come by after this three-year point through bargaining with local garages, carefully searching auto wreckers' yards, or looking on the Internet. And a reconditioned or used part usually costs one-third to half the price of a new part. There's generally no difference in the quality of reconditioned mechanical components, and they're often guaranteed for as long as, or longer than, new ones. In fact, some savvy shoppers use the ratings in Part Three of this guide to see which parts have a short life and then buy those parts from retailers who give lifetime warranties on their brakes, exhaust systems, tires, batteries, and so on.

Buying from discount outlets or independent garages, or ordering through mail-order houses, can save you big bucks (30–35 percent) on the cost of new parts and another 15 percent on labour when compared with dealer charges. Mass merchandisers like Costco are another good source of savings; they cut prices and add free services and lifetime warranties (on brakes, mufflers, and transmissions).

Body parts are a different story. Although car company repair parts cost 60 percent more than certified generic aftermarket parts, buyers would be wise to buy only original equipment manufacturer (OEM) parts supplied by automakers in order to get body panels that fit well, protect better in collisions, and have maximum rust resistance, says *Consumer Reports* magazine. Insurance appraisers often substitute cheaper, lower-quality aftermarket body parts in collision repairs, but *Consumer Reports* found that 71 percent of those policyholders who requested OEM parts got them with little or no hassle. The magazine suggests that consumers complain to their provincial Superintendent of Insurance if OEM parts aren't provided.

With some European models, you can count on a lot of aggravation and expense caused by the unacceptably slow distribution of parts and by the high markup. Because these companies have a quasi-monopoly on replacement parts, there are few independent suppliers you can turn to for help. And junkyards, the last-chance repository for inexpensive car parts, are unlikely to carry foreign parts for vehicles that are more than three years old or are manufactured in small numbers.

Finding parts for Asian and domestic cars and trucks is no problem because of the large number of vehicles produced, the presence of hundreds of independent suppliers, the ease with which relatively simple parts can be interchanged from one model to another, and the large reservoir of used parts stocked by junkyards.

Insurance Costs Less

The price you pay for insurance can vary significantly, not only between insurance companies but also within the same company over time. But one thing does remain constant: The insurance for used vehicles is a lot cheaper than new-car coverage, and through careful comparison shopping, insurance premium payouts can be substantially reduced.

Beware of "captive" brokers

Although the cost of insurance premiums for used cars is often one-third to half the cost of the premiums you would pay for a new vehicle, using the Internet to find the lowest auto insurance quote and accepting a large deductible are critical to keeping premiums low.

Use InsuranceHotline.com

InsuranceHotline.com is the largest online quoting service for car insurance in Ontario and car insurance in Canada. *InsuranceHotline.com* represents 80 percent of the Canadian auto insurance, home insurance, and life insurance market for consumers searching for the lowest rate. At no charge, the agency will run applicants' profiles through its database of 30 insurance companies to find the insurer with the lowest rate.

Surprisingly, some of the vehicles with the poorest reliability, durability, and fuel economy ratings, such as GM's Hummer, have good insurance rates and don't see the same multiplication of premiums in the case of a ticket or accident (in which case, your premiums can almost quadruple). When rates for a 2006 Hummer and a 2006 Honda Civic were calculated, the Civic driver saved only $49 compared to the Hummer premium. But add a police ticket and accident to the equation, and the Civic owner could pay over $2,500 more.

Here are some other *InsuranceHotline.com* findings:

- A family car under $35,000 can cost more to insure than one over $35,000.
- SUVs under $35,000 don't always cost more to insure than a family car or a small luxury model.
- Luxury cars mean luxury premiums, costing on average about $500 more annually to insure than family cars, SUVs, muscle cars, or hybrids.
- Hybrids' fuel savings can be wiped out by higher-cost insurance premiums that rival what you would pay to insure a muscle car.

Auto theft in Canada: The list you don't want to be on

According to the Insurance Bureau of Canada, automobile theft costs Canadians close to $1 billion every year, including $542 million for insurers to fix or replace stolen cars, $250 million in police, health care, and court system costs, and millions more for correctional services.

Thieves generally steal cars for one of four reasons:

1. For sale abroad: Stolen cars are often immediately packed—with their vehicle identification numbers (VINs) still intact—and shipped abroad, where they are sold for many times their original market value.
2. For sale to unsuspecting consumers: Stolen cars may be given a new identity with false vehicle identification plates, and then sold to unsuspecting consumers. They can also be dismantled and sold for parts.
3. To get somewhere: This is commonly, but inappropriately, referred to as "joyriding." Auto theft of any kind is still a crime, and innocent people do get hurt or killed as a result.
4. To commit another crime: Stolen cars used to commit other crimes are often recovered—abandoned and badly damaged—within 48 hours of their theft.

CANADA'S TOP 10 MOST STOLEN VEHICLES OF 2010

1. 2000 Honda Civic SiR two-door
2. 1999 Honda Civic SiR two-door
3. 2002 Cadillac Escalade four-door 4×4
4. 2004 Cadillac Escalade four-door 4×4
5. 2005 Acura RSX Type S two-door
6. 1997 Acura Integra two-door
7. 2000 Audi S4 Quattro four-door AWD
8. 2003 Hummer H2 four-door AWD
9. 2006 Acura RSX Type S two-door
10. 2004 Hummer H2 four-door AWD

Note: While Honda Civics sit in the top two spots, the appearance of high-end models like the Cadillac Escalade and Hummer H2 on the list reflects the increasing involvement of organized crime in auto theft.

"Although many high-end, four-wheel-drive vehicles like the BMW X6, Toyota RAV4, and Lexus RX350 don't appear in the top ten," says Rick Dubin, Vice-President, Investigations at the Insurance Bureau of Canada, "thieves are stealing them in greater numbers than ever before. There is a demand for vehicles like these in Ghana, Nigeria, Dubai, Lebanon, the Middle East, and Eastern Europe. Organized criminals are shipping the vehicles overseas, and as a result, the recovery rate for stolen vehicles in Canada continues to decline, even though there are fewer thefts in total."

Auto theft by the numbers:

- In 2008, auto theft cost Canadian insurers $465 million, which averages out to about $30 per auto insurance policy.
- According to Statistics Canada, 125,271 vehicles were stolen in Canada in 2008, a drop of 15 percent from 2007, which is attributed to better alarm systems.
- In 2009, Insurance Bureau investigators working in partnership with law enforcement stopped 300 stolen vehicles from leaving Canadian ports and repatriated 72 vehicles from abroad, with a total value of approximately $11 million.

CANADA'S 10 LEAST STOLEN VEHICLES OF 2008

1. 2003 Cadillac Deville four-door (tied for first)
2. 2002 Lincoln Continental four-door (tied for first)
3. 2001 Lincoln Town Car four-door (tied for first)
4. 2007 Chevrolet Impala four-door
5. 2001 Toyota Avalon four-door (tied for fifth)
6. 1999 Toyota Tacoma 4×2 (tied for fifth)
7. 2005 Buick Terraza EXT (tied for seventh)
8. 2003 Buick Regal four-door (tied for seventh)
9. 2002 Toyota Highlander four-door 4×2 (tied for seventh)
10. 2000 Ford/Mercury Taurus/Sable Wagon (tied for seventh)

The Insurance Bureau of Canada claims that individuals steal less expensive cars because they are easier to steal and tend not to have alarm systems. More data on which vehicles are stolen the most and least and accident claims stats on a model and year basis are just a click away at *www.ibc.ca*.

Insured collision repairs

The Automobile Repair Regulatory Council says the owner of a motor vehicle damaged in an accident has the right to choose the shop that will do the repairs. Do not waste your time or that of several shops getting several estimates. Select a repair facility you feel comfortable with, then notify your agent or insurance company, or ask the shop to call on your behalf. Your insurance adjuster may require that the damage to the vehicle be inspected. This can be done at an insurance drive-in claim centre or at the shop you have chosen.

Here are some things to inspect yourself, before driving away:

- Check the appearance of the repaired area close up and at a distance.
- Examine the paint for colour match, texture, and overspray.
- Take a test drive to check mechanical repairs.
- Check that the vehicle is clean.

If you are not satisfied, mention your concerns immediately and follow up with a written claim and a time period for the work to be completed.

Notify your insurance company

Before you sign any work orders, notify your insurance company or agent, and tell them where the damaged vehicle can be inspected. Most collision and repair centres guarantee their work to some degree, which may not include the paint job. Ask to see a copy of the shop's guarantee and have any information you do not understand clarified. As for the paint warranty: Try to get at least a one-year guarantee.

Choosing a qualified repair shop

Look for signs that indicate repair technician certification and training. Membership in professional trade associations indicates that the shop is keeping up with the latest repair procedures. Also, affiliation with automobile associations like the AMA, BCAA, or CAA is a plus, because you can use the association to exert pressure when the repair takes too long, or the work isn't done properly. In Part Two you will find jurisprudence where one auto club was found liable for the negligence of one of its member garages (page 112).

Defects Can't Hide

You can easily avoid any nasty surprises by having your chosen used vehicle checked out by an independent mechanic (for $85–$100) before you purchase.

This examination protects you against any of the vehicle's potential hidden defects. It's also a tremendous negotiating tool, since you can use the cost of any needed repairs to bargain down the purchase price.

It's easier to get permission to have the vehicle inspected if you promise to give the seller a copy of the inspection report should you decide not to buy it. If you still can't get permission to have the vehicle inspected elsewhere, walk away from the deal, no matter how tempting the selling price. The seller is obviously trying to put one over on you. Ignore the standard excuses that the vehicle isn't insured, that the registration plates have expired, or that the vehicle has a dead battery.

You Know the Past, Present, and Future

Smart customers can easily run an Internet history check on a vehicle and its owners through CarProof ($50) and then read through *Lemon-Aid* to get answers to the following questions before signing a contract: What did the vehicle first sell for, and what is its present insured value? Who serviced it? Has it had accident repairs? Are parts easily available? How much of the original warranty or repair warranties are left? Does the vehicle have a history of costly performance-related defects? What free repairs are available through "goodwill" warranty extensions? (See "Secret Warranties/Internal Bulletins/Service Tips" in Part Three.)

Justice Is Cheap and Easy

Lawyers win, regardless of whether you win or lose. And you're likely to lose more than you'll ever get back using the traditional court system in a used-car dispute.

But if you're just a bit creative, you'll discover there are many federal and provincial consumer-protection laws that go far beyond whatever protection may be offered by the standard new-vehicle warranty. In fact, Nova Scotia just passed its own Lemon Law. Furthermore, buyers of used vehicles don't usually have to conform to any arbitrary rules or service guidelines to get this protection.

Let's say you do get stuck with a vehicle that's unreliable, has undisclosed accident damage, or doesn't perform as promised. Fortunately, small claims courts have a jurisdiction limit of $10,000–$25,000–more than enough to cover the cost of repairs, or compensate you if the vehicle is taken back. That way, any dispute between buyer and seller can be settled within a few months, without lawyers or excessive court costs. Furthermore, you're not likely to face a battery of lawyers standing in for the automaker and dealer in front of a stern-faced judge. You may not even have to face a judge at all, since many cases are settled through court-imposed mediators at a pretrial meeting that's usually scheduled a month or two after filing.

Choosing Safe "Wheels"

Looking through Part Three can help you make a list of safe and reliable buys you can consider before you even leave the house.

The best indicator of a car's overall safety is the NHTSA's front, side, rollover, and roof strength crashworthiness ratings, applicable to most vehicles made and sold over the past several decades in North America. You will then want to compare NHTSA scores with ratings from the Insurance Institute for Highway Safety, which crashes vehicles differently and rates head restraint effectiveness. Results from these two agencies are posted for each model rated in Part Three.

2008 Smart Fortwo: Front- and side-impact results and rollover findings are worrisome.

However, there are many other national and international testing agencies that you may consult, and they can be found at *www. crashtest.com/netindex.htm*. This site shows the results of early crash tests of cars that were sold in Australia, Europe, and Japan and that are just now coming to the North American market. Take the Mercedes Smart Car as an example: Nowhere in Mercedes' or Chrysler's sales brochures did I see a reference to the Smart's unimpressive "Acceptable" frontal crash test rating for early models, or any mention that during the 2008 Smart Fortwo's side-impact test the driver-side door unlatched and opened. A door opening during a side-impact crash increases the likelihood of occupant ejection and massive injuries or death.

Of course, no one expects to be in a collision, but NHTSA estimates that every vehicle will be in two accidents of varying severity during its lifetime. So why not put the averages on your side?

Reliable, Cheap, and "Green" Buys

Consider these important points when making your choice:

- The more than 20 million cars and light-duty trucks on Canada's roads today are responsible for 12 percent of the nation's greenhouse gas emissions.
- Nationwide, 5,000 deaths per year are attributed to smog pollutants, which alone cost the Ontario economy $10 billion in health care costs and business losses, according to the Ontario Medical Association.
- By purchasing a used vehicle, you are already doing a lot for the environment by not adding to the vehicle population. Nevertheless, in choosing a fuel-efficient, safe small car, you are also protecting your life and your wallet.

Unfortunately, our federal and provincial governments have wasted millions of dollars in giving cash incentives in several misguided attempts to encourage motorists to buy small cars, to promote the use of ethanol, and to scrap cars and trucks that are 10 years or older.

The Canadian House of Commons' Standing Committee on Industry, Science and Technology confirmed "Cash for Clunkers" rebates would not help the environment and would waste money. In its *Study of the Crisis in the Automotive Sector in Canada,* which it released in March 2009, the Committee concluded that the only "green" that would result would be the dollars going from car buyers' wallets into car dealers' pockets:

> The Automotive Industries Association of Canada (AIA) claimed that a scrappage program either as an environmental or safety measure was flawed. Although its members supported the federal government in offering incentives for Canadians to purchase new vehicles, it opposed taking older cars off the road for a number of economic reasons:
>
> - Replacement parts purchased for repair of older cars are often recycled or remanufactured components which keep replacement parts prices competitive and are good for the environment by reducing waste and saving energy costs;
> - A strong inventory of recycled and remanufactured parts keeps repair prices down for consumers and provides options for keeping their cars on the road. Motorists in this economic downturn do not want to take on more debt and added insurance costs with the purchase of a new vehicle;
> - Scrappage incentives would hurt thousands of independent repair shops, auto restorers, customizers and their customers across the country who depend on the used car market. The automotive aftermarket provides thousands of Canadian jobs and generates millions of dollars in local, provincial and federal tax revenues;
> - The program will reduce the number of used vehicles available for low-income individuals and drive up the cost of the remaining vehicles; and
> - The premise that existing trucks and SUVs must be scrapped in order to save energy is short-sighted. The reduced "carbon footprint" argument does not factor-in the energy and natural resources expended in manufacturing the existing car, spent scrapping it and manufacturing a replacement car.

Here are *Lemon-Aid*'s picks of the top environmentally friendly, reliable, and cheap used cars, SUVs, trucks, and vans. Regrettably, no vehicles made by Chrysler or General Motors made this list, due to their poor quality.

Ford Escape/Mazda Tribute—A gas-saver; Escape Hybrid is outstanding but pricey.

Ford Focus—model years 2005–09 are more reliable and fuel-efficient; earlier buys are toxic.

Ford Fusion—Similar to the Lincoln MKZ and Mercury Milan, this family-sized car offers good fuel economy, better-than-average reliability, and a reasonable retail price. The gas/electric hybrid is particularly fuel-efficient.

Honda Civic—A reliable fuel miser; pricey, but dealers will haggle.

Honda Fit—A good-performing minicar; 2009 model year vehicles get power and interior upgrades.

Honda Odyssey—Better engineered and better performing than Toyota's Sienna; some price haggling.

Hyundai Accent—Cheap, with good fuel economy, but not-so-great acceleration.

Hyundai Elantra/Tiburon—Reliable, cheap, roomy; gives fair gas mileage.

Hyundai Sonata—In exchange for good fuel economy, you put up with a busy ride and numb steering.

Hyundai Tucson—A reliable and versatile downsized SUV; horsepower may be overstated.

Mazda5—A mini-minivan that carries six passengers and burns fuel like a compact car.

Nissan Sentra—Reasonably priced, reliable, and provides average fuel economy.

Nissan Versa—A reliable "jumbo shrimp"; roomy for a small car, and hoards fuel; a bit pricey.

Suzuki Aerio and Swift—Cheap, cheap, and cheap; for urban dwellers only.

Toyota Corolla—Reliable, spacious, and comfortable; 1997–2009 models were not as well built.

Toyota Echo—Economical and bland, but more reliable and cheaper than a Yaris.

Toyota Tercel—A cheap fuel-sipper that's not as refined as a Honda Fit or Nissan Versa.

VW TDI—Cheap to run, and simple to service through the 2007 models.

Note: We don't recommend gas-electric engine hybrids (except for the Ford Escape Hybrid SUV), such as the Toyota Prius, Honda Insight, or Civic Hybrid. Their fuel economy can be 20–40 percent worse than the automakers' reports, their long-term reliability is unimpressive, battery replacement costs may be $3,000, and their retail prices are almost double what a Toyota Corolla would cost. A 2009 Prius that originally sold for $27,400 is now worth a paltry $20,000, while a $14,565 2009 Corolla CE will command $11,000. Hmm... And, with the Corolla, you won't ever need to buy a battery pack. Oh, what a feeling!

Fuel Economy Fantasies

Consumer Reports recently discovered what *Lemon-Aid* has known for the past several decades: The mileage promised on car stickers is grossly inflated, sometimes by as much as 40 percent. *CR* admitted that hybrids alone account for fuel consumption discrepancies that average 12 L/100 km (19 mpg) worse than the city-driving rating given by the U.S. Environmental Protection Agency and Transport Canada.

But Chrysler, Ford, GM, Honda, Lexus, and Toyota don't tell the average buyer that their so-called fuel-frugal hybrids and ethanol-friendly or diesel-powered vehicles are simply high-tech, feel-good PR machines that often don't hold their values as well as conventionally powered comparable models. Not only does it cost much more than advertised to run vehicles equipped with special engines and alternate fuels, but poor reliability and higher servicing costs also give these "green" vehicles a decidedly lemony flavour.

Yet most public environmental protection groups and government agencies, seconded by the major automobile clubs, genuflect whenever the hybrid, ethanol, or diesel alternative is proposed.

Once again, we have to be wary of the lies. Toyota, for example, seldom mentions the fact that its hybrid battery packs can cost about $3,000 (U.S.) to replace, or that *Automotive News, Car and Driver,* and Edmunds have also found that diesel and hybrid fuel consumption figures can be 30–40 percent more than advertised.

Why am I so hard on ethanol? After all, in its 2007 budget the federal Conservative government committed $2 billion in incentives for ethanol, made from wheat and corn, and for biodiesel. The Canadian Renewable Fuels Association says ethanol is "good for the environment," a position echoed by the Manitoba and Saskatchewan governments, which emphasize that ethanol "burns cleaner" than gasoline.

Hogwash! Environment Canada's own unpublished research says ethanol "burns no cleaner than gasoline."

Scientists at Environment Canada studied four vehicles of recent makes, testing their emissions in a range of driving conditions and temperatures. "Looking at tailpipe emissions, from a greenhouse gas perspective, there really isn't much difference between ethanol and gasoline," said Greg Rideout, head of Environment Canada's toxic emissions research. The study was broadcast by CBC on March 30, 2007, and can be found at *www.cbc.ca.*

Scientists found no statistical difference between the greenhouse gas emissions of regular unleaded fuel and 10 percent ethanol blended fuel. Although they did note a reduction in carbon monoxide, a pollutant that forms smog, emissions of some other gases, such as hydrocarbons, actually increased under certain conditions.

Other drawbacks of ethanol: It's hard to find (there are only two outlets in all of Canada), it eats fuel line and gas tank components, it performs poorly in cold climates, it gives you 25–30 percent less fuel economy than gasoline, and it adds to world hunger (the crop used to produce one SUV fill-up of ethanol could feed a person for a year).

Smart drivers should continue to ignore automaker gas-saving hype, hunker down, and keep their paid-for, reliable, gas-guzzling used vehicles, because the depreciation savings will more than offset the increased cost of fuel.

Courts Blast Fuel Economy Fibs

Car owners, panicked over soaring fuel prices in early 2008, were being scammed by retailers with bogus gas-saving devices and additives, while salespeople and automakers lied about the fuel economy of the vehicles they sold.

Fortunately, Canadian courts are cracking down on lying dealers who use false gas consumption figures to sell their cars. Ontario's revised *Consumer Protection Act, 2002* (available through the province's searchable law database, *www.e-laws.gov. on.ca*) for example, lets consumers cancel a contract within one year of entering into the agreement if a dealer makes a false, misleading, deceptive, or unconscionable representation. This includes false fuel economy claims.

Dealers cannot make the excuse that they were fooled or that they were simply providing data supplied by the manufacturer. The law clearly states that both parties are jointly liable, and therefore the dealer is *presumed* to know the history, quality, and true performance of what is sold.

According to the precedent-setting decision in *Sidney v. 1011067 Ontario Inc. (c.o.b. Southside Motors)*, fuel economy misrepresentation can lead to a contract's cancellation if the dealer gives a higher-than-actual figure, even if they claim it was an innocent misrepresentation. In *Sidney*, the buyer was awarded $11,424.51 plus prejudgment interest because of a false representation made by the defendant regarding fuel efficiency. The plaintiff claimed that the defendant advised him that the vehicle could run 800–900 km per tank of fuel, when in fact the maximum distance was only 500 km per tank.

This consumer victory is particularly important as fuel savings are misrepresented by everyone from automakers to sellers of ineffective gas-saving gadgets and hawkers of "miracle" additives who make outlandishly false fuel economy claims.

When and Where to Buy

When to Buy

In the fall, dealer stocks of quality trade-ins and off-lease returns are at their highest level, and private sellers are moderately active. Prices are higher, but you'll have greater choice of vehicles. In winter, prices decline substantially, and dealers and private sellers are generally easier to bargain with because buyers are scarce and weather conditions don't allow sellers to present their wares in the best light. In spring and summer, prices go up a bit as private sellers become more active and increased new-car rebates bring in more trade-ins.

Private Sellers

Private sellers are your best source for a cheap and reliable used vehicle because you're on an equal bargaining level with a vendor who isn't trying to profit from your inexperience. A good private sale price would be about 5 percent *more* than the rock-bottom wholesale price, or approximately 20 percent *less* than the retail price advertised by local dealers. You can find estimated wholesale and retail prices in Part Three.

Remember, no seller, be it a dealer or a private party, expects to get his or her asking price. As with price reductions on home listings, a 10–20 percent reduction on the advertised price is common with private sellers. Dealers usually won't cut more than 10 percent off their advertised price.

It is also a good idea to draw up a bill of sale that gives all the pertinent details of your used-car transaction. See the following page for one that you may use as your guide.

Buying with Confidence

No matter whom you're buying a used vehicle from, there are a few rules you should follow to get the best deal.

First, have a good idea of what you want and the price you're willing to pay. If you have a preapproved line of credit, that will keep the number crunching and extra fees to a minimum. Finally, be resolute and polite, but make it clear that you are a serious buyer and won't participate in any "showroom shakedowns."

PLEASE PRINT CLEARLY

Bill of Sale

- **Sections 1 and 2 must be completed** in order to make this Bill of Sale acceptable for vehicle registration. Completion of section 3, on the back of this form, is optional.
- Two copies of this Bill of Sale should be completed. The buyer keeps the original and the seller keeps the copy.
- Alterations or corrections made while completing the vehicle information section should be initialled by the buyer and seller.

SECTION 1

SELLER(S) INFORMATION			
Name(s) *(Last, First, Second)*			Telephone Number ( )
Address Street	City / Town	Province / State	Postal Code / Zip Code
Personal Identification:			

VEHICLE INFORMATION			
Year	Make	Model or Series	Style
Vehicle Identification Number (VIN) / Serial Number	Body Color	Roof Color	Odometer Reading

BUYER(S) INFORMATION			
Name(s) *(Last, First, Second)*			Telephone Number ( )
Address Street	City / Town	Province / State	Postal Code / Zip Code
Personal Identification:			

This vehicle was sold for the sum of:

_____ Dollars $ _____

(Sum written in full)

(Subject to the terms and special conditions which appear in Section 3 on the back of this form)

SECTION 2

Dated at: _____

| City / Town | Province / State | Country |

on _____ .

I certify that all information shown above is true to the best of my knowledge.

_____	_____
Signature of Buyer	Signature of Seller
_____	_____
Signature of Buyer	Signature of Seller
_____	_____
Signature of Witness	Signature of Witness

REG3126 (2008/09)

Here's a successful real-world technique used by Kurt Binnie, a frequent *Lemon-Aid* tipster:

> Imagine the surprise of the used-car salesman when I pulled out my BlackBerry and did a VIN search right in front of him using Carfax. Threw him right off balance. Carfax results for Ontario vehicles give a good indication, but not the complete MTO [Ministry of Transportation, Ontario] history. I bought the UVIP [Used Vehicle Information Package]…before closing the deal. For the car I ended up buying, I didn't even tell the sales staff that I was running the VIN while I was there. I was able to see it wasn't an auction vehicle or a write-off. This technique should work with pretty much any WAP [Wireless Application Protocol] enabled phone.

Kurt's letter goes on to describe how he avoids negotiations with sales staff and managers. He figures out the price he's willing to pay beforehand, using a combination of book values and the prices listed at *www.autotrader.ca*. He then test drives the vehicle, runs the VIN through his BlackBerry, and then makes a point-blank, one-time offer to the dealer. He has also found that used-car staff often have no knowledge about the vehicles on their lots beyond their asking price, and they make no distinction between cars manufactured early or late in the model year. An alert buyer could get a car built in August 2002 for the same price as one from September 2001, since they're both used 2002 cars.

Primary Precautions

Get a printed sales agreement, even if it's just handwritten, that includes a clause stating that there are no outstanding traffic violations or liens against the vehicle. It doesn't make a great deal of difference whether the car will be purchased "as is" or certified under provincial regulation. A vehicle sold as safety certified can still turn into a lemon or be dangerous to drive. The certification process can be sabotaged if a minimal number of components are checked, the mechanic is incompetent, or the instruments are poorly calibrated. "Certified" is not the same as having a warranty to protect you from engine seizure or transmission failure. It means only that the vehicle met the minimum safety standards on the day it was tested.

Make sure the vehicle is lien-free and has not been damaged in a flood or written off after an accident. Flood damage can be hard to see, but it impairs ABS, power steering, and airbag functioning (making deployment 10 times slower).

Canada has become a haven for rebuilt U.S. wrecks. Write-offs are also shipped from provinces where there are stringent disclosure regulations to provinces where there are lax rules or no rules at all.

If you suspect your vehicle is flood-damaged, is a rebuilt wreck from the States, or was once a taxi, there's a useful Canadian search agency called CarProof that can give you within a day a complete history of any vehicle.

CarProof (*www.carproof.com*)

Operating out of London, Ontario, CarProof's services cost $34.95, $49.95, or $64.95, plus taxes, per report. Information requests can be completed overnight—or sometimes within minutes—online. Contact the company through its website, or if you prefer to talk, call 519-675-1415.

In most provinces, you can do a lien and registration search yourself, but it's hardly worth the effort considering the low cost and comprehensive nature of CarProof's services.

If a lien does exist, you should contact the creditor(s) listed to find out whether any debts have been paid. If a debt is outstanding, you should arrange with the vendor to pay the creditor the outstanding balance, or agree that you can put the purchase price in a trust account to pay the lender. If the debt is larger than the purchase price of the car, it's up to you to decide whether you wish to complete the deal. If the seller agrees to clear the title personally, make sure that you receive a written relinquishment of title from the creditor before transferring any money to the seller. Make sure the title doesn't show an "R" for "restored," since this indicates that the vehicle was written off as a total loss and may not have been properly repaired.

Even if all documents are in order, ask the seller to show you the vehicle's original sales contract and a few repair bills in order to ascertain how well it was maintained. The bills will show you if the odometer was turned back and will also indicate which repairs are still guaranteed. If none of these can be found, leave. If the contract shows that the car was financed, verify that the loan was paid. If you're still not sure that the vehicle is free of liens, ask your bank or credit union manager to check for you. If no clear answer is forthcoming, look for something else.

Don't Pay Too Much

Prices for used large and mid-sized cars, trucks, and SUVs are falling as gas prices go higher. But this price drop hasn't been as severe with small cars and trucks, mini-minivans, downsized SUVs, or wagon crossovers. Their prices on the used-car market are relatively stable and are expected to stay that way through the summer.

If you'd like to save even more when buying used, consider these tips:

- Choose a vehicle that's five years old or more and has a good reliability and durability record. Don't buy an extended warranty that may become worthless. The money you save from the extra years' depreciation and lower insurance premiums will make up for some additional maintenance costs.
- Look for discounted off-lease vehicles with low mileage and a good reputation.
- Buy a vehicle that's depreciated more than average simply because of its bland styling, unpopular colour (dark blue, white, and champagne are out; silver is in), lack of high-performance features, or discontinuation.
- Buy a cheaper twin or rebadged model like a fully loaded Camry instead of a Lexus ES, a Toyota Matrix in lieu of a Pontiac Vibe, or a Chevrolet Silverado instead of a GMC Sierra.
- Buy a fully equipped gas hog. Your $30,000 savings on a large SUV or pickup will pay the gas bill many times over, and the vehicle can be easily resold a few years down the road, with only moderate depreciation.

Price Guides

The best way to determine the price range for a particular model is to read the *Lemon-Aid* values found in Part Three. From there, you may wish to get a free second opinion by accessing Vehicle Market Research International's Canadian used-car prices at *www.vmrcanada.com*. It is one of the few free sources that list wholesale and retail values for used cars in Canada. The site even includes a handy calculator that adjusts a vehicle's value according to model, mileage, and a variety of options.

Black Book and *Red Book* price guides, found in most libraries, banks, and credit unions, are essential to anyone buying or selling a used vehicle. Both guides are easily accessible on the Internet. To read the *Canadian Black Book* values, simply copy the following URL into your web browser: *www.canadianblackbook.com/used-cars.html*. This site lists the vehicle's trade-in and future value, as well as the asking price based upon your Canadian postal code. No other identification is required.

Now, if you want to use the *Canadian Red Book Vehicle Valuation Guide*, which seems more attuned to Quebec and Ontario sales, you can order single copies of their used car and light truck wholesale and retail price guide for $19.95 at *www.canadianredbook.com* (an annual subscription costs $105). There are no restrictions as to who may subscribe.

You may also go to *Auto Trader* magazine's website at *www.autotrader.ca* to see at what prices other Canadians are trying to sell your chosen vehicle.

Don't be surprised to find that many national price guides have an Eastern Ontario and Quebec price bias, especially the *Red Book*. They often list unrealistically low prices compared with what you'll see in the eastern and western provinces and in rural areas, where good used cars are often sold for outrageously high prices or are simply passed down through the family for an average of eight to 10 years. Other price guides may list prices that are much higher than those found in your region.

Consequently, use whichever price guide lists the highest value when selling your trade-in or negotiating a write-off value with an insurer. When buying, use the guide with the lowest values as your bargaining tool.

Cross-Border Sales

Shopping in the States for a used car or truck won't save you much money with cheaper, entry-level small cars. However, sports cars, luxury vehicles, SUVs, large trucks, and vans bought in the States can save you tens of thousands of dollars, now that the Canadian dollar is flirting with parity to the American greenback.

Here's what to do:

1. Check with Ottawa to see if the used vehicle you covet can be imported into Canada (call the Registrar of Imported Vehicles at 1-888-848-8240, or visit their website at *www.riv.ca*).
2. Take a trip across the border to scout out what is available from all dealers. Compare your findings with what's offered by Canadian cross-border brokers.
3. Verify if the price is fair once taxes and transport charges are considered.

Hire a broker or deal directly with the dealer. Be wary of private sellers, because your legal rights may be more limited in cross-border transactions.

Rental and Leased Vehicles

Next to buying privately, the second-best choice for getting a good used vehicle is a rental company or leasing agency. Due to our slumping economy, Budget, Hertz, Avis, and National are selling, at cut-rate prices, vehicles that have one to two years of service and approximately 80,000–100,000 km on the odometer. These rental companies will gladly provide a vehicle's complete history and allow an independent inspection by a qualified mechanic of the buyer's choice, as well as arrange for competitive financing.

Rental vehicles are generally well maintained, sell for a few thousand dollars more than privately sold vehicles, and come with strong guarantees, like Budget's 30-day money-back guarantee at some of its retail outlets (including three in B.C.). Rental-car companies also usually settle customer complaints without much hassle so as not to tarnish their images with rental customers.

Rental agencies tend to keep their stock of cars on the outskirts of town near the airport (particularly in Alberta and B.C.) and advertise in the local papers. Sales are held year-round as inventory is replenished. Late summer and early fall are usually the best times to see a wide selection because the new rentals arrive during this time period.

Vehicles that have just come off a three- or five-year lease are much more competitively priced than rentals, generally have less mileage, and are usually as well maintained. You're also likely to get a better price if you buy directly from the

Even rental agencies are in the used-car business.

lessee, rather than going through the dealership or an independent agency. But remember that you won't have the dealer's leverage to extract post-warranty "goodwill" repairs from the automaker.

Repossessed Vehicles

Repossessed vehicles frequently come from bankrupt small businesses or subprime borrowers who failed to make their finance payments. They are usually found at auctions, but finance companies and banks sometimes sell them as well. Canadian courts have held that financial institutions are legally responsible for defects found in what they sell, so don't be at all surprised by the disclosure paperwork that will be shoved under your nose. Also, as with rental car company transactions, the combination of these companies' deep pockets and their abhorrence of bad publicity means you'll likely get your money back if you make a bad buy. The biggest problem with repossessed sport-utilities and pickups is that they may have been damaged by off-roading or neglected by their financially troubled owners. Although you rarely get to test drive or closely examine these vehicles, a local dealer may be able to produce a vehicle maintenance history by running the VIN through their manufacturer's database.

New-Car Dealers

New-car dealerships aren't bad places to pick up good used cars or trucks. Sure, prices are about 20 percent higher than those for vehicles sold privately, but rebates and zero percent financing plans can trim used-car prices dramatically. Plus, dealers are insured against selling stolen vehicles or vehicles with finance or other liens owing. They also usually allow prospective buyers to have the vehicle inspected by an independent garage, offer a much wider choice of models, and have their own repair facilities to do warranty work. Also, if there's a possibility of getting post-warranty "goodwill" compensation from the manufacturer, your dealer can provide additional leverage, particularly if the dealership is a franchisee for the model you have purchased. Finally, if things do go terribly wrong, dealers have deeper pockets than private sellers, so there's a better chance of winning a court judgment.

Provinces are also cracking down on dealers who sell defective used cars. In addition to Nova Scotia's recently enacted "Lemon Law," Alberta now requires a thorough mechanical inspection of every used car sold by dealers. Under the revised regulations, a mechanical assessment will be completed by licensed journeyman technician with a trade certificate as an Automotive Service Technician or Heavy Equipment Technician under the *Apprenticeship and Industry Training Act.*

MECHANICAL FITNESS ASSESSMENT
As required by Vehicle Inspection Regulation (A/R 211/2006)

ALBERTA MOTOR VEHICLE INDUSTRY COUNCIL

Dealer: _____ AMVIC License Number: _____

Address: _____

VEHICLE INFORMATION

Year: _____ Make: _____ Model: _____ Previous Province of Registration: _____

Vehicle Identification Number: _____ Odometer Reading: _____ ☐ (km / mi ☐

☐ Truck ☐ Motorcycle ☐ Bus ☐ Van ☐ Light Truck ☐ Auto ☐ Motorized RV ☐ Other

Please check mark (✓) each item as C = Complies   N = Non-Compliant   N/A=Not Applicable

Powertrain	C	N
Accelerator		
Fuel System		
Exhaust		
Transmission		
Front/Rear/Spindles Axles		
Clutch		
Fluid Levels (power steering, brake)		
CV Joints		

Lamps	C	N
Head Lamp Hi Beam		
Head Lamp Lo Beam		
Head Lamp Location		
Daytime Running Lamps		
Tail Lamps		
Brake Lamps		
Turn Signal Lamps		
Hazard Warning Lamps		
Licence Plate Lamp		

Instruments	C	N
Speedometer/Odometer		
Indicator Lamps		
Horn		
Hi Beam Indicator		

Technician Comments

Brakes	C	N
Parking/Emergency Brake		
Hydraulic System		
Vacuum System		
Drum Brakes		
Disc Brakes		
Shoes/Pads		
Anti-Lock (if OEM equipped)		

Steering	C	N
Steering Lash		
Steering Linkage		
Rack & Pinion		
Power Steering System		
King Pin		
Ball Joints		

Suspension	C	N
Leaf springs		
Struts and Shocks		
Coil spring		
Torsion Bar		
Independent/Multilink Rear		
Computer Controlled		
Diagnostic Trouble Codes		

Frame & Body	C	N
Hood Latch		
Door Latches & Hinges		
Bumpers		
Windshield Wipers & Washer		
Rear Wiper & Washer		
Windshield		
Windows		
Defrost/Heaters		
Mirrors		
Seats		
Seat Belts/Airbags		
Mudguards		
Window Glazing		
Structural Integrity		

Tires & Wheels	C	N
Tread Depth		
Tread Section		
Sidewalls		
Wheels		

Electrical	C	N
Wiring		
Battery		
Switches		
Alternator		

Alberta's Mechanical Fitness Assessment is a good template of the kind of inspection buyers should demand from independent garages anywhere in Canada before they purchase a used vehicle.

mechanical fitness assessment will be valid for 120 days from the time of completion. This is a change from 14 days for the previous certificate. The extended time period recognizes the broader nature of the assessment. More information about the amendments to the vehicle inspection regulation is available on the Alberta Transportation website at *www.transportation.alberta.ca* (under the "Drivers and Vehicles" tab).

"Certified" vehicles

The word "certified" doesn't mean much. Ideally, it tells us the vehicle has undergone some reconditioning that was monitored by the manufacturer. Of course, some dealers don't do anything but slap a "certified" sticker on the car and then inflate the selling price. Sometimes, an auto association will certify a vehicle that has been inspected and has had the designated defects corrected.

Used-car leasing

It isn't a good idea to lease either new or used vehicles. Leasing has been touted as a method of making the high cost of vehicle ownership more affordable, but don't you believe it. Leasing is generally costlier than an outright purchase, and, for most people, the pitfalls far outweigh any advantages. If you must lease, do so for the shortest time possible and make sure the lease is close-ended (meaning that you walk away from the vehicle when the lease period ends). Also, make sure there's a maximum mileage allowance of at least 25,000 km per year and that the charge per excess kilometre is no higher than 8–10 cents.

Used-Car Dealers

Used-car dealers usually sell their vehicles for a bit less than what new-car dealers charge. However, their vehicles may be worth a lot less because they don't get the first pick of top-quality trade-ins. Many independent urban dealerships are marginal operations that can't invest much money in reconditioning their vehicles, which are often collected from auctions and new-car dealers reluctant to sell the vehicles to their own customers. And used-car dealers don't always have repair facilities to honour the warranties they do provide. Often, their credit terms are easier (but more expensive) than those offered by franchised new-car dealers.

That said, used-car dealers operating in small towns are an entirely different breed. These small, often family-run businesses recondition and resell cars and trucks that usually come from within their communities. Routine servicing is usually done in-house, and more complicated repairs are subcontracted out to specialized garages nearby. On one hand, these small outlets survive by word-of-mouth advertising and wouldn't last long if they didn't deal fairly with local townsfolk. On the other hand, their prices will likely be higher than elsewhere due to the better quality of their used vehicles and the cost of reconditioning and repairing what they sell under warranty.

Auctions

First of all, make sure it's a legitimate auction. Many are fronts for used-car lots where sleazy dealers put fake ads in complicit newspapers, pretending to hold auctions that are no more than weekend selling sprees.

Furthermore, you'll need lots of patience, smarts, and luck to pick up anything worthwhile. Government auctions—places where the mythical $50 Jeeps are sold—are fun to attend but highly overrated as places to find bargains. Look at the odds against you: It's impossible to determine the condition of the vehicles put up for bid, prices can go way out of control, and auction employees, professional sellers, their relatives, and their friends usually pick over the good stuff long before you ever see it.

To attend commercial auctions is to swim with the piranhas. They are frequented by "ringers" who bid up the prices, and by professional dealers who pick up cheap, worn-out vehicles unloaded by new-car dealers and independents. There are no guarantees, cash is required, and quality is apt to be as low as the price. Remember, too, that auction purchases are subject to provincial and federal sales taxes, the auction's sales commission (3–5 percent), and, in some cases, an administrative fee of $75–$100.

If you are interested in shopping at an auto auction, remember that certain days are reserved for dealers only, so call ahead. You'll find the vehicles locked in a compound, but you should have ample opportunity to inspect them and, in some cases, take a short drive around the property before the auction begins.

The Internet

The Internet is a risky place to buy a used car. You don't know the seller, and you know even less about the car. It's easy for an individual to sell a car they don't own, and it's even easier to create a virtual dealership, with photos of a huge inventory and a modern showroom, when the operation is likely made up of one guy working out of his basement.

Rating systems are unreliable too. Ratings from "happy customers" may be nothing but ploys—fictitious postings created by the seller to give out five-star ratings and the appearance that the company is honest and reliable.

If you must use the Internet, get the seller's full name and a copy of their driver's licence, plus lots of references. Then go see the vehicle, take a road test, and have a mechanic verify if the car is roadworthy and able to pass a safety inspection.

Although you take an even bigger risk buying out-of-province or in the States, there are a few precautions you can take to protect yourself. First off, compare shipping fees with a Canadian automobile transporter like Hansen's (*www.lhf.com*), and put your money into an escrow account until the vehicle is delivered in satisfactory condition.

If the car is located in the United States, print out the tips found on eBay's website at *http://pages.ebay.ca/ebaymotors/explained/checklist/howtobuyUS.html*. The website takes you through each step in detail and will tell you if the vehicle is admissible in Canada and the likely modification requirements. If the vehicle needs modification, you should check with a mechanic for an estimate. You will also need to get a recall clearance letter from the dealer or automaker in order to pass federal inspection. Additional information can be obtained from the Registrar of Imported Vehicles (1-888-848-8240 or *www.riv.ca*).

Beware of phony eBay solicitations that are sent via doctored emails selling out-of-province vehicles. In the email the "owner" will even promise to deliver the car to you at no extra cost. Rather than paying through the relatively secure PayPal used in most legitimate transactions, you will be instructed to send payment through a Western Union or MoneyGram money transfer.

How prevalent is this scam? About a third of the ads in *Canadian Auto Trader* checked out several years ago by the non-profit Automobile Protection Association turned out to be phony. The most obvious indications these ads were placed by scam artists is that the same email address kept reappearing, or the listed phone number was a dummy.

Most of the fraudulent advertisements were placed outside of Canada, apparently without the knowledge of the online sites that published them. Nevertheless, it's hard not to suspect some complicity because the ads are quite easy to verify by the hosting site. For example, *Wheels.ca* staffers refuse advertisers with an IP address outside of Canada and ad claims and contact information are constantly checked.

Another fraud is committed by phony overseas used-car buyers who take the delivery of the car and pay for it with a worthless cashier's cheque. Again, using PayPal will protect you from this scam.

There is some government help available to catch Internet used-car swindlers. PhoneBusters, the federal-provincial agency set up to deal with telephone and Internet scams (1-888-495-8501) has ties to the RCMP and OPP, and will investigate and arrest these high-tech crooks.

Here are some more tips for selling or purchasing vehicles online:

- Check out the listed phone number and ask for an address and independent reference.
- Insist that the car be inspected by a third party before closing the deal.
- Search the VIN or ad description using Google or *www.carproof.com*. Often the same wording or VIN will appear on different sites.
- Never use a money transfer service.
- Call the online escrow agency and speak with a representative before divulging any personal financial information.
- Be skeptical of eBay "second chance" offers.
- Always use the eBay "contact seller" process.
- Report all shady deals to the local RCMP detachment. Then, file a complaint with your local police service and at the same time voice your concerns with the Internet service provider (ISP) hosting the offensive material. The Canadian Association of Internet Providers (*www.caip.ca*) would also welcome your comments or concerns in regards to Canadian ISPs.

Canadian car sales websites
- *AMVOQ.ca*—Quebec used-car classifieds (in French)
- *AutoHunter.ca*—Alberta used-car classifieds
- *Autonet.ca*—New and used cars and trucks, new-car dealers, new-car prices, and reviews

- *AutoTrader.ca*—Used-car classifieds from all across Canada
- *BuySell.com*—Classifieds from all across Canada
- eBay Motors Canada (*http://cars.eBay.ca*)—The premiere site for used cars located in Canada or anywhere in the world
- North American Automobile Trade Association (*www.naata.org*)—This trade association lists dealers and brokers who will help you find a new or used cross-border bargain
- *RedFlagDeals.com*—A compendium of shopping tips, as well as advice on dealing with the federal and provincial governments
- Used Cars Ontario (*www.usedcarsontario.com*)—Used-car classifieds for major cities in Ontario, with links and articles

U.S. car sales websites
- *AutoTrader.com*—New- and used-car classifieds
- *Cars.com*—Ditto, except there's an "Advanced Search" option
- *CarsDirect.com*—One of the largest car-buying sites
- eBay Motors U.S. (*www.motors.ebay.com*)—Similar to the Canadian site
- *Edmunds.com*—Lots of price quotes and articles
- The Big Lot! (*www.thebiglot.com*)—Another large car-buying site

Financing Choices

You shouldn't spend more than 30 percent of your annual gross income on the purchase of a new or used vehicle. By keeping the initial cost low, there is less risk to you, and you may be able to pay mostly in cash. This can be an effective bargaining tool to use with private sellers, but dealers are less impressed by cash sales because they lose their kickbacks from the finance companies.

Credit Unions

A credit union is the best place to borrow money for a used car at competitive interest rates and with easy repayment terms. In fact, credit unions are jumping into car financing as the major auto-makers pull back. You'll have to join the credit union or have an account with it before the loan is approved. You'll also probably have to come up with a larger down payment.

Banks

Financing a car through a bank can mean either applying for a car loan or a line of credit. A loan will require a lien on your car and fixed monthly payments

INTEREST RATES FOR A $15,000 CAR LOAN

	Months		
	36	48	60
Bank of Nova Scotia	6.84	6.51	6.65
Caisses Desjardins	7.59	7.59	7.59
CIBC	7.25	7.50	7.75
Comtech Credit Union	5.99	5.99	5.99
DUCA Credit Union	5.46	5.56	5.66
National Bank	8.75	9.00	9.30
Ont. Civil Service Credit Union	4.99	4.99	4.99
PACE Savings and Credit Union	6.00	6.00	6.00
TD Canada Trust	7.50	7.50	7.50

Source: *Canoe.ca*; March 28, 2011

until the end of the term. Interest rates on car loans often vary considerably. According to *www.bankrate.com/funnel/auto*, the cost of a car loan taken out for three years in Miami, Florida, goes from a low of 3.2 percent to a high of almost 12.99 percent with a $50–$200 spurious "document fee" added. The average new-car loan interest rate in the States is 5.913 percent (*www.bankrate.com/funnel/auto*).

In Canada, loans vary between 4.99 and 9.5 percent (*http://money.canoe.ca/rates/en/carloans.html*).

You can get a good idea on the different car-loan interest rates through an online comparison of bank rates. For purchases in the States, go to *www.bankrate.com*; Canadian loan interest rates are updated at *http://money.canoe.ca/rates/carloans.html*.

Since you are already online, email the lowest-interest lenders and get a loan commitment first, before you start shopping and the dealer's sales agent starts throwing different figures at you. Simply Google the bank's name and add "car loan interest rates."

Lines of credit, on the other hand, require no lien and offer the ability to pay a minimum each month, or as much as you can afford. The rates are often lower than traditional bank loans and there are no penalties for paying it off early, making it the preferred route for many car buyers.

Banks are always leery of financing used cars, but they generally charge rates that are competitive with what dealers offer.

In your quest for a bank loan, keep in mind that the loan officer will be impressed by a prepared budget and sound references, particularly if you seek out a loan before choosing a vehicle. If you don't have a preapproved loan, it wouldn't hurt to buy from a local dealer, since banks like to encourage businesses in their area.

The Internet offers help for people who need an auto loan and want quick approval but don't want to face a banker. For example, the Royal Bank website has a selected list of dealers who are empowered to process Royal Bank loans at their dealerships (see *www.rbcroyalbank.com/products/personalloans/installment_loan.html*).

Dealers

Cash may be king with some Canadian retailers, but not at your local car dealership. It's a myth that dealers will treat you better if you pay cash. Dealers want you to buy a fully loaded vehicle and finance the whole deal. And, now that auto loans are easier to get than they were in 2008 and 2009, dealers are financing everything in sight—especially used cars.

Still, not that many buyers have that kind of extra green lying around anyway. Fewer than eight percent of all car sales are cash deals, so that leaves financing through the dealer or a bank as the only options for most of us.

Dealer financing isn't the rip-off it once was, but still be watchful for all the expensive little extras the dealer may try to pencil into the contract, because, believe it or not, dealers make far more of a profit on used-car sales than on new car deals. Don't write them off for financing, though—if they want to, dealers can finance your purchase at rates that compete with those of banks and finance companies, because they agree to take back the vehicle if the creditor defaults on the loan. Some dealers mislead their customers into thinking they can get financing at rates far below the prime rate. Actually, the dealer jacks up the base price of the vehicle to compensate for the lower interest charges. As bank and other financing choices dry up in some areas, a credit union or cash may be your only alternatives.

Dealer Scams

Most dealer sales scams are so obvious, they're laughable. But like the "Nigerian lost fortune" email rip-off, enough stupid people get sucked in to make these flim-flam practices profitable.

One of the more common tricks is to not identify the previous owner because the vehicle was used commercially, was problem-prone, or had been written off as a total loss after an accident. It's also not uncommon to discover that the mileage has been turned back, particularly if the vehicle was part of a company's fleet. Your best defence? Demand the name of the vehicle's previous owner and then run a VIN check through CarProof as a prerequisite for purchasing.

It would be impossible to list all the dishonest tricks employed in used vehicle sales. As soon as the public is alerted to one scheme, crooked sellers use other, more elaborate frauds. Nevertheless, under industry-financed provincial compensation funds, buyers can get substantial refunds if defrauded by a dealer.

Here are some of the more common fraudulent practices you're likely to encounter.

Evading Sales Tax by Trimming the Price

Here's where your own greed will do you in. In a tactic used almost exclusively by small, independent dealers and some private sellers, the buyer is told that he or she can pay less sales tax by listing a lower selling price on the contract. But what if the vehicle turns out to be a lemon, or the sales agent has falsified the model year or mileage? The hapless buyer is offered a refund on the fictitious purchase price indicated on the contract. If the buyer wanted to take the dealer to court, it's quite unlikely that he or she would get any more than the contract price. Moreover, both the buyer and dealer could be prosecuted for making a false declaration to avoid paying sales tax.

Phony Private Sales ("Curbsiders")

Individual transactions account for about three times as many used-vehicle sales as dealer sales, and crooked dealers get in on the action by posing as private sellers. Called "curbsiders," these scammers lure unsuspecting buyers through lower prices, cheat the federal government out of tax money, and routinely violate provincial registration and consumer protection regulations. Bob Beattie, executive director of the Used Car Dealers Association of Ontario (*www.ucda.org*), once estimated that about 20 percent of so-called private sellers in Ontario are actually curbsiders. Dealers in large cities like Toronto, Calgary, and Vancouver believe curbsiders sell half of the cars advertised in the local papers. This scam is easy to detect if the seller can't produce the original sales contract or show repair bills made out over a long period of time in his or her own name. You can usually identify a car dealer in the want ads section of the newspaper—just check to see if the same telephone number is repeated in many different ads. Sometimes you can trip up a curbsider by requesting information on the phone, without identifying the specific vehicle. If the seller asks you which car you are considering, you know you're dealing with a curbsider.

Legitimate car dealers claim to deplore the dishonesty of curbsider crooks, yet they are their chief suppliers. Dealership sales managers, auto auction employees, and newspaper classified ad sellers all know the names, addresses, and phone numbers of these thieves but don't act on the information. Newspapers want the ad dollars, auctions want the action, and dealers want someplace they can unload their wrecked, rust-cankered, and odometer-tricked junkers with impunity. Talk about hypocrisy, eh?

Curbsiders are particularly active in Western Canada, importing vehicles from other provinces where they were sold by dealers, wreckers, insurance companies, and junkyards (after having been written off as total losses). They then place private classified ads in B.C. and Alberta papers, sell their stock, and then import more.

Buyers taken in by these scam artists should sue both the seller and the newspaper that carried the original classified ad in small claims court. When just a few cases are won in court and the paper's competitors play up the story, the practice will cease.

"Free-Exchange" Privilege

Dealers get a lot of sales mileage out of this deceptive offer. The dealer offers to exchange any defective vehicle for any other vehicle in stock. What really happens, though, is that the dealer won't have anything else selling for the same price and so will demand a cash bonus for the exchange—or you may get the dubious privilege of exchanging one lemon for another.

"Money-Back" Guarantee

Once again, the purchaser feels safe in buying a used car with this kind of guarantee. After all, what could be more honest than a money-back guarantee? Dealers using this technique often charge exorbitant handling charges, rental fees, or mechanical repair costs to the customer who's bought one of these vehicles and then returned it.

"50/50" Guarantee

This can be a trap. Essentially, the dealer will pay half of the repair costs over a limited period of time. It's a fair offer if an independent garage does the repairs. If not, the dealer can always inflate the repair costs to double their actual worth and then write up a bill for that amount (a scam sometimes used in "goodwill" settlements). The buyer winds up paying the full price of repairs that would probably have been much cheaper at an independent garage. The best kind of used-vehicle warranty is 100 percent with full coverage for a fixed term, even if that term is relatively short.

"As Is" and "No Warranty"

You will see from the jurisprudence in Part Two that these phrases are pure bluff, whether used in a dealer or private sale. Sellers insert these clauses much like parking lot owners or coat checkers at restaurants do when they put up signs warning that they have no responsibility to indemnify your losses. In fact, when you pay for a custodial service or a used vehicle, the commission the seller of that service or product receives requires that you be protected.

Remember, every vehicle carries a provincial legal warranty protecting you from misrepresentation and the premature failure of key mechanical or body components. Nevertheless, sellers often write "as is" or "no warranty" in the contract in the hope of dissuading buyers from pressing legitimate claims.

Generally, when "as is" has been written into the contract or bill of sale, it usually means that you're aware of mechanical defects, you're prepared to accept the responsibility for any damage or injuries caused by the vehicle, and you're agreeing to pay all repair costs. However, the courts have held that the "as is" clause is not a blank cheque to cheat buyers, and must be interpreted in light of the seller's true intent. Was there an attempt to deceive the buyer by including this clause? Did the buyer really know what the "as is" clause could do to his or her future legal rights? It's also been held that the courts may consider oral representations ("parole evidence") as an expressed warranty, even though they were never written into the formal contract. So, if a seller makes claims as to the fine quality of the used vehicle, these claims can be used as evidence. Courts generally ignore "as is" clauses when the vehicle has been intentionally misrepresented, when the dealer is the seller, or when the defects are so serious that the seller is presumed to have known of their existence. Private sellers are usually given more latitude than dealers or their agents.

Odometer Fraud

Who says crime doesn't pay? It most certainly does if you turn back odometers for a living in Canada. Here is what one casual observer reported (*http://conscience-daily.com*) seeing at a Toronto shipper exporting cars to Nigeria:

> I want the public to know that these people from Toronto are buying high mileage unsafe cars most with over 200,000 km and many over 300,000 km and rolling back the mileage to less than 100,000 km, they even remove the check engine and brake lights on dash so your people have no idea what they are driving. I see it happen every day as I work next door to a shipper, I watch them roll back the kilometers to at least 20 cars a day and that only this one shipper in Mississauga on Tompkin and Kamato. Innocent people from Nigeria are being ripped off by their own people from Toronto and they are being endangered because they have no idea what shape their car is really in. I want to inform the Nigerian public that they can check on websites the real mileage of their cars such as Carfax and [CarProof] which gives the cars actual kilometers and if it's been in a accident....

> Do you know how many Toyota Camry Corolla Sienna, Honda Accord CR-V and Odyssey models from years 1998-2005 go from Toronto Mississauga to Nigeria with less than 100,000 km? Hundreds every week. The shippers and exporters both roll back the mileage to maximize their profits.

Readers Digest Canada reports in an exposé written by Hal Karp (*www.readersdigest.ca/mag/2001/04/lemon.html*):

> In Edmonton, a former employee of an auto auction house that serves dealers recalls a saying among fellow employees: "There are two kinds of vehicles at auction: those tampered with and those that are going to be tampered with." Says AMVIC [Alberta Motor Vehicle Industry Council] investigator Del Huget, "There's potentially big money in spinning–$3,000 to $6,000 per vehicle, right into the seller's pocket."

> Why is odometer fraud so rampant in Canada? Because vehicle histories nationwide fail to include easily accessible mileage records. You might record the mileage when registering your car, but that information is rarely entered into computer databases.

Estimates are that each year close to 90,000 vehicles with tampered odometers reach the Canadian marketplace—at a cost to Canadians of more than $3.56 million. This is about double the incidents one would expect based on a 2002 U.S. National Highway Traffic Safety Administration study that pegs odometer fraud at 450,000 vehicles annually. NHTSA estimates that half of the cars with reset odometers are relatively new high-mileage rental cars or fleet vehicles.

Odometer fraud is a pernicious crime that robs thousands of dollars from each victim it touches. See, for example, *United States v. Whitlow*, 979 F.2d 1008, 1012 (5th Cir. 1992) (under sentencing guidelines, the court affirmed the estimate that consumers lost $4,000 per vehicle). The television news magazine *60 Minutes* once characterized it as the largest consumer fraud in America. Victims of this fraud are commonly the least able to afford it, since buyers of used cars include large numbers of low-income people. In addition, consumers generally are unaware of being victimized.

Odometer tampering involves several interrelated activities. Late-model, high-mileage vehicles are purchased at a low price. The vehicles are "reconditioned" or "detailed" to remove many outward appearances of long use. Finally, odometers are reset, typically removing more than 40,000 miles (64,000 km).

Does anyone really believe this 1975 Pontiac Trans Am only has only 11,000 miles on the "clock"?

In addition to the cosmetic "reconditioning" of the car, the odometer tamperer "reconditions" the car's paperwork. Automobile titles include a declaration of mileage statement to be completed when ownership is transferred. To hide the actual mileage that is declared on the title when the car is sold to an odometer tamperer, the tamperer must take steps to conceal this information. These steps vary from simple alteration of mileage figures to creating transfers to fictitious "straw" dealerships to make it unclear who was responsible for the odometer rollback and title alteration. Alternatively, the odometer tamperers frequently destroy original title documents indicating high mileage and obtain duplicate certificates of title from state motor vehicle departments, upon which the false, lower mileage figures are entered.

Odometer fraud is practiced by a variety of people, including:

- Organizations that roll back (or "clock") the odometers on thousands of cars, wholesaling them to dealers who resell them to the public.
- Groups of individuals (commonly called "curbstoners") who buy cars, clock them, and sell them through the classifieds, passing them off as cars of a friend or relative ("I'm selling Aunt Sally's Buick for her").
- Individuals who only clock their own car to defeat a lease provision or cheat on a warranty.

Gangs of odometer scammers ply their trade in Canada because it seems as if no one cares what they do, and they stand to gain thousands of dollars, or 10 cents profit for each mile erased from the odometer on the resale value of a doctored car. Moreover, electronic digital odometers make tampering child's play for anyone with a laptop computer, or anyone who has sufficient skill to simply replace the dashboard's instrument panel.

Think: When was the last time you heard of a Canadian dealership being charged with odometer fraud? Probably a long time ago, if at all. And what is the punishment for those dealers convicted of defrauding buyers? Not jail time or loss of their franchise. More than likely, it'll be just a small fine.

Not so in the States. There, many victims can get compensation from dealers who sold cars with altered odometers, regardless of who was responsible for the alteration. For business and legal reasons, dealers frequently compensate consumers who purchased vehicles with altered odometers. U.S. federal law permits consumers to obtain treble damages or $1,500, whichever is greater, when they are victims of odometer fraud (49 U.S.C. section 32710). The courts have been liberal in protecting consumers in these kinds of lawsuits against dealers.

How to spot a car that's been to a "spin doctor":

- When calling a supposedly private seller, ask to see the car in the ad, without specifying which one.
- Ask the seller for a copy of the contract showing the name of the selling dealer and previous owner.
- Check the history of the car through CarProof.
- Look for uneven paint or body panels that don't line up. Do the doors, hood and trunk open and close easily? Do the bumpers and fenders sit squarely?
- Examine brake and gas pedal wear as well as the driver's door sill. Does their wear match the kilometres? An average tire lasts 80,000 kilometres; any premature wear signals an odometer turnback or chassis misalignment.
- Check to see if the numbers on the odometer are lined up and snug. If they jiggle when you bang your hand on the dash, have an expert check for fraud.
- Have the car inspected by a franchised dealer for that make of vehicle, and ask for a copy of the service records, noting the mileage each time the vehicle was serviced.

Misrepresentation

Used vehicles can be misrepresented in a variety of ways. A used airport commuter minivan may be represented as having been used by a Sunday school class. A mechanically defective sports car that's been rebuilt after several major accidents may have plastic filler in the body panels to muffle the rattles or hide the rust damage, heavy oil in the motor to stifle the clanks, and cheap retread tires to eliminate the thumps. Your best protection against these dirty tricks is to have the vehicle's quality completely verified by an independent mechanic before completing the sale. Of course, you can still cancel the sale if you learn of the misrepresentation only after taking the vehicle home, but your chances of successfully doing so dwindle as time passes.

Private Scams

A lot of space in this guide is dedicated to describing how used-car dealers and scam artists cheat uninformed buyers. Of course, private individuals can be dishonest, too. In either case, protect yourself at the outset by keeping your deposit small and by getting as much information as possible about the vehicle you're considering. Then, after a test drive, you may sign a written agreement to purchase the vehicle and give a deposit of sufficient value to cover the seller's advertising costs, subject to cancellation if the automobile fails its inspection. After you've taken these precautions, watch out for the following private sellers' tricks.

Vehicles That Are Stolen or Have Finance Owing

Many used vehicles are sold privately without free title because the original auto loan was never repaid. You can avoid being cheated by asking for proof of purchase and payment from a private seller. Be especially wary of any individual who offers to sell a used vehicle for an incredibly low price. Check the sales contract to determine who granted the original loan, and call the lender to see if it's been repaid. Place a call to the provincial Ministry of Transportation to ascertain whether the car is registered in the seller's name. Find out if a finance company is named as beneficiary on the auto insurance policy. Finally, contact the original dealer to determine whether there are any outstanding claims.

In Ontario, all private sellers must purchase a Used Vehicle Information Package at one of 300 provincial Driver and Vehicle Licence Issuing Offices, or online at *www.mto.gov.on.ca/english/dandv/vehicle/used.htm*. This package, which costs $20, contains the vehicle's registration history in Ontario; the vehicle's lien information (i.e., if there are any liens registered on the vehicle); the fair market value on which the minimum tax payable will apply; and other information such as consumer tips, vehicle safety standards inspection guidelines, retail sales tax information, and forms for bills of sale.

In other provinces, buyers don't have easy access to this information. Generally, you have to contact the provincial office that registers property and then pay a small fee for a computer printout that may or may not be accurate. You'll be asked for the current owner's name and the car's VIN, which is usually found on the driver's side of the dashboard.

There are two high-tech ways to get the goods on a dishonest seller. First, have a dealer of that particular model run a vehicle history check through the automaker's online network. This will tell you who the previous owners and dealers were, what warranty and recall repairs were carried out, and what other free repair programs may still apply. Second, you can use CarProof (*www.carproof.com*) to carry out a background check.

Wrong Registration

Make sure the seller's vehicle has been properly registered with provincial transport authorities; if it isn't, it may be stolen, or you could be dealing with a curbsider.

Summary: Be a Tough Customer

You can get a reliable used car, truck, or minivan at a reasonable price—it just takes some patience and homework. Prevent potential headaches by becoming thoroughly familiar with your legal rights, as outlined in Part Two, and by buying a vehicle recommended in Part Three. The following is a summary of the steps to take to keep your level of risk to a minimum:

1. Keep your present vehicle for at least 10 years. Don't get panicked over high fuel costs—depreciation is a greater threat to your pocketbook.
2. Sell to a dealer if the reduction in applicable taxes on your next purchase is greater than the potential profit of selling privately.
3. Sell privately if you can get at least 15 percent more than what the dealer offered.
4. Buy from a private party, rental car outlet, or dealer (in that order).
5. Use an auto broker to save time and money, but pay a set fee, not a commission.
6. Buy only a *Lemon-Aid*-recommended three- to five-year-old vehicle with some original warranty left that can be transferred.
7. Carefully inspect front-drive vehicles that have reached their fifth year. Pay particular attention to the engine intake manifold and head gasket, CV joints, steering box, and brakes. Make sure the spare tire and tire jack haven't been removed.
8. Buy a full-sized, rear-drive delivery van and then add the convenience features that you would like (seats, sound system, etc.) instead of opting for a more-expensive, smaller, less-powerful minivan.
9. Buy a vehicle recommended by *Lemon-Aid*, thereby foregoing the need to purchase a $1,500–$2,000 extended warranty; many of these warranty providers may be headed for bankruptcy.
10. Have maintenance repairs done by independent garages that offer lifetime warranties on brakes, exhaust systems, and automatic transmissions.
11. Install used or reconditioned mechanical parts, demand that original parts be used for body repairs, and insist upon choosing your own repairer.
12. Keep all the previous owner's repair bills to facilitate warranty claims and to let mechanics know what's already been replaced or repaired.
13. Upon delivery, adjust mirrors to reduce blind spots and adjust head restraints to prevent your head from snapping back in the event of a collision. On airbag-equipped vehicles, move the seat backward more than half its travel distance and sit at least 30 cm away from the airbag housing.
14. Ensure that the side airbags include head protection.

15. Make sure that both the dealer and automaker have your name in their computers as the new owner of record. Ask for a copy of your vehicle's history, which is stored in the same computer. Buy a $26.95 (U.S.) one-year subscription ($44.95 for five years) Internet download or data disc of all your vehicle's service bulletins from ALLDATA (*www.alldatadiy.com/buy*). This will keep you current as to the latest secret warranties, recalls, and troubleshooting tips for correcting factory screw-ups.

Part Two

FIGHTING BACK!

Chrysler Canada: Profits Before Safety

"In this case, the quantum ought to be sufficiently high as to correct the defendants' behaviour. In particular, Chrysler's corporate policy to place profits ahead of the potential danger to its customers' safety and personal property must be punished. And when such corporate policy includes a refusal to comply with the provisions of the Act and a refusal to provide any relief to the plaintiff, I find an award of $25,000 for exemplary damages to be appropriate. I therefore order Chrysler and Dodge City to pay: Damages in the sum of $41,969.83; Exemplary damages in the sum of $25,000; Party and party costs."

JUSTICE ROTHERY

PREBUSHEWSKI V. DODGE CITY AUTO (1984) LTD. AND CHRYSLER CANADA LTD.

(2001 SKQB 537; QB1215/99JCS)

Think of this part of *Lemon-Aid* as your free legal assistant to help you fight against the lies and consumer abuses found in the auto industry.

Here's 40 years' worth of information on strategy, tactics, negotiation tools, and jurisprudence you may cite to hang tough and get an out-of-court settlement, or to win your case without spending a fortune on lawyers. If you do end up using a lawyer, the following roundup of successful lawsuits from French and English courts in Canada, as well as some important American decisions, will save you lots of research time and money.

Broken Promises

Used cars can turn out to be bad buys for various reasons: They were misrepresented by the seller (covered up damage, odometer turned back, inflated fuel economy, not really driven only on Sundays by a little old lady, etc.), or they are afflicted with factory-induced defects like sudden acceleration or brake failures. In some cases, abusive driving or poor maintenance can make a vehicle unreliable or dangerous to drive. Misrepresentation is relatively easy to prove: you simply have to show the vehicle doesn't conform to the oral or written sales representations made before or during the time of purchase. These representations include sales brochures and newspaper, radio, and television ads. Omission of key information can also fall under misrepresentation.

Private sales can easily be cancelled if the vehicle's mileage has been turned back, if accident damage hasn't been disclosed, or if the seller is really a dealer in disguise. Even descriptive phrases like "well-maintained," "driven by a woman"

In *Prebushewski v. Dodge City Auto (1984) Ltd. and Chrysler Canada Ltd.,* the Supreme Court ordered Chrysler to pay $25,000 in punitive damages for denying a Saskatoon Dodge Ram owner's refund request following a truck fire.

(whatever *that*'s supposed to imply), or "excellent condition" can get the seller into trouble if misrepresentation was intended.

Defects are usually confirmed by an independent garage examination that shows either that the deficiencies are premature, factory-related, or not maintenance-related or that they were hidden at the time of purchase. It doesn't matter if the vehicle was sold new or used. In fact, many of the small claims court victories against automakers relating to defective paint, engines, and transmissions were won by owners who bought their vehicles used and then sued both the seller and the automaker.

Sure, automakers will sometimes plead they are not part of the chain of responsibility because they didn't sell the product to the plaintiff. Fortunately, as you will learn reading this section, Canadian judges do not buy that argument. Particularly if the defect was obviously factory-related and caused an injury or death.

Cases involving these kinds of failures are not that difficult to win in Canada under the doctrine of *res ipsa loquitur*, meaning "the thing speaks for itself," or in negligence cases, the liability is shown by the failure itself. Planes shouldn't fall and cars shouldn't suddenly accelerate or fail to stop. Under *res ipsa loquitur,* you don't have to pinpoint the exact cause of the failure and judges are free to award damages by weighing the "balance of probabilities" as to fault.

This advantage found in Canadian law was laid out succinctly in the July 1, 1998, issue of the *Journal of Small Business Management* in its comparison of product liability laws on both sides of the border (see "Effects of Product Liability Laws on Small Business" at *www.allbusiness.com*):

> Although in theory the Canadian consumer must prove all of the elements of negligence (*Farro v. Nutone Electrical Ltd. 1990*; Ontario Law Reform Commission 1979; Thomas 1989), most Canadian courts allow injured consumers to use a procedural aid known as *res ipsa loquitur* to prove their cases (*Nicholson v. John Deere Ltd. 1986*; *McMorran v. Dom. S tores Ltd. 1977*). Under *res ipsa loquitur*, plaintiffs must only prove that they were injured in a way that would not ordinarily occur without the defendant's negligence. It is then the responsibility of the defendant to prove that he was not negligent. As proving the negative is extremely difficult, this Canadian reversal of the burden of proof usually results in an outcome functionally equivalent to strict product liability (*Phillips v. Ford Motor Co. of Canada Ltd. 1971*; Murray 1988). This concept is reinforced by the principal that a Canadian manufacturer does not have the right to manufacture an inherently dangerous product when a method exists to manufacture that product without risk of harm. To do so subjects the manufacturer to liability even if the safer method is more expensive (*Nicholson v. John Deere Ltd. 1986*).

In *Jarvis v. Ford* (United States Second Circuit Court of Appeal, February 7, 2002), a judgment was rendered in favour of a driver who was injured when her six-day-old Ford Aerostar minivan suddenly accelerated as it was started and put into gear. What makes this decision unique is that the jury had no specific proof of a defect. The Court of Appeal agreed with the jury award, and Justice Sotomayor (now a Supreme Court Justice) gave these reasons for the court's verdict:

> A product may be found to be defective without proof of the specific malfunction: It may be inferred that the harm sustained by the plaintiff was caused by a product defect existing at the time of sale or distribution, without proof of a specific defect, when the incident that harmed the plaintiff: (a) was of a kind that ordinarily occurs as a result of product defect; and (b) was not, in the particular case, solely the result of causes other than product defect existing at the time of sale or distribution.
>
> Restatement (Third) of Torts: Product Liability § 3 (1998). In comment c to this section, the Restatement notes:
>
> [There is] *no requirement that plaintiff prove what aspect of the product was defective*. The inference of defect may be drawn under this Section without proof of the specific defect. Furthermore, quite apart from the question of what type of defect was involved, the plaintiff need not explain specifically what constituent part of the product failed. For example, if an inference of defect can be appropriately drawn in connection with the catastrophic failure of an airplane, the plaintiff need not establish whether the failure is attributable to fuel-tank explosion or engine malfunction.

The jury awarded Ms. Jarvis $24,568 in past medical insurance premiums, $340,338 in lost earnings, and $200,000 in pain and suffering. For future damages, the jury awarded $22,955 in medical insurance premiums, $648,944 in lost earnings, and $300,000 for pain and suffering.

Two Warranties

Used-vehicle defects are covered by two warranties: the *expressed* or *written* warranty, which has a fixed time limit, and the *implied* or *legal* warranty, the application of which is entirely up to a judge's discretion based upon the vehicle's cost, how it was maintained, manufacturer and dealer assertions, the severity of the failure, and the extent of that failure's consequences.

Expressed

The expressed warranty given by the seller is often full of empty promises, and it allows the dealer and manufacturer to act as judge and jury when deciding whether a vehicle was misrepresented or is afflicted by defects they'll pay to correct. Rarely does it provide a money-back guarantee.

Some of the more familiar lame excuses used in denying expressed warranty claims are "You abused the car," "It was poorly maintained," "It's normal wear and tear," "It's rusting from the outside, not the inside," and "It passed the safety inspection." Ironically, the expressed warranty sometimes says there is no warranty at all, or that the vehicle is sold "as is." Fortunately, courts usually throw out these exclusions by upholding two legal concepts:

1. The vehicle must be fit for the purpose for which it was purchased.
2. The vehicle must be of merchantable quality when sold.

Not surprisingly, sellers use the expressed warranty to reject claims, while smart plaintiffs ignore the expressed warranty and argue for a refund under the implied warranty instead.

Implied

The implied warranty ("of fitness") is your ace in the hole. As clearly stated in the under-reported Saskatchewan decision *Maureen Frank v. General Motors of Canada Limited* (see also page 83), in which the judge declared that paint discoloration and peeling shouldn't occur within 11 years of the purchase of the vehicle, the implied warranty is an important legal principle. It is solidly supported by a large body of federal and provincial laws, regulations, and jurisprudence, and it protects you primarily from hidden defects that may be either dealer- or factory-related. But the concept also includes misrepresentation and a host of other scams.

This warranty also holds dealers to a higher standard of conduct than private sellers because, unlike private sellers, dealers and auto manufacturers are presumed to be aware of the defects present in the vehicles they sell. That way,

EXPRESSED WARRANTY "WEASEL WORDS"

We are not responsible:

For any damage and/or breakdown resulting from freezing, rust or corrosion, water or flood, acts of god, salt, environmental damage, chemicals, contamination of fluids, fuels, coolants or lubricants.

For any breakdown caused by misuse, abuse, negligence, lack of normal maintenance, or improper servicing or repairs subsequent to purchase. For any breakdown caused by contaminants resulting from your failure to perform recommended maintenance services, or failure to maintain proper levels of lubricants and/or coolants, or failure to protect your vehicle from further damage when a breakdown has occurred or failure to have your vehicle towed to the service facility when continued operation may result in further damage. Continued operation includes your failure to observe warning lights, gauges, or any other signs of overheating or component failure, such as fluid leakage, slipping, knocking, or smoking, and not protecting your vehicle by continuing to drive creating damage beyond the initial failure.

For any repair or replacement of any covered part if a breakdown has not occurred or if the wear on that part has not exceeded the field tolerances allowed by the manufacturer.

For loss of use, time, profit, inconvenience, or any other consequential loss and any consequential damage to a non-covered part that results from a breakdown.

When the responsibility for the repair is covered by a manufacturer and/or dealer customer assistance program.

For any pre-existing condition known to you or for any breakdown occurring before coverage takes effect or prior to the contract purchase date.

---

they can't just pass the ball to the previous owner and then walk away from the dispute.

Dealers are also expected to disclose defects that have been repaired. For instance, in British Columbia, provincial law (the *Motor Dealer Act*) says that a dealer must disclose damages that cost more than $2,000 to fix. This is a good law to cite in other jurisdictions.

In spite of all your precautions, there's still a 10 percent chance you'll buy a lemon, says mobility services company Runzheimer International (a figure also cited by former GM VP Bob Lutz, who confirms that one out of every 10 vehicles produced by the Detroit automakers is likely to be a lemon).

Why the implied warranty is so effective

- It establishes the concept of reasonable durability (see "How Long Should a Part or Repair Last?" following), meaning that parts are expected to last for a reasonable period of time, as stated in jurisprudence, judged by independent mechanics, or expressed in extended warranties given by the automaker in the past (7–10 years/160,000 km for engines and transmissions).

- It covers the entire vehicle and can be applied for whatever period of time the judge decides.
- It can order that the vehicle be taken back, or a major repair cost be refunded. One *Lemon-Aid* reader writes:

    > I wanted to let you and your readers know that the information you publish about Ford's paint failure problem is invaluable. Having read through your "how-to guide" on addressing this issue, I filed suit against Ford for the "latent" paint defect. The day prior to our court date, I received a settlement offer by phone for 75 percent of what I was initially asking for.

- It can order that plaintiffs be given compensation for supplementary transportation, inconvenience, mental distress, missed work, screwed-up vacations, insurance paid while the vehicle was in the repair shop, repairs done by other repairers, and exemplary, or punitive, damages in cases where the seller was a real weasel.
- It is often used by small claims court judges to give refunds to plaintiffs "in equity" (out of fairness), rather than through a strict interpretation of contract law.

How Long Should a Part or Repair Last?

How do you know when a part or service hasn't lasted as long as it should and whether you should seek a full or partial refund? Sure, you have a gut feeling based on the use of the vehicle, the way you maintained it, and the extent of work that was carried out. But you'll need more than emotion to win compensation from garages and automakers.

You can definitely get a refund if a repair or part lasts beyond its guarantee but not as long as is generally expected. You'll have to show what the auto industry considers to be "reasonable durability," however.

This isn't all that difficult if you use the conservative benchmarks that automakers, mechanics, and the courts have recognized over the years—see the "Reasonable Part Durability" chart on the following page.

Much of the chart's guidelines are extrapolated from the terms of automaker payouts to dissatisfied customers within the past three decades, and from Chrysler's original seven-year powertrain warranty, applicable from 1991 to 1995 and then reapplied since then. Other sources for this table include the following:

- Ford and GM transmission warranties, which are outlined in their secret warranties
- Ford, GM, and Toyota engine "goodwill" programs, which are laid out in their internal service bulletins
- Court judgments where judges have given their own guidelines as to what constitutes reasonable durability

REASONABLE PART DURABILITY

ACCESSORIES

Air conditioner	7 years
Cruise control	5 years/100,000 km
Power doors, windows	5 years
Radio	5 years

BODY

Paint (peeling)	7–11 years
Rust (perforations)	7–11 years
Rust (surface)	5 years
Water/wind/air leaks	5 years

BRAKE SYSTEM

Brake drum	120,000 km
Brake drum linings	35,000 km
Brake rotor	60,000 km
Brake calipers/pads	30,000 km
Master cylinder	100,000 km
Wheel cylinder	80,000 km

ENGINE AND DRIVETRAIN

CV joint	6 years/160,000 km
Differential	7 years/160,000 km
Engine (diesel)	15 years/350,000 km
Engine (gas)	7 years/160,000 km
Motor	7 years/112,000 km
Radiator	4 years/80,000 km
Transfer case	7 years/160,000 km
Transmission (auto.)	7 years/160,000 km
Transmission (man.)	10 years/250,000 km
Transmission oil cooler	5 years/100,000 km

EXHAUST SYSTEM

Catalytic converter	5 years/100,000 km or more
Muffler	2 years/40,000 km
Tailpipe	3 years/60,000 km

IGNITION SYSTEM

Cable set	60,000 km
Electronic module	5 years/80,000 km
Retiming	20,000 km
Spark plugs	20,000 km
Tune-up	20,000 km

SAFETY COMPONENTS

Airbags	life of vehicle
ABS brakes	7 years/160,000 km
ABS computer	10 years/160,000 km
Seat belts	life of vehicle

STEERING AND SUSPENSION

Alignment	1 year/20,000 km
Ball joints	10 years/160,000 km
Coil springs	10 years/160,000 km
Power steering	5 years/80,000 km
Shock absorber	2 years/40,000 km
Struts	5 years/80,000 km
Tires (radial)	5 years/80,000 km
Wheel bearing	3 years/60,000 km

VISIBILITY

Halogen/fog lights	3 years
Sealed beam	2 years
Windshield wiper	5 years

Airbags

Airbags usually carry a four-year warranty in Canada; however, automakers routinely offer "goodwill" warranty extensions for up to 10 years/100,000 miles. Mercedes-Benz Canada, for example, sent off a dealer notification on December 2010 advising dealers that it would cover airbag replacement or correct a faulty wiring harness connection for free on 2005 through 2008 models up to 10 years or 100,000 miles (160,000 km). The affected vehicles are model years 2005–06 ML (164), SLK (171), C (203), CLK (209), E (211), CLS (219), R (251), and 2005–08 G (463).

Owners who paid for the repair will be refunded their money upon presentation of an acceptable receipt from a Mercedes-Benz dealer. Independent garage receipts will likely be accepted if you push hard enough.

Here is part of a letter that was sent out to U.S. owners:

> Dear Mercedes-Benz Owner,
>
> Daimler AG (DAG), the manufacturer of Mercedes-Benz vehicles, has determined that due to a production quality issue electrical resistance variations may be detected within your driver's air bag wiring harness. If this situation occurs in your vehicle, the vehicle's diagnostic system will detect this situation, the "Air Bag" light will be illuminated in the instrument cluster, and Diagnostic Trouble Code 9103 or 9123 will be stored in your vehicle's air bag system memory. The air bag control unit and all air bag systems remain fully functional as designed to protect you even if this situation occurs. It is important to note, however, that any time the "Air Bag" light is illuminated that you immediately bring your vehicle to an authorized Mercedes-Benz dealer for a full diagnosis. The vehicles potentially affected are Model Years 2005–2006 ML, SLK, C, CLK, E, CLS, R-Class and Model Years 2005–2008 G-Class vehicles.
>
> In our continuing efforts to assure the proper performance of Mercedes-Benz products and to ensure the satisfaction of our customers, Mercedes-Benz USA, LLC (MBUSA) has decided to extend the warranty for the driver's air bag wiring…from the original 4 years/50,000 miles (whichever occurs first) to 10 years/100,000 miles (whichever occurs first). This warranty extension applies to these vehicles regardless of ownership. If, during this period, your vehicle should experience an illumination of the "Air Bag" light as described above, this warranty extension would cover the necessary repairs to correct those conditions.
>
> RALPH S. FISHER
> MERCEDES-BENZ USA, LLC
> GENERAL MANAGER, CUSTOMER ASSISTANCE CENTER
> DECEMBER 2010

Mercedes-Benz's admission that airbag systems should be trouble-free for 10 years/100,000 miles serves as an important benchmark for owners experiencing airbag-related failures. Owners of any make or model of vehicle can use this durability standard (what the automaker considers "reasonable durability") to haggle for a "goodwill" settlement or to win a small claims court petition.

Airbags cost thousands of dollars to fix or replace. They are one of the most failure-prone components found on late model vehicles. Insurance companies won't cover their replacement or repair cost unless a collision is involved. But even if they did refund the repair cost, why should you pay a higher insurance fee for a failure caused by the automaker's poor design or use of inferior quality electronics?

Inadvertent deployment may occur after passing over a bump in the road or slamming the car door, or, in some Chrysler minivans, simply by putting the key in the ignition. This happens more often than you might imagine, judging by the hundreds of recalls and thousands of complaints recorded on the National Highway Traffic Safety Administration (NHTSA) website.

Forget the assurances of auto manufacturers and the safety establishment. Airbag deployment can cause massive face and chest trauma, ruin your hearing and eyesight, and break bones. Granted, any personal injuries or cabin-area damages caused by airbag deployment are covered by your accident insurance policy. However, if the airbag fails to deploy, or there is a sudden deployment for no apparent reason, the automaker and the dealer should be held jointly responsible for all injuries and damages caused by the failure.

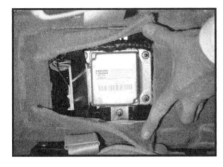
Almost all vehicles have a data recorder.

How do you prove that the airbag deployed improperly? Download the data from your "black box" Electronic Data Recorder (EDR) *immediately* after the incident. Further driving of the vehicle may cause the EDR crash data record to be overwritten by the addition of new data.

You can use the car's data recorder (see pages 91–93) to prove that the airbag, brakes, or throttle control failed prior to an accident. Simply hook a computer up and then download the data from your vehicle's EDR. This will likely lead to a more generous settlement from the two parties and will prevent your insurance premiums from being jacked up.

Once you get all of your proof assembled, including photos of interior damage or injuries caused by the airbag's inadvertent deployment, or non-deployment, file suit in provincial court if it's obvious no settlement is in the offing. If your insurance company decides to pay all of your damages and doesn't want to subrogate your case before the courts, make sure you state that they cannot raise your rates following their decision not to sue.

If you do decide to sue, follow the template lawyers have used in the following Statement of Claim against Toyota for inadvertent airbag deployment.

Emissions Components

Car companies have repeatedly gotten themselves into hot water for refusing to replace emissions parts free of charge. These parts are covered by the emissions warranty, a relatively generous warranty set up several decades ago by automakers with the approval of the U.S. Environmental Protection Agency, which also monitors how fairly the warranty is applied. Canada has approved the same warranty, but leaves enforcement to the States and the courts. The EPA has fined

IN THE PROVINCIAL COURT OF ALBERTA
JUDICIAL DISTRICT OF EDMONTON

BETWEEN:

███████

Plaintiff

- and -

**TOYOTA CANADA INC., COMPANY #1,
COMPANY #2 and COMPANY #3**

Defendants

Schedule "A"

CIVIL CLAIM

1. The Plaintiff, ███████ ("the Plaintiff"), was at all material times to this action a resident of the City of Edmonton, in the Province of Alberta.

2. The Defendant, TOYOTA CANADA INC. ("Toyota"), is a body corporate incorporated under the laws of the Dominion of Canada and is in the business of designing, manufacturing, selling and repairing motor vehicles. At all material times to this action, Toyota was carrying on business in Canada and in the Province of Alberta.

3. The Defendant, COMPANY #1, is a body corporate and is in the business of manufacturing and supplying air bags and air bag assemblies to Toyota including the Supplementary Restraint System ("SRS").

4. The Defendant, COMPANY #2, is a body corporate and is in the business of manufacturing and supplying electrical systems to Toyota including the Electronic Control Unit ("ECU").

5. The Defendant, COMPANY #3, is a body corporate and is in the business of manufacturing and supplying sensing and diagnostic modules to Toyota including the Event Date Recorder ("EDR").

6. On or about the 11th day of July, 2009, the Plaintiff was operating his motor vehicle, a 2005 Toyota 4Runner ("the vehicle"), registration number JTEBT17R058022580, and while entering his driveway the driver and passenger side curtain airbags of the vehicle deployed and the driver's seat belt pretensioner deployed. The odometer reading at the time of deployment was 99,100 kilometres.

7. The said vehicle was purchased on April 4, 2005, and was subject to Toyota's New Vehicle Warranty (the "Warranty"). The Warranty covers repairs needed on any seatbelt or air bag system supplied by Toyota that is defective in material or workmanship and includes coverage for a period of 60 months or up to 100,000 kilometres, whichever comes first. On July 11, 2009, the said vehicle was within the Warranty period of 60 months and had an odometer reading of 99,100 kilometres.

8. Following the deployment of the air bags, the vehicle was examined by a Field Technical Consultant ("FTC") from Toyota. The inspection by the FTC included diagnostic testing on the ECU and SRS. Toyota concluded from the inspection that the incident was the result of the rollover sensor detecting the onset of a rollover event and not the result of a vehicle defect. No malfunction of the SRS was identified. Based on the inspection and conclusion of the FTC, Toyota has denied and continues to deny warranty coverage for the vehicle.

9. The said vehicle was equipped with an EDR. The EDR contains data useful for troubleshooting and records data in a crash or near car crash event. Data from the EDR, if obtained, could support or dispute the conclusion reached by Toyota through the inspection of the ECU and SRS. Toyota did not have a proper readout tool and was unable to download the vehicle's EDR and the EDR was not inspected.

10. As a result of Toyota's decision not to cover the vehicle under the Warranty, the Plaintiff has suffered damages including the cost of repairing the vehicle and reinstalling new air bags.

11. The damages to the Plaintiff were caused jointly and/or severally by the negligence of the Defendants, some particulars of which include the following:

    a. Failing to properly install the said air bags in the vehicle;

    b. Failing to properly test the said air bags of the vehicle;

    c. Using faulty products to manufacture the air bag, the SRS, the ECU and the EDR;

    d. Failing to properly test the SRS, ECU and EDR;

    e. Failing to properly inspect the SRS and the ECU;

    f. Failing to inspect the EDR and failing to make available and/or update information allowing for a reading of the EDR;

continued on p. 70

g. Failing to properly advise the Plaintiff that the air bags or air bag assembly may be deficient and as a result of the deficiency, could reasonably and foreseeably cause the Plaintiff injury;

h. Failing to inspect all available tools and vehicle systems which could provide essential data relating to the sudden deployment of the air bags in the said vehicle; and

i. Such further and other particulars of negligence which may be proven at the trial of this action.

12. As a result of the negligence and the resulting deployment of the air bags, the Plaintiff has suffered special damages including but not limited to:

a. Repair costs in the sum of $6,436.65;

b. Towing costs in the sum of $317.63;

c. Alternate Transportation costs in the sum of $1,500;

d. Corporate Search requests in the sum of $33.00;

e. Postage fees for Registered Mail in the sum of $51.33.

13. The Plaintiff has demanded that Toyota cover the above noted loss for the repairs to the vehicle however, Toyota denies and continues to deny responsibility for the said loss to the Plaintiff and continues to refuse Warranty coverage for the repairs.

14. As a further result of the negligence of the Defendants, or any of them, and the resulting necessary repairs, the Plaintiff has been required to be absent from his place of employment and has suffered a loss of income.

15. As a further consequence of the negligence of the Defendants, or any of them, the Plaintiff may incur special damages and will seek leave at the Trial of this action to amend the Civil Claim herein to include a claim for these damages.

16. As a further consequence of the negligence of the Defendants, or any of them, the Plaintiff seeks punitive damages in the sum of $5,000.00 for the failure to ensure all appropriate measures were undertaken to fully and properly inspect the vehicle for defects. Specifically, Toyota has failed to rule out a vehicle defect as the cause for the sudden deployment of air bags causing concern to the Plaintiff relating to the continued use and safety of the vehicle. Toyota's failure to inspect the EDR and the refusal to provide Warranty coverage falls below the standard of care expected by consumers.

17. The Plaintiff pleads and relies upon the provisions of the Excise Tax Act, R.S.C. 1985, c. E-14, Part IXX, and amendments thereto, insofar as Goods and Services Tax is payable in respect of the Plaintiff's claim or in respect of his costs.

18. The Plaintiff proposes that the trial of this action be held at the Law Courts Building, at the City of Edmonton, in the Province of Alberta.

WHEREFORE THE PLAINTIFF CLAIMS AGAINST THE DEFENDANT:

(a) Judgment in the sum of $13,338.61;

(b) Damages for loss of income in an amount to be determined at trial;

(c) Interest pursuant to the Judgment Interest Act, R.S.A. 2000, c. J-1, as amended;

(d) Such other relief as the nature of this case may require and which this Honourable Court shall deem just;

(e) Costs of this action.

DATED at the City of Edmonton, in the Province of Alberta, this 16th day of February, AD., 2010.

Toyota claims in its standard, boilerplate denial of responsibility that it operated within a reasonable standard of care and that the deployment of the airbags was caused by the negligence of the plaintiff.

both Ford and Chrysler for rejecting legitimate claims for failed emissions parts covered by the EPA and thereby violating the warranty's provisions. The EPA has aggressively gone after other automakers and have entered into consent agreements with them to respect owner warranty rights (see "Emissions-Control Warranties," following).

Use the manufacturer's emissions warranty as your primary guideline for the expected durability of high-tech electronic and mechanical pollution-control components, such as powertrain control modules and catalytic converters. These guidelines are usually found in bulletins dealing with sudden acceleration, stalling, hard starts, foul exhaust odours, and excessive tailpipe emissions. First look at your owner's manual for an indication of which parts on your vehicle are covered. Buttress that information with what the U.S. government's Internet copy of the service bulletin says is covered (the service bulletins are available under the "Vehicle Owners" tab at *www.safercar.gov*). If you don't come up with much detailed parts information, ask the auto manufacturer for a list of specific components covered by the emissions warranty. If you're stonewalled, invest $26.95 (U.S.) in an ALLDATA service bulletin subscription (available for 1982–2011 models).

Emissions-Control Warranties

These little-publicized warranties can save you big bucks if major engine or exhaust components fail prematurely. They come with all new vehicles and cover major components of the emissions-control system for up to 8 years/130,000 km no matter how many times the vehicle is sold. Unfortunately, although owner's manuals vaguely mention the emissions warranty, most don't specify which parts are covered. The U.S. Environmental Protection Agency has intervened on several occasions with hefty fines against Chrysler and Ford and ruled that all major motor and fuel-system components are covered. The components covered include fuel metering, ignition spark advance, restart, evaporative emissions, positive crankcase ventilation, engine electronics (computer modules), and catalytic converters, as well as hoses, clamps, brackets, pipes, gaskets, belts, seals, and connectors.

Unlike the United States, Canada has no government-defined list of parts that must be covered. Nevertheless, Environment Canada and the Canadian Vehicle Manufacturers' Association do have a Memorandum of Understanding that says emissions warranties will be identical on both sides of the border (see *www.dieselnet.com/standards/ca*).

Many of the confidential technical service bulletins (TSBs) listed in Part Three show parts failures that are covered under the eight-year emissions warranty, even though motorists are routinely charged for their replacement.

Make sure to get your emissions system checked out thoroughly by a dealer or an independent garage before the emissions warranty expires and before having the vehicle inspected by provincial emissions inspectors. In addition to ensuring you pass provincial tests, this precaution could save you up to $1,000 if both your catalytic converter and other emissions components are faulty.

Following are sample emissions warranty bulletins from Ford, GM, and Toyota.

FORD STEADY 30–50 MPH CRUISE SURGE

BULLETIN NO.: TSB 05-23-13   DATE: NOVEMBER 28, 2005

2006 Focus

ISSUE: Some 2006 focus vehicles, equipped with the 2.0L non-PZEV engine and 4F27E automatic transaxle, may exhibit a minor hesitation and/or surge at a steady state cruise between 30 to 50 mph (48 to 80 km/h) with no diagnostic trouble codes (DTCs) present in the powertrain control module (PCM).

ACTION: Reprogram the PCM to the latest level.

WARRANTY STATUS: Eligible Under Provisions Of New Vehicle Limited Warranty Coverage And Emissions Warranty Coverage

OPERATION	DESCRIPTION	TIME
052313A	2006 Focus 2.0L: Check Diagnostic Trouble Codes And Reprogram Powertrain Control Module	0.4 Hr.

This simple $100 repair is covered by the eight-year emissions warranty as well as Ford's base three-year warranty.

GM EMISSIONS WARRANTY
EMISSIONS PROGRAMMING WARRANTY COVERAGE

BULLETIN NO.: 04-06-04-036E   DATE: MAY 8, 2008

2009 and Prior GM Passenger Cars and Trucks (Including Saturn); 2003–09 HUMMER H2; 2006–09 HUMMER H3; 2009 and Prior Saab Vehicles (Canada Only). Attention: This bulletin applies only to dealers in the United States and Canada.

The coverage for emission-related reprogramming has the same coverage as the emission controller under the emission controller warranty—8 years/80,000 miles (130,000 km).

TOYOTA EMISSIONS WARRANTY
UPDATE FOR SHIFT IMPROVEMENTS

BULLETIN NO.: TSB-0068-08   DATE: MAY 21, 2008

ECM CALIBRATION: ENHANCEMENT TO SHIFTING PERFORMANCE & SMOOTHNESS

YEAR(S)	MODEL(S)	ADDITIONAL INFORMATION
2007–2009	Camry	Engine(s): 2AZ Transmission(s): 5MT, 5AT VDS(S): BE46K
2007–2008	Solara	Engine(s): 2AZ Transmission(s): 5MT, 5AT VDS(s): CE30P

INTRODUCTION: To enhance shifting performance and smoothness during acceleration the Engine Control Module/ECM (SAE term: Powertrain Control Module/PCM) calibration has been revised.

APPLICABLE WARRANTY: This repair is covered under the Toyota Federal Emission Warranty. This warranty is in effect for 96 months or 80,000 miles, whichever occurs first, from the vehicle's in-service date. Warranty application is limited to correction of a problem based upon a customer's specific complaint.

Remember, you can avoid the ALLDATA fee by accessing bulletin numbers and titles at *www.alldatadiy.com/recalls*, or NHTSA's free service bulletin summary at *www.safercar.gov* (see under "Vehicle Owners"; you can search for the complete bulletin by its number or by the car model and year).

Contact the Right People

Before we go any further, let's get one thing straight: A telephone call to a service manager or automaker usually won't get you much help. Auto manufacturers and their dealers want to make money, not give it back. Customer service advisors are paid to *apply* the warranty policy; don't expect them to *make* policy due to your claim's extenuating circumstances.

To get action, if you suspect a secret warranty applies or that your vehicle has a factory-related defect, you have to kick your claim upstairs, where the company representatives have more power. This can usually be accomplished by sending your claim to the legal affairs department (typically found in Ontario). It should be a registered letter, fax, or email—something that creates a paper trail and gets attention. What's more, that letter must contain the threat that you will use the implied warranty against the dealer and manufacturer and cite convincing juris-prudence to win your small claims court action in the same region where that business operates.

On the following pages are two sample complaint letters that show the type of ammunition you'll need in order to invoke the implied warranty and get a refund for a bad car or ineffective repairs.

Legal "Secrets" Only Lawyers Know

Send a claim letter to both the seller (if it's a dealer) and the automaker to let them work out together how much they will refund to you. Make sure you keep plenty of copies of the complaint and indicate how you can most easily be reached.

Unfair Contract Clauses

Don't let anyone tell you that contracts are iron-clad and cannot be broken. In fact, a judge can cancel an unfair sales contract at any time, even though corporate lawyers spend countless hours protecting their clients with one-sided standard-form contracts. Judges look upon these agreements, called "contracts of adhesion," with a great deal of skepticism. They know these loan documents, insurance contracts, and automobile leases grant consumers little or no bargaining power. So when a dispute arises over terms or language, provincial consumer protection statutes require that judges interpret these contracts in the way most favourable to the consumer. Simply put, ignorance can sometimes be a good defence.

Hearsay and Courtroom Tactics

Judges have considerable latitude in allowing hearsay evidence if it's introduced properly. But it is essential that printed evidence and/or witnesses (relatives are

USED-VEHICLE COMPLAINT LETTER/FAX/EMAIL

WITHOUT PREJUDICE

Date: _____
Name: _____

Please be advised that I am dissatisfied with my used vehicle, a (state model), for the following reasons:

1.
2.
3.
4.
5.

In compliance with the provincial consumer protection laws and the "implied warranty" set down by the Supreme Court of Canada in *Donoghue v. Stevenson, Wharton v. GM*, and *Sharman v. Ford Canada*, I hereby request that these defects be repaired without charge. This vehicle has not been reasonably durable and is, therefore, not as represented to me.

Should you fail to repair these defects in a satisfactory manner and within a reasonable period of time, I shall get an estimate of the repairs from an independent source and claim them in court, without further delay. I also reserve my right to claim up to $1 million for punitive damages, pursuant to the Supreme Court of Canada's February 22, 2002, ruling in *Whiten v. Pilot*.

I have dealt with your company because of its honesty, competence, and sincere regard for its clients. I am sure that my case is the exception and not the rule.

A positive response within the next five (5) days would be appreciated.

(signed with telephone number, fax number, or email address)

not excluded) be available to confirm that a false representation actually occurred, that a part is failure-prone, or that its replacement is covered by a secret warranty or internal service bulletin alert. If you can't find an independent expert, introduce this evidence through the automaker reps and dealership service personnel who have to be at the trial anyhow. They know all about the service bulletins and extended warranty programs cited in *Lemon-Aid* and will probably contradict each other, particularly if they are excluded from the courtroom prior to testifying. Incidentally, you may wish to have the court clerk send a subpoena requiring the deposition of the documents you intend to cite, all warranty extensions relevant to your problem, and other lawsuits filed against the company for similar failures. This will make the fur fly in Oshawa, Oakville, and Windsor, and will likely lead to an out-of-court settlement. Sometimes, the service manager or company

SECRET WARRANTY CLAIM LETTER/FAX/EMAIL

WITHOUT PREJUDICE

Date: _____
Name: _____

Please be advised that I am dissatisfied with my vehicle, a _____, bought from
you on _____.

It has had the following recurring problems that I believe are factory-related defects, as
confirmed by internal service bulletins sent to dealers, and are covered by your "goodwill" policies:

1.
2.
3.

If your "goodwill" program has ended, I ask that my claim be accepted nevertheless,
inasmuch as I was never informed of your policy while it was in effect and should not be
penalized for not knowing it existed.

I hereby formally put you on notice under federal and provincial consumer protection
statutes that your refusal to apply this extended warranty coverage in my case would be
an unfair warranty practice within the purview of the above-cited laws.

Your actions also violate the "implied warranty" set down by the Supreme Court of
Canada (*Donoghue v. Stevenson* and *Longpre v. St. Jacques Automobile*) and repeatedly
reaffirmed by provincial consumer protection laws (*Lowe v. Chrysler, Dufour v. Ford du
Canada*, and *Frank v. GM*).

I have enclosed several estimates (my bill) showing that this problem is factory related
and will (has) cost $_____ to correct. I would appreciate your refunding me
the estimated (paid) amount, failing which, I reserve the right to have the repair done
elsewhere and claim reimbursement in court without further delay. I also reserve the
right to claim up to $1 million for punitive damages, pursuant to the Supreme Court of
Canada's February 22, 2002, ruling in *Whiten v. Pilot*.

A positive response within the next five (5) days would be appreciated.

(signed with telephone number, fax number, or email address) representative will make key admissions if questioned closely by you, a court mediator, or the trial judge. Here are some questions to ask: Is this a common problem? Do you recognize this service bulletin? Is there a case-by-case "goodwill" plan covering this repair?

Automakers often blame owners for having pushed their vehicle beyond its limits. Therefore, when you seek to set aside the contract or get repair work reimbursed, it's essential that you get an independent mechanic or your co-workers to prove the vehicle was well maintained and driven prudently.

Reasonable Diligence

When asking for a refund, keep in mind the "reasonable diligence" rule that requires that a suit be filed within a reasonable amount of time after the purchase, which usually means less than a year. Because many factory-related deficiencies take years to appear, the courts have ruled that the reasonable diligence clock starts clicking only after the defect is confirmed to be manufacturer- or dealer-related (powertrain, paint, etc.). For powertrain components like engines and transmissions, this allows you to make a claim for up to seven years after the vehicle was originally put into service, regardless of whether it was bought new or used. Body failures like paint delamination (see *Frank v. GM*) are reimbursable for up to 11 years. If there have been negotiations with the dealer or the automaker, or if either the dealer or the automaker has been promising to correct the defects for some time or has carried out repeated unsuccessful repairs, the deadline for filing the lawsuit can be extended.

Extra, Punitive Damages

Yes, you can claim for hotel and travel costs or compensation for general inconvenience. Fortunately, when legal action is threatened—usually through small claims court—automakers quickly up their out-of-court offer to include most of the owner's expenses because they know the courts will be far more generous. For example, a British Columbia court's decision gave $2,257 for hotel and travel costs, and then capped it off with a $5,000 award for "inconvenience and loss of enjoyment of their luxury vehicle" to a motorist who was fed up with his lemon Cadillac (see *Wharton v. Tom Harris Chevrolet Oldsmobile Cadillac Ltd. and General Motors of Canada Limited*; B.C. Supreme Court, Vancouver; 1999/12/02; Docket C982104). In the *Sharman v. Ford* case (see page 116), the judge gave the plaintiff $7,500 for "mental distress" caused by the fear that his children would fall out of his 2000 Windstar equipped with a faulty sliding door.

As of March 19, 2005, the Supreme Court of Canada confirmed that car owners can ask for punitive, or exemplary, damages when they feel the seller's or the automaker's conduct has been so outrageously bad that the court should protect society by awarding a sum of money large enough to dissuade others from engaging in similar immoral, unethical conduct. I call this the "weasel-whacker" law. In *Prebushewski v. Dodge City Auto (1984) Ltd. and Chrysler Canada Ltd.* (2001 SKQB 537; QB1215/99JCS), the plaintiff got $25,000 in a judgment handed down

December 6, 2001, in Saskatoon. The award followed testimony from Chrysler's expert witness that the company was aware of many cases where daytime running lights shorted and caused 1996 Ram pickups to catch fire. The plaintiff's truck had burned to the ground, and Chrysler refused the owner's claim, saying it had fulfilled its expressed warranty obligations, in spite of its knowledge that fires were commonplace. The plaintiff sued on the grounds that there was an implied warranty that the vehicle would be safe. Justice Rothery gave this stinging rebuke in his judgment against Chrysler and its dealer:

> Not only did Chrysler know about the problems of the defective daytime running light modules, it did not advise the plaintiff of this. It simply chose to ignore the plaintiff's requests for compensation and told her to seek recovery from her insurance company. Chrysler had replaced thousands of these modules since 1988. But it had also made a business decision to neither advise its customers of the problem nor to recall the vehicles to replace the modules. While the cost would have been about $250 to replace each module, there were at least one million customers. Chrysler was not prepared to spend $250 million, even though it knew what the defective module might do.

> Counsel for the defendants argues that this matter had to be resolved by litigation because the plaintiff and the defendants simply had a difference of opinion on whether the plaintiff should be compensated by the defendants. Had the defendants some dispute as to the cause of the fire, that may have been sufficient to prove that they had not willfully violated this part of the *Act*. They did not. They knew about the defective daytime running light module. They did nothing to replace the burned truck for the plaintiff. They offered the plaintiff no compensation for her loss. Counsel's position that the definition of the return of the purchase price is an arguable point is not sufficient to negate the defendants' violation of this part of the *Act*. I find the violation of the defendants to be willful. Thus, I find that exemplary damages are appropriate on the facts of this case.

> In this case, the quantum ought to be sufficiently high as to correct the defendants' behaviour. In particular, Chrysler's corporate policy to place profits ahead of the potential danger to its customers' safety and personal property must be punished. And when such corporate policy includes a refusal to comply with the provisions of the *Act* and a refusal to provide any relief to the plaintiff, I find an award of $25,000 for exemplary damages to be appropriate. I therefore order Chrysler and Dodge City to pay: Damages in the sum of $41,969.83; Exemplary damages in the sum of $25,000; Party and party costs.

Warranty Rights

The manufacturer's or dealer's warranty is a written legal promise that a vehicle will be reasonably reliable, subject to certain conditions. Regardless of the number of subsequent owners, this promise remains in force as long as the warranty's original time/kilometre limits haven't expired. Tires aren't usually covered by car manufacturers' warranties; they're warranted instead by the tiremaker on a prorated basis. This isn't such a good deal, because the manufacturer is making a profit by charging you the full list price. If you were to buy the same replacement tire from a discount store, you'd likely pay less, without the prorated rebate.

But consumers have gained additional rights following Bridgestone/Firestone's massive recall in 2001 of its defective ATX II and Wilderness tires. Because of the confusion and chaos surrounding Firestone's handling of the recall, Ford's 575 Canadian dealers stepped into the breach and replaced the tires with any equivalent tires they had in stock, no questions asked. This is an important precedent that tears down the traditional wall separating tire manufacturers from automakers in product liability claims. In essence, whoever sells the product can now be held liable for damages. In the future, Canadian consumers will have an easier time holding the dealer, the automaker, and the tire manufacturer liable, not just for recalled products but also for any defect that affects the safety or reasonable durability of that product.

This is particularly true now that the Supreme Court of Canada (*Winnipeg Condominium v. Bird Construction* [1995] 1 S.C.R. 85) has ruled that defendants are liable in negligence for any designs that result in a risk to the public's safety or health. Sometimes automakers plead that their compliance with federal automobile safety laws immunizes them from product liability claims, but this argument has been shot down countless times by the courts. (Type "auto safety standards liability" into an Internet search engine.)

Other Warranties

In the U.S., safety restraints such as airbags and safety belts have warranty coverage extended for the lifetime of the vehicle, following an informal agreement made between automakers and NHTSA. In Canada, however, some automakers have tried to dodge this responsibility, alleging that they are separate entities, their vehicles are different, and no U.S. agreement or service bulletin can bind them. That distinction is both disingenuous and dishonest and wouldn't likely hold up in small claims court—probably the reason why most automakers relent when threatened with legal action.

Aftermarket products and services—such as gas-saving gadgets, rustproofing, and paint protectors—can render the manufacturer's warranty invalid, so make sure you're in the clear before purchasing any optional equipment or services from an independent supplier.

How fairly a warranty is applied is more important than how long it remains in effect. Once you know the normal wear rate for a mechanical component or body part, you can demand proportional compensation when you get less than normal durability—no matter what the original warranty says. Some dealers tell customers that they need to have original equipment parts installed in order to maintain their warranty. A variation on this theme requires that the selling dealer does routine servicing—including tune-ups and oil changes (with a certain brand of oil)—or the warranty is invalidated. Nothing could be further from the truth.

Canadian law stipulates that whoever issues a warranty cannot make that warranty conditional on the use of any specific brand of motor oil, oil filter, or any other component, unless it's provided to the customer free of charge.

Sometimes dealers will do all sorts of minor repairs that don't correct the problem, and then after the warranty runs out, they'll tell you that major repairs are needed. You can avoid this nasty surprise by repeatedly bringing your vehicle to the dealership before the warranty ends. During each visit, insist that a written work order include the specific nature of the problem, as you see it, and a statement that this is the second, third, or fourth time the same problem has been brought to the dealer's attention. Write this down yourself, if need be. This allows you to show a pattern of non-performance by the dealer during the warranty period and establishes that the problem is both serious and chronic. When the warranty expires, you have the legal right to demand that it be extended on those items consistently reappearing on your handful of work orders. *Lowe v. Fairview Chrysler* (see page 113) is an excellent judgment that reinforces this important principle. In another lawsuit, *François Chong v. Marine Drive Imported Cars Ltd. and Honda Canada Inc.* (see page 113), a Honda owner forced Honda to fix his engine six times—until they got it right.

A retired GM service manager suggests another effective tactic when you're not sure that a dealer's warranty "repairs" will actually correct the problem for a reasonable period of time after the warranty expires. Here's what he says you should do:

> When you pick up the vehicle after the warranty repair has been done, hand the service manager a note to be put in your file that says you appreciate the warranty repair, however, you intend to return and ask for further warranty coverage if the problem reappears before a reasonable amount of time has elapsed—even if the original warranty has expired. A copy of the same note should be sent to the automaker.... Keep your copy of the note in the glove compartment as cheap insurance against paying for a repair that wasn't fixed correctly the first time.

Extra-Cost Warranties

When a company goes bankrupt, its extended warranties become worthless unless successfully litigated. At best, payouts will be parsimonious. Supplementary warranties providing extended coverage may be sold by the manufacturer, the dealer, or an independent third party and are automatically transferred when the vehicle is sold. They cost between $1,500 and $2,000 and are usually a waste of money. You can protect yourself better by steering clear of vehicles that have a reputation for being unreliable or expensive to service (see Part Three), and using the threat of small claims courts when factory-related trouble arises. Don't let the dealer pressure you into deciding right away.

Generally, you can purchase an extended warranty any time during the period in which the manufacturer's warranty is in effect or, in some cases, shortly after buying the vehicle from a used-car dealer. An automaker's supplementary warranty will likely cost about a third more than warranties sold by independents. And in some parts of the country, notably B.C., dealers have a quasi monopoly on selling warranties, with little competition from the independents.

Dealers love to sell extended warranties, whether you need them or not, because dealer markup represents up to 60 percent of the warranty's cost. Out of the remaining 40 percent comes the sponsor's administration costs and profit margin, calculated at another 15 percent. What's left to pay for repairs is a paltry 25 percent of the original amount. The only reason that automakers and independent warranty companies haven't been busted for this Ponzi scheme is that only half of the car buyers who purchase extended service contracts actually use them.

It's often difficult to collect on supplementary warranties because independent companies frequently go out of business or limit the warranty's coverage through subsequent mailings. Provincial laws cover both situations. If the bankrupt warranty company's insurance policy won't cover your claim, take the dealer to small claims court and ask for repair costs and the refund of the original warranty payment. Your argument for holding the dealer responsible is a simple one: By accepting a commission to act as an agent of the defunct company, the dealer took on the obligations of the company as well. As for limiting the coverage after you have bought the warranty policy, this is illegal, and it allows you to sue both the dealer and the warranty company for a refund of both the warranty and the repair costs.

Psst..."Secret" Warranties Are Everywhere

Automakers are reluctant to make free repair programs public because they feel that doing so would weaken confidence in their product and increase their legal liability. The closest they come to an admission is sending a "goodwill policy," "product improvement program," or "special policy" technical service bulletin (TSB) to dealers or first owners of record. Consequently, the only motorists who find out about these policies are the original owners who haven't changed their addresses or leased their vehicles. The other motorists who get compensated for repairs are the ones who read *Lemon-Aid* each year, staple TSBs to their work orders, and yell the loudest.

Remember, vehicles on their second owners and repairs done by independent garages are included in these secret warranty programs. Large, costly repairs, such as blown engines, burned transmissions, and peeling paint, are often covered. Even mundane little repairs, which can still cost you $100 or more, are frequently included in these programs. If you have a TSB but you're still refused compensation, keep in mind that secret warranties are an admission of manufacturing negligence. Here are a few examples of secret warranties that may save you thousands of dollars. More extensive listings are found in Part Three's model ratings.

Audi

2002–06 S4 and A6 equipped with 2.7L turbocharged V6 engines

Problem: Defective auxiliary coolant pump leaks coolant from the pump body. When the pump fails, the coolant light will come on, warning that continued driving could cause serious engine damage. **Warranty coverage:** VW will install a Repair Kit free of charge up to 7 years/160,000 km. See TSB #05-05, published October 28, 2005.

Audi, Chrysler, Mercedes-Benz, Saab, Toyota, and VW

1997–2004 Audi A4; 1999–2002 Chrysler models equipped with a 2.7L V6; 1998–2002 Mercedes-Benz vehicles; 1998–2003 Saab 9-3 and 9-5 models; 1997–2002 Toyota and Lexus vehicles with 2.2L 4-cylinder or 3.0L V6 engines; and 1997–2004 VW Passat

Problem: Engine sludge. **Warranty coverage:** Varies; usually 7–10 years/160,000 km. Automakers can't automatically deny this free repair if you don't have proof of all of your oil changes, unless they can show that the sludge was caused by a missed oil change (which, according to independent mechanics, is impossible to do). Remember, the warranty has been extended to fix a factory-related problem that occurs despite regular oil changes. That's why it's the automaker's responsibility.

Service bulletins, press releases, and dealer memos are all admissions of responsibility. From there, the legal doctrine of "the balance of probabilities" applies. To wit, a defect *definitely* causes engine sludge, while a missed oil change *may* cause engine sludge. Therefore, it is more probable that the defect caused the sludge.

Once the sludge condition is diagnosed, the dealer and automobile manufacturer are jointly liable for all corrective repairs plus additional damages for your inconvenience, your loss of use or the cost of a loaner vehicle, and the cost to replace the oil. The automaker's owner notification letter may not have gone out to Canadian owners, since it is not required by any Canadian recall or by statute. If a letter goes out, it is usually sent only to first owners of record. And in the case of Chrysler's engine, no customer notification letters have been sent to anyone.

Some automakers say owners must use a special, more-expensive oil to prevent sludge. This after-sale stipulation is illegal and can also provide owners with a reason to ask for damages, or even a refund, since it wasn't disclosed at the time of sale. All of the letter restrictions and decisions made by the dealer and the manufacturer can easily be appealed to the small claims court, where the sludge letter is powerful proof of the automaker's negligence.

BMW
2007–10 models equipped with a high-pressure fuel pump
Problem: Premature failure. **Warranty coverage:** BMW has extended the emissions warranty to 10 years/120,000 mi. (193,000 km), according to bulletin #SI B13 03 09, announced in BMW's November 2010 dealer letter.

Chrysler
2007–08 Avenger and Sebring
Problem: A broken transmission gearshift-lever interlock spring retainer hook will "freeze" the lever in the Park position. **Warranty coverage:** A steel reinforcement clip will be installed for free, if needed, says Customer Satisfaction Notification Program K16, dated August 2010.

Chrysler, Ford, General Motors, and the Asian Automakers
All years, all models
Problem: Faulty automatic transmissions that self-destruct, shift erratically, gear down to "limp mode," are slow to shift in or out of Reverse, or are noisy. **Warranty coverage:** If you have the assistance of your dealer's service manager, or some internal service bulletin that confirms the automatic transmission may be defective, expect an offer of 50–75 percent (about $2,500) if you threaten to sue in small claims court. Acura, Honda, Hyundai, Lexus, and Toyota coverage varies between seven and eight years.

> I've just been told that I need my fourth transmission on my '96 Town & Country minivan with 132,000 miles [212,000 km] on it. I've driven many cars well past that mileage with only *one* transmission. The dealer asked Chrysler, who said they would not help me. My appeals to Chrysler's customer service department yielded me the same result.... Chrysler split some of the costs with me on the previous rebuilt replacements.

All years, all models
Problem: Premature wearout of brake pads, calipers, and rotors. Produces excessive vibration, noise, and pulling to one side when braking. **Warranty coverage:** *Calipers and pads:* "Goodwill" settlements confirm that brake calipers and pads that fail to last 2 years/40,000 km will be replaced for half the repair

cost; components not lasting 1 year/20,000 km will be replaced for free. *Rotors:* If they last less than 3 years/60,000 km, they will be replaced at half price; replacement is free up to 2 years/40,000 km.

Chrysler, Ford, General Motors, and Honda

All years, all models

Problem: Faulty paint jobs that cause paint to turn white and peel off in horizontal panels. **Warranty coverage:** Automakers will offer a free paint job or partial compensation for up to six years (no mileage limitation). Thereafter, most manufacturers will offer 50–75 percent refunds on the small claims courthouse's front steps.

In *Maureen Frank v. General Motors of Canada Limited*, the Saskatchewan small claims court judge ruled that paint finishes should last for 11 years. Three other Canadian small claims judgments have likewise extended the benchmark for second owners and to pickups. In those cases, the courts judged that seven years was an appropriate extension.

Although the automakers' attempts to blame paint delamination on the sun, acid rain, tree sap, bird droppings, and owners' lack of care appear comical at first, professional car washers are not laughing. In 2003, the International Carwash Association advised its members to inform drivers that the paint defect is due to a poor factory paint job—not the soap or brushes used in car washes (see "ICA warns of paint problems with some GM vehicles" at *www.carwash.com*).

Ford

1992–2004 Aerostar, Focus, Sable, Taurus, and Windstar

Problem: Defective front coil springs may suddenly break, puncturing the front tire and leading to loss of steering control. **Warranty coverage:** Under a "Safety Improvement Campaign" negotiated with NHTSA, Ford will replace *broken* coil springs at no charge up to 10 years/unlimited mileage. The company initially said that it wouldn't replace the springs until they had broken—if you survived to submit a claim, that is—but it relented when threatened with a lawsuit. Since then, customer complaints have trailed off. Ford has placed a recall on 1997–98 models that are registered in rust-belt states or in Canada for the installation of a protective shield (called a "spring catcher bracket" in the Canadian recall) to prevent a broken spring from shredding the front tire.

2008–09 F-250 through F-550 trucks equipped with a 6.4L diesel engine

Problem: Premature wearout of the fuel injector O-rings. **Warranty coverage:** Under Customer Satisfaction Program #09B08, Ford said it would replace the faulty injectors for free through August 31, 2010. Presently, dealer service managers are continuing the expired program on a case-by-case basis as a "goodwill" gesture.

1998–2003 Windstar; 2004 Freestar

Problem: Defective rear axles may suddenly break, throwing the vehicle out of control. **Warranty coverage:** Ford was repairing these vehicles free of charge on a "goodwill" case-by-case basis. However, NHTSA forced Ford to recall the affected Windstars in August 2010. The downside is that parts won't be available until well into 2011 and the 2004 Freestar may be afflicted with the same defective axle.

General Motors

2009 Acadia, Enclave, Outlook, and Traverse

Problem: Temporary reduction in power brake assist in extreme cold weather. **Warranty coverage:** GM will repair or replace the power brake assist for free up to June 30, 2011.

2006–07 Cobalt, G4/G5, and Ion

Problem: A faulty fuel pump module may produce a fuel odour or spotting on the ground. **Warranty coverage:** GM has extended the fuel pump warranty to 10 years/120,000 mi. (193,000 km), says TSB #09275A, issued March 3, 2010.

2009 Cobalt, HHR, Pursuit, and Ion

Problem: A faulty Engine Control Module could cause the vehicle to fail the provincial pollution inspection. **Warranty coverage:** GM has extended the ECM warranty to 15 years/150,000 mi. (240,000 km), says TSB #09014, issued September 9, 2009.

2005–06 Corvette

Problem: Roof delaminates and separates from the frame. **Warranty coverage:** GM will repair or replace affected roofs for free. (See the text box on the following page.)

2002–06 Buick Rendezvous; 2000–05 Cadillac DeVille; 2003–06 Cadillac CTS; 2004–06 Cadillac SRX; 2005–06 Cadillac STS; 2006 Cadillac DTS

Problem: Roof rust perforation. **Warranty coverage:** GM will replace, repair, or repaint the roof for free up to 6 years/100,000 km.

2007 Cadillac Escalade, ESV, EXT, Avalanche, Sierra, Silverado, Suburban, Tahoe, Yukon, and Yukon XL

Problem: Peeling of the interior chrome door handles. **Warranty coverage:** GM will replace the door handles for free up to 10 years/100,000 mi. (160,000 km).

2002–05 Ion; 2003–04 Vue

Problem: VTi automatic transmission failure. **Warranty coverage:** GM will pay 50 percent of the repair, or give the owner $5,000 (U.S.) toward the purchase of a new GM model up to 8 years/100,000 mi. (160,000 km). This Special Policy is detailed in TSB #09280, published November 5, 2009.

2006–07 Malibu and G6

Problem: Catalytic Converter failure. **Warranty coverage:** Under Special Coverage Adjustment #10134, dated November 17, 2010, GM will replace the converter free of charge up to 10 years/120,000 mi. (193,000 km).

2005–06 G6, Malibu, and Malibu Maxx; 2008 G6, Malibu, Malibu Maxx, and Aura

Problem: Loss of power-steering assist. **Warranty coverage:** Under Special Coverage Adjustment #10183, dated July 20, 2010, GM will replace the failed components free of charge up to 10 years/100,000 mi. (160,000 km).

2008–09 Grand G8

Problem: A vapour leak at the fuel tank filler cap may cause the instrument cluster Check Engine light to remain lit. **Warranty coverage:** The fuel filler cap will be replaced free of charge and be guaranteed for 10 years/120,000 mi. (193,000 km).

2001–02 Grand Prix, Impala, Monte Carlo, and Regal

Problem: Defective catalytic converters may cause vehicle to lose power or the dash warning light to come on. **Warranty coverage:** The converter warranty is extended to 10 years. Owners will also be reimbursed for previous converter/OBD system repairs or replacements.

2006–07 Solstice; 2007 Sky

Problem: Premature caralytic converter failure. **Warranty coverage:** GM will replace for free the converter for a period of 10 years/120,000 mi. (193,000 km).

Honda

2006–09 Civic

Problem: Engine overheats or leaks coolant because the engine block is cracking at the coolant passages. **Warranty coverage:** Honda will install a new engine block assembly free of charge under a "goodwill policy," as stated in its TSB #10-048, issued August 17, 2010.

1999–2003 Odyssey and Pilot

Problem: EGR valve contamination or EGR port clogging may cause engine surging or stalling. **Warranty coverage:** Honda will install a new EGR valve and a valve kit under a "goodwill" program applicable up to 8 years/160,000 km (TSB #05-026; Date: July 20, 2005).

2003–05 Odyssey

Problem: Premature paint peeling on vehicles painted dark blue. **Warranty coverage:** Honda will repaint the affected areas free of charge up to seven years, with no mileage limit. This warranty extension is covered in Honda Service Bulletin #08-031, issued May 21, 2008.

Infiniti

2003–04 G35

Problem: The seat-mounted side airbag harness may be defective, causing the Airbag light to stay lit. **Warranty coverage:** Infiniti will relocate and secure the seat-mounted side airbag connectors under Voluntary Service Campaign #P0339 as detailed in TSB #ITB10-034a, issued July 21, 2010. No time or mileage restrictions are indicated.

Kia

2006–10 Sedona

Problem: Faulty door latch. **Warranty coverage:** Kia will install a free door latch kit to prevent the sliding door from binding under Service Action #SA058, issued November 2010.

Lexus

2007–09 RX 350

Problem: The rubber portion of the oil supply hose may degrade over time. This condition may cause the oil to leak from the oil hose, producing abnormal engine noise and resulting in the Oil Pressure light illuminating. **Warranty coverage:** Lexus will replace the oil hose under Limited Service Campaign #9LH, issued November 16, 2009. No time or mileage restrictions are indicated.

Toyota

2004–07 Prius

Problem: Faulty electric water pump. **Warranty coverage:** According to Limited Service Campaign #A0N, Toyota will replace the water pump free of charge until November 30, 2013. There is no mileage limitation.

1995–2000 Tacoma and Tundra

Problem: Rust-damaged structural frames. The excessive rusting is caused by inadequate anti-corrosion undercoating applied at the factory. **Warranty coverage:** According to the April 14, 2008, edition of *Automotive News*, Toyota will repair or buy back the affected pickups. Dealers will inspect all affected Tacomas and Tundras free of charge and apply an extended 15-year frame-rust warranty. Trucks with minor frame pitting will be repaired for free; trucks with more serious damage will be bought back at 150 percent of the "excellent" value listed in the U.S.-published *Kelley Blue Book* guide, regardless of the truck's condition.

Volvo

2007–10 S8; 2008–10 V70 and XC70, and 2010 XC60

Problem: Leaking coolant from the cylinder-head bleeder hose. Leakage may cause the engine to run hot and cause severe engine damage. **Warranty coverage:** According to Volvo Service Campaign #232, as announced in the company's November 30, 2010, internal dealer service bulletin, Volvo will replace the engine cylinder-head bleeder hose free of charge until November 30, 2012.

Free Recall Repairs

Vehicles are recalled for one of two reasons: Either they are potentially unsafe or they don't conform to federal pollution control regulations. Whatever the reason, recalls are a great way to get free repairs—if you know which ones apply to you and you have the patience of Job.

In North America, over 300 million unsafe vehicles have been recalled by automakers for the free correction of safety-related defects since American recall legislation was passed in 1966 (a weaker Canadian law was enacted in 1971). During that time, about one-third of the recalled vehicles never made it back to the dealership for repairs, because owners were never informed, didn't consider the defect to be that hazardous, or gave up waiting for corrective parts.

Subsequent American legislation targets automakers that drag their feet in making recall repairs. Owners on both sides of the border may wish to cite the NHTSA guidelines (left) for support.

If you've moved or bought a used vehicle, it's smart to pay a visit to your local dealership, give them your address, and get a report card on which recalls, warranties, and free service campaigns apply to your vehicle. Simply give the service advisor the vehicle identification number—found on your insurance card, or on your dash just below the windshield on the driver's side—and have the number run through the automaker's computer system. Ask for a computer printout of the vehicle's history (have it emailed to you or a friend), and make sure you're listed in the automaker's computer as the new owner. This ensures that you'll receive notices of warranty extensions and emissions and safety recalls.

Regional Recalls

Don't let any dealer refuse you recall repairs because of where you live.

In order to cut recall costs, many automakers try to limit a recall to vehicles in a certain designated region. This practice doesn't make sense, since cars are mobile and an unsafe, rust-cankered steering unit can be found anywhere—not just in certain rust-belt provinces or American states.

For instance, in 2001, Ford attempted to limit to five American states its recall of faulty Firestone tires. Public ridicule of the company's proposal led to an extension of the recall throughout North America.

Common safety defects

Wherever you live or drive, don't expect to be welcomed with open arms when your vehicle develops a safety- or emissions-related problem that's not yet part of a recall campaign.

For example, both Ford and Toyota have been cited for stonewalling customer safety complaints. In 2010, NHTSA hit Toyotoa with three fines, each for the maximum $16.4 million (U.S.), for dragging its feet on three different recalls.

More fines are expected as Washington looks more closely into when Toyota first became aware of its sudden acceleration problems.

Ford is in deeper trouble with axle breakage on its 1998–2003 Windstar minivans, and NHTSA will have to share the blame. Although some 200 owners of 1999–2003 Ford Windstar minivans had filed complaints about broken rear axles years ago, NHTSA never opened a safety investigation after Ford assured safety investigators in Washington and Ottawa that even if the axle broke, drivers wouldn't lose steering control. Yet NHTSA's own driving tests not only showed a loss of steering but also concluded the Windstar would likely roll over. Still NHTSA did not open a formal inquiry. Only after the *New York Times* did a story on the axle defect in May did the safety agency begin a formal investigation, saying it had received 234 complaints and reports of two accidents. The axle failures were linked to corrosion damage primarily in snowbelt states where roads are salted in winter.

Industry insiders say Ford will likely join Toyota and be forced to pay the maximum $16.4 million for delaying its axle recall.

In late August, Ford finally recalled 612,000 Windstars from the 1998–2003 model years in the United States and Canada, and in November the safety agency issued an unusual warning to Windstar owners: Get rusty rear axles fixed quickly before they break.

Only one problem with that advice: Ford stopped production of Windstars in 2003 and replacement axles won't be available until well into 2011.

Ford and Toyota aren't all that different from other automakers in putting profits before safety, except for the egregious nature of the scam perpetrated by these two automakers. Ford sold the fire-prone Pinto long after the fire danger was evident, and Toyota hushed up its Prius brake failures and sudden acceleration on almost their entire lineup of vehicles in order to generate windfall profits. In fact, Toyota internal documents boasted at one sales meeting that its lobbying of NHTSA saved the automaker $100 million (U.S.).

Let's do the math: Toyota has been fined a total of almost $50 million. On the other hand, Toyota saves $100 million by pressuring the government to drop or delay inquiries into the safety of its vehicles. Result: a $50 million U.S. profit from lobbying NHTSA alone.

No wonder automobile manufacturers and dealers take a restrictive view of what constitutes a safety or emissions defect and frequently charge for repairs that should be free under federal safety or emissions legislation. To counter this tendency, look at the following list of typical defects that are clearly safety-related. If you experience similar problems, insist that the automaker fix the problem at no expense to yourself, including paying for a car rental while corrective repairs are done.

- Airbag malfunctions
- Corrosion affecting safe operation
- Disconnected or stuck accelerators
- Electrical shorts
- Faulty windshield wipers
- Fuel leaks
- Problems with original axles, driveshafts, seats, seat recliners, or defrosters
- Seat belt problems
- Stalling or sudden acceleration
- Sudden steering or brake loss
- Suspension failures
- Trailer coupling failures

Recall campaigns in the U.S. force automakers to pay the entire cost of fixing a vehicle's safety-related defect for any vehicle purchased up to eight years before the recall's announcement. A reasonable period beyond that time is usually a slam dunk in small claims court.

Voluntary recall campaigns, frequently called "Special Service" or "Safety Improvement Campaigns," are a real problem, though. The government doesn't monitor the notification of owners; dealers and automakers routinely deny there's a recall, thereby dissuading most claimants; and the company's so-called fix, not authorized by any governing body, may not correct the hazard at all. Also, the voluntary recall may leave out many of the affected models, or unreasonably exclude certain owners.

Safety Defect Information

If you wish to report a safety defect or want recall info, you may access Transport Canada's website at *www.tc.gc.ca/roadsafety/recalls/search_e.asp*. Recall information is available in French and English, as is general information relating to road safety and importing a vehicle into Canada. Web surfers can now access the recall database for 1970–2008 model year vehicles, but, unlike NHTSA's website, the Transport Canada website doesn't list owner complaints, doesn't disclose defect investigations, doesn't show "voluntary warranty extensions" (read "secret warranties"), and doesn't provide service bulletin summaries. You can also call Transport Canada at 1-800-333-0510 (toll-free within Canada) or 613-993-9851 (within the Ottawa region or outside Canada) to get additional information.

If you aren't happy with Ottawa's treatment of your recall inquiry, try NHTSA's website. It's more complete than Transport Canada's (NHTSA's database is updated daily and covers vehicles built since 1952). You can search the database for your vehicle or tires at *www.nhtsa.dot.gov/cars/problems*. You'll get immediate access to four essential database categories applicable to your vehicle and model year: the latest recalls, current and past defect investigations, complaints reported by other owners, and a brief summary of TSBs.

"Black Box" Data Recorders

If your car has an airbag, it's probably spying on you. And if you get into an accident caused by a mechanical malfunction, you will be glad that it is.

Event data recorders (EDRs) the size of a VCR tape have been hidden near the engine, under the seat, or in the centre consoles of about 30 million airbag-equipped Ford and GM vehicles since the early '90s. Almost all domestic and imported cars now carry them. To find out if your car or truck carries an EDR, read your owner's manual, contact the regional office of your car's manufacturer, or go to *www.harristechnical.com/downloads/cdrlist.pdf.*

The data recorders operate in a similar fashion to flight data recorders used in airplanes: They record data from the last five seconds before impact, including the force of the collision, the airbag's performance, when the brakes were applied, engine and vehicle speed, gas pedal position, and whether the driver was wearing a seat belt.

Getting EDR Data

In the past, automakers have systematically hidden their collected data from government and insurance researchers, citing concerns for drivers' privacy. This argument, however, has been roundly rejected by law enforcement agencies, the courts, and car owners who need the independent information to prove negligence or simply to keep track of how and where their vehicles are driven. Car owners, rental agencies, and fleet administrators are also using EDR data to pin legal liability on automakers for accidents caused by the failure of safety components, such as airbags that don't deploy when they should (or do deploy when they shouldn't) and anti-lock brakes that don't brake.

One handy portable tool for downloading EDR data to any PC is made by the Vetronix Corporation and sells for $2,500 (U.S.). It's presently marketed to accident reconstructionists, safety researchers, law enforcement agencies, and insurance companies as a tool to assess culpability in criminal and civil trials. Car owners who wish to dispute criminal charges, oppose their insurer's decision as to fault, or hold an automaker responsible for a safety device's failure (airbags, seat belts, or brakes) will find this data invaluable—if the data hasn't been wiped clean by the dealer!

A Tool for Parents

One of the scariest days for parents is when their teenager passes the driver's licence exam. Today there are cell phones, satellite radios, flip-down DVD players, and other entertainment options to distract even the most seasoned drivers. Teenagers just learning the rules of the road are especially susceptible to these distractions, and even more so when other teens are in the car.

Electronic monitors are a constant reminder to teens that driving is a privilege that can be taken away if they don't drive safely. No more "he said, she said"!

It's now possible to electronically monitor your teenager's driving habits and the places he or she visits with a device called the Road Safety RS-1000 On-Board Computer (see *www.techedu. com/RoadSafety_RS-1000.asp*). It is a relatively inexpensive device that plugs into the data recorder and sets off an audible alarm when the driver exceeds a preset speed limit. The device also uses an accelerometer, similar to those used in automotive testing, to measure vehicle G-forces that are created by aggressive driving. As G-forces become excessive, an audible warning immediately tells the driver to back off. The only way to prevent hearing the audible warning (and feeling the embarrassment when friends are in the vehicle) is to drive safely.

The RS-1000 black box tells you how and when your teen was driving on a second-by-second basis. If you say, "I don't want you speeding on the freeway," and your teen does it anyway, you will know it. If curfew is at midnight and your darling gets home at 1:00 a.m., you will know it. The data is always accessible: Just pop the memory card out of the RS-1000 black box and plug it into your family's computer to display the reports and graphs.

The RS-1000 can be bought through Road Safety International's website. Devices cost $295 (U.S.). For vehicles manufactured in 1996 or later, anyone can install the system by simply plugging the on-board computer into the vehicle's OBD-II connector. The device will also work in 1995 and older vehicles, but it will require hard-wire installation by a qualified automotive technician. For more information, contact the company at *rsi@roadsafety.com* or 805-498-9444.

Another useful monitoring gadget is the CarChip Pro (see *www.davisnet.com/drive/ products/carchip_products.asp*). It costs $99 (U.S.) and can be used with any PC using Windows 98SE and above.

Safety Benefits

EDRs are not simply good tools for collecting safety data; they have also had a positive effect on accident prevention. A 1992 study by the European Union, cited by the Canada Safety Council, found that EDRs reduced the collision rate by 28 percent and costs by 40 percent in police fleets where drivers knew that they were being monitored.

The recorders are particularly helpful in getting compensation for accident victims, prompting automaker recalls, and punishing dangerous drivers—even if one such driver happens to be a U.S. Congressmen. In January 2004, South Dakota Congressman Bill Janklow was convicted of manslaughter for speeding through a stop sign—his EDR readout proved he was driving faster than the speed limit, although slower than police had estimated.

In October 2003, Montreal police won their first dangerous driving conviction using EDR data (*R. v. Gauthier*; 2003/05/27 QC C.Q. Dossier: 500-01-013375-016; available at *www.canlii.org*). In June 2003, Edwin Matos of Pembroke Pines, Florida, was sentenced to 30 years in prison for killing two teenage girls after crashing into their car at more than 160 km. The recorder's speed data convicted him. A chronological list of dozens of Canadian and American court cases related to automotive EDRs has been prepared by the traffic accident reconstructionists at Harris Technical Services (see "EDR Case Law" at *www.harristechnical.com*).

The Art of Complaining

Step 1: Can We Talk?

Not likely. You can try phoning the seller or automaker, but don't expect to get much out of the call. Private sellers won't want to talk with you, and dealer customer service agents will tell you the vehicle was sold "as is." They simply apply the dealership's policy, knowing that 90 percent of complainers will drop their claims after venting their anger.

Still, try to work things out by contacting someone higher up who can change the policy to satisfy your request. In your attempt to reach a settlement, ask only for what is fair and don't try to make anyone look bad.

Speak in a calm, polite manner, and try to avoid polarizing the issue. Talk about cooperating to solve the problem. Let a compromise emerge—don't come in with a rigid set of demands. Don't insist on getting the settlement offer in writing, but make sure that you're accompanied by a friend or relative who can confirm the offer in court if it isn't honoured. Be prepared to act upon the offer without delay so that your hesitancy won't be blamed if the seller or automaker withdraws it.

Service manager help

Service managers have more power than you may realize. They make the first determination of what work is covered under warranty or through post-warranty "goodwill" programs, and they are directly responsible to the dealer and manufacturer for that decision (dealers hate manufacturer audits that force them to pay back questionable warranty decisions). Service managers are paid both to save the dealer and automaker money and to mollify irate clients—almost an impossible balancing act. Nevertheless, when a service manager agrees to extend warranty coverage, it's because you've raised solid issues that neither the dealer nor the automaker can ignore. All the more reason to present your argument in a confident, forthright manner with your vehicle's service history and *Lemon-Aid's* "Reasonable Part Durability" table on hand (refer to page 66). Also, bring as many TSBs and owner complaint printouts as you can find from NHTSA's website and similar sources. It's not important that they apply directly to your problem; they establish parameters for giving out after-warranty assistance, or "goodwill."

Don't use your salesperson as a runner, since the sales staff are generally quite distant from the service staff and usually have less pull than you do. If the service manager can't or won't set things right, your next step is to convene a mini-summit with the service manager, the dealership principal, and the automaker's service rep, if he or she represents that make. Regional service representatives are technicians who are regularly sent out by the manufacturer to help dealers with technical problems. By getting the automaker involved, you can often get an agreement where the seller and the automaker pay two-thirds of the repair cost, even though the vehicle was bought used.

Get an independent estimate

Dealers who sell a brand of vehicle used that they don't sell new will give you less latitude. You have to make the case that the vehicle's defects were present at the time of purchase or should have been apparent to the seller, or that the vehicle doesn't conform to the representations made when it was purchased. Emphasize that you intend to use the courts if necessary to obtain a refund—most sellers would rather settle than risk a lawsuit with all the attendant publicity. An independent estimate of the vehicle's defects and repair costs is essential if you want to convince the seller that you're serious in your claim and that you stand a good chance of winning your case in court. Come prepared with an estimated cost of repairs to challenge the dealer who agrees to pay half the repair costs and then jacks up the price 100 percent so that you wind up paying the whole shot.

Step 2: Create a Paper Trail

If you haven't sent a written claim letter, fax, or email, you really haven't complained—or at least, that's the auto industry's mindset. If your vehicle was misrepresented, has major defects, or wasn't properly repaired under warranty, the first thing you should do is give the seller a written summary of the outstanding problems and stipulate a time period within which the seller can fix the vehicle or refund your money. Follow the format of the sample complaint letters on pages 74–75.

Remember, you can ask for compensation for repairs that have been done or need to be done, insurance costs while the vehicle is being repaired, towing charges, supplementary transportation costs such as taxis and rented cars, and damages for inconvenience. If no satisfactory offer is made, ask for mediation, arbitration, or a formal hearing in your provincial small claims court. Make the manufacturer a party to the lawsuit, especially if the emissions warranty, a secret warranty extension, a safety recall campaign, or extensive chassis rusting is involved.

Step 3: Mediation and Arbitration

If the formality of a courtroom puts you off, or you're not sure that your claim is all that solid and don't want to pay legal costs to find out, consider using mediation or arbitration. These services are sponsored by the Better Business Bureau, the Automobile Protection Association, the Canadian Automobile Association, and by many small claims courts where compulsory mediation is a prerequisite to going to trial.

Getting Outside Help

Don't lose your case because of poor preparation. Ask government or independent consumer protection agencies to evaluate how well you've prepared before going to your first hearing. Also, use the Internet to ferret out additional facts and gather support (*www.lemonaidcars.com* and its links are good places to start).

Pressure Tactics

You can put additional pressure on a seller or garage, and have fun at the same time, by putting a lemon sign on your car and parking it in front of the dealer or garage, by creating a "lemon" website, or by forming a self-help group. Angry Chrysler and Ford owners, for example, have received sizeable settlements in Canada by forming their own Chrysler Lemon Owners Group and Ford Lemon Owners Group.

Use your website or place a newspaper ad to gather data from others who may have experienced a problem similar to your own. This can help you set the foundation for a meeting with the automaker, or even for a class action lawsuit, and it pressures the dealer or manufacturer to settle. Websites are often the subject of news stories, so the media may pick up on yours.

Here's some more advice from this consumer advocate with hundreds of pickets and mass demonstrations under his belt: Keep a sense of humour, and never break off the negotiations.

Finally, don't be scared off by threats that it's illegal to criticize a product or company. Unions, environmentalists, and consumer groups do it regularly (it's called informational picketing), and the Supreme Court of Canada in *R. v. Guinard* reaffirmed this right in February 2002. In that judgment, an insured posted a sign on his barn claiming the Commerce Insurance Company was unfairly refusing his claim. The municipality of Saint-Hyacinthe, Quebec, told him to take the sign down. He refused, maintaining that he had the right to state his opinion. The Supreme Court agreed.

This judgment means that consumer protests, signs, and websites that criticize the actions of corporations or government cannot be shut up or taken down simply because they say unpleasant things. However, what you say must be true, and your intent must be to inform, without malice.

Even if you do respectfully protest your treatment following a used car purchase from a dealer, on rare occasions that dealer may file suit against you for defamation or libel. Generally, Canadian courts take a dim view of consumers and non-government organizations, like unions and environmental groups, being sued for protesting, or even picketing. Nevertheless, some dealers will sue, as you can see in the typical filing shown on the following page.

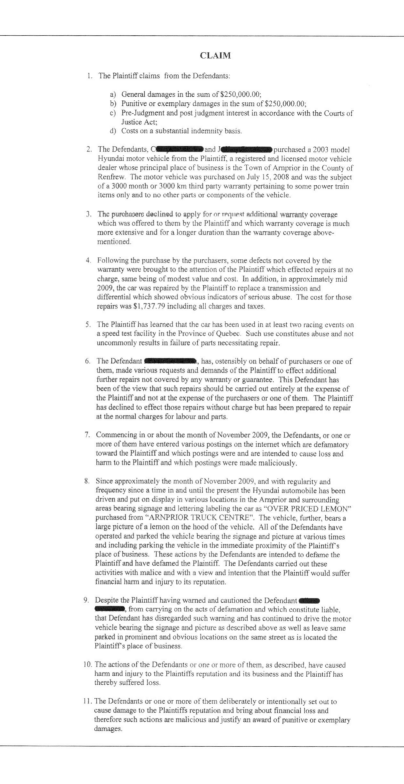

CLAIM

1. The Plaintiff claims from the Defendants:

    a) General damages in the sum of $250,000.00;
    b) Punitive or exemplary damages in the sum of $250,000.00;
    c) Pre-Judgment and post judgment interest in accordance with the Courts of Justice Act;
    d) Costs on a substantial indemnity basis.

2. The Defendants, C█████████████ and J█████████████ purchased a 2003 model Hyundai motor vehicle from the Plaintiff, a registered and licensed motor vehicle dealer whose principal place of business is the Town of Arnprior in the County of Renfrew. The motor vehicle was purchased on July 15, 2008 and was the subject of a 3000 month or 3000 km third party warranty pertaining to some power train items only and to no other parts or components of the vehicle.

3. The purchasers declined to apply for or request additional warranty coverage which was offered to them by the Plaintiff and which warranty coverage is much more extensive and for a longer duration than the warranty coverage above-mentioned.

4. Following the purchase by the purchasers, some defects not covered by the warranty were brought to the attention of the Plaintiff which effected repairs at no charge, same being of modest value and cost. In addition, in approximately mid 2009, the car was repaired by the Plaintiff to replace a transmission and differential which showed obvious indicators of serious abuse. The cost for those repairs was $1,737.79 including all charges and taxes.

5. The Plaintiff has learned that the car has been used in at least two racing events on a speed test facility in the Province of Quebec. Such use constitutes abuse and not uncommonly results in failure of parts necessitating repair.

6. The Defendant ███████████████, has, ostensibly on behalf of purchasers or one of them, made various requests and demands of the Plaintiff to effect additional further repairs not covered by any warranty or guarantee. This Defendant has been of the view that such repairs should be carried out entirely at the expense of the Plaintiff and not at the expense of the purchasers or one of them. The Plaintiff has declined to effect those repairs without charge but has been prepared to repair at the normal charges for labour and parts.

7. Commencing in or about the month of November 2009, the Defendants, or one or more of them have entered various postings on the internet which are defamatory toward the Plaintiff and which postings were and are intended to cause loss and harm to the Plaintiff and which postings were made maliciously.

8. Since approximately the month of November 2009, and with regularity and frequency since a time in and until the present the Hyundai automobile has been driven and put on display in various locations in the Arnprior and surrounding areas bearing signage and lettering labeling the car as "OVER PRICED LEMON" purchased from "ARNPRIOR TRUCK CENTRE". The vehicle, further, bears a large picture of a lemon on the hood of the vehicle. All of the Defendants have operated and parked the vehicle bearing the signage and picture at various times and including parking the vehicle in the immediate proximity of the Plaintiff's place of business. These actions by the Defendants are intended to defame the Plaintiff and have defamed the Plaintiff. The Defendants carried out these activities with malice and with a view and intention that the Plaintiff would suffer financial harm and injury to its reputation.

9. Despite the Plaintiff having warned and cautioned the Defendant █████ ███████, from carrying on the acts of defamation and which constitute liable, that Defendant has disregarded such warning and has continued to drive the motor vehicle bearing the signage and picture as described above as well as leave same parked in prominent and obvious locations on the same street as is located the Plaintiff's place of business.

10. The actions of the Defendants or one or more of them, as described, have caused harm and injury to the Plaintiffs reputation and its business and the Plaintiff has thereby suffered loss.

11. The Defendants or one or more of them deliberately or intentionally set out to cause damage to the Plaintiffs reputation and bring about financial loss and therefore such actions are malicious and justify an award of punitive or exemplary damages.

Fortunately, two other Supreme Court decisions buttress a citizen's right to engage in information protests or picketing. This assumes the protest is done without infringing upon the rights of others through actions such as assault, restricting access, defacing property, or harassing others.

The first decision overturned a lower court award of $1.5 million to a forestry executive who sued *The Toronto Star*. The *Star* alleged he had used political connections to get approval for a golf course expansion (*Grant v. Torstar Corp.*).

The Supreme Court struck down the judgment against the newspaper because that judgment had failed to give adequate weight to the value of freedom of expression. The court announced a new defense of "responsible communication on matters of public interest." In the court's opinion, anyone (journalists, bloggers, unions, picketers, etc.) can avoid liability if they can show that the information they communicated—whether true or false—was of public interest and they tried their best to verify it.

In another case, again involving a major Canadian newspaper, a former Ontario police officer sued *The Ottawa Citizen* after it reported he had misrepresented his search-and-rescue work at Ground Zero in New York City after the attacks of September 11, 2001. The Supreme Court reversed the $100,000 jury award because the judges felt the article was in the public interest (*Quan v. Cusson*).

Safety Failures

Incidents of sudden acceleration and chronic stalling are quite common. However, they are very difficult to diagnose, and individual cases can be treated very differently by federal safety agencies. Sudden acceleration is considered to be a safety-related problem—stalling isn't. Never mind that a vehicle's sudden loss of power on a busy highway (as happens with 2001–05 Toyota and Lexus models) puts everyone's lives at risk. The same problem exists with engine and transmission powertrain failures, which are only occasionally considered to be safety-related. ABS and airbag failures are universally considered to be life-threatening defects. If your vehicle manifests any of these conditions, here's what you need to do:

1. Get independent witnesses to confirm the problem exists. Confirmation includes verification by an independent mechanic, passenger testimony, downloaded data from your vehicle's data recorder, and lots of Internet browsing using *www.lemonaidcars.com* and a search engine like Google. Notify the dealer or manufacturer by fax, email, or registered letter that you consider the problem to be a factory-induced, safety-related defect. Make sure you address your correspondence to the manufacturer's product liability or legal affairs department. At the dealership's service bay, make sure that every work order clearly states the problem as well as the number of previous attempts to fix it. (You should end up with a few complaint letters and a handful of work orders confirming that this is an ongoing deficiency.) If the dealer won't give you a copy of the work order because the work is a warranty claim, ask for a

copy of the order number "in case your estate wishes to file a claim, pursuant to an accident." (This will get the service manager's attention.) Leaving a paper trail is crucial for any later claim, because it shows your concern and persistence and clearly indicates that the dealer and manufacturer had ample time to correct the defect.

2. Note on the work order that you expect the problem to be diagnosed and corrected under the emissions warranty or a "goodwill" program. It also wouldn't hurt to add the phrase on the work order or in your claim letters that "any deaths, injuries, or damage caused by the defect will be the dealer's and manufacturer's responsibility" since this work order (or letter, fax, or email) constitutes you putting them on formal notice.

3. If the dealer does the necessary repairs at little or no cost to you, send a follow-up confirmation saying that you appreciate the assistance. Also, emphasize that you'll be back if the problem reappears, even if the warranty has expired, because the repair renews your warranty rights applicable to that defect. In other words, the warranty clock is set back to its original position. You won't likely get a copy of the repair bill, because dealers don't like to admit that there was a serious defect present. Keep in mind, however, that you can get your complete vehicle file from the dealer and manufacturer by issuing a subpoena, which costs about $75 (refundable), if the case goes to small claims or a higher court. This request has produced many out-of-court settlements when the internal documents show extensive work was carried out to correct the problem.

4. If the problem persists, send a letter, fax, or email to the dealer and manufacturer saying so, look for ALLDATA service bulletins to confirm that your vehicle's defects are factory-related, and call Transport Canada or NHTSA, or log onto NHTSA's website, to report the failure. Also, contact the Center for Auto Safety in Washington, D.C. at 202-328-7700 or visit *www.autosafety.org* for a lawyer referral and an information sheet covering the problem. To find an expert Canadian lawyer familiar with auto defects and sales scams, contact the non-profit Automobile Protection Association (contact info available at *www.APA.ca*).

5. Now come two crucial questions: Should you repair the defect now or later, and should you use the dealer or an independent? Generally, it's smart to use an independent garage if you know the dealer isn't pushing for free corrective repairs from the manufacturer, if weeks or months have passed without any resolution of your claim, if the dealer keeps claiming that it's a maintenance item, or if you know an independent mechanic who will give you a detailed work order showing the defect is factory-related and not a result of poor maintenance. Don't mention that a court case may ensue, since this will scare the dickens out of your only independent witness. A bonus of using an independent garage is that the repair charges will be about half of what a dealer would demand. Incidentally, if the automaker later denies warranty "goodwill" because you used an independent repairer, use the argument that the defect's safety implications required emergency repairs to be carried out by whoever could see you first.

6. Take note of the manufacturer's own safety warnings. Dashboard-mounted warning lights usually come on prior to airbags suddenly deploying, ABS brakes failing, or engine glitches causing the vehicle to stall out. (Sudden acceleration, however, usually occurs without warning.) Automakers consider these lights to be critical safety warnings and generally advise drivers to immediately have the vehicle serviced to correct the problem (advice that can be found in the owner's manual) when any of the above lights come on. This bolsters the argument that your life was threatened, emergency repairs were required, and your request for another vehicle or a complete refund isn't out of line.

7. Use the balance of probabilities. Sudden acceleration can have multiple causes, is difficult to prove because it isn't easy to duplicate, and is often blamed on the driver mistaking the accelerator for the brakes or failing to perform proper maintenance. Yet NHTSA data shows that factory-related defects are often the culprit. For example, 1997–2004 Lexus ES 300/330s and Toyota Camrys may have a faulty transmission that may cause engine surging. So how do you satisfy the burden of proof showing that the problem exists and is the automaker's responsibility? Use the legal doctrine called "the balance of probabilities" (refer to page 61) by eliminating all of the possible dodges the dealer or manufacturer may employ. Show that proper maintenance has been carried out, that you're a safe driver, and that the incident occurs frequently and without warning.

8. If any of the above defects causes an accident, the airbag fails to deploy, or you're injured by its deployment, ask your insurance company to have the vehicle towed to a neutral location and clearly state that neither the dealer nor the automaker should touch the vehicle until your insurance company and Transport Canada have completed their investigation. Also, get as many witnesses as possible and immediately go to the hospital for a check-up, even if you're feeling okay. You may be injured and not know it because the adrenalin coursing through your veins is masking your injuries. A hospital exam will easily confirm that your injuries are related to the accident, which is essential in court or for future settlement negotiations.

9. Peruse NHTSA's online accident database to find reports of other accidents caused by the same failure.

10. Don't let your insurance company settle the case if you're sure the accident was caused by a mechanical failure. Even if an engineering analysis fails to directly implicate the manufacturer or dealer, you can always plead the aforementioned balance of probabilities. If the insurance company settles, your insurance premiums will probably increase.

Paint and Body Defects

The following tips on making a successful claim apply mainly to paint defects, water and air leaks, and subpar fit and finish, but you can use the same strategy for any other vehicle defect that you believe is the automaker's or dealer's responsibility. If you're not sure whether the problem is a factory-related deficiency or a maintenance item, have it checked out by an independent garage or get a TSB summary for your vehicle. The summary may include specific bulletins relating to the diagnosis, correction, and ordering of upgraded parts needed to fix your problem.

1. If you know that your vehicle's paint problem is factory-related, take your vehicle to the dealer and ask for a written, signed estimate. When you're handed the estimate, ask if the paint job can be covered by some "goodwill" assistance. (Ford's euphemism for this secret warranty is "Owner Notification Program" or "Owner Dialogue Program"; GM's term is "Special Policy"; and Chrysler simply calls it an "Owner Satisfaction Notice." Don't use the term "secret warranty" yet. You'll just make everyone angry and evasive.)

2. Your request will probably be met with a refusal, an offer to repaint the vehicle for half the cost, or (if you're lucky) an agreement to repaint the vehicle free of charge. If you accept the half-cost offer, make sure that it's based on the original estimate you have in hand, since some dealers jack up their estimates so that your 50 percent is really 100 percent of the true cost.

3. If the dealer or automaker has already refused your claim and the repair hasn't been done yet, get an additional estimate from an independent garage that shows the problem is factory-related.

4. If the repair has yet to be done, mail or fax a registered claim to the automaker (and send a copy to the dealer) claiming the average of both estimates. If the repair has been done at your expense, mail or fax a registered claim with a copy of your bill.

5. If you don't receive a satisfactory response within a week, deposit a copy of the estimate or paid bill and claim letter/fax before the small claims court and await a trial date. This means that the automaker/dealer will have to appear, no lawyer is required, and costs should be minimal (under $100). Usually, an informal pretrial mediation hearing with the two parties and a court clerk will be scheduled within a few months, followed by a trial a few weeks later (the time varies depending on region). Most cases are settled at the mediation stage. You can help your case by collecting photographs, maintenance work orders, previous work orders dealing with your problem, and TSBs and by speaking to an independent expert (the garage or body shop that did the estimate or repair is best, but you can also use a local teacher who teaches automotive repair). Remember, service bulletins can be helpful, but they aren't critical to a successful claim.

Other situations

- If the vehicle has just been repainted or repaired but the dealer says that "goodwill" coverage was denied by the automaker, pay for the repair with a certified cheque and write "under protest" on the cheque. Remember, though, if the dealer does the repair, you won't have an independent expert who can affirm that the problem was factory-related or that it was a result of premature wearout. Plus, the dealer can say that you or the environment caused the paint problem. In these cases, TSBs can make or break your case.

- If the dealer or automaker offers a partial repair or refund, take it. Then sue for the rest. Remember, if a partial repair has been done under warranty, it counts as an admission of responsibility, no matter what "goodwill" euphemism is used. Also, the repaired component or body panel should be just as durable as if it were new. Hence the clock starts ticking from the time of the repair until you reach the original warranty parameter—no matter what the dealer's repair warranty limit says.

Very seldom do automakers contest these paint claims before small claims court, instead opting to settle once the court claim is bounced from their customer relations people to their legal affairs department. At that time, you'll probably be offered an out-of-court settlement for 50–75 percent of your claim.

Stand fast, and make reference to the service bulletins you intend to subpoena in order to publicly contest in court the unfair nature of this "secret warranty" program (automakers' lawyers cringe at the idea of trying to explain why consumers aren't made aware of these bulletins)—100 percent restitution will probably follow.

Four favourable paint judgments

Dunlop v. Ford of Canada (No. 58475/04; Ontario Superior Court of Justice, Richmond Hill Small Claims Court; January 5, 2005; Deputy Judge M.J. Winer). The owner of a 1996 Lincoln Town Car purchased used in 1999 for $27,000 was awarded $4,091.64. Judge Winer cited the *Shields* decision (following) and gave these reasons for finding Ford of Canada liable:

> Evidence was given by the Plaintiff's witness, Terry Bonar, an experienced paint auto technician. He gave evidence that the [paint] delamination may be both a manufacturing defect and can be caused or speeded up by atmospheric conditions. He also says that [the paint on] a car like this should last ten to 15 years, [or even for] the life of the vehicle....
>
> It is my view that the presence of ultraviolet light is an environmental condition to which the vehicle is subject. If it cannot withstand this environmental condition, it is defective in my view.

Shields v. General Motors of Canada (No. 1398/96; Ontario Court, General Division; Oshawa Small Claims Court; July 24, 1997; Deputy Judge Robert Zochodne). The owner of a 1991 Pontiac Grand Prix purchased the vehicle used with over 100,000 km on its odometer. Beginning in 1995, the paint began to bubble and flake and eventually peeled off. Deputy Judge Robert Zochodne awarded the plaintiff $1,205.72 and struck down every one of GM's environmental/acid rain/ UV rays arguments. Here are the other important aspects of this 12-page judgment that GM did not appeal:

1. The judge admitted many of the TSBs referred to in *Lemon-Aid* as proof of GM's negligence.
2. Although the vehicle already had 156,000 km on it when the case went to court, GM still offered to pay for 50 percent of the paint repairs if the plaintiff dropped his suit.
3. The judge ruled that the failure to protect the paint from the damaging effects of UV rays is akin to engineering a car that won't start in cold weather. In essence, vehicles must be built to withstand the rigours of the environment.
4. Here's an interesting twist: The original warranty covered defects that were present at the time it was in effect. The judge, taking statements found in the GM technical service bulletins, ruled that the UV problem was factory-related, existed during the warranty period, and represented a latent defect that appeared once the warranty expired.
5. The subsequent purchaser was not prevented from making the warranty claim, even though the warranty had long since expired from a time and mileage standpoint and he was the second owner.

Bentley v. Dave Wheaton Pontiac Buick GMC Ltd. and General Motors of Canada (Victoria Registry No. 24779; British Columbia Small Claims Court; December 1, 1998; Judge Higinbotham). This small claims judgment builds on the Ontario *Shields v. General Motors of Canada* decision and cites other jurisprudence as to how long paint should last on a car. If you're wondering why Ford and Chrysler haven't been hit by similar judgments, remember that they usually settle out of court.

Maureen Frank v. General Motors of Canada Limited (No. SC#12 (2001); Saskatchewan Provincial Court; October 17, 2001; Provincial Court Judge H.G. Dirauf). I discuss this case on page 83.

Other paint and rust cases

Whittaker v. Ford Motor Company (1979) (24 O.R. (2d), 344). A new Ford developed serious corrosion problems in spite of having been rustproofed by the dealer. The court ruled that the dealer, not Ford, was liable for the damage for having sold the rustproofing product at the time of purchase. This is an important judgment to use when a rustproofer or paint protector goes out of business or refuses to pay a claim, since the decision holds the dealer jointly responsible.

Martin v. Honda Canada Inc. (March 17, 1986; Ontario Small Claims Court, Scarborough; Judge Sigurdson). The original owner of a 1981 Honda Civic sought compensation for the premature "bubbling, pitting, [and] cracking of the paint and rusting of the Civic after five years of ownership." Judge Sigurdson agreed with the owner and ordered Honda to pay $1,163.95.

Thauberger v. Simon Fraser Sales and Mazda Motors (3 B.C.L.R., 193). This Mazda owner sued for damages caused by the premature rusting of his 1977 Mazda GLC. The court awarded him $1,000. Thauberger had previously sued General Motors for a prematurely rusted Blazer truck and was also awarded $1,000 in the same court. Both judges ruled that the defects could not be excluded from the automaker's expressed warranty or from the implied warranty granted by British Columbia's *Sale of Goods Act.*

See also:

- *Danson v. Chateau Ford (1976) C.P.* (Quebec Small Claims Court; No. 32-00001898-757; Judge Lande)
- *Doyle v. Vital Automotive Systems* (May 16, 1977; Ontario Small Claims Court, Toronto; Judge Turner)
- *Lacroix v. Ford* (April 1980; Ontario Small Claims Court, Toronto; Judge Tierney)
- *Marinovich v. Riverside Chrysler* (April 1, 1987; District Court of Ontario; No. 1030/85; Judge Stortini)

Using the Courts

Nova Scotia's Used-Car "Lemon Law"

By the summer of 2011, Nova Scotia will be the first Canadian province to require that used-car dealers identify rebuilt or previously damaged vehicles by placing labels on their windshields. Acting on consumer complaints, the provincial government introduced changes to the *Motor Vehicle Act* last November to ensure consumers know a used vehicle's history before they buy it.

Under the new law, dealers must clearly label vehicles that have been deemed unrepairable, are manufacturers' buybacks, or have been involved in a serious collision in Canada or the United States. Sellers who do not comply with the new legislation will be fined up to $1,000 per vehicle.

Unfortunately, the fines are ridiculously low and the new rules will not apply to private auto sales or trade-ins.

Sue as a Last Resort

If the seller you've been negotiating with agrees to make things right, give him or her a deadline and then have an independent garage check the repairs. If no offer is made within 10 working days, file suit in court. Make the manufacturer a party to the lawsuit only if the original, unexpired warranty was transferred to you; if your claim falls under the emissions warranty, a TSB, a secret warranty extension, or a safety recall campaign; or if there is extensive chassis rusting due to poor engineering.

Choosing the Right Court

You must decide what remedy to pursue: a partial refund or a cancellation of the sale. To determine the refund amount, add the estimated cost of repairing existing mechanical defects to the cost of prior repairs. Don't exaggerate your losses or claim for repairs that are considered routine maintenance. A suit for cancellation of sale involves practical problems. The court requires that the vehicle be "tendered," or taken back to the seller, at the time the lawsuit is filed. This means that you are without transportation for as long as the case continues, unless you purchase another vehicle in the interim. If you lose the case, you must then take back the old vehicle and pay storage fees. You could go from having no vehicle to having two, one of which is a clunker.

Generally, if the cost of repairs or the sales contract amount falls within the small claims court limit, file the case there to keep costs to a minimum and to get a speedy hearing. Small claims court judgments aren't easily appealed, lawyers aren't necessary, filing fees are minimal (about $125), and cases are usually heard within a few months.

Watch what you ask for. If you claim more than the small claims court limit, you'll have to go to a higher court—where costs quickly add up and delays of a few years or more are commonplace.

Small Claims Courts

Crooked automakers scurry away from small claims courts like cockroaches from bug spray, not because the courts can issue million-dollar judgments or force litigants to spend millions in legal fees (they can't), but because they can award sizeable sums to plaintiffs and make jurisprudence that other judges on the same bench are likely to follow.

For example, in *Dawe v. Courtesy Chrysler* (Dartmouth Nova Scotia Small Claims Court; SCCH #206825; July 30, 2004), Judge Patrick L Casey, Q.C., rendered an impressive 21-page decision citing key automobile product liability cases over the past 80 years. He awarded $5,037 to the owner of a new 2001 Cummins-equipped Ram pickup that suffered from myriad ailments. The truck shifted erratically, lost braking ability, wandered all over the road, lost power or jerked and bucked, bottomed out when passing over bumps, allowed water to leak into the cab, produced a burnt-wire and oil smell as the lights would dim, and produced a rear-end whine and wind noise around the doors and under the dash. Dawe had sold the vehicle and reduced his claim to meet the small claims threshold.

There are small claims courts in most counties of every province, and you can make a claim either in the county where the problem happened or in the county where the defendant lives and conducts business. Simply go to the small claims court office and ask for a claim form. Instructions on how to fill it out accompany the form. Remember, you must identify the defendant correctly, and this may require some help from the court clerk or a law student because some automakers name local attorneys to handle suits (look for other recent lawsuits naming the same party). Crooks often change their company's name to escape liability; for example, it would be impossible to sue Joe's Garage (2008) if your contract is with Joe's Garage Inc. (2004).

At this point, it wouldn't hurt to hire a lawyer or a paralegal for a brief walk-through of small claims procedures to ensure that you've prepared your case properly and that you know what objections the other side will likely raise. If you'd like a lawyer to do all the work for you, there are a number of law firms around the country that specialize in small claims litigation. "Small claims" doesn't mean small legal fees, however. In Toronto, some law offices charge a flat fee of $1,000 for a basic small claims lawsuit and trial.

Remember that you're entitled to bring to court any evidence relevant to your case, including written documents such as a bill of sale, receipt, contract, or letter. If your car has developed severe rust problems, bring a photograph (signed and dated by the photographer) to court. You may also have witnesses testify, but it's important to discuss witness testimony prior to the court date. If a witness can't attend the court date, he or she can write a report and sign it for representation in court. This situation usually applies to an expert witness, such as an independent mechanic who has evaluated your car's problems.

If you lose your case in spite of all your preparation and research, some small claims court statutes allow cases to be retried, at a nominal cost, in exceptional circumstances. If a new witness has come forward, additional evidence has been discovered, or key documents that were previously not available have become accessible, apply for a retrial. In Ontario, this little-known provision is Rule 18.4 (1).B.

Alan MacDonald, a *Lemon-Aid* reader who won his case in small claims court, gives the following tips on beating Ford (*MacDonald v. Highbury Ford Sales Limited*, Ontario Superior Court of Justice in the Small Claims Court London, June 6, 2000, Court File #0001/00, Judge J. D. Searle):

> In 1999 after only 105,000 km the automatic transmission went. I took [my 1994 Ford Taurus wagon] to Highbury Ford to have it repaired. We paid $2,070 to have the transmission fixed, but protested and felt the transmission failed prematurely. We contacted Ford, but to no avail: their reply was we were out of warranty period. The transmission was so poorly repaired (and we went back to Highbury Ford several times) that we had to go to Mr. Transmission to have the transmission fixed again nine months later at a further $1,906.02....

> My observations with going through small claims court involved the following: I filed in January of 2000, the trial took place on June 1 and the judgment was issued June 6.

> At pretrial, a representative of Ford (Ann Sroda) and a representative from Highbury Ford were present. I came with one binder for each of the defendants, the court, and one for myself (each binder was about 3 inches thick–containing your reports on Ford Taurus automatic transmissions, ALLDATA Service Bulletins, [and extracts from the following websites:] Taurus Transmissions Victims (Bradley website), Center for Auto Safety...Read This Before Buying a Taurus...and the Ford Vent Page....

The representative from Ford asked a lot of questions (I think she was trying to find out if I had read the contents of the information I was relying on). The Ford representative then offered a 50 percent settlement based on the initial transmission work done at Highbury Ford. The release allowed me to still sue Highbury Ford with regards to the necessity of going to Mr. Transmission because of the faulty repair done by the dealer. Highbury Ford displayed no interest in settling the case, and so I had to go to court.

For court, I prepared by issuing a summons to the manager at Mr. Transmission, who did the second transmission repair, as an expert witness…. Next, I went to the law school library in London and received a great deal of assistance in researching cases pertinent to car repairs. I was told that judgments in your home province (in my case, Ontario) were binding on the court; that cases outside of the home province could be considered, but not binding, on the Judge.

The cases I used for trial involved *Pelleray v. Heritage Ford Sales Ltd.*, Ontario Small Claims Court (Scarborough) SC7688/91 March 22, 1993; *Phillips et al. v. Ford Motor Co. of Canada Ltd. et al*, Ontario Reports 1970, 15th January 1970; *Gregorio v. Intrans-Corp.*, Ontario Court of Appeal, May 19, 1994; *Collier v. MacMaster's Auto Sales*, New Brunswick Court of Queen's Bench, April 26, 1991; *Sigurdson v. Hillcrest Service & Acklands (1977)*, Saskatchewan Queen's Bench; *White v. Sweetland*, Newfoundland District Court, Judicial Centre of Gander, November 8, 1978; *Raiches Steel Works v. J. Clark & Son*, New Brunswick Supreme Court, March 7, 1977; *Mudge v. Corner Brook Garage Ltd.*, Newfoundland Supreme Court, July 17, 1975; *Sylvain v. Carroseries d'Automobiles Guy Inc. (1981)*, C.P. 333, Judge Page; and *Gagnon v. Ford Motor Company of Canada, Limited et Marineau Automobile Co. Ltée. (1974)*, C.S. 422–423.

In court, I had prepared the case, as indicated above, and had my expert witness and two other witnesses who had driven the vehicle (my wife and my 18-year-old son). As you can see by the judgment, we won our case and I was awarded $1,756.52, including prejudgment interest and costs.

Key Court Decisions

The following Canadian and U.S. lawsuits and judgments cover typical problems that are likely to arise. Use them as leverage when negotiating a settlement or as a reference should your claim go to trial. Legal principles applying to Canadian and American law are similar; Quebec court decisions, however, may be based on legal principles that don't apply outside of that province. Nevertheless, you can find a comprehensive listing of Canadian decisions from small claims courts all the way to the Supreme Court of Canada at *www.legalresearch.org* or *www.canlii.org*.

You can find additional court judgments in the legal reference section of your city's main public library or at a nearby university law library. Ask the librarian for help in choosing the legal phrases that best describe your claim. LexisNexis (*www.lexisnexis.com*) and FindLaw (*www.findlaw.com*) are two useful Internet sites for legal research. Their main drawback, though, is that you may need to subscribe or use a lawyer's subscription to access jurisprudence and other areas of the sites.

Some of the small claims court cases cited in *Lemon-Aid* may not be reported. If that happens, contact the office of the presiding judge named in the decision and ask his or her assistant to send you a copy of the judgment. If the judge or assistant isn't available, ask for the court clerk of that jurisdiction to search for the case file and date referenced in *Lemon-Aid*.

An excellent reference book that will give you plenty of tips on filing, pleading, and collecting your judgment is Judge Marvin Zuker's *Ontario Small Claims Court Practice 2011, 30th Anniversary Edition* (Carswell, 2010). Judge Zuker's book is easily understood by non-lawyers and uses court decisions from across Canada to help you plead your case successfully in almost any Canadian court. It costs $91 (CDN) and can be ordered from *www.fedpubs.com/subject/law/sm_claims.htm*.

Product Liability

Almost three decades ago, in *Kravitz v. GM* (the first case where I was called as a pro bono expert witness), the Supreme Court of Canada clearly affirmed that automakers and their dealers are jointly liable for the replacement or repair of a vehicle if independent testimony shows that it is afflicted with factory-related defects that compromise its safety or performance. The existence of a secret warranty extension or TSB also helps prove that the vehicle's problems are the automaker's responsibility. For example, in *Lowe v. Fairview Chrysler* (see page 113), technical service bulletins were instrumental in showing an Ontario small claims court judge that Chrysler's history of automatic transmission failures went back to 1989.

In addition to replacing or repairing the vehicle, an automaker can also be held responsible for any damages arising from the defect. This means that loss of wages, supplementary transportation costs, and damages for personal inconvenience can be awarded. In the States, product liability damage awards often exceed millions of dollars. Canadian courts, however, are far less generous.

Implied Warranty Rulings

Reasonable durability

As outlined near the beginning of the chapter, this is that powerful "other" warranty that they never tell you about. It applies during and after the expiration of the manufacturer's or dealer's expressed or written warranty and requires that a part or repair will last a reasonable period of time. What is reasonable depends in a large part on benchmarks used in the industry, the price of the vehicle, and how it was driven and maintained. Look at the "Reasonable Part Durability" table on page 66 for some guidelines as to what you should expect. Judges usually apply the implied or legal warranty when the manufacturer's expressed warranty has expired and the vehicle's manufacturing defects remain uncorrected.

Chevrier v. General Motors du Canada (October 18, 2006; Quebec Small Claims Court, Joliette District (Repentigny) No. 730-32-004876-046; Justice Georges Massol). You can find the full judgment (French) at *www.canlii.org*.

The plaintiff leased and then bought a 2000 Montana minivan. At 71,000 km the automatic transmission failed and two GM dealers estimated the repairs to be between $2,200 and $2,500. They refused warranty coverage because the warranty had expired after the third year of ownership or 60,000 km of use. The owner repaired the transmission at an independent garage for $1,869 and kept the old parts, which GM refused to examine.

A small claims court lawsuit was filed, and Judge Massol gave the following reasons for ruling against GM's two arguments that (1) there was no warning that a claim would be filed, and (2) all warranties had expired:

- GM filed a voluminous record of jurisprudence in its favour, relative to other lawsuits that were rejected because they were filed without prior notice. But the judge reasoned that GM could not plead a "failure to notify," because the owner went to several dealers who were essentially agents of the manufacturer.
- The judge also reasoned that the expiration of GM's written warranty does not nullify the legal warranty set out in articles 38 and 39 of the *Consumer Protection Act*. The legal warranty requires that all products be "reasonably durable," which did not appear to be the case with the plaintiff's vehicle, given its low mileage and number of years of use.

GM was ordered to pay the entire repair costs, plus interest, and the $90 filing fee.

Dufour v. Ford Canada Ltd. (April 10, 2001; Quebec Small Claims Court, Hull; No. 550-32-008335-009; Justice P. Chevalier). Ford was forced to reimburse the cost of engine head gasket repairs carried out on a 1996 Windstar 3.8L engine—a vehicle not covered by the automaker's Owner Notification Program, which cut off assistance after the '95 model year.

Schaffler v. Ford Motor Company Limited and Embrun Ford Sales Ltd. (Ontario Superior Court of Justice; L'Orignal Small Claims Court; Court File No. 59-2003; July 22, 2003; Justice Gerald Langlois). The plaintiff bought a used 1995 Windstar in 1998. Its engine head gasket was repaired for free three years later, under Ford's seven-year extended warranty. In 2002, at 109,600 km, the head gasket failed again, seriously damaging the engine. Ford refused a second repair. Justice Langlois ruled that Ford's warranty extension bulletin listed signs and symptoms of the covered defect that were identical to the problems written on the second work order ("persistent and/or chronic engine overheating; heavy white smoke evident from the exhaust tailpipe; flashing 'low coolant' instrument panel light even after coolant refill; and constant loss of engine coolant"). Judge Langlois concluded that "the problem was brought to the attention of the dealer well within the warranty period; the dealer was negligent." The plaintiff was awarded $4,941 plus 5 percent interest. This judgment included $1,070 for two months' car rental.

John R. Reid and Laurie M. McCall v. Ford Motor Company of Canada (Superior Court of Justice; Ottawa Small Claims Court; Claim No: #02-SC-077344; July 11, 2003; Justice Tiernay). A 1996 Windstar, bought used in 1997, experienced engine head gasket failure in October 2001 at 159,000 km. Judge Tiernay awarded the plaintiffs $4,145 for the following reason:

> A Technical Service Bulletin dated June 28, 1999, was circulated to Ford dealers. It dealt specifically with "undetermined loss of coolant" and "engine oil contaminated with coolant" in the 1996–98 Windstar and five other models of Ford vehicles. I conclude that Ford owed a duty of care to the Plaintiff to equip this vehicle with a cylinder head gasket of sufficient sturdiness and durability that would function trouble-free for at least seven years, given normal driving and proper maintenance conditions. I find that Ford is answerable in damages for the consequences of its negligence.

Dawe v. Courtesy Chrysler (Dartmouth Nova Scotia Small Claims Court; SCCH #206825; July 30, 2004; Judge Patrick L Casey, Q.C.). "Small claims" doesn't necessarily mean small judgments. This 21-page, unreported Nova Scotia small claims court decision is impressive in its clarity and thoroughness. It applies *Donoghue, Kravitz, Davis, et al.* in awarding a 2001 Dodge Ram owner over $5,000 in damages. Anyone with engine, transmission, and suspension problems or water leaking into the interior will find this judgment particularly useful.

Fissel v. Ideal Auto Sales Ltd. (1991) (91 Sask. R. 266). Shortly after the vehicle was purchased, its motor seized and the dealer refused to replace it, even though the car was returned on several occasions. The court ruled that the dealer had breached the statutory warranties in sections 11 (4) and (7) of the *Consumer Products Warranties Act*. The purchasers were entitled to cancel the sale and recover the full purchase price.

Friskin v. Chevrolet Oldsmobile (72 D.L.R. (3d), 289). A Manitoba used-car buyer asked that his contract be cancelled because of his car's chronic stalling problem. The garage owner did his best to correct it. Despite the seller's good intentions, the *Manitoba Consumer Protection Act* allowed for cancellation.

Graves v. C&R Motors Ltd. (April 8, 1980; British Columbia County Court; Judge Skipp). The plaintiff bought a used car on the condition that certain deficiencies be remedied. They never were, and he was promised a refund, but it never arrived. The plaintiff brought suit, claiming that the dealer's deceptive activities violated the provincial *Trade Practices Act*. The court agreed, concluding that a deceptive act that occurs before, during, or after the transaction can lead to the cancellation of the contract.

Hachey v. Galbraith Equipment Company (1991) (33 M.V.R. (2d) 242). The plaintiff bought a used truck from the dealer to haul gravel. Shortly thereafter, the steering failed. The plaintiff's suit was successful because expert testimony showed that the truck wasn't roadworthy. The dealer was found liable for damages for being in breach of the implied condition of fitness for the purpose for which the truck was purchased, as set out in section 15(a) of the New Brunswick *Sale of Goods Act*.

Henzel v. Brussels Motors (1973) (1 O.R., 339 (C.C.)). The dealer sold a used car, brandishing a copy of the mechanical fitness certificate as proof that the car was in good shape. The plaintiff was awarded his money back because the court held the certificate to be a warranty that was breached by the car's subsequent defects.

Johnston v. Bodasing Corporation Limited (February 23, 1983; Ontario County Court, Bruce; No. 15/11/83; Judge McKay). The plaintiff bought a used 1979 Buick Riviera that was represented as being "reliable" for $8,500. Two weeks after purchase, the motor self-destructed. Judge McKay awarded the plaintiff $2,318 as compensation to fix the Riviera's defects. One feature of this particular decision is that the trial judge found that the *Sale of Goods Act* applied, notwithstanding the fact that the vendor used a standard contract that said there were no warranties or representations. The judge also accepted the decision in *Kendall v. Lillico* (1969) (2 Appeal Cases 31), which indicates that the *Sale of Goods Act* covers not only defects that the seller ought to have detected but also latent defects that even his or her utmost skill and judgment could not have detected. This places a very heavy onus on the vendor, and it should prove useful in actions of this type in other common-law provinces with laws similar to Ontario's *Sale of Goods Act*.

General Motors Products of Canada Ltd. v. Kravitz, (1979) (1 S.C.R. 790). The court said the seller's warranty of quality was an accessory to the property and was transferred with it on successive sales. Accordingly, subsequent buyers could invoke the contractual warranty of quality against the manufacturer, even though they did not contract directly with it. This precedent was then codified in articles 1434, 1442, and 1730 of Quebec's *Civil Code*.

Morrison v. Hillside Motors (1973) Ltd. (1981; 35 Nfld. & P.E.I.R. 361). A used car advertised to be in "A1" condition and carrying a 50/50 warranty developed a number of problems. The court decided that the purchaser should be partially compensated because of the ad's claim. In deciding how much compensation to award, the presiding judge considered the warranty's wording, the amount paid for the vehicle, the model year of the vehicle, the vehicle's average life, the type of defect that occurred, and the length of time the purchaser had use of the vehicle before its defects became evident. Although this judgment was rendered in Newfoundland, judges throughout Canada have used a similar approach for more than a decade.

Neilson v. Maclin Motors (71 D.L.R. (3d), 744). The plaintiff bought a used truck on the strength of the seller's allegations that the motor had been rebuilt and that it had 210 hp. The engine failed. The judge awarded damages and cancelled the contract because the transmission was defective and the motor had not been rebuilt and did not have 210 hp.

Parent v. Le Grand Trianon and Ford Credit (1982) (C.P., 194; Judge Bertrand Gagnon). Nineteen months after paying $3,300 for a used 1974 LTD, the plaintiff sued the Ford dealer for his money back because the car was prematurely rusted out. The dealer replied that rust was normal, there was no warranty, and the claim was too late. The court held that the garage was still responsible. The plaintiff was awarded $1,500 for the cost of rust repairs.

Narbonne v. Glendale Recreational Véhicules (Quebec Small Claims Court; June 2, 2008; Reference: 2008 QCCQ 5325; Judge Richard Landry). Three years after the plaintiff purchased a travel trailer, the manufacturer sent a recall notice to the wrong address. Seven years after that, the vehicle broke down when the recalled part failed. The manufacturer said it had done its part in sending out the recall notice. The judge disagreed, and found the company responsible for the full cost of the repairs, lodging, and $500 for general inconvenience, for a total of $5,792.

"As is" clauses

Since 1907, Canadian courts have ruled that a seller can't exclude the implied warranty as to fitness by including such phrases as "there are no other warranties or guarantees, promises, or agreements than those contained herein." See *Sawyer-Massey Co. v. Thibault* (1907; 5 W.L.R. 241).

Adams v. J&D's Used Cars Ltd. (1983) (26 Sask. R. 40 Q.B.). Shortly after the plaintiff purchased a car, its engine and transmission failed. The court ruled that the inclusion of "as is" in the sales contract had no legal effect. The dealer breached the implied warranty set out in Saskatchewan's *Consumer Products Warranties Act.* The sale was cancelled, and all monies were refunded.

Leasing

Ford Motor Credit v. Bothwell (December 3, 1979; Ontario County Court, Middlesex; No. 9226-T; Judge Macnab). The defendant leased a 1977 Ford truck that had frequent engine problems, characterized by stalling and hard starting. After complaining for one year and driving 35,000 km, the defendant cancelled the lease. Ford Credit sued for the money owing on the lease. Judge Macnab cancelled the lease and ordered Ford Credit to repay 70 percent of the amount paid during the leasing period. Ford Credit was also ordered to refund repair costs, even though the corporation claimed that it should not be held responsible for Ford's failure to honour its warranty.

Salvador v. Setay Motors/Queenstown Chev-Olds (Hamilton Small Claims Court; Case No.1621/95). The plaintiff was awarded $2,000, plus costs, from Queenstown Leasing. The court found that the company should have tried harder to sell the leased vehicle, and at a higher price, when the "open lease" expired.

Schryvers v. Richport Ford Sales (May 18, 1993; B.C.S.C.; No. C917060; Justice Tysoe). The court awarded $17,578.47, plus costs, to a couple who paid thousands of dollars more in unfair and hidden leasing charges than if they had simply purchased their Ford Explorer and Escort. The court found that this price difference constituted a deceptive, unconscionable act or practice, in contravention of the *Trade Practices Act*, R.S.B.C. 1979, c. 406.

Judge Tysoe concluded that the total general damages awarded to the Schryvers for both vehicles would be $11,578.47. He then proceeded to give the following reasons for awarding an additional $6,000 in punitive damages:

> Little wonder Richport Ford had a contest for the salesperson who could persuade the most customers to acquire their vehicles by way of a lease transaction. I consider the actions of Richport Ford to be sufficiently flagrant and high handed to warrant an award of punitive damages.
>
> There must be a disincentive to suppliers in respect of intentionally deceptive trade practices. If no punitive damages are awarded for intentional violations of the legislation, suppliers will continue to conduct their businesses in a manner that involves deceptive trade practices because they will have nothing to lose. In this case I believe that the appropriate amount of punitive damages is the extra profit Richport Ford endeavoured to make as a result of its deceptive acts. I therefore award punitive damages against Richport Ford in the amount of $6,000.

See also:

- *Barber v. Inland Truck Sales* (11 D.L.R. (3rd), No. 469)
- *Canadian-Dominion Leasing v. Suburban Super Drug Ltd. (1966)* (56 D.L.R. (2nd), No. 43)
- *Neilson v. Atlantic Rentals Ltd. (1974)* (8 N.B.R. (2d), No. 594)
- *Volvo Canada v. Fox* (December 13, 1979; New Brunswick Court of Queen's Bench; No. 1698/77/C; Judge Stevenson)
- *Western Tractor v. Dyck* (7 D.L.R. (3rd), No. 535)

Repairs: Faulty Diagnosis

Davies v. Alberta Motor Association (August 13, 1991; Alberta Provincial Court; Civil Division; No. P9090106097; Judge Moore). The plaintiff had the AMA's Vehicle Inspection Service check out a used 1985 Nissan Pulsar NX prior to buying it. The car passed with flying colours. A month later, the clutch was replaced and numerous electrical problems ensued. At that time, another garage discovered that the car had been involved in a major accident, had a bent frame and a leaking radiator, and was unsafe to drive. The court awarded the plaintiff $1,578.40 plus three years' interest. The judge held that the AMA set itself out as an expert and should have spotted the car's defects. The AMA's defence—that it was not responsible for errors—was thrown out. The court held that a disclaimer clause could not protect the association from a fundamental breach of contract.

Secret Warranty Rulings

It's common practice for manufacturers to secretly extend their warranties to cover components with a high failure rate. Customers who complain vigorously get extended warranty compensation in the form of "goodwill" adjustments.

François Chong v. Marine Drive Imported Cars Ltd. and Honda Canada Inc. (May 17, 1994; British Columbia Provincial Small Claims Court; No. 92-06760; Judge C.L. Bagnall). The plaintiff was the first owner of a 1983 Honda Accord with 134,000 km on the odometer. He had six engine camshafts replaced—four under Honda "goodwill" programs, one where he paid part of the repairs, and one via this small claims court judgment.

In his ruling, Judge Bagnall agreed with Chong and ordered Honda and the dealer to each pay half of the $835.81 repair bill for the following reasons:

> The defendants assert that the warranty, which was part of the contract for purchase of the car, encompassed the entirety of their obligation to the claimant, and that it expired in February 1985. The replacements of the camshaft after that date were paid for wholly or in part by Honda as a "goodwill gesture." The time has come for these gestures to cease, according to the witness for Honda. As well, he pointed out to me that the most recent replacement of the camshaft was paid for by Honda and that, therefore, the work would not be covered by Honda's usual warranty of 12 months from date of repair. Mr. Wall, who testified for Honda, told me there was no question that this situation with Mr. Chong's engine was an unusual state of affairs. He said that a camshaft properly maintained can last anywhere from 24,000 to 500,000 km. He could not offer any suggestion as to why the car keeps having this problem.

> The claimant has convinced me that the problems he is having with rapid breakdown of camshafts in his car is due to a defect, which was present in the engine at the time that he purchased the car. The problem first arose during the warranty period and in my view has never been properly identified nor repaired.

Automatic Transmission Failures (Chrysler)

Lowe v. Fairview Chrysler-Dodge Limited and Chrysler Canada Limited (May 14, 1996; Ontario Court, General Division; Burlington Small Claims Court; No. 1224/95). This judgment, in the plaintiff's favour, raises important legal principles relative to Chrysler:

- Technical dealer service bulletins are admissible in court to prove that a problem exists and that certain parts should be checked out.
- If a problem is reported prior to a warranty's expiration, warranty coverage for the problematic component(s) is automatically carried over after the warranty ends.
- It's not up to the car owner to tell the dealer/automaker what the specific problem is.
- Repairs carried out by an independent garage can be refunded if the dealer/automaker unfairly refuses to apply the warranty.
- The dealer/automaker cannot dispute the cost of the independent repair if they fail to cross-examine the independent repairer.
- Auto owners can ask for and win compensation for their inconvenience, which in this judgment amounted to $150.

Court awards quickly add up. The plaintiff was given $1,985.94, with the addition of court costs and prejudgment interest, plus costs of inconvenience fixed at $150. The final award amounted to $2,266.04.

Tire Failures: Premature Wear

Blackwood v. Ford Motor Company of Canada Ltd., 2006 (Provincial Court of Alberta, Civil Division; Docket: PO690101722; Registry: Canmore; 2006/12/08; Honourable J. Shriar). This four-page judgment gives important guidelines as to how a plaintiff can successfully claim a refund for a defective tire.

The plaintiff bought a new 2005 Ford Focus. After 10 months and 22,000 km, his dealer said all four tires needed replacing at a cost of $560.68. Both the dealer and Ford refused to cover the expense under the 3-year/60,000 km manufacturer's tire warranty, alleging that the wear was "normal wear and tear." Judge Shriar disagreed and awarded the plaintiff the full cost of the replacement tires, plus the filing fee and costs related to the registered mail and corporate records address check. An additional $100 was awarded for court costs, plus interest on the total amount from the date of the filing.

False Advertising

Misrepresentation

Goldie v. Golden Ears Motors (1980) Ltd (Port Coquitlam; June 27, 2000; British Columbia Small Claims Court; Case No. CO8287; Justice Warren). In a well-written, eight-page judgment, the court awarded plaintiff Goldie $5,000 for engine repairs on a 1990 Ford F-150 pickup in addition to $236 court costs. The dealer was found to have misrepresented the mileage and sold a used vehicle that didn't meet Section 8.01 of the provincial *Motor Vehicle Act Regulations* due to its unsafe tires and defective exhaust and headlights.

In rejecting the seller's defence that he disclosed all information "to the best of his knowledge and belief" as stipulated in the sales contract, Justice Warren stated,

> The words "to the best of your knowledge and belief" do not allow someone to be willfully blind to defects or to provide incorrect information. I find as a fact that the business made no effort to fulfill its duty to comply with the requirements of this form.... The defendant has been reckless in its actions. More likely, it has actively deceived the claimant into entering into this contract. I find the conduct of the defendant has been reprehensible throughout the dealings with the claimant.

This judgment closes a loophole that sellers have used to justify their misrepresentation, and it allows for cancellation of the sale and damages if the vehicle doesn't meet highway safety regulations.

MacDonald v. Equilease Co. Ltd. (January 18, 1979; Ontario Supreme Court; Judge O'Driscoll). The plaintiff leased a truck that was misrepresented as having an axle stronger than it really was. The court awarded the plaintiff damages for repairs and set aside the lease.

Seich v. Festival Ford Sales Ltd. (1978) (6 Alta. L.R. (2nd), No. 262). The plaintiff bought a used truck from the defendant after being assured that it had a new motor and transmission. It didn't, and the court awarded the plaintiff $6,400.

Used car sold as new (demonstrator)

Bilodeau v. Sud Auto (Quebec Court of Appeal; No. 09-000751-73; Judge Tremblay). This appeals court cancelled the contract and held that a car can't be sold as new or as a demonstrator if it has ever been rented, leased, sold, or titled to anyone other than the dealer.

Rourke v. Gilmore (January 16, 1928; as found in *Ontario Weekly Notes,* vol. XXXIII, p. 292). Before discovering that his new car was really used, the plaintiff drove it for over a year. For this reason, the contract couldn't be cancelled. However, the appeals court instead awarded damages for $500, which was quite a sum in 1928!

Vehicle not as ordered

Whether you're buying new or used, the seller can't misrepresent the vehicle. Anything that varies from what one would commonly expect, or from the seller's representation, must be disclosed prior to signing the contract. Typical misrepresentation scenarios include odometer turnbacks, undisclosed accident damage, used or leased cars being sold as new, new vehicles that are the wrong colour or the wrong model year, and vehicles that lack promised options or standard features.

Chenel v. Bel Automobile (1981) Inc. (August 27, 1976; Quebec Superior Court, Quebec City; Judge Desmeules). The plaintiff didn't receive his new Ford truck with the Jacob brakes essential for transporting sand in hilly regions. The court awarded the plaintiff $27,000, representing the purchase price of the vehicle less the money he earned while using the truck.

Lasky v. Royal City Chrysler Plymouth (February 18, 1987; Ontario High Court of Justice; 59 O.R. (2nd), No. 323). The plaintiff bought a 4-cylinder 1983 Dodge 600 that was represented by the salesman as being a 6-cylinder model. After putting 40,000 km on the vehicle over a 22-month period, the buyer was given her money back, without interest, under the provincial *Business Practices Act.*

Punitive Damages

Punitive damages (also known as "exemplary damages") awards the plaintiff compensation that exceeds his or her losses in order to deter those who carry out dishonest or negligent practices. These kinds of judgments have been quite common in the U.S. for almost 50 years, and they sometimes reach hundreds of millions of dollars.

Punitive damages are rarely awarded in Canadian courts and are almost never used against automakers. When they are given out, it's usually for sums less than $100,000. During the past decade, though, our courts have cracked down on business abuses and awarded plaintiffs amounts varying from $5,000 to $1 million.

In February 2002, the Supreme Court of Canada let stand an unprecedented million-dollar award against what one of the justices called "the insurer from hell." In *Whiten v. Pilot Insurance Co.*, the couple's home burned down and the insurer refused to pay the claim. The jury was so outraged that it ordered the company to pay $345,000 for the loss, plus $320,000 for legal costs and $1 million in punitive damages, making it the largest punitive damage award in Canadian history. The Supreme Court refused to overturn the jury's decision. This judgment scares the dickens out of insurers, who fear that they face huge punitive damage awards if they don't pay promptly.

In May 2005, the Supreme Court of Canada once again reaffirmed the use of punitive damages in *Prebushewski v. Dodge City Auto (1984) Ltd. and Chrysler Canada Ltd.* (2001 SKQB 537; Q.B. No. 1215). The Court backed the Saskatchewan court's $25,000 punitive damage award against Chrysler, rendered in Saskatoon on December 6, 2001, which cited egregious violations of provincial consumer protection statutes (see part of the judgment on page 77). The Supreme Court of Canada's confirmation of the judgment can be found at *http://scc.lexum.umontreal.ca*.

Canadian courts have become more generous in awarding plaintiffs money for mental distress experienced when defects aren't repaired properly under warranty. In *Sharman v. Formula Ford Sales Limited, Ford Credit Limited, and Ford Motor Company of Canada Limited*, Justice Sheppard of the Ontario Superior Court in Oakville awarded the owner of a 2000 Windstar $7,500 for mental distress resulting from the breach of the implied warranty of fitness, plus $7,207 for breach of contract and breach of warranty. The Windstar's sliding door wasn't secure and leaked air and water after many attempts to repair it. Interestingly, the judge cited the *Wharton* decision as support for his award for mental distress:

> The plaintiff and his family have had three years of aggravation, inconvenience, worry, and concern about their safety and that of their children. Generally speaking, our contract law did not allow for compensation for what may be mental distress, but that may be changing. I am indebted to counsel for providing me with the decision of the British Columbia Court of Appeal in *Wharton v. Tom Harris Chevrolet Oldsmobile Cadillac Ltd.*, [2002] B.C.J. No. 233, 2002 BCCA 78. This decision was recently followed in *T'avra v. Victoria Ford Alliance Ltd.*, [2003] B, CJ No. 1957.
>
> In *Wharton*, the purchaser of a Cadillac Eldorado claimed damages against the dealer because the car's sound system emitted an annoying buzzing noise and the purchaser had to return the car to the dealer for repair numerous times over two and a half years. The trial court awarded damages of $2,257.17 for breach of warranty with respect to the sound system, and $5,000 in non-pecuniary damages for loss of enjoyment of

their luxury vehicle and for inconvenience, for a total award of $7,257.17. The Court of Appeal upheld the decision of the trial judge and Levine J.A. spent considerable time reviewing the law, but in particular the law relating to damages for breach of implied warranty of fitness: "The principles applicable to an award of damages for mental distress resulting from a breach of contract were thoroughly and helpfully analyzed in the recent judgment of the House of Lords in *Farley v. Skinner*, [2001] 3 W.L.R. 899, [2001] H.L.J. No. 49, affirming and clarifying the decision of the English Court of Appeal in *Watts v. Morrow*, [1991] I W.L.R. 142 1. Both of those cases concerned a claim by a buyer of a house against a surveyor who failed to report matters concerning the house as required by the contract. In *Watts*, the surveyor was negligent in failing to report defects in the house, and non-pecuniary damages of $6,750 were awarded to each of the owners for the inconvenience and discomfort experienced by them during repairs. In *Farley*, the surveyor was negligent in failing to discover, as he specifically undertook to do, that the property was adversely affected by aircraft noise. The House of Lords upheld the trial judge's award of non-pecuniary damages of $610,000, reversing the Court of Appeal, principally on the grounds that the object of the contract was to provide 'pleasure, relaxation, peace of mind, or freedom from molestation' and also because the plaintiff had suffered physical discomfort and inconvenience from the aircraft noise."

•

The reasons for judgment in *Farley* provide a summary and survey of the law as it has developed, in England, to date. They are helpful in analyzing and summarizing the principles derived from *Watts*, which are, in my view, applicable to the case at bar. In summary they are (borrowing the language from both *Watts* and *Farley*):

(a) A contract-breaker is not in general liable for any distress, frustration, anxiety, displeasure, vexation, tension, or aggravation which the breach of contract may cause to the innocent party.
(b) The rule is not absolute. Where a major or important part of the contract is to give pleasure, relaxation or peace of mind, damages will be awarded if the fruit of the contract is not provided or if the contrary result is instead procured.
(c) In cases not falling within the "peace of mind" category, damages are recoverable for inconvenience and discomfort caused by the breach and the mental suffering directly related to the inconvenience and discomfort. However, the cause of the inconvenience or discomfort must be a sensory experience as opposed to mere disappointment that the contract has been broken. If those effects are foreseeably suffered during a period when defects are repaired, they create damages even though the cost of repairs are not recoverable as such.

Application of Law to the Facts of This Case

In the *Wharton* case, the respondent contracted for a "luxury" vehicle for pleasure use. It included a sound system that the appellant's service manager described as "high end." The respondent's husband described the purchase of the car in this way:

"[W]e bought a luxury car that was supposed to give us a luxury ride and be a quiet vehicle, and we had nothing but difficulty with it from the very day it was delivered with this problem that nobody seemed to be able to fix…. So basically we had a luxury product that gave us no luxury for the whole time that we had it."

It is clear that an important object of the contract was to obtain a vehicle that was luxurious and a pleasure to operate. Furthermore, the buzzing noise was the cause of physical, in the sense of sensory, discomfort to the respondent and her husband. The trial judge found it inhibited listening to the sound system and was irritating in normal conversation. The respondent and her husband also bore the physical inconvenience of taking the vehicle to the appellant on numerous occasions for repairs. The inconvenience and discomfort was, in my view, reasonably foreseeable, if the defect in the sound system had been known at the date of the contract. The fact that it was not then known is, of course, irrelevant.

The award of damages for breach of the implied warranty of fitness satisfies both exceptions from the general rule that damages are not awarded for mental distress for breach of contract, set out in *Watts* as amplified in *Farley*.

The justice continued and said at para. 63 "…awards for mental distress arising from a breach of contract should be restrained and modest."

The court upheld the trial judge's award of $5,000 in *Wharton* where the issue was a buzzing in the sound system.

In my view, a defect in manufacture which goes to the safety of the vehicle deserves a modest increase. I would assess the plaintiff's damage for mental distress resulting from the breach of the implied warranty of fitness at $7,500.

Judgment to issue in favour of the plaintiff against the defendants, except Ford Credit, on a joint and several basis for $14,707, plus interest and costs….

Provincial business practices acts and consumer protection statutes prohibit false, misleading, or deceptive representations and allow for punitive damages should the unfair practice toward the consumer amount to an unconscionable representation (see *Canadian Encyclopedic Digest* (3d) s. 76, pp. 140–45). "Unconscionable" is defined as "where the consumer is not reasonably able to protect his or her interest because of physical infirmity, ignorance, illiteracy, or inability to understand the language of an agreement or similar factors." This concept has been successfully used in consumer, environmental, and labour law.

- Exemplary damages are justified where compensatory damages are insufficient to deter and punish. See *Walker et al. v. CFTO Ltd. et al. (1978)* (59 O.R. (2nd), No. 104; Ontario Court of Appeal).
- Exemplary damages can be awarded in cases where the defendant's conduct was "cavalier." See *Ronald Elwyn Lister Ltd. et al. v. Dayton Tire Canada Ltd. (1985)* (52 O.R. (2nd), No. 89; Ontario Court of Appeal).

- The primary purpose of exemplary damages is to prevent the defendant and all others from doing similar wrongs. See *Fleming v. Spracklin* (1921).
- Disregard of the public's interest, lack of preventive measures, and a callous attitude all merit exemplary damages. See *Coughlin v. Kuntz* (1989) (2 C.C.L.T. (2nd); B.C.C.A.).
- Punitive damages can be awarded for mental distress. See *Ribeiro v. Canadian Imperial Bank of Commerce* (1992) (Ontario Reports 13 3rd) and *Brown v. Waterloo Regional Board of Commissioners of Police* (1992) (37 O.R. 2nd).

In the States, punitive damage awards have been particularly generous. Whenever big business complains of an "unrestrained judiciary," it trots out a 20-year-old case where an Alabama BMW 500 series owner was awarded $4 million because his new car had been repainted before he bought it and the seller didn't tell him so. Under appeal, the owner was offered $50,000.

The case was *BMW of North America, Inc. v. Gore* (517 U.S. 559; 116 S. Ct. 1589; 1996). In this case, the Supreme Court cut the damages award and established standards for jury awards of punitive damages. Nevertheless, million-dollar awards continue to be quite common. In the following example, an Oregon dealer learned that a $1 million punitive damages award was not excessive under *Gore* and under Oregon law.

The Oregon Supreme Court determined that the standard it set in *Oberg v. Honda Motor Company* (888 P.2d 8; 1996), on remand from the Supreme Court, survived the Supreme Court's subsequent ruling in *Gore*. The court held that the jury's $1 million punitive damages award, 87 times larger than the plaintiff's compensatory damages in *Parrott v. Carr Chevrolet, Inc.* (2001 Ore. LEXIS; 1 January 11, 2001), wasn't excessive. In that case, Mark Parrott sued Carr Chevrolet, Inc. over a used 1983 Chevrolet Suburban under Oregon's *Unlawful Trade Practices Act*. The jury awarded Parrott $11,496 in compensatory damages and $1 million in punitive damages because the dealer failed to disclose collision damage to a new-car buyer.

See also:

- *Vlchek v. Koshel (1988)* (44 C.C.L.T. 314; B.C.S.C., No. B842974)
- *Granek v. Reiter* (Ontario Court, General Division; No. 35/741)
- *Morrison v. Sharp* (Ontario Court, General Division; No. 43/548)
- *Schryvers v. Richport Ford Sales* (May 18, 1993; B.C.S.C., No. C917060; Judge Tysoe)
- *Varleg v. Angeloni* (B.C.S.C., No. 41/301)
- *Grabinski v. Blue Springs Ford Sales, Inc.* (U.S. App. LEXIS 2073; 8th Cir. W.D. MO; February 16, 2000)

Part Three

1980–2009 LEMONS, CHERRIES, AND CITROËNS

The Little Citroën That Could

1957 Citroën 2CV, 350,000 miles (563,000 km)—Tom Anderson of Summerland, British Columbia, paid less than $1,000 in 1961 for his used Citroen. Priced new at $1,200, the Belgian-built 2CV was sold with 50,000 miles (80,000 km) on the clock. Now, 50 years later, Tom still enjoys the car's astounding reliability, cheap maintenance, impressive versatility, and "go anywhere" toughness, all accomplished with the scintillating speed of a 12-horsepower engine that gets 68 miles per Canadian gallon (4.2 L/100 km).

Says Tom:

"A story about my 2CV aired on the program *As It Happens* in 1990. Except for the minor engine repair mentioned in the story, all other work on the car has been done by me alone. But that hasn't amounted to much—mostly just replacing tires and other rubber parts, damaged top, seat pads, etc. The car runs amazingly well,

considering how worn the engine is. I bought all the parts needed to rebuild it many years ago, but other 2CV owners have advised, 'If it's running okay, don't mess with it.' So the parts are just sitting here in the corner of my bedroom, gathering dust. I don't really need a car where I live, so I drive it very little nowadays—mainly just fun trips into the mountains and along backcountry trails. Not really into pet names. I expect my car is grateful for that."

Big Savings, Small Problems

Of course, few used car buyers get a car as outstanding as Tom Anderson's little Citroën, but most buyers do quite well. Still, no matter if you buy American, Asian, or European, new or used, you are taking on someone else's problems: the dealer's and automaker's, or the previous owner's. Fortunately, you likely already saved $10,000 (on the average three-year-old American family sedan) or more buying used, so you'll have plenty of cash reserve to repair run-of-the-mill glitches at cheaper, independent shops.

Plus, there's not much that can surprise you on a well-inspected vehicle that has been widely sold and can be easily serviced. There's a safety advantage as well, since the vehicle's crashworthiness has likely been tested and retested by a handful of different agencies and about 75 percent of the recalls have been carried out. Best of all, there's the peace of mind knowing you won't get left in the lurch if the dealer or automaker goes bust—again.

A Good 15-Year-Old

Primarily, you buy used to save money and to have reliable transportation for a decade or more. A good used car or truck should cost you no more than one-third to one-half of its original selling price ($7,500–$15,000) and should be between three and five years old. A "new" used car must meet your everyday driving needs and have high crashworthiness and reliability scores. Annual maintenance should cost no more than the CAA-and-DesRosiers-estimated average of $800–$1,100, and the depreciation rate should have levelled off, so that subsequent years won't cut the car's price by more than a couple thousand dollars over the next few years, leaving you with some resale equity. Parts and servicing costs shouldn't be excessive either, which means checking out maintenance costs before you buy.

Fuel economy isn't all that important when you are buying used, since all of your other savings should easily compensate for the extra fuel costs. We don't recommend most gas-electric engine hybrids: their retail prices are incredibly high; long-term reliability is problematic; fuel economy can be 40 percent worse than the automakers' reports; their expensive motors are predicted to have a high failure rate due to corrosion; battery replacement costs are estimated to run as high as $3,000 (U.S.) for the Toyota Prius and $10,000 for other makes; and their eight-year resale values are no better than similar vehicles equipped with conventional engines. Look again at a 2005 Toyota Prius that originally sold for $30,330. It is now valued at a disappointing $9,500, less than a third of its original price (and we're coming up to the expiration of that battery-pack warranty).

Compare that to the price of a fully equipped 2005 Camry XLE V6, which sells for about $1,000 more—with no $3,000 battery-pack surcharge.

Depreciation Is Your Friend

Not all cars and trucks are born with equal attributes, and they age (depreciate) at different rates. When buying new, you want a reliable model that depreciates slowly; when buying used, consider a vehicle that has prematurely lost much of its value but is still dependable and inexpensive to maintain. Fortunately, there are plenty of the latter on the market due to poor vehicle sales during the 2008 and 2009 model years.

On the other hand, used vehicles that hold their value well after four years aren't bargains now, but they'll have considerable equity in them should you have to sell due to a cash emergency. And yes, models that depreciate slowly are usually the more dependable vehicles that hold up better in the long run.

During the past year, rebates, cut-rate financing, subsidized leasing, and fluctuating fuel costs, along with poor reputations for quality, have depressed the residual values of most American cars and trucks. According to the *Automotive Lease Guide* (*www.alg.com*), Detroit-made vehicles that come off lease barely keep 37 percent of their sticker values after three years. As we go through the present recession, values are hovering near 30 percent.

THE 10 BEST AND 10 WORST VEHICLES FOR HOLDING VALUE OVER FIVE YEARS

BEST VALUE-HOLDERS		WORST VALUE-HOLDERS	
1. Volkswagen R32	6. Toyota RAV4*	1. Hyundai Entourage*	6. Kia Rio
2. Jeep Wrangler*	7. Infiniti G35/G37*	2. Chevrolet Malibu Classic*	7. Suzuki Reno
3. BMW MINI Cooper*	8. Dodge Viper*	3. Kia Optima	8. Kia Spectra
4. Toyota Scion xB	9. BMW 1 Series*	4. Suzuki Forenza	9. Chevrolet Uplander
5. Honda CR-V*	10. Nissan Rogue*	5. Hyundai Accent*	10. Lincoln Town Car*

Source: ALG; August 2008.

Lemon-Aid has rated these models highly over the years, but they have been downgraded due to recent negative owner reports and the shifting sands in the automaker desert.

Judging "Quality Ratings"

Lemon-Aid has been giving honest, independent, and dependable auto ratings for 38 years by following these simple rules:

- Ratings should be used primarily as a comparative database when the low-ranked or recommended models reappear in different driving tests and owner surveys. The best rating approach is to combine a driving test with an owners' survey of past models (only *Consumer Reports* does this).
- We use the database of owner complaints collected by the NHTSA's *safercar. gov*. It's a treasure trove of auto-failure anecdotes that show which cars have

repeated failures, outstanding recalls, or are part of an ongoing safety probe, and which particular component is faulty. It even suggests ways to get a free warranty extension to cover the repair, or to get a free replacement part.

On this free webpage you can find auto recalls and service bulletins, or post a complaint and view complaints posted by other owners of the same vehicle, for over 30 years of production.

- The responses must come from a large owner pool (1.2 million responses from *Consumer Reports* subscribers, for example). Anecdotal responses should then be cross-referenced, updated, and given depth and specificity through NHTSA's safety complaint prism. Responses must be cross-referenced again through automaker internal service bulletins to determine the extent of the defect over a specific model and model-year range and to alert owners to problems likely to occur. This is how we discovered that millions of GM 1995–2004 cars and minivans had defective engine intake manifold gaskets and millions of Ford trucks and Lincolns had faulty fuel gauges.

- Rankings should be predicated on important characteristics measured over a significant period of time, unlike Car of the Year contests, owner-perceived values, or J.D. Power–surveyed problems assessed after only three months of ownership.

- Ratings must come from unimpeachable sources. There should be no conflicts of interest due to ties with advertisers or consultants, and no results gathered from self-serving tests done under ideal conditions, like previous years' Transport Canada and U.S. Environmental Protection Agency (EPA) fuel economy tests.

- Tested cars must be bought, not borrowed, and serviced, not pampered as part of a journalists' fleet lent out for ranking purposes. Also, all automakers need to be judged equally. (Toyota at one time did not accept weekend car journalist "roundup" tests as valid and refused to lend its vehicles to the events; thus, they were penalized.) Automakers must not be members of the ranking body.

- Again, we are wary of self-administered fuel economy ratings used by automakers in complicity with the federal government. *Automotive News* recently added its name to the list of skeptics when it found that Honda and Toyota

ERRATIC FUEL GAUGE

BULLETIN NO.: TSB 08-2-9   **DATE: APRIL 2, 2008**

FUEL GAUGE OPERATION—MIL ON—DTCS P0460/P0463 OR INSTRUMENT CLUSTER MODULE DTC B1201

FORD: 2004–08 F-150; LINCOLN: 2006–08 Mark LT

ISSUE: Some 2004–08 F-150 and 2006–08 Mark LT vehicles, built before 12/3/2007, may exhibit erratic fuel gauge operation or illuminated malfunction indicator lamp (MIL) with diagnostic trouble codes (DTCs) P0460 or P0463, and/or Instrument Cluster Module DTC B1201. This may be caused by sulphur contamination in the fuel causing an open or high resistance in the fuel level sender.

ACTION: Follow the Service Procedure steps to correct the condition.

SERVICE PROCEDURE: Install a new fuel level sender following the service procedure instruction sheet provided in the fuel sender kit.

WARRANTY STATUS: Eligible Under Provisions Of New Vehicle Limited Warranty Coverage And Emissions Warranty Coverage. IMPORTANT: Warranty coverage limits/policies are not altered by a TSB. Warranty coverage limits are determined by the identified causal part.

hybrids get 20–40 percent less real-world gas mileage than advertised. The car industry publication discovered that hybrids need to be driven in a particular way in order to be fuel efficient, use more fuel than ordinary cars on short trips or when using air conditioning, and are affected by colder climates, resulting in increased fuel consumption way beyond what the ratings figures indicate. The EPA has admitted its fuel economy calculations were overestimated and has set up a website at *www.fueleconomy.gov* that contains recalculated figures for 1985–2007 model year vehicles that will leave you scratching your head.

Definitions of Terms

We rate vehicles on a scale of one to five stars, with five stars being our top ranking. Models are designated as "Recommended," "Above Average," "Average," "Below Average," or "Not Recommended," with the most recent year's rating indicated by the number of stars beside the vehicle's name.

Recommended

We don't give this rating out very often, and we are quick to drop it if safety, servicing, or overall quality control decline. We don't believe for one moment that the more you spend, the better performing, more reliable, or safer the vehicle. For example, most Hondas are as good as Acuras, which cost thousands of dollars more for their luxury cachet. The same is true when you compare Toyota and Lexus. Even more surprising, some luxury makes, such as Jaguar, are "pseudo-luxe," because they may be merely dressed-up ordinary Fords sold at a luxury-car price. The extra money only buys you more features of dubious value and newer, unproven technology, such as rear-mounted video cameras, backing up "beepers," and other failure-prone electronic gadgetry.

In fact, the simplest choice is often the best buy. Chrysler's minivans and small Jeeps, Ford's Mustang, and Hyundai's Elantra and Tiburon get positive ratings because they are easy to find, fairly reliable, and reasonably priced—not the case with many overpriced Hondas and Toyotas.

Above Average/Average

Vehicles that are given an Above Average or Average rating are good second choices if a Recommended vehicle isn't your first choice, isn't available, or isn't within budget.

Below Average/Not Recommended

Many vehicles are given a Below Average rating by *Lemon-Aid* because we know they will likely be troublesome; however, we also believe their low price and reasonably priced servicing may make them acceptable buys to some do-it-yourselfers who have put aside sufficient money saved from the transaction to cover expected failures.

Vehicles with a history of unforseeable, recurring, and expensive defects are most likely to be given a Not Recommended rating. They are best avoided altogether, no matter how low the price, because they're so likely to suffer from many durability and performance problems that you may never stop paying for repairs. Sometimes, however, a Not Recommended model will improve over several model years and garner a better rating (as the Ford Focus and Hyundai's Sonata and SUVs have done).

Incidentally, for those owners who wonder how I can stop recommending model years I once recommended, let me be clear: As vehicles age, their ratings change to reflect new information from owners and from service bulletins relating to durability and the automaker's warranty performance. For example, Nissan's Quest, Toyota's Sienna, and BMW's Mini have been downgraded for some years because new service bulletins and additional owner complaints show some disturbing trends in dependability and servicing performance. Unlike car columnists who can't change their ratings due to automaker pressure, I quickly warn shoppers of rating downgrades as soon as they're made through subsequent editions of *Lemon-Aid* and updates to my website, *www.lemonaidcars.com*.

For 38 years, I have been an *active* consumer advocate, not a *passive* auto journalist. When I uncover fraud, unsafe designs, or failure-prone components, I first denounce the problem. Then I take a second step, one rarely taken by journalists: I become part of the story by mobilizing owners, lawyers, and independent mechanics to force an automaker to recall or reimburse.

My proudest achievement? Getting GM Canada to pay back millions of dollars to Canadian car owners stuck with "cooked" V6 engines afflicted by warped intake manifold gaskets in GM's 1995–2005 models. GM paid Canadians an estimated

$40 million in repairs because the automaker used faulty engine gaskets made out of plastic to save a few pennies per car.

Throughout the year, I get refunds for buyers cheated by dealers and automakers. I lobby automakers to compensate owners of out-of-warranty vehicles either through formal warranty extension programs or on a case-by-case basis. I also publish little-known lawsuits, judgments, and settlements in *Lemon-Aid* to help car owners win their cases or get a fair settlement without my personal assistance.

Reliability data is compiled from a number of sources, including confidential technical service bulletins, owner complaints sent to me each year by *Lemon-Aid* readers, owners' comments posted on the Internet, and survey reports and tests done by auto associations, consumer groups, and government organizations. Some auto columnists feel this isn't a scientific sampling, and they're quite right. Nevertheless, the results have been mostly on the mark over the past four decades.

Not all cars and trucks are profiled; those that are new to the market or relatively rare may receive only an abbreviated mention until sufficient owner or service bulletin information becomes available. Best and worst buys for each model category (e.g., "Small Cars," "Medium Cars," and so on) are listed in a summary at the beginning of each rating section.

Strengths and Weaknesses

With the Detroit automakers, engine head gasket, automatic transmission, brake, steering, and electrical failures are omnipresent. South Korean vehicles have weak transmissions, electrical systems, and electronic control modules. Japanese makes are noted mostly for their brake, door, AC, window, sound system, electrical, and fuel delivery glitches, though engine and transmission failures have been appearing more frequently, especially with Toyota and Lexus models built during the past decade. Finally, the European automakers are in a high-tech bind: Electronic demons constantly bedevil Audi, BMW, Jaguar, Land Rover, Mercedes, Saab, Volvo, and VW products, making them unreliable and costly to service after only a few years of ownership; plus, these vehicles are so complicated to diagnose and service that many mechanics simply throw up their hands in dismay. And with Volvo sold to the Chinese, Saab to the Dutch, and Jaguar/Land Rover now an Indian subsidiary, servicing can only get worse.

Unlike other auto guides, *Lemon-Aid* knows where automotive skeletons are buried and pinpoints potential parts failures, explains why those parts fail, and advises you as to your chances of getting a repair refund under a "goodwill warranty" program. We also give parts numbers for upgraded parts (why replace poor-quality brake pads with the same failure-prone part?) and offer troubleshooting tips direct from the automakers' bulletins so that your mechanic won't replace parts unrelated to your troubles before coming upon the defective component that is actually responsible.

Parts supply can be a real problem. It's a myth that automakers have to keep a supply of parts sufficient to service what they sell, as any buyer of a Cadillac Catera, a front-drive Lincoln Continental, or a Ford Tempo/Topaz will quickly tell you. Additionally, apart from *Lemon-Aid*, there's no consumer database that warns prospective purchasers as to which models are "parts-challenged."

The "Secret Warranties/Internal Bulletins/Service Tips" sections and vehicle profile tables show a vehicle's overall reliability and safety, providing details as to which specific model years pose the most risk and why. This helps you direct an independent mechanic to check out the likely trouble spots before you make your purchase.

Vehicle History

This section outlines a vehicle's differences between model years, including major redesigns and other modifications. If a model is unchanged from one model year to the next, why pay a premium for it simply because it is one year newer? Or, if a vehicle was redesigned a few years ago, don't you want that vehicle a year after the redesign, when most of the factory kinks have been ironed out?

Safety Summary

Ongoing safety investigations, safety-related complaints, and safety probes make up this section. National Highway Traffic Safety Administration (NHTSA) complaints are summarized by model year, even though they aren't all safety-related. The summary will help you spot a defect trend (sudden acceleration, brake failures, and airbag deployment malfunctions being the top three defect categories) before a recall or bulletin is issued. You can also prove that a part failure is widespread and factory-related and then use that information for free "goodwill" repairs or in litigation involving accident damage, injuries, or death.

NHTSA records indicate other common safety-related failures that include vehicles with collapsing axles (Ford Windstar/Freestar, et al.), vehicles rolling away with the transmission in Park, sliding minivan doors that don't open when they should or open when they shouldn't, or electronic computer modules that cause a vehicle to "lag and lurch." The vehicle won't accelerate from a stop for a few seconds, and then it will lurch out into traffic after the accelerator has been floored to get the vehicle out of harm's way (hello, Toyota!).

Several years ago, a Calgary mother left her two-year-old daughter in an idling SUV to run a quick errand. The child was strangled by the power-assisted window. A passerby extricated her from the window and left to call the police. The mother returned and saw what she thought was the child asleep in the rear seat. Almost an hour later, she realized her daughter was dead. Safety researchers know of at least eight other incidents like this in North America. Yet parents assume a window or door will retract automatically if a hand or neck is caught in its path.

Be wary. You are dealing with an industry that ignores cars suddenly accelerating out of control with no brakes, pickups that corrode so badly their suspension is unsafe, steering wheels that fly off, and, with GM Corvettes, steering assemblies that suddenly lock up and roofs that take flight once the car is underway.

In a nutshell, the auto industry continues to put profits before safety, unions value jobs over integrity, and all that governments care about is getting back their auto bailout investment.

If *Lemon-Aid* doesn't list a problem you have experienced, go to the NHTSA website's database at *www.safercar.gov/Vehicle+Owners* or *www.safercar.gov/Vehicle+Shoppers* for an update. Your vehicle may be currently under investigation, or may have been recalled since this year's guide was published.

Automotive News says an estimated 72 percent of the 25 million vehicles recalled in 2005 were fixed, which is an improvement over the earlier 65 percent fix rate. *Lemon-Aid* doesn't list most recalls because there are so many, and the info can be easily obtained either from NHTSA at the above-listed sites or from Transport Canada (*www.tc.gc.ca/roadsafety/recalls/search_e.asp*). Dealers willingly give out recall info when they run a vehicle history search through their computers, since they hope to snag the extra repair dollars. Just make sure you ask the dealer to also check for a "customer satisfaction program," a "service policy," a "goodwill" warranty extension, or a free emissions warranty service.

Secret Warranties/Internal Bulletins/Service Tips

It's not enough to know which parts on your vehicle are likely to fail. You should also know which repairs will be done for free by the dealer and automaker, even though you aren't the original owner and the manufacturer's warranty has long since expired.

Welcome to the hidden world of secret warranties, found in confidential technical service bulletins (TSBs) or gleaned from owners' feedback.

Over the years, I've grown tired of service managers denying that service bulletins exist to correct factory-related defects free of charge. That's why I pore over thousands of bulletins each year and summarize or reproduce in *Lemon-Aid* the important ones for each model year, along with improved parts numbers. These bulletins target defects related to safety, emissions, and performance that service managers would have you believe either don't exist or are your responsibility to fix. If you photocopy the applicable service bulletin included in *Lemon-Aid*, you'll have a better chance of getting the dealer or automaker to cover all or part of the repair costs. Bulletins taken from *Lemon-Aid* have also been instrumental in helping claimants win in small claims court mediation and trials (remember, judges like to have the bulletins validated by an independent mechanic or the dealer/automaker witness you are suing).

Service bulletins listed in *Lemon-Aid* cover repairs that may be eligible for expressed or implied warranty coverage in one or more of the following five categories (although the description of the repairs is not always specific):

1. Emissions expressed warranty (5–8 years/80,000–130,000 km)
2. Safety component expressed warranty (this covers seat belts, ABS, and airbags, and usually lasts from eight years to the lifetime of the vehicle)
3. Body expressed warranty (paint: six years; rust perforations: seven years)
4. Secret implied warranty (coverage varies from five to 10 years)
5. Factory defect/implied legal warranty (depends on mileage, use, and repair cost; may be as high as 11 years, according to GM paint delamination jurisprudence)

Use these bulletins to get free repairs—even if the vehicle has changed hands several times—and to alert an independent mechanic about defects to look for. They're also great tools for getting compensation from automakers and dealer service managers after the warranty has expired, since they prove that a failure is factory-related and, therefore, not part of routine maintenance or caused by a caustic environmental substance such as bird droppings or acid rain. In small claims court, the argument that bird droppings caused a paint problem usually loses credibility when only certain models or certain years are shown to be affected, pointing the finger at the paint process and quality.

Automakers' "bird poop" defence doesn't explain why birds apparently defecate only on certain model vehicles (Chrysler Caravans, Ford's Taurus and Sable, GM minivans, etc.). Nevertheless, the implied warranty requires that all automakers use the same durability standard or disclose at the time of sale that their vehicles aren't "bird-proofed."

The diagnostic shortcuts and lists of upgraded parts found in many service bulletins make them invaluable in helping mechanics and do-it-yourselfers to troubleshoot problems inexpensively and to replace the correct part the first time. Auto owners can also use the TSBs listed here to verify that a repair was diagnosed correctly, that the correct upgraded replacement part was used, and that the labour costs were fair.

Each annual edition of *Lemon-Aid* lists of safety-related failures, crashworthiness scores, service bulletins, and prices of a range of model years. If your vehicle, perhaps a 1997 model, isn't included in this year's guide (which provides detailed information on 2001–2011 models), consult an earlier edition.

Summaries of service bulletins relating to 1982–2011 vehicles can be obtained for free from the ALLDATA or NHTSA websites, but they are worded so cryptically that you really need the bulletins themselves. If you have a vehicle that's off warranty, you should get copies of the hundreds of pages of bulletins applicable to your model year, listing factory-related defects and diagnostic shortcuts. These bulletins can be ordered and downloaded from the Internet for $26.95 (U.S.)

through ALLDATA at *www.alldatadiy.com/buy/index.html*. Or you can get the bulletin title for free from ALLDATA and then search for it on the Internet through a search engine such as Google.

Vehicle Profile Tables

These tables cover the various aspects of vehicle ownership at a glance. Included for each model year are the vehicle's original selling price (the manufacturer's suggested retail price, or MSRP), the wholesale and retail prices you can expect to pay, reliability ratings (specific defective parts are listed in the "Strengths and Weaknesses" section), and details on crashworthiness.

Prices

Dealer profit margins on used cars vary considerably—giving lots of room to negotiate a fair price if you take the time to find out what the vehicle is really worth. Three prices are given for each model year: the vehicle's selling price when new, as suggested by the manufacturer; its maximum used price (▲), which is often the starting price with dealers; and its lowest used price (▼), more commonly found with private sellers.

The original selling price is given as a reality check for greedy sellers who inflate prices on some vehicles (mostly Japanese imports, minivans, and sport-utilities) in order to get back some of the money they overpaid in the first place. This happens particularly often in the Prairie provinces and British Columbia.

Used prices are based on sales recorded as of February 2010. Prices are for the lowest-priced standard model that is in good condition with a maximum of 20,000 km for each calendar year. Watch for price differences reflecting each model's equipment upgrades, designated by a numerical or alphabetical abbreviation. For example, L, LX, and LXT usually mean more standard features are included, progressively, in each model. Numerical progression usually relates to engine size.

Prices reflect the auto markets in Quebec and Ontario, where the majority of used-vehicle transactions take place. Residents of Eastern Canada should add 10 percent, and Western Canadians should add at least 15–20 percent to the listed price. Why the higher costs? Less competition, combined with inflated new-vehicle prices in these regions. Don't be too disheartened, though; you'll recoup some of what you overpaid down the road when you sell the vehicle.

Why are *Lemon-Aid*'s prices sometimes lower than the prices found in dealer guides such as *Red Book*? The answer is simple: Much like a homeowner selling a house, dealers inflate their prices so that you can bargain the price down and wind up convinced that you made a great deal.

I use newspaper classified ads from Quebec, Ontario, and B.C., as well as auction reports, to calculate my used-vehicle values. I then check these figures against *Red Book* and *Black Book*. I don't start with *Red Book*'s retail or wholesale figures because their prices are inflated about 10 percent for wholesale/private sales and almost 20 percent for retail/dealer sales (compare the two, and you'll see what I mean). I then project what the value will be by mid-model year, and that lowers my prices further. I'll almost always fall way under *Red Book*'s value, but not far under *Black Book*'s prices.

I include a top and bottom price to give you some margin for negotiation as well as to account for the regional differences in prices, the sudden popularity of certain models or vehicle classes, and the generally depreciated value of used vehicles.

Most new cars depreciate 50–60 percent during the first three years of ownership, despite the fact that good-quality used cars are in high demand. On the other hand, some minivans and most vans, pickups, and SUVs lose barely 40 percent of their value, even after four years of ownership.

Since no evaluation method is foolproof, check dealer prices against newspaper- and Internet-sourced private classified ads and then add the option values listed on the next page to come up with a fairly representative offer. Don't forget to bargain the price down further if the odometer shows a cumulative reading of more than 20,000 km per calendar year. Interestingly, the value of anti-lock brakes in trade-ins plummeted during the last few years as they became a standard feature on many entry-level vehicles.

It will be easier to match the lower used prices if you buy privately. Dealers rarely sell much below the maximum prices; they claim that they need the full price to cover the costs of reconditioning and paying future warranty claims. If you can come within 5–10 percent of this guide's price, you'll have done well.

In the table on p. 132, take note that some options—such as paint protector, rust-proofing, and tinted windows—have little worth on the resale market, though they may make your vehicle easier to sell.

Reliability

The older a vehicle gets (at five to seven years old), the greater the chance that major components, such as the engine and transmission, will fail as the result of high mileage and environmental wear and tear. Surprisingly, a host of other expensive-to-repair failures are just as likely to occur in new vehicles as in older ones. The air conditioning, electronic computer modules, electrical systems, and brakes are the most troublesome components, manifesting problems early in a vehicle's life. Other deficiencies that will appear early, due to sloppy manufacturing and harsh environments, include failure-prone body hardware (trim, finish, locks, doors, and windows), susceptibility to water leakage or wind noise, and peeling and/or discoloured paint. The following legend shows a vehicle's relative degree of overall reliability; the numbers lighten as the rating becomes more positive:

VALUE OF OPTIONS BY MODEL YEAR

OPTION	2001	2002	2003	2004	2005	2006	2007	2008	2009
Air conditioning	$200	$300	$300	$400	$500	$600	$700	$800	$950
AM/FM radio & CD player	100	100	100	150	175	200	300	500	600
Anti-lock brakes	0	50	100	125	150	175	300	300	400
Automatic transmission	150	200	250	275	300	400	500	700	800
Cruise control	0	50	50	75	100	125	225	300	350
Electric six-way seat	0	50	100	125	150	175	200	400	450
Leather upholstery	50	100	200	225	325	400	500	800	900
Level control (suspension)	0	50	75	100	125	150	250	350	450
Paint protector	50	50	50	50	50	50	50	50	50
Power antenna	0	0	0	0	0	75	75	75	75
Power door locks	0	50	100	125	150	175	200	250	250
Power windows	0	50	100	125	150	175	225	250	250
Rustproofing	0	0	0	0	25	25	50	50	50
Stability control	0	50	100	125	150	175	225	275	300
Sunroof	0	50	50	75	125	150	300	500	500
T-top roof	150	200	300	400	500	700	800	1,000	1,000
Tilt steering	0	50	50	75	75	100	175	250	200
Tinted windows	0	0	0	0	25	50	50	50	50
Tires (Firestone)	–100	–100	–100	–100	–100	–150	–150	–150	–150
Traction control	50	100	125	150	175	275	400	500	500
Wire wheels/locks	50	75	100	125	150	175	275	300	350

1	**2**	**3**	**4**	**5**
Unacceptable	Below Average	Average	Above Average	Excellent

Crashworthiness

Some of the main factors weighed in the safety ratings are a model's crashworthiness, its front and rear visibility, and the availability of safety features such as seat belt pretensioners, depowered airbags, airbag disablers, adjustable brake and accelerator pedals, integrated child safety seats, effective head restraints, and assisted stability and traction control.

NHTSA CRASH TESTS: Front, side, and roof crash protection figures are taken from NHTSA's New Car Assessment Program. For the front crash test, vehicles are crashed head-on at 57 km/h (35 mph) into a fixed barrier. NHTSA uses star rankings to show the likelihood, expressed as a percentage, of belted occupants surviving a crash without serious injury—the higher the number, the greater the protection.

SIDE CRASHWORTHINESS: NHTSA's side crash test represents an intersection-type collision with a 1,368 kg (3,015 lb.) barrier moving at 62 km/h (38.5 mph) into a standing vehicle. The moving barrier is covered with material that has give in order to replicate the front of a car.

ROOF STRENGTH: In May of 2009, NHTSA amended Federal Motor Vehicle Safety Standard 216, Roof Crush Resistance, to improve roof strength as part of a comprehensive plan for addressing rollover crashes, which account for more than 10,000 fatalities annually. The agency's plan was to include actions to reduce the occurrence of rollover, mitigate ejection, and increase protection for occupants in a rollover event.

Under the regulation, roofs of light passenger vehicles weighing up to 6,000 pounds are required to withstand up to three times the weight of the vehicle (a strength-to-weight ratio of 3) on both the driver's and passenger's side of the vehicle. Heavier light-duty vehicles weighing 6,000 to 10,000 pounds need only withstand 1.5 times their own weight on the roof.

The Center for Auto Safety, Advocates for Highway and Auto Safety, and others say that the same protections afforded people in lighter vehicles should apply to those riding in heavier ones. NHTSA, in its petition denial, pointed out that relatively few vehicles weigh more than 6,000 pounds (and those are usually commercial vehicles). They tend to afford more headspace to start with, and the cost of reinforcing those vehicles' roofs would outweigh the benefits. (Only a handful of vehicles tested weigh that much—some heavy-duty pickups and a small number of the largest SUVs.)

Another contentious point argued by independent safety advocates is that gently applying weight to a vehicle's roof—which is how current "static" rollover testing is done—is not a proper approximation of what happens when a speeding car rolls over, especially one that rolls over several times before coming to rest. The problem, says NHTSA, is devising a testing mechanism that actually throws a car onto its roof with repeatable results.

IIHS CRASH TESTS: The Insurance Institute for Highway Safety (IIHS) rates vehicles' frontal offset, side, and head-restraint/rear crash protection as "Good," "Acceptable," "Marginal," or "Poor." Head restraints may be rated for both front- and rear-seat occupants.
In the Institute's 64 km/h (40 mph) frontal offset test, 40 percent of the total width of each vehicle strikes a barrier on the driver's side. The barrier's deformable face is made of aluminum honeycomb, which makes the forces in the test similar to those involved in a frontal offset crash between two vehicles of the same weight, each going just less than 64 km/h.

IIHS's 50 km/h (31 mph) side-impact test is carried out at a slower speed than NHTSA's test; however, the barrier uses a front end that is shaped to simulate the typical front end of a pickup or SUV, which is deemed to give truer results. The Institute also includes the degree of frontal-impact head injury in its ratings.

While many automakers are making improvements, a few are going in the wrong direction. Seat/head restraints in recent Chrysler 300, Kia Amanti, and Nissan Altima tests have earned Marginal ratings, compared with Acceptable ratings for their earlier designs, which were tested in 2004. Furthermore, a disappointingly large number of other models have been rated Poor. They include the Acura TSX, BMW 5 Series, Buick LaCrosse (Allure in Canada) and Lucerne, Cadillac CTS and DTS, Chevrolet Aveo, Honda Accord and Fit, Hyundai Accent, Infiniti M35, Jaguar X-Type, Kia Rio, Mitsubishi Galant, Pontiac Grand Prix, Toyota Avalon and Corolla, and Suzuki Forenza and Reno.

ROLLOVERS: A vehicle's rollover resistance rating is an estimate of its risk of rolling over in a single-vehicle crash, not a prediction of the likelihood of a crash. The lowest-rated vehicles (one star) are at least four times more likely to roll over than the highest-rated vehicles (five stars) when involved in a single-vehicle crash.

Safest Used Cars

Just as with quality, purchase price is no indication of how well a car will protect occupants in a collision. To be included in the list that follows, a vehicle must be fairly cheap, have two frontal crash test ratings and two side crash test ratings, and have earned four- and five-star ratings across the board. In addition, any vehicle meeting our pricing criteria and having five-star ratings across the board, as well as vehicles with three five-star ratings and one four-star rating, were also guaranteed a spot on the list.

Ford—Escape, Mustang

Honda—Accord, Civic, Element

Hyundai—Accent, Elantra

Mazda—Mazda3, Tribute

Mitsubishi—Galant

Nissan—Frontier, Sentra

Suzuki—Aerio

Toyota—Corolla, Echo

Extended Warranties

Can an Average or Above Average vehicle become Recommended through the purchase of a strong extended warranty?

Hardly. At some point in time a powertrain or computer malfunction will recur, repair costs will go through the roof, and you will be faced with several abusive clauses that will render the extended warranty useless. Here are some of the most common "weasel" clauses:

1. Vehicle was not properly maintained, and the requested repairs are a maintenance item not covered by this extended warranty.
2. Repairs are normal wear and tear, which is excluded from coverage.
3. Vehicle was abused by the owner, and repairs were not inspected or carried out by the warrantor's service agency.

Some vehicles are total "lemons," like Ford's Windstar/Freestar minivans, or GM's front-drive minivans. No amount of warranty protection will save you from broken axles, sudden loss of steering, burned-up transmissions, blown engines, or "demonic" sliding doors opening and closing while the vehicle is underway.

GM's front-drive minivans (Montana, Relay, Silhouette, Terraza, Uplander, and Venture) have experienced four times as many failures as Ford's Windstar, simply because GM sold four times as many models. Used-van buyers are taken in by the GM minivans' modern styling touches and loaded instrumentation and convenience features.

Recommended vehicles don't need optional, extra-cost ($2,000–$3,000) extended warranties. Sometimes, though, an extended warranty is advisable for those model years that aren't rated because they are too new on the market or too few were sold to get reliable owner feedback.

A good rule to follow is that you really shouldn't buy these low-rated vehicles in the first place. Still, if you want extra protection, don't buy too much warranty. For example, if the vehicle has a history of powertrain problems, like Chrysler's entire Dodge and Jeep lineup, buy the cheaper powertrain warranty only—not the bumper-to-bumper product that is double the powertrain-only cost.

Also, invest in only enough extra warranty to get you through the critical period when the vehicle is five to 10 years old. Don't be surprised to discover that dealers have the market practically sewn up and profit by about 65 percent on most warranty contracts sold. This advantage comes from their backing by insurance and claims funds supported by the auto manufacturers, and this gives dealers tremendous marketing leverage. Sometimes you can bargain the price down by getting competing dealers to bid against each other; contact them by fax or through their websites.

Be careful with extended warranty companies that aren't backed by major insurers; most left the market in 2008–09 when auto sales soured, but some remnants of these agencies are still floating around, promising "universal" coverage until the first claim arrives. Protect yourself by looking for "weasel words" in the contract; having the dealer write in the contract that his or her agency will underwrite any warranty claim unfairly rejected by the warrantor. Check out the warrantor's record on the Internet, and ask to see the repair facility used by the warrantor to judge and repair submitted claims.

SMALL CARS

When buying a used car, punch the buttons on the radio. If all the stations are rock and roll, there's a good chance the transmission is shot.

LARRY LUJACK

When Cheap Is Too Cheap

Your biggest risk in buying a small car is that, mesmerized by the low prices, you'll buy a bare-bones model that's too cheap. Sure, the extra dollars will feel great in your pocket and the fuel economy will be worth bragging about—until the engine blows, the tranny packs it in, the throwaway battery leaves you stranded, insufficient sound insulation drives you to distraction, or the skimpy seat padding becomes literally a pain in the butt. Yet, for just a few dollars more you could have gotten a newer version of the same model that would be much more durable and incorporate additional safety, performance, and convenience upgrades.

On the other hand, be wary of formerly Recommended cars that are past their prime. Take the Toyota Yaris, for example. It has been one of the top compact car picks in Canada for years. But Toyota hasn't added much to the car over that time, while Honda, Hyundai, and Mazda, among others, now sell small feature-packed, entry-level cars that cost less and outperform Toyota's stand-pat Yaris.

Yaris has less power than the Ford Fiesta, Honda Fit, and Kia Rio5, with a 0–100 km/h time that is beaten by most of the competition. Plus, the Toyota's 4-speed automatic transmission is noisy and the car gets worse fuel economy than the Ford.

Small cars are mostly entry-level vehicles that attract budget-conscious shoppers and young, first-time buyers who eschew cachet for more cash savings. These customers want an affordable vehicle for daily commuting and don't need a lot of cargo or passenger space. Plus, a small car's tidy size makes it a sensible choice for buyers who drive and park in congested urban areas.

Therefore, it's a no-brainer that your first line of defence against high fuel prices isn't buying a Toyota Prius, a Honda Insight hybrid, or GM's $40,000 2011 Volt electric car. What you want instead is a cheap, small, crashworthy, reliable, and easy-to-repair used car. In the bargain, you'll be following the "reduce, reuse, and recycle" environmentalist creed.

Indeed, fuel-frugal 4-cylinder compact cars are primarily for city dwellers who want good fuel economy in the city/highway range of 9.3/5.9 L/100 km (30/48 mpg), easy manoeuvrability in urban areas, a relatively low retail price, and modest depreciation. In exchange, owners must accept a cramped interior that may carry only two passengers in comfort, an engine that can take eons to merge with traffic or pass other cars, and insufficient luggage capacity (hatchbacks, however, make the best use of what room there is). As well, engine and road noise are fairly excessive on base models.

In response to these shortcomings, many cars in this class, such as the Honda Civic and Toyota Echo, have been replaced during the past decade by much larger, more stylish iterations that rival the size of Honda's early Accord and Toyota's Camry. This upsizing makes room for new "micro" small cars like the Honda Fit, Hyundai Accent, and Nissan Versa, which vary in size between Mercedes-Benz's Smart Car and BMW's Mini Cooper.

Safety is a mixed bag, however.

One of the more alarming characteristics of a small car's highway performance is its extreme vulnerability to strong lateral winds, which may make the car difficult to keep on course and require constant steering corrections that are both distracting and tiresome. On the other hand, crashworthiness is not necessarily compromised by a small size. In fact, evidence suggests that lighter-weight vehicles can be as safe as heavier ones.

In the October 17, 2005, edition of *Automotive News*, Robert Hall, professor emeritus of operations management at Indiana University, said the following:

> In the last 40 years, auto-racing speeds have increased, yet deaths have decreased significantly while the weights of the vehicles have gone down progressively. Why? Crushable fronts that absorb impact, "tubs" that shelter drivers after the entire car has disintegrated, a relocation of the front axle and, yes, crash bags. In this case, lighter is markedly safer.

Many newer small cars incorporate a body structure that deflects crash forces away from occupants, making these cars more crashworthy than some larger vehicles. The Smart Car is a good example: It offers acceptable, though not impressive, crashworthiness through a well-designed restraint system and the use of a stiff chassis design that minimizes intrusion.

The Smart Car sandwiches its powerplant under the floor—raising the passenger compartment above the impact area in a collision with another passenger car. The powertrain is mounted on a sliding rack to diminish the force of a collision.

Although most small cars are similar in appearance, the Japanese and South Koreans have brought out subcompacts with flashy new designs that have added much-needed flair to functionality.

Traditional "ho-hum" small car styling was thrown out the window when the Nissan Cube debuted as a late-2009 model, and the Kia Soul joined the class as an

The Nissan Cube (*left*) is an Average buy; the cheaper Kia Soul (*right*) is rated Above Average.

early 2010. Both are tall four-door wagons that boast outstanding cargo and passenger space, thanks to their upright body architecture. A 2009 Cube that originally sold for $16,998 now goes for $11,500; a 2010 Soul that sold for $15,495 is now worth $10,500.

2011 Prices

Up and down.

Automakers have added lots of safety and performance features to their small cars and this has driven up base prices substantially, but this isn't always the case, as we can see with the value-added 2011 Hyundai Accent, which comes in at under $10,500. On the other hand, the completely redesigned 2011 Ford Mustang V6 ($27,000) is well worth its $1,500 price increase this year, even though the car's many improvements make earlier models obsolete and practically worthless.

As safer, better-performing models hit showrooms for 2011, they will drive down prices of previous models. If the improvements aren't that important, the cheaper, earlier models can be excellent buys.

SMALL CAR RATINGS

Recommended

Honda Fit (2009)
Hyundai Elantra (2007–09)
Mazda3 (2006–09)

Suzuki SX4 (2007–09)
Toyota Echo (2000–05)

Above Average

Ford Focus (2005–09)
Honda Fit (2007–08)
Hyundai Accent (2006–09)

Mazda Protegé (1999–2003)
Nissan Sentra (2007–09)
Subaru Forester (2003–09)

Hyundai Elantra (1999–2006)
Mazda3 (2004–05)
Mazda5 (2006–09)

Subaru Legacy, Outback (1999–2009)
Suzuki Aerio (2003–07)
Suzuki Swift, Swift+ (1999–2009)

Average

BMW Mini Cooper (2008–09)
Chrysler Neon, SX 2.0, SRT4 (2004–05)
Honda Civic (1999–2009)
Hyundai Accent (2004–05)
Kia Rio, Rio5, Spectra, Spectra5 (2009)
Nissan Cube (2009)
Nissan Sentra (2001–06)
Nissan Versa (2007–09)

Subaru Forester (1999–2002)
Subaru Impreza (1999–2009)
Suzuki Esteem (1999–2002)
Suzuki Verona (2004–06)
Toyota Yaris (2006–09)
Toyota/General Motors Matrix/Vibe (2009)

Below Average

BMW Mini Cooper (2002–07)
Chrysler Neon (2001–03)
Daewoo/General Motors Aveo, Aveo5,
    Lanos, Wave (2004–09)
Hyundai Accent (2001–03)
Kia Rio, Rio5, Spectra, Spectra5
    (2006–08)

Mercedes-Benz Smart Fortwo (2009)
Toyota Corolla (1997–2009)
Toyota/General Motors Matrix/Vibe (2003–08)
Volkswagen diesel models (1999–2006)
Volkswagen Golf, Rabbit, Jetta, Cabrio (1999–2009)

Not Recommended

Chrysler Caliber (2007–09)
Daewoo Lanos, Nubira, Leganza
    (2000–02)
Daewoo/General Motors Optra,
    Optra5 (2004–08)
Ford Focus (2000–04)
General Motors Saturn S-Series, L-Series,
    ION (1999–2007)

Honda Civic Hybrid (2003–09)
Honda Insight (2001–06)
Kia Rio, Rio5, Spectra/Sephia, Spectra5
    (2000–05)
Mercedes-Benz Smart Fortwo (2005–08)
Subaru WRX/STi (2002–09)
Volkswagen diesel models (2007–09)

BMW

| MINI COOPER | ★★★ |

RATING: Average (2008–09); Below Average (2002–07). "High performance" means low quality. With the Mini, you choose performance and cuteness over reasonable reliability and cheap, convenient servicing. **Ideal model year:** The 2008 Cooper convertible. Originally sold for $31,600; now priced at $10,000 less. **"Real" city/highway fuel economy:** *Manual 5-speed:* 9.0/6.2 L/100 km. *Manual 6-speed:* 7.3/5.4 L/100 km. *Automatic 6-speed:* 7.8/5.9 L/100 km.

BMW's Mini: A "cute" low-quality performer.

Maintenance/repair costs: Outrageously higher than average. **Parts:** Expensive and sometimes rare; God help you if the supercharger goes. BMW's Pony Express parts distribution system gives preference to 2008 and later model years, and dealers find it more profitable to stock 2008 or later model year parts. This is characteristic of every model that is redesigned every three years or so. Older parts are back ordered until they run out. **Extended warranty:** A good idea, but no solution to the slow parts delivery. **Best alternatives:** *For performance:* Ford Mustang, Honda Civic Si, and Mazda3. *For fuel economy/ reliability:* Honda Civic; Hyundai Accent or Elantra; Mazda Protegé; Nissan Sentra; Suzuki Aerio, Esteem, or Swift; and Toyota Corolla. **Helpful websites:** *www.northamericanmotoring.com* and *www.mini2.com.*

Strengths and Weaknesses

Base hatchbacks come with a 118 hp 4-cylinder engine, while S versions are equipped with a turbocharged 172 hp variant. Convertibles feature a standard 115 hp 4-banger, while the S sports a 168 hp version of the same powerplant. A 6-speed manual is standard on most models, but the 2007 added a 6-speed automatic that replaced the previous year's continuously variable transmission (CVT) and manifested many of the factory and supplier defects that often follow such upgrades. The 2007 hatchbacks come with front side airbags and side curtain airbags; convertibles are equipped with front side airbags with head and torso protection.

This is a typical fun-to-drive, small European car that doesn't sacrifice power and handling for fuel economy. Handling is a breeze: The car performs responsibly in all speed ranges with precise steering, minimal body lean, and hardly any front-end noseplow. The 2007 redesign smoothed out the car's choppy ride a bit but made the audio and climate controls more confusing than ever. The ride is still harsh, road and engine noise are omnipresent, body glitches are common, and rear interior room and comfort are sadly lacking. The 2007 Mini is 7.5 cm (3 in.) longer than the 2006 model. However, *CarsDirect.com* says the 2007 has 5 cm (2 in.) less rear leg room (73.5 vs. 79 cm; 29 vs. 31 in.) and 1 square foot less luggage space when the rear seats are folded down (24 vs. 25 sq. ft.).

According to *Automotive.com*, the 2007 S model with the turbocharger has 4 more horsepower than the 2006 S model with a supercharger; it also gets 16 percent better city gas mileage. Gone is the scream of the supercharger, and you'll have to live with the annoying engine hesitation caused by turbo lag.

About 90 percent of the 2008's components are new or upgraded, and the 2008 Mini is 19.5 cm (7.5 in.) longer and 4.4 cm (1.7 in.) wider for increased driver and passenger space. Another plus: 10 percent quicker steering makes the car a bit more nimble, while the slightly longer wheelbase improves performance.

The 2009 convertible was redesigned and given a power fabric top and heated-glass rear window. JCW models come with a 208 hp turbocharged 4-banger along with stronger brakes, a performance suspension, specific exhaust tuning, and 17-inch wheels.

Reliability and quality control are problematic with 2007 and earlier Minis. *Consumer Reports* and *Lemon-Aid* have had different views on this matter over the years. I disagreed with *Consumer Reports'* earlier rating of this car as having above-average reliability. It does not.

In its 2010 report, however, *CR* toughened its assessment, calling the non-turbo models only "Average" for reliability and giving a "Below Average" designation to the Cooper S.

What are the big problems afflicting this little car?

Owner complaints and internal service bulletins point to major highway performance and safety deficiencies on the 2002–07 models that are obviously factory-related. Owners report chronic stalling, CVT breakdowns, power-steering failures, automatic window electrical shorts, prematurely worn side struts and brake calipers and rotors, constantly cracking windshields, and poor fit and finish and body design (for example, the hood scoop deforms due to heat from the turbo)—as well as expensive servicing and long waits for parts.

The picture isn't totally bleak: 2008–09 models are much better built, with only a few complaints concerning the engine, the fuel system, premature clutch wear, poor-quality body hardware, spontaneous sunroof shattering, and the speedometer being off by about 10 percent.

Safety Summary

All models: 2002—Fire ignited under the dashboard. • Airbag failed to deploy. • Frequent power-steering failures. • Automatic window failures. • Many early automatic transmission, clutch, and cable replacements:

> The automatic transmission of my 2002 MINI Cooper failed while my friend was driving my car. She was on a winding coastal road and the car died on a blind curve, putting her at great danger. Fortunately nobody was hurt. The car was towed to the San Francisco BMW dealership, where I was informed I needed a $8,500 "refurbished" transmission, as the transmission is not even made anymore. Research on line shows that this [is] becoming a frequent problem with "first generation" MINIs with the "CVT" automatic transmission.

2003—CVT and steering failures continue. • In one incident, power-steering pump caught fire; in other reported incidents, it simply stopped working. • Electrical shorts cause inside lights and gauges to operate erratically. • Power windows open on their own. **2004**—Vent fan in motor catches fire. • More transmission trouble. • Power steering fails:

> www.mini2.com has reports of around 1 in 4 vehicles having this pump fail prematurely. I believe an investigation is important due to member reports of fires starting under the hood.

• Manual transmission failure. • Power window doesn't roll down. • Windshield is easily cracked:

> While driving normally a very very small pebble size stone hits underneath the windshield wiper on the passenger's side. The windshield [immediately] spiders all over the window. I've been told all the problems with the BMW windshields were corrected, but I've heard from over 20 fellow MINI owners of random cracking and failures within the first 2,000 miles [3,200 km]!

• Brake failure. • Hard to find horn button's "sweet spot." **2005**—Power-steering pump, transmission, clutch, and strut failures continue unabated:

> Complete catastrophic failure of the front passenger strut, strut tower, mount and lower control arm bushing caused by an imperfection on a public, well traveled road. Reports on enthusiast forums of over 216 others suffering the same failure on the same model car and a report in the Sept–Oct 2007 edition of MC^2 magazine citing the need to look for these common flaws on this model car when considering purchasing a used one.

• Car continually loses power when cruising; owner is told the problem is a loose gas cap, but it isn't. • Windshield spontaneously cracks. • Sudden stalling ("limp home" mode) on the highway; DME component needs to be reprogrammed. • Front wheel rubbing noises when turning hard left or hard right. • One vehicle lost three out of four lug nuts on the front driver-side wheel. **2006**—Vehicle suddenly stalls on the highway. • Both strut mounts fail. • ABS and DSC systems don't work properly. • Speedometer registers 7 percent faster than the actual speed; odometer registers 1 percent more than the actual mileage. • Passenger-side seatback won't lock in the upright position. • "Mushrooming" struts:

> "Mushrooming" is when the car gets a hard hit and the strut tower pushes up the metal where it is attached to [create] a bubble and damage the alignment. How can the strut tower [make] this damage without damaging the rim first?

• Stalling and then sudden acceleration. • Engine seizes after driving through a rain puddle. • Windshield cracked (stress fracture) while one car was parked overnight; many other complaints of cracks, while BMW denies all liability. • One car suddenly veered out of control on the highway when brakes were applied. BMW experts say it was due to brake rotor "unexpected separation." Again, BMW denies all liability. • Plastic fuel tank is easily punctured by road debris. **2006–07**—Passenger-side airbag is disabled when average-sized adult is seated. • Tailpipe sticks out too far, burns leg as driver unloads packages from the rear; a common hazard with the Mini:

> The tailpipes, when hot, apparently protrude enough to cause severe burns to the leg. My 7-year-old daughter sustained a serious burn this way when getting something out of the hatchback.
>
> •
>
> After a 30 minute drive, I parked and then pulled something out of the trunk. While reaching in, I burned my left shin on the tailpipe. I showed it a couple of days later to our burn unit director and he told me that it was a functional full thickness burn in an extremely dangerous location (because of the poor blood perfusion to the shin, healing is impaired and infection risk is high).... It is a very common problem (a simple Google search will show this).

• Ongoing problems with transmission and fuel-pump failures and with windshield stress fractures. • Hood scoop deforms due to extreme heat. • Excessive heat in driver's footwell near the centre pillar. • Dunlop run-flat radial tubeless tires have side wall bubbling. **2008**—Legs continue to get burned by the protruding tailpipe; recall doesn't cover all the affected cars. • Passenger airbag is disabled even though a full-sized adult is seated. • Multiple transmission failures. • Premature tire failure. **2008–09**—Sunroof suddenly shatters:

> The back sunroof just exploded, sending fragment shards of glass blowing into my car. Drove to nearest gas station and covered the gaping hole in the sunroof. When I got home, I noticed that all edges of the broken glass point outward. I did not hit anything for this to have happened. The explosion was instantaneous and frightening.

Cooper S: **2009**—Electrical fire started in the dashboard area. • Airbag failed to deploy. • Several incidents where the engine timing belt tensioner failed. • Loud knocking diesel sound on a cold start. • Engine tends to lag and lurch when accelerating from a stop. *JCW:* **2009**—Cold start rattle or knock. • Deflectors under front bumpers are too rigid and fail at the seam where the rubber is fused to the hard plastic. • When it rains, front windows open on their own. • Passenger-side Disable Airbag warning light comes on when an average-sized adult is seated. *Clubman:* **2009**—Excessive engine rattling:

> Engine makes a loud rattling noise like it has no oil pressure. Not just on startup but for as long as a few blocks of driving. It has done this 6 times in the first 2,000 miles [3,200 km] of ownership. I am concerned that severe internal damage is being done to the engine if I continue to drive it this way. Dealer says they are aware of problem but have no fix from BMW, or do not have a fix that actually solves the problem.

Secret Warranties/Internal Bulletins/Service Tips

All models: 2002–05—CVT automatic transmission "howling." **2002–06**—Engine flaring on acceleration. • Stiff diagonal gear shifts. • Noise from air recirculation door motors. • Hydraulic fluid leakage from the engine mount. **2004–06**—A secret warranty extension affecting the Emissions Warranty will cover the free replacement of engine oxygen sensors up to 10 years or 100,000 miles (M120409090801-003). **2005–06**—Troubleshooting instrument panel creaking. **2006–09**—Remedies for a squealing engine drivebelt. **2007**—No-crank, no-start. • Free crankcase breather retrofit and engine-cooling-fan fuse replacement. • Cruise control cuts out at 110 km/h. • Automatic transmission fluid leak. • Various drivability complaints. • An inoperative navigation system may require the replacement of the HIP module under warranty. • Diagnosing and repairing various electrical malfunctions. • Inoperative electric steering lock. • Steering rattles. • Front-end clunking when passing over bumps. • Rear axle knocking. • Water leaks onto the front carpet. • Tailgate hard to open or close. • Speedometer buzzes and sunroof squeaks. • Sunroof sunshade opens on its own. • Sunroof wind noise. • Instrument panel rattle. • Windshield whistling noise. **2007–08**—Fuel gauge brightness fluctuations. **2008**—A front-end knocking noise may be caused by a defective engine mounting bracket. • BMW says an engine knocking noise may simply mean the engine vacuum pump is working as it should (what?). • Headlights flickering or moving up or down on their own is likely caused by a chaffed headlight wiring harness. **2009**—Surging in traffic traced to a fuel pressure pump/shaft defect. • A rear suspension knock or rattle may indicate that the inner diameter of the stabilizer bar mounts is too large.

MINI COOPER PROFILE

	2002	2003	2004	2005	2006	2007	2008	2009
Cost Price ($)								
Cooper	25,200	25,200	22,700	23,500	23,500	23,950	22,800	22,800
Clubman	—	—	—	—	—	—	26,400	26,400
S	29,950	29,950	29,950	30,500	30,600	30,600	29,900	29,900
Convertible	29,950	29,950	29,950	30,500	30,600	30,600	31,600	31,600

Used Values ($)								
Cooper ▲	5,000	6,000	7,500	8,500	9,500	13,000	15,000	17,000
Cooper ▼	4,000	5,000	6,500	7,500	8,500	12,000	14,000	16,000
Clubman ▲	—	—	—	—	—	—	17,000	20,000
Clubman ▼	—	—	—	—	—	—	15,500	18,500
S ▲	6,500	7,500	9,500	11,500	13,000	16,500	19,500	23,000
S ▼	5,500	6,500	8,500	10,500	12,000	15,000	18,000	22,000
Convertible ▲	—	—	—	—	14,500	17,000	21,000	24,500
Convertible ▼	—	—	—	—	13,000	16,500	19,500	23,000

Reliability	2	2	2	2	2	2	3	3
Crash Safety (F)	4	4	4	4	4	—	5	4
Side	4	4	4	4	4	—	4	5
IIHS Side	—	—	—	—	3	3	3	3
Offset	5	5	5	5	5	5	5	5
Roof Strength	—	—	—	—	—	3	3	3
Head Restraints (F)	2	2	2	2	2	3	3	5
Rollover Resistance	4	4	4	4	4	—	5	5

Chrysler

CALIBER ★

bad buy

RATING: Not Recommended (2007–09). An unsafe, quality-challenged, underpowered fuel hog that will soon be replaced by an entirely new car based on the Fiat Alfa Romeo Giulietta. **"Real" city/highway fuel economy:** Very poor; in the 15.0/14.0 L/100 km range. **Maintenance/repair costs:** Likely to be higher than average once the warranty expires and Fiat takes over the dealer network. **Parts:** Easily found and relatively inexpensive now, but expected to be in short supply in the near future. High-performance powertrain parts for the SRT4 are already in short supply and quite costly. **Extended warranty:** A good idea. **Best alternatives:** The Chevrolet HHR; Honda Civic; Hyundai Accent; Mazda3; Nissan Versa; Suzuki SX4; and Toyota Corolla, Echo, or Tercel. The 2008 SE 2.0L costs $8,000, or half its original selling price, but it is underpowered and fuel-thirsty. The $1,000-cheaper 1.6L engine–equipped model is entirely out of its league, although the 5-speed manual transmission is a better performer than the CVT. **Helpful websites:** *www.caliberforumz.com.*

Strengths and Weaknesses

This small four-door hatchback provides a good view of the road, thanks to its SUV-like raised seats. The ride is acceptable; however, handling is poor, and the noisy 1.8L, 2.0L, and 2.4L engines (148, 158, and 172 hp, respectively) lack low-end power for merging with traffic—which would be acceptable if there was a trade-off for good fuel economy, but there isn't. Gas consumption (regular or premium)

All ratings on a numbered scale where ▨ is good and **1** is bad. See page 132 for a more detailed description.

is quite high for a car this small. Many powertrain and fit and finish problems have been reported in these first-generation models. A more powerful 280 hp SRT4 debuted in 2008, but 2009 was its last year.

Reliability has never been Chrysler's strong suit, and the Caliber duplicates many of the quality and performance failures of Chrysler's earlier models. Interestingly, the AWD version is much less reliable than the front drive versions. Nevertheless, expect numerous powertrain defects, like chronic stalling followed by sudden lurching and oxygen sensor and throttle bushing failures that cause the engine to run roughly or the throttle to stick. Here's how one owner explains it at *www.caliberforumz.com*:

> My 2007 2.0 has had the throttle stick three times. Once when accelerating off a highway on ramp and once when leaving a stop light. Today I installed bosch Iridium spark plugs. After a 20 mile [32 km] drive I decided to reset the electronic throttle. After pressing the pedal to the floor and releasing, I started the car and the throttle was stuck. I instantly shut off the ignition and got down on my knees to inspect the pedal assembly. I found two bronze bushings on the floor near the pedal and when I moved the pedal it returned to the idle position.

Brake and electrical problems abound. The air conditioning system is failure-prone and costly to repair. Paint easily peels off at the car wash, and windshield cracks at the windshield wiper mounting are common. The tie rod end, 4-cylinder engine gaskets, and automatic transmission module fail. The suspension struts are of poor quality (four replacements in one year, reports one owner); owners also report excessive vibration caused by a defective idler pulley. Interior noise is omnipresent, and includes tire thumping; engine rattles; window-crank, door-hinge, and driver-seat squeaks; and radio-speaker and fender rattles (the fender may be missing a bolt). Poor body fit allows for wind and water to enter the car practically everywhere, but especially through the sunroof area when the drain gets "kinked."

Safety-related factory defects are legion, though crashworthiness is fairly good. NHTSA awarded the 2007–09 Caliber five stars for front- and side-impact occupant protection and four stars for rollover resistance. IIHS, however, concluded that although the Caliber gives Good frontal offset crash protection, side protection is rated Marginal. No roof strength tests have been carried out, but head-restraint protection has been rated as Marginal.

Caliber prices have fallen dramatically since the car was launched as a 2007 model. Buyers are afraid of the car's reputation for poor quality and are waiting to see the Fiat platform changeover coming up in 2012. Higher fuel prices may cause a small spike in the Caliber's selling price, but this will erode as the 2012 models approach. A 2009 base SE now costs $7,000–$8,000, the RT front-drive is valued at $9,500–$10,500, and the RT AWD will cost $11,500–$13,000. The 2008 models are worth $1,500–$2,000 less. SRT4 models have lost the most value since they were dropped in 2009: selling originally for $25,000, a 2009 version can now be bought for $11,500; a 2008 will run $15,000 less than its original price.

Safety Summary

All models: 2007—Constant stalling. • There's an off-idle hesitation when pulling away from a traffic stop. • Tailpipe is cut too short; allows fumes to enter the cabin. • Firestone tire-tread separation; 15-inch Dunlop tire defects. • Premature wheel bearing replacement. • AC/heater produces a nauseating smell when activated. • Excessive highway vibration. • Gas-pedal bushing falls out, causing engine to surge; in one case, the assembly fell under the brake pedal, preventing braking. • ABS failure can cause an accident. • Cold, rainy weather prevents the power windows from rolling down. • Automatic door locks can lock you out if you exit the vehicle to close the garage door, for example. • Cold water, then hot water, drips onto passengers from the heater core:

> Hot water leaking from under the steering wheel. Husband sustained second and third degree burns.... It was determined that the AC condensation drain hose was clogged with debris which caused hot water to get inside the vehicle.

• If a passenger's head is resting near the lock button when the door is unlocked, the force of the spring can injure the passenger. • One cannot drive with the rear windows down without hearing a painful, helicopter-like roar. **2007–08**—Airbags fail to deploy. **2008**—Seat belts often become unlatched because occupants mistakenly put the tongue into the latch housing. • Vehicle pulls sharply to the right when accelerating. • Stalling problem traced to a malfunctioning wireless control module. • Intermittent failure of the turn signals and fog lights. • Inaccurate fuel gauge. • Water collects in the tail lights. • As with the BMW Mini, the Caliber's tailpipe can burn the unwary:

> The exhaust pipe protrudes too far from the rear of the vehicle making it possible for small children to receive injury when the vehicle is hot. A small child in our home received a second degree burn when walking around the vehicle.

2009—In a collision, seat belt unlatched and airbag failed to deploy. • Accelerator pedal fell off while car was changing lanes:

> It became necessary for me to punch the gas pedal in order to make a lane change. When I did this, the accelerator pedal broke off just below the spring-action pivot point and the accelerator became useless because the spring (which is wired to the engine's accelerator and receives acceleration input from the pedal to which it is attached) was no longer (obviously) attached to the pedal.

The Caliber is a "tire-eater":

> 2009 Dodge Caliber has no adjustments for rear camber and requires an after-market bolt installation for front. My 2009 Dodge Caliber 1B3HB28C69D116544, has eaten the inside edges off all 4 tires (scooped). This was written off as tire wear—ok on

each Chrysler service. I noticed that the insides of the tires were scooped out when the wheels were turned out when I parked recently. Essentially, you as the owner get to replace four tires every 24,000 miles [38,600 km] and there seems to be no solid repair. My car has 17,425 miles [28,000 km] and I am disgusted that this is a problem that essentially has no repair. The bolt they installed in the R front allows for a + or −1 degree adjustment. What happens if the owner doesn't find the problem? Blowouts and crashes.

Many engine head gasket and automatic transmission failures. • Transmission line suddenly burst; Chrysler billed owner $450 U.S. for repairs. • Transmission slippage. *SRT4:* Poor braking performance.

Secret Warranties/Internal Bulletins/Service Tips

All models: 2007—A sticking accelerator pedal involves inspecting the accelerator pedal assembly bushings and replacing under warranty the pedal assembly, if necessary. • AC compressor noise or housing damage. • Water leaking from headliner. • Windshield crack diagnosis for warranty approval. **2007–08**— Engine won't start with wireless key feature. • Excessive engine vibration at idle may also be fixed by reprogramming the control module. • Squeak or groan sound when raising or lowering door glass. • Seat creak or squawk. • Whistling sound from the left side mirror. • Horizontal panel paint etching. **2008**—Manual transmission gear clashing. • Clutch pedal squeak troubleshooting. *SRT4:* **All years:** A "limp-in condition" or lack of turbo boost may require that the injector be replaced and the powertrain control module be erased and reprogrammed. **2007–09**—Poor handling, a rough ride, or leaky struts requires that the jounce bumper and dust shield be replaced with a new design. Obviously, this should be done under warranty.

NEON, SX 2.0, SRT4	★ ★ ★

RATING: Average (2004–05); Below Average (2001–03). A low-quality, fuel-thirsty small car. This "econobox" eats engine head gaskets and brake calipers, so what savings you realized from its low resale price will be lost through high maintenance and depreciation costs that will creep even higher as the parts supply dries up. **"Real" city/highway fuel economy:** Owners report extremely poor fuel economy in the 11.0/12.5 L/100 km range. **Maintenance/repair costs:** Costlier than average. **Parts:** Not yet hard to find and still relatively inexpensive. However, Chrysler is particularly slow in distributing parts for cars it no longer makes; waits of several months are commonplace. **Extended warranty:** Too many things will go wrong. Choose a different model, not an extended warranty. **Best alternatives:** Honda Civic; Hyundai Accent; Mazda3 or Protegé; Suzuki Esteem or SX4; and Toyota Corolla or Echo. **Helpful websites:** *http://forums.neons.org.*

Strengths and Weaknesses

A small, noisy car with big quality problems in its first-generation models, the Neon does offer a spacious interior and responsive steering and handling. Nevertheless, it's seriously handicapped by an antiquated, feeble, and fuel-thirsty 3-speed automatic gearbox, a DOHC 4-cylinder 150 hp powerplant that has to be pushed hard to do as well as the SOHC 132 hp engine, and a mushy base suspension.

The 2003 Neon was renamed the SX 2.0 in Canada. It is roomy and reasonably powered for urban use, and later refinements gave it a softer, quieter ride while enhancing the car's handling and powertrain performance. Quality didn't improve that much, though.

Chrysler has tried to make its low-end cars more appealing and more profitable by adding high-performance features that quickly lose their value as the vehicle ages and are a nightmare to service. For example, the 2004 SRT4 equipped with a turbocharged 215 hp 2.4L 4-cylinder engine hooked to a manual 4-speed transmission sold originally for $26,950; it's now worth $4,000.

Reliability has always bedevilled the Neon. Owners have reported costly automatic transmission failures and a gearbox that frequently slams into gear, engine motor mounts that last only a few years, an AC system noted for condenser and compressor failures, a plethora of electrical short circuits, interior noise and water leaks, and uneven fit and finish, along with poor-quality trim items.

The 2004–05 models are not better made. They continue to have plenty of engine, transmission, and body deficiencies. Engine stalling is a recurring problem, mostly caused by poorly calibrated computer modules (an 8-year/130,000 km emissions warranty item). Failure of the front control arms and suspension bushings, paint delamination, and cracked dashboards also afflict all Neon model years.

Owners of newer models also say the brakes squeak constantly; early starter rust-out causes no-starts; the automatic transmission shudders when shifting; the AC fails to cool the vehicle adequately; when the car is passing through puddles, the engine can ingest water though the air-intake port; and the engine noticeably loses power when windows are lowered, the sunroof is open, or the AC is engaged. Owners also complain of overall poor fuel economy.

VEHICLE HISTORY: 2002—An upgraded automatic transmission (reliability remains poor). **2003**—New steering wheels, front and rear fascias, and engine mounts to smooth out engine roughness. A taller Fifth gear is used in the manual transmission. **2004**—High-performance versions get a small 15 hp boost and a limited-slip differential. **2005**—The SRT4 gets a specially tuned sport suspension, improved brakes, and sport seats.

Safety Summary

All years: Fires. • "Inappropriate" airbag deployment or failure to deploy. • Sudden acceleration. • Chronic stalling. • No-starts because of rusted-out starter. • Throttle system failures. • Faulty cruise control. • Steering loss. • Steering locks up when it rains. • Chronic transmission failures and slippage. • Transmission suddenly downshifts to First gear when accelerating at 90 km/h. • ABS failures. • Defective brake master cylinder. • Premature front brake pad/rotor wearout. • Excessive vibration. • Small horn buttons are hard to find in an emergency. • Trunk lid or hood may fall. • Headlight switch is a hide-and-seek affair. • Axle shafts may suddenly collapse. **2001**—Electrical shorts (lights and gauges). • Engine damage caused by water ingested through the air-intake system. • Annoying reflection in the front windshield. **2002**—Stalling caused by the engine ingesting water when it rains. • Transmission slips between First and Second gear. • Vehicle pulls when cruising or on acceleration, and tends to wobble side to side at low speeds. • Difficult to maintain control of vehicle because of excessive steering-wheel vibration. **2003**—Engine manifold failure. • Poor braking. **2004**—Seat belts fail to lock during a collision. • In one instance, unoccupied passenger seat flew off its track during a collision. • Electrical system suddenly shuts down. • Rusted, prematurely worn brake rotors. **2005**—Airbags failed to deploy. • Radio catches fire. • Hard starting, followed by engine surging. • Manual transmission self-destructs. • Automatic transmission control module failures. • CV joint failure. • Brake pedal goes to the floor without effect. • Lower control arm bushings separate from their housing. • Faulty multifunction switch causes the battery to fail and fog lights to flicker. • Ignition switch won't free up the key. • Motor mounts often fail. • Corners of both front doors are abnormally sharp:

> On two occasions, an occupant on the front passenger side was cut on her face when attempting to enter the vehicle.

Secret Warranties/Internal Bulletins/Service Tips

All years: Paint delamination, peeling, or fading. • Tips on getting rid of the AC's musty smell. **2000–05**—Headlight water condensation. • TSB #M19-07-05 admits that a clicking noise heard when turning may be due to a misaligned or defective steering column. A similar clicking may emanate from the drivetrain. **2001**—Engine hesitation. • No-starts in cold weather. • Rear window may not go all the way down. **2002**—Poor engine and AC performance caused by miscalibrated or faulty computer modules. **2002–03**—Delayed shifts may require the installation of a new automatic transmission front pump assembly. **2003–04**—TSB #09-007-04 says an engine snapping sound is Chrysler's fault and can be remedied by chamfering the bore radius on cam bearing caps L2 through L5 and R2 through R5. **2004**—Hard starts. • Acceleration stumble. **2005**—Rough, shuddering 1–2 upshifts. • Engine runs poorly.

	2001	2002	2003	2004	2005
Cost Price ($)					
Base	18,375	18,505	—	—	—
Sport/SX 2.0	—	—	14,995	15,195	15,605
SRT4	—	—	—	26,950	27,380
Used Values ($)					
Base ▲	1,200	2,000	—	—	—
Base ▼	1,000	1,500	—	—	—
Sport/SX 2.0 ▲	—	—	1,300	2,000	2,500
Sport/SX 2.0 ▼	—	—	1,000	1,800	2,000
SRT4 ▲	—	—	—	4,000	6,000
SRT4 ▼	—	—	—	3,000	5,000
Reliability	1	1	1	2	2
Crash Safety (F)	4	4	4	4	4
Side	3	3	3	3	3
IIHS Side	1	1	1	1	1
Offset	2	2	2	2	2
Head Restraints (F)	1	1	1	1	1
Rollover Resistance	4	4	4	4	4

Daewoo

Lemon-Aid does not recommend any cars by South Korean automaker Daewoo. The manufacturer marketed three cars in Canada from 2000 to 2002: the Lanos subcompact, the Nubira compact sedan and wagon, and the Leganza luxury sedan. All of these cars are rated Not Recommended because they are unreliable and expensive to maintain. Daewoo entered the North American car market in 1988, declared bankruptcy a year later, and was bought by General Motors in 2002. General Motors brought up production quality, but it was too little, too late. Today, Daewoo/GM continues to run in the rear of the pack. By the way, Daewoo depreciation is mind-boggling: An entry-level, $13,395 2002 Lanos is now worth less than $1,000, and the top-of-the-line 2002 Leganza CDX that originally sold for $25,495 now sells for about $1,500.

Daewoo/General Motors

Daewoo skipped the 2003 model year in Canada and brought out three models under the GM banner as 2004 models. Chevrolet dealers sell the entry-level Aveo (a Lanos spin-off); the Optra, a compact based on the Daewoo Lacetti; and the Epica, a mid-sized vehicle based on Daewoo's Magnos. Suzuki sells the subcompact Swift+, based on the Kalos, and the Verona for GM.

RATING: Below Average (2004–09). A failure-prone small car that has improved only marginally since General Motors bought Daewoo. Best used as a bare-bones urban runabout. Aveo5 is a similarly priced four-door hatchback base model. **Ideal model year:** The 2008 Wave5 costs only $5,000 and would be good for light urban chores. **"Real" city/highway fuel economy:** 8.8/6.1 L/100 km. Owners report fuel savings may undershoot this estimate by about 10 percent. **Maintenance/repair costs:** Higher than average. **Parts:** Easily found and relatively inexpensive. **Extended warranty:** A toss-up. **Best alternatives:** The Ford Focus (post-2007); Honda Civic or Fit; Hyundai Accent; Mazda3 or Protegé; Suzuki Aerio, Esteem, Swift+, or SX4; and Toyota Corolla or Echo. **Helpful websites:** *www.automotiveforums.com/f1439-aveo.html.*

Strengths and Weaknesses

First launched by Daewoo as the Lanos, this nondescript, cheaply made, small South Korean car had few redeeming qualities. Both cars carry an underpowered 103 hp 1.6L 4-cylinder engine mated with a 5-speed manual or a 4-speed automatic. The powertrain and overall performance lack the refinement found with many other bantamweights anchoring the compact-car division. The engine is particularly noisy and strains going uphill with its maximum four-passenger load. Four *small* passengers. Around town, though, the car is peppy and nimble.

The 2004 Aveo's $2,000 price tag is very reasonable for a four-door that originally sold for $13,480. It saves buyers $1,000 over a $3,000 Toyota Echo that's comparatively priced new but depreciates slower. Don't worry if you pay a bit extra for a better-performing and more reliable Honda, Hyundai, Mazda, or Toyota—the difference means nothing when spread out over a number of years, and it will likely be refunded through a higher resale price.

Lanos owners complain of an unending series of powertrain failures, serious fit and finish deficiencies, and electrical short circuits. These problems have continued with the 2004 and later versions built under GM's supervision. Even up through the past few years, Daewoo DNA still causes transmissions to burn out, electrical systems to short-circuit, engines to stall, and brakes to fail. Fit and finish is about average for a stagecoach; owners report persistent water leaks and an unending symphony of squeaks, grunts, and rattles.

VEHICLE HISTORY: 2001—The SE hatchback and SX four-door sedan are dropped, and a gussied-up sport hatchback is launched. **2002**—Daewoo goes bankrupt. After Ford dithers for almost a year, GM buys Daewoo's assets and dumps the dealers, who finally get a few crumbs in an out-of-court settlement. **2004**—Aveo launches in early 2004 with a slightly longer sedan, the same puny engine, optional ABS, and no side airbags. **2006**—Standard front side airbags and larger optional wheels. GM-imposed quality improvements here and there mirror Hyundai's puny efforts to address similar Kia deficiencies during the fateful 2005 model year. **2007**—7.5 cm (3 in.) longer and slightly restyled.

🚗 Safety Summary

All years: Airbags fail to deploy:

> The driver stated that in a front end collision the airbags did not deploy. Vehicle was travelling about 50 mph [80 km/h] and went under a truck. Most of the impact was to the hood, rooftop, and windshield. The steering wheel was completely damaged. There was no substantial damage to the bumper. The driver sustained the following injuries: the nose was fractured, left eyeball went out of orbit, and the cheekbone was crushed. The manufacturer stated all three sensors have to be hit simultaneously for the airbags to deploy.

Sudden acceleration. • Stalling. • Brake failures. • Premature brake pad/rotor wearout. **2004–05**—Transmission failures. • Excessive on-road vibration felt in the front end and steering. • Accelerator and brake pedal are mounted too close to each other. • Clutch overheats and fails. • Snapped side shock bolt. • Plastic thermostat splits, allowing engine to overheat. • Windshield cracking. • Door lock falls into the door's interior. **2006**—Early coil spring replacement. **2006–08**—Passenger-side airbag is disabled by an average-sized seated adult. **2007**—Spark plug cables rub on engine bolt and cause the engine to misfire. • Cruise control works erratically. • Premature alternator failure:

> Dealer claims that Aveo has the problem with alternators, but they are not covered under warranty. Alternator causes massive electrical problems throughout car. One car lost battery, dome light, radio, wipers, throttle sensor due to malfunctioning alternator.

• Difficulty in shifting the vehicle out of Park. • Premature rotor wearout. • More windshield cracks after chipping at the base:

> A pinhead size chip on the passenger side windshield base has created a crack spreading across the middle of the windshield. I believe this is a flaw in the windshield design, factory installation, and/or aerodynamic design. My web research has shown that other Chevrolet owners have had this problem with the Aveo and other models.

• A voltage spike burns out the headlights. • Automatic door locks won't open from the inside. • Faulty gas gauge. • Tires provide poor traction. **2008**—Passenger-side Airbag light remains lit even though a fully grown adult is seated. • Hood pops open while car is underway; secondary hood latch keeps hood from flying away. • Bent wheel rims cause excessive front-end vibration. • Sharp door handles on the driver's side can cut one's hand. • Door lock failures:

> After locking the doors, they sometimes do not open from within the passenger compartment. The contact carries a hammer in the vehicle in case she has to break the windows to exit the vehicle.

• Brakes warp prematurely, causing excessive shuddering when braking; rear drums don't last long, either.• Instrument panel lights shut down. • Faulty tire pressure sensors. **2009**—Chronic stalling, loss of power:

Out of the blue the engine will lose power again, there are never any warnings or Check Engine lights.... We have taken the car to 3 different Chevrolet dealerships.... None of the Chevrolet dealers could get it to duplicate or find any codes in the 10 days they had the car. The problem seems to be getting worse.... The problem has occurred at all speeds, including when on the freeway. We have already spent over $600 on various (so-called) fixes; including a complete fuel system cleaning (including the throttle body cleaning) none have ever helped. I was told by a Chevrolet dealer it was a bad O2 sensor (but no Check Engine light had ever came on). O2 sensors always cause a Check Engine light to come on. I think it may be the entire ECU computer; but no dealer wants to admit that.

Secret Warranties/Internal Bulletins/Service Tips

2000–11—If the tire slowly goes flat, check first for aluminum wheel bead seat corrosion as the cause. • Troubleshooting shifting clunk noise. **2004**—Engine runs poorly when first started. **2004–06**—Can't shift out of Park or remove ignition key. **2004–07**—Engine front end leaks oil. • Suspension squawk, rubbing noise on bumps. **2004–09**—Hoot, whistle, moan noise from the windshield/door area. **2004–10**—Front-end rattling when passing over bumpy roads. • Remedy for an erratic AC blower motor. **2005–08**—Radiator coolant leak correction. **2005–11**—If the Reduced Power dash light remains lit for no reason, chances are water has seeped into the system. **2006–08**—Troubleshooting a sticking throttle. **2007–08**—What to do when the vehicle won't shift out of Park.

AVEO, AVEO5, LANOS, WAVE PROFILE

	2001	2002	2004	2005	2006	2007	2008	2009
Cost Price ($)								
Aveo/Wave	—	—	13,480	13,595	11,995	12,995	12,995	13,970
Aveo5/Wave5			13,820	14,705	12,195	12,995	13,000	13,770
Lanos	12,900	13,395	—	—	—	—	—	—
Used Values ($)								
Aveo/Aveo5 ▲	—	—	2,000	2,500	3,000	5,000	6,500	8,000
Aveo/Aveo5 ▼	—	—	1,500	2,000	2,500	4,000	5,500	7,000
Lanos ▲	600	700	—	—	—	—	—	—
Lanos ▼	500	600	—	—	—	—	—	—
Wave/Wave5 ▲	—	—	—	2,500	3,000	4,500	6,000	7,500
Wave/Wave5 ▼	—	—	—	2,000	2,500	4,000	5,000	6,500
Reliability	1	1	2	2	2	2	2	2
Crash Safety (F)	—	—	5	5	5	5	5	5
Side	—	—	3	3	4	4	4	4
IIHS Side	—	—	—	—	—	2	2	2
Offset	—	—	—	—	—	3	3	3
Head Restraints	—	—	—	—	—	1	1	1
Roof Strength	—	—	—	—	—	—	—	2
Rollover Resistance	—	—	—	3	4	3	3	3

bad buy

RATING: Not Recommended (2004–08). A bit larger Daewoo *cum* Chevrolet, the Optra isn't versatile or reliable enough to compete against the Honda Civic, Hyundai Elantra, Mazda3, and Toyota Echo or Tercel. **"Real" city/highway fuel economy:** 11.0/7.1 L/100 km. Owners report fuel savings may undershoot this estimate by at least 15 percent. **Maintenance/repair costs:** Average. **Parts:** Often in short supply. **Extended warranty:** Not needed, due to the few complaints recorded. **Best alternatives:** Honda Fit or Civic; Hyundai Accent; Mazda3 or Protégé; and Toyota Echo or Tercel. **Helpful websites:** *www.cargurus. com/Cars/autoclub/forum-chevrolet-optra-ac1377* and The Chevrolet Optra Forum on Facebook.

Strengths and Weaknesses

Depreciation has hit these models hard. Known in the U.S. as the Suzuki Forenza, the 2004 Optra was a uniquely Canadian car that sold for $16,190, or almost $3,000 more than the same model-year Aveo. Presently, a 2004 Optra or Optra5 hatchback is worth between $2,500 and $3,000, while a 2004 Aveo, originally priced at $13,480, now costs only $1,000 less ($1,500–$2,000).

The Optra/Forenza is a reasonably equipped compact sedan that carries a puny 119 hp 2.0L 4-cylinder engine that has only 16 more horses than the entry-level Aveo. Standard features include a four-wheel independent MacPherson strut suspension, an AM/FM/CD stereo and four speakers, front power windows, power door locks, variable intermittent wipers, folding rear seats, a tachometer, a tilt steering wheel, 15-inch tires and wheels, and a driver's seat that is height-adjustable and includes a lumbar adjustment. The car has a nicely finished interior, but seating is comfortable for up to four passengers only.

Safety Summary

2004—Airbags fail to deploy. • Passenger-side wheel shears off. • Chronic stalling and hard starts. • Premature tire wear; vehicle easily hydroplanes. **2005**—Back wheel shears off. • Sudden loss of power. • Erratic transmission shifting. • Passenger-side airbag is disabled when an average-sized passenger is seated. • Driver-side seat belt suddenly unlatches. • Wipers operate too slowly. **2006**—Fire ignites near the engine wiring harness. • Airbags deploy and catch fire. • In one incident, airbags failed to deploy and seat belts didn't lock up. • Airbag alert stays lit for no reason. • Early failures of the engine timing chain, valves, and cylinder head. • Sudden acceleration. • Automatic transmission sticks in Second gear, and is slow to accelerate and revs high when shifting. • Jerky transmission shifts. • Hard starts. • Electrical short causes headlight flickering; recall doesn't include many vehicles with the defect. • Inside door handles are easily broken (a $150 repair). **2006–07**—Automatic transmission speed sensor has a high failure rate (car kicks into Neutral while moving). **2007**—Airbags fail to deploy. • Automatic transmission failures continue:

A few weeks ago, I noticed it was not shifting gears right. Then it got worse and would actually stop moving and just rev up. I almost was in an accident because of this. Luckily the truck had good brakes. I took my car in and the cashier told me what it probably was before they even looked at it and she made a statement that all the Forenzas are having this problem, not to mention there were 14 in the service area. Anyway, the shop told me it was my transmission range sensor [and] it was not covered by my powertrain warranty. Go figure. So, I paid $215.00 out of pocket.

• Engine lag and lurch and throttle body failures. • Electrical failures cause the tail lights to fail or the brake lights to remain lit and the transmission to malfunction. • Rear struts wear out prematurely. • Front windshield is defective. • Dash overheats. • Door handles keep breaking. • Faulty tire sensors. **2008**—Airbags fail to deploy. • Airbag alert is constantly lit. • Passenger-side airbag is disabled when an average-sized adult is seated. • Original-equipment Kumho Ecsta HP4 tires fail prematurely. • Tire pressure sensors often malfunction.

Secret Warranties/Internal Bulletins/Service Tips

All years: Loose shifter (automatic transmission), and key sticks in the ignition. • Front-end suspension noise. **2004**—Door frame paint peeling. **2004–05**—Rough idle and stalling. • Free water pump pulley inspection (see Customer Service Campaign "KQ"). • Excessive rear brake noise. • Door lock falls into door. **2004–06**—Steering components rubbing and growling. • Can't shift out of Park or remove ignition key. **2004–08**—Troubleshooting an engine rubbing noise. • Loss of engine power. • Harsh shifting. • Manual transmission sticks in Fifth gear. **2005–08**—Inoperative rear window washer. **2006**—Free door handle replacement (see Campaign "KS"):

Dealers are to replace all four black plastic inside door handles with new part number handles on all affected in-stock and customer vehicles regardless of vehicle age, mileage or date of visit. Please check under the engine hood at the core support for the red "KS" sticker or the vehicle warranty history to verify if the repair is already done. Please refer to the Campaign Bulletin SC-36 for claim submission instructions and labor times.

2006–07—Fuel odour in the passenger compartment. **2008**—AC suction hose replacement (Campaign "NJ").

OPTRA, OPTRA5 PROFILE

	2004	2005	2006	2007	2008
Cost Price ($)					
Optra	16,190	15,550	15,630	15,330	15,395
Optra5	16,191	15,551	14,630	14,330	14,395
Used Values ($)					
Optra ▲	3,000	3,500	5,000	6,000	8,000
Optra ▼	2,500	3,000	4,000	5,000	6,500

	3,000	3,500	4,500	6,000	7,500
Optra5 ▲	3,000	3,500	4,500	6,000	7,500
Optra5 ▼	2,500	3,000	4,000	5,000	6,000
Reliability	1	1	1	1	1
Crash Safety (F)	4	4	4	4	4
IIHS Offset	4	4	4	4	4
Side	4	4	4	4	4
IIHS Side	3	—	—	—	—
Head Restraints	1	1	1	1	1
Rollover Resistance	4	4	4	4	4

Ford

FOCUS ★★★★

Ford's Focus went from frog to prince after five years of quality "debugging."

RATING: Above Average (2005–09); Not Recommended (2000–04). This is a Dr. Jekyll and Mr. Hyde car: Its first five years of production turned out unreliable, problem-prone vehicles that cost thousands of dollars to fix, when a correction could be found. Some models couldn't be driven through puddles because the low-mounted air-intake hose ingested water into the engine ($5,000 repair). Chronic stalling and powertrain breakdowns have also been a major problem. Owners say their Focus seems "possessed": It eats ignition keys and locks and unlocks doors on its own. Yet 2005 and later model vehicles have shown incremental improvement each year to the point that the latest versions are fuel-thrifty, handle well, and offer generous cargo space (hatchback). They are acceptable buys selling for exceptionally low prices. **Ideal model year:** A 2006 ZX4 ST for about

$6,000. It originally cost $23,000 and comes loaded with safety, performance, and convenience features. **"Real" city/highway fuel economy:** *Manual:* 8.6/6.1 L/100 km. *Automatic:* 9.0/6.7 L/100 km. *SVT:* 11.3/7.8 L/100 km, but owners say the automatic transmission cuts fuel economy by over 20 percent. **Maintenance/repair costs:** Average for the 2005 and later versions; quite high for earlier models. **Parts:** Again, expensive and sometimes hard to find on early models. **Extended warranty:** Having a bumper-to bumper warranty, or a rich uncle, is a prerequisite to owning a 2000–04 Focus. **Best alternatives:** Asian small cars are your best bet. Try the Honda Civic (it's softer-riding, quieter, and has a smoother-running engine) or Fit; Hyundai Accent or Elantra; Mazda3 or Protegé; Suzuki Aerio, Esteem, or Swift; and Toyota Corolla, Echo, or Tercel. **Helpful websites:** *www.focusfanatics.com.*

Strengths and Weaknesses

Hailed as Europe's 1999 Car of the Year (a big mistake), Ford's 2000 Focus came to North America shortly thereafter as a premium small car. Its base engine, a 110 hp 2.0L 4-cylinder, was carried over to the Focus LX and SE, while the 130 hp twin-cam 2.0L (also used on the Escort ZX2 coupe) became the standard powerplant on the ZTS and ZX3. Both engines were given more power with the 2005 models and the beefed-up 151 hp 2.3L 4-cylinder.

VEHICLE HISTORY: 2002—Debut of a high-performance 170 hp SVT Focus with sport suspension and 17-inch wheels, and the ZX5, a four-door hatchback. **2004**—No more anti-skid system, and a 145 hp 2.3L 4-cylinder is added. **2005–07**—Totally revamped with a horsepower boost, new exterior and interior styling, and durable, more reliable components. ZX4 ST models offer standard ABS and traction control. **2008**—Restyled, with a number of new features. Hatchback and wagon models were dropped. **2009**—Carried over mostly unchanged.

While early models are agile and fun to drive, the 130 hp 2.0L powerplant is barely sufficient for highway cruising, where passing and merging require a bit more power. The 2005–08 2.0L and 2.3L engines are a bit stronger and more reliable performers, but acceleration and overall road performance with the standard powertrain remain unimpressive. You can also expect an omnipresent engine buzz and some hard shifting with the automatic gearbox at any decent speed. Brakes grind when applied, and the front suspension creaks constantly. Uneven terrain causes the car to bounce about, as if it were a baby harnessed in a Jolly Jumper.

This small car does handle well in city traffic, thanks to its tight turning radius and nimble steering. The small back-corner windows are also handy for keeping the rear visibility unobstructed. The car's unusually tall roofline gives ample headroom and allows for a higher, more upright riding position than you'll see with traditional small cars. Front and rear legroom is impressive as well, as long as the front passengers don't push their seats too far back.

The disappointing build quality of this car is highlighted by its easily broken, plasticky components. The car has convenient grab-and-pull door handles, but the centre armrest may be too high for some.

Fuel, electrical, powertrain, and brake system failures are commonplace for all model years. Service bulletins are replete with special instructions telling dealers how to practically rebuild the car to make it tolerably driveable. Expect excessive vibration; poor engine and transmission performance; chronic stalling (covered up to 10 years by a secret warranty); and 2003 SVT flywheel, pressure plate, and clutch assembly failures. Other problems: trunk and AC leaks; power-window failures; door mouldings that fall off; a fuel-door lid that breaks in half; hood latches that break off when the hood is closed; a trunk latch that sticks or suddenly opens; premature rotor and brake pad wear and squeaking; a seatback bar that digs into the driver's back; a driver's door that won't open from the inside (help!); interior panels that don't fit or align properly; excessive wheel, brake, engine, suspension, and steering-column noise; and a failure-prone ignition switch that won't turn, locks up, and eats keys (unlocking costs $300).

The Focus can also be a threat to your wallet and your genitalia:

> The 2004 Focus cigarette lighter after being pushed in and getting hot popped out of the holder and landed either on the occupant's lap or on the carpeting. When this was shown to the rental company, and a demonstration was done, the lighter burned the representative's legs.

Safety Summary

2000–01—Ford admits to chronic stalling and extends engine computer warranty to 10 years (see "Secret Warranties/Internal Bulletins/Service Tips"). **2000–02**—Many complaints of chronic stalling with loss of brakes and steering. • Defective speed control causes sudden acceleration in spite of corrective recall. • Other sudden acceleration incidents ascribed to faulty power control module and driver's shoe being caught under the plastic console. • Sudden acceleration in Reverse. • Collapse of tie rod and axle, leading to loss of control. • Defective axle wheel bearing. • Sudden pull to the left when turning left. • Clutch pedal spring pops out, injuring driver. • Pedal falls on floorboard. • Transmission slippage and failure. • Smoking electrical wiring in dash. • In one instance, under-hood fire ignited after AC engaged. • Driver-side seat belt won't deploy. • Emergency brake often fails to engage because button on handle stays depressed. • One vehicle was cruising at 110 km/h when gas pedal fell off its mounting. • Frayed accelerator throttle cable snaps; cable also kinks, causing hesitation, acceleration, and surging. • Stabilizer bar suddenly breaks. • One car left in Park rolled downhill. • Rear end is very unstable in snow, feels wobbly under normal conditions, and throws rear passengers about. • Sudden, unintended acceleration, and then engine cuts out. • Engine shuts down while cruising on the highway. • New engine needed after rainwater ingested into engine because of low air-intake valve. • Transmission hard to shift into Second or Reverse in cold weather. • Fuel-tank leak due to cracked filler pipe. • No brakes. • No steering. • Steering wheel locks while driving. • Broken rack and pinion. • Tie rod suddenly breaks off. • Front and rear wheels buckle. • Collapsed front wheel:

> My 2002 Ford Focus lost control due to the front control arm fracturing. My right front tire ended up totally unattached to the control arm and only staying attached to the vehicle by the hold of the tie rod. My vehicle swerved into the median and into the oncoming traffic (thankfully no traffic was around).

• Rear hatch opens on its own. • Faulty rear wheel bearings cause wheel to wobble and wander. • Original equipment Firestone tires wear out prematurely. • Dash lights flicker, then quit. **2003**—Chronic stalling. • Reports of severe back trauma from seatback failure in rear-enders. • Transmission and axle failures. • Excessive vibration. • Trunk latch suddenly releases. **2004**—Car fire believed to be caused by faulty fuel-line connection. • Cruise control self-activates, causing vehicle to surge suddenly. • One car's hood flew up, shattering windshield while car was cruising on the highway. • Automatic transmission, bearings, and throttle body replaced during first year. • Total brake failure and frequent rotor, pad, and caliper replacements:

> Brakes failed on our 2004 Ford Focus ZX5 4-door hatchback as my wife went to stop at a stop sign leaving our development and was broadsided by a truck. This resulted in a total loss of vehicle and injuries sustained to my wife.

• Chronic stalling and surging continues to be a problem. • Bent steering tie rod makes vehicle wander all over the road. • Wheel bearing failure. • No-start because ignition cylinder seized:

> I drove and parked the 2004 Ford Focus about 40 mins from my home. About 2 hours later, I went to get in my car and the steering wheel was locked. I inserted the key and it would not turn. Several people tried jiggling the steering wheel, stepping on the brake all to no avail.

• Water entry destroys the horn. • Snow kills the windshield wiper motor. **2004–05**—Sudden, unintended acceleration. **2005**—Airbags fail to deploy. • Key won't turn in the ignition. • Broken motor mounts. • Sudden transmission clutch failure. • Fuel pump fuse blows repeatedly. • Decorative wheel lug nuts fly off. • Door locks and unlocks on its own. • Early wearout of rear brakes and tires. **2005–06**—Airbag light stays on for no reason. **2006**—Stuck accelerator. • Key still sticks in the ignition. • Driver's seatback suddenly falls backwards. • Running lamp fuses blow constantly. • Brake calipers cut into the rotor. • Wheel lug nuts break off. • Rear passenger door opens suddenly while car is underway:

The rear passenger door opened unexpectedly. The contact pulled over to the side of the road and attempted to close the door; however, it failed to close and had to be tightly secured with a bungee cord. In addition, the latches failed to secure the rear liftgate. On two separate occasions, the vehicle was taken to an independent mechanic for repairs.

• Tail light bulb melts the plastic cover assembly. • Dashboard lights short out. **2007**—Airbag deploys for no reason. • One vehicle's front right wheel flew off with its struts attached. • Transmission suddenly downshifts or shifts into Neutral when cruising on the highway. • "Chopped" rear tires due to a faulty suspension. • Engine cylinders overheat and burn out the spark plugs. • Defective alternators:

2007 Ford Focus loses all power, lights, signals, speedometer, etc., while driving. Make it to dealership at great risk with no brake lights, turn signals, etc. Told alternator is bad, dealer to replace under extended warranty. Ford has a really bad design issue here, as it also happened with my 2003 Focus.

• Keys continue to stick in the ignition:

My 2007 Ford Focus key is stuck in my ignition and it's a security and safety hazard. Ford wants to charge 400–500 dollars to fix their own common problem. The consequence of this is I will probably stop stimulating the economy along with others and not buy an American-made car. I refuse to correct a problem Ford will not correct for free so I am buying another car.

• Tire rim stem fails, causing a blowout in one instance (this is a common Ford problem with tire stems imported from China and used on most of Ford's vehicles). **2008**—Airbags fail to deploy. • Failure of the tire pressure warning system. • Faulty throttle body:

The throttle body leans [messes up] the fuel mixture causing the car to lose all power, but it still idles, keeping your power steering and brakes. You then have to pull over, turn the car off and restart car only to have it every 50 miles [80 km] or so.

• Defective power door locks. • Premature wearout of original equipment Pirelli tires. • Missing spare tire, jack, and lug wrench:

The dealer stated that the vehicles do not come with spare tires, jacks or lug wrenches. The dealer attempted to locate a jack, spare tire, and wrench, but the manufacturer did not design a spare tire or jack for the 2008 two-door Ford Focus.

Secret Warranties/Internal Bulletins/Service Tips

2000–01—Reuters News Service reported on November 20, 2003, that a faulty fuel delivery module linked to chronic engine stalling would be replaced free of charge by Ford up to 10 years, without any mileage limitation (Campaign #03N01). **2000–02**—Low power. • Stalling. • AC evaporator case/cowl leaks

WATER LEAKS/A/C CONDENSATION LEAKS AT FRONT FLOOR AREA

2000–05 Focus

ISSUE: Some 2000–05 Focus vehicles may exhibit a difficult to diagnose or difficult to repair water leak or AC system condensation leak condition in the front floor area. This may be caused by sealer skips, loose grommets, mis-positioned seals or condensation leaking from the A/C evaporator case.

ACTION: Determine if the concern is an A/C condensation leak or a water leak and repair as necessary. Some common water leak locations and repair recommendations are listed in this article to help reduce repair time and increase repair effectiveness.

water into the interior. • Repeated heater core failure. **2000–03**—Troubleshooting rear-end water leaks. **2000–04**—Remedy for front suspension creak, crunch, grinding, or rattle. **2000–05**—Getting a little wet, are you? The following bulletin looks at some of the reasons why. • What to do if the key sticks in the ignition. **2000–07**—Vehicle drifts or pulls to one side due to a misalignment of the front subframe. **2001**—Difficult to shift out of Park. • 2.0L Zetec engines may hesitate, surge, or idle roughly in cold weather. • Intermittent stalling, hesitation, or lack of power. • Troubleshooting the Check Engine light. • Ignition key may be difficult to turn in cylinder. **2003–05**—If doors lock or unlock when they shouldn't, try cleaning the door-latch connectors. **2003–06**—Premature manual clutch wearout. • AC fluid leaks. **2004**—Customer Satisfaction Program #04B16 will pay for the correction of faulty front-seat heater element pads. **2005–07**—Slow fuel fill or early shut off. **2006–07**—Rear-end rattling. • Water leaks onto the front/rear floor area. • Manual transmission fluid leaks. **2006–08**—Power steering fluid leaks. **2006–10**—If the trunk lid won't latch, the solenoid is the likely culprit, requiring that the latch assembly be replaced. **2007–08**—Tire valve stem free inspection or pro-rata tire replacement (see bulletin on the following page). **2008**—No Third or Fourth gear (automatic). • Water leaks onto the rear floor. • Front-end pop/click. • Interior door handle pulls loose. **2008–10**—Remedy for front-end noise when passing over rough roads. • An engine fuel rail or injector malfunction may be the cause of an idle ticking noise. • A click/pop noise heard from the front end may be caused by faulty front stabilizer bar end links in the front upper strut bearing area, and/or by the lower control arm. • The steering column lock may need replacing if the ignition key binds in the ignition cylinder. • Although Ford is emphatic that paint abrasion on the side of the car is the owner's responsibility, TSB #09-17-5, issued 09/07/09, says the affected area (rocker panels, or door bottoms) will be repainted under warranty.

TIRE VALVE STEM INSPECTION AND MAINTENANCE REMINDER

BULLETIN NO.: 09L03   DATE: APRIL 8, 2009

REASON FOR THIS ACTION: A recent Ford Motor Company and National Highway Traffic Safety Administration (NHTSA) investigation into reports of valve stem cracks and air leaks has prompted Ford to develop a "Tire Valve Stem Inspection and Maintenance Reminder" letter that will be mailed to owners of certain 2007 and 2008 model year vehicles. This letter reminds owners of proper tire maintenance and provides instructions that will enable them to perform valve stem inspections on their own vehicles. We expect most owners will be able to perform this inspection; however, some will return to the dealership for assistance.

AFFECTED VEHICLES

Vehicles	Model Years	Assembly Plant	Build Date Range
Escape, Mariner	2007–08*	Kansas City	11/01/06–5/31/07
Focus	2007–08*	Wayne	11/01/06–5/31/07
F150	2007–08*	Dearborn	11/01/06–5/31/07
F150	2007	Norfolk	11/01/06–5/31/07
F150	2007–08*	Kansas City	11/01/06–5/31/07
Montego, Sable, Five Hundred, Taurus	2007–08*	Chicago	11/01/06–5/31/07
Fusion, MKZ, Milan	2007–08*	Hermosillo	11/01/06–5/31/07
Navigator, Expedition	2007–08*	Michigan	11/01/06–5/31/07
Mark LT	2007–08*	Dearborn	11/01/06–5/31/07
Edge, MKX	2007–08*	Oakville	11/01/06–5/31/07
Mustang	2007–08*	Flatrock	11/01/06–5/22/07
Crown Victoria, Grand Marquis	2007–08*	St. Thomas	11/20/06–5/31/07
Ranger	2007–08*	Twin Cities	11/20/06–5/31/07
Explorer, Mountaineer, Sport Trac	2007–08*	Louisville	11/06/06–5/31/07
Freestar	2007	Oakville	11/01/06–11/08/06
Freestyle	2007	Chicago	11/01/06–4/13/07
Taurus X	2008*	Chicago	12/07/06–5/25/07

*Only a small percentage of early built 2008 model year vehicles are affected.

FOCUS PROFILE

	2001	2002	2003	2004	2005	2006	2007	2008	2009
Cost Price ($)									
LX/S	16,015	15,970	16,275	16,475	—	—	14,799	15,999	14,799
ZX3S	16,690	17,390	17,550	17,775	17,555	17,599	—	—	—
ZX4 ST	—	—	—	—	—	22,995	—	—	—
Wagon SE	17,695	17,271	18,995	19,165	19,365	19,565	17,099	—	—
Used Values									
LX/S ▲	1,500	2,000	3,000	3,500	—	—	8,000	9,000	10,500
LX/S ▼	1,000	1,500	2,500	3,000	—	—	7,000	8,500	9,500
ZX3S ▲	2,000	2,500	3,500	4,000	5,000	6,000	—	—	—
ZX3S ▼	1,500	2,000	3,000	3,500	4,500	5,000	—	—	—

All ratings on a numbered scale where ☐ is good and **1** is bad. See page 132 for a more detailed description.

ZX4 ST ▲	—	—	—	—	—	6,500	—	—	—
ZX4 ST ▼	—	—	—	—	—	5,500	—	—	—
Wagon SE ▲	2,500	3,000	3,500	4,500	5,000	6,500	7,500	—	—
Wagon SE ▼	2,000	2,500	3,000	4,000	4,500	5,500	7,000	—	—
Reliability	1	1	1	1	3	3	4	4	4
Crash Safety (F)		4	4	4	4	4	4	5	5
4d	4							4	4
Side	4	3	4	4	3	3	3	3	3
4d	3	4	3	3	3	3	3	5	5
IIHS Side	1	1	1	1	1	1	1	5	5
Offset								5	5
Head Restraints	2	2	2	2	2	3	3	5	5
Rollover Resistance	—	4	4	4	4	4	4	4	4
4d	4	4	4	4	4	4	4	4	4

General Motors

SATURN S-SERIES, L-SERIES, ION ★

bad buy

RATING: Not Recommended (1999–2007). Gone and best forgotten; although some secret warranties are still in effect. GM shut down Saturn after discovering no one would buy the division. Everyone knows Saturn lost billions of dollars because its early models were late to market, bland, and lacklustre performers. Most important, quality control was the pits, especially as it related to powertrain dependability. Even GM's less-pretentious models, like the Cavalier and Sunfire or the minuscule Metro and Firefly, offered better quality and value for your money. Saturn's latest entries, like the Aura, Sky, and Outlook SUV, are marginally better from a performance and styling perspective, but in the end, they are just as problem-plagued. Now that Saturn has been closed, parts like the CVT transmission and powertrain components will be hard to find at a fair price. **"Real" city/highway fuel economy:** *SL 1.9L:* 9.4/6.2 L/100 km. *ION 1.9L:* 10.2/6.8 L/100 km, though owners report that the automatic transmission burns almost 20 percent more fuel. **Maintenance/repair costs:** Much higher than average; many repairs are dealer-dependent. Saturn "goodwill" refunds will be of short duration, if applied at all, and parts like the CVT will be hard to find and cost an arm and a leg. **Parts:** Best bet is to scour junkyards. CVTs are hellacious to troubleshoot. **Extended warranty:** A comprehensive extended warranty will be of little help; there are too many things that can go wrong, and parts will always be back ordered. **Best alternatives:** Honda Civic LX, Hyundai Elantra, Mazda3, Ford Focus (2005 and later), Nissan Sentra or Versa, and Toyota Corolla. **Helpful websites:** *www.saturnfans.com* and *www.saturnspot.com/f38*.

Strengths and Weaknesses

S-Series

This entry-level model will cost no more than $1,000, tops. It's as low-tech as they come and remained virtually unchanged until replaced by the 2003 ION. The base model provides a comfortable driving position, adequate instrumentation and controls, unobstructed visibility, good braking, dent-resistant body panels, and better-than-average crashworthiness scores. But, balancing these advantages, buyers have to contend with excessive engine noise, limited rear seatroom, glitch-prone anti-lock brakes and serious factory-related deficiencies.

L-Series

In an attempt to save money by adapting a European car to the American market, Saturn brought out the LS sedan and LW wagon, derivatives of GM's own quality-challenged Opel Vectra. Some major differences, however, include a lengthened body, a softer-riding chassis for a more comfortable ride, and the use of a homegrown 137 hp 2.2L 4-banger constructed with failure-prone aluminum components. The higher-priced models have a roomy interior with a full range of convenience features, plus a good V6 powertrain matchup that provides a firm ride and impressive high-speed stability and braking.

ION

A larger, more comfortable, and more powerful vehicle than its S-Series predecessor, the early IONs were powered by a 140 hp 2.2L 4-cylinder engine. The ION 2 and 3 came with a 145 hp 4-cylinder and an optional 175 hp 4-cylinder. The Red Line coupe used a supercharged 205 hp 4-cylinder engine hooked to a manual transmission.

The ION's many deficiencies mirror those of the S-Series coupe and its L-Series big brother. The only added wrinkle is the CVT, which, despite an extended warranty following widespread quality complaints, is only good for the trash heap. In the meantime, ION and VUE SUV owners are likely to face long servicing waits and mind-boggling depreciation.

VEHICLE HISTORY: *L-Series:* **2002**—Standard side curtain airbags. **2003**—Four-wheel disc brakes. **2004**—Standard ABS and traction control; the 5-speed manual transmission is no more. *ION:* **2003**—ION arrives with a CVT. After first extending the warranty in 2003, Saturn drops the CVT in its 2005 models because of quality problems. **2004**—Upgraded interior materials, and a high-performance Red Line model sporting a 205 hp 4-cylinder engine and sundry other performance features. **2005**—The 5-speed automatic is replaced by a 4-speed automatic. Suspension and steering are also upgraded. Improved seating for the ION 1 and ION 2 versions. **2006**—The ION 1 sedan is dropped, and the ION 3 gets a 175 hp 4-cylinder engine.

TSBs and owner complaints indicate that a variety of major quality problems are likely to crop up throughout all model years. These include self-destructing engines; poorly welded exhaust systems; failure-prone Firestone tires; alternator and AC compressor failures; chronically malfunctioning automatic transmissions; a host of body defects, led by paint delamination, rattles, and wind and water leaks; and failure-prone brake, ignition, fuel, and electrical systems (are flickering, dimming lights your cup of tea?).

Safety Summary

All years: Reports of stuck accelerators. • Airbag fails to deploy. • Seat belt fails to restrain driver in collision. • Hard starts, surging, and chronic stalling. • Gear lever slips out of gear and is hard to put into Reverse. • Manual transmission jumps out of Third and Fifth gears; automatic transmission is failure-prone and parts (CVT) cost more than the car is worth, when you can find them. • Frequent brake failures. • Brake rotor warpage and frequent pad replacement. • Sudden head gasket failure causes other engine components to self-destruct. • Loss of steering control. • Poor horn and radio performance. • Steering failures:

> Steering failure during static and very slow turning exercises. This is a consistent problem with the vehicle. We teach new drivers and re-train elderly drivers and this is a major issue for a training vehicle.

2005—Electrical fire ignites near the battery. • Complete loss of braking:

> I was driving my 2005 Saturn ION-2 and the brakes totally failed when I depressed the clutch on my 5 speed transmission. After taking it in for service the mechanic told me that the slave cylinder was leaking and allowed air into the brake system because the brakes and clutch have a shared hydraulic fluid reservoir. I couldn't downshift because the clutch failed and I couldn't brake because the brakes failed. The warning system failed because there was still some fluid in the shared reservoir.

• Defective rear brake rotors and drums (drums will warp if car isn't driven for several weeks). • Shifter knob falls off; shifter shaft replaced. • Dash gauges fail suddenly. • Door panels crack. • Driver's window falls into the door. • Water leaks into headlights. **2007**—Sudden acceleration. • Fuel leakage; fuel-pump fuel line leaks. • Key sticks in the ignition; won't turn. • Sudden steering loss; steering fuses blow constantly:

> We have a 2007 Saturn ION with 45,000 miles [72,400 km]. Yesterday the power steering motor went out. Motor is part of the steering column so we have to have it all replaced. Quote by a Saturn dealer is $1,000.

Secret Warranties/Internal Bulletins/Service Tips

All models/years: Reprogramming of the power control module (PCM) and engine control module (ECM) now have equal coverage under the emission warranty up to 8 years/130,000 km, per TSB #04-1-08, published June 2004. **All**

models: 2003–04—Engine coolant leakage into oil. *ION:* 2003–04—Intermittent no-starts may be caused by solidified grease in the ignition switch; a new switch must be installed. • Low-speed grinding noise or hesitation requires the installation of a new transaxle control module (TCM) or its recalibration, says TSB #03-07-30-051. • Automatic transmission delay and surging requires the replacement of the control-valve body and recalibration of the ECM (TSB #03-07-30-052). • No movement in Drive may require a new VT25E transaxle assembly, per TSB #04-07-30-024. • If you're lucky, the TCM may only need to be reprogrammed to cure upshift delays, harsh downshifts, or erratic gear engagement. • Coolant leak from water-pump plug; get an upgraded water pump. • Rear-door cracking. 2003–07—Remedy for incomplete rear-window defogging. Fix for loose seat cushion cover. 2004–07—A defective power steering assist control module will be replaced free of charge up to 10 years/160,000 km, says GM Service Bulletin #10187, issued July 20, 2010. If GM balks, ask for a small claims refund since GM's bulletin commitment was made after its bankruptcy:

CAMPAIGN—POWER STEERING LOSS OF POWER ASSIST

BULLETIN NO.: 10187   DATE: JULY 20, 2010

SPECIAL COVERAGE ADJUSTMENT—POWER STEERING ASSIST

2004–07 Saturn ION

CONDITION: Some customers of 2004–07 model year Saturn ION vehicles, equipped with electric power steering, may experience a sudden loss of power steering assist, which could occur at any time while driving the vehicle.

SPECIAL COVERAGE ADJUSTMENT: This special coverage covers the condition described above for a period of 10 years or 100,000 miles (160,000 km), whichever occurs first, from the date the vehicle was originally placed in service, regardless of ownership.

Retailers are to replace the power steering motor. The repairs will be made at no charge to the customer.

2006–07—A similar free replacement program exists for the 2006–07 fuel pump module. Again if GM balks, or says the policy only covers certain regions, get your money from small claims court using the service bulletin below:

CAMPAIGN—FUEL PUMP WARRANTY EXTENSION

BULLETIN NO.: 09275A   DATE: MARCH 3, 2010

SPECIAL COVERAGE ADJUSTMENT—FUEL ODOR OR SPOTTING ON GROUND—REPLACE FUEL PUMP MODULE.

2006–07 Chevrolet Cobalt; 2006 Pontiac G4; 2006–07 Saturn ION; and 2007 Pontiac G5

The plastic supply or return port on the modular reservoir assembly (MRA) may crack. If either of these ports develop a crack, fuel will leak from the area. The customer may notice a fuel odor while the vehicle is being driven or after it is parked. If the crack becomes large enough, fuel may be observed dripping onto the ground and vehicle performance may be affected.

SPECIAL COVERAGE ADJUSTMENT: This special coverage covers the condition described above for a period of 10 years or 120,000 miles (193,000 km), whichever occurs first, from the date the vehicle was originally placed in service, regardless of ownership. Dealers are to replace the fuel pump module. The repairs will be made at no charge to the customer.

	2001	2002	2003	2004	2005	2006	2007
Cost Price ($)							
SL	14,358	14,245	—	—	—	—	—
SC	16,763	16,765	—	—	—	—	—
LS/L100	20,065	21,125	—	—	—	—	—
LW/LW200	25,235	23,325	23,480	—	—	—	—
L300	—	—	—	23,030	24,995	—	—
ION	—	—	15,495	14,775	14,935	15,995	15,665
Red Line	—	—	—	—	—	23,995	24,075
Used Values ($)							
SL ▲	1,300	1,800	—	—	—	—	—
SL ▼	1,100	1,300	—	—	—	—	—
SC ▲	1,500	2,000	—	—	—	—	—
SC ▼	1,300	1,500	—	—	—	—	—
LS/L100 ▲	3,000	3,500	—	—	—	—	—
LS/L100 ▼	2,500	3,000	—	—	—	—	—
LW/LW200 ▲	3,500	4,000	4,500	—	—	—	—
LW/LW200 ▼	3,000	3,500	4,000	—	—	—	—
L300 ▲	—	—	—	5,000	6,000	—	—
L300 ▼	—	—	—	4,500	5,000	—	—
ION ▲	—	—	2,000	2,500	3,000	4,000	5,000
ION ▼	—	1,500	2,000	3,000	3,500	4,500	
Red Line ▲	—	—	—	—	—	5,500	7,000
Red Line ▼	—	—	—	—	—	5,000	6,000
Reliability	2	2	2	2	2	3	3
Crash Safety (F)							
L-Series	4	5	4	4	4	—	—
ION	—	—	5	5	5	5	5
Side	—	—	—	—	—	—	—
L-Series	2	3	3	3	3	—	—
ION	—	—	3	3	3	4	4
IIHS Side							
L-Series	1	1	1	1	1	—	—
ION	—	—	1	1	1	1	1
Offset	3	—	—	—	—	—	—
L-Series	3	3	3	3	3	—	—
ION	—	—	—	3	3	3	3
Head Restraints	1	1	—	—	—	—	—
L-Series	1	1	1	1	1	—	—
ION	—	—	1	1	2	2	2
Rollover Resistance	4	4	4	4	4	4	4

Honda

CIVIC, INSIGHT, CIVIC HYBRID ★★★/★

RATING: *Civic:* Average (1999–2009). Civics have been downgraded from Above Average to Average due to their higher incidence of failures, highlighted by cracked engine blocks, a tire-eating rear suspension, and "in your face" sun visors, among other quality deficiencies. When Honda announces publicly that the company will extend its warranty to cover these defects and others listed further on, *Lemon-Aid* will raise the Civic's rating. *Civic Hybrid:* Not Recommended (2003–09). *Insight:* Not Recommended (2001–06). **Ideal model year:** A fully equipped 2006 Civic EX sedan that originally sold for $22,180 and now lists for about $9,500. **"Real" city/highway fuel economy:** *Civic manual:* 7.5/5.7 L/100 km. *Civic automatic:* 8.0/5.7 L/100 km, though owners report they burn about 10 percent more. *High-performance SiR versions:* 9.2/7.0 L/100 km. *Hybrids:* These models get nowhere near their estimated 4.7/4.3 L/100 km fuel consumption; expect to burn as much as 30 percent more. **Maintenance/repair costs:** Average. Independent garages can carry out repairs, but the 16-valve engine's complexity means that more-expensive dealer servicing may be unavoidable. Owners should check the engine timing belt every 3 years/60,000 km and replace it every 100,000 km ($300). **Parts:** A bit more expensive than with most other cars in this class; airbag control modules and body panels may be back ordered for weeks. **Extended warranty:** A waste of money. **Best alternatives:** Honda Fit; Hyundai Accent or Elantra; Mazda3 or Protegé; Nissan Sentra; Suzuki Aerio, Esteem, or Swift; and VW Golf or Jetta TDI. **Helpful websites:** *www.civicforums. com* and *www.honda-tech.com.*

 ## Strengths and Weaknesses

Canada's top-selling small car, Civics have distinguished themselves by providing sports car acceleration and handling with excellent fuel economy and quality control that is far better than what American, European, and most other Asian automakers can deliver. Other advantages: a comfortable ride; a roomy, practical trunk; high-quality construction; good front and rear visibility; bulletproof reliability; simple, inexpensive maintenance; and a smooth-shifting automatic transmission. Also, these cars can be easily and inexpensively customized for better driving performance, or to gain a racier allure.

Si models are Honda's factory hot rods (the Acura 1.6 EL is a Si clone), providing lots of high-performance thrills without the bills. Despite four-wheel disc brakes, the Si's mediocre braking and its lack of low-end torque are the car's main performance flaws. Its suspension may be too firm for some, and its spoiler may block rear visibility.

The 2001–04 Civic models move from the subcompact to the compact class and increase interior volume while providing seats that are wider and higher. They are also marginally better performers than earlier models from a power and handling standpoint. Although steering feedback is a bit vague and over-assisted, the softly sprung suspension still gives the base car a floating feel, and there's excessive body lean when cornering at high speeds (EX and Si models have a firmer stance). Drivers will find that parking is more of a chore because the car's increased size makes it difficult to see its rear corners.

Honda quality control, like Toyota, has gone steadily downhill for well over a decade. Having said this, Honda's lineup has always been better-made than the rest of the Asian competition and much better built than what Detroit offers. Heading the list of owner complaints are engine crankshaft failures, transmission malfunctions, weak front springs and shocks, and early strut failure resulting in degraded handling. Owners also complain of AC failures, chronic water leaks, delaminated paint, suspension knocks and squeaks, erratic fuel gauge readings, a subpar stereo system, a constantly lit Check Engine light, fuel and electrical system failures frequent brake repairs (rotor warpage and pad replacement), trunk hinges that steal storage room and damage cargo, a faulty engine computer module and oxygen sensor, and early replacement of the crankshaft pulley and timing belt.

Other common problems include windshield air leaks and noise; warped windshield mouldings; hard-to-access horn buttons; windows that fall off their tracks; side mirrors that vibrate excessively; headlights that can't be focused properly and are prone to water leaks; gas-tank fumes that leak into the interior; and premature rusting, uneven paint application, chalky spots, and paint peeling off. Here's what owners of 2001–07 Civics report:

> I have researched and found many other people complaining about the paint and having the same issues as me. I believe Honda's paint is defective and should be investigated. I have never had a car's paint be so soft and of poor quality The guy at the body shop said that he had to repaint 4 Honda vans that have the blue paint because the paint was defective.

Insight and Civic Hybrid

Stay away from used hybrids. Build quality is inconsistent, the electrical and braking systems can be quite hazardous, maintenance is highly dealer-dependent, depreciation is a bit faster than with comparable makes, and fuel economy is illusory. *Consumer Reports* says the Civic Hybrid's fuel economy may fall short by at least 25 percent. Says this owner of a 2003 Civic Hybrid:

> The Hybrid is supposed to get 48 mpg/city [4.9 L/100 km] and 47 mpg/highway [5.0 L/100 km]. Even the fine print states that the actual mileage should range between 40–56 [4.2–5.9 L/100 km] in the city and 39–55 [4.3–6.0 L/100 km] on the highway.

Honda was the first automaker to introduce gas-electric hybrid technology to North American consumers when it launched the Honda Insight in the States in December 1999, followed by the Civic Hybrid in March 2002. Neither vehicle has sold as well as the Toyota Prius.

The first-generation Insight is a two-passenger hatchback coupe that uses a small electric motor to assist the 3-cylinder gasoline engine during hard acceleration. The engine recharges the battery pack when coasting or braking and returns to battery power when the car is stopped. The car is slow to accelerate, is tossed about by moderate crosswinds, has a harsh ride and little soundproofing, and has very little interior room and poor rear visibility. Toyota's Prius seats four and uses a more-versatile hybrid system, wherein the electric motor is dominant and gasoline and electric power vary, depending upon driving conditions.

Insight's 2010 second-generation model sells for $2,100 less than the 2006 fist-generation series and is a much better-built hybrid with more features than the previous model. A used model goes for about $19,000, while a 2006 Insight sells for half as much. The 2010 is the better buy.

The Civic Hybrid looks and feels just like a regular Civic, both inside and out. It carries a 3 year/60,000 km base warranty, a 5 year/100,000 km powertrain warranty, an 8 year/160,000 km battery pack warranty, and emissions-related equipment that's covered by a more extensive warranty. It does offer some fuel savings—plus it's smooth-shifting, gives a comfortable ride, and provides good front and rear visibility—but it comes in second to the Ford Escape and Toyota Prius, two more-refined hybrids. If your main goal is fuel economy, good alternatives are the 2005 or later Ford Focus, the Civic DX and EX (equipped with a manual transmission), Mazda3 Touring, and Volkswagen Golf TDI.

Hybrid cold weather performance isn't as fuel-efficient as advertised, hilly terrain eats into fuel savings, and the AC increases gas consumption and shuts off at stoplights, encouraging drivers to sneak up on lights. *Car and Driver* magazine concluded in its September 2004 issue that one would have to drive a Toyota or Honda hybrid 265,500 km to amortize its higher costs. Furthermore, the car's unique dual powerplants can make for risky driving and erratic braking, as this Hybrid owner warns:

so that the car slid across the road and into a snow bank and concrete abutment, causing $6,000 (U.S.) in damage. If there had been oncoming traffic, there could have been serious injuries or fatalities.

There's limited long-term reliability data, repairs and servicing are very complicated to perform, and rescuers are wary of cutting through the 500-volt electrical system to save occupants. Honda Hybrid performance and overall quality issues include chipped paint, rough shifting; a rotten-egg smell that intrudes into the cabin; premature brake and rear strut wear; a constantly lit Airbag light; poor-quality radio speakers; and a rear bumper cover that may fall off, be misaligned, or come loose.

VEHICLE HISTORY: 2001—More interior room, additional horsepower, and fresh styling; no more hatchback; Insight hybrid is launched in Canada a year after its American debut. **2002**—The 160 hp SiR sporty hatchback arrives. Improved fit and finish, a firmer suspension, and a rear stabilizer bar (except on the base model). Front suspension uses MacPherson struts, which increases interior space while watering down the car's sporty performance. Insight is given a CVT. **2003**—New gauges, a CD player for the HX, and the Civic Hybrid arrives. **2006**—Redesigned with an emphasis on new styling, new safety equipment, and more power. The sedan is larger outside and somewhat smaller inside; the coupe is a bit smaller overall. Side curtain airbags and ABS are standard features. **2007**—A sedan version of the sporty Si coupe arrives. **2008**—A new EX-L and high-performance MUGEN Si sedan are added to the lineup. **2009**—A minor restyling inside and out.

Safety Summary

All models/years: Spoiler and head restraints restrict rear visibility, and large rear-view mirror restricts forward visibility for tall drivers. • Numerous safety defects, including sudden acceleration and stalling, and a sticking accelerator pedal:

> All of a sudden the car lurched at a high speed three times, and I was trying to brake it to make it quit and it wouldn't quit or brake. My car bashed in the window of the 7/11 and my foot was not on the gas...it was a horrible experience. However, Honda dealer is saying they cannot find anything wrong with it. I was just on the forum and there are lurching problems.

• Engine and transmission failures. • Airbags that fail to deploy, deploy inadvertently, or deploy with such force they cause severe injuries:

> My 2002 Honda Civic EX hit another vehicle squarely in the rear end while traveling approximately 15 mph [24 km/h]. Neither of the front airbags deployed! The collision repair centre could find nothing wrong with my airbags. The tow truck operator and the collision repair centre told me that there was some sort of alert out for 2001 and 2002 Honda Civics where the airbags didn't deploy after a front-end collision.

• Ball joints don't have a castellated nut to secure the ball in position; the nut can back off, and the ball pulls out of the steering arm. • Dangerous instability on wet roads. • Faulty cruise control. • ABS failures and constant rotor and pad replacement. • Defective automatic transmissions. • Transmission may suddenly jump into Reverse. • Surging when brakes are applied. • Vehicle may roll away when parked on an incline. • Original-equipment tire failures. • Hood and trunk lids that come crashing down. • Inoperative door locks. • Cracked windshields. • Headlights and interior lights that suddenly go out. • Vehicle wanders all over the road:

> Civic drifts to the side while driving. All of the uneven, worn out tires were replaced as well as the rims. Even though the tires and rims were replaced, it still did not correct the problem.

All models: 2005—Early alternator and battery failures. • The smallest pebble can puncture the AC condenser. • Faulty speedometer. **2006**—More than 450 safety-related incidents reported to NHTSA—twice as many as one would normally expect. • Defective upper rear control arms. **2006–07**—Sun visor split at the seam:

> I went online and found several blogs: *www.usrecallnews.com and www.civicforums. com and www.honda-tech.com*, filled with complaints from other Honda owners having identical problems.

2006–08—Cracked engine block:

> There is a big engine block crack with a lot of 2006–08 Honda Civics, many of the owners have already posted their problems on many forums. Many owners took the car back to the Honda dealership and Honda did repair it for free. But! I still think the government should do an inspection on it and tell Honda to set up a recall on this problem. Honda will fix the problem only if it's under the warranty.... It is a manufacturer's fault for using bad heating material on engine blocks. Here's a link to a forum site: *http://8thcivic.com/forums/mechanical-problems-technical-chat/42339-my-r18-block-cracked-check-yours.html*.

2007—Faulty upper rear control arms suddenly fall off or simply chew up the rear tires:

> My rear control arm broke for absolutely no reason. It snapped in half.... the quality of material used to put together the rear control arm was completely unsafe.... I did not hit anything on the road, and the piece just snapped.... Fortunately, I did not crash. This has been an experience that has been completely traumatic to myself, and I am in complete fear of driving any Honda now. I haven't had the money to replace the parts on my vehicle, because my car is out of warranty. This particular piece of the car should have definitely been in a recall.

•

Uneven rear tire wear that is noticeable at 5,000 miles [8,000 km] and cups rear tires so bad by 10,000 miles [16,100 km] that there is so much noise in vehicle it sounds like the wheel bearings are shot. By 15,000 miles [24,100 km] the tires are showing cords because of uneven wear. Took it to dealer and they replaced arms on rear, sold me new tires for rear, and realigned vehicle. Said problem was corrected. Now have 11,000 miles [17,700 km] on new tires installed with same problem on new rear tires. Dealer will not fix problem. Looked on Internet at same complaints on same year Honda Civic about uneven tire wear. Same problem across country with dealer not knowing how to fix.

• Early wheel bearing failures. • Brakes detach from their mounts. • Tire side wall cracks and splits from the rim. • Airbag warning light comes on for no reason. • Windshield water leaks. 2008—Airbags fail to deploy. • Vehicle lunges forward when the brakes are applied. • Sun visors continue to melt, crack, or fall down due to a faulty hinge.• Rodents snack on Honda wiring:

Rodents eat wires, fuel, brake lines. It seems the car companies have started using a newer material to replace the common plastic used in wire insulation and tubing with a soy-based product.

2009—Sudden, unintended acceleration with the steering locked:

We then hit the third and final curb, the car went airborne again slamming into the building at about six feet high on the wall. All airbags deployed, the passenger window shattered and windshield cracked. Immediately after the crash I proceeded to place the car into park when the shifter itself came out. The car was still trying to drive itself through the building when we crashed.

• Airbags deploy for no reason. • Sudden failure of the driver-side axle. • Prematurely worn-out brake pads and glazed rotors continue to be a common problem along with rapid tire wear and tire "cupping." • Poor rain performance and excessive wear with Turanza tires:

I began researching the Bridgestone Turanza EL400 tires online. There are numerous consumer complaints for the same exact problem that I am having. I find it quite odd that Honda says no one else has complained, but there are so many complaints posted online about these same tires. I find them to be a safety hazard. I have to drive under 55 mph [89 km/h] if it is raining. If I do not, my car hydroplanes all over the road.

• Early wearout of the front strut assemblies. • Reports of brake failures after passing over rough or bumpy roads. • Snow and ice accumulate on the inner walls of the front wheels, causing them to be out of balance; this makes the Civic practically uncontrollable at 80 km/h. • Road debris can easily damage the AC condenser; other vehicles have a protective screen:

I was told that a rock hit my AC condenser. I was told that I would have to pay 700 dollars to fix it. While doing some research, I found out that this has happened to plenty of other Honda owners. I went back to the dealership and told them about the plenty of other Honda owners who suffered the same problem. I was still told that I would have to pay for it. When plenty of people have suffered the same problem, there is obviously a design flaw and we should not be punished for it and have to pay 700 dollars to fix it.

• Loose steering rack bolts cause a clunking noise when turning. • Intermittent no-starts. • Sun visors continue falling down or "exploding":

While driving at 70 mph [113 km/h] in interstate. The sun visor literally "exploded". Pieces of plastic from the back seam fell and the visor [dropped] right in my view almost causing me to have an accident. Had to pull over to keep it together as out of nowhere this thing [cracked] and fell on my face.

• Seat head restraints force short occupants' chins into their chests. • Windshield distorts visibility. *Insight:* **2001–06**—Random events of power loss cause significant reduction of engine power when it is most needed. • CVT failure. • Steering becomes abnormally unstable when vehicle is driven above 50 km/h over uneven or grooved roadways. • Vehicle is prone to hydroplaning on wet roads. • Tire-tread separation. *Civic Hybrid:* **2003**—One vehicle lost all forward power while cruising on the highway. • Chronic stalling. • Excessive brake vibration; vigorous brake pumping needed to get adequate braking. • Hazardous braking system. • Seat belt locks up. • In cold weather, power windows won't roll back up until vehicle warms up. • Prematurely worn shock absorbers. • Driver's seat design can cause serious back pain. • The vehicle's strong electromagnetic field may be a health hazard:

With the use of a gaussmeter, an instrument used to measure electro magnetic fields, the consumer found that vehicle had a high electromagnetic field. The highest level occurred when the engine draws power from the battery via the integrated motor assist or when the battery was charging.

2005—Transmission slippage and frequent failures. **2007**—Windows cannot be rolled down while underway without producing a roar. **2007–09**—Front door glass comes out of its channel.

Secret Warranties/Internal Bulletins/Service Tips

All models/years: Most Honda TSBs allow for special warranty consideration on a "goodwill" basis, even after the warranty has expired or the car has changed hands. Referring to the "goodwill" euphemism will increase your chances of getting some kind of refund for repairs that are obviously related to a factory defect. • Seat belts that are slow to retract will be replaced for free under Honda's seat belt lifetime warranty, says TSB #03-062, issued September 16, 2003. • Vehicle pulling or drifting to one side. **All models: 1999–2005**—Warped/deformed windshield moulding. • Harsh shifts. **2001–04**—If vehicle won't move in Drive, it's likely caused by excessive Second clutch wear. **2001–05**—Starter grinds while engine cranks. • Inoperative or erratically operating power windows. • Driver's seat rocks back and forth. • Water leaks into the trunk. • Automatic transmission warranty extension:

2003–04—Sticking door lock cylinder. • Inaccurate fuel gauge. *Insight:* **2001–02**—Water leaks into the trunk. *Civic Hybrid:* **2003**—A CVT update. **2003–04**—Deformed windshield moulding. **2003–05**—Inoperative or erratically operating power windows. **2004**—Hard-to-close trunk lid. • A-pillar rattles. **2006**—Honda will replace for free until 2012 the defective auto-tensioner pivot bolt and reroute the drivebelt to prevent loss of steering or excessive noise. **2006–07**—Honda admits that rapid, uneven rear tire wear is caused by a manufacturing defect. The company will install for free a rear upper control arm kit, replace the flange bolts, and pay (prorated) for the replaced worn tires (TSB # 08-001, published July 22, 2009). • Water pump pulley bolts come loose (dealer will install a water pump pulley kit free of charge). • Front-end noise. • Front door glass comes out of the channel. **2006–08**—Engine overheats or loses coolant; Honda will replace the engine at no charge under a "goodwill" warranty (see TSB on the following page). • Honda admits that its sun visors split or come apart in TSB #08-023, published August 8, 2008. • Rear suspension noise. • Poor A/C performance on acceleration. **2007–09**—Engine oil leak at the timing cover. • Inoperative power windows. **2008**—Engine oil leak from the oil/air separator. **2008–09**—A front-end click, pop, or clunk when turning may signal that the steering gearbox mounting bolts are not torqued correctly. **2009**—A front-end rattle can be silenced by inserting a plastic washer between the bumper and fender.

ENGINE OVERHEATS/LOSES COOLANT

BULLETIN NO.: 08-044 **DATE: JULY 30, 2009**

ENGINE OVERHEATS OR LEAKS COOLANT

2006–08 Civic — ALL except GX, Hybrid, and Si

SYMPTOM: The engine is leaking coolant and may be overheating.

PROBABLE CAUSE: The engine block is cracking at the coolant passages.

CORRECTIVE ACTION: Install a new engine block assembly.

WARRANTY CLAIM INFORMATION

OP#	Description	FRT
111100	Install a new engine block assembly	12.0
Q	Add for alignment	0.4

IN WARRANTY: The normal warranty applies.

FAILED PART: P/N 10002-RNA-A00

H/C 8143323

DEFECT CODE: 07601

OUT OF WARRANTY: Any repair performed after warranty expiration may be eligible for goodwill consideration by the District Parts and Service Manager or your Zone Office. You must request consideration, and get a decision, before starting work.

CIVIC, INSIGHT, CIVIC HYBRID PROFILE

	2001	2002	2003	2004	2005	2006	2007	2008	2009
Cost Price ($)									
Civic	15,800	15,900	16,000	16,150	16,200	17,180	17,180	16,990	16,990
Si	19,800	19,902	20,700	20,800	21,600	25,880	26,380	26,680	26,680
SiR	—	—	25,500	25,500	—	—	—	—	—
Insight	26,000	26,000	26,000	26,000	26,000	26,000			
Hybrid	—	—	28,500	28,500	28,500	25,800	26,250	26,350	26,350
Used Values ($)									
Civic ▲	3,000	3,500	4,000	4,500	5,500	7,000	8,500	10,000	12,000
Civic ▼	2,500	3,000	3,500	4,000	4,500	6,000	7,500	9,000	10,500
Si ▲	5,000	6,000	6,500	7,500	8,500	10,000	12,500	15,500	18,500
Si ▼	4,000	5,500	6,000	6,500	8,000	9,000	11,000	14,000	17,000
SiR ▲	—	—	8,500	9,500	—	—	—	—	—
SiR ▼	—	—	7,500	8,500	—	—	—	—	—
Insight ▲	4,500	5,500	6,000	7,500	8,500	10,000	—	—	—
Insight ▼	3,500	4,500	5,500	6,500	7,500	9,000	—	—	—
Hybrid ▲	—	—	6,500	8,000	9,000	10,500	12,500	15,500	18,000
Hybrid ▼	—	—	6,000	7,000	8,000	9,500	11,500	14,000	16,500

All ratings on a numbered scale where 5 is good and **1** is bad. See page 132 for a more detailed description.

Reliability	3	3	3	3	3	3	3	3	3
Insight	—	—	3	3	3	3	—	—	—
Hybrid	—	—	—	—	4	4	4	4	4
Crash Safety (F)	—	—	5	5	5	5	5	5	5
4d	3	—	5	5	5	5	5	5	5
Insight	4	4	4	4	4	4	—	—	—
Side	**2**	**2**	5	4	4	4	4	4	4
4d	—	—	—	—	4	4	4	4	4
Insight	4	4	4	4	4	4	—	—	—
IIHS Side	—	—	—	—	—	3	3	3	3
Offset	—	—	—	—	—	5	5	5	5
Head Restraints	**2**	—	**2**	**3**	**1**	5	5	5	5
4d	—	—	**1**	**1**	**1**	5	5	5	5
Hybrid	—	—	**1**	**1**	—	5	5	5	5
Rollover Resistance	—	—	4	4	4	4	4	4	4
Insight	—	—	4	4	4	4	—	—	—

FIT

best buy

★★★★★

RATING: Recommended (2009); Above Average (2007–08). The Fit is a competent urban econocar that saves fuel without sacrificing reliability or driving performance. **Ideal model year:** The redesigned 2009 LX version. It sold originally for $17,380 and now goes for about $12,000. **"Real" city/highway fuel economy:** 7.1/5.7 L/100 km. Very few complaints that actual fuel consumption doesn't match fuel economy claims. **Maintenance/repair costs:** Lower-than-average maintenance costs. **Parts:** Reasonably available and relatively inexpensive. **Extended warranty:** A waste of money; the Fit is fairly dependable as is. **Best alternatives:** Honda Civic; Hyundai Accent, Elantra, or Tiburon; Mazda3 or Protegé; Nissan Sentra; Suzuki Esteem or Swift; and VW TDI. **Helpful websites:** *www.fitfreak.net.*

Strengths and Weaknesses

The Fit, launched as a 2007 model, is Honda's newest entry-level four-door hatchback. Powered by a 118 hp 1.5L 4-cylinder engine and coupled to a 5-speed manual or automatic transmission, this small car provides better fuel economy than the Nissan Versa, is easily accessed, and has a surprisingly large interior for cargo, thanks to the clever seating arrangement (only a bit less room than in a Civic sedan). Highway performance is fairly good, with sufficient power and agile handling; city handling is better than with the larger Versa. Side curtain airbags and ABS are standard, and the Fit's reliability scores are a few points better than the Versa's.

The redesigned 2009 Honda Fit gained size and engine strength with an increase of 8 horsepower. A 5-speed manual transmission is standard, and a 5-speed automatic is optional; Sport models with an automatic transmission get steering wheel–mounted shift paddles this year, along with more aerodynamic styling, upgraded trim, and 16-inch alloy wheels. Safety features include ABS, traction control, an anti-skid system (new for 2009), front side airbags, and side curtain airbags.

Fit depreciation has been moderate. A 2008 base Fit DX hatchback sold new for $14,980 and is now worth $9,000–$10,000; an LX sold for $17,380 and now fetches $11,000–$12,000. The all-dressed 2008 Sport version retailed for $19,580 and is now worth $12,000–$13,000.

NHTSA awarded the 2007–09 Fit five stars for occupant protection in a frontal impact, five stars for side crashworthiness, and four stars for rollover prevention— better-than-average scores for a small car. IIHS gave the 2007–09 Fit its top rating for occupant protection in both frontal offset and side collisions. Roof strength was judged Acceptable on the 2009–11 models, and head-restraint protection was rated Poor on the 2007–08 models but Good for the 2009–11 versions.

A few complaints: Owners have endured gas-tank fuel sloshing underneath the driver's seat, automatic transmission gears that fail to engage smoothly, rear-bumper paint chipping, and the front side bumper falling off the vehicle. Many owners warn that the AC condenser is highly vulnerable to pebble damage:

> Rock damage to condenser caused AC failure due to aluminum grade condenser and lack of adequate protection. Aluminum condenser can be crushed by finger force, clearly not designed to hold up to road projectiles, such as pebbles or small rocks impacting at interstate speeds. First repair on vehicle less than 1 year old and under 14K miles [22,530 km]. No protection offered to prevent [the problem] from occurring again. Out $700 to repair condenser. Modifications to protect condenser will void warranty.

 ## Safety Summary

2007—Engine raced and brakes failed after one vehicle passed over a speed bump.
• Sudden steering loss:

> 2007 Honda Fit lost power steering without warning, becoming very hard to steer. Dealer reports code #61-04. There is a July 2009 service bulletin on this problem suggesting replacement of the EPS control unit, which has been done. An Internet search suggests this problem is common—there should be a recall, as serious accidents could occur as a result of sudden loss of power steering.

• Power-steering control unit often fails when turning, causing a sudden loss of steering. • While one driver made a right-hand turn, the steering locked up because the ignition key was stuck in the steering-column orifice. • Turning the steering wheel right or left, or applying the brakes, may cause the engine to increase rpms. • After making a right turn, the automatic transmission fails to engage while the engine races for five seconds. • Automatic transmission hesitates when gearing down from 10 to 5 km/h in rolling stops for yield signs. • Sudden loss of engine power and sputtering said to be caused by defective coil packs. • Significant forward and rearward blind spots. • Angle at which foot must depress accelerator pedal can be painful; driver's seat position blamed. • Headlights are aimed too low, reducing visibility. • Failure of the right axle lift bearing. • Tires leak air. **2007–08**—Airbags fail to deploy:

> My son was involved in an auto accident in his 2007 Honda Fit Sport. He hit a truck stopped in the street while trying to avoid the truck. The impact occurred on the left driver's side of the Honda Fit. The driver's side of the Fit was heavily damaged and the car was a total loss. My son had a serious head injury and was flown by Life Flight to a trauma center where he was hospitalized with a serious brain injury. None of the car's airbags deployed. Had the side curtain airbag on the driver's side deployed, his injury would have been greatly reduced. Before the accident, the car was in excellent condition with 38,000 miles [61,000 km] on it. The insurance company placed the salvage value at $1,100. Why didn't the airbags work in such a serious accident?

> •

> After a tear down by the body shop it was determined that the [airbag] sensors were installed at the sides at the front end of the frame rail. This is a very low position on this car since it's already low to the ground…. Had these sensors been placed at a higher elevation…the airbags would [likely] have gone off and the injuries would have been…minor. This design decision seems like it was developed to satisfy the frontal crash tests conducted by the Insurance Institute for Highway Safety. During those tests the cars are evaluated for crashes to a solid object anchored to the ground. The airbags would not deploy in a crash scenario with any vehicle that would not be a compact car.

2008—Sudden engine surging at low speeds when the brakes are applied. • Dash lights stay on even if the headlights are off. • The placement of the gas and brake pedals causes leg cramping. • Tire jack bends sideways when used to lift the vehicle. **2009**—Sudden, unintended acceleration. • Faulty Bridgestone Turanza EL470 tires (they develop side wall blisters). • Dunlop SP Sport tires show excessive treadwear and are prone to side wall bubbling. • Sun reflection from the dash impairs driver's view. • Headlight low beams do not engage. • Rodents eat up the Fit's wiring but leave alone a Honda Element parked nearby:

> I did a Google search ["automobile wiring and rodents" / "Honda wiring and rodents"]. The search turned up many references to this problem in Honda automobiles and other manufacturer's automobiles. The search also uncovered many references to the recent use of soy in automobile wiring covering. If this is true it could explain why my 2005 Element has not been attacked while my 2009 Fit has been. It would also indicate a glaring defect in some auto electrical wiring. I am now dealing with the problem by leaving my Fit in with my dogs and letting them urinate on the tires. As of now this seems to be working. Obviously this is a lousy solution to the problem.

2007—Windshield wiper chatter. • Passenger seat won't slide. • Wind noise at top of windshield. **2007–08**—Steering may be more difficult due to a malfunctioning EPS control unit, says Honda Service Bulletin #09-043, published June 23, 2009. • Remedy for vehicles that pull or drift to one side of the road. • Tips on silencing under-dash gurgling noises. **2009**—Cracked front armrest repair. • Displayed fuel mileage is too high. • Troubleshooting a dash rattle. **2009–10**—Fuel filler door may not open.

Hyundai

ACCENT	★ ★ ★ ★

RATING: Above Average (2006–09); Average (2004–05); Below Average (2001–03). Having dumped and then abandoned its lemon grove of Ponys, Stellars, and Excels in the '80s, Hyundai has used the past decade to leapfrog the competition and create high-quality, fuel-efficient, and reasonably priced vehicles. They got the product right, even if it did take them almost a decade and involved them pirating away Toyota's quality-control engineers. Just as Honda and Nissan have improved since phasing out their '70s rustbuckets, Hyundai has learned from its mistakes (with the help of quality-control documents purloined from Toyota). Hyundai now makes highly reliable cars with better warranties—at bargain prices. The absence of ABS is no big loss and should lead to cheaper maintenance costs as the Accent ages. However, the skinny tires and small engine relegate the car to an urban environment. **Ideal model year:** Look for a loaded $5,500 2006 GL model. It originally sold for $13,995. **"Real" city/highway fuel economy:** 8.9/6.2 L/100 km. Owners report fuel savings may undershoot this estimate by about 10 percent. **Maintenance/repair costs:** Average. **Parts:** Reasonably priced and easily found. **Extended warranty:** Consider getting an optional powertrain warranty as protection from occasional engine head gasket and tranny failures. **Best alternatives:** Honda Civic; Hyundai Elantra; Mazda3 or Protegé; Nissan Sentra; Suzuki Esteem; and Toyota Echo or Tercel. **Helpful websites:** *www.hyundaiforum.com.*

 ## Strengths and Weaknesses

Launched as a '95 model, the early Accent was basically an Excel that had been substantially upgraded to provide decent performance and reliability at a phenomenally low price. Since that time, the car has increased in size and Hyundai has added more equipment and performance features while increasing the car's overall quality and reliability. Of course, with its small 4-cylinder engine, the Accent is no tire-burner, but it will do nicely for urban commuting and grocery shopping. Consider investing in larger wheels and tires that equip the GT for safer highway handling. Overall, the Accent offers lots of performance for a very low price brought about by a faster than average rate of depreciation.

Other major drawbacks are so-so acceleration with the automatic transmission, little steering feedback, and limited rear seat access, especially with the hatchback versions.

VEHICLE HISTORY: 2001—Engine gets 16 more horses. **2003**—A slightly larger engine; restyled front and rear ends. **2006**—Redesigned to be safer, larger, and more powerful (six more horses). Front side airbags, side curtain airbags, ABS, and four-wheel disc brakes are standard features. **2007**—ABS becomes an optional feature—ho-hum. **2008**—An upgraded instrument panel comes on board.

Owner complaints are surprisingly rare; however, the following problem areas have been noted: faulty engine cooling system and cylinder head gaskets (engine overheating), engine sputtering, Check Engine light constantly comes on, and chronic automatic transmission failures (an extended transmission warranty is suggested for models no longer under warranty). One owner says the car cannot be aligned in the rear because there are no "adjustments" allowing for it. Owners also frequently complain of excessive front-end vibration; wheel bearing, fuel system, and electrical component failures; premature front brake wear; and excessive noise when braking, particularly an annoying clicking emanating from the rear brake drums. Paint, trim, and body hardware have also been subpar.

Recent models have been surprisingly trouble-free apart from a smattering of reports related to chronic stalling, loss of power when accelerating, excessive road vibrations (mostly a tire balance problem), prematurely worn Kumho original-equipment tires, and a transmission delay similar to Toyota's "lag and lurch" that causes the vehicle to lunge into gear:

> These few seconds that I wait for it to engage have caused problems in traffic, which I feel will result in an accident. When it does engage it shifts very abruptly or basically "lunging" into drive.... Upon exiting the highway if the car does not have sufficient time to send the signal from the computer to the transmission, it searches for the signal or abruptly shifts into drive or hangs in a semi neutral "zone" before engaging. If this is a normal operation of this car, someone is going to be hurt or killed as a result of it.

Safety Summary

All years: Airbags fail to deploy, or deploy inadvertently:

> The contact owns a 2009 Hyundai Accent. While driving 45 mph [72 km/h] and slid on ice his vehicle crashed into a ditch, roll over twice and the air bags did not deploy. He was not injured and the weather was raining cold and icy. The vehicle was totalled and a police report is available if needed. The insurance company towed the vehicle for inspection. There was no maintenance on the air bags prior to the accident. The manufacturer was contacted but offered no assistance. The failure mileage was 10,000 [16,000 km].

• Horn controls may be hard to find in an emergency. • Rear head restraints appear to be too low to protect occupants. **2002**—Throttle body sensor failure causes car to accelerate on its own; intermittent high engine revs. • Chronic stalling. • Automatic transmission failures characterized by slippage, free-wheeling, jerky shifts, and a clunking noise. • When stopped, brake pedal sinks slowly to the floor and car rolls away (possibly faulty brake master cylinder). • Manual windows fall down. **2003**—Under-hood fire. **2004**—Sudden stalling and total loss of power while driving. • Airbag deploys when passing over railroad tracks. • Small original-equipment wheels and tires make the car unstable at high speeds or when cornering. • Automatic transmission downshifts abruptly or won't shift at all. **2005**—Fire ignites in the engine compartment. • Fuel sloshes out from the fuel-filler pipe. • Rear window shattered as one car was warming up. **2006**—Windshield wiper bolt constantly works loose. **2007**—Sudden acceleration. • One car sped forward when parking in a garage. **2007–08**—Passenger-side airbag is disabled even though seat occupant is an adult. **2008**—Vehicle "wobbles" when driven. • Condensation in both tail lights. • Motor surges when vehicle stops at a stoplight:

> Occasionally when I brake to stop for traffic or for a red light the car engine would surge and you had to press hard on the brake to keep it from moving. The engine would surge to 2000 rpms while in drive, and when I shifted it to Neutral once it surged to 5000 or 6000 rpms.

• Front bumper spoiler flew off while one car was underway. • Turn signal switch malfunctions. • Groundhogs love to snack on Hyundai wiring:

> My 2008 Accent I bought in February has groundhog problems. Two weeks ago, I saw a groundhog go under my car and several times after. About ten days ago, the transmission would stay in First gear and would not shift (when starting). When it finally did shift, at about 4K rpm, the transmission would remain in the higher gears. Trying to stop from a dead stop is quite slow. The Check Engine light also came on. I took the car into the dealer's. The repair man said that 3 of the cables were chewed. One for the trans., one for the brake level indicator, and one for the speedometer. The damage was not covered by Hyundai's warranty. They replaced the wires at $402.00. It's eight days later. I've lost the speedometer cable. For some reason these wires attract groundhogs.

Secret Warranties/Internal Bulletins/Service Tips

All years: Tips on troubleshooting excessive brake noise. • Apparent slow acceleration on cold starts is dismissed as normal. • A new AC "refresher" will control AC odours. **1999–2001**—TSB #03-40-018 says a defective kickdown servo switch could cause automatic transmission malfunctions. **1999–2004**—A defective pulse generator may cause harsh, delayed, and erratic shifting, says TSB #03-40-022. • A TSB published in March 2004 says many automatic transmission breakdowns can be traced to faulty transaxle solenoids. **1999–2008**—Troubleshooting tips on correcting a steering pull or drift to one side and silencing a steering pump whine. **2000–06**—Automatic transaxle oil leak behind the torque converter. **2002**—Harsh or delayed automatic transmission shifting. **2006–09**—silencing a creaking idle (manual transmissions) by replacing the clutch release lever fulcrum and applying grease to the clutch release bearing. **2007**—Remedy for a rough cold start/idle. • Free replacement of the clutch pedal ignition lock switch (service campaign T38). • Free Engine Control Module update. **2007–09**—Troubleshooting tips for a rough idle. **2008**—Sunroof clicking or ticking.

ACCENT PROFILE

	2001	2002	2003	2004	2005	2006	2007	2008	2009
Cost Price ($)									
L/GS	11,995	12,395	12,395	12,895	12,995	12,995	13,495	14,295	13,595
GL 4d	13,595	13,795	13,795	14,195	13,995	13,495	14,295	15,745	15,295
Used Values ($)									
L/GS ▲	2,000	2,500	2,500	3,000	3,500	4,500	5,500	7,000	8,500
L/GS ▼	1,500	2,000	2,000	2,500	3,000	3,500	4,500	6,000	7,000
GL 4d ▲	2,500	3,500	4,000	4,500	5,000	5,500	6,000	7,500	9,000
GL 4d ▼	2,500	3,000	3,500	4,000	4,500	5,000	5,500	6,500	8,000
Reliability	1	1	1	4	4	5	5	5	5
Crash Safety (F)	—	—	—	5	5	5	5	—	—
4d	—	4	4	4	4	5	5	5	5
Offset	—	—	—	—	—	3	3	3	3
Side	—	3	—	4	4	4	4	—	—
4d	3	3	3	5	5	4	4	4	4
IIHS Side	—	—	—	—	—	1	1	1	1
Head Restraints	3	3	3	—	—	1	1	1	1
Roof Strength	—	—	—	—	—	3	3	3	3
Rollover Resistance	4	4	4	4	4	4	4	4	4

ELANTRA ★★★★★

RATING: Recommended (2007–09); Above Average (1999–2006). What hypocrisy! This is the car auto columnists laugh at in their columns and then buy for their families. They know that over the past decade Hyundai's quality has become the best from South Korea, on par with the Japanese, and is generally much better than what Detroit offers. Another advantage is that the Accent, Elantra, and Tiburon fly under the radar for most buyers, meaning that more of them are available and they're much more reasonably priced than better-known brands. There's only a $3,000 difference between the high-end and entry-level 2008 model. **Ideal model year:** For about $9,500, look for a 2007 GLS equipped with side curtain airbags, electronic stability control, and an unexpired warranty. If not available, go for a 2008 version. **"Real" city/highway fuel economy:** *Manual:*

8.9/6.4 L/100 km. *Automatic:* 9.6/6.7 L/100 km. **Maintenance/repair costs:** Average. Dealer servicing has improved considerably, and independent garages find the Elantra's simple mechanical layout quite easy to diagnose and service. **Parts:** Reasonably priced and easily found. **Extended warranty:** Yes, for the transmission, mainly. **Best alternatives:** Honda Civic or Accord; Hyundai Accent; Mazda3, Mazda5, or Protegé; Nissan Sentra; Suzuki Aerio, Esteem, or Swift; and Toyota Echo. **Helpful websites:** *www.hyundaiforum.com.*

Strengths and Weaknesses

This conservatively styled, "high-end" front-drive sedan was first launched as a 1992 model. It was only marginally larger than the failure-prone Hyundai Excel, but its overall reliability is much better, making it a credible alternative to GM Saturns and the Mazda Protegé, Nissan Sentra, and Toyota Corolla. The redesigned 1996 and 2007 versions actually narrow the size, handling, and performance gap with the segment leader, Honda's Civic.

There is some excessive body lean when cornering, but overall handling is fairly good, mainly because of a relatively long wheelbase and sophisticated suspension. Brakes are adequate, though sometimes difficult to modulate. Conservative styling makes the Elantra look a bit like an underfed Accord, but there's plenty of room for four average-sized occupants.

VEHICLE HISTORY: 2001—A revision makes the wagon disappear, increases interior and engine size (now a 140 hp 2.0L 4-cylinder), and adds four-wheel disc brakes and ABS. **2002**—Debut of a GT hatchback, which is a bargain when one totes up the cost of its standard features. **2003**—The GT adds a four-door sedan. **2005**—A new base GLS hatchback comes online. **2006**—The sporty GT sedan is gone; front side airbags are standard, but no side curtain airbags. **2007**—Totally redesigned, restyled, and better-equipped, with more standard safety features. Elantra now comes only as a four-door sedan and gains width and height on a wheelbase that's 4 cm longer. All models use a 4-cylinder engine with a manual transmission or an optional 4-speed automatic. ABS is standard, but traction control has been dropped. Side curtain airbags and front side airbags are now standard. **2008**—Given electronic stability control and brake assist; no more Limited version.

As with most Hyundai products, transmission failures are commonplace and have been the subject of numerous service bulletins (see the Accent "Secret Warranties/Internal Bulletins/Service Tips") and recalls. Airbag failures are another frequent complaint. Other problem areas include body deficiencies (fit, finish, and assembly), a leaking sunroof, paint cracking, engine misfire, oil leaks (some oil burning), hard starting, and warped brake rotors. The passing power in post-'95 automatics is perpetually unimpressive, and the trunk's narrow opening makes for a relatively small storage space.

That being said, the above-noted problems are in no way as severe or as frequent as what you would find with the Detroit competition.

The 2001–07 Elantras are noted for chronic stalling; early manual transmission clutch burnout; prematurely worn-out rear brake drums, cylinders, and shoes; and excessive brake noise and chassis vibration. Brake rotors are particularly vulnerable to rusting and premature wearout. Writes one owner from Nova Scotia:

> I am writing to express my dissatisfaction at having to again replace two front wheel rotors (this time plus a "seized up" caliper in a back wheel) on a 2003 Elantra. Three and a half years ago I had to replace all four rotors, in both cases at considerable cost.

Owners also complain of tire thumping, paint/clearcoat cracking, delayed window defrosting, the dash front-panel console squeaking, rainwater seeping in under the door, the steering wheel covering peeling away, a humming noise emanating from the corners of the windshield, and wind howling in the interior when encountering a crosswind.

Problems reported on the 2008 Elantra relate mostly to airbag malfunctions, early brake repairs, and a faulty fuel delivery system that causes chronic stalling even after the fuel pump is replaced under a recall program. Body squeaks and rattles are still omnipresent. 2009 vehicles are mostly afflicted with airbag, brake, and powertrain problems.

Safety Summary

All years: Airbags fail to deploy, or deploy for no reason. • Chronic stalling. • Erratic transmission shifting and excessive noise. • Sudden brake loss. • Warped front brake rotors, and master cylinder failure. • Gas and brake pedals are mounted too close together. • Passenger seat belt retracts and locks so that passengers are unable to move. **2001**—Sudden, unintended acceleration. • In one incident, a child had to be cut free from jammed rear centre seat belt. • Seat belt fails to lock up in a collision. • Brakes randomly engage by themselves and overheat/pulsate. • Rear doors freeze shut in cold weather. **2002**—Seatback failure when one car was rear-ended. • While driving in a rainstorm, all interior and exterior lights shut off. **2003**—Engine surging while on the highway. • Vehicle suddenly loses all power. • Complete loss of brakes. • Headlights will read "dim" but will actually be on high. • Distracting windshield glare. • Seat belts fail to lock. **2004**—Under-hood fire:

> Vehicle caught on fire in the engine compartment while driving 40 mph [64 km/h]. The local fire department arrived to extinguish the fire. Dealer and the manufacturer were notified. The consumer stated that she smelled smoke coming through the vents while driving. The engine light came on, and the vehicle lost all power. Vehicle brakes went out. The consumer stopped the vehicle, and her and the passengers got out of the vehicle within seconds of flames.

• Many complaints that the passenger-side front airbag is disabled when an average-sized adult is seated; recall doesn't correct the problem for all claimants:

> Repeated intermittent illumination of "passenger airbag off" beginning within days of purchase. Failures occur when anyone sits in passenger seat. Adults weighing 190, 170, and 140 have turned airbags off. Poodle weighing 9 lbs turned airbags on!

• Chronic stalling. • Back cover on passenger seat pops out. • Faulty crankshaft position sensor causes the engine to stall. • Engine surging. • Stabilizer bar snaps, causing vehicle to fishtail. • Warped brake rotors. • Defective batteries corrode cables and leak acid. • In one incident, passenger seat collapsed in a frontal collision at moderate speed. • In another, the roof buckled while the car was underway. • Seat belt extenders not available. **2004–05**—Sudden, unintended acceleration. **2005**—Rear brake wheel-cylinder fluid leaks. **2005–06**—Faulty sensor continues to disable airbag when the seat is occupied; it is designed to disable the system only when an underweight occupant is seated. **2006**—Seat belt fails to lock in a collision. • Automatic transmission slippage. • Snow builds up in the wheels, causing severe vibration above 50 km/h. • Excessive vibration reported for other reasons. • Sunroof explodes for no reason. • Frequent headlight failures. • Faulty speedometer. **2007**—Car suddenly accelerates while parking. • Chronic stalling due to a faulty fuel pump; stalling often occurs after a fill-up. • One vehicle swerved and went out of control while changing lanes. • Rear end sways, especially when carrying a full load. • Camber settings make the car oversteer. • Transmission shift lever locks in Drive or Park. • Seatback collapses in a collision. • Passenger seat belt may not unlatch. • Brake light suddenly goes out. **2008**—Sudden acceleration (sticking throttle sensor). • Gas pedal sticks under the floor mat. • Cruise control often resets itself at a much higher speed. • Car suddenly shuts off while underway, especially when turning; brakes don't work. • Airbag alert comes on for no discernable reason. • Chronic stalling continues even after fuel pump recall. • Horn cuts out. • Faulty brake light switch prevents shifting; earlier models were recalled for this problem. • Car doesn't downshift properly. • Emergency brakes don't hold the car on a hill. • Batteries frequently lose their charge. • Sudden steering loss. • Tire pressure sensor gives false alerts.

2009—Airbags failed to deploy. • Gas pedal can get stuck under the floormat. • Stalling out due to a faulty fuel injector. • Brakes lock up when driving on loose, wet snow. • Vehicle oversteers when making steering corrections. • Inner sides of the front tires wear out prematurely. • Owners say original-equipment Solus all-weather tires constantly slide and lose contact with the road, causing the ABS to repeatedly engage.

Secret Warranties/Internal Bulletins/Service Tips

2001–02—Troubleshooting 2–3 shift flaring usually requires a simple updating of the TCM, says TSB #02-40-001. **2001–05**—Automatic transaxle oil leak behind the torque converter. **2001–06**—Automatic transmission delayed/harsh shifting into Park or Drive. **2002–03**—Excessive chassis vibration when cruising. **2002–04**—Poor engine performance when driving in high-altitude regions may require an upgraded fuel pump. **2003**—Automatic transmission sticks in Second gear. • Harsh shifts into Drive or Reverse. • Rough-running engine may require an upgraded fuel pump. • Corrosion in the front-door wiring connector. **2006–07**—Remedy for harsh/delayed transmission shifts. **2007**—Automatic transmission cannot be shifted into or out of Park. • Glove box damper replacement is covered by a secret warranty. • Windshield water leaks are covered by a secret warranty:

CAMPAIGN T39—POTENTIAL WINDSHIELD WATER LEAK

BULLETIN NO.: 07-01-004-2   **DATE: FEBRUARY 2007**

Elantra 2007

SUBJECT: Windshield glass water leak (Service Campaign T39).

IMPORTANT: Dealers must perform this campaign on all affected vehicles prior to customer retail delivery and whenever an affected vehicle is in the shop for any maintenance or repair.

2007–08—Silencing accelerator cable noise. • Automatic transmission defaults into "limp home" Third gear. **2008–09**—A front strut noise heard when passing over bumps signals means the front struts need to be changed.

ELANTRA PROFILE

	2001	2002	2003	2004	2005	2006	2007	2008	2009
Cost Price ($)									
GL	14,875	15,295	15,295	15,630	14,995	14,995	15,595	15,895	15,845
GLS/VE	17,075	16,995	16,995	17,525	17,365	17,365	23,095	20,595	20,595
GT	—	18,495	18,495	19,015	19,895	19,985	—	—	—
Used Values ($)									
GL ▲	2,500	3,000	3,500	4,000	5,000	6,500	7,500	8,700	11,500
GL ▼	2,000	2,500	3,000	3,500	4,000	5,000	6,000	8,000	10,000
GLS/VE ▲	3,500	4,500	5,000	5,500	6,000	7,500	10,000	11,500	14,000
GLS/VE ▼	3,000	4,000	4,500	5,000	5,500	6,000	9,000	10,500	13,000
GT ▲	—	4,500	5,000	,5,500	6,000	8,000	—	—	—
GT ▼	—	4,000	4,500	5,500	5,500	6,500	—	—	—

Reliability	4	4	4	4	4	4	5	5	5
Crash Safety (F)	4	4	4	5	5	5	5	5	5
Side	5	5	5	5	5	5	4	4	4
IIHS Side	**1**	**1**	**1**	**1**	**1**	**1**	**2**	**2**	**2**
Offset	**1**	**1**	**1**	5	5	5	5	5	5
Head Restraints	**1**	**1**	**1**	**1**	**1**	**1**	**3**	**3**	**3**
Rollover Resistance	—	—	4	4	4	4	4	4	4

Kia

After going bankrupt in 1998, Kia was bought by Hyundai and now sells a full lineup that includes small cars, mid-sized sedans, a minivan, and several sport-utility vehicles. Hyundai's infusion of cash and better-quality components has ratcheted up the quality control on Kia's 2006 and later Optima and Sportage models and made them relatively dependable performers. On the other hand, the quality of the Amanti, Sedona, Sorento, and Spectra continues to be caught in a downward spiral that hasn't abated.

Earlier Kias were poison. Known mainly for their cheap price tags, poor quality control, and below-average crashworthiness scores, they usually anchored the bottom rung of most owner satisfaction surveys. Mediocre highway performance and malfunctioning automatic transmissions (a Daewoo bugaboo, too) have also been well-known Kia traits.

RIO, RIO5, SPECTRA/SEPHIA, SPECTRA5 ★★★

RATING: Average (2009); Below Average (2006–08); Not Recommended (2000–05). The 2006 and later models have more safety and performance features but are lacking in quality. The early Spectras and Rios don't offer even a modicum of the crashworthiness, safety features, performance, or reliability that other cars deliver for the same price or less. **Ideal model year:** Nothing stands out, but the 2009 models have improved a bit. **"Real" city/highway fuel economy:** *Manual:* 8.9/6.6 L/100 km. *Automatic:* 9.3/6.7 L/100. **Maintenance/repair costs:** Average. **Parts:** Average costs, and parts are easily found. **Extended warranty:** A bumper-to-bumper warranty is a must-buy on 2005 and earlier models, which wipes out your low sales-price savings. **Best alternatives:** *Rio, Spectra/ Sephia:* Honda Fit or Civic; Hyundai Accent or Elantra; Mazda3 or Protegé; Nissan Sentra; and Toyota Corolla, Echo, Tercel, or Yaris. *Spectra GS-X:* Hyundai Elantra GT; Mazda3, Mazda5, or Protegé; and VW Golf. **Helpful websites:** *www.kia-forums.com.*

Strengths and Weaknesses

A bit smaller than the earlier Kia Sephia and Spectra, the Rio was originally a South Korean spin-off of the Aspire, marketed from 1995 to 1997 under the Ford nameplate. It's one of the cheapest cars on the market and offers both sedan and wagon versions, a limited number of standard safety and performance features, and cheap interior and exterior materials. Versions from 2005 and earlier put a low base price before safety, reliability, and performance.

Rios are equipped with a puny 104 hp 1.6L 4-cylinder engine that gives adequate power when teamed with a 5-speed manual transmission. Add an automatic transmission, and you'll need an hourglass to clock your speed. Options available include a 4-speed automatic transaxle; ABS; air conditioning; power steering, door locks, and windows; and fog lights. Side airbags are offered on only the most recent models.

Rios are highly manoeuvrable in city traffic and quite fuel efficient, but early models equipped with the 1.5L 4-cylinder engine are poorly suited for highway cruising or driving situations that require quick merging with traffic. Kia's true horsepower ratings may be just as inflated as Hyundai's during its early years, and reports of chronic stalling have sapped owner confidence even more. The Rio's Poor head-restraint rating from IIHS through 2009 and its Acceptable score for frontal collision crashworthiness on its 2006–09 models are also worrisome. Two-star side crashworthiness scores from NHTSA on many model years aren't very reassuring, either. On the other hand, NHTSA has given mostly four and five stars to the Rio for occupant crash protection.

Rio owners report problems with the automatic transmission, seat belts, and electrical and fuel systems; frequent front-end alignments; unreliable tires; and weak, prematurely worn, noisy brakes.

Other areas of complaint include tire thumping; a busy, harsh ride; small door openings; small audio controls; a missing remote trunk release; weak and noisy engine performance; problematic entry and exit; slow and imprecise highway handling; low-budget interior materials; an optional tilt steering wheel that doesn't tilt much; limited passenger room, with little rear headroom or legroom; a small dealer network that complicates servicing and warranty performance; a small trunk opening that doesn't take bulky items and doesn't offer a pass-through for large objects; and poor body construction (stagnant water collects in the dash on the 2006 model).

Spectra/Sephia

The 2000–01 Sephia is a four-door sedan that bears a passing resemblance to the Toyota Corolla. Braking is barely adequate, fit and finish is deplorable, and it's powered by a 125 hp 1.8L inline 4-cylinder engine that is woefully weak.

The Sephia became the Spectra in 2002. This five-passenger four-door came with new styling, an upgraded interior, and a new hatchback/four-door sedan body style based on the Mazda Protegé platform, housing Mazda's 4-cylinder powertrain.

In the spring of 2004, revamped Spectra models arrived with new styling, more power, and additional safety features, but they kept the 2004 designation. The

GSX hatchback is a well-equipped, sporty version of the Spectra, powered by a 125 hp 1.8L engine. It has more storage space and performs adequately on the highway. On the other hand, the engine is quite noisy, braking is subpar, and fit and finish is unbelievably bad.

Spectra owners' litany of complaints is similar to those of Rio owners: chronic stalling and surging, airbag failures, steering malfunctions, premature brake wear, brake failures, and fit and finish that is highlighted by poor-quality materials and slapdash workmanship.

Kia's products, unlike Daewoo's, do have a track record—and it's not good. In fact, *Consumer Reports* commented on the cars' debut in its April 1999 New Car edition, "You'd have to search far and wide to find a car that's worse than this small Korean model." And the proportionally large number of safety-related complaints recorded by NHTSA through 2005 confirms *CR*'s early conclusion.

VEHICLE HISTORY: *Rio:* **2003**—Subtle styling changes, a slightly larger engine, and extra standard and optional features. **2006**—A complete redesign gives the car more room, power, and safety features. A four-door hatchback called the Rio5 joins the lineup. The sole engine is a 110 hp 4-cylinder mated with a standard 5-speed manual transmission; a 4-speed automatic is optional. Front side airbags and side curtain airbags are standard, though anti-lock four-wheel disc brakes are optional. *Spectra:* **Mid-2004**—Considerably upgraded. **2005**—The Spectra5 hatchback arrives. **2006**—Standard cruise control on the SX and Spectra5. **2007**—A revised interior and a plug-in for digital audio players.

 **Safety Summary**

All models/years: Airbags fail to deploy. • Chronic stalling and engine surging. **All models: 2001–03**—Defective fuel line ignites an under-hood fire. • One vehicle's hood flew up and broke the front windshield. • Vehicle disengages from Overdrive because of a missing transmission control modulator. • Transmission jumps out of gear when brakes applied. • Brakes stick and pedal goes to the floor without vehicle stopping. • Brakes are noisy. • Excessive shaking and vibration. • Vehicle swerves all over the road. • Rear seat belt shreds or jams. • Steering binds and grinds when turned; on other occasions, it's too loose. • Premature tire wear. • Various mechanical and electrical problems, including clock spring failure. • Check Engine light, Airbag light, and Fuel light constantly stay lit. • Bent wheel rims. **2003**—Sudden steering loss. • No-starts, particularly in cold weather, due to faulty engine computer module. • Premature failure of the engine and transmission. • In damp weather, brakes grab abruptly and won't release, or they don't "catch" at all:

> The brake fell off the pad. In most normal cars the brakes are held on with a pop rivet. Not this car. They are held on with thin pieces of aluminum. Everyone knows how easy aluminum bends and twists and that's exactly how mine were. And the brake is held onto the pad with glue!!!

• Steering-column bolt snaps. • Seat belt cuts across the driver's and passenger's throats. • Wheel lug nuts shear off. • Windshield wiper nuts often come off. **2004**—Mass airflow sensor failures are the likely cause of chronic stalling. • Windshield wiper nut loosens and causes the wiper to fail:

> The retaining nut on the windshield-wiper arm loosens, causing the windshield wipers not to function. The dealership inspected and tightened the retaining nut, but the problem still exists.

2005—Airbag deploys for no reason. • Manual transmission clutch replaced at 9,000 km. • Child safety door lock failure (door could not be opened). **2006–07**—Passenger-side airbag is disabled when an average-sized adult is seated. **2007**—Sudden brake failure. *Spectra:* **2005**—Steering locks up. • Defective tie rods, struts, and sway bar linkage cause the vehicle to constantly pull to one side. • Key sticks in the ignition. • Cigarette lighter pops out of its housing and can start a fire in the cabin. • Front seat belt latches detach on their own. • Headlights frequently burn out. • Premature tire wearout. **2006**—One vehicle's side airbag deployed as door was closing. • Stalling caused by faulty alternators or malfunctioning engine computer. • Rear brakes suddenly lock up while cruising on the highway. • Early tire failures. • Front windshield moulding blows out while cruising. *Rio:* **2007**—Engine fire ignites while vehicle is underway. • Sudden acceleration when brakes are applied. • Passenger-side airbag is disabled for no reason. • Leaking gas tank; chronic stalling:

> Problems with the fuel tank and purge canister system. The normal operation of fueling the vehicle can cause the purge system to become filled with fuel. This created a dangerous situation by allowing fuel to be expelled or leak out of the tank or what the dealer called overflow onto the floor in my garage.

• Sudden brake loss. • Brake lights stay on after releasing the brake pedal, or don't come on at all. • Driver's side floor mats are not securely anchored. • Doors lock on their own:

> The contact exited the vehicle and shut the door with the keys still in the ignition. After a few seconds, all of the doors locked automatically with her 11-month-old child still in the vehicle.

• AC can leak Freon. • Faulty sway bar links. **2008**—Fire ignites in battery/fuse box area. • Airbag is disabled when the passenger seat is occupied. • Parking lights come on after vehicle is exited, causing battery to lose its charge.

Secret Warranties/Internal Bulletins/Service Tips

All models: 2003–04—TSB #013 addresses different remedies for curing hard starts in cold weather (reprogramming software is one field fix). *Rio:* **2006–07**—More remedies for poor cold starts or a rough idle. • Rear seatback may stick in the folded position. **2007**—Electronic control module upgrade to correct a rough idle. • Special campaign to silence rear-door glass-run channel wind noise. **2008**—Special campaign to replace prematurely worn door weatherstrip. • Troubleshooting a rough idle. **2009**—"Goodwill" campaign to replace the fuel cap. *Spectra:* **2006**—Key sticks in the ignition. **2006–07**—Troubleshooting tips for automatic transmission 2–3 gearshift shock, slip, or flare. **2006–08**—Correcting a rough idle. **2009**—"Goodwill" campaign to replace the fuel cap and fix the window crank handle.

RIO, SPECTRA/SEPHIA PROFILE

	2001	2002	2003	2004	2005	2006	2007	2008	2009
Cost Price ($)									
S/EX	11,995	12,095	12,351	12,650	12,995	13,295	13,595	13,995	13,595
RS	12,995	13,095	13,251	13,550	13,995	—	—	—	—
Sephia	13,845	—	—	—	—	—	—	—	—
Spectra	—	14,595	14,795	14,995	15,995	15,595	15,995	15,995	15,695
GSX	—	17,595	17,795	17,995	—	—	—	—	—
Used Values ($)									
S/EX ▲	1,500	2,000	3,000	3,500	4,500	5,000	6,000	7,500	8,500
S/EX ▼	1,000	1,500	2,500	3,000	4,000	4,500	5,000	6,500	7,500
RS ▲	2,000	2,500	3,500	4,000	4,500	—	—	—	—
RS ▼	1,500	2,000	3,000	3,500	4,500		—	—	—
Sephia ▲	1,000	—	—	—	—	—	—	—	—
Sephia ▼	700	—	—	—	—	—	—	—	—
Spectra ▲	—	3,000	4,000	5,000	6,000	7,000	8,500	9,500	10,500
Spectra ▼	—	2,500	3,500	4,500	5,000	6,000	7,500	8,500	9,500
GSX ▲	—	3,500	4,500	5,500	—	—	—	—	—
GSX ▼	—	3,000	4,000	4.500	—	—	—	—	—
Reliability	2	2	2	2	2	3	3	3	3
Crash Safety (F)	—	4	4	4	4	4	4	4	4
Side	3	3	2	2	2	4	4	4	4
IIHS Side	—	—	—	—	—	1	1	1	1
Spectra	—	—	—	1	1	1	1	2	2
Offset	—	—	—	1	3	3	3	3	3
Spectra	—	—	—	1	3	3	3	3	3
Head Restraints	1	1	1	1	1	1	1	1	1
Spectra	—	—	—	—	3	3	3	3	3
Roof Strength	—	—	—	—	—	3	3	3	3
Rollover Resistance	—	4	4	4	4	4	4	4	4

Mazda

MAZDA3, MAZDA5, PROTEGÉ ★★★★/★★★★

The Mazda3.

RATING: *Mazda3:* Recommended (2006–09); Above Average (2004–05). Owner complaints continue to be remarkably few in number. Nevertheless, make sure the AC cools the car sufficiently and the brake calipers and rotors are sound. *Mazda5:* Above Average (2006–09). Many of these small minivans are coming off-lease at bargain prices. *Protegé:* Above Average (1999–2003). These cars are plentiful at bargain prices. **Ideal model year:** A 2007 MazdaSpeed3. This sporty car delivers driving thrills without the garage bay bills. It's lightning-fast, user-friendly, European-stiff, and yet tame enough to handle that ultimate driver's challenge: stop-and-go city traffic. Cost? $30,995. But only if you bought new. Today, you drive it away for $13,500 to $14,500. Only one caveat: Engine power has been known to loosen the engine mount bolt on the driver's side. A recall applies. The MazdaSpeed3 gives you all of the Mazda3 GT features, plus traction control system, dynamic stability control, 18-inch alloy wheels with summer tires, and a six-CD Bose stereo with four speakers, two tweeters, and a subwoofer. Shoppers looking for the best Mazda5 choice should consider the 2008 Mazda5 GT for its sporty powertrain and refined performance. Originally sold for $24,600, it's now worth about $13,000. **"Real" city/highway fuel economy:** There isn't a lot of variation in fuel economy among the different model years, except for the turbocharged engine that wastes gas at a rate of 10.0/7.3 L/100 km. Owners say they burn about 10 percent more fuel than the following estimates indicate. *Mazda3 2.0L manual:*

8.5/6.2 L/100 km. *Mazda3 2.0L automatic:* 9.1/6.4 L/100 km. *Mazda3 2.3L manual:* 9.2/6.7 L/100 km. *Mazda3 2.3L automatic:* 9.8/7.5 L/100 km. *Mazda5 2.3L manual:* 10.6/8.0 L/100 km. *Mazda5 2.3L automatic:* 11.2/8.3 L/100 km. *Protegé manual 1.6L:* 8.5/6.7 L/100 km. *Protegé automatic 1.6L:* 9.3/6.9 L/100 km. *Protegé 2.0L manual:* 9.6/7.3 L/100 km. *Protegé 2.0L automatic:* 9.9/7.4 L/100 km. **Maintenance/repair costs:** Average. **Parts:** Reasonably priced and easily found. **Extended warranty:** Not necessary. **Best alternatives:** *Mazda3, Protegé:* Honda Civic; Hyundai Accent or Elantra; Nissan Sentra; Suzuki Aerio, Esteem, or Swift; and Toyota Echo or Tercel. *Mazda5:* Honda Odyssey, Hyundai Entourage, and Kia Sedona. **Helpful websites:** *www.mazdas247.com/forum/index.php.*

 ## Strengths and Weaknesses

Protegé

Although 1996–2003 Protegés are far more reliable than most American-made small cars, automatic transmissions are their weakest link (a problem also seen with Ford's Escort and Hyundai's lineup), characterized by erratic shifting and locking up in Fifth gear. Owners also endure fuel-system glitches, electrical problems, front brake vibration, rotor warping, and premature pad wear. Other generic deficiencies are weak rear defrosting, chronic engine stalling (a secret warranty applies, up to seven years), AC failures, and body defects, including wind and water leaks into the interior.

Mazda3

An econobox with flair, the front-drive 2004 Mazda3 is the entry-level small car that replaced the Protegé. With considerable engineering help from Ford and Volvo, these cars use a platform and 4-cylinder engines that will also serve future iterations of the Ford Focus and Volvo S40. These pocket rockets are powered by three different 4-cylinder powerplants: a base 148 hp 2.0L, a 167 hp 2.5L, or a 263 hp 2.3L 4 turbo. Coupled with either a 5-speed manual or a 4-speed Sport-mode automatic transmission, the car offers spirited acceleration and smooth, sporty shifting. Handling is enhanced with a highly rigid body structure, front and rear stabilizer bars, a multi-link rear suspension, and four-wheel disc brakes. Interior room is also quite ample with the car's relatively long 263.9 cm (103.9 in.) wheelbase, extra width, and straight sides, which maximize headroom, legroom, and shoulder room.

The Mazda3 is a breeze to break into. Bizarre, but true—all it takes is a blow to the door on either side of any 2004–07 model, and the lock pops. The Internet is full of reports telling how easily the cars and their contents are stolen. This information first came to light in the fall of 2006 in Western Canada, and now police and insurers like the Insurance Corporation of British Columbia are scrambling to answer complaints coming in from all over the country.

Mazda3 owner complaints are about average in number, which is still too high for a vehicle that is this simply made. There are some electrical shorts as well as numerous minor fit and finish deficiencies, and sporadic reports of prematurely worn-out transmission clutch assemblies. The rear seats provide limited footroom; the high deck reduces rear visibility; early brake pad and rotor replacements continue unabated; some drivers say the car's standard engine could use more passing power; and some Mazda dealers have been accused of overcharging for scheduled maintenance. Other reported problems: dashboards crack; window regulators break; the steering box makes a clicking/ticking sound; the dash and driver's door rattle; AC performance is wimpy; the driver's right knee rubs the console; there's excess brake dust on rear wheels; the Door Ajar light comes on for no reason; the gas and brake pedal are too close together; a front-end clunk is felt on hard acceleration; paint is unusually thin and aluminum rims peel; the passenger-side wiper may not clean the windshield sufficiently; fuel consumption is excessive, about 10 percent more than advertised; the 5-speed manual gearbox sometimes has trouble shifting from First to Second gear; a popping/creaking/rattling noise emanates from the rear end (hatch struts may be the culprit); and drivers easily catch the side of their shoe against the brake when accelerating (consider getting customized racing pedals). Original-equipment and Goodyear tires perform poorly in rain and slush (Michelin Pilot and Hakkapeliitta winter tires are better performers; check with *www.tirerack.com* for the best tire combination).

Mazda5

The Mazda5 is mainly a compact miniwagon that's based broadly on the Mazda3 and carries six passengers in three rows of seats. Used mostly for urban errands and light commuting, the "5" employs a peppy though fuel-frugal 153 hp 2.3L 4-cylinder engine hooked to a standard 5-speed manual transmission or a 4-speed automatic.

Since it debuted as a 2006 model, the Mazda5 has had few problems. It has all the advantages of a small minivan without the handling or fuel penalties. Furthermore, it's reasonably priced used and provides a comfortable ride and relatively quiet interior (except for omnipresent road noise—a common trait with small wagons). There are a few minuses, however. The small 4-cylinder engine doesn't have much torque for heavy loads or hill climbing, and towing isn't recommended. There isn't much room for two passengers in the third-row seat, either. There's also a history of automatic transmission and electrical malfunctions (but much fewer than with Honda or Toyota), prematurely worn-out brake rotors and pads, and fit and finish deficiencies.

So far, only a few dozen complaints have been reported to NHTSA concerning transmission malfunctions, the vehicle rolling downhill with the parking brake engaged, poor wet-road traction, and premature tire wear. However, one serious complaint that is repeated dozens of times in NHTSA's logs is the sudden loss of steering on both the Mazda3 and Mazda5. Apparently, both cars have been recalled to correct this defect, but owners say the problem persists.

VEHICLE HISTORY: *Protegé:* **1999–2003**—Totally revamped, with a restyled interior and exterior and a more-powerful engine lineup; handling, acceleration with the automatic tranny, and entry/exit are improved. Better-performing than earlier versions. **2001**—A restyled front end, optional disc brakes, and a 130 hp 2.0L engine is offered. **2003**—A turbocharged 170 hp MazdaSpeed Protegé debuts and is sold in small quantities. **2004**—Protegé is replaced by the 2004 Mazda3. *Mazda3:* **2004–07**—Mazda3 launches with two 4-cylinder engines: a base 148 hp 2.0L and a 160 hp 2.3L. **2007**—A new performance model equipped with the highly recommended traction/anti-skid control feature. *Mazda5:* **2006**—Mazda5's first model year. **2007**—A more upscale wagon arrives. **2008**—A restyled interior and exterior and a 5-speed automatic transmission.

Safety Summary

All models/years: Airbags fail to deploy. • Chronic stalling. • Transmission failures and malfunctions. • If you stop or park on an incline, vehicle will likely roll away even with brakes applied. • Metal rods in driver's seat could cause severe back injuries in a rear-end collision. • Brake pedal pad is too narrow. **All models: 2001**—Loss of brakes. • Gearshift lever jumps from Drive to Neutral while driving. • Defective steering-column coupling. • Broken rear axle causes severe pulling to one side. • **2003**—Brake pedal pushed almost to the floor before brakes work; they produce excessive noise. *Mazda3:* **2004**—Premature wearout of brake pads and rotors. • The transmission can be hard to shift, especially from Third to Fourth gear. • Transmission needs replacing during the first year. • Huge accumulation of brake dust on the rear wheels. • Brake rotors are prematurely grooved. • Chronic hard starts, stalling, and poor idling. **2004–05**—AC is inadequate; it doesn't cool the car and compromises acceleration. **2005**—When car stalls on the highway, both steering and brakes fail. • Brake failures. • Windshield wiper flies off the car. **2006**—Sudden acceleration when using the cruise control. • Engine failure due to defective lower engine rod. • Vehicle goes into Reverse when shifted into Fourth gear. • Brake and accelerator pedal mounted too close together. • Early rear brake pad and rotor replacement. • On one occasion, driver's seatback collapsed in a rear collision. • Tire rims are easily damaged when passing over potholes. **2007**—Gas tank puncture. • Warped front brake rotors. • Large rear blind spot. • Xenon headlights provide poor visibility. • Toyo tire side walls blow out. • Sudden failure of the MazdaSpeed3 engine:

> Mazda Speed3 2007 has been having problems with engine mounting failures. It seems the engine mount is not bolted correctly or the bolt itself to the engine is defective. Mazda3 Forums [h]as some picture[s] provided by actual consumers who had this [happen] to their cars: *www.mazda3forums.com/index.php?topic=68463.0.*

2008—Parking brake won't hold the car on an incline. • Original-equipment Goodyear Eagle all-season tires don't give sufficient traction and wear out quickly. • Incorrect negative rear camber setting causes rear tires to wear out prematurely:

The dealership and zone office will replace the defective part but I am having difficulty having them pay for replacement tires. The tires have been affected by the defective part therefore the warranty should cover the full cost of replacement tires.

• ABS goes on and off. • Power steering failure:

In the power steering system the fuse that controls this valve blew for the first time on May 11, 2009. It has blown 2 additional times, including today in rush hour traffic. Unlike other manufacturers, when this fuse blows, the valve closes, cutting off all flow to the rack, disabling the power assist. When the fuse blew today, I was in the middle of an intersection, turning left. I had to struggle to turn sharp enough to avoid hitting a car waiting to go straight. The valve should have been designed to stay open when power is removed.

• Fuel cap sticks. • Severe engine and steering wheel shake • Cabin air may be contaminated by toxic gases:

I bought a 2008 Mazda3 4 months ago. The car began making me sick—bad headaches and loss of concentration.... I sent for a formaldehyde testing kit from a lab and tested the car after driving and getting really sick. The results came back positive with a .075 ppm (almost exact FEMA trailer litigation average). This testing was done on a 60–65 degree [15.5–18.3 degrees Celsius] ambient temperature day. The formaldehyde levels seem to get worse the warmer it gets. I took car to dealer, dealer inspected, wrote it up as an air leak—could not duplicate. I filed a formal complaint with Mazda. I sought help from the BBB [Better Business Bureau]. I took the car back to the dealer. The dealer took the car and did nothing.

2008—Prematurely worn original equipment rear tires. • Many complaints of sudden steering failures:

On a few separate occasions (approximately three) during especially hot weather, the power steering has failed while driving my 2009 Mazda 3. One especially concerning instance occurred while driving on a highway in very heavy traffic. Each time I have pulled over, shut the car off, and turned it back on, following the instructions in the owner's manual. This has been successful for the most part. However, on one occasion, which occurred in 100+ degree weather, the power steering did not return and the car had to be left in a parking structure to cool down.

• Recalled steering repair parts are unavailable, for many. • Mazda aluminum tire valve stems are weak, vulnerable to corrosion, and will interfere with the low-pressure alert feature. • Gas cap seizing. Mazda5: 2006—Driver's seat collapses in a rear-end collision. • Chronic engine overheating (faulty AC compressor?). • Hesitation when shifting. • Stalling in traffic believed to be caused by a defective PCM. • Leaking casing requires a transmission replacement. • Brake failures. • Sudden power-steering failure. • Leaking front struts. • Shocks, front stabilizer bushing, and damper wear out early. • Prematurely worn original tires (cupping). • Weak side walls on Dunlop Sport Signature tires. • Very poor traction on wet roads. • AC compressor failure. • Doors freeze shut. 2007—Car parked 3 metres from the house with the engine running suddenly accelerated, damaging the house. • Third-row safety belt anchor is placed too far forward to secure the passenger. • Fob-controlled door locks don't work. **2008**—Loose bolts in the rear right suspension. • Premature rear tire wear ("cupping"). • Power steering goes out sporadically. • Floor mat can catch the clutch pedal during gear changes. • Sunroof suddenly explodes while closed. **2009**—Engine compartment fire caused by improper length of wire in harness causing a loose connection to the controller unit. • Gas pedal stuck three times. • Frequent sudden power steering failures that return to normal if the car is restarted (recalled parts are on national back order). • Parked vehicle rolled down a hill even though the emergency brake was applied. • Premature wearout of Toyo rear tires. • Loose nut connecting the right rear anti-sway bar to the suspension. • Goodyear Eagle RS tires perform poorly in light snow conditions. • Broken fuel cap is a common problem:

> Tried to unscrew fuel cap to fuel vehicle. It would not come off. Tried several times until it broke off. A quick Internet search found dozens of similar incidents with Mazda 3's and Mazda 5's. The cap has 2 parts, the outer part is what broke off, while the inner part remains stuck. After the outer part breaks off, it becomes evident the inner part is mistreated, something not evident while the cap is intact.

Secret Warranties/Internal Bulletins/Service Tips

All models: 1999–2007—Troubleshooting tips for eliminating wind noise around windows. *Mazda3:* **2004**—Poor AC performance. • Mazda-upgraded shock absorbers will reduce suspension knocking when passing over bumps. • A splashing sound comes from the dash area. • Trunk lid difficult to open. • Power-window failures require a new window motor. • Fix for squeaking rear brakes. **2004–05**—Hard starts and poor idle are tackled in TSB #01-013/05, and the correction is covered by the warranty. • Engine stalls at low rpms. • Possible causes for a noisy, smelly engine coming from any Mazda3 equipped with a manual transmission. • Installing countermeasure washers can stop drivetrain clicking. • Excessive engine vibration fix. • Rear brake squeal and grinding has been remedied with upgraded brake pads, says TSB #04-003/05. • Modified pads and a mounting support for the front brake calipers to correct front brake squeaking. • Front-door rattle correction guidelines. • One-touch window stops halfway down. **2004–06**—Hard starts in cold weather require a software recalibration under warranty. • Rough idle and engine hesitation. • Troubleshooting a snap or clunk noise when operating the windows. **2004–07**—Body vibration at cruising speed. • High power-steering effort. • Corroded wiper arm hinges. • Inability to adjust driver-seat manual lift. **2004–08**—No-start in Park. • Manual transmission grinding noise; pops out of gear. • Rough idle; engine stalls. • How to deal with brake noise, judder, and dragging. **2004–09**—Engine knocking noise on start or shutdown. • Front power window noise. • Cracked centre dash. • Vibration at cruising speed can be eliminated by installing countermeasure engine mount rubbers made by Mazda. This should be a free "goodwill" repair because the problem is of Mazda's own making. • Water in lights. **2004–10**—Front head restraint rattling. **2006–07**—Idle dip when AC cycles on. • Engine stalls or hesitates after a hot start (reprogram the PCM). **2006–08**—Coolant leaks. **2006–09**—AC no longer cools after a long drive. **2007–08**—Measures to correct difficult steering. • Clunking brakes. **2007–09**—High steering effort. **2008**—Silencing a ticking noise from the purge solenoid valve. **2009**—Engine oil leak between the engine and the automatic transmission bell housing. • Excessive noise generated by the manual transmission. *Mazda5:* **2004–08**—Moisture in lights. **2006–07**—Stiff steering. • Intermittent engine stumble. • Engine stalls at low rpms. • Idle fluctuation and engine vibration. • Body vibration at cruising speeds. • Front suspension squeak, knock, or rattle. • Outer mirror wind noise. **2006–08**—Clunking brakes. • Rough idle, stalling. • Eliminating brake noise, judder, and dragging. **2006–09**—Engine knocking noise on start or shutdown. • AC no longer cools after a long drive. **2006–10**—Front power window noise. • Front head restraint rattling. **2008**—Coolant leaks.

MAZDA3, MAZDA5, PROTEGÉ PROFILE

	2001	2002	2003	2004	2005	2006	2007	2008	2009
Cost Price ($)									
Protegé	15,795	15,795	15,795	—	—	—	—	—	—
Mazda3	—	—	—	16,195	16,295	16,495	16,795	16,895	14,895
MazdaSpeed3	—	—	—	—	—	—	30,995	31,095	29,360
Mazda5 GS	—	—	—	—	—	19,995	19,995	20,795	19,995
Mazda5 GT	—	—	—	—	—	22,795	22,895	24,815	23,295
Used Values ($)									
Protegé ▲	3,000	4,000	5,000	—	—	—	—	—	—
Protegé ▼	2,500	3,500	4,000	—	—	—	—	—	—
Mazda3 ▲	—	—	—	5,500	6,500	7,500	9,000	10,000	11,500
Mazda3 ▼	—	—	—	4,500	5,500	6,500	8,000	9,000	10,500
MazdaSpeed3 ▲	—	—	—	—	—	—	14,500	18,000	21,000
MazdaSpeed3 ▼	—	—	—	—	—	—	13,500	16,500	19,500
Mazda5 GS▲	—	—	—	—	—	8,500	10,000	11,500	14,000
Mazda5 GS▼	—	—	—	—	—	7,000	9,000	10,000	12,500
Mazda5 GT▲	—	—	—	—	—	9,500	11,500	13,000	16,000
Mazda5 GT ▼	—	—	—	—	—	8,000	10,000	11,500	14,500
Reliability	5	5	5	3	4	4	4	5	5
Crash Safety (F)	5	5	5	4	4	4	4	4	4
Side	3	3	3	3	3	3	3	3	—
IIHS Side	—	—	—	—	1	1	1	1	—
Offset	3	3	3	5	5	5	5	5	5
Head Restraints (F)	3	3	3	2	2	2	2	2	2
Rear	2	2	2	2	2	—	—	—	—
Rollover Resistance	—	—	4	4	4	4	4	4	4

Mercedes-Benz

Rating: Below Average (2009); Not Recommended (2005–08). Although the post-2008s are a bit improved in performance and quality control, there are many cheaper, more reliable Asian-, European-, and Detroit-hailed small cars—like the Honda Fit and Civic (the older the better); the Mazda3, soon to be joined by the Mazda2; the Nissan Sentra; and the VW TDI. These are all frugal-runners that are more refined and easier to service and repair. **Ideal model year:** For pure fuel economy in an urban environment: any one of the older diesel versions. **Maintenance/repair costs:** Extraordinarily high; Why should dealers give you the lowest prices and best service if you have no where else to go? Servicing bays are closing down as dealers focus on high-end Mercedes products. So don't be surprised if your servicing complaints are met with Gallic indifference. Service bulletins, which some enterprising do-it-yourselfers find essential, aren't widely distributed. **Parts:** Rare and expensive. Smart sales have been terrible with only 4,000 sales in the States during the first seven months of 2010. As a result, few independent suppliers stock Smart parts, and dealers find it more profitable to sell high-profit Mercedes parts and servicing than looking for some obscure "cheapo" Smart part in the back of the warehouse. **Extended warranty:** An expensive requirement for such a cheap car. It'll only keep you longer in a dealer network that doesn't want you. **Best alternatives:** Ford Fiesta or post-2004 Focus; Honda Civic or Fit; Hyundai Accent; Mazda3, Mazda5, or Protegé; Nissan Sentra; Suzuki Forsa, Swift, Esteem, or Aerio; and any VW TDI. **Helpful websites:** *www.451s. com* and *www.smartcarofamerica.com.*

 ## Strengths and Weaknesses

Not a "smart" idea when the competition is cheaper and performs much better on the highway and in city congestion. Daimler has lost billions on the Smart since its 1998 European debut, and the company has lost its shirt trying to sell Smarts in the States through the 70 dealers belonging to the Penske Automotive Group since 2008. Without a burst of American expansion, Canadian Smart owners may be restricted to Canadian roads if they're at all worried about servicing. And even if they stay home, parts supply and servicing will likely dry up as dealers forsake these "green" cars for greener pastures of their own.

Actually, the Smart is not as green as its boosters pretend, since its estimated 41 miles per U.S. gallon (premium) (5.7L/100 km) is no climate changer, though the diesel fuel economy at an estimated 74 mpg (3.2L/100 km) is impressive. Nevertheless, Asian microcars are cheaper by a few thousand dollars and are all-around better performers. Even the much-vaunted Ford Fiesta sells for $2,000 less, while almost matching the Smart's fuel economy.

The Smart, sold in most of Canada's Mercedes-Benz dealerships, is fuel-frugal and distinctively styled. On the other hand, you will pay new $14,999 for a rudimentary European minicar that is not suited for North American roads and will lose more than half its original value after three years of use. If you are cruising at 120 km/h you're killing its little 1.0L 3-banger. Plus, there's the Smart's lethargic acceleration, tiny wheels that transform small potholes into moon craters, and stiff-riding short wheel base that compromises emergency handling. Owners also have to contend with highly dealer-dependent servicing (trips must be planned carefully for servicing accessibility) and parts that are often back ordered.

Many Smart cars won't go into or get out of Park or Reverse. See *www.smartcarofamerica.com/forums/f25/gear-knob-button-stuck-4454*; *www.smartcarofamerica.com/forums/f25/diy-gear-shift-removal-lube-short-video-5428*. This appears to be a serious problem.

The Smart's poor highway performance has been confirmed by a number of independent auto publications, including the following:

> Beyond the Fortwo's safety concerns, it also has sluggish acceleration, even for a subcompact car. It is low on utility since it offers seating for just two and only 12 cubic feet of cargo space (and that's only if you're willing to obscure the rear window). Test drivers also complain loudly about the car's sluggish transmission and the fact that the engine requires premium gasoline.
>
> U.S. NEWS AND WORLD REPORT
> JULY 21, 2010

> Herky-jerky automatic gearbox, seats only two, gets buffeted on the highway by stiff crosswinds and big trucks.
>
> EDMUNDS.COM

> So the Smart is an unpleasant-to-drive, one-trick pony. And yet there are plenty of people—some 30k American early adopters at last count—who couldn't care less about its dreadful driving dynamics.
>
> THE TRUTH ABOUT CARS
> NOVEMBER 2, 2007

Smarts depreciate much too quickly for a small car that one would imagine to be in high demand by fuel-frugal drivers. For example, sold new for $16,500, a used 2005 entry-level Smart Fortwo Coupe now goes for $3,000 to $4,000; a new $19,500 2005 entry-level convertible now sells for between $5,500 and $6,500.

Smarts were originally powered by an 800 cubic centimetre 3-cylinder turbodiesel motor that produced 41 hp—nowhere near the 108 horses offered by Toyota's smallest car, the $13,165 2008 Yaris. Today's versions carry a 1.0L, 3-cylinder engine that uses premium fuel. Furthermore, the Smart is only 2.5 metres long and weighs in at only 730 kg, which is very light when compared to the Toyota Echo or Yaris. These factors combine to give the Smart an estimated 4.4 L/100 km rating, much better than the Toyota Echo's estimated city/highway fuel economy of 6.7/5.2 L/100 km (with a manual transmission), and much more frugal than the outrageously inaccurate fuel-savings claims bandied about by Honda and Toyota when they hype their hybrids.

After dismal sales in the States, Roger Penske Enterprises (300 dealerships) gave back to Mercedes-Benz the U.S. Smart distribution rights. Smart North American sales tumbled 38 percent during 2009, despite a $1,700 price cut. In January 2011, only 82 Smart cars were sold in Canada (6 percent less than a month earlier). Like Fiat, Lada, Peugeot, and Renault—four automakers that abandoned Canada after failing to expand into the States—Mercedes may leave Smart owners high and dry if it decides Smart cannot compete successfully against the existing and forthcoming wave of European and Asian economy cars. Mercedes wouldn't hesitate to "flip the switch," as it did when it dumped Chrysler in May 2007. In fact, you have to admit that Mercedes doesn't have a great record with small entry-level models. Remember the "Baby Benz" models, such as the 190 model that was introduced over a decade ago and then quickly abandoned, or the C-Class hatchback that was quickly dropped? This wouldn't be much of a problem if Smarts were conventional small cars backed by an extensive dealer network and a large parts inventory. But that's not the case. Furthermore, unlike old MGs and Triumphs, there isn't a body of independent repairers and part suppliers who can step into the breach.

As for reliability and safety concerns, the Smart receives mixed reviews. Reliability figures on the 2008 model compiled by *Consumer Reports* magazine show serious deficiencies affecting the transmission, body hardware, fuel and electrical systems, and overall fit and finish.

As for crashworthiness, NHTSA has given the 2008 through 2010 Smart Fortwo (2-door) a four-star rating for frontal protection and a five-star score for side occupant crash protection. Rollover resistance was given three stars for those same model years. IIHS has given the 2008 through 2010 Smart a Good rating for frontal and side-impact occupant protection as well as roof strength. Head-restraint effectiveness was judged Acceptable. During the NHTSA side-impact test, the driver's door unlatched and opened. A door opening during a side-impact crash increases the likelihood of occupant ejection. Second-generation models come with standard electronic stability control and side curtain airbags. For reliability and overall highway performance, all first-generation Fortwos (built through 2007) come up far short. The 41 hp turbodiesel that powers these vehicles (up to 2008, when a 71 hp 1.0L gasoline engine took over) is clearly inadequate for merging in highway traffic; passengers will find the ride to be jiggly and unsettling and handling to be barely competent. Shifting also requires a great deal of patience and foresight because there can be considerable "lag and lurch."

Common complaints include chronic stalling; the transmission "hanging up" in gear during hard acceleration or sticking in Park so the car must be towed; myriad shortcircuits (most common: door locks that won't lock and interior lights that behave erratically); premature ball joint wear; blower motor failures; the ABS warning light coming on due to a faulty brake light switch; defective tire valve stems; inaccurate fuel gauge readings; polycarbonate roof panels that often need replacing (spider cracks); and an assortment of other body glitches.

SMART FORTWO PROFILE

	2005	2006	2007	2008	2009
Cost Price ($)					
Coupe	16,500	16,700	16,700	14,990	14,990
Convertible	19,500	19,700	19,700	21,250	21,250
Used Values ($)					
Coupe ▲	4,000	5,500	7,000	9,500	11,000
Coupe ▼	3,000	4,500	6,500	8,000	9,500
Convertible ▲	6,500	8,000	10,500	13,500	15,500
Convertible ▼	5,500	6,500	9,000	12,000	14,000

Nissan

SENTRA ★★★★

RATING: Above Average (2007–09); Average (2001–06). The pre-2007 Sentras have been downgraded for their numerous safety and quality problems. Note the below-average side and head-restraint crashworthiness scores up to the 2006 models. **Ideal model year:** A 2007 SE-R or 2008 2.0 SL. **"Real" city/highway fuel economy:** *Manual 1.8L:* 8.5/6.1 L/100 km. *Automatic 1.8L:* 8.3/6.2 L/100 km. *Manual 2.5L:* 10.2/7.3 L/100 km. *Automatic 2.5L:* 10.2/7.7 L/100 km. Owners report fuel economy is much less than these estimates. **Maintenance/repair costs:** Average costs and availability; anyone can repair these cars, although the high-performance versions require special skill. **Parts:** Owners report waiting weeks for recall-related parts. **Extended warranty:** A good idea. **Best alternatives:** Honda Civic; Hyundai Elantra or Tiburon; Mazda3 or Protegé; Suzuki Esteem or Swift; and Toyota Echo or Tercel. High-performance enthusiasts should consider Sentra's 2007 and later SE-R and Spec V models, although the Honda Civic Si and MazdaSpeed are still the benchmark for the most performance for your dollar. **Helpful websites:** *http://forums.nicoclub.com/technical.html.*

Strengths and Weaknesses

Owner complaints for 1995–2002 models concern stalling and hard starting; engine rattles; electrical glitches; premature brake wear and excessive brake noise; an automatic transmission whine; AC solenoid failures, and an AC that blows hot air or freezes up; and malfunctioning accessories. Owners have also had to contend with a recurrent steering clunk noise as well as clutch, clutch-switch, suspension-strut, wheel bearing, and catalytic converter failures. Crank position sensor malfunctions may prevent the vehicle from starting. Body assembly is also a problem, with some complaints of loose windshield mouldings, poor body fits, paint defects, and air and water leaks into the interior through the trunk and doors.

The 2003–06 models are just as problem-prone. One gets the impression Nissan held back many quality improvements for later inclusion in the 2007 model redesign. Owners of these versions are plagued by cylinder head gasket leaks; cracked #4 cylinder heads on the 1.8L engine; a misfiring #3 cylinder; early replacement of the engine serpentine belt; engine pinging and rattling; and automatic transmission, fuel-system, and electrical problems.

Front brake pads and rotors also wear out quickly; there's excessive noise, bouncing, and vibration caused by prematurely worn struts and control-arm bushings; the doors vibrate noisily; passenger-side windows leak; the hood allows water to leak onto the drivebelt; rear bumpers may fall off; there is excessive wind noise around the windshield moulding; and a poor AC design wastes fuel.

The 2007–09 Sentras are much improved from a quality control and crashworthiness standpoint, but some serious problems remain and new ones have appeared. The CVT is smooth and usually very responsive (though cold weather may adversely affect its performance), the ride is more comfortable, the interior trim has gone upscale, there are handy flip-forward rear-seat cushions and flat-folding rear seatbacks, and more attention has been paid to fit and finish. On the minus side, get used to limited passing power on the highway with base models, excessive engine noise in the higher revs, numb steering, mediocre manual shifting, instrument gauges that wash out in sunlight, and tight rear seating.

Quality is still problematic. Owners report that the engine may overheat without any warning lights coming on, or that the front brake calipers and warped brake rotors require frequent replacing. As well, fuel-delivery system glitches cause loss of power, hard starting, and stalling. Other problems: power steering failures, defective rear beam axles, and premature rear tire wear due to faulty rear alignment.

VEHICLE HISTORY: 2000—A major redesign produces more powerful engines, a better ride, and enhanced handling. **2002**—The 145 hp SE model was replaced at the top of the line by the SE-R and SE-R Spec V; the latter offers a 180 hp engine, a limited-slip differential, and a sport-tuned suspension to compete against the Honda Civic SiR and Mazda's high-performance spin-offs. Four-wheel disc brakes also become a standard feature. **2003**—Arrival of the GXE, equipped with ABS, a 165 hp 2.5L engine, and front side airbags. **2007**—Redesigned with fresh styling, more power, a longer wheelbase, and added standard features, such as AC, side curtain airbags, four-wheel disc brakes (Spec V), ABS on higher-end models, a 6-speed manual transmission, an automatic CVT (2.0 SL), a 140 hp 2.0L that boosts horsepower by 14, and a sizzling 177 hp 2.5L 4-cylinder powerplant (SE-R) that's pumped up to 200 horses on the Spec V.

Safety Summary

All years: Chronic stalling. • Sudden acceleration. • Complete brake failures. • Brake and accelerator pedals are set too close together. • Airbags fail to deploy or deploy inadvertently. • Steering lock-up or failures. • Premature tire wear. • Horn blows on its own. **2004**—Erratic, rough idling. • Early automatic transmission replacement. • Keyless remote doesn't work, and back door doesn't open from the inside, apparently due to a short in the electrical system. **2005**—Rear wheel lock-up. • Warped rear brake drums. • Front seatback collapsed from a rear-end collision in one incident. • Frequent horn malfunctions. • Inoperative driver's door handle. **2006**—Automatic transmission stays in Neutral, or slips out of gear. • Door locks with the keys in the ignition. • Faulty front wheel bearings. • Defective window regulators. • Gas tank pressure forces fuel out of the tank:

> A new gas tank and fuel filter were needed. The vehicle is currently being repaired at the dealer. They covered half of the repair costs. The failure is identical to NHTSA Campaign ID Number 05v269000 (Fuel System, Gasoline: Storage) for an earlier model of the same vehicle; however, the VIN was not included in the recall.

2007—One vehicle caught fire while driving on the highway. • Broken motor mounts and steering-column bolts (steering wheel turns without effect). • Cracked engine block. • Frequent power steering failures:

> The issue occurs more often in the cold weather, and the power steering has been failing almost daily this winter. Typically, after the car is restarted several times the PS light will turn off and the power steering will again operate correctly. Often I have had to drive the vehicle without functional power steering, and it is very difficult to maneuver the car. Because this issue is worsened by the cold weather, the roads may be icy or snowy, adding to the danger of operating without proper functioning steering. It was difficult for me to have this issue diagnosed by my mechanic, as I had to get the car to him while the PS light was on, and when he ran it through the computer it gave him the code C1606. Having done research online, I see that I am not the only person having this recurring problem with this particular vehicle, but Nissan has not issued any recall. It is an expensive fix (estimated at $2,500).

• Original tires are poor winter performers. • False illumination of the Low Tire Pressure light. • Poor crossmember design eats tires:

A manufacturing defect of the rear cross member does not allow adjustment for toe alignment which resulted in excessive tire wear creating an incalculable risk of failure.

•

We are experiencing severe rear tire wear. Dealership refused to acknowledge problem until the third visit when we went with handful of testimonials (printed from car review sites on Internet) from other people experiencing this same problem with their Nissan 2007–2008 Sentra.

2008—Vehicle bangs into gear after hesitating. • Rear-end toe out cannot be adjusted, making the rear end unstable on wet roads and gouging out the rear tires:

I noticed the rear wheels tilt in at the top, especially the left rear wheel, at least 5 degrees negative camber (I am an insurance auto appraiser). It also appears to have slight [toe] in. This is a fixed non-adjustable beam axle that was set up wrong in the assembly jig and welded up wrong. After some research, [I discovered] this affects 07 and 08 models. The tires will wear out quickly on the inside of the tread (not too noticeable from the outside of the car), and may blow out. At best I will be replacing rear tires all the time. I complained to the dealer 7/29/08 the week after delivery and he said Nissan is aware of the problem and is working on it. They were aware of this in 2007 and have done nothing so far, and are still shipping cars with defective rear beam axles.

• Front struts wear out quickly. • Faulty original-equipment Bridgestone tires:

Anyone with these tires should do a Google search of "Bridgestone Turanza problems" and "Bridgestone Turanza EL400 complaints." I have seen complaints from Toyota, BMW, Mercedes, Honda, and Nissan owners about these tires.

• Tire Pressure warning sensor often comes on for no reason. • Seat belt buckle snaps back with excessive force, injuring occupants. • Bottom of the windshield is distorted. • Faulty rear- view mirror design:

Blinded by the early morning sun and automatically reached for my sun visor. When I tried to pull it down it hit the rear view mirror and stopped in a position that blocked my entire forward view except for a few feet…. These auto dimming mirrors were 10.5 inches [26.7 cm] wide as opposed to the standard day/nights' 9.5 inches [24.1 cm] on other 2008 Sentras. I advised the service manager of this and he and others verified that all the Sentras with this option had the same too-large mirror.

2009—Car accelerated forward even with driver's foot on the brake. • Front passenger airbag isn't disabled when a child is seated in the front seat. • Owners say vehicle swerves too much on the freeway. • Bridgestone Turanza tires keep setting off the low-tire-pressure sensor.

Secret Warranties/Internal Bulletins/Service Tips

2000–04—TSB #AT04-002, published March 10, 2004, says abnormal shifting of the automatic transmission is likely due to a defective control valve assembly. **2000–05**—Alternator chirping or squealing is caused by a defective alternator drivebelt; "goodwill" adjustment available. **2000–06**—Front-door windows may not work properly. **2002–05**—A 2–3 shift chirping noise can be silenced by pouring in two bottles of Nissan's special ATF transmission treatment fluid. Do this first, before spending big bucks on unneeded repairs, inspections, etc. **2004–08**—Leaking tire pressure sensors. **2005**—Fix for cold engine stumbling and stalling. **2007**—Doors are hard to open with the outside handle in cold weather. • Hard-to-close trunk lid. **2007–08**—AC compressor noise, poor cooling, and window fogging. **2007–09**—Coolant leaks from reservoir hoses. • Steering, suspension pop or clunk when turning. • Fixing an erratically operating sunroof. • Inoperative power-window "Auto Up" function. • Squeaking front seats. **2007–10**—Erratic fuel gauge readings usually indicate a need to replace the fuel level sensor unit. • Diagnostic steps to troubleshoot drivebelt noise.

SENTRA PROFILE

	2001	2002	2003	2004	2005	2006	2007	2008	2009
Cost Price ($)									
Sentra	15,298	15,598	15,598	15,798	15,598	16,698	16,798	16,798	14,798
SE-R	—	19,998	20,498	21,498	21,498	21,698	—	—	—
Spec V	—	21,498	21,998	21,998	21,998	22,198	24,298	22,798	22,048
Used Values ($)									
Sentra ▲	2,500	3,500	4,000	5,000	6,000	6,500	7,500	9,000	10,500
Sentra ▼	2,000	3,000	3,500	4,500	5,000	5,500	6,500	7,500	9,500
SE-R ▲	—	4,500	5,000	6,000	7,000	8,500	—	—	
SE-R ▼	—	4,000	4,500	5,500	6,000	7,500	—	—	—
Spec V ▲	—	5,500	6,000	7,500	8,500	10,000	12,000	14,000	16,000
Spec V ▼	—	5,000	5,500	6,500	7,500	8,500	10,500	12,500	15,000
Reliability	3	3	3	3	3	3	3	4	4
Crash Safety (F)	4	4	4	4	4	4	5	5	5
Side	—	—	2	2	2	2	5	5	5
IIHS Side	1	1	1	1	1	1	5	5	5
Offset	3	3	3	3	3	3	5	5	5
Head Restraints	2	1	1	1	1	1	5	5	5
Rollover Resistance	—	4	4	4	4	4	4	4	4

RATING: Average (2007–09). **Ideal model year:** A 2008 SL Hatchback for $8,500 to $9,500 will steer you away from first-year production glitches, offer the best performance and fuel economy, likely have some of the original manufacturer's warranty left, and cost less than half what the car sold for new. **"Real" city/ highway fuel economy:** 7.9/6.1 L/100 km. Owners have taken to task "puffed up" fuel economy claims. Drivers say that the Versa's fuel consumption is about 10 percent higher than what Canadian government figures show:

> This is a 2007 Nissan Versa and [it has] been getting only about 22 to 24 miles per gallon [9.8–10.7 L/100 km] in town. Sticker says the car gets 30 miles per gallon [7.8 L/100 km] in town. I have never gotten close to that. Took car to dealer and they said the air intake temp was 165 degrees [74°C] and they replaced the sensor. Gas mileage is still not what it should be.

Maintenance/repair costs: Lower-than-average maintenance costs (predicted). **Parts:** Several weeks' delay for some parts (fuel pump and airbag). **Extended warranty:** Not needed. **Best alternatives:** Honda Civic or Fit; Hyundai Elantra or Tiburon; Mazda3 or Protegé; Suzuki Esteem or Swift; and Toyota Corolla or Echo. **Helpful websites:** *http://forums.nicoclub.com* and *www.nissanclub.com/ forums/nissan-versa.*

Strengths and Weaknesses

Versa is Nissan's entry-level small hatchback and sedan, first launched as a 2007 model. The 2008–09 models were carried over with few important changes. Entry-level versions are powered by a 107 hp 1.6L 4-cylinder engine, while the SL models get a 122 hp 1.8L 4-banger. Coupled to a 6-speed manual transmission or a 4-speed automatic CVT, this small car gives decent fuel economy and a comfortable ride, is easily accessed, and is one of the roomiest econocars on the market. Side curtain airbags are standard, and first-year reliability has been acceptable. On the downside, the manual tranny isn't as smooth as the automatic CVT, handling is only so-so, wind and road noise are annoyingly loud, and brakes squeak continuously.

A 2007 base Versa S Hatchback sold new for $14,498 and is now worth $5,500–$7,000; a 2008 version sells for $7,000–$8,000; and a 2009 S will fetch about $8,000–$9,000. An all-dressed 2007 SL Hatchback sold for $17,098 and is now worth $7,000–$8,000, and the 2009 is worth between $10,000 and $11,500. The top-of-the-line SL Sed,an is priced similarly as the SL Hatchback.

NHTSA awarded the 2007 four-door Versa hatchback four stars for occupant protection in a frontal impact, five stars in a side collision, and four stars for rollover prevention, which are better-than-average scores for a small car. The 2008 hatchback and four-door earned four stars for front, side, and rollover protection. IIHS gave the 2007–09 Versa its top rating for occupant protection in both frontal offset and side collisions and for head-restraint protection.

Safety-related complaints include hard starts and stalling, some premature brake replacements, and poor performance of the original-equipment tires. Other areas of complaint concern faulty water pumps; front-end "popping" when turning, despite changing the right front strut and bushing and sway bar; a front bumper that will dislodge while the vehicle is underway; sunroof drain ducts that leak inside the passenger compartment; and other body hardware deficiencies.

🚗 Safety Summary

2007—A fire ignited in the rear wheelwell of one vehicle. • Airbag cover comes out of the dash. • No brakes. • In one incident, the vehicle shut down while cruising and the airbag deployed, knocking the driver unconscious. • The steering column of another vehicle had to be replaced twice. • Car veers left or right while cruising. • Car suddenly swerves out of control for no apparent reason. • Tie rod suddenly snaps, pulling the vehicle sharply to the right. • Gasoline spurts out of the filler neck when refuelling. **2007–08**—A fire in one vehicle originated in the front console area; other fires reported after the Check Engine light lit. • Vehicle seat belts fail to lock up in a sudden stop. • Airbags don't deploy when they should, or deploy when they shouldn't:

> Suddenly the airbag came out, she was scared, she applied the brakes and the car sped up, and she grabbed the emergency brake lever. The car stopped but she already hit other car, she had to go out through the passenger door.

• Driver's side window "guillotine hazard": Express-up window doesn't easily retract and could strangle a child. • Doors lock/unlock on their own. • Vehicle stalls out after cruising 200 km. • Many sudden front strut separations (suspension and steering loss). • CVT failures:

> Front axles "click" when making turns. CVT transmission cuts out or stalls when making turns and/or accelerating from a stop. Occurrence is 3–5 [times] weekly. I have taken this vehicle in for service 9–10 times. They have replaced the front axles and transmission with no improvement.

• Faulty fuel pump and malfunctioning mass air flow sensor cause total loss of power while underway. • Windshield cracks first appear at the base on the passenger side and move upward. • Inadequate defrosting. • Instrument panel gauges wash out in daylight. • Horn doesn't blow unless it is tapped at exactly the right spot. • Hubcaps often fly off. • Original equipment Continental tire shredding. • Many complaints that the Tire Pressure warning light comes on even though the tires are properly inflated. **2009**—Airbags failed to deploy during a rear-end collision. • Loss of all braking capability. • Poor braking performance on ice. • Frequent replacement of prematurely worn brake rotors and pads. • Hard starts or no-starts even after the fuel pump and fuel pressure regulator were replaced. • Sudden stalling due to a faulty fuel pump. • Heater/defroster failure due to a faulty fan resistor. • Speedometer is difficult to read in daylight:

• Vehicle tends to wander on the highway. • Early wearout of original equipment Continental Conti Pro Contact tires. • Tire air pressure sensor failures. • Noisy steering and delayed steering response when turning (see *http://x.nissanhelp.com/forums/versa/3861-versa-turning-right-problem-steering-column.html*).

Secret Warranties/Internal Bulletins/Service Tips

2007—Front airbag cover not flush. • Inoperative driver-door mirror. **2007–08**—Tips on installing a child safety seat. • AC compressor noise and window fogging. • Hard starting; long cranking time. • Front-end pop. • Water leaks onto driver's side floor and front floor carpet. • Squeaking front seats and rear brakes. **2007–09**—A long crank time before starts is traced to a faulty fuel pressure regulator. • Coolant leaks from reservoir hoses. • Water leaks onto driver's side floor. • AC compressor noise in very cold weather. • Steering, suspension pop or clunk when turning. • Fixing an erratically operating sunroof. • Inoperative power-window "Auto Up" function. • Squeaking front seats. • Loose cowl end mouldings. **2007–10**—Tips on silencing rear brake squealing. • Front axle clicking when accelerating from a stop. • Erratic fuel gauge readings usually indicate a need to replace the fuel level sensor unit. • Front seatbacks won't recline. • Front seat has too much "play," or won't move forward or backward. **2008**—A sill cover plate will be installed at no charge to prevent water from entering the cabin.

Subaru

FORESTER, IMPREZA, WRX/STI	★★★★/★★★/★

RATING: *Forester:* Above Average (2003–09); Average (1999–2002). *Impreza:* Average (1999–2009). *WRX/STi:* Not Recommended (2002–09). The WRX has tricky handling and serious, costly reliability issues (powertrain, brake, and steering). Except for the Forester, Subaru's model lineup is mostly the bland leading the bland. There's nothing remarkable about Subaru except for its early use of AWD for its entire lineup as a desperate move to stave off bankruptcy in the mid-'90s. This was a smart move because it gave buyers AWD versatility without the fuel penalty seen with larger engines. **Ideal model year:** Get a 2006 or 2009 Forester for its upgraded performance and safety features and depreciated prices. The same advice applies to the 2009 Impreza WRX performance model, although diehard high performance enthusiasts may well want to invest in a 2004 WRX STi sedan. In either case, a thorough WRX drivetrain and brake inspection is warranted, judging by past failures. Buyers of the base Impreza would do well to stick to the upgraded 2006 and 2009 versions. **"Real" city/highway fuel**

Subaru's WRX and STi are more "no-performance" than "high-performance"—be wary.

economy: *Forester turbocharged manual:* 13.0/9.3 L/100 km. *Forester turbocharged automatic:* 12.5/9.3 L/100 km. Generally, owners report the turbocharged Forester's actual gas consumption is often 20 percent higher than the above estimates. *Impreza 2.5L manual:* 11.2/7.7 L/100 km. *Impreza 2.5L automatic:* 10.6/7.6 L/100 km. *Forester:* 10.9/7.9 L/100 km. *WRX:* 11.8/8.0 L/100 km. **Maintenance/repair costs:** Average. Subaru sales have done relatively well in 2009, keeping dealers in the fold and buying sufficient inventory. Expensive servicing is still sometimes hard to overcome because independent garages can't service key AWD components. **Parts:** Only powertrain parts are hard to find and costly. **Extended warranty:** Only for the powertrain. **Best alternatives:** If you don't need the AWD capability, you're wasting your money. Here are some front-drives worth considering: Honda Civic; Hyundai Elantra; Mazda3 or Protegé; Nissan Sentra; Suzuki Aerio, Esteem, or Swift; and Toyota Corolla, Echo, or Yaris. Some recommended small vehicles with 4×4 capability that are set on a car's frame, not a truck's (to provide more carlike handling and better fuel economy), include the GM Vibe, Honda CR-V, Hyundai Tucson, and Toyota Matrix. **Helpful websites:** *http://forums.nasioc.com.*

Strengths and Weaknesses

These well-equipped small cars have one of the most refined AWD drivetrains you'll find. With their four-wheel traction, they provide lots of storage space with the wagons, along with good fuel economy and responsive handling without any torque steer. On the other hand, Subaru makes you pay dearly for its seamless AWD capability: Expect clutch failures, poor body fit and finish, and unreliable braking that can get downright scary. Furthermore, small doors and entryways restrict rear access, the coupe's narrow rear window and large rear pillars hinder rear visibility, heat and air distribution is often inadequate, and legroom may be insufficient for tall drivers and passengers. Without their AWD capability, these cars would be back-of-the-pack used-car picks.

The full-time AWD Impreza is essentially a shorter Legacy with additional convenience features. It comes as a four-door sedan, a wagon, and an Outback Sport wagon, all powered by a 135 hp 2.2L or a 165 hp 2.5L 4-cylinder engine. The 2.5L performs much better with the Impreza and Forester than with the Legacy Outback. It is smooth and powerful, with lots of low-end torque for serious off-road use. The automatic transmission shifts smoothly. The manual transmission's "hill holder" clutch prevents the car from rolling backward when starting out. These Subarus hurtle through corners effortlessly, with a flat, solid stance and plenty of grip. Tight cornering at highway speeds is done with minimal body lean and no loss of control, and steering is precise and predictable.

Forester

Another Subaru spin-off, the Forester is a cross between a tall wagon and a sport-utility. Based on the shorter Impreza, the Forester added eight horses to the Legacy Outback's 165 hp 2.5L engine and coupled it to a 5-speed manual transmission or an optional 4-speed automatic; the turbocharged variant produces 223 horsepower. Its road manners are more subdued, and its engine provides more power and torque for off-roading than do most vehicles its size. One minus: cramped rear seating. The Forester isn't perfect, but it beats most AWDs hands down.

WRX

An AWD car for the high-performance crowd, the WRX first showed up in 2001 as a 2002 model. It debuted as a goofy-looking, squat little wagon/SUV with a large rear end, a 227 hp 2.0L 4-cylinder engine mated to a high-boost turbocharger, lots of standard performance features, a sport suspension, an aluminum hood with a functional scoop, and higher-quality instruments, controls, trim, and seats. As time has passed, the engines have become more powerful and less reliable. Clutches have also become quite problematic. Subaru blames both of the above design deficiencies on driver abuse when the manufacturer turns down warranty repairs or grudgingly accept to pay half the repair cost with a "goodwill" arrangement:

> My 09 WRX, purchased in October, spun a bearing rod just over a month ago (had 6,001 miles [9,600 km] on it at the time). I live at altitude (8,200 ft.) and drive a roughly paved mountain road each day. This is not good on my tires, not one bit. Mike Shaw Subaru in Thorton, Colorado has finally gotten around to fixing the car. Took them one month, and I had a rental car for one week, but, they replaced the turbo and engine. One major repair is not covered by Subaru's limited warranty due to the "abusive or aggressive driving habits and/or vehicle modifications." Because of tire wear? Really? Now, my warranty is shot for any future engine work, the dealership itself told me. I refused to sign any of their papers, and will be aggressively pursuing litigation if I do not get this decision reversed or at least have someone knowledgeable explain to me how I "abused" my car.

VEHICLE HISTORY: All models: 2002—2.2L 4-cylinder is dropped, along with Subaru's pretensions for making affordable entry-level cars. Totally redesigned models include the 2.5 TS Sport Wagon, 2.5 RS sedan, Outback Sport Wagon, the WRX sporty sedan, and the Sport Wagon. There is no longer a two-door version available. *Forester:* **2003**—Improved interior materials, an upgraded suspension, and enhanced handling and ride quality. You'll also find larger tires and fenders, and revised head restraints and side-impact airbags. **2004**—A turbocharged 210 hp 2.5L 4-banger and a racier appearance. **2006**—More power and a slightly restyled interior and exterior. The 2006 turbocharged XT adds 20

The Subaru Forester.

hp, now up to 230 hp via a redesigned engine intake manifold (this could be troublesome in the future); other models get eight more horses, for a total of 173 hp. A retuned suspension enhances ride smoothness and handling response, and there's improved braking feel on all models. Ground clearance is slightly increased, and an alarm system is now standard. **2007**—17-inch wheels replace the 16-inchers. *Impreza:* **2004**—New front end with larger headlights and a restyled interior and exterior. **2006**—A small horsepower increase, enhanced front end, additional airbags, and a freshened interior. **2008**—Fresh styling and additional safety features that include side curtain airbags. **2009**—Most models were substantially upgraded with added power, safety, and convenience features. *WRX:* **2004**—A 300 hp engine comes on the scene. **2006**—2.5L gets 20 extra horses (up to 230 hp). **2009**—WRX got 41 more horses and a sportier performance suspension. STi was given a similar suspension upgrade.

Subarus are noted for only average quality control, spotty, expensive servicing, and serious automatic transmission and brake deficiencies. There's also a history of premature clutch failures and shuddering, particularly after a cold start-up. Owners report paint peeling; poor engine idling; rear wheel bearing failures; doors that don't latch properly; a sunroof that won't close properly; frequent cold-weather stalling; catalytic converter failures; minor electrical short circuits; manual transmission malfunctions; excessive vibration caused by the alloy wheels; a windshield that cracks and scratches too easily; premature exhaust system rust-out and early brake caliper and rotor scoring and wear; and body panel and trim fit and finish deficiencies characterized by water leaks and condensation problems from the top of the windshield or sunroof.

In addition to the paint peeling from delamination, owners report that Subaru paint chips much too easily:

> My Subaru Forester 2006 has paint chips all over. Dealer says they are rock chips. I took it to [an] auto body paint shop and one of the techs said it's very odd for there to be rock chips all over the car since we live in the city.

All models/years: Common complaints include sudden, unintended acceleration, stalling, transmission failures, steering loss, and airbag and brake malfunctions. • A mountain of complaints relative to loss of braking and premature wearout of key brake components. • Floor runner railings allow the front seats to unexpectedly move fore and aft. • Windshield is easily cracked, especially in freezing weather. **All models: 2001**—ABS overreacts when braking over an irregular surface. • Rear wheel bearings fail repeatedly. **2002**—Many reports of blown transmissions. **2003**—Very poor braking when passing over rough surfaces:

> On my 2003 Subaru Impreza Outback Sport, the anti-lock brakes are dangerous. If you hit a bump while braking, it will trigger the ABS—and result in an almost complete loss of braking ability. I notice a bulletin is listed for the WRX only, but this is a major problem in my car as well.

• Seat belt ratchets tighter; refuses to unlock. **2004**—Vehicle won't go into gear. • Raw fuel smell in the cabin. • Car wanders all over the road because of defective suspension struts. **2005**—Chronic rear strut failure. • Fuel odour inside the cabin. • Side window shatters spontaneously. *Impreza, Forester:* **2000**—One driver burned from airbag deployment. • Sudden loss of transmission fluid. • Driver's seatback may suddenly recline because seat belt gets tangled up in the recliner lever. • Frequent wheel bearing failures. • Fuel-filler cap design is too complicated for some gas station attendants to put on properly, which causes the Check Engine light to come on; driver has to pay dealer to reset it. **2001**—Rear wheel bearings break. • Brake and accelerator pedals are too close together. • In one collision, airbags failed to deploy and seat belt didn't restrain occupant. • In a similar incident, shoulder belt allowed driver's head to hit the windshield. • Headlights don't illuminate the edge of the road and are either too bright on High or too dim on Low. • Alarm system self-activated, trapping a baby inside one vehicle until fire rescue arrived. **2002**—Dangerous delay, then surging, when accelerating forward or in Reverse. • Surging at highway speeds, and stalling at lower rpm. • Transmission failure; gears lock in Park intermittently. • Open wheel design allows snow and debris to pack in the area and throw wheel out of balance, creating dangerous vibration. • High hood allows water onto the engine. *Forester:* **2003**—Five doors but only one keyhole makes for difficult access when the keyless entry fails. **2004**—Automatic fuel pumps overfill the fuel tank. • Premature wheel bearing replacements. • Hood latch released while one Forester was underway. **2005**—Car is too flimsy to protect occupants in a rollover (recent models have been given top ratings):

> The symmetrical all wheel drive system of my 2005 Subaru Forrester XT failed, the vehicle fishtailed and drifted, resulting in a rollover, and severe bodily injury. The vehicle was so flimsy, it was disgusting. Every door and window opening collapsed, glass flew everywhere. The ceiling collapsed on the passengers' heads.

• Car hesitates and bucks in cold weather. • Cruise control fails to disengage. • ABS sticks. • Windshield wipers often won't work. **2006**—One driver's seatback collapsed when vehicle was rear-ended. • Engine surges and sags, especially after a cold start. • Oil leaks onto the exhaust system. • Rear tailgate hydraulic struts fail, and the tailgate falls. • Gas station pumps don't shut off automatically when the car is fuelled. • Low-beam headlights fail to provide adequate illumination. **2006–07**—Passenger-side airbag disabled when an average-sized passenger is seated. • Several reports that original-equipment Yokohama tires' side walls blow out, plus they're poor winter performers and wear out quickly. **2007**—Cruise control fails to disengage. • Engine surges when vehicle goes downhill. • Vehicle surges forward as driver shifts the manual transmission from First to Second gear. • Transmission locks up. **2008**—Floor mat slides about and bunches up near the accelerator pedal. • Prematurely worn wheel bearings and hub assembly. • Steering over-corrects when turning. • No keyhole on the liftgate; in the event of an electrical failure, there is no way to open the trunk. *WRX:* **2002–03**—Chronic ABS failures. • Fuel smell in the cabin caused by fuel pooling in the engine manifold recess. **2003**—Increased braking distance when brakes are applied on an uneven surface. **2004**—Turbocharger failure. • Loss of power on the highway. • Failure-prone, clunking struts will not rebound, causing the rear end to sag and degrading handling. **2004–05**—Difficulty shifting into Fifth gear:

> I discovered that this is a common problem in 2004 and 2005 STIs. Apparently, Subaru of America put an inferior synchro in 5th gear. 1st, 2nd, 3rd, 4th, and 6th all have upgraded synchros. Starting in 2006, Subaru began putting the upgraded synchros in all 6 gears.

2005—Tricky handling. **2006**—Cracked oil pickup tube:

> Broken oil pickup tube, driving home from work the pickup tube broke causing the oil in the oilpan to not circulate through the system. This destroyed all internal bearings and likely fatigued many other engine internals. The dealership replaced all bearings under warranty but did not replace any other engine block.

• Premature manual transmission clutch failure. • Fuel-system lines and hoses continue to leak fuel:

> Fuel system lines and hoses become unstable, leaking fuel and fuel odors are present in cabin of vehicle. The nature of this complaint follows NHTSA recall campaign number: PE04002. That report found that the condition manifested in "very cold" temperatures. However, it has started in 45–50 degree F. The undersigned request that the investigation be reopened. Further, the problem does not resolve itself upon engine warm up. Smell of fuel lingers in and around the vehicle even while parked in garage. Noticeable loss in range of car upon full tank of gas.

2008–09—Frequent early engine failures involving "blown" rods and pistons:

My STi had cracked ringlands on the # 2 and 4 pistons. Before I purchased this car Subaru issued a stop sale on all 2008 WRX's. [T]he car was repaired at a local dealership under a goodwill repair. In Mar 2010. Recently the engine has developed a knock. The dealership says that the rod bearing on CYL #4 had failed. This is the same issue that prompted Subaru to place a stop sale on the vehicles.

•

The Subaru STi series known at the GR is prone to breaking piston ringlands if detonation ever occurs, which happens easily on this engine, which is now tuned for more power yet fewer emissions. The ringland breakage results in power loss and extreme oil consumption due to blowby and if not noticed in time will lead to engine seizing. If driven aggressively enough, this seizing due to oil loss can happen in as few as 10 minutes. It is also possible for the ringland breakage to be so severe that that engine spray-coats a large section of roadway, making for the equivalent of a black ice condition for other traffic. A potential safety hazard I'm not aware of happening with this vehicle yet but still possible is not only the loss of control should the engine seize and the driver not be mechanically savvy enough to know disengaging the clutch will give him [or her] back some control and reduce the chances of being rear-ended when the car tries to stop very rapidly without the brakes and therefore the brakelights being used. Despite the large numbers of these failures being reported, Subaru denies a problem exists.

Secret Warranties/Internal Bulletins/Service Tips

All models/years: Automatic transmission pops out of gear. • At least three bulletins deal with manual transmission malfunctions. • Diagnostic and repair tips for transfer clutch binding and/or bucking on turns. • Troubleshooting a sticking anti-lock brake relay; this problem is characterized by a lit ABS light or the ABS motor continuing to run and buzz when the ignition is turned off. • Premature brake pad, caliper, and rotor wear. • A rotten-egg smell could be caused by a defective catalytic converter. It will be replaced, after a bit of arguing, free of charge for up to five years, as per the emissions warranty. **All models: 2003**—Defective 4EAT transmission parking pawl rod. **2008–09**—Difficult fuel fill-up in cold weather. • Premature rusting around the liftgate area. • Front stabilizer bar rubbing noise. • Click noise heard coming from the bottom of the A-pillar. • Water leak onto the front floor. *WRX:* **2004–05**—Tips on silencing a noisy rear differential. **2007**—Remedy for hard acceleration surge. **2008**—High idle with clutch disengaged. • Rear quarter panel paint chipping.

FORESTER, IMPREZA, WRX PROFILE

	2001	2002	2003	2004	2005	2006	2007	2008	2009
Cost Price ($)									
Forester	28,395	28,395	28,395	27,995	27,995	27,995	26,995	26,995	25,795
Impreza	22,196	21,995	22,995	22,995	22,995	23,495	22,695	20,695	20,995
WRX	—	34,995	34,995	35,495	35,495	35,495	35,495	32,995	30,995

Used Values ($)

Forester ▲	4,500	5,500	7,000	8,500	10,000	11,000	14,500	17,000	20,000
Forester ▼	4,000	5,000	6,000	7,500	9,000	10,000	13,000	15,500	18,500
Impreza ▲	3,000	3,500	5,500	6,500	7,500	9,500	11,500	13,500	15,000
Impreza ▼	2,500	3,000	4,500	6,000	6,500	8,500	10,000	12,000	13,500
WRX ▲	—	7,500	8,500	9,500	12,500	15,000	16,500	19,500	22,500
WRX ▼	—	6,500	8,000	8,500	11,000	13,500	15,000	18,000	21,000

Reliability	3	4	4	4	4	4	4	4	4
WRX, STi	2	2	2	2	2	1	1	1	1
Crash Safety (F)									
Forester	4	4	5	5	5	5	5	5	5
Impreza	—	4	4	—	—	4	4	5	5
Side (Forester)	5	5	5	5	5	5	5	5	5
Impreza	—	4	4	—	—	4	4	5	5
IIHS Side	—	—	5	5	5	5	5	5	5
Offset	—	5	5	5	5	5	5	5	5
Forester	5	5	5	5	5	5	5	5	5
Head Restraints	2	3	3	—	5	5	5	5	5
Forester	3	—	—			5	5	5	5
WRX	—	—	—	2	2	2	2	3	3
Roof Strength	—	—	—	—	—	—	—	5	5
Rollover Resistance									
Forester	3	3	3	4	4	4	4	4	4
Impreza	—	4	4	—	—	4	4	4	4

LEGACY, OUTBACK ★★★★

RATING: Above Average (1999–2009). An overpriced, competent full-time AWD performer for drivers who want to move up in size, comfort, and features. Available as a four-door sedan or five-door wagon, the Legacy is cleanly and conventionally styled, with a hint of the Acura Legend in its rear end. The AWD is what this car is all about. It handles difficult terrain without the fuel penalty or clumsiness of many truck-based SUVs, although it is a bit ponderous traversing normal highways. The Outback is a marketing coup that stretches the definition of "sport-utility" by simply customizing the all-wheel-drive Legacy to give it more of an outdoorsy flair. Interestingly, what was a $10,000 gap between the high-end and entry-level model narrows to a couple thousand dollars after a few years. **Ideal model year:** A 2008 Legacy offers the best combination of reliability, standard features, and an attractive price. **"Real" city/highway fuel economy:** *Manual:* 11.0/7.8 L/100 km. *Automatic:* 10.9/7.9 L/100 km. *3.0L 6-cylinder:* 12.4/8.4 L/100 km. Owners say their fuel consumption is about 15 percent more than these estimates. **Maintenance/repair costs:** Higher than average (imagine a $50 "reset" charge for each tire sensor recalibration and $35 for each tire stem). Repairs are dealer-dependent due to the unique AWD mechanism. **Parts:**

Powertrain parts aren't easily found and can be costly. **Extended warranty:** Get an extended warranty to cover powertrain deficiencies after the base warranty has expired. **Best alternatives:** Honda CR-V and Hyundai Tucson or Santa Fe. **Helpful websites:** *www.subaruoutback.org.*

Strengths and Weaknesses

Costing a bit more than the smaller Impreza, these Subaru models are well-appointed, provide a comfortable ride and acceptable handling with the right options, and have lots of cargo room. On the downside, owners report problematic automatic transmission performance when it's hooked to the base engine; sluggish performance from the 2.5L, undoubtedly because of the car's heft; sloppy handling on base models; excessive 4-cylinder engine noise; cramped back seats, with a tight fit for the middle rear-seat passenger; limited rear headroom for tall passengers; trunk hinges that can damage cargo and cut into storage space; seat belts that may be too short for large occupants; and very dealer-dependent servicing.

First launched in 1989 as front-drives, these compacts are a bit slow off the mark. The 5-speed is a bit "notchy," and the automatic gearbox is slow to downshift, has difficulty staying in Overdrive, and is failure-prone. Early Legacy models are noisy, fuel-thirsty cars with bland styling that masks their solid, dependable AWD performance. Actually, the availability of a proven 4×4 powertrain in a compact family sedan or wagon makes these cars appealing for special use.

VEHICLE HISTORY: 2001—Two new Outback wagons, featuring a more-powerful 3.0L engine, join the lineup. **2002**—The H6-3.0 VDC Outback sedan, equipped with a standard 3.0L engine, joins the lineup. **2003**—New front-end styling; GT gets an upgraded engine and a semi-manual Sport Shift; Outback suspension is upgraded to improve cornering and reduce front-end plow. **2005**—Subaru's mid-sized cars are restyled and have larger dimensions, additional features, and more power. In fact, 2.5i models use a 168 hp 4-cylinder with a manual transmission or optional 4-speed automatic. However, a new 250 hp turbocharged version of that engine powers the Legacy 2.5 GT/GT Limited and Outback 2.5 XT models, and it's mated with a manual or an optional 5-speed automatic. The Outback 3.0 R sedan, L.L. Bean Edition wagon, and VDC Limited wagon come with only the 5-speed automatic and a 250 hp 3.0L 6-cylinder engine (up from 212 hp). The automatic transmissions include a manual-shift feature. On the safety front, all these Subarus have anti-lock brakes, front side airbags, and side curtain airbags. An anti-skid system is standard on the Outback 3.0 R VDC wagon but is otherwise unavailable. **2006**—A new sporty version of the GT, called the spec.B. **2007**—A 60/40 split-folding rear seatback. A slight restyling, revised dash, and the addition of the 3.0 R Limited, equipped with a 245 hp 6-cylinder engine. The automatic is standard on the 3.0. Automatic transmission–equipped 2008 Legacies also include steering wheel shift paddles. A wagon body style is no longer offered. **2008**—A slightly restyled interior and exterior, plus a new 3.0 R model carrying a 245 hp 6-cylinder engine. Steering wheel-mounted automatic transmission shift paddles are new.

The 6-cylinder engine is adequate but doesn't feel as if it has much in reserve. The automatic transmission shifts into too high a gear to adequately exploit the engine's power, and it's reluctant to downshift into the proper gear. On pre-2005 models, the 2.5L engine is a better performer with the manual gearbox, although its shift linkage isn't suitable for rapid gear changes. The 4-cylinder has several drawbacks as well: It's noisy and rough-running, and it's tuned more for low-end torque than speedy acceleration.

Base models don't handle well. They bounce around on uneven pavement, the rear end tends to swing out during high-speed cornering, and there's too much body lean in turns at lesser speeds. Higher-end models handle well, though there's some excessive lean when cornering. The GT's firmer suspension exhibits above-average handling.

The Legacy and Outback have had more than their share of reliability problems over the years. Powertrain defects can sideline the car for days. Engine and transmission problems keep showing up. Servicing can be awkward because of the crowded engine compartment, particularly on turbocharged versions.

Automatic transmission front seals and clutch breakdowns are most common through 2008; the transmission sometimes downshifts abruptly while descending a long grade or travelling on snow-packed highways, or suddenly shifts into Neutral when the car is underway; and the front brakes require frequent attention. Check Engine, Tire Pressure, and ABS warning lights come on constantly, for no reason. Shock absorbers, constant velocity joints, and catalytic converters also often wear out prematurely. Other problems that appear over most model years include chronic electrical and fuel-system malfunctions; hard starting, surging, and stalling in cold weather; starter and ignition relay failures; and snow packing inside the wheelwells, binding steering. Misadjusted door strikers make for hard closing/opening. Tire valve stems are expensive to replace (dealer charges $50 a pop), and there is no reset system for the Tire Pressure warning light so most owners simply let it stay lit. Owners also report that headlight illumination is inadequate, particularly with the 2008 Outback:

> When going downhill you can't see more than 20 feet [6 metres] ahead of the car. We immediately stopped for fear of hitting something in the road and not being able to see if the road stayed straight or turned ....This car has the new projector lights and even on level road you can see a very definitive line of demarcation when driving at night.

Safety Summary

All models/years: Many reports of sudden acceleration in Drive and in Reverse, constant stalling followed by engine surging, severe pulling to one side, ABS brake failures, and the premature wearout of brake components. • Small horn buttons may be hard to find in an emergency. **All models: 1999**—When accelerating or decelerating, vehicle will begin to jerk because of excessive play in the front axle. • Front bumper skirt catches on parking blocks, resulting in the bumper twisting and ripping off. **1999–2001**—A cracked #2 piston may cause major engine failure. • The centre rear seat belt's poor design prohibits the installation of many types of child safety seats. **2000–01**—Cruise control fails to disengage when brake pedal is depressed. • During a collision, airbags deploy but fail to inflate. • Steering locks up while vehicle is underway. • Vehicle's rear end bounces about when passing over bumps. • Cracked seat belt buckle. • **2002**—While idling in Park, vehicle suddenly jumps into Drive. **2004**—Automatic transmission failure. • Seat belt comes undone during a collision. **2005**—Cruise-control failure. **2006**—Oil pickup tube shears off, causing major engine damage. • Fuel-pump fuse burns out repeatedly. • Early wearout of the rear brakes (front and rear rotors warped). • Windshield wipers come on and go off on their own, as if possessed. **2006–07**—Airbags fail to deploy. **2007**   Oil return line cracks and ignites a fire in the engine compartment:

> Two weeks later same problem same oil line and its cracked again. This is obviously a manufacturing defect among these parts and a design flaw as well.

•

> The contact owns a 2007 Subaru Legacy. While driving 15 mph [24 km/h], oil leaked on the exhaust and caused a small engine fire. The dealer replaced the oil line.

2008—Shift shock when going from Second to Third or Third to Second. • High idle with clutch disengaged. • Gear slippage. • Premature wheel bearing failures. • When cruising downhill, headlights don't illuminate enough of the roadway to provide adequate lighting. • Vehicle rolled backward while in Park with the engine running. • Uncomfortable head restraints. • AC cycles erratically; the problem is so bad, the cabin won't cool:

> The manufacturer, Subaru of America has determined this is a "normal characteristic of the vehicle" although it took them over a month to come to this conclusion. Many other Subaru Legacy owners report this same problem online, however no fix seems to be coming.

2009—Airbag failed to deploy and seat belt failed to sufficiently restrain the driver.

Secret Warranties/Internal Bulletins/Service Tips

All models/years: Troubleshooting tips on a sticking anti-lock brake relay; this problem is characterized by a lit ABS light or the ABS motor continuing to run/buzz when the ignition is turned off. • Diagnostic and repair tips for transfer clutch binding and/or bucking on turns. **All models: 2002**—Excessive blower motor noise. • Countermeasures to reduce brake squeal. **2003**—Defective engine water pump. • Improved Sport Shift cold-weather operation. • Defective transmission parking pawl rod. • Premature suspension corrosion:

Certain rear suspension subframe components were produced with poor paint quality, which, after continued exposure to corrosive road salts for a period of several years, could result in rust-out of the component and possible breakage of the subframe. If such breakage occurs while the vehicle is being operated, control of the vehicle could be affected, increasing the risk of a crash. Remedy: Dealers will clean and rustproof the rear suspension subframe under a special service campaign.

2004—Possible causes of transfer clutch binding when cornering. **2005**—Seat belt warning chimes when seat is unoccupied. • Water leak from AC evaporator drain hose. **2005–06**—Radiator cooling fan relay #2 replacement. • Troubleshooting instrument panel squeaks. **2005–07**—How to fix front-door rattles and a right front wheel bearing squeak, squeal. **2005–08**—Sunroof sunshade rattles. **2005–09**—Water leaks onto the passenger-side floor. **2006**—Fixing rattles from the liftgate area. **2007**—Rear differential vent oil leak. • Transmission Temperature light flashing. • Rubbing noise when turning steering wheel. **2007–08**—Transmission shift-lever boot cracking. • Rear differential oil seepage. **2007–09**—Hesitation when accelerating. **2008**— Condensation buildup in the headlights is the likely cause of flickering headlights.

LEGACY, OUTBACK PROFILE

	2001	2002	2003	2004	2005	2006	2007	2008	2009
Cost Price ($)									
Legacy	24,295	27,395	27,295	27,295	27,995	28,495	26,996	26,996	26,995
Outback	35,195	31,995	37,995	26,995	32,995	32,995	30,995	30,995	30,995
Used Values ($)									
Legacy ▲	4,000	5,500	7,000	8,500	9,500	10,500	13,000	17,000	17,500
Legacy ▼	3,500	5,000	6,000	7,500	9,000	9,500	11,500	15,500	16,000
Outback ▲	6,500	7,500	8,500	10,500	11,500	13,000	14,000	17,500	20,500
Outback ▼	5,500	7,000	8,000	9,000	10,500	11,500	13,000	16,000	19,000
Reliability	3	3	3	3	3	4	4	5	5
Crash Safety (F)									
Legacy 4d	4	4	4	4	5	5	5	5	5
Side	4	4	3	4	—	—	5	5	5
Wagon	—	—	4	4	—	—	5	—	—
IIHS Side	—	—	—	—	2	5	5	5	5
Offset	5	5	5	5	5	5	5	5	5
Head Restraints	3	3	3	4	3	5	5	5	5
Rollover Resistance	—	4	4	4	—	—	4	4	4

Note: Roof strength test results carried out by IIHS on 2010 and 2011 Legacys were qualified as Good (5 stars).

Suzuki

AERIO, ESTEEM, SWIFT, SWIFT+, SX4, VERONA ★★★★/★★★/★★★★★

The Suzuki SX4.

RATING: *Aerio:* Above Average (2003–07). *Esteem:* Average (1999–2002). *Swift, Swift+:* Above Average (1999–2009). *Verona:* Average (2004–06). *SX4:* Recommended (2007–09). Suzuki's earlier lineup has been downgraded one level because its poor sales and constant reorganization make sales and servicing more problematic for older cars. Getting the most horsepower bang for your buck means shopping for a sport model or looking at the upgraded model from 2000 or later. Wagons are especially versatile and reasonably priced for the equipment provided. Both the base GL and upscale GLX come loaded with standard features that cost extra on other models. **Ideal model year:** Getting the most horsepower bang for your buck means shopping for a sport model or looking at the upgraded 2000+ model years. Wagons are especially versatile and reasonably priced for the equipment provided. Both the SX4 JX and upscale JLX depreciate quickly and come loaded with standard features that cost extra on other models. A loaded 2008 JLX AWD, for example, costs $11,500 to $12,500, or just about half its original price. **"Real" city/highway fuel economy:** *Aerio manual:* 9.4/7.0 L/100 km. *Aerio automatic:* 9.3/7.0 L/100 km. *Aerio AWD automatic:* 9.9/7.6 L/100 km. *Swift manual:* 8.9/5.9 L/100 km. *Esteem manual:* 8.3/6.0 L/100 km. *Esteem automatic:* 9.0/6.3 L/100 km. *Swift automatic:* 9.1/6.3 L/100 km. *SX4 AWD manual:* 10.1/7.6 L/100 km. *SX4 AWD automatic:* 9.9/7.1 L/100 km. *Verona automatic:*

12.0/7.9 L/100 km. **Maintenance/repair costs:** Cheap to keep up and repair. **Parts:** Average costs, and most parts are easily found. **Extended warranty:** A toss-up. Some long-term powertrain protection would be helpful; buy your brakes from independents who give long warranties. **Best alternatives:** Honda Civic; Hyundai Accent or Elantra/Tiburon; Mazda3 or Protegé; Nissan Sentra; and Toyota Corolla or Echo. **Helpful websites:** *www.suzuki-forums.com* and *www. sx4club.com.*

Strengths and Weaknesses

The Esteem is a small four-door sedan that is a step up from the Swift. Smaller than the Honda Civic and Chrysler Neon, it has a fairly spacious interior, offering rear accommodation (for two adults) that is comparable to or better than most cars in its class. It stands out with its European-styled body and large array of such standard features as AC, a fold-down back seat, and remote trunk and fuel-door releases. The roomy cabin has lots of front and rear headroom and legroom. Cargo space is fairly good with the sedan and exceptional with the wagon's rear seats folded.

The small engine delivers respectable acceleration, and overall performance is acceptable, thanks to the Esteem's four-wheel independent suspension, which gives just the right balance between a comfortable ride and no-surprise handling.

Suzuki's entry-level Aerio front-drive sedan and wagon replaced the Esteem for the 2003 model year. Equipped with optional all-wheel drive, it is one of the lowest-priced AWD vehicles available in Canada. Both models come with a 145 hp 4-cylinder engine that's among the most powerful standard engines in this class. Every Aerio comes with AC, power windows and mirrors, a tilt steering wheel, a CD player, and split-folding rear seats.

Suzuki's Swift was built at CAMI Automotive in Ingersoll, Ontario, and was first launched in 1995 for the American and Canadian markets. It was dropped in the States in 2001 but continues to be sold in Canada as the Swift and the Swift+. The Swift+, essentially a GM/Daewoo Aveo knock-off, was first launched as a 2004 model. It has posted good reliability scores, though crashworthiness info is quite sparse.

SX4

Launched as a 2007 model, the SX4 arrived with a 143 hp 4-cylinder engine and a 5-speed manual transmission, or optional 4-speed automatic. The SX4 is good for urban chores, although the engine could use more freeway power. The AWD system lacks low-range gearing, but it can be set for front-wheel drive only, for AWD, or for a locked-in front/rear power split. For extra safety, there's standard ABS with all-disc braking, Sport models have added traction/antiskid control, and all models have front and curtain side airbags.

Overall, the SX4 is well-equipped, fairly reliable, and relatively fuel-efficient. It handles well, gives a comfortable ride, provides generous cargo room, and has an adequate powerplant if not pushed. Things not to like: Rear seating is a bit tight, and engine and road noise intrude into the cabin area. Good alternative models are the Honda Fit or Hyundai Accent.

VEHICLE HISTORY: 2003—Aerio makes its debut. **2004**—The 145 hp 2.0L is replaced by a 155 hp 2.3L engine. Swift+ debuts. **2005**—Standard front side airbags and a host of new exterior styling touches. **2006**—ABS becomes a standard item. **2007**—Suzuki's smallest car, the Aerio, drops its hatchback, leaving a four-door sedan in base and premium trims. All Aerios still have a 155 hp 4-cylinder engine. Automatic-transmission models are available with all-wheel drive. ABS and front side airbags are standard, but side curtain airbags are not available. **2008**—Suzuki SX4 adds a sedan model to the existing four-door hatchback. The new sedan, called SX4 Sport, replaces Suzuki's Aerio sedan and comes with front-wheel drive only. **2009**—The SX4 hatchback adopts front-drive.

Here are some of the drawbacks to owning one of these econoboxes: small tires compromise handling; power steering doesn't transmit much road feedback; the automatic transmission may shift harshly and vibrate excessively between gear changes; and braking is mediocre for a car this light.

During the relatively short time the Esteem was around, it proved to be a high-quality, reliable small car. In this respect, it competes well with its Detroit-built rivals such as the Chevrolet Cavalier, Dodge Neon, and Ford Escort, while being outclassed by the Honda Civic, Mazda3 and Protegé, and Toyota Corolla, Echo, and Yaris. Problems reported by Esteem and Aerio owners include paint delamination/peeling; fragile body panels and trim items; occasional electrical short circuits; premature clutch, tire, brake, and transmission wear; noisy front brakes and early wearout of brake pads and rotors; and wind and water intrusion into the engine and passenger compartment through the Aerio's air-intake breather.

Safety Summary

Aerio: **2001**—Automatic transmission sticks in lower gear. • Brake failure. **2002**—Brake caliper may leak fluid; early rotor wear. • Faulty wheel bearings. • Ball joints may fall out. • Lower control arm snaps. • Loose heat shield bolts. **2003**—Many complaints of broken, cracked, or bent aluminum wheel rims and wheel bearing failures. • Delayed shifts. • Vehicle refuses to go into Reverse gear. • CV axle joint separation. • Misaligned power-steering bracket. • Trunk pops up while driving. **2004**—Sudden, unintended acceleration. **2005**—Prematurely worn brakes tops the list of owner complaints. • Passenger-side airbag deploys for no reason. • Front brake failure; faulty brake pads. • Excessive body shake caused by defective stabilizer bushing, bracket, and mount. • Engine was damaged after one Aerio was driven through a puddle of water. **2006**—Driver-side airbag deploys for no reason. • Brake pads often need changing. • Emergency Brake light comes on for no reason. • Premature engine failures. • Serpentine belt failures (early symptom is excessive squealing). • Air intake sucks up water on flooded streets and causes serious engine damage, stalling:

> While driving 25 mph [40 km/h] on a rainy day, the vehicle shut off when it drove over a puddle. The vehicle was towed to the dealer and they stated that the failure was caused by water intrusion. They further stated that the rod failed and went through the aluminum motor. Both times the rod went through the motor, the water intrusion was caused by the air [breather] positioned under the motor.

2007—Premature wearout of the brake caliper may lead to brake failure. • Hard starting. • Brakes and tires continue to wear out prematurely. *SX4:* **2007**— Inadvertant airbag deployment. • Airbag light comes on for no reason (dealers charge over $80 to scan the system for what is a common Suzuki owner complaint). • When going uphill, the car downshifts a couple of times, then when passing over the crest, it resumes cruise control at an ever-increasing speed. • Sudden loss of brakes as engine surged. • Faulty tire pressure sensors. • Condensation drips/pours out of the AC unit. • **2007–09**—Faulty airbag sensor for the passenger front seat:

> Took to dealer, computer reset done. Lasted only 4 days, AIR BAG SYS FAULT lights on again. Taken back to dealer, service dept said the front passenger seat air bag sensor was faulty. Mileage 54,442 [87,600 km] not covered under warranty. Over $2,400 U.S. to fix issue (a quick review of the Internet reveals this to be a common problem. *www.sx4club.com/forums.* Search SX4 airbag light).

2008—When traction control kicks in, the car may fishtail. • Jack storage mount is easily broken in a collision, allowing the jack to fly about with potential deadly effect. **2008–09**—Airbags fail to deploy. **2009**—Several underhood fires reported. • Steering column locked while vehicle was underway.

Secret Warranties/Internal Bulletins/Service Tips

All models: Pops out of gear when driving (Fifth gear in manual trannies). • Battery discharge can be avoided by installing an upgraded alternator, says TSB #TS-03-06304. **2002–03**—Popping noise when turning. **2002–04**—Loose door mirrors. • Left driveshaft pops out of final drive. • Instruments don't display. **2004–06**—Suzuki admits that its own faulty suspension may cause abnormal tire wear (TSB #TS 05-11225). **2005**—The stabilizer-bar mount bushing may cause a clunking sound coming from underneath the vehicle. **2007**—AC water leak on the passenger side. **2007–08**—Extended cranking to start. • Abnormal vibration can be felt with the shift lever when driving in Third gear. *SX4:* **2007**—Pops out of Fifth gear while driving. • Cold engine stall. • AC doesn't cool because the compressor clutch fails to engage. • Clicking noise from the front hub area. **2007–08**—Extended cranking time to start. • Manual transmission Third gear vibration. **2007–09**—Water drips on the passenger floor when using the AC. **2009**—Countermeasures to apply when the Airbag warning light comes on for no reason.

AERIO, ESTEEM, SWIFT, SWIFT+, SX4, VERONA PROFILE

	2001	2002	2003	2004	2005	2006	2007	2008	2009
Cost Price ($)									
Aerio sedan	—	—	15,785	15,995	17,995	18,595	18,995	—	—
Aerio SX (AWD)	—	—	—	20,495	23,995	22,995	—	—	—
Esteem GL	15,695	16,195	—	—	—	—	—	—	—
Esteem GLX	18,795	19,795	—	—	—	—	—	—	—
Swift	11,595	—	—	—	—	—	—	—	—
Swift+	—	—	—	13,495	13,595	13,745	13,895	13,995	14,495
SX4 Sedan/ Hatchback	—		—	—	—		15,995	17,195	17,395
SX4 JX	—	—	—	—	—	—	18,195	18,695	19,995
SX4 JLX AWD	—	—	—	—	—	—	21,495	22,695	23,195
Verona	—	—	—	22,995	22,995	22,995	—	—	—
Used Values ($)									
Aerio sedan ▲	—	—	3,500	5,000	6,500	7,500	9,500	—	—
Aerio sedan ▼	—	—	3,000	3,500	5,000	6,500	8,000	—	—
Aerio SX (AWD) ▲	—	—	—	6,500	7,500	8,500	—	—	—
Aerio SX (AWD) ▼	—	—	—	5,000	6,500	8,000	—	—	—
Esteem GL ▲	2,500	3,500	—	—	—	—	—	—	—
Esteem GL ▼	2,000	3,000	—	—	—	—	—	—	—
Esteem GLX ▲	3,500	4,000	—	—	—	—	—	—	—
Esteem GLX ▼	3,000	3,500	—	—	—	—	—	—	—
Swift ▲	2,500	—	—	—	—	—	—	—	—
Swift ▼	2,000	—	—	—	—	—	—	—	—
Swift+ ▲	—	—	—	3,500	4,500	5,000	6,000	7,500	9,000
Swift+ ▼	—	—	—	3,000	4,000	4,500	5,000	6,500	7,500
SX4 ▲	—	—	—	—	—	—	8,000	10,000	12,000
SX4 ▼	—	—	—	—	—	—	7,000	9,000	10,500
SX4 JX ▲	—	—	—	—	—	—	8,500	10,500	12,500
SX4 JX ▼	—	—	—	—	—	—	7,000	9,500	11,500
SX4 JLX AWD ▲	—	—	—	—	—	—	9,500	12,500	15,500
SX4 JLX AWD ▼	—	—	—	—	—	—	8,500	11,500	14,000
Verona ▲	—	—	—	4,000	4,500	6,000	—	—	—
Verona ▼	—	—	—	3,500	4,500	5,000	—	—	—
Reliability	4	4	4	4	4	4	4	5	5
Crash Safety (F)									
Aerio	—	—	—	4	4	—	—	—	—
SX4	—	—	—	—	—	—	—	4	4
Side (Aerio)	—	—	—	5	5	—	—	—	—
SX4	—	—	—	—	—	—	5	5	5
IIHS Side	—	—	—	—	**1**	**1**	**1**	—	—
SX4	—	—	—	—	—	—	5	5	5
Offset	—	5	5	5	5	5	5	5	5
Head Restraints	—	**2**	**2**	**2**	**2**	**2**	**2**	**2**	**2**
Rollover Resistance	—	—	—	—	—	—	—	4	4

All ratings on a numbered scale where ⑤ is good and **1** is bad. See page 132 for a more detailed description.

Toyota/General Motors

COROLLA, MATRIX/VIBE ★★/★★★

RATING· *Corolla:* Below Average (1997–2009). Corollas are no longer paragons of high quality and bulletproof reliability, so be wary of serious safety deficiencies (see "Strengths and Weaknesses"). Since the 1997 model was "de-contented" through the use of lower-quality materials, less soundproofing, and fewer standard features, there has been a noticeable reduction in quality control—though their horsepower-enhanced engines make them better performers than earlier versions. Be sure to ditch the poor-performing or failure-prone Bridgestone, Firestone Affinity, and Goodyear Integrity tires. *Matrix/Vibe:* Average (2009); Below Average (2003–08). Aimed at the youth market, these versatile spin-offs don't provide enough horsepower to justify their sporty pretensions, and they aren't suitable for any place more rugged than Ontario's Highway 401. **Ideal model year:** If you want standard traction control, search out a 2010 version. Another good buy is the 2009 Vibe. It sells for $9,500 to $10,500 (original price: $15,995) and comes with new styling, more power, and all-wheel drive. Try to get a model with some unexpired warranty coverage, even though fewer owner complaints have been posted against the Vibe than against either the Matrix or Corolla. **"Real" city/highway fuel economy:** *Corolla manual:* 7.1/5.3 L/100 km. *Corolla automatic:* 8.1/5.8 L/100 km. *Matrix manual:* 7.7/6.0 L/100. *Matrix automatic:* 8.3/6.4 L/100 km. *Matrix 6-speed manual:* 9.5/6.8 L/100 km. *Vibe manual:* 7.7/6.0 L/100 km. *Vibe automatic:* 8.3/6.4 L/100 km. *Matrix/Vibe AWD:* 9.1/6.9 L/100 km. Owners report that their fuel consumption is about 10 percent higher than these estimates. **Maintenance/repair costs:** *Corolla:* Lower than average, and repairs can be done anywhere. *Matrix/Vibe:* Powertrain and body part supply is a bit problematic now that GM has closed down so many dealers, plus owners complain that they cost more than similar parts used on other models. **Parts:** Electronic and powertrain parts can be expensive at the dealership, and there are few independent suppliers who carry these parts. **Extended warranty:** Not needed. But you will be limited to Toyota dealers now that GM has shut down Pontiac. **Best alternatives:** Matrix/Vibe third-year depreciation is brutal—a bargain for buyers, but disappointing come trade-in time. Consider the Hyundai Accent or Elantra; Mazda3, Mazda5, or Protegé; Nissan Sentra; and Suzuki Aerio or SX4. For extra cabin storage space and all-wheel drive, check out the Suzuki Aerio AWD and Subaru Forester. **Helpful websites:** *www.toyotanation.com* and *www.toyotaownersclub.com.*

Strengths and Weaknesses

A step up from the Tercel, Echo, and Yaris, the Corolla has long been Toyota's standard-bearer in the compact-sedan class—many late '80s Corollas are still on our roads after 20+ years. Over the years, however, the car has grown in size, price, and refinement to the point where it can now be considered a small family sedan. All Corollas ride on a front-drive platform with independent suspension on all wheels.

For over a decade, Corollas have been afflicted by serious quality problems that include chronic stalling; brake and tire failures; an easily cracked windshield and windshield reflections; faulty strut assemblies; sudden acceleration; engine hesitation and surging; the suspension bottoming out; warped brake rotors and early brake pad wearout; poor steering (vehicle wanders all over the road); seat belt failures; hard starting; dash gauge "washout"; airbag malfunctions; poorly designed headlights that misdirect the light beam; and the transmission popping out of Drive into Neutral or refusing to shift at all.

VEHICLE HISTORY: 2001—A slight facelift, and a new sport-oriented variant called the Corolla S is added. The VE is dropped, and the formerly mid-level CE replaces it, carrying fewer standard features. The LE is dropped to the CE's former level and is also "de-contented," losing its standard AC and power windows, locks, and mirrors. 2003—Corolla is redesigned to be taller, wider, and longer; it gets a new 4-speed automatic transmission and five more horses. Matrix/Vibe launches. 2005—A light restyling, and side curtain airbags are optional for all models. Toyota also launches its new high-performance Corolla XRS sedan. 2007— Matrix/Vibe loses all-wheel drive. All sporty models are dropped. 2009—Vibe is redesigned with new styling, more power, and the return of all-wheel drive; then it gets axed.

Matrix/Vibe

Redesigned for 2009 with a new look and more performance, these practically identical small front-drive or all-wheel-drive sporty wagons are crosses between mini-SUVs and station wagons, but they're packaged like small minivans. Unlike the Matrix, which has soldiered on, GM dropped Vibe from its lineup when it shut down the Pontiac division. Toyota's Cambridge, Ontario, plant still manufactures the Matrix, alongside the Corolla, whose platform it shares. The Matrix is expected to soldier on for another year.

The front-drive Matrix/Vibe is equipped with a 1.8L 132 hp engine, a 5-speed manual overdrive transmission, and lots of standard features; however, the weak, buzzy base engine can be felt throughout the car. The AWD models are about 10 percent heavier and are woefully power-challenged. Says *Forbes* magazine:

> [B]oth all-wheel-drive cars are saddled with a really wretched 4-speed automatic that almost has to be shifted manually to get the car moving. To put it bluntly, the AWD Vibe and Matrix are so pokey, they feel like they're towing Winnebagos. To boot, the 1.8L engine doesn't hit its paltry torque peak...until a screaming 4200 rpm, at which point the vibration—did somebody say Vibe?—in the cabin is worse than a little off-putting.

If you really need a bit more horsepower, get a model equipped with the 2.4L 158-hp 4-cylinder, but keep in mind that there are safer, better-quality high-performance choices out there, such as the Honda Civic Si, Mazda5, or a base Acura RSX. Other front-drives worth considering are the Ford Focus, Honda Civic, Hyundai Elantra or Tiburon, Mazda3, Nissan Sentra, and Suzuki SX4. The Subaru Impreza and Forester are two other good choices for the AWD variant.

Safety Summary

All models/years: Chronic airbag malfunctions; they deploy when they shouldn't, or don't deploy when they should:

> [Our] [t]hirteen-year-old daughter sustained [a] severe traumatic brain injury after [a] head-on collision. Her airbag deployed, [but the] top of passenger-side airbag was completely blown apart from one side to the other, allowing her head to strike [the] dash. We both had seat belts on. I sustained bruising of [my] hips and right rib. She was in [a] coma and [is] just now beginning to move [her] left side. She still cannot sit up, stand, walk, talk coherently, eat, or do anything for herself.

• Sudden, unintended acceleration:

> While at a stop sign, the sudden acceleration happened again, and I was unable to immediately stop my car from lurching forward. It moved several inches into oncoming (perpendicular) traffic before I finally threw it into Park and pulled the emergency brake to stop it.
>
> •
>
> I have a 2007 Toyota Matrix and have 3 incidents of uncontrolled acceleration of over 70 mph [113 km/h] and uncontrolled deceleration when going 35 to 60 mph [56 to 97 km/h] in heavy traffic. I have been lucky enough to have avoided any accidents but last week came very close to hitting a tree. My car is not part of the recall. I have had trouble with my floor mats but this is not the problem with the accelerator. I took the car to the dealership and they said that there is nothing wrong with the accelerator.

• Engine hesitation and surging. • Poor headlight illumination. • Engine compartment fires. • Gas fumes in the interior. • Brake and power-steering failures. • Excessive drifting and high-speed instability. • Premature control arm failure. • Seat belt releases in accident. • Rear wheel breaks at the axle. • Windshield cracks easily. • Premature tire side wall shredding. *Corolla:* **2001**— Stuck accelerator pedal. • In one incident, rear driver-side axle sheared in half; vehicle rolled over. • Excessive front brake pad wear; premature failure of the brake proportioning valve and rear brake shoes. • Hole in the oil pan. **2002**—Fuel leakage:

> On 04/29/02 consumer discovered that vehicle was leaking fuel. Vehicle was repaired by dealer who advised consumer that the fuel lines had come loose. On 07/29/02 while driving, engine compartment caught on fire as a result of fuel leaking.

• While using cruise control, gas pedal suddenly goes to the floor. • Weak climate-control system. **2002–03**—Unable to shift out of Park. **2003**—Fire ignites because of loose fuel line. • One vehicle suddenly shut down while underway at 100 km/h; in another case, vehicle suddenly accelerated while cruise control was engaged. • Several owners report that a hole in the oil pan causes vehicle to stall. • Faulty seat belt wiring could cause a fire. • Floormat catches accelerator pedal. • Pedal goes soft when brakes are applied, and brakes lock up when coming to a gradual stop, resulting in extended stopping distances. • Rear welding breaks away from the frame, resulting in complete loss of control. • Shifter refuses to go into gear while driving; transmission sometimes goes from Drive to Neutral while driving. • In windy conditions, vehicle becomes hard to steer, veering left or right. • Glow-in-the-dark inside trunk release doesn't glow in the dark because it is rarely exposed to light (owner actually crawled inside trunk to test it out!). • Sunlight washes out dash readings. **2004**—Hand brake doesn't hold very well. • Front passenger-side windshield frame obstructs visibility. • Sun visor interferes with the rear-view mirror. • One vehicle's sunroof came unglued from the metal frame; glass from the sunroof flew off. **2004–05**—Brake and gas pedals mounted too close together. **2005**—Passenger-seat sensor is too sensitive and rings an alarm when there is the slightest pressure on the seat. • Water pools in the ventilation system:

> [S]evere mildew growth has occurred in ventilation system. This mildew creates an awful sewage smell, and is extremely irritating to my allergies. Dealer sprayed Lysol disinfectant in ventilation intake. The problem came back a week later. To this day, I continually must spray Lysol in the ventilation system. Many types of mildew can be toxic to any human (not just allergy sufferers), and are known to cause cancer, which is very concerning to me.... I personally know other 2005 Corolla owners, and their Corollas suffer from the same problem.

• Car will not slow down when foot is taken off the accelerator pedal. • Low engine intake ingests water when going through puddles, causing severe engine damage. • Steering-wheel lock-up. • Excessive play in rear hub bearings. **2006**—AC condenser destroyed by small rocks:

> What really ticks me off is Toyota knows about the problem and released it in their technical service bulletin AC002-06. Which I'm just now finding out about on the Internet.

> •

> Toyota has issued a technical service bulletin indicating that the A/C condenser is not properly protected. The number for this problem is AC002-06. Additionally, the Toyota has redesigned the Corolla to correct this in 2007 by properly protecting the A/C condenser leaving the 2005–2006 customers in the dust. This problem appears to occur just outside of warranty. I discovered my condenser was not working (causing no air conditioning) 16 days after my warranty expired. I now live in the southwest and the type of heat experienced and lack of A/C could be considered a health hazard. Toyota refuses to replace the condenser and wants to charge customers the full $600 for replacement.

• Gas pedal sticks under the floormat. **2006–07**—A defective throttle sensor/ECM unit is blamed for lurching acceleration, surging, stalling, and no starts:

> Many people complain about the same problem on the Internet and describe such cases where either the car's engine dies in the middle of the road, or the car leaves people in the middle of nowhere and won't start at all (*www.toyotanation.com/forum/showthread.php?t=201631*). Toyota has issued a technical service bulletin about this problem: TSB EG042-07 (*www.tundrasolutions.com/forums/attachments/corolla-matrix/27763d1201041193-2006-obdii-code-po607-06-corolla-tsb.pdf*). Information on the Internet suggests that faulty solenoids on the ECM board are causing the computer to go crazy. Given the severity of the problem, I don't believe that Toyota should be leaving all Corolla and Matrix drivers [to] get stuck on the road before replacing the faulty parts.

•

> At approximately 70–75 miles per hour [113–121 km/h] in the fast lane, probably while on cruise control, car began to accelerate, [I] hit the brake which had no effect, and if it had been on cruise control, it did not override the acceleration. I began to get closer to the car in front of me. I do not believe I initially tried to put the car into neutral. I turned off the car engine, the acceleration stopped, I hit the brake somewhat to get it down to a regular speed, put the car into neutral, started it while coasting, put it back into gear (manual transmission), and the crisis was over.

2008—Chronic stalling. • Poor steering. • Driver-side axle suddenly snapped:

> The driver heard a loud bang as she slowly made a left turn. The vehicle was towed to the dealer. According to the work order, the end of the axle was broken off in the differential and the axle seal was leaking.

• Tire and rim fly off vehicle while underway. • The rear heat shield mount between the exhaust and the fuel tank may rust out. • Driver's express window rollup feature doesn't have a safety mechanism to retract; it could possibly amputate a finger or strangle a child. • Normal braking causes the wheels to lock up. • Car window suddenly shattered while one vehicle was parked in mild weather. • Odometer/speedometer is hard to read in daylight. **2009**—Normally, NHTSA posts an average of 50 safety-related complaints per year for each model. The 2009 Corolla has racked up over 729 complaints, where about 75 would have been the norm over a year and a half. Most of the complaints are for sudden acceleration, no brakes, steering failures, and many of the other failures already listed for previous model years. Some new and unusual failures have also appeared, however. • Vehicle seems to float all over the road, hydroplanes, or swerves right to left. • Steering lock-up while vehicle is underway. • Water on the driver's side floor. • Premature wearout of Firestone Affinity Touring tires. *Matrix:* **2003**—Excessive steering wander; some torque steer (twisting) evident, especially on wet roads. • The manual shift lever's upward and forward position is counterintuitive and feels a bit ragged. • Instrument panel lights are dimmed by automatic sensor to the point where they are unreadable in twilight hours. • Automatic headlights turn on and go off for no apparent reason. **2004**—Hand brake doesn't hold very well. • Clutch failures with the manual transmission. • Car drifts out of control and crashes; steering is non-responsive:

> Matrix drifted to the left while driving, resulting in the consumer losing control and the vehicle flipping over. As the consumer attempted once more to gain control of the steering, the vehicle veered off to the left, hit a ditch, went airborne, and flipped. Toyota determined that there were steering problems.

Dealers have blamed a defective steering yoke and poor-quality original-equipment tires for this instability and steering loss. • Warped front brake rotors. • Dashboard reflects onto the windshield. • Front bumper/spoiler drags on the ground over any uneven surface. • Ice collects in wheel rims, throwing tires out of balance. **2005**—Hard starting and chronic stalling. • Engine begins racing while vehicle is stopped. • Alloy wheel splits in half. **2006**—Frequent replacement of the engine control module, throttle body assembly, transmission, and clutch. **2006–07**—Original-equipment tires are notorious for premature wearout; faulty shocks, poor differential alignment, and a too-light rear end are blamed. **2007**—Gasoline fumes in the cabin caused by failure of the fuel-pressure regulator and fuel-injector seals. • Power-steering failure. • Goodyear Eagle original-equipment tires crack at the side wall. **2008**—Vehicle stalls out due to a defective computer module. • The left rear passenger window in one vehicle suddenly exploded. • On another occasion, entire rear quarter window spontaneously shattered. • Premature rear tire wear blamed on inaccurate rear alignment. **2009**—Stalling while underway. • Automatic transmission struggles going into First and Reverse. • Fuel gauge registers empty when the tank is actually full. *Vibe:* **2003**—Vehicle will roll while in Park. • Faulty ABS. • Dash gauges unreadable when driver wears sunglasses. • Automatic headlight sensor turns the headlights on and off about 20 times per day, depending on sun and shade variations. • When the lights go on, dash lights become unreadable. • Transmission indicator unlit at night. • After start-up, 15–20 seconds elapse before the automatic headlights and tail lights turn on. • Sunroof suddenly explodes. • Excessive condensation on interior glass. • Refuelling impossible without a large amount of fuel spitting out. • Rear outboard seat belts constantly tighten. **2004**—Too much steering play, making the Vibe, like its Toyota counterpart, highly unstable on the highway. • Rear-passenger seat belt may be hazardous to children:

> The rear-passenger seat belt twisted around the child's abdomen and would not release. Every time the child moved, it clicked tighter. The child had to be cut out of the seat belt.

• Automatic door locks may not secure the door shut. • Instrument-cluster chrome finish reflects into windshield. • Power side window cracks as it is being raised. • Speedometer needle can't be seen on sunny days. • Wheel lug nuts may fail. • Many electrical shorts. • Loose firewall shield screws. **2005**—Poor rear visibility. • Hard starts. • Severe pulling to one side when accelerating or braking. • Mice can crawl into the dash, air vents. **2006**—Sudden loss of power due to a malfunctioning powertrain control module. • Driver-side window doesn't roll down completely; when it is lowered, it interferes with the door's operation. • Annoying dash reflection onto the windshield. **2007**—Stalling, hard starting caused by a defective throttle body/ECM. • Accelerator pedal too sensitive, leading to jerky acceleration. • Vehicle pulls to the left when underway, due to a misaligned rear end. • Windshield distortion. **2008–09**—About 100 complaints posted by NHTSA and most of these were carryovers from the sudden acceleration, brake failures, premature tire wear, and steering issues mentioned above. • Uneven wear of rear brake pads:

> Passenger side outer pad is positioned in an angle which causes premature wear of that pad while all other pads are wearing evenly. Such defect (caliper position) causes rotor damage and possible wheel lock. This is a second Vibe with the same problem that I've seen. The passenger side rear caliper needs to be adjusted and repositioned.

Secret Warranties/Internal Bulletins/Service Tips

All models/years: Steering-column noise may require the replacement of the steering-column assembly. • Toyota has developed special procedures for eliminating AC odours and excessive wind noise. These problems are covered in TSBs #AC00297 and #BO00397, respectively. *Corolla:* **2002–04**—Troubleshooting tips for fixing a poorly performing AC. **2002–07**—Repair tips for correcting a severe pull to one side when underway (TSB #ST005-01). **2003–05**—Ways to silence front- and rear-door wind noise and a rear hub axle bearing humming. **2003–07**—Remedy for engine compartment squeaks and rattles. • Rear hatch is slow to open. **2003–08**—Tips on silencing windshield, automatic transmission whistle or hoot, wind noise, and front brake rattling. **2003–11**—Remedy for a windshield ticking noise. **2004–06**—Front-seat movement correction. **2004–10**—Fixing front-seat squeaking. **2005–06**—Engine vibration/drone when accelerating. • Toyota's correction for hard starts (TSB #EGO53-06). • Grill mesh available to protect the AC condenser from road debris. **2005–07**—Troubleshooting tips to fix a harsh-shifting automatic transmission and hard starts. **2009–10**—Poor steering feel. • Steering clunk, pop noise. A-pillar rattles. • Premature front brake pad wear (see TSB on following page). *Matrix, Vibe:* **2003**—Loose or deformed front or rear glass door run. • AC doesn't sufficiently cool the vehicle. • Headlights come on when turned off. **2003–06**—Correction for rear-end whining, humming, or growling. **2005–06**—Troubleshooting no-starts. **2009**—Harsh downshift when stopping. • Instrument panel rattling. **2009–10**—No starts. • Condensation dripping from the dome lamp. *Vibe:* **2003**—Transmission shifts too early when accelerating at full throttle and the engine is cold. • Harsh shifting. • Water leak from the A-pillar or headliner area. **2003–04**—Harsh 1–2 upshifts. • Slipping transmission. **2003–08**—Silencing a hoot or whistle heard on light acceleration (replace the automatic transaxle cooler hoses).

BRAKES—PREMATURE FRONT BRAKE PAD WEAR

BULLETIN NO.: T-SB-0392-09   DATE: DECEMBER 3, 2009

YEAR(S)	MODEL(S)	ADDITIONAL INFORMATION
2009–2010	Corolla	

APPLICABILITY: Some 2009–2010 model year Corolla vehicles may exhibit premature pad wear. Use the following replacement pads to address this condition.

PREVIOUS PART NUMBER	CURRENT PART NUMBER	PART NAME	QTY
04465-02240 (NAP)	04465-12630	Pad, Kit Disc Brake, Front	1
04465-02220 (JPP)			
04945-12100 (NAP)	Same	Shim, Anti-Squeal, Front	1
04945-02150 (JPP)	Same		1
N/A	08887-80609	Disc Brake Caliper Grease (50 g Tube)	1

PARTS INFORMATION

OP CODE	DESCRIPTION	TIME	OFP	T1	T2
473301	R & R Pad Kit and Shims	0.7	43512-02240 (NAP) 43512-12710 (JPP)	87	19

WARRANTY INFORMATION: This repair is covered under the Toyota Comprehensive Warranty. This warranty is in effect for 36 months or 36,000 miles.

COROLLA, MATRIX/VIBE PROFILE

	2001	2002	2003	2004	2005	2006	2007	2008	2009
Cost Price ($)									
Base Corolla	15,625	15,765	15,290	15,410	15,490	15,715	15,785	14,565	14,565
Matrix	—	—	16,745	16,745	16,925	17,200	17,200	17,200	15,705
XR AWD	—	—	24,115	24,210	24,550	24,825	21,465	21,465	19,180
XRS AWD	—	—	24,540	24,640	25,560	25,835	—	—	25,220
Vibe	—	—	20,995	21,150	19,900	19,900	19,950	19,210	15,995
GT AWD	—	—	27,000	27,140	25,670	25,670	—	—	24,995
Used Values ($)									
Base Corolla ▲	2,500	3,000	3,500	4,500	5,500	6,000	7,500	9,000	11,000
Base Corolla ▼	2,000	2,500	3,000	4,000	5,000	5,500	6,000	7,500	9,500
Matrix ▲	—	—	5,000	5,500	6,500	7,000	9,000	11,000	12,500
Matrix ▼	—	—	4,500	5,000	6,000	6,500	7,500	10,000	11,500
XR AWD ▲	—	—	5,000	6,000	7,500	9,500	—	14,500	16,000
XR AWD ▼	—	—	4,000	5,500	6,000	8,500	—	13,000	14,500
XRS AWD ▲	—	—	7,500	8,000	9,500	10,500	—	—	20,000
XRS AWD ▼	—	—	6,500	7,000	8,500	9,500	—	—	18,500

All ratings on a numbered scale where ▓ is good and **1** is bad. See page 132 for a more detailed description.

Vibe ▲	—	—	3,000	4,000	5,000	6,000	8,000	9,000	10,500
Vibe ▼	—	—	2,500	3,000	4,500	5,000	6,500	8,000	9,500
GT AWD ▲	—	—	4,000	4,500	5,500	7,500	—	—	13,500
GT AWD ▼	—	—	3,500	4,000	4,500	6,500	—	—	12,500
Reliability	3	3	3	3	2	2	2	2	2
Crash Safety (F)	4	4	5	5	5	5	5	5	4
Matrix	—	—	5	5	5	5	5	5	5
Vibe	—	—	5	5	5	5	5	5	5
Side	4	4	4	4	4	4	4	4	5
Matrix	—	—	5	5	3	3	3	3	5
Vibe	—	—	5	5	3	3	3	3	5
IIHS Side	—	—	1	1	3	3	3	3	5
Offset	3	3	5	5	5	5	5	5	5
Head Restraints	2	2	3	3	1	1	1	1	3
Matrix/Vibe	—	—	—	—	—	—	—	—	3
Roof Strength	—	—	—	—	—	—	—	—	5
Rollover Resistance	3	3	4	4	4	4	4	4	4

Toyota

ECHO, YARIS ★★★★★/★★★

RATING: *Echo:* Recommended (2000–05). *Yaris:* Average (2006–09). Both cars are practical and cheap, if you can get past the tall, function-over-form styling and rust-damaged ABS brakes of the newer Yaris. The Echo is an excellent alternative to the similarly styled, glitch-ridden early Ford Focus models and the discontinued Chrysler Neon and PT Cruiser. Now that the Echo has been replaced by the larger Yaris, Echo resale values have declined markedly. **Ideal model year:** A 2007 Base Yaris for $5,500 to $6,500 (less than half its original price) with some unexpired warranty. For new safety and performance features, like traction control and an anti-skid system, look for a high-mileage, upgraded 2010 version with some factory warranty left. **"Real" city/highway fuel economy:** *Echo manual:* 6.7/5.2 L/100 km. *Echo automatic:* 7.1/5.5 L/100 km. *Yaris manual:* 7.0/5.5 L/100 km. *Yaris automatic:* 7.0/5.6 L/100 km. Owners say fuel economy can sometimes be almost 30 percent less than advertised. **Maintenance/repair costs:** Low, except for 2007–08 Yaris brake corrosion problems. **Parts:** Easily found and cheap. **Extended warranty:** A waste of money. **Best alternatives:** Honda Civic; Hyundai Accent; Mazda3, Mazda5, or Protegé; Nissan Sentra; and Suzuki Aerio. **Helpful websites:** *www.toyotanation.com* and *www.toyotaownersclub.com*.

Strengths and Weaknesses

Echo

Toyota scrapped its highly recommended Tercel in favour of the 2000 Echo for a six-year run before it was replaced by the Yaris. Echo is an entry-level, five-passenger econocar that usually gives good fuel economy without sacrificing performance. Both two- and four-door models are available, and the car costs substantially less than the Corolla. The Echo also offers about the same passenger space as the Corolla, thanks to a high roof and low floor height.

The Echo is powered by a 108 hp 1.5L DOHC 4-cylinder engine, featuring variable valve timing (VVT) cylinder-head technology. Normally, an engine this small would provide wimpy acceleration, but thanks to the Echo's light weight, acceleration is more than adequate with the manual gearbox and acceptable with the automatic.

Standard safety features include five three-point seat belts (front seat belts have pretensioners and force limiters), two front airbags (sadly, side airbags are not available), four height-adjustable head restraints, rear child-seat tether anchors, and rear door locks.

The Echo has more usable power than the Tercel and provides excellent fuel economy and lots of interior space. There's plenty of passenger room, along with an incredible array of storage areas, including a huge trunk and standard 60/40 split-folding rear seats. All models are reasonably well equipped with good-quality materials, well-designed instruments and controls, comfortable seating, easy rear access, and excellent fore and aft visibility. It's quite nimble when cornering, very stable on the highway, and surprisingly quiet for an economy car. The car hasn't changed much after its 2000 model debut and generates few complaints—an amazing feat when compared with the quality decline in Corollas, Camrys, and Siennas since 1997.

The Echo's base tires provide poor wet traction, its narrow body limits rear bench seating to two adults, its tall profile and light weight make it vulnerable to side-wind buffeting, and its excessive torque steer makes for sudden pulling to one side when accelerating. There have also been a few complaints about rough idling, hard transmission shifts, broken door latches, leaking shock absorbers, engine ticking and rattling, some interior and brake squeaks, and a high-pitched whine and pulling to the right when underway.

Yaris

Although it's not very refined mechanically or stylistically when compared with the Honda and Mazda competition, you can't beat a Yaris for giving good fuel economy and offering reasonable reliability. It does provide a comfortable ride, but rear entry/exit is a pain, handling is surprisingly sloppy, engine and road noise is omnipresent, adequate acceleration is not one of the options offered, and the car can be hard to control when buffeted about by side winds or when it gathers speed (hatchbacks, especially). Braking is another drawback. Stops seem to take forever without the optional anti-lock brakes. Acceleration with the 106 hp 1.5L 4-cylinder engine is acceptable, but you will have to contend with lots of engine and road noise entering into the cabin area as the car picks up speed. The positioning of the steering wheel and centre-mounted dash gauges may be hard for some drivers to accept, as well. Yaris models are selling at discount now that the Ford Fiesta, Honda Fit, and Mazda3 are eating into the small-car market, which Toyota once practically owned.

VEHICLE HISTORY: *Echo:* **2003**—A major restyling adds 4 cm to overall length, via new front and rear sheet metal, as well as revised bumpers, hood, front fenders, headlights, tail lights, trunk lid, and grille. *Yaris:* **2006**—Replaced Echo as a new 2006 model. **2008**—A "sporty" S hatchback arrives with the generic 106 hp 1.5L 4-cylinder engine hooked to a 5-speed manual or 4-speed automatic transmission. **2009**—A 4-door hatchback joins the lineup.

Safety Summary

Echo: **All years:** Airbag malfunctions. • Several incidents of sudden, unintended acceleration:

> While driving, the Echo will accelerate to 60 mph [100 km/h] without [my] hitting the gas pedal. I have to put the vehicle in Neutral to stop it. I contacted [the] dealer, but he cannot locate the cause. The sudden acceleration incident occurred three times. The dealer was unable to duplicate the problem in test-driving, but removed the cruise control. The problem was not corrected by removing the cruise control.

2000–01—Brake pedal mounted too close to the accelerator pedal. **2001**—Partial brake loss. • Fuel line comes undone or cracks. • Driver's seat belt fails to lock in a collision. **2002**—In one incident, sudden steering loss led to crash. • Vehicle often jumps out of Drive into Neutral. **2003**—Engine hesitates when shifting gears. • Chronic stalling when decelerating. • Dash lights not bright enough. **2005**—Brake failure caused by a warped brake rotor. • Vehicle won't remain in Overdrive. • Gasoline smell permeates the cabin. • Leaking shock absorbers. • Broken door latches. *Yaris:* **2006**—Dashboard fire. • Sudden acceleration. • Total brake failure. • Intermediate steering shaft fails. **2007**—Airbag deploys and seat belt locks for no reason. • Seat belt fails to retract. • In one incident, a child had to be cut free from a seat belt that continued to tighten around the child's body. • In cold weather, the manual transmission sticks in First gear. • On a hill, First gear will not prevent the vehicle from backing down the hill while parked. • Floormat can jam the accelerator. • Vehicle pulls to the left and the right when reaching 100 km/h. • Trunk lid may suddenly fall. • Driver's side door window explodes for no reason. • Original-equipment tires aren't durable. **2007–08**—Airbags fail to deploy. **2008**—Sudden, unintended acceleration. • Accelerator pedal sticks. • Frequent stalling. • No brakes, or brakes lock up. • Car cannot be refuelled without gas overflowing. • Poor wiper design:

In snowy conditions the right wiper will ice up and attach itself to the windshield, therefore, making the left one not work either. The only thing to do is to pull over and clear it or ride it to an exit to clear it with absolutely no visibility.

2009—Sudden unintended acceleration caused vehicle to crash, and airbags failed to deploy. • Passenger-side airbag is disabled even when an average-sized passenger is seated. • Cruise control won't deactivate unless one stomps on the brake pedal. • Inaccurate fuel gauge reading shuts down the car. • Random stalling with manual transmission. • Brake failures. • AC produces disagreeable odours. • Ignition key sticks in the ignition and burns up the starter.

Secret Warranties/Internal Bulletins/Service Tips

All models: 2003–11—Eliminating a windshield ticking noise. **2004–10**—Front seat squeak. *Echo:* **2002–05**—Fixes for a vehicle that pulls to one side. **2003–05**—AC evaporator leaks water into the cabin. *Yaris:* **2006–07**—Front windshield ticking noise. **2006–09**—Inability to shift out of Park. **2007**—Trunk lid full-open improvement. • Engine compartment rattle heard when car is put in Reverse. • Intermittent odour in the cabin. • Paint staining along horizontal surfaces. **2007–08**—Water on front and rear carpets. • Noise, vibration with the blower motor on. • Rattle from the upper instrument panel area. • ABS light stays on (corrosion alert). • Noise, vibration on acceleration, or when shifting gears. **2007–09**—Engine noise, vibration when vehicle accelerates. • Automatic transmission shift cable rattles in when car in Reverse. **2007–10**—AC blower motor noise and vibration.

ECHO, YARIS PROFILE

	2001	2002	2003	2004	2005	2006	2007	2008	2009
Cost Price ($)									
Echo hatch	13,980	14,084	13,690	12,995	12,995	—	—	—	—
Yaris	—	—	—	—	—	13,580	13,725	13,165	13,210
Used Values ($)									
Echo hatch ▲	2,000	2,500	3,000	3,500	4,000	—	—	—	—
Echo hatch ▼	1,500	2,000	2,500	3,000	3,500	—	—	—	—
Yaris ▲	—	—	—	—	—	5,000	6,500	8,000	9,500
Yaris ▼	—	—	—	—	—	4,500	5,500	7,000	8,500
Reliability	4	4	4	4	4	4	3	3	3
Crash Safety (F)	4	4	4	4	4	—	4	4	4
Yaris hatch	—	—	—	—	—	—	—	5	—
Side	3	3	3	3	3	—	3	3	4
IIHS Side (Yaris)	—	—	—	—	—	—	1	1	5
Offset (Yaris)	—	—	—	—	—	—	5	5	5
Head Restraints (Yaris)	—	—	—	—	—	—	2	2	2
Roof Strength	—	—	—	—	—	—	3	3	3
Rollover Resistance	4	4	4	4	4	—	4	4	—

Volkswagen

GOLF, RABBIT, JETTA, CABRIO, EOS/DIESEL MODELS ★★★/★

RATING: Below Average (1999–2009). Warning: Volkswagens equipped with a D3G manual transmission are failure-prone and lag and lurch in any gear. These small cars are far less reliable than they were in the past. Golfs are entry-level models that are the cheapest of the lot and depreciate fairly rapidly. A Jetta is a Golf with a trunk, the most popular configuration, which fetches fair resale prices. A Cabrio is a Golf without a roof; it depreciates steeply after its first five years. An Eos is an overpriced 2007 or later Cabrio; it's a car for impatient buyers with big wallets—expect a $10,000 depreciation after its first year on the market. *Diesel models:* Not Recommended (2007–09); Average (1999–2006). Servicing for the new diesel system in these recent models takes considerable skill, and fixes don't last long. **Ideal model year:** Old-technology, pre-2007 diesels present fewer quality problems and are more reasonably priced, but they are only the best of a bad lot. The diesel system is less complicated than the newer units and if you want to junk the car after a few years, you can do so with minimal depreciation loss. Be careful of the newer TDIs: a 2009 Jetta TDI Wagon costing between $16,000 and $17,500 can easily hit you with a $10,000 engine repair bill and a forced diet of expensive new tires. **"Real" city/highway fuel economy:** *City Golf manual:* 9.8/7.1 L/100 km. *City Golf automatic:* 9.6/7.2 L/100 km. *Golf manual:* 9.8/7.2 L/100 km. *Golf automatic:* 9.6/7.2 L/100. *Golf TDI manual:* 6.2/4.6 L/100 km. *Golf TDI automatic:* 7.1/4.2 L/100 km. *GTI manual:* 9.8/6.9 L/100 km, or 11.1/7.3 L/100 km with the 6-speed. *Jetta 1.8 manual:* 9.9/6.9 L/100 km. *Jetta 1.8 automatic:* 10.8/7.4 L/100 km. *Jetta 2.0 manual:* 9.8/7.0 L/100 km. *Jetta 2.0 automatic:* 9.6/7.2 L/100 km. *Jetta 2.8 manual:* 11.1/7.3 L/100 km. *Jetta TDI manual:* 6.2/4.6 L/100 km. *Jetta TDI automatic:* 7.1/4.9 L/100 km. *Eos 2.0 manual:* 10.1/6.8 L/100 km. *Eos 2.0 automatic:* 10.3/6.9 L/100 km. *Eos 3.2 V6 automatic:* 10.8/7.5 L/100 km. *Diesel versions:* Although owners of gasoline-fuelled vehicles report that their consumption is about 15 percent higher than the estimates listed above, the TDI engine still burns about 30 percent less fuel than an equivalent 4-cylinder gasoline engine and has an impressive range of 1,000 km (600 mi.) or more. You'll need that range, however, since only one fuel station out of three or four sells diesel fuel. Plus, diesel fuel is usually much more expensive than gasoline. **Maintenance/repair costs:** Maintenance costs are unreasonably high; for example, TDIClub (*www.tdiclub.com*) warns that power-steering fluid, brake fluid, and special automatic transmission fluid should be purchased only from the dealer for optimal performance, even though the VW power-steering fluid is many times more expensive than fluid sold by independents. Repairs have always been dealer-dependent, and even more so since VW changed its diesel technology in 2007. **Parts:** Expensive, and not generally available from independent suppliers. Recall campaign parts may be back ordered for months. **Extended warranty:** A smart idea. "Goodwill" warranty repairs are practically nonexistent in Canada. **Best**

alternatives: Any small car that doesn't punish backseat passengers as much as this VW trio does. Try the Honda Civic; Hyundai Elantra or Tiburon; Mazda3, Mazda5, or Protegé; and Nissan Sentra. The only viable diesel alternative is a Jeep Liberty—a small SUV that has performed quite well. If a convertible tickles your fancy, buy a Mazda Miata. **Helpful websites:** *http://forums.vwvortex.com* and *http://volkswagenownersclub.com/vw*.

Strengths and Weaknesses

Like most European imports, these small cars give a comfortable ride, are fun to drive, and provide good fuel economy. On the other hand, rear passenger room is fairly restricted, and some models, like the GLI, don't provide enough power for most tastes. Both engines are easily started in cold weather, but here's the rub: Golfs and Jettas, like the failure-prone Rabbit, aren't reliable once the warranty expires. What you save with less fuel consumption, you lose in the car's high retail price and higher diesel fuel costs. Also, the ever-mounting maintenance costs as the vehicle gains years and mileage will easily wear you down. Finding a qualified independent repairer can offset the high maintenance charges, but qualified independents are rarer than hen's teeth. And 2007 and later models use new diesel technology that offer drivers a steep learning curve.

VEHICLE HISTORY: **2001**—A 150 hp 1.8L turbo-four available for the GLS and is standard in the base GTI; Jetta wagon is added, along with steering-mounted audio controls on some models. **2002**—Debut of the more-powerful 1.8L 4-cylinder engine, a 5-speed automatic transmission, and an optional 6-speed manual transmission; 2.8L V6 horsepower boosted (200 hp). **2003**—Anti-skid system becomes standard with the V6 engine; GL gets power windows, heated power mirrors, and cruise control; GLS versions come with alloy wheels and a sunroof. **2004**—All-wheel-drive Golf arrives. **2005**—Jetta's GLI VR6 sedan and the limited-edition all-wheel-drive V6 Golf R32 are ditched. Mid-year, revamped Jettas with a larger platform, 150 hp 5-cylinder engine, four-wheel ABS disc brakes, and head-protecting side airbags arrive. **2006**—Turbocharged gasoline engine and rear side airbags. The Jetta 2.0T and GLI get the 200 hp turbocharged 4-cylinder and 6-speed manual transmission. Frequently stolen Xenon headlights are standard on the GLI and optional for the 2.0T. The Golf is renamed the Rabbit (the Rabbit name was last used in 1983). These hatchbacks are redesigned for 2006 and are accompanied by a sporty two-door called the GTI. **2007**—Jetta GL's suspension is lowered by 2 cm (0.8 in.). Wolfsburg Edition joins the lineup with its sunroof, heated front seats, and 5-cylinder engine. **2008**—Jetta gets more power and a new model lineup that includes S, SE, and SEL versions, instead of the Base and 2.5. The GLI now carries a base 170 hp 2.5L 5-cylinder engine, an increase of 20 hp from 2007. GLI uses a turbocharged 200 hp 2.0L 4-cylinder. S and SE versions are available with a 5-speed manual transmission. GLIs use a 6-speed manual. A 6-speed automatic is standard on the SEL and optional on all other Jettas. The Rabbit gets 20 more horses. **2009**—Jetta adds a wagon and an available 140-hp 2.0L 4-cylinder turbodiesel engine.

Jettas and Golfs rust prematurely, usually around areas where panels join or chrome strips have been placed. Undercarriages suffer from deterioration and increasingly frequent mechanical/electrical failures after their fourth year in service. For example, starters often burn out because they are vulnerable to engine heat; fuel pumps self-destruct. As well, sunroofs leak, door locks jam, window cranks break, and windows bind. Owners also report engine head gasket leaks as well as water-pump and heater-core breakdowns. It's axiomatic that all diesels are slow to accelerate, but VW's Fourth gear often can't handle highway speeds above 90 km/h. Engine noise can be deafening when shifting down from Fourth gear.

VW reliability is below average and repair charges are onerous. Invariably, VW service managers blame owners, never the car. Still, it's hardly a secret that VW powertrains, brake components, and fuel and electrical systems have the half-life of a fruit fly, requiring expensive repairs that are often ineffective. Exhaust systems aren't very durable, body hardware and dashboard controls are fragile, the paint often discolours and is easily chipped, and window regulators constantly fail.

Similar quality shortcomings afflict Volkswagen's other divisions: Audis and Porsches are undoubtedly top-performing vehicles, but they're cursed by using similar failure-prone VW components (did someone mention the DSG transmission?) that can't be diagnosed or repaired at the corner garage. When the faulty part is found, it will likely be back ordered for weeks. Owners endure chronic electrical short circuits; heater/defroster resistor and motor failures; leaking transmission and stub-axle seals; and defective valve-pan gaskets, head gaskets, timing belts, steering assemblies, suspension components, and alternator pulleys. Body problems are legion, including air and water leaks, faulty catalytic converters, inoperative locks and latches, poor-quality body construction and paint, and cheap, easily broken accessories and trim items.

Owners also complain of noisy brakes and wheel bearings; malfunctioning gauges and accessories; fragile bumpers that become brittle and crack as the temperature falls; chronic automatic transmission/clutch and diesel-engine turbocharger problems; and leaky sunroofs and assorted water leaks from other areas (when it rains, both the front and rear floors are soaked).

Eos

A four-seater Jetta with a folding metal hardtop, the Eos is a pricey convertible that doesn't provide sporty handling and has limited rear passenger room. Powered by a peppy 200 hp 2.0L turbocharged 4-cylinder or a torquier 250 hp 3.2L V6 coupled to either a standard 6-speed manual or an automated manual DSG transmission (yikes!), the Eos provides the same superb handling and ride comfort as the Jetta—without the wind buffeting, wind and water leaks, and chassis flexing found with many convertibles. The 2008 models returned relatively unchanged. The 2009 Eos dropped the VR6 version; all models now carry the ubiquitous 200 hp turbocharged 2.0L 4-cylinder.

People who buy a diesel-powered vehicle such as VW's TDI usually cite at least one of these three reasons for their decision: lower fuel costs, lower maintenance costs, and the popular notion that diesel engines are more durable. Unfortunately, none of these reasons stand up under close scrutiny:

> 2009 VW Jetta TDI fuel pump explodes sending metal shavings into the fuel system and engine. Causing the vehicle to stall in the middle of the interstate while driving. Dealership gave me repair quote of $10,000. I don't have the money to get my car fixed. I was told that this is an ongoing issue with these cars.

Higher operating costs

Diesel-fuelled vehicles do provide 20–30 percent better fuel economy than gasoline burners. But those savings are being progressively wiped out by higher diesel fuel prices and added maintenance costs (learn to say, "Top off the urea, please"). Regular gas in Ontario, for example, sells for 102.9–125.9 cents per litre, while a litre of diesel fuel in the same area goes for an average price of 108.9–119.9 cents. Diesel fuel costs are expected to go even higher as North American refiners are forced to produce cleaner, more expensive fuel.

Servicing price gouging

Diesel owners decry the high cost of regular maintenance and claim that parts and fluids can cost many times what a non-diesel engine requires. Furthermore, dealerships' service personnel are in a monopolist "take it or leave it" position because there are few independent mechanics available to service diesel cars— good diesel mechanics are rare in most dealerships, and diesel engine diagnostic tools and parts inventories are often wanting.

Reliability: The dark side of diesels

Automakers promote diesel engines are for their fuel-efficient and dependable performance; however, recent studies and owner complaints indicate diesels burn more fuel than advertised, are more likely to break down than gasoline-powered engines, and produce emissions that exacerbate lung diseases like emphysema.

With the latest urea-dependent, cleaner-burning diesel system installed within the past few model years, no one knows what the final verdict on diesels will be. One thing is sure, though: Servicing will be more complicated and expensive, and you will be the dealership's captive customer because few independent mechanics will have the experience, tools, fluids, and service codes needed to service these new systems.

J.D. Power's 2004 Vehicle Dependability Study found that the most fuel-efficient vehicles—diesels and gas-electric hybrids—had more engine problems than similar gasoline-powered vehicles. It's instructive to note that this survey polled owners of vehicles equipped with relatively uncomplicated diesel systems. And its conclusions are backed by automaker service bulletins and owner complaints sent to NHTSA. The diesel deficiencies are an eye-opener:

- Ford and Chevrolet diesel pickups had more engine problems than similar gas-powered models, while Dodge and GMC trucks were better overall.
- Owners of Volkswagen diesels reported up to twice as many engine problems than did owners of VWs that burn gas

Safety Summary

All models/years: Golfs and Jettas, as well as many Audis, are easily stolen due to a flawed door lock mechanism design, reports *Lemon-Aid* reader and British Columbia resident Susan O.:

> Basically, it is a factory-installed flaw in the design that if you pop the silver cylinder off the only keyed door, you can remove the lock mechanism, which allows anyone to get into the vehicle. Further to that, you are also able to deactivate the alarm, so the VW/Audi owner would not hear anyone gaining entry.

• NHTSA's database shows repeated reports of the following problems: fires; lights that go out; self-activating alarms; inadequate defrosting; AC mould and mildew smell; brake, tire, and AC failures; early replacement of brake pads; window regulator failure; inadvertent airbag deployment; transmission and wheel bearing failures; poor-quality body components; inoperable power windows; erratic cruise-control operation; Airbag light stays on for no apparent reason; electrical malfunctions leading to chronic stalling; airbags fail to deploy or cause severe injuries when they go off; and DSG manual transmission pops out of gear or tends to lag and lurch. Also, doors may open suddenly; hoods suddenly fly up; locks jam shut, fall out, or freeze; power-window motors and regulators self-destruct; cigarette lighters pop out of their holders while lit; the seat heater may burn a hole in the driver's seat; and battery acid can leak onto the power-steering reservoir and cause sudden steering loss. **All models: 2000–03**—Airbag cover pops off while driving. • Cracked oil pan. • Engine burns oil. • Hard starting. • Noisy, prematurely worn brakes. • Sudden headlight failure; poor headlight illumination. • Faulty power-window regulators cause windows to fall down into door panels. **2002**—Sudden, unintended acceleration. • Vehicle hesitates on acceleration. **2003**—One vehicle's driver's seat burst into flames. **2004**—Golf totally destroyed by a fire of unknown origin. • Jetta fire ignited in the seat-heater control, which was shut off at the time. • VW says engines need a special oil to prevent engine sludge. • Transmission clutch slipping. • There is such a long delay when shifting the automatic transmission in Reverse or Drive, the vehicle is free to roll as if it were in Neutral. • Harsh downshifts. • Transmission locks up between Third and Fourth gears. • Frequent electrical shorts (windows, lights, gauges, alarm system, etc.). • Dash gauges cannot be read in sunlight. • Distracting reflection from the chrome shifter panel. **2005**—Engine surges when shifted into Reverse. • Faulty fuel gauges. • Driver's seat becomes unattached. **2006**—Fuel doesn't get to the engine. • Full throttle will only make the vehicle idle. • Engine is always ready to stall out. **2007**—Faulty water pump impeller causes the car to overheat. **2008**—"Lag and lurch": vehicle feels like it is going to stall out, and then it suddenly surges:

> There has been an intermittent fuel shutoff problem that results in a stall or a lurch that results in a near-stop. This occurs in low-speed, heavy traffic situations with trailing throttle (typically no brake application)...I have since found identical complaints on several VW-interest forums on the web including Carspace Automatic forums and VWVortex forums, VW Rabbit Owners Club and Edmunds.com. This is a disgrace and an example of corporate irresponsibility.

• Windshield wipers stop when the brakes are applied. • Faulty Continental tires. **2009**—Chronic stalling at all speeds. • Faulty steering box may cause excessive steering wheel shake (some, but not all, units were recalled). • Steering locks up while vehicle was underway; freed up when car was restarted. Dealer changed the steering unit. • Vehicle wanders ("floats") all over the road. • In one vehicle the Check Engine and Fuel Cap warning lights came on inexplicably; the fuel tank imploded while dealer was looking for the cause. • RPMs suddenly spike and then the vehicle stalls out. • Car shifts into Neutral while underway. • While the car is in Drive, driver can remove the ignition key and the car will roll freely on any sort of slope. • Driver-side rear door may not unlock. • *TDI:* **2004**—Many reports of engine overheating, chronic stalling, and EGR/turbocharger failures:

> TDI engine will stall at times due to coolant leaking internally into [the] intake manifold through [a] faulty EGR cooler, causing vehicle to lose steering and brake assist. I have looked on VW web forums, and many owners have had a similar incident.

•

> TDI engine and manual transmission: While driving, vehicle lost power intermittently. Pressed accelerator; no change in rpm—just idled. [The] "glow plug" flashed and [the] Engine Warning light...lit after [the] first two occasions, not on [the] third. Re-start solves problem for 30 seconds. Dealership was notified, but did not resolve the problem in two attempts. Vehicle is in for third attempt.

The EGR problem is so rampant and expensive to correct that VW owners are pleading for relief. Enterprising independent repair shops are seizing the opportunity to make a profit by offering cheaper fixes for the well-known turbocharger problems. • Stripped manifold bolts are another cause of the turbo's demise. **2005**—Clutch disengages from the flywheel. • TDI's fuel-filler pipe is too small for most truck stop gas stations. • Chronic surging and stalling. • Sunroof's drains clog, causing serious electrical problems and mould growth:

> Sunroof drains clog causing backup of water to settle on floors ruining carpet, causing mold. Water gets into door frames causing buckling of doors during winter months. Water damage also caused an electrical wiring short which caused an airbag failure as well as ruined two batteries. I have not used or opened the sunroof since for fear of

more problems. I was informed that the cost to replace the carpeting again would be charged to me if the car had another water problem again due to the clogged drains.

2006—In a rear-ender, the driver's seatback collapsed and the airbag failed to deploy. • The vehicle stalls out when the accelerator pedal is depressed. Intercooler leaks oil:

> Chaffing of the aluminum intercooler pipes by the perpendicular piece of plastic that extends to it from the front passenger side grill and touches the intercooler. Over time, the plastic rubs against the intercooler and eventually creates holes where oil leaks out. If left unchecked, this would lead to continued loss of oil, loss of boost and eventually failure of the turbo. Numerous Internet searches and looking on *www. TDIClub.com* show many occurrences of this problem. It is specific to the TDI version of the Golf since it has a turbo. At a minimum, the plastic needs to be trimmed and a piece of foam or something soft needs to be inserted so nothing hard can rub against the aluminum intercooler pipes.

2008—DSG automatic transmission–equipped cars may buck or jerk when accelerating; there is often a one- or two-second delay after the gas pedal is pressed. VW has recalled the 2008 and 2009 models for transmission failures:

> The car would lunge forward from a starting position while in Drive or lunch backwards from a starting position while in Reverse. The car makes very jerky, jolty movements forward.

> •

> This issue is more prevalent when the car is warmed up, like after driving for 20 or 30 minutes or so. My car (VW Jetta '08 DSG) automatic tranny operation fails usually when in First gear (while in "D" mode) or in reverse so that you experience very bad "lurching" and surging effect. The car would suddenly rev and jump forward a foot or two then feel like it was idling wrong and feel like it was going to die, then run fine then do it all over again.

• Premature wear of rear pads and rotors. • Mould buildup due to a defective trunk gasket seal. **2009**—TDI chronic stalling and shutdown; diesel $10,000 failure due to shards of metal in the fuel lines:

> Car had to be towed to VW. Upon receipt of the car, VW tried to accuse me of using "bad fuel" but then changed their story, once they did more research (and they found that many people across the US are having this problem). Volkswagen states that there is a complete fuel pump failure, with metal particulate in the fuel filters and system, and all components must be replaced (see *www.tdi-issues.com/hpfp-cases-tac68/2010-vw-jetta-tdi-gap186.htm#comment344*).

• Faulty fuel pump blamed on owner:

After being in the shop now for six weeks the dealer has informed me that the problem is with the fuel system and that the fuel pump has failed. They say there is rust and other contamination in it and there must have been water in the system. VW has refused to cover it under the warranty. The cost of replacing the entire fuel system will be $8,000–$10,000. Having researched the issue online I have found that this is an often reported occurrence and a known problem with the 2009 Jetta TDIs. It appears that VW is covering the problem in many cases but not in others.... This problem is a point of discussion on numerous forums see *http://forums.tdiclub. com/showthread.php?t=286380*.... VW is trying to foist it off on the customers rather than taking responsibility for it. I may well need to file suit against the dealership to get this issue resolved.

• Hard cold weather starts. • Premature, uneven rear brake wearout:

Brakes need to be replaced at 25,000 miles [40,200 km] and 50% of the miles were highway miles. Spongy brake pedal and heavy rear wheel brake dust reported to dealer 3 times when new and at the normal service intervals. VW dealer service manager said all 09 Jetta's rear brakes are wearing out between 20,000 and 30,000 miles [32,200–48,300 km]. Either rear brake design or materials are defective causing premature wear and failure.

• Quirky, failure-prone DSG transmission doesn't supply needed power to the car.

I own a 2009 Jetta TDI with a DSG transmission. I feel like I am going to get hit when I start from a stop. The transmission jumps and hesitates. I [have] been to the dealer without [it] being fixed. It is terrifying to drive a car that may or may not accelerate which also jumps in and out of gear!

Secret Warranties/Internal Bulletins/Service Tips

All models/years: It's surprising that, despite the many owner complaints, VW has issued few service bulletins. This means these problems don't exist in Volkswagen's opinion, or the automaker doesn't have corrective fixes to apply and will simply carry on as if all systems are "normal." **All models: 1999–2006**—Possible reasons why the car won't start or is hard to start. **1999–2008**—Inoperative window regulator. • Noisy, binding sunroof. • Repair tips on fixing heated rear windshield lines that are inoperative. **1999–2010**—Troubleshooting brake pedal vibration, pulsation. **2000–08**—Fuel-related driveability issues. **2003–10**—Causes for excessive vibration when braking (a warranty item, admits VW). **2004–06**—Shift delay upon acceleration. **2005–07**—Engine knocking noise. • Rattle from front passenger-side floor area. **2005–08**—How to silence front and rear suspension and front-seat creaks. • Troubleshooting sound system malfunctions. • Fix for an inoperative seat heater. • Seized AC compressor. **2005–10**—Cooling fan runs on after ignition shut off. • Poor heater output. **2006**—Faulty door lock cylinders. **2006–08**—AC isn't cold enough. **2007**—Water pump may fail, causing the engine to suddenly overheat; replace the pump with an upgraded one that uses a metallic impeller. **2008**—

Loose door mirrors; incorrect fold functions. • Engine cooling fan stays on. **2009–10**—No start, runs rough. *Rabbit, GTI, R32:* **2006–08**— Ice deforms leading edge of doors.

GOLF, RABBIT, JETTA, CABRIO, EOS PROFILE

	2001	2002	2003	2004	2005	2006	2007	2008	2009
Cost Price ($)									
Cabrio/Eos	28,530	28,530	—	—	—	—	36,900	35,975	35,975
Golf/City	19,040	19,230	17,950	18,300	18,530	18,530	14,900	15,300	15,300
Jetta/City	21,280	21,490	24,260	24,520	24,750	24,975	16,700	16,900	16,900
Jetta TDI	23,100	23,220	23,450	25,860	26,080	26,310	—	—	24,275
Jetta TDI wagon	—	—	—	25,860	27, 550	27,780	—	—	25,775
Rabbit	—	—	—	—	—	—	19,990	19,975	19,975
Used Values ($)									
Cabrio/Eos ▲	5,000	6,500	—	—	—	—	19,000	23,000	26,000
Cabrio/Eos ▼	4,500	5,500	—	—	—	—	17,500	21,500	24,500
Golf/City ▲	3,000	3,500	4,500	5,500	6,500	7,500	8,000	9,500	11,000
Golf/City ▼	2,500	3,000	4,000	4,500	5,500	6,500	7,500	8,500	10,000
Jetta/City ▲	4,500	5,500	6,000	6,500	8,000	9,000	10,500	11,500	13,500
Jetta/City ▼	4,000	5,000	5,500	6,000	7,000	8,500	9,500	10,500	12,000
Jetta TDI ▲	6,000	7,000	8,500	9,000	11,000	14,000	—	—	18,500
Jetta TDI ▼	5,500	6,000	7,000	8,000	9,500	13,000	—	—	17,000
Jetta TDI Wagon ▲	—	—	7,500	8,500	10,500	14,500	—	—	17,500
Jetta TDI Wagon ▼	—	—	6,000	7,500	9,000	13,000	—	—	16,000
Rabbit ▲	—	—	—	—	—	—	11,500	13,500	15,500
Rabbit ▼	—	—	—	—	—	—	10,000	12,000	14,500
Reliability	2	2	2	2	2	2	2	2	2
Crash Safety (F)									
Golf	5	5	5	5	5	5	—	—	—
Jetta	5	5	5	3	5	4	4	—	—
Rabbit	—	—	—	—	—	—	4	4	4
Side									
Golf	—	—	4	4	4	4	—	—	—
Jetta	—	4	4	5	5	5	5	—	—
Rabbit	—	—	—	—	—	—	—	5	5
IIHS Side (Golf)	5	5	5	5	5	—	—	—	—
Eos	—	—	—	—	—	—	5	5	5
Rabbit	—	—	—	—	—	5	5	5	5
Jetta	—	—	—	—	5	5	5	5	5
Offset									
Eos	—	—	—	—	—	—	5	5	5
Rabbit	—	—	—	—	—	5	5	5	5
Jetta	—	—	—	—	5	5	5	5	5

Head Restraints (F)									
Golf 2d					—	—	—	—	—
Golf 4d	3	3	3	3	—	—	—	—	—
Jetta	3	3	3	3	3	3			
Eos	—	—	—	—	—	—	2	2	
Rabbit	—	—	—	—	—	3	2	2	
Roof Strength (Rabbit)	—	—	—	—	—				
Rollover Resistance	4	4	4	4		4	—	—	
Rabbit	—	—	—	—	—	—	4	4	4

MEDIUM CARS

The most popular size car sold in North America today, medium- or mid-size vehicles usually have wheelbases between 105 inches (267 cm) and 110 inches (279 cm). A mid-size car is a trade-off between size and fuel economy, offering more room and convenience features but a bit less fuel economy than a small car. Owners also get a full complement of important safety features like side curtain airbags and electronic stability control. As a result of their versatility, as well as both upsizing and downsizing through the years, these vehicles overlap with several car niches and encompass small trucks and downsized SUVs as well.

For example, in 1985 the U.S. Environmental Protection Agency classified the Honda Accord and Toyota Camry as compact, but since the 1990s, both have been classified as mid-size.

These cars are best for combined city and highway driving, with the top choices traditionally dominated by Japanese automakers: the Honda Accord; the Mazda5, Mazda6, and 626; and the Toyota Camry. South Korean automakers, however, are catching up fast, both in good times and bad, with Hyundai's Elantra and Sonata leading the pack.

Hyundai's 1996–09 Sonata is as good a mid-size car as you can find.

But there are lots of bad cars in this group, too, and they belong mostly to the Detroit automakers. Take the Ford Taurus and Sable, for example. Bestsellers for many years and easily found for a few thousand dollars at most, these two models don't cost much because they are no longer built and have a well-deserved reputation for being lemons. Engine, transmission, brake, electrical, and body problems are legion, and repair costs for the automatic transmission alone can easily run about $3,500.

GM's mid-sized lineup is only marginally better. Cars like the Chevrolet front-drive Impala and Malibu are decent highway performers and relatively fuel-frugal, but their reliability is the pits. Chrysler is the Detroit automaker with the worst quality-control record of all. The Avenger, Dakota, Durango, Sebring, and most of their Jeeps and minivans have declined dramatically in quality during the past decade and are mediocre highway performers. Cheap, they are. But that's mainly because their upkeep costs so much. The only Chrysler model that may be a good buy if priced low enough is a Dodge truck (with an early diesel engine).

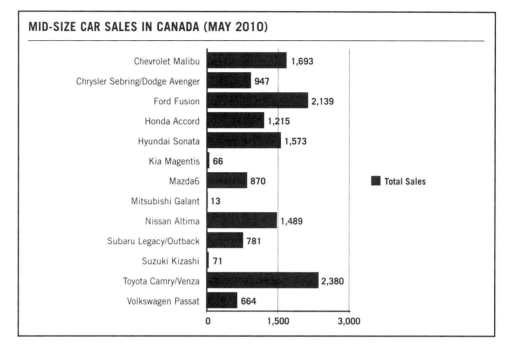

MID-SIZE CAR SALES IN CANADA (MAY 2010)

Model	Total Sales
Chevrolet Malibu	1,693
Chrysler Sebring/Dodge Avenger	947
Ford Fusion	2,139
Honda Accord	1,215
Hyundai Sonata	1,573
Kia Magentis	66
Mazda6	870
Mitsubishi Galant	13
Nissan Altima	1,489
Subaru Legacy/Outback	781
Suzuki Kizashi	71
Toyota Camry/Venza	2,380
Volkswagen Passat	664

Ford's Fusion has led Detroit's mid-size car revival.

Bottom line? Stick with the Asian models, not only for their dependability and solid highway performance but also for the odds that their manufacturers won't go bankrupt in 2011.

MEDIUM CAR RATINGS

Recommended

Acura 1.6 EL, 1.7L EL (1999–2005)
Hyundai Sonata (2009)

Above Average

Acura CSX (2006–09)
Honda Accord Hybrid (2004–07)
Hyundai Sonata (2006–08)

Mazda6 (2006–09)
Nissan Altima (2008–09)
Toyota Solara (2006–08)

Average

Chrysler Avenger, Sebring (2007–09)
General Motors Grand Prix,
   Impala, Malibu, Malibu Hybrid
   (2008–09)

Hyundai Sonata (1999–2005)
Mazda6 (2003–05)
Mazda 626 (1999–2002)
Nissan Altima (2002–07)

Honda Accord (2007)   Nissan Altima Hybrid (2007–09)
Honda Accord Hybrid (2003)   Toyota Solara (1999–2005)

Below Average

Chrysler Avenger, Sebring (1999–2007)   Honda Accord (2008–09; 1999–2006)
General Motors Bonneville, Grand Prix,   Toyota Prius (2001–09)
   Impala, Intrigue, LeSabre, Lumina,   Volkswagen New Beetle (2008–09)
   Malibu, Monte Carlo,   Volkswagen Passat (1999–2009)
   Regal (1999–2007)

Not Recommended

Ford Sable, Taurus (1999–2006)   Volkswagen New Beetle (1999–2007)
Toyota Camry (1996–2009)
Toyota Camry Hybrid (2007–09)

Acura

1.6 EL, 1.7 EL, CSX ★★★★/★★★★★

best buy

The Acura CSX.

RATING: *1.6 EL, 1.7 EL:* Recommended (1999–2005). The first Japanese automobile built exclusively in and for the Canadian market (manufactured in Alliston, Ontario), the EL is basically a gussied-up Honda Civic sold under the Acura moniker. The redesigned 2001 EL and later models offer the most reliability and performance for the least amount of money. They are the cheapest Acuras available and offer more features and a slightly more powerful, torquier engine than the Civic. As the Civic grew in size from a subcompact to a compact during the past decade, so did the EL. *CSX: Above Average (2006–09),* but watch out for transmission glitches. The 2006–09 CSX is a twin of the Civic Si, borrowing the engine and drivetrain from the Si but adding some luxury options, including leather seating. The CSX also features distinctive front and rear fascias. **Ideal model year:** If you want the performance thrills without the acquisition bills, seriously consider getting a $16,000 to $17,500 2007 Type-S. You will be paying half the car's original cost. If you aren't bowled over by the Acura moniker, then choose a 2007 Honda Civic Si Coupe for about $12,500. **"Real" city/highway fuel economy:** *1.6L manual: 7.8/6.1 L/100 km. 1.6L automatic: 7.9/6.0 L/100 km. 1.7L manual: 8.1/6.3 L/100 km. 1.7L automatic: 7.9/6.0 L/100 km.* **Maintenance/repair costs:** Average. Repairs aren't dealer-dependent. **Parts:** Average costs, thanks to the use of generic Civic parts sold through more price-competitive independent suppliers. **Extended warranty:** Not needed. **Best alternatives:** Ford Fusion; Honda Civic EX or Si; Hyundai Elantra or Sonata; Mazda3, 5, or 6; and the Suzuki SX4. **Helpful websites:** *www.8thcivic.com/forums/mechanical-problems-technical-chat.*

Strengths and Weaknesses

As a new car purchase, *Lemon-Aid* suggests buying the cheaper Civic version and keeping it "forever." However, once depreciation has taken its toll on both models, the higher cost of an Acura may be a small premium to pay for the Acura cachet.

VEHICLE HISTORY: 2001—Roomier, more fuel-efficient, and better equipped. Buyers get standard side airbags, four-wheel disc brakes, and front seat belt pretensioners. The standard 5-speed manual transmission is revised for smoother shifts and quieter operation, and the 4-speed automatic transmission boosts fuel economy. Even though horsepower remains the same, torque increases by almost 8 percent. **2003**—A retuned suspension and steering system for better handling and enhanced ride comfort reduce engine vibration through improved engine mounts and upgraded brakes. New features: adjustable head restraints and upgraded instrument clusters, armrests, and front seats. **2006**—CSX is launched. **2007**—Arrival of the high-performance Type-S, selling at a premium over the base CSX. The extra money buys 42 more horses, plenty of torque, a 3000 rpm redline, and a 6-speed close-ratio manual gearbox. The car also gets stiffer springs, larger stabilizer bars front and rear, and a sport-tuned suspension system. **2008**—Electronic stability control is a big plus.

EL

First generation ELs come with a peppy 127 hp VTEC 1.6L 4-banger that's both reliable and economical to run. Add the Civic's chassis and upgraded suspension components, and you have competent performance that's as good as or better than the Civic Si's. Weak points: a narrow interior, with seats and seatbacks that are not to everyone's liking; emergency braking that's only average; head restraints rated Poor by IIHS; an overly soft suspension; and excessive engine noise intruding in the passenger compartment.

The 1.6 and 1.7 EL have done quite well over the years they've been on the market. The cabin is quieter than the Civic's, the steering is quick and responsive, handling is quite nimble with 15-inch tires versus the Civic's 14-inchers, and the suspension is firmer. Braking and acceleration have also improved; however, the engine's maximum torque is reached at only about 5000 rpm, which means lots of downshifting with a full load of passengers and cargo. Interestingly, Honda recommends premium gasoline, yet the equivalent Civic gets by with regular fuel. One major safety complaint targets premature strut failures that degrade handling. Otherwise, the few owner complaints recorded have typically concerned premature suspension wear (mostly springs and bushings), merely adequate engine power, wind noise, easily dented body panels, malfunctioning accessories (AC, audio system, electrical components, etc.), and fragile trim items.

CSX

The CSX went on sale in November 2005 as a 2006 model replacement for the 1.7 EL and a template for the JDM Civic. Still a Civic spin-off, the CSX is a luxury compact for penny pinchers who can't afford the high prices and servicing costs of competitive German luxe performers. Acura differentiates the car from the Civic through exterior upgrades that include Acura rims, a double exhaust, chrome wheels and door handles, and a restyled front fascia. Other differences: The manumatic comes with cheap-feeling thin paddles mounted on the steering column, plus there are Lilliputian instrument controls, as well as heated leather seats.

A 155 hp 2.0L 4-cylinder engine, also used in the RSX, delivers power smoothly; however, acceleration times are merely middle of the pack. The BMW Mini Cooper and 128i, Volvo C30, Audi A3 2.0T, and similarly priced Civic Si all give faster takeoffs.

Secret Warranties/Internal Bulletins/Service Tips

All models/years: Most Honda/Acura TSBs allow for special warranty consideration on a "goodwill" basis even after the warranty has expired or the car has changed hands. Referring to this euphemism will increase your chances of getting some kind of refund for repairs that are obviously related to a factory defect. Keep in mind that many Honda bulletins often apply to Acuras as well. So check out the Civic's and Accord's TSBs and safety complaints before assuming that the manufacturer doesn't recognize a particular Acura problem, or that it's your responsibility. • Should you have a tranny breakdown within 7 years/160,000 km, don't hesitate to cite Honda's latest transmission extended warranty, applicable to the Civic and Accord, to back up your claim (see the following page). **All models: 2003–04**—A soft brake pedal feel or any noise from the brake assembly when braking may indicate a problem with the brake-booster master cylinder. *CSX:* **2006**—*Lemon-Aid* reader Larry says:

> The alloy wheels have a huge design flaw—the wheels have a groove in them on the inside. Stones, dirt, ice accumulate in here and throw off the balance which in turn

wrecks the tires. I had to throw out a perfectly good set of tires last year (tires get cupped when you do traveling on unbalanced wheels) and it looks like I will probably have to throw this set out as well (maybe 15,000 km on them if I am lucky).

2006–08—Manual transmission Third gear failures:

HONDA (3RD GEAR)	
BULLETIN NO.: 08-020	DATE: APRIL 12, 2008

TRANSMISSION GRINDS WHEN SHIFTING INTO 3RD GEAR, POPS OUT OF 3RD GEAR, OR IS HARD TO SHIFT INTO 3RD GEAR

2003–07 Accord V6 with M/T: ALL; 2008 Accord V6 with M/T; 2006–07 Civic Si; 2007 Civic Si 4-Door; and 2008 Civic Si 4-Door.

SYMPTOM: The 6-speed manual transmission grinds when shifting into 3rd gear, pops out of 3rd gear, or is hard to shift into 3rd gear. NOTE: These symptoms can be intermittent and sometimes more noticeable in colder climates.

PROBABLE CAUSE: A faulty 3rd gear synchronizer or 3-4 shift sleeve.

CORRECTIVE ACTION: Replace the 3rd gear set.

1.6 EL, 1.7 EL, CSX PROFILE

	2001	2002	2003	2004	2005	2006	2007	2008	2009
Cost Price ($)									
1.6/1.7 EL	21,500	21,700	22,000	22,200	23,000	—	—	—	—
CSX	—	—	—	—	—	25,400	25,900	26,990	26,990
CSX Type-S	—	—	—	—	—	—	33,400	33,400	33,400
Used Values ($)									
1.6/1.7 EL ▲	5,000	6,000	8,000	9,500	11,000	—	—	—	—
1.6/1.7 EL ▼	4,500	5,000	7,000	8,500	9,500	—	—	—	—
CSX ▲	—	—	—	—	—	12,000	14,500	18,000	20,000
CSX ▼	—	—	—	—	—	10,500	13,000	16,500	18,500
CSX Type-S ▲	—	—	—	—	—	—	17,500	20,500	23,000
CSX Type-S ▼	—	—	—	—	—	—	16,000	19,000	22,000
Reliability									

Note: These vehicles have not been crash tested, but should perform as well as the Civic.

Chrysler

AVENGER, SEBRING ★★★

RATING: Average (2007–09); Below Average (1999–2006). The Avenger and its better-appointed Sebring twin are not great performers, but they are so cheap and easily fixed, it's not hard to give them the nod as inexpensive basic transporters. Drive a hard bargain, though, because the money you save you'll need to keep in a cookie jar for upcoming transmission, brake and fuel system, and AC evaporator repair bills. The Sebring convertible is an attractively styled bargain ragtop that comes with water leaks and a symphony of squeaks and rattles due to the chassis flexing. **Ideal model year:** None. If you don't mind taking a "leap into the abyss" with your fingers crossed, shop around for a $15,000 to $16,000 Sebring LX Convertible. The number of complaints against this car registered with NHTSA is amazingly small (44). You can get used to water leaks, right? Stay away from the AWD models. **"Real" city/highway fuel economy:** *Sebring convertible manual:* 11.9/7.9 L/100 km. *Sebring convertible automatic:* 11.2/7.8 L/100 km. *2.4L sedan:* 11.1/7.7 L/100 km. *2.7L sedan:* 10.6/7.3 L/100 km. Fuel savings may be lower by about 15 percent. **Maintenance/repair costs:** Average. **Parts:** Reasonably priced and good availability. **Extended warranty:** Yes, an extra $2,000 expense for an extended powertrain warranty. **Best alternatives:** Ford Fusion, Honda Accord, Hyundai Elantra or Sonata, and Mazda5 or Mazda6. **Helpful websites:** *www.chryslerforum.com/forum* and *www.topix.com/forum/autos/chrysler-sebring*.

Strengths and Weaknesses

These coupes, sedans, and convertibles are mediocre buys mainly because they're so underpowered and basic. Defects affect body and mechanical components equally, and lead to serious long-term reliability and durability problems. On the positive side, these cars are dirt cheap because the public has little confidence in the reliability of Chrysler products or in the solvency of the automaker itself. As Chrysler drifts toward another bankruptcy, servicing won't be affected much due to the length of time these cars have been on the market with the same simple design and parts. For example, powertrains, platforms, safety features, and other mechanical components are shared among the entire lineup and can be bought easily from independent suppliers for much less than dealers charge.

VEHICLE HISTORY: 2001—The redesigned Sebring adds a sedan, a more-powerful V6, and a premium sound system. The Avenger is dropped. **2002**—Sebrings are joined by a 200 hp 2.7L V6 R/T sedan equipped with a manual 5-speed gearbox. **2003**—Four-wheel disc brakes. **2006**—Coupes are dropped. **2007**—The sedan is completely redesigned and the convertible is dropped for one model year. The sedan is a bit wider and 10 cm taller, offers more interior room (especially rear legroom) and a taller seating position, and has slightly less cargo volume. Buyers have a choice of three engines: a 2.4L 4-cylinder hooked to the ubiquitous gas-guzzling 4-speed automatic transmission; a 2.7L V6, also coupled to the 4-speed; and a more powerful, better performing 3.5L V6 mated to a 6-speed manumatic transmission. **2008**—A revamped Sebring convertible is resurrected with the 2007 Sebring upgrades. An optional AWD Limited sedan is offered. Sebring's sister car, the Dodge Avenger, returns as a four-door sports sedan after an eight-year absence; it had sold from 1995 to 2000 as a two-door coupe. **2009**—AWD model is axed.

The 3.5L V6 is the engine of choice to overcome the power-hungry automatic transmission and to avoid a persistent 4-cylinder engine head gasket defect affecting all model years. In theory, the 6-speed transmission should be more economical; however, with the V6 it's overkill and it tends to shift too much, negating the fuel savings one would expect. Handling is so-so, and the ride is generally comfortable.

The 2.7L V6 would normally be a good alternative to the small 4-cylinder; however, it is subject to oil sludging and early failures of the engine primary timing-chain tensioner and tensioner O-ring. Opt for the 2.4L instead. Over the past decade, Avenger/Sebring owners report widespread automatic transmission failures, grinding when shifting, shuddering from a stop, and defaulting to Second gear. Other deficiencies in need of attention include loss of steering; engine oil leaks; sunroof malfunctions; premature brake wear, brake failures, and suspension replacement; ignition, electrical system, and PCM glitches; sloppy body construction (water leaks and lots of wind noise); and a clanking or rattling heard when turning over rough pavement. The driver-seat motor frequently burns out; replacement cost: $2,000. Scrapyard price: $200!

As with 2005–06 Corvettes, Sebring convertible tops can fly off on early models, plus they leak water and air and operate erratically. A faulty window regulator lets the window run off its track; poor design and sloppy construction allow water into the vehicle when the window is partly opened; and rear windshield sealant lets water leak into the vehicle. The side door mouldings melt; there's excessive brake dust; the chrome wheels and airbag coating peel; wheel rims are easily bent and leak air from normal driving; and a black goo oozes from body panels and the undercarriage.

2007–09 models have been beset by some brake, fuel system, and body defects, however, few safety-related complaints have been recorded for these model years. The upgraded 2007s improved brake performance and give a quieter ride. And while the 2.4L 4-cylinder coupled to the 4-speed automatic works hard, the acceleration is woefully unresponsive; the 6-speed transmission hooked to the 3.5L V6 works much more smoothly and delivers the power that's needed, but with excess noise in the process. Post-2006 models also give a busy ride, respond slowly to steering corrections, and feel ponderous and ungainly on the road.

 **Safety Summary**

All years: Sudden, unintended acceleration. • Airbags fail to deploy. • Chronic stalling. • Electrical short-circuits. • Horn blows on its own. • Steering and automatic transmission failures. • Brake failures. • Early replacement of brake pads and rotors. • Brake and gas pedals too close together. • Exploding windows. **2003**—Driver's airbag deploys for no reason. • Tapping brakes locks them up. • ABS failure. • Rodents can get into the heater blower area. • Headlights dim and shut off intermittently. **2004**—Electrical wiring in the rear defroster catches fire. • Firewall fuel line leakage. • Engine overheating. • Transmission slippage—not engaging the gear selected and shifting to a higher and then a lower gear, making the car surge. • Transmission sticks in Park. • Seat heater overheats. • Dash lights flicker, and headlights may suddenly go off. • Key sticks in the ignition. • Chrome door handles can cut fingers. • Bumper falls off. **2005**—Airbags deploy and start a fire. • Delayed shifts. • Steering failure caused by broken steering knuckle. • Left front wheel breaks away from vehicle. • Filler pipe collapses while vehicle is refuelling. • Inaccurate fuel gauge readings. • Horn sounds on its own; costs $700 to fix. **2006**—More self-activating horn incidents; beating on the steering wheel won't shut it off. Then, when you need the horn, it remains silent. Fixes don't last. • Varmints chew on the soy-based electrical wiring (control sensor), which makes the engine lose power when the car accelerates. • Engine crankshaft seal failure at 74,000 km (46,000 mi.). • Fuel pump ($500) sends too much fuel to the engine, causing stalling and lagging when accelerating. • Water collects on the floor of the rear passenger area. • When one car reached 100 km/h, the convertible top blew away. **2007**—Four engine compartment fires reported; one fire attributed to a faulty cooling fan. • Airbag alert light will not turn off. • Chronic stalling and lurching. • Excessive steering shimmy when braking. • ABS and traction control engage for no reason, almost pulling car off the road. • Cruise control failures. • One 4-speed automatic could not be shifted out of Park. • Fuel odour in the cabin. • Instrument panel cluster won't illuminate, or dims unexpectedly. • While underway, the hood suddenly opens and flies backwards. **2008**—Convertible engine compartment fire. • Engine surges when the brake pedal is depressed. • Car accelerates and the cruise control fails to disengage when brakes are applied. • Defective PCM computer module. • Incorrect fuel gauge readings are one-quarter off when the fuel tank is almost empty. **2009**—Emergency brake didn't hold the car in Park. • All four TPS valve stems leaked and caused all four tires to go flat. • Vehicle loses power and then stalls; starter grinds. • Even at its highest setting, driver's seat is too low for driver to see over the hood. • Side window glare obstructs driver's vision. • Hard to secure child safety seats due to restricted accessibility and clearance.

Secret Warranties/Internal Bulletins/Service Tips

2002–04—Delayed gear engagement. **2003–04**—Harsh downshifts. **2004**—Driveability improvements to fix engine stumbling and rough running, idle fluctuations, and surging when at idle or coming to a stop. • Harsh 4–3 downshifts. • Low-speed transmission bumps. • Pop/clunk sound from front of vehicle; engine snapping noise. • Steering-column click. • Revised suspension lateral-control links. • Door clunk noise. • Power seat won't adjust; front seat movement. • Intermittent loss of accessories. **2004–05**—Inoperative AC. **2007–08**—Tips on silencing noisy seats and rear suspension rattles. • Sunroof water leaks. • Rear-door glass comes out of its track; won't roll up. • Front door glass flutter or rattle. • Engine surge or gear hunting upon deceleration. • Steering honk, moan, or grinding sound when making left turns (replace the power steering fluid reservoir). **2007–09**—AC leaks water onto passenger floor. • Difficult to fill fuel; nozzle shut off. • Honk, moan on hard left-hand turns. **2008**—Hard starts; no-starts.

AVENGER, SEBRING PROFILE

	2001	2002	2003	2004	2005	2006	2007	2008	2009
Cost Price ($)									
Avenger SE	—	—	—	—	—	—	—	21,195	21,995
Avenger AWD	—	—	—	—	—	—	—	30,760	—
Sebring	23,240	23,320	23,610	24,115	24,560	24,880	22,995	22,995	22,995
Sebring V6	30,095	27,380	27,795	28,415	28,855	—	—	—	—
Convertible	33,595	33,580	34,305	35,195	35,795	36,115	—	29,995	29,995
Used Values ($)									
Avenger SE ▲	—	—	—	—	—	—	—	11,500	13,500
Avenger SE ▼	—	—	—	—	—	—	—	10,000	12,000
Avenger AWD ▲	—	—	—	—	—	—	—	13,500	—
Avenger AWD ▼	—	—	—	—	—	—	—	12,000	—
Sebring ▲	3,000	3,500	4,000	4,500	5,000	6,500	9,000	11,500	13,500
Sebring ▼	2,500	3,000	3,500	4,000	4,500	5,000	7,500	10,000	12,000
Sebring V6 ▲	4,000	4,500	5,000	6,000	7,000	—	—	—	—
Sebring V6 ▼	3,500	4,000	4,500	5,500	6,500	—	—	—	—
Convertible ▲	4,500	5,000	6,000	6,500	7,000	8,500	—	15,500	18,500
Convertible ▼	4,000	4,500	5,500	6,000	6,500	7,500	—	14,000	17,000
Reliability	2	2	2	2	2	2	3	3	3
Crash Safety (F)									
Avenger	—	—	—	—	—	—	—	5	5
Sebring 2d	4	4	4	4	4	—	—	—	—
Sebring 4d	5	5	5	5	5	5	5	5	5
Sebring cvt.	3	3	3	3	3	3	—	4	4
Side									
Avenger	—	—	—	—	—	—	—	5	5
Sebring	3	3	3	3	3	—	—	—	—
Sebring 4d	3	3	3	3	3	3	5	5	5
Sebring cvt.	3	3	3	3	3	—	—	5	5
IIHS Side									
Avenger	—	—	—	—	—	—	—	5	5
Sebring	1	1	1	1	1	1	5	5	5

All ratings on a numbered scale where ☐ is good and **1** is bad. See page 132 for a more detailed description.

Offset									
Avenger	—	—	—	—	—	—	—	5	5
Sebring	3	3	3	3	3	3	5	5	5
Head Restraints									
Avenger	—	—	—	—	—	—	—	3	3
Sebring	2	3	1	1	1	1	3	3	3
Sebring cvt.	—	—	—		—	—	—	2	2
Roof Strength	—	—	—	—	—	—	—	5	5
Rollover Resistance									
Avenger	—	—	—	—	—	—	—	4	4
Sebring 4d	—	—	4	4	4	—	—	4	4
Sebring cvt.	—	—	5	5	5	5	—	4	4

Ford

bad buy

TAURUS ★

RATING: Not Recommended (1999–2006). This would be the worst car *Lemon-Aid* has rated in 41 years, if it weren't for its big brother, the Ford Windstar. Wow! A 2006 Taurus for $5,000—a car that originally sold for $25,099. Is that a bargain, or what? No! Both the Taurus and the Sable, its unindicted co-conspirator, are bargain-basement traps that will quickly deplete your savings, make you take forced marches, and give you a crash course in making emergency electrical and powertrain repairs. These quintessential lemons make the Ford "You Light Up My Life" Pinto and Vauxhall Firenza look good. They are easy to find and dirt cheap because their owners can't wait to get rid of them before they pay another $4,000 in powertrain repairs (if they're lucky). And the extra engine and transmission warranty protection you'll have to buy will wipe out any savings realized from the low selling price. The restyled and upgraded 2008 Ford Five Hundred and Ford Freestyle have been renamed the Taurus and Taurus X, respectively. Don't confuse them with the 2006 and earlier Taurus; they are much better buys than their older cousins. **"Real" city/highway fuel economy:** *3.0L automatic:* 12.4/8.2 L/100 km. These Fords are real gas hogs; don't believe the fuel-economy claims. **Maintenance/repair costs:** Astronomical, but you have some wiggle room to get a better price because repairs aren't dealer-dependent. Shopping at engine, transmission, brake, and muffler shops offering lifetime warranties can prevent some repeat repair costs. **Parts:** Average costs (independent suppliers sell for much less). Parts are very easy to find, except for Taurus parts, such as the fuel pumps and electrical components needed to correct chronic stalling and electrical shorts. **Extended warranty:** Nothing less than a bumper-to-bumper extended warranty will do. Even with additional protection, you're taking a huge risk with your wallet. **Best alternatives:** No, another front-drive Detroit-built family-sized car like the GM Malibu or Impala is not a good idea. It would simply amount to exchanging a chalice of hemlock for sips of arsenic. Instead, choose a Honda Civic or Accord, Hyundai Elantra wagon or Sonata, Mazda6, or 2005 or 2006 Toyota Camry. **Helpful websites:** *www.fordforums.com* and *www.2carpros. com/makes/ford/taurus*.

Strengths and Weaknesses

Although they lack pickup with the standard 4-cylinder engine, these mid-sized sedans and wagons are competent family cars, offering lots of interior room, nice handling, a good crash rating, and many convenience features. From a performance standpoint, the best powertrain combination for all driving conditions is the 3.0L V6 hooked to a 4-speed on the family sedan.

The first generation Taurus LX was *Motor Trend* magazine's Car of the Year for 1986 and placed on *Car and Driver*'s annual Ten Best list from 1986 to 1991. Two examples of why most automobile journalists can't be trusted.

These cars are extremely risky buys, and they are getting worse as they age. To see just how badly time is taking its toll, look up Sable or Taurus on NHTSA's website (*www.nhtsa.dot.gov*). Chronic engine head gasket/intake manifold and automatic transmission failures; a plethora of hazardous airbag, fuel-system, brake, suspension, and steering defects; and chronic paint/rust problems are the main reasons these cars' ratings are so low. Owners also report that engine and transmission repairs don't last: Some owners are routinely putting in new engines or transmissions every few years.

Up until 2001, Ford's "goodwill" programs usually compensated owners for most of the above-noted failures once the warranty had expired. Unfortunately, these refund programs have dried up. Owners routinely face $3,000 engine or automatic transmission repair bills in addition to thousands of dollars in repairs for defective fuel systems, brakes, and suspension and steering assemblies. Ford rejects many owner complaints on the grounds that repairs were done by independent agencies, or the vehicle was bought used, or it is no longer under the original warranty—three reasons often rejected by small claims court judges.

The 4-cylinder engine is a dog that no amount of servicing can change. It's slow, noisy, prone to stalling and surging, and actually consumes more gas than the V6. The 3.0L 6-cylinder is noted for engine head bolt failures and piston scuffing and is characterized by hard starting, stalling, excessive engine noise, and poor fuel economy. Transmission cooler lines leak and often lead to the unnecessary repair or replacement of the transmission.

Other things to look out for are blown heater hoses, malfunctioning fuel gauge sending units, and brakes that need constant attention—they're noisy, pulsate excessively, tend to wear out prematurely, require a great deal of pedal effort, and are hard to modulate. Master cylinders need replacing at around 100,000 km.

VEHICLE HISTORY: 2000—Redesigned and restyled to provide a more comfortable ride, a quieter and more powerful powertrain, upgraded airbags, adjustable pedals, seat belt pretensioners, and improved child safety seat anchors. Ford drops the oval design. **2005**—LX and SES versions are dropped. **2006**—The wagon and 201 hp V6 engine are ditched.

Fourth-generation 2000–06 models use an adequate, though dated, base 155 hp 3.0L Vulcan V6. The suspension was softened, and the better-performing four-wheel disc brakes were eliminated. These cars are generally quiet running, but the handling and road holding are mediocre, and the ride is floaty.

Some other minuses include insufficient storage space, limited rear headroom and access, and an ongoing history of transmission and engine breakdowns. Engine intake manifolds have a three- to five-year lifespan. The automatic transmission often shifts too soon out of First gear, shifts slowly, constantly bangs through the gears, and frequently chooses the wrong gear. Also expect AC failures; chronic warped brake rotors; extremely poor fit and finish; electrical system shorts (lots of blown fuses); uncomfortable seats and hard plastics everywhere; and steering, front suspension, fuel (faulty fuel pumps), and brake system deficiencies. You will also have to get used to water leaks throughout the interior and a never-ending symphony of rattles, buzzes, whines, and moans to keep you company on long drives.

Safety Summary

All years: Tie rod may collapse suddenly. Although the 1992 models were recalled to fix this defect, many other model years are affected and haven't been recalled. • Front coil springs may fracture because of excessive corrosion. Ford has replaced many coils for free under a secret warranty. Interestingly, Ford's Windstars have the same problem and benefitted from the same 10-year extended warranty, which has now turned into an open-ended recall campaign (see page 477). Use that recall as your argument for compensation. • Strong fuel odour seeps into the interior. • Power steering suddenly fails. • These vehicles eat brake rotors, calipers, and pads every 8,000 km. • Transmission slips out of Park. • Frequent complaints of sudden acceleration or high idle when taking the foot off the gas pedal at a standstill, shifting into Reverse, slowly accelerating, or applying the brakes. • Chronic stalling and brake failures. • Airbag fails to deploy, or is accidentally deployed. • Dash reflects onto windshield. **2002**—Engine compartment fire. • Sudden acceleration. • Vehicle surges and then shuts off when fuel tank is filled. • Frequent stalling, hard starts, and poor idle caused by chronic fuel-pump failures or a contaminated fuel-pressure sensor. • Fuel gauge gets stuck on Full. • Fuel tank is easily punctured • Seat belts may not reel out or retract. • In one incident, the seat belt continually tightened around a child and had to be cut. • Rear brake lines rub together. • High beam lights are too dim. • Cigarette lighter pops out and falls under passenger seat. **2003–06**—Cowl water leaks short out the heater/AC and other climate-control items:

I have a 03 Taurus which leaked water onto the passenger floor board also causing my AC blower motor to short out. I could not get Ford to act even though a related recall existed under 03v087000. I have found many others with this problem.

2005—Engine compartment fire. • Transmission shifts erratically:

The transmission started slipping around 38,500 miles [62,000 km]. It has been repaired 3 times. I was almost hit twice because the transmission slipped from 50 mph to 25 mph [80 to 40 km/h] in a matter of seconds. The vehicles behind me had to slam on brakes and jump lanes to keep from hitting me.

• Vehicle wanders all over the road. • Side windows implode while underway. • Inaccurate fuel gauge. **2006**—Airbags fail to deploy, or deploy while vehicle is parked. • Sudden acceleration while stopped at a stop sign. • Car accelerates on its own when cruise control is engaged. • Transmission failure. • Defective power-steering pump replaced via a "goodwill" warranty extension (expect this policy to continue up to 7 years/160,000 km). • Head restraints force occupants' heads down into their chins. • Water leaks into the driver-side floor area, causing mould buildup. • More water leaks from the cowl area into the front-passenger area, where it short-circuits the climate controls and blower. • Rear brake lights work intermittently. • Sudden failure of all the instrument panel gauges • Hard starts; no-starts.

Secret Warranties/Internal Bulletins/Service Tips

All years: Many reports of sudden coil spring breakage puncturing tires and throwing vehicles out of control. Writes the owner of a 1999 Taurus SE in 2004:

Driver side coil spring failed, cutting the tire in half. Not too bad at 60 km/h but would have been a disaster at 100 km/h. Seems there were "not enough failures" to require recall earlier, but ANOTHER investigation has been opened by [the] government. Dealer said it was a "common" failure!!! I would not drive a Taurus/Windstar until I put something other than Ford springs on them. There are also reports of similar failures in Contours, Escorts, Focus, and F-150s. Problems with Ford coil springs and corrosion date from at least 1993. So, 11 years later, they clearly have done NOTHING to fix the problem. The corrosion where my spring broke was NOT visible externally, but was clearly rusted internally at the point where it broke.

• Repeated heater core leaks. • A buzz or rattle from the exhaust system may be caused by a loose heat shield catalyst. • A sloshing noise from the fuel tank when accelerating or stopping requires the installation of an upgraded tank. • Paint delamination, fading, and peeling. **1999–2003**—Repair tips for when the torque converter clutch doesn't engage. **1999–2006**—Remedy for chronic heater core leaks. **2000–06**—An inaccurate fuel gauge will be repaired under the emissions warranty on a case-by-case basis up to eight years. • Aluminum body panels may be afflicted with early corrosion. • Vibration or booming at idle. • Seat belt is slow to retract. **2001–05**—Tips on eliminating an engine ticking noise. **2002–05**—

Troubleshooting transmission malfunctions. • Engine cooling fan cause of body boom. • Incorrectly installed gear-driven camshaft-position-sensor synchronizer assemblies may cause engine surge, loss of power, or MIL to light. **2003**—Transmission may not go into Reverse. **2003–06**—Inoperative AC compressor. **2004**—3.0L engine oil leaks; hard cold start, no-start, and surging. • Hesitation when accelerating. • Wipers won't shut off. • Inoperative rear window defroster. • Accelerator pedal vibration. • Speedometer malfunctions. • Wheel cover and front suspension noise. **2005–06**—Troubleshooting a misfiring engine.

TAURUS PROFILE

	2001	2002	2003	2004	2005	2006
Cost Price ($)						
Taurus LX	24,250	24,550	24,750	24,995	—	—
GL/SE Wagon	26,555	27,285	27,630	28,355	26,345	25,099
Used Values ($)						
Taurus LX ▲	3,000	3,500	3,500	5,000	—	—
Taurus LX ▼	3,000	3,000	3,500	4,000	—	—
GL/SE Wagon ▲	3,500	3,500	4,000	4,500	5,000	7,000
GL/SE Wagon ▼	3,000	3,500	4,000	4,000	4,500	5,500
Reliability	2	2	2	2	2	—
Crash Safety (F)	5	5	4	4	4	—
Side	3	3	3	3	3	—
Offset	5	5	5	5	5	—
Head Restraints (F)	5	2	3	2	2	—
Rear	3	3	—	—	—	—
Rollover Resistance	4	4	4	4	4	—

General Motors

BONNEVILLE, GRAND PRIX, IMPALA, INTRIGUE, LESABRE, LUMINA, MALIBU, MALIBU HYBRID, MONTE CARLO, REGAL ★★★

RATING: Average (2008–09); Below Average (1999–2007). These are the mid-size cars that pushed GM into bankruptcy a few years back: Their blandness, poor fuel economy, non-existent quality control, and mediocre highway performance made the cars so unwanted that even fleet buyers were turning them down. By the time GM began improving the 2008 Malibu and Impala, the company had lost the public's confidence. **Ideal model year:** An upgraded 2008 Malibu 2LT for $13,500 to $15,000. **"Real" city/highway fuel economy:** *Malibu 2.2L automatic: 9.9/6.6 L/100 km. Malibu 3.5L 6-cylinder automatic: 10.4/6.8 L/100 km. LeSabre, Bonneville 3.8L 6-cylinder automatic: 11.9/7.3 L/100 km. Monte Carlo 3.4L 6-cylinder automatic: 11.8/7.1 L/100 km.* Owners report gas consumption isn't as good as the above figures. **Maintenance/repair costs:** Higher than average. **Parts:** Parts are more difficult to find and are more costly because GM's bankruptcy has curtailed inventories for older models everywhere. Fortunately, repairs and parts procurement for the newer front-drive Impala and Malibu aren't as dealer-dependent. **Extended warranty:** Yes, mainly for the engine and automatic transmission. **Best alternatives:** Acura Integra or TSX; Ford Fusion; Honda Civic or Accord (choose the model year carefully and check out the tranny); Hyundai Elantra or Sonata; and a Mazda5 or 6. **Helpful websites:** *www.gminsidenews.com/forums* and *www.topix.com/forum/com/gm.*

Strengths and Weaknesses

The following problems are common to all models and most years: engine oil pan leaks; sudden loss of power steering; harsh shifting, with harsh 1–2 upshifts; poor engine performance and transmission slipping; delayed shifts, slips, flares, or extended shifts in cold weather; poor braking, and frequent replacement of the brake rotor pads; moaning, leaking steering assembly (bad spool and input seals are the likely culprits); and no-start or no-crank conditions caused by a defective ignition and start switch assembly.

Body assembly on all models is notoriously poor, evidenced by premature paint peeling and rusting, squeaks and rattles, wind and road noise, and water leaks:

> Water leaks into the vehicle on the passenger side through the fuse box panel. The failure creates a puddle of water on the passenger floor and also affects the electrical system, especially the window motors.

Accessories are also plagued by problems, with defective door locks, radios, cruise control, alarm systems, and power antennas leading the pack. Premature automatic transmission failures and excessive noise when shifting have been endemic. Engine intake manifold gaskets have a high failure rate and were covered by a 7-year/120,000 km out-of-court settlement in Canada affecting the 1995 through 2004 models equipped with 6-cylinder engines (see *www.merchantlaw.com/classactions/gmmanifoldgasket.php* for the Settlement Administrator's contact information).

GM front-drives

The rear-drive versions of these cars have been off the market for over a decade (but if you can get your hands on an early "classic" one (1984–87), they're highly recommended). The rear-drives were competent and comfortable cars, but they definitely came from a time when handling wasn't a priority and fuel economy was unimportant. Front-drive technology is not GM's proudest achievement.

Phased into the lineup in the '80s, GM front-drives are a different breed of car: less reliable and more expensive to repair than rear-drives, with a considerable number of mechanical (e.g., brake, steering, and suspension component) deficiencies directly related to their front-drive configuration. Nevertheless, acceleration is adequate, fuel economy is good, and handling is better than with their rear-drive cousins—except in emergencies, when their brakes frequently lock up or fail, notwithstanding ABS technology. The Detroit automakers' front-drive designs and manufacturing weaknesses make for unimpressive high-speed performance, a poor reliability record, and expensive maintenance costs. That's why most fleets and police agencies use rear-drives when they can get them, and GM is banking on supplying that clientele with new rear-drive police cars, similar to the old Caprice, sometime in 2012.

GM's medium-sized front-drives aren't particularly driver-friendly. Many models have a dash that's replete with confusing push buttons and gauges that are washed out in sunlight or reflect annoyingly upon the windshield. At other times, there are retro touches, like the Intrigue's dash-mounted ignition, that simply seem out of place. The keyless entry system often fails, the radio's memory is frequently forgetful, and the fuel light comes on when the tank is just below the one-half fuel-level mark. The electronic climate control frequently malfunctions, and owners report that warm air doesn't reach the driver-side heating vents. Servicing, especially for the electronic engine controls, is complicated and expensive, forcing many owners to drive around with their Airbag, Service Engine, and ABS warning lights constantly lit.

Other major problem areas include weak shocks; warping rotors; leaking oil pans; rear brake/wheel lock-ups; excessive front brake pad wear; faulty electronic modules; rack-and-pinion steering failures; seizure of the rear brake calipers; early replacement of the suspension struts; automatic transmission failures and clunking; leaking and malfunctioning AC systems (due mainly to defective AC modules); and myriad electrical failures requiring replacement of the computer module.

The high-performance 3.4L V6, available since 1991, gives out plenty of power, but only at high engine speeds. Overall, the 3.8L V6 is a more suitable compromise. One major powertrain problem found in 1995–2008 models carrying 3.1L, 3.4L, 3.5L, 3.8L, and 3.9L V6 engines is head gasket leaks caused by cracking plastic intake manifolds.

Other deficiencies: Lots of road and wind noise comes through the side windows, thanks to the inadequately soundproofed chassis. Seating isn't very comfortable because of the lack of support caused by low-density foam and knees-in-your-face low seats combined with the ramrod-straight rear backrest. The ride is acceptable with a light load, but when fully loaded, the car's back end sags and the ride deteriorates.

On the one hand, 2002–05 models do have a comfortable ride; a nice array of standard features; an easily accessed, roomy interior; and a good choice of powertrains that includes a supercharged 3.8L engine. But on the minus side, they continue to have bland styling, noisy engines at high speeds, rear seating that's uncomfortable for three, and obstructed rear visibility because of a high-tail rear end.

Except for the automatic transmission upgrade, owners report that newer versions still have many of the same shortcomings seen on earlier front-drive models. Body construction is still below par, with loose door panel mouldings, poorly fitted door fabric, misaligned panels, and water accumulation in the backup lights. Other common problems are fuel-pump whistling, frequent stalling, vague steering, premature paint peeling on the hood and trunk, heavy accumulation of hard-to-remove brake dust inside the honeycomb-design wheels, scraped fenders from contact with the front tires when the wheel is turned, and hard starts due to delayed cranking.

The 3.1L engine is still problematic. Engine controls, faulty intake manifold gaskets (a chronic problem affecting the entire model lineup; see "Secret Warranties/Internal Bulletins/Service Tips"), and electronic fuel-injection systems have created many problems for GM owners. The 4-speed automatic transmission shifts erratically and sometimes slams into gear. The front brakes wear quickly, as do the MacPherson struts, shock absorbers, and tie-rod ends. Steering assemblies tend to fail prematurely, the electrical system is temperamental, the sunroof motor is failure-prone, and owners report water leaks from the front windshield. Front-end squeaks may require the replacement of the exhaust manifold pipe springs with dampers.

VEHICLE HISTORY: *Bonneville:* **2000**—Restyled similarly to the Buick LeSabre, with a larger wheelbase and longer platform but less headroom. Also new this year: standard front seat side-impact airbags, four-wheel disc ABS, a tire-inflation monitor, and an anti-skid system (SSEi). **2001**—SLE is given standard traction control. **2004**—A 275 hp V8 arrives; the 240 hp V6 is dropped. *Malibu:* **2004**—Completely redesigned. The sedan uses Saab's 9-3 platform and a base 145 hp 4-cylinder engine (a 200 hp V6 comes with the LS and LT) hooked to a 4-speed automatic transmission. A Maxx hatchback uses the same powertrain but adds a sliding rear seat with a reclining seatback, a cargo cover that transforms into a tailgate table, a glass skylight, four-wheel disc brakes, and head-protecting side curtain airbags. **2008**—The smaller of Chevy's two midsize sedans, the 2008 Malibu was redesigned with new styling, more available power, and added safety features, like an anti-skid system. A gas/electric Hybrid makes its appearance. A standard 169 hp 2.4L 4-cylinder engine teams with a 4-speed automatic transmission on the entry-level models, though a 6-speed automatic comes with the LTZ Four. Optional on the LT and standard on the LTZ is a 252 hp 3.6L V6 that also teams with the 6-speed automatic. **2009**—Power-adjusted pedals are dropped. *Impala:* **2004**—An SS model equipped with a 240 hp supercharged V6. **2007**—A 3.9L V6 with a tire-pressure monitor and GM's Active Fuel Management, which deactivates some cylinders to save fuel. Both features are surefire extra maintenance items as the Impala ages. **2008**—Engine tweaked to run on E85 ethanol-blended fuel. *Monte Carlo:* **2001**—Standard OnStar, traction control, driver-side airbag, and emergency inside trunk release. **2004**—A supercharged 3.8L SS. *Impala, Monte Carlo:* **2006**—Chevrolet updates its largest sedan and Monte Carlo coupe with new engines, upgraded suspensions, and revised exterior styling. The 3.5 models come with a 211 hp 3.5L V6 (an increase of 30 hp); LTZ sedans carry a 242 hp 3.9L V6; and Chevrolet SS models are equipped with a potent 303 hp V8 with Displacement on Demand, which cuts off four cylinders under light throttle conditions to save fuel. Supercharged models are dropped. All come with a 4-speed automatic transmission. Except for the SS, all models use bench seats for six-passenger capacity. The SS comes with front bucket seats only. Head-protecting side curtain airbags are standard in Impalas but unavailable in the Monte Carlo.

1995–2005 Impala, Lumina, and Monte Carlo

These models are popular two- and four-door versions of Chevy's "large" mid-sized cars, featuring standard dual airbags, ABS, and 160 hp V6 power. Powertrain enhancements have increased horsepower and fuel efficiency. A 3.1L V6 is the base engine, a standard 3.4L 210 hp V6 powers the coupe and is optional with the LS Lumina, and a 3.8L V6 equips the more upscale versions. The 2004 SS comes with a supercharged 3.8L engine that's hard to service and keep in parts.

1997–2003 Malibu

This front-drive medium-sized sedan is a boringly styled car that uses a rigid body structure to cut down on noise and improve handling. Standard mechanicals include a 2.4L twin-cam 4-cylinder engine and an optional 3.1L V6. The Malibu offers plenty of passenger and luggage space. Although headroom is tight, it can carry three rear passengers and gives much more legroom than either the Cavalier or Lumina.

Here are other points to consider: The base 4-cylinder is loud, handling isn't on par with the Japanese competition, there's lots of body lean in turns, outside mirrors are too small, there's no traction control, and the ignition switch is mounted on the dash (a throwback to your dad's Oldsmobile).

Malibu was redesigned for the 2004 model year, adding a companion hatchback body style and new features that include remote control engine starting and a rear seat that slides seven inches fore and aft. Its new platform houses a 145 hp 4-cylinder engine, while the LS and LT sedans carry a 200 hp V6. The hatchback Maxx has a 6-inch-longer wheelbase and a bit shorter body. All of these design changes failed to improve the car's overall reliability.

1998–2002 Intrigue

Strikingly similar to the Alero, the Oldsmobile Intrigue was GM's replacement for the Cutlass Supreme and represents the most refined iteration of the front-drive platform once shared by the Century, Grand Prix, Lumina, and Regal. It's more luxurious than the Lumina and performs as well as the Accord, Camry, or Maxima. Its rigid chassis has fewer shakes and rattles than with GM's other models, and its 3.8L engine provides lots of low-end grunt but lacks the top-end power that makes the Japanese competition so much fun to toss around. The '99 versions got a torquier 3.5L V6 coupled with standard traction control. This engine's a bit more refined, but it's still not smooth, and the automatic transmission still struggles to get past its first two gears. The 2001 models dropped standard traction control and added automatic headlights.

2004–09 Impala and Malibu

Impalas and Malibus perform quite similarly and share most of the same performance and quality problems. However, the Impala's poor suspension geometry and rear misalignment in the factory chews up tires and makes the vehicle difficult to control on slick highways:

> I made a left turn after being stopped at a stop light going approximately 5–10 mph [8–16 km/h] and back end continued the turn and car spun 180 degrees. Went to an Internet discussion board and noticed I'm not the only driver experiencing problem.

Two vehicles were sold as Malibus: the "old" Malibu (N-body) that was renamed the Classic, and the redesigned (Z-body) Malibu. The latter Malibu's engine feels underpowered for highway cruising, with constant shifting by a not-so-frugal 4-speed automatic transmission that slips and bangs into gear. The ride is a bit firm and seating in the rear is knees-to-chin.

In addition to the generic front-drive problems listed previously, owners also report the following deficiencies with some of the latest Impalas and Malibus: side window whistling; failure-prone transmissions; unpredictable steering; annoyingly loud brake squeal; poor headlight illumination; excessive vibration at any speed; sensors failing throughout the vehicle; fuel-injector deposits that cause chronic stalling, poor idling, or hard starts; early wearout of the tires, brakes, alternator, steering assembly, and tire-pressure sensor; premature suspension strut failures (vehicle bottoms out with four or more passengers aboard); and early failures of the exhaust and intake manifold gaskets, now afflicting the 2006 through 2008 models equipped with 3.5L and 3.9L V6 engines.

Malibu Hybrid

The Malibu Hybrid arrived as a 2008 model and uses a 2.4L 4-cylinder gas engine with an electric motor/generator. The four-banger is mated to a 4-speed automatic. It is classified as a "mild" hybrid because it can't run solely on its battery. Despite its complexity, there have been few owner complaints targeting the hybrid models. The biggest disappointment so far is that the car's gas consumption is far higher than the figures touted by Environment Canada and GM (8.5/6.2 L/100 km). *CanadianDriver.com* tested the Hybrid and found it burned an average of 11.0 L/100 km.

Other complaints posted relate to generic Malibu problems: premature brake wear, transmission breakdowns, and electrical shorts.

Safety Summary

All models/years: Airbag fails to deploy. • Sudden engine failure or overheating (faulty intake manifold). • Vehicle suddenly accelerates or stalls in traffic. •

Frequent loss of braking, and premature rotor warpage and pad wearout. • Vehicle rolls downhill when parked on an incline. • Many incidents of total loss of steering or power steering. • Dash reflection in the windshield obstructs view. • Automatic trunk lid flies up and falls down on one's head. • Improper headlight illumination. • Horn is difficult to activate because of the hand pressure required. **All models: 2003**—Fire ignites when defogger activated. • Fire erupts in the rear deck speaker. • Shifter can be moved without key in the ignition or brakes applied. *Impala:* **2003**—Frequent complaints of dash area and engine compartment fires. • Front harness wires overheat; excessive current load from fuel pump may burn the ignition block wire terminal; inhalation injuries caused by the melting of the wiring harness plastic. • Electrically heated seat burns the driver's back. • The connection that goes to the brake pedal piston collapses, causing total brake failure. • When traction control is activated, wheel slip computer is also activated, and security system kills the engine and prevents it from restarting. • Driver-side wheels fall off. • Steering, ball joint, and lower, left, and right control arm failures. • AC refrigerant leaks into car interior. • In one incident, the driver-seat adjuster failed and the seat suddenly moved backward, causing loss of vehicle control. • Design of the rubber seal on the windows allows road salt to enter and short-circuit the window mechanism. • Front driver-side windshield wiper doesn't clean the windshield completely; poor design allows dirty windshield washer fluid to be deflected off the windshield and cuts the view from the side windows. **2004**—Crankshaft position sensor failures cause vehicle to stall and not restart. • Vehicle can be shifted out of Park without applying the brakes. • Vehicle hydroplanes easily, wanders all over the road, and jerks to one side when braking. • Steering wheel suddenly jerks to one side and resists driver's pull in the other direction. • Unreliable steering assembly. • Lights dim when power windows are raised or lowered. • Poorly designed daytime running lights blind oncoming drivers. • Fuel-tank failures. **2005**—Inadvertent airbag deployment:

> A 2005 Chevy Impala police car was traveling on a gravel road in rural Ogle County, Illinois, when both front air bags deployed, the car never made contact with anything, there are at least 30 pictures of the car and the roadway. Since the 30th I personally have called General Motors about my concerns involving the rest of my 2005 squad cars, I've called every day since the 30th, with no response.

• Fuel-pressure regulator may leak fuel. • Intermediate steering shaft is a sealed unit, yet requires frequent lubrication. • Steering-pump failure. • The transmission fails to hold the vehicle in Park or in Reverse on an incline. • Car can be shifted into any gear without depressing the brake pedal. • ABS failure. • Frequent traction-control system failures. • Automatic window could easily kill a child:

> The way that the window switch is designed it can easily shut on a child's body or body part.... When the consumer's son leaned his head out the window, his elbow hit the switch, and the window began to go up. The consumer suggested that a different type of switch be installed, the type that one would have to pull in order to close the window.

• Inadequate headlight illumination. • AC blower seizes, causing an electrical fire. *Impala, Malibu:* **2006**—Seat belts fray and tear under normal use. • Frequent water-pump and power-steering-hose failures. • Steering freezes while cruising:

> The power steering mechanism was replaced with a newly designed system. The mechanic informed me that this was the 6th replacement of such a device for the Impala.

• Early tie-rod replacements. • Doors unlock or lock on their own. • Car cannot be shut off. • Melted wiring harness. • Tire side walls blow out. **2007**—In one incident, airbags didn't deploy in a collision, despite OnStar being alerted that they had deployed. • One driver's seatback collapsed twice. • Automatic transmission slips, then bangs into gear. • In cold weather, shifter sticks in Park. • Brake rotors and pads wear out prematurely, and vehicle shakes excessively when braking. • Parking brake doesn't hold in Reverse or when parked on a slight incline. • Broken exterior door handle. • Faulty tire-pressure sensors ($600). • Original-equipment tire failures (Goodyear Eagle F1), and early wear on the inner sides of the rear tires:

> Talked to dealers. They said it was not a reported problem. Found out later that was BS. It's a suspension problem. So much so there is an aftermarket kit to correct the problem. I had to take car to tire dealer where they corrected problem. Reported problem to GM and got more BS.
>
> •
>
> I am now buying the third set of rear tires in less than a year. The inside tread wears down to the wires every 13–16,000 miles [21,000–26,000 km]. The VIN on my car falls within the VINs listed on GM TSB 8032, however this car is not a police car. GM states that I must be hitting a pothole causing alignment problems. I must be hitting the same pothole at the same mileage all three times and it only affects the rear tires.

• Intermediate steering shaft failures and steering lockups are quite common. • Tire pressure monitoring system gives incorrect readings. • Headlights and instruments lights intermittently dim or go out completely (see TSB #07-08-42-008). **2008**—Airbag alert light stays on for no reason. • Engine lags and lurches. • Automatic transmission line failure. • All seat belts fail to tension properly when vehicle stops abruptly. • When vehicle is shut off, it continues running. • Squirrely steering is still a problem due to the car's poor tracking. • Excessive tire wear (back tires first, then front tires) due to all four wheels being constantly out of alignment. • Steering shake. • Steering may freeze in cold weather. • Steering wheel jerks to the side. • Brake rotor warpage. • Remote starter won't work in cold weather. • Brake master cylinder leak. • Inadequate rear defroster. • Key jams in the ignition. • Water leak under the dashboard. • Sunroof explodes. • Hubcaps snap off the wheels. • Doors lock and unlock on their own; door lock motors burn out:

The door locks on both back doors and the passenger door started malfunctioning a few months ago, and now even the driver door lock is inoperable. I have changed the batteries in the fobs, to no avail. I had OnStar also do the Auto Unlock, but this too is unsuccessful.

2009—Transmission lag and lurch. • Excessive steering shake; sudden loss of steering capability. • Frequent replacement of the steering sway bar components. • Rear wheel bearing failures. • Doors lock and unlock on their own. • Power windows won't operate. • Poorly designed driver's seat causes severe back pain. • Bent wheel rims:

I have lived in the same location for 17 years and have owned or driven 10 different automobiles in that time, never experiencing problems with bent rims. Both the dealer and GM have been told of the problem but they both deny any responsibility for the damaged rims. They say that this a driver problem and bad road conditions in the area where I live.... I have been advised that this problem exists on the Saturn Aura, which is the same basic car as the Malibu. These bent rims cause a severe out of balance condition and can affect the low tire sensors, causing a false reading.

Secret Warranties/Internal Bulletins/Service Tips

All models/years: Reverse servo cover seal leak (transmission). • Keep in mind that some of the following service bulletins may apply to subsequent model years. **All models: 1999–2001**—Troubleshooting engine oil pan leaks. **1999–2004**—Five GM service bulletins confirm a pattern of engine intake manifold gasket defects, which are covered by a 7-year/120,000 km out-of-court settlement (contact information for the Settlement Administrator is available at *www.merchantlaw.com/classactions/gmmanifoldgasket.php*). • TSB #01-08-42-001A covers the causes and remedies for moisture in the headlights. **2001–02**—Poor engine performance and erratic shifting. • Intermittent no-starts. **2001–04**—Erratic shifting, slipping transmission. • Troubleshooting a noisy blower motor. **2001–05**—Harsh 1–2 upshifts. **2001–07**—Correcting a shift shudder during light acceleration. **2003–05**—Remedy for side window binding. **2004–05**—Troubleshooting an inoperative horn. **2004–06**—Assorted steering noises. **2004–10**—Finding the source of a front end clunk, rattle, or knock when turning or passing over bumps. **2005**—AC compressor noise. **2005–06**—Engine knocking, ticking requires replacement of the flexplate and torque converter. **2006–07**—Troubleshooting tips to stop coolant loss and leaks from the 3.5L engine. **2006–08**—Correcting engine coolant loss and leaks, and a rear brake rattle. **2008–09**—Wet carpet on the passenger side. **2008–10**—Automatic transmission refuses to go into gear (see the following page). *Malibu:* **1999–2002**—Troubleshooting tips for plugging water leaks into the trunk and interior. **1999–2003**—Inoperative tail lights due to water intrusion. • Automatic transmission flaring. **2003**—Firm shifts, shudder, or no downshifts. **2004**—Noisy steering column, and lack of steering assist. • Ignition key hard to remove in cold weather. • Instrument panel rattle or buzz. **2004–05**—Steering pop or snap noise when turning. • Hood won't latch in the primary position. • A special lube must be applied to prevent door latches from

---

A/T—NO REVERSE/3RD OR 5TH GEAR

BULLETIN NO.: 09-07-30-012A   **DATE: JANUARY 12, 2010**

NO REVERSE, 3RD OR 5TH, CHECK ENGINE LIGHT ILLUMINATED, DTC P0776 (REPLACE 3-5 REVERSE CLUTCH PLATE (WAVED)

2008–09 Buick Enclave

2008–09 Chevrolet Equinox, Malibu

2009 Chevrolet Traverse

2007–09 GMC Acadia

2007–09 Pontiac G6

2008–09 Pontiac Torrent

2007–09 Saturn Aura, Outlook

2008–09 Saturn VUE

All Equipped with 6T70/75 6-Speed Automatic Transmission (RPOs MH2, MH4, MH6 or MY9)

CONDITION: Some customers may comment about an SES light and/or no reverse and may also comment on a slip/flare or harsh shifts in drive range 3rd and/or 5th gear.

CAUSE: This condition may be caused by a broken 35R clutch wave plate allowing the apply piston to overstroke, causing the piston to leak and causing loss of apply. This normally will not occur before approximately 32,000 km (20,000 mi). Debris generated by the condition can affect the operation of the speed sensors and other clutches.

---

freezing. **2004–06**—Poor instrument panel backlighting. • Inoperative tail/turn lights. **2004–08**—Front-end clunk or rattle when passing over small bumps at low speeds. **2005–07**—Rear brake creak or squeak. *Impala:* **2006–08**—GM bulletin #08-06-04-039, published August 7, 2008, says that if the car cranks but won't start, the likely culprit is a blown fuel pump fuse, which will be replaced under warranty. • Coolant leaks that can cause engine overheating usually require that the engine head gasket be replaced. Again, this is a warranty item that is often covered up to 7 years/160,000 km under "goodwill" warranty extensions:

ENGINE—COOLANT LEAK/COOLANT LOSS

BULLETIN NO.: 08-06-01-012A   **DATE: NOVEMBER 19, 2008**

ENGINE COOLANT LEAK, LOSS OF COOLANT (REPLACE AFFECTED CYLINDER HEAD GASKET)

2006–07 Buick Terraza; 2006–07 Chevrolet Monte Carlo; 2006–08 Chevrolet Impala, Uplander; 2008 Chevrolet Malibu; 2006–08 Pontiac G6, Montana SV6; 2006–08 Saturn Relay; and the 2007–08 Saturn Aura All with a 3.5L or 3.9L engine

CONDITION: Some customers may comment on a coolant leak. The comments may range from spots on the driveway to having to add more coolant. Upon inspection, the technician may find that there is an external coolant leak coming from the top end of either cylinder head.

CORRECTION: If a leak is found to be coming from a cylinder head gasket, the gasket must be replaced. When replacing the gasket be advised that larger flange hex head bolts are now to be used at locations 5 and 8. The larger flange hex bolts are the same as the ones used at the other six locations. When installing the two large flange hex head bolts at locations 5 and 8 a new style lower intake manifold gasket that has provisions to allow for the larger flange bolts must be used. Caution: Failure to use the new lower intake manifold gaskets when installing the larger flange hex head bolts at locations 5 and 8 may result in the lower intake manifold not fitting properly, which may result in a leak condition.

2006–09—Rear suspension creak, clunk, pop noise. • Power-steering noise reduction measures. **2007**—Troubleshooting wind/road noise. **2007–08**— Engine squealing on start-up. • AC won't maintain desired temperature. • Ignition key cannot be removed. • No shift out of Park. • Undercar noises. • Rear speaker rattling. **2008**—Inaccurate fuel gauge readings.

BONNEVILLE, GRAND PRIX, IMPALA, INTRIGUE, LESABRE, LUMINA, MALIBU, MALIBU HYBRID, MONTE CARLO, REGAL PROFILE

	2001	2002	2003	2004	2005	2006	2007	2008	2009
Cost Price ($)									
Bonneville	32,065	32,365	33,430	34,345	35,310	—	—	—	—
Grand Prix	28,110	28,050	28,277	28,125	27,865	25,885	25,595	26,230	—
Impala	24,490	24,875	26,020	26,810	26,405	24,685	25,230	25,695	26,625
Intrigue	28,450	28,365	—						
LeSabre	32,120	32,960	33,720	33,935	34,550	—	—	—	—
Malibu	22,495	22,760	22,980	22,370	22,375	21,995	20,230	22,995	23,395
Malibu Hybrid	—	—	—	—	—	—	—	26,995	28,295
Malibu Maxx	—	—	—	26,320	26,495	25,595	25,930	—	—
Monte Carlo	26,165	26,525	27,620	28,200	27,840	24,685	25,231	—	—
Regal	28,895	29,080	29,980	29,975	—	—	—	—	—
Used Values ($)									
Bonneville ▲	3,000	3,500	4,000	4,500	5,500	—	—	—	—
Bonneville ▼	3,000	3,500	3,500	4,000	4,500	—	—	—	—
Grand Prix ▲	3,000	4,500	5,000	5,500	6,500	8,000	11,000	13,500	—
Grand Prix ▼	2,500	3,500	4,500	5,000	5,500	6,500	9,500	12,000	—
Impala ▲	3,500	4,500	5,500	6,500	7,500	9,000	10,500	13,000	15,500
Impala ▼	3,000	4,000	5,000	5,500	6,500	8,000	9,500	12,000	14,000
Intrigue ▲	2,500	3,000	—	—	—	—	—	—	—
Intrigue ▼	2,000	2,500	—	—	—	—	—	—	—
LeSabre ▲	3,500	4,000	5,000	6,500	7,000	—	—	—	—
LeSabre ▼	3,000	3,500	4,400	5,500	6,500	—	—	—	—
Malibu ▲	3,000	3,500	4,500	5,000	6,500	8,000	9,500	12,000	14,500
Malibu ▼	2,500	3,000	4,000	4,500	5,500	7,000	8,500	10,500	13,000
Malibu Hybrid ▲	—	—	—	—	—	—	—	15,000	18,000
Malibu Hybrid ▼	—	—	—	—	—	—	—	13,500	16,500
Malibu Maxx ▲	—	—	—	4,500	5,500	8,000	9,500	—	—
Malibu Maxx ▼	—	—	—	4,500	5,500	7,000	8,500	—	—
Monte Carlo ▲	3,000	4,000	5,500	6,000	7,000	8,500	10,000	—	—
Monte Carlo ▼	2,500	3,500	5,000	5,500	6,500	7,500	9,000	—	—
Regal ▲	4,000	4,500	5,500	6,500	—	—	—	—	—
Regal ▼	3,500	4,000	5,500	6,000	—	—	—	—	—

Reliability	2	2	2	2	2	2	2	2	2
Crash Safety (F)									
Bonneville 4d	4	4	4	4	—	—	—	—	—
Grand Prix 4d	4	4	4	3	3	5	5	5	—
Impala	5	5	5	5	5	5	5	5	5
LeSabre 4d	4	4	4	4	—	—	—	—	—
Malibu	4	4	4	4	5	5	5	5	5
Monte Carlo	5	—	5	5	5	5	—	—	—
Regal 4d	4	4	4	—	—	—	—	—	—
Side									
Bonneville 4d	4	4	4	4	—	—	—	—	—
Grand Prix	2	2	3	3	3	3	3	3	—
Impala	4	4	4	4	4	5	5	5	5
Intrigue	3	—	—	—	—	—	—	—	—
LeSabre 4d	4	4	5	4	—	—	—	—	—
Malibu	3	3	4	4	5	5	5	5	5
Monte Carlo	3	—	3	3	3	3	—	—	—
Regal 4d	3	3	3	—	—	—	—	—	—
IIHS Side									
Grand Prix	—	—	—	2	2	2	2	2	—
Impala	—	—	—	—	—	5	5	5	5
Malibu 4d	—	—	—	5	5	5	5	5	—
Offset									
Bonneville 4d	5	5	5	5	5	—	—	—	—
Grand Prix 4d	3	3	3	5	5	5	5	5	—
Impala	5	5	5	5	5	3	3	3	3
Intrigue	3	—	—	—	—	—	—	—	—
LeSabre	5	5	5	5	5	—	—	—	—
Malibu	—	—	—	1	1	1	5	5	—
Regal	3	3	3	—	—	—	—	—	—
Head Restraints									
Bonneville	—	1	1	1	—	—	—	—	—
Grand Prix	2	2	2	1	1	1	1	1	—
Intrigue	1	—	—	—	—	—	—	—	—
Impala	1	1	1	1	1	2	2	2	3
LeSabre 4d	—	1	1	1	—	—	—	—	—
Malibu	2	2	1	3	3	3	3	2	2
Malibu Classic	—	1	1	1	—	—	—	—	—
Monte Carlo	2	2	2	—	—	—	—	—	—
Regal 4d	1	1	1	—	—	—	—	—	—
Rollover Resistance									
Bonneville	—	5	5	5	—	—	—	—	—
Grand Prix	—	4	4	4	4	4	4	—	—

All ratings on a numbered scale where 5 is good and **1** is bad. See page 132 for a more detailed description.

Impala	4	4	4	4	4	4	4	—	4
LeSabre	—	—	—	5	—	—	—	—	—
Malibu	—	4	4	4	4	4	4	4	4
Monte Carlo	—	—	4	4	4	4	—	—	—

Honda

ACCORD/ACCORD HYBRID ★ ★ / ★ ★ ★ ★

RATING: *Accord:* Below Average (2008–09; 1999–2006); Average (2007). *Accord Hybrid:* Above Average (2004–07); Average (2003). The Hybrid's first model year production had a larger number of factory-related snafus than later models. It has been off the market for four years, which seriously compromises servicing and parts availability. Thoroughly check the automatic transmission, rear suspension, and brakes on all Accords. The number of safety-related defects on 2008 and 2009 models is many times that of the average for most cars. Most knee-jerk "anything Japanese is good" car guides give the Honda Accord and Toyota Camry equally positive ratings. Not *Lemon-Aid*. We know after looking through reams of confidential service bulletins and owner complaints that for the past decade Toyota has been asleep at the switch and allowed quality to decline in its lineup. Now we are seeing the same low quality in Honda models. Defects aside (and that's asking a lot), the Accord is one of the most driver-friendly, versatile compacts you can find. Think of it as a better-performing Toyota Camry that welcomes driver input and is an all-around good road performer. Nevertheless, *Lemon-Aid* has downgraded the ranking for 2008–09 models because of their many factory-related and redesign glitches. These deficiencies include expensive powertrain failures, sudden acceleration and stalling, loss of brakes, and airbag malfunctions. **"Real" city/highway fuel economy:** *2.4L manual:* 9.4/6.4 L/100 km. *2.4L automatic:* 9.5/6.4 L/100 km. *3.0L 6-speed manual:* 11.4/7.2 L/100 km. *3.0L automatic:* 11.5/7.5 L/100 km. *3.5L V6 6-speed manual:* 12.2/7.8 L/100 km. *3.5L V6 automatic:* 11.0/6.9 L/100 km. *Hybrid:* 8.2/6.1 L/100 km. **Maintenance/repair costs:** Average. Except for the Hybrid, repairs aren't dealer-dependent. Recall repairs have been delayed on some models because corrective parts are often unavailable. **Parts:** Higher-than-average costs, but non-Hybrid parts can be easily found for much less from independent suppliers. **Extended warranty:** Not needed, unless you are buying the Hybrid. **Best alternatives:** Acura CSX, EL, or Integra; Ford Fusion or Mercury Milan; post-2006 Honda Civic; Hyundai Elantra wagon, Sonata, or Tiburon; Kia Rondo; Mazda5 or Mazda6; Nissan Sentra; and 2005 or 2006 Toyota Camry. *Hybrids:* Ford Escape. **Ideal model year:** A 2007 SE V6 costing between $15,000 and $16,000 is your best bet. It has worked out earlier revamping glitches from the 2006 redesign and dodges the new set of problems inherent in the reworked 2008 model. **Helpful websites:** *www. honda-tech.com* and *www.hondaaccordforum.com/forum*.

Strengths and Weaknesses

Fast and nimble even without a V6, this is the mid-sized sedan of choice for drivers who want maximum fuel economy and comfort along with lots of space for grocery hauling and occasional highway cruising. With the optional V6, the Accord is one of the most versatile mid-sized cars you can find.

The gasoline-powered Accord doesn't really excel in any particular area; it's just very, very good at everything. It's smooth, quiet, mannerly, and competent, with acceptable fit and finish inside and out. Other strong points are comfort, ergonomics, and driveability. Like Toyota's lineup, there are powertrain and brake problems, and in recent years (2008–09 models especially) there have been an unusually large number of serious safety-related complaints reported to NHTSA. In this sense, Honda is mirroring Toyota's quality decline, although Honda's hasn't been as steep, and unlike Toyota's, consists almost entirely of automatic transmission and suspension/alignment failures.

Accord Hybrid

After successfully launching its 2003 Civic Hybrid, Honda introduced the 2005 Accord Hybrid. Equipped with a 255 hp V6 engine, the Hybrid is assisted as needed by an electric motor and a 5-speed automatic transmission. An innovative Variable Cylinder Management System automatically deactivates three cylinders when cruising or on deceleration. Like the Civic Hybrid, the Accord Hybrid can't be driven on electricity alone.

The primary complaint of Hybrid owners is that the vehicle gets nowhere near the advertised gas mileage; owners say it's about 30 percent worse than promised. Other Hybrid-specific complaints involve electrical short circuits and premature brake wear. Overall, though, there are proportionately fewer complaints from Accord Hybrid owners than from Toyota Prius and GM Malibu Hybrid owners, and the complaints are less serious in nature. Nevertheless, due to slow Hybrid sales, 2007 was the car's last model year.

VEHICLE HISTORY: 2001—A restyled exterior, dual side airbags, V6 traction control, and improved soundproofing. **2003**—This larger, totally restyled model offers a V6 and 6-speed manual tranny combo, and increased 4-cylinder and V6 horsepower (160 and 240 hp, respectively) with better fuel economy. **2004**—V6 models add traction control. Head-protecting side curtain airbags are standard on EX V6 models. **2005**—Honda introduces the Hybrid sedan and standard side curtain-type airbags, along with front torso airbags and better interior soundproofing. **2006**—Revised front and rear styling. **2008**—More power and passenger space; no more Hybrid. Two engines are offered: A 2.4 L four with 177–190 horsepower, and a 3.5-L V6 that is rated at 268 horsepower. The V6 uses Honda's Variable Cylinder Management while cruising to conserve fuel. A standard four-cylinder engine hooked to a 5-speed manual or a 5-speed automatic transmission powers all models, though EX and EX-L sedans also provided a V6 coupled to either a 5-speed automatic or a 6-speed manual tranny. Standard safety features included antilock brakes, traction control, an antiskid system, curtain side airbags, and front side airbags. **2009**—The Accord's 2008 redesign sent safety complaints skyrocketing for both the 2008 and 2009 models. Apparently, Honda had trouble fixing its redesign glitches in a timely manner.

Owners of 2001 and 2002 models report that sudden, unintended acceleration remains a serious problem and can occur at any time. Other performance related problems include automatic transmission breakdowns, expensive and frequent servicing of the brake rotors and pads, and electrical glitches.

The 2003 redesign manifested a continued decline in quality through the 2006 model year, resulting in the Accord losing its Recommended rating for all those years. Honda promised us better-performing, more durable transmissions in its redesigned 2003 models, but the company lied, and then later reluctantly extended the warranty up to eight years. Furthermore, some 2003–06 model year Accord owners say their cars have similar problems but haven't been included in the extended "goodwiil" warranty program; others complain that the corrective repairs haven't fixed the tranny problems and that they were forced to pay a high deductible, which should be Honda's responsibility.

Other problems related to the 2003 and later models' redesign: roof buckling; defective paint; frequent hard starts; warped brake rotors; erratic transmission shifts; a steering-column ticking; a defective CD changer; coolant in the engine oil pan; windshield creaks in cold, dry weather; brake shuddering, grinding, and squealing; a moonroof that doesn't close all the way; a popping noise heard when accelerating; wrinkled, bubbling door window moulding; doors closing on occupants as they leave the vehicle; an AC condenser that's easily punctured by road debris; stereo speaker hum or popping and frequent speaker blowouts; passenger-side seat heater coming on by itself and overheating; non-stop rattles, squeaks, and vibrations in door panels, tops of windows, and rear shelves, and in the B-pillars around the top seat belt anchor; engine-oil leaks onto the manual transmission clutch, causing shifting slippage (the problem is caused by a low vent valve on the 6-speed tranny); and the rear headliner becoming unglued and sagging, causing water to leak into the cabin and trunk (the carpeting and rear seat are saturated after moderate rainstorms).

The increase in engine, transmission, and brake failures is worrisome. To its credit, Honda puts a "goodwill" clause in almost all of its service bulletins, allowing service managers to submit any claim to the company long after the original warranty period has elapsed. Powertrain and brake repairs have often been covered by these secret warranties—after a little verbal jousting.

The Accord's 2008 redesign, carried over in 2009, has also sent safety complaints skyrocketing. Just one example: Owners report that the car's faulty suspension/ steering geometry makes the vehicle dangerously unstable and chews up rear tires, accounting for a sixfold increase in NHTSA complaints for those model years.

All models/years: Sudden acceleration, stalling. • Automatic transmission failures:

> Independent mechanic says Honda transmissions are poorly designed in that first the filter is hard to get to and that there is a very small hole for fluid to flow through and that once clogged with no fluid the transmission fails. Now he's rebuilding it and our supposed trusty Honda is going to cost us $2400.

• Airbags fail to deploy, or deploy for no reason. • Check Engine light is always on. • AC failure due to a punctured condenser. • Premature front/rear brake wear. **All models: 2001**—Excessive front-end vibration and wandering over the highway. • Automatic transmission leaks and jerks into gear. • Rear stabilizer bar links break. • Vehicle rolls back when stopped on an incline. • Complete brake loss. • Incorrect fuel gauge readings. **2002**—Seat belt won't retract, or continually tightens; in one incident, child had to be cut free. • Child safety seat can't be installed because buckle latch is located too far into the seat. • Partial brake failure; brakes fail to catch at first, then suddenly grab. • Vehicle pulls sharply when braking. • Trunk lid may suddenly fall. **2003**—Axle suddenly snaps. • Severe pulling to the right. • Power-steering groan believed to be caused by the steering pump. • Console overheats and smells burnt. • Keys overheat in the ignition. • Complete brake failure. • ABS and Traction Control lights stay lit, and corrective parts aren't easily found. • Rear vision is obstructed by head restraints, high rear deck, and roof pillar. **2004**—Higher than average number of safety-related incidents registered (487). Faulty airbags, brake, and automatic transmission failures lead the complaint list. • Several reports of fires igniting in the insulation material. • One report of fire igniting behind the right front tire while vehicle was underway. • Brake light bulb drops down into the trunk area and burns through luggage. • Axle collapses while vehicle is underway. • Vehicle accelerates when brakes are applied. • Engine surges when gears are shifted. • Complete brake failure; Brake Alert light is constantly lit. • In one incident, brakes were applied, car jerked to the side, there was total loss of braking (other complainants say the brakes lock up), and the Accord hit a guardrail. • Steering suddenly locks up. • Seat belt failed to retract in a rear-end collision; several complaints allege the front seat belts failed to restrain occupants in frontal collisions. • Passenger-side mirror slipped off; another one "exploded." • Steering pulls to one side while driving. • Side window shatters after morning moisture is wiped off. • Side airbag sensor won't warn you if passengers are improperly seated. • If you put your purse on the front passenger-side seat, the airbag is disabled. The same thing occurred when a driver's 90-pound daughter sat in the same seat. • Driver's seat moves forward on its own. • Carbon monoxide fumes invade the passenger compartment. • Defogger causes condensation on inside windshield, which then freezes. **2005**—Automatic transmission regularly slips out of gear and sometimes violently downshifts to Second. • Passenger-seat Airbag warning light came on even though seat was unoccupied. • Right front wheel comes apart. • Cracks in the steering wheel just above the airbag. • Power-steering pump failures. • Intermittent power-steering failure. • Honda's jack is a knuckle-buster that won't hold the car. • Shifter slips by

Drive mode into D3, or sticks in Second gear. • Inoperative inside door handles trap occupants. **2006**—Less than average number of complaints posted (143). • Car will roll away in Park, unless emergency brake is set. Brake failures, noise, and premature wearout. • Ignition key can be removed while vehicle is in gear. • Sharp door handles can cut occupants' hands. **2007**—Fewer than average safety-related defects reported (164). • Driver-side seat catches fire. • When accelerating, engine hesitates and then surges; sudden acceleration when vehicle is in Park:

> While parking my car in my garage, I had put it in Park and took my foot off the brake pedal, my 2007 Honda Accord sedan lunged forward hitting my drywall, solar water heater, washer and dryer, then it jumped back and stopped. I was so stunned as I didn't know what was happening here. Instantly the car decided to go in Reverse at an accelerated rate down the hill of my driveway hitting the concrete side of my neighbor's garage, their car, and bounced forward up the hill to hit my house again and stopped at the crest of the hill.

• Manual transmission pops out of Third gear, or grinds when going into Third gear. • Vehicle vibrates so badly that hands on the steering wheel go numb. • Rear brake pad pins become so rusted they won't let the brake pads release. • The dash lights are illuminated and the daytime running lights are lit, but the headlights aren't automatically activated, as with most cars. • Dash lights and headlights flicker when the AC compressor cycles; compressor is also easily damaged by pebbles on the highway, due to Honda's poor design. Honda says it's an insurance issue, but no—it's Honda's responsibility. • Intermittent failure of the power door locks, especially when it rains. • Serious blind spots due to the design of the front windshield pillars. • Horn may not sound in cold weather. • Michelin tires bubble on the side wall (a frequent complaint over many model years). • Check Gas Cap warning will light if cap isn't tightened with three clicks. • LED tail lights are nausea-inducing for drivers behind you. **2008**—More than 815 safety-related incidents have been reported to the U.S. government; 150 complaints would have been the norm over a three-year span. Most of these problems relate to sudden, unintended acceleration and brake failures. Other brake issues are brake squeaking, screeching, and grinding and the uneven and premature wearout of brake pads, calipers, and rotors:

> It is my understanding that for 2008 and 2009, Honda went to smaller rear pads and rotors and that's why they wear out so fast.... I looked at one web site, *carcomplaints.com*, and there are 517 complaints regarding premature brake wear for 2008 and 2009 Honda Accords, with a severity rating of 7.8 out of 10. Also car magazine *Motor Trend* had the same problem: *www.motortrend.com/roadtests/oneyear/112_0910_2008_honda_accord_test_verdict/index.html*.

•

> Over 1100 complaints about this car on *Beef.com* are we going to wait for something terrible to happen before this is addressed? Dealer repaired 2 times at my expense. Honda is aware of this issue but will not correct permanently.

• Poorly designed head restraints results in painful "chin-to-chest" driving. • Lights dim or flicker; owner afraid of road rage retaliation. • Clearcoat used by Honda on its wheel rims causes the rims to corrode prematurely. • Door locks won't open when key fob is activated. • Defective rear door handles; doors can be opened only from the outside. **2009**—NHTSA has posted 246 safety failures similar to those listed for the 2008 model Accords (50 would have been normal in a single year). A large part of these complaints concern faulty airbags, front and rear brake failures (premature pad, caliper, and rotor wear), and uncomfortable head restraints:

> The feature to move the headrest forward in the event of a rear-end collision puts the upper-back region of the seat too far forward, creating a very uncomfortable region with little lower-back support. I find that my lower-back aches after an hour of driving, and needed to lean up against the steering wheel while driving to relieve the pain. I believe this is unsafe if the airbag deployed. I have resorted to putting a bolster pillow in the lumbar region but this again places me too close to the airbag, on the edge of the sat, and no more seat adjustment is possible. I have seen these comments on-line as well, and some have been cutting into the seats to disable the headrest feature.

• Engine surging; sudden acceleration. • In one incident, side airbag deployed five minutes after driver shut the door. • Broken axle. • Headlights dim or blink intermittently. • AC blows hot air. • AC condenser damaged by road debris. • Seat wobbles back and forth. • Head restraint blocks rear view. • Sunroof glass was sucked out of the car during highway cruising. • Defective lock/unlock remote control. • Michelin Pilot tire side wall blistering. Tire pressure sensor gives false alerts. *Hybrid:* **2005**—Transmission failure ($4,000 U.S.). • Defective motor mount. • Defective speedometer. • Instead of a spare tire, owners are given a can of sealant that won't work if the puncture is located outside the tread. **2006**—Car accelerates when brakes are applied. • Long hesitation when accelerating invites a rear-end accident. • Brake failure. • Engine MIL and other instrument panel warning lights come on for no reason. **2007**—Only one reported safety-related failure. • Much like the Toyota Prius, Accord Hybrid brakes fail after passing over a bump:

> Brakes have failed to stop car when I've gone over a bump—they vibrate and make noise, but do not stop the car. This has led to near accidents four times since I bought the car new over three years ago. A similar problem has occurred when brakes are wet and I'm trying to stop at low speed.

Secret Warranties/Internal Bulletins/Service Tips

All models/years: Accord service bulletins may also apply to the Hybrid. • Troubleshooting tips for vehicles that pull sharply to one side. **All models: 1999–2004**—V6 engine oil leaks (an extension of a problem first noticed on 1994–97 models). **1999–2006**—Vehicles with broken rear stabilizer links are eligible for a free replacement under a Honda "goodwill" program. • Repair tips applicable to vehicles that pull/drift to one side. **2003**—"Goodwill" campaigns to replace automatic transmissions and multiplex integrated control units that regulate door locks, trunk alarm, etc. • Corrective action for coolant leakage into the engine oil pan; oil leaks at the cylinder head cover. • A faulty air-intake air-breather pipe hose may cause the Engine warning light to remain lit. • An automatic transmission that won't go into Reverse is eligible for a free correction under a Honda "goodwill" campaign (TSB #03-042). • Automatic transmission leaks on the cooler lines. • Troubleshooting calipers, rotors, and pads, following complaints of excessive brake vibration. • Troubleshooting ABS light illumination. • Inaccurate gauges. • Doors don't unlock in cold weather. • Dash or pillar creaking or clicking. • Roof moulding channel leaks water; roof water leak fix. **2003–04**—If the brake pedal is stiff, a new booster vacuum hose may be required. • Loose steering or clunky steering response. **2003–05**—Low Fuel warning is activated even though fuel tank is a quarter full. **2003–06**—Guidelines for fixing dashboard/A-pillar creaks and clicks. **2003–07**—Drivetrain ping, rattle, squeal when accelerating. • Brake pedal is low and feels soft. **2003–08**—The 6-speed manual transmission grinds when shifted into Third gear, pops out of Third gear, or is hard to shift into Third gear. **2003–09**—Power-steering moan/whine. **2004**—Excessive engine vibration in idle. • Noisy steering. • No-starts and faulty power windows. • Door rattles. • Wheel bearing humming or growling. **2005–10**—Silencing a chirp coming from the engine timing belt area. **2007**—A fix for the manual transmission grinding or popping out of Third gear (TSB #08-020, dated 07/18/08). • Inadequate AC cooling. • Noisy rear window regulator. **2008**—The tire pressure warning system may give invalid warnings. • Engine rattles on cold start-up. • Blower motor noisy or inoperative. • Carpet on the passenger's side pulls out from under the door sill trim. • If an owner reports a front brake squeal or judder, Honda will refinish the front brake discs and install new brake pads under a "goodwill" warranty, says Honda Service Bulletin #09-096, published December 24, 2009. **2008–09**—Troubleshooting an engine whining noise and a steering clicking. • Fix for an engine that ticks or knocks at idle. **2008–10**—Honda extends its brake repair up to the 2010 models and states the normal warranty applies. However, take a close look at the bulletin below where it says "Failed Part" and "Defect Code." This admission of a part failure or of a "defect" gives rise to Honda's liability beyond its normal warranty limitations under the legal *implied* warranty. That's the case to make in small claims court, should Honda be silly enough to reject your claim:

BRAKES—FRONT BRAKES SQUEAL/JUDDER

BULLETIN NO.: 09-096	DATE: MAY 28, 2010

2008–10 Accord

SYMPTOM: When the brakes are applied normally, the driver feels a juddering vibration through the steering wheel or brake pedal, and/or hears a squealing noise.

THE NORMAL WARRANTY APPLIES: Operation Number: 410820; Flat Rate Time: 0.9 hour; Failed Part: P/N 45022-SEA-J11; Defect Code: 00504; Symptom Code: 03503.

Hybrid: **2006–07**—Hybrids that lose power when accelerating need three different software updates. This will be done under a "goodwill" warranty at no charge to the customer, says Honda Service Bulletin #09-058, published July 30, 2009. • Correcting a popping noise, similar to a backfire, heard when accelerating.

ACCORD, ACCORD HYBRID PROFILE

	2001	2002	2003	2004	2005	2006	2007	2008	2009
Cost Price ($)									
LX/SE sedan	22,800	23,000	25,000	25,100	25,500	26,301	26,501	25,090	25,090
EXi/EX V6	30,800	31,100	32,500	32,900	33,600	34,100	34,90	31,690	31,690
Hybrid	—	—	—	—	36,990	38,900	38,100	—	—
Used Values ($)									
LX/SE sedan ▲	4,000	5,000	6,000	7,500	9,500	11,500	14,500	17,000	19,000
LX/SE sedan ▼	3,500	4,500	5,500	6,000	8,000	10,500	13,000	15,500	17,500
EXi/EX V6 ▲	6,000	7,000	8,500	10,000	11,500	14,000	17,000	20,000	23,500
CXi/CX V6 ▼	5,000	6,500	7,500	8,500	10,000	12,500	16,000	18,500	22,000
Hybrid ▲	—	—	—	—	11,500	13,000	17,000	—	—
Hybrid ▼	—	—	—	—	10,000	11,500	25,500	—	—
Reliability	3	3	3	3	3	3	4	2	2
Crash Safety (F)									
4d									
Side (2d)	4	4		4	4	4	4	4	
4d	4	4			4	4	4	3	3
IIHS Side	—	—	**1**	**1**					
Offset	3	3							
Head Restraints (2d)	—	—	**1**	**1**	**1**	**1**	**1**		
Roof Strength	—	—	—	—	—	—	—	3	3
Rollover Resistance	5	5	4	4	4	4	4	5	5

Note: The Accord's relatively rapid rate of depreciation is similar to that of the Civic Hybrid and Toyota Prius. Although some head restraints offer good crash protection, their poor design results in painful "chin-to-chest" driving.

Hyundai

SONATA ★★★★★

RATING: Recommended (2009); Above Average (2006–08); Average (1999–2005). Recent iterations of the Sonata haven't registered one-half the number of safety complaints of the highly rated Honda Accord or Toyota Camry. On the other hand, Sonata's crashworthiness ratings aren't impressive for some model years. For maximum savings and crash safety, I suggest you buy a 2007 version, keep it at least five years to amortize the depreciation, and put some of the savings on the purchase price into a comprehensive supplementary warranty to protect yourself when the warranty ends. **Ideal model year:** Shop around for a 2009 V6 version to get the newest safety, comfort, and performance features. A 2009 GL V6 will cost about $16,500 (original price: $27,795). If you want the cheaper, earlier upgraded models, look for a base 2007 Sonata for $9,000 to $10,500. By purchasing the 2007 version, you are avoiding many of the glitches found in the

2006's first year redesign and saving about $4,500 over a newer, 2009 model. **"Real" city/highway fuel economy:** *2.4 automatic: 10.9/7.2 L/100 km. 2.7 6-cylinder automatic: 12.3/7.9 L/100 km. 3.5 6-cylinder automatic: 13.9/8.4 L/100 km.* Owners report fuel savings may undershoot these estimates by at least 10 percent, or up to 20 percent with the 3.5L engine. **Maintenance/repair costs:** Higher than average. Repairs aren't dealer-dependent. **Parts:** Average part costs; most parts are quickly found. **Extended warranty:** An extended transmission warranty is a smart buy. **Best alternatives:** Acura Integra, Honda Accord, Hyundai Elantra wagon, or the Mazda6 or 626. **Helpful websites:** *www.hyundai-forums.com* and *www.hyundai-forums.com/f70-4g-2006-sonata.htm.*

Strengths and Weaknesses

This mid-sized front-drive sedan went from bad to good in an incredibly short period. Could it be just a coincidence that major Hyundai quality improvements were initiated almost a decade ago, once Hyundai hired away a gang of Toyota's top quality-control engineers? Apparently, the pirated employees brought with them a bushel basket of internal quality reports that listed prominently Toyota's sudden acceleration, brake loss, lag and lurch powertrain, and truck corrosion issues. It's a moot point now. The papers were returned to Toyota's lawyers several years ago, following threats of legal action. Hyundai assured Toyota the documents went unread (wink, wink; nudge, nudge).

Corporate intrigue aside, the Sonata is a decent performer in most areas, with some notable exceptions, like the brakes, fuel system, and fit and finish. Acceleration is impressive with the manual gearbox and passable with the automatic, if equipped with the 6-cylinder engine. Handling and performance are also fairly good, although emergency handling isn't confidence-inspiring, particularly because of the imprecise steering and excessive lean when cornering. As with early Hyundai models, reports for 2006–08 models continue to note the erratically shifting automatic transmission, the jamming manual tranny clutches, and endemic brake loss and premature wear.

VEHICLE HISTORY: 2002—GL is given four-wheel disc brakes. **2003**—Standard front side airbags. **2006**—A major redesign gives the Sonata new looks, more passenger room (especially rear-seat legroom), additional trunk space, and more power. The new 162 hp 2.4L 4-cylinder adds 24 more horses, while the 235 hp 2.7L V6 puts out 65 more horses. Traction and stability control, anti-lock four-wheel disc brakes, front side airbags, and head-protecting side curtain airbags are standard features. **2009**—Retuned suspension, redesigned interior, and a restyled exterior. The 4-cylinder gained 13 hp to 175, while the V6 added 15 hp to 249. Previous to 2009, 4-cylinder models also got the smoother-performing 5-speed automatic transmission used by the V6 models.

Throughout the Sonata's history, Hyundai's technical service bulletins have been replete with references to automatic transmissions that exhibit what Hyundai describes as "shift shock" as well as delayed shifting.

The 2006 through 2009 Sonatas have elicited very few quality-control and safety complaints, and represent the best buys. Nevertheless, airbags, steering, sun visors, suspension struts, power door locks, brakes (rotors and pads), automatic transmissions, and fuel- and electrical-system components still top the list of parts most vulnerable to premature failure or malfunctioning. Highway performance for some owners has also come under serious criticism:

> Bad pull to the left, replaced front strut. Assorted spring noises while driving. Tires feathering. No stability while driving; any kind of bumps mean you are wandering all over the road. Shimmy in steering wheel. With two passengers in the back seat the car lifts up in front and stability while driving is even worse. This has been occurring since it was new. Easy to lose control of vehicle, dealership acknowledges all tires feathering but say they cant fix it.

Fit and finish continue to be problematic. Interestingly, some of these problems, like disabled passenger-side airbags, short circuits, premature brake wear, and inadequate headlight illumination, have apparently been carried over to a lesser extent to the 2009 model year, according to NHTSA owner complaint records.

Safety Summary

All years: Airbags don't deploy when they should, or deploy when they shouldn't. • Frequent automatic transmission failures. • Poor design of the car's anti-fogging feature:

> Sonata Hyundai windows fog quickly, completely and frequently blinding the driver necessitating distracting changes to be made to balance multiple changes in outside to inside temps along roads. Defogging is achieved—only—with outside air intake vents open. Life threatening maneuvers to drive safely are distractions designed into the Hyundai instrument control system.

2002—Axle (U-bolt) fails while car is underway. • Seat belt latch releases when jostled by passenger's elbow. **2003**—Driver-side seat belt buckle suddenly releases. • Large rear-view mirror obstructs the view. **2004**—Gas fumes enter the cabin. • Stalling because of a faulty throttle sensor. • Early clutch failure. • Automatic transmission slippage and seizure. • Complete brake loss. • Rear wheel bearing seizure. • Seat belt comes loose during a collision. **2004–06**—Sudden, unintended acceleration. **2005**—Failure of the passenger-side front suspension. • No brakes. • Loose front passenger seat. • Vibration caused by loose engine mount bolts. • Excessive heat generated under the driver-side dash. **2006–07**—Sunroof glass explodes. **2006–08**—After recall repairs, front passenger-side airbag is still disabled even though an adult is seated. • Driver-side sun visor sags and continually drops down. **2007**—In one incident, cruise control would not disengage when the brakes were applied. • Vehicle rolls back on an incline while in Drive. • Headlights don't give enough light, and both the headlights and rear lights burn out quickly. **2007–08**—Premature brake pad and rotor wear:

This condition is reported online by many other owners with as little as 20K [mi.] [32,000 km]. Dealer will not cover under warranty. Hyundai USA will only consider reimbursement after it is repaired first and preferably by a dealer. My dealer said it's a "design flaw with the pad retainer;" those online report corroded caliper mounting pins as the cause.

• Rear brake pad comes apart. • Rear calipers freeze against the brake rotors. **2008**—Fire ignites from the wires in the trunk. • Driver's seat belt release latch doesn't operate properly. • Vehicle suddenly loses power when cruising at 100 km/h (throttle position sensor suspected). • When cruising in Third, transmission suddenly downshifts into First. **2009**—In two separate frontal collisions, front seat belts failed to tighten. • Sudden, unintended acceleration. • Clutch pedal will sometimes jam or not engage:

The clutch on my 5 speed 2009 Hyundai Sonata is sporadically dropping to the floor and not allowing me to change gears. I was nearly hit from behind, as the car behind me assumed I'd be accelerating, but when the clutch drops (without much resistance) the linkage locks and I can't change gears.... I removed the floor mat when I went to pick up my car, and, in their parking log, going from 1st to 2nd gear, the clutch pedal dropped to the floor and I could not change gears, until I hit the clutch a few more times! Apparently, Hyundai is having lots of problems with their clutches, but they refuse to fix it, because it is costly to take apart the transmission to see what is wrong.

• After cruise control is deactivated, it resumes at a higher speed. • Worn out and noisy rear brakes:

They told me there is uneven wear on rear break pads and that the sliders are sticking causing the pads to stay compressed to rotor. They offered to "lube" them for me and replace pads for over $200.00

• Wiring harness caught fire. • Intermittent electrical short kills the dash lights. • Faulty throttle position sensor causes hard starts, loss of power, and stall-outs. • AC drains poorly, produces a musty smell. • Low-beam headlights have too narrow a beam. • Windshield suddenly shattered without cause:

Rear window shattered while commuting into work this morning on Interstate I-95. The glass repair man stated new cars sometimes have a faulty wire that causes these windows to shatter. I was using the heater & had the defrost activated. [O]utside temperature: 27 degrees C.

Secret Warranties/Internal Bulletins/Service Tips

All years: Troubleshooting tips for delayed engagement of the automatic transmission. • Harsh shifting when coming to a stop or upon initial acceleration likely caused by an improperly adjusted accelerator pedal switch transmission control unit. • Troubleshooting hard, delayed shifts. • A faulty air exhaust plug could cause harsh shifting into Second and Fourth gears on vehicles with automatic transmissions. • Brake pedal pulsation can be corrected by installing upgraded front discs and pads. • Troubleshooting tips for reducing brake noise. **1999–2006**—Troubleshooting tips for differential seal oil leaks. **2001–02**—Hyundai will fix a noisy rear suspension by replacing the rear stabilizer bar bushing. **2002**—Troubleshooting poor shifting and torque converter clutch malfunctions. • 2–3 shift flare. • Erratic operation of the automatic climate control. • Sticks in Second gear. **2003–04**—Low-speed driveline "bump." **2004**—Engine hesitation requires a reprogrammed PCM. **2005**—Oil leak from the bell housing/torque converter area. **2006**—Front drive axle snapping noise. **2006–07**—Front windshield creak or squeak. **2006–08**—Engine hesitation and misfire repair tips. • Remedy for seat creaking, squeaking. **2006–09**—Oil temperature sensor may leak. **2006–10**—Steering squeaks when turning. **2007–10**—Troubleshooting hard starts or a rough idle. **2008**—Correction for a steering wheel shimmy/vibration. **2009–10**—A water leak onto the passenger side front floor is likely due to a kinked AC drain hose.

SONATA PROFILE

	2001	2002	2003	2004	2005	2006	2007	2008	2009
Cost Price ($)									
Base	20,495	21,195	21,595	22,395	22,395	21,900	23,595	22,295	21,995
Used Values ($)									
Base ▲	3,500	4,500	5,000	5,500	7,000	9,500	10,500	13,000	15,000
Base ▼	3,000	4,000	4,500	5,000	6,000	8,500	9,000	11,500	13,500
Reliability	2	2	2	3	3	3	3	3	3
Crash Safety (F)	—	4	4	4	4	5	5	5	5
Side	4	4	4	4	4	5	5	5	5
IIHS Side	1	1	1	1	1	3	3	3	3
Offset	3	3	3	3	3	5	5	5	5
Head Restraints (F)	1	1	1	1	1	5	5	5	5
Roof Strength	—	—	—	—	—	2	2	2	2
Rollover Resistance	—	5	5	5	5	4	4	4	4

Mazda

MAZDA6, 626 ★★★★/★★★

RATING: *Mazda6*: Above Average (2006–09); Average (2003–05). *626*: Average (1999–2002). Tall drivers should be wary of the low headrests, which can be hazardous in a collision, and short drivers will want to ensure they can see adequately without getting dangerously close to the airbag housing. **Ideal model year:** For enhanced highway performance, safety, and comfort, pick an upgraded 2007 GT for $12,000 to $13,000; a 2005 Mazda6 for $8,000 to $9,500 is another good choice. It will give you anti-lock braking and traction control, as well as a 6-speed automatic transmission on some versions. **"Real" city/highway fuel economy:** *Mazda6 2.3 manual: 9.6/6.7 L/100 km. Mazda6 2.3 automatic: 10.4/ 7.5 L/100 km. Mazda6 3.0 manual: 12.1/8.1 L/100 km. Mazda6 3.0 automatic: 12.3/8.1 L/100 km. Mazda 626 2.0 manual: 9.4/6.8 L/100 km. Mazda 626 2.0 automatic: 11.3/7.9 L/100 km. Mazda 626 2.5 6-cyl. manual: 11.8/8.5 L/100 km. Mazda 626 2.5 6-cyl. automatic: 12.2/8.5 L/100 km.* There isn't a lot of difference in fuel consumption rates between these models. Although the newer versions are a bit more fuel-frugal, their higher price tag means any savings are illusory. Gas mileage may be 15 percent lower than advertised. **Maintenance/repair costs:** Average. Repairs aren't dealer-dependent, however, so save bagfuls of loonies by frequenting independent repair shops. **Parts:** Easily found, but sometimes costly; compare prices with independent suppliers. **Extended warranty:** An extended powertrain warranty is recommended as protection against mostly automatic transmission failures. **Best alternatives:** Acura CSX or RSX; Honda Accord; and the Hyundai Elantra, Sonata, or Tucson. **Helpful websites:** *www.mazdaforum. com/forum* and *www.mazdas247.com/forum/index.php.*

Strengths and Weaknesses

626

Although far from being high-performance vehicles, these cars ride and handle fairly well and still manage to accommodate four people in comfort. They have changed little over the years and are still easy-riding, fairly responsive, and not hard on gas. On the downside, complaints posted up to the 2002 model year for the 626 and on later Mazda6 versions point out that there's too much body lean in turns; road noise intrudes into the cabin; the rear spoiler blocks rear visibility; the car is hard-riding over uneven pavement; the trunk opening isn't conducive to loading large objects; excessive torque steer (pulling) to the right often occurs when accelerating; and shifting isn't all that smooth, nor is the automatic gearbox very reliable.

Mazda6

The 2003 through 2009 Mazda6 offers the following powerplants: a 156 hp inline 4-cylinder, a 2.5L 170 hp inline 4-cylinder, a 212 hp V6, and a 272 turbocharged V6. All are adequate for most tasks but come up short for fuel economy. Either Mazda engine can be hooked to a 5-speed or 6-speed manual or automatic transmission.

Don't get the idea that this is a warmed-over 626. It's set on an entirely new platform and carries safety and convenience features never seen by its predecessor, such as two-stage airbags and a chassis engineered to deflect crash forces away from occupants. The Mazda6's interior also allows for a comfortable ride and carries an unusually large trunk.

During its first year on the market, there was a wide range of owner complaints that have become fewer with more recent models. Owners mention various water leaks, omnipresent interior and exterior clunks (suspension), and a number of driveability concerns that include poor engine and transmission performance (clutch failures, predominantly).

Also, the 5-speed transmission is sometimes difficult to shift in its lower gears, hesitates when accelerating or decelerating, and gets stuck in gear. Many owners report dash rattles, paint bubbling, window motor failures, chronic stalling and hard starts, defective engine knock sensors, electrical shorts everywhere, noisy and prematurely worn brakes and steering, separation of the radiator's bottom seam, excessive condensation on the inside bottom of the front windshield, and waits of a month or more for replacement parts.

VEHICLE HISTORY: *626:* **2000**—Restyled and substantially improved with a small horsepower boost (5 hp) and enhanced handling, steering, and interior appointments. The 626 carried on until 2002, but there were no changes. *Mazda6:* **2004**—A four-door hatchback and wagon are added, along with passenger-side airbags. **2005**—Standard anti-lock braking and traction control; a 6-speed automatic transmission replaces the 5-speed unit for S models. **2007**—Standard side curtain airbags. **2008**—No more wagon or MazdaSpeed models. **2009**—Larger, with sportier handling.

 ## Safety Summary

All models/years: The 626's different iterations have registered far fewer complaints than their Asian, European, or American counterparts. • Inadvertent airbag deployments, or airbags that fail to deploy in a collision. • Sudden, unintended acceleration. • Frequent automatic transmission malfunctions and failures. *626:* **2001**—Seat belts fail to retract. **2002**—One vehicle's driver-side seat belt unlatched during an accident. *Mazda6:* **2003**—Hard starts. • Steering failures. **2004**—Fuel line detaches from engine, even after fix:

> I have had two incidents where the fuel line has detached from inside the engine and the car has stalled and gasoline has poured out from underneath the car. The first time, the dealership told me that there was a recall and I should receive [notification] in the mail. I later found out there was no recall. They then fixed the car supposedly, and three months later it happened again.

• Dangerous automatic transmission design cuts engine power when passing another vehicle. • Total brake failure. • Early severe brake rotor warpage. • Airbag light comes on due to cracked front sensors that short out from water ingress. • Rear windshield shatters because the defroster shorts out. • Electronic door lock often will not allow occupant to open car door from the inside (help!). **2005**—Harsh shifts, automatic transmission slippage, getting stuck in gear (has to be put into manual mode), and dropping into the next lower gear for no reason. • Manual transmission seizure. **2006**—Automatic transmission failure took a month to be repaired, in one incident. • Chronic stalling. • Car loses power when accelerating in cold weather (see *forum.mazda6club.com/index.php?showtopic=65171&st=0*). • Frequent replacement of brake pads and rotor. • Vehicle shifts from Sixth gear down to Third gear. **2007**—Hesitation when shifting gears. • Engine rear main seal oil leak; complete transmission failure due to a leaking seal at the torque converter. • One vehicle's engine threw a rod at 66,000 miles (106,000 km). • Lights and remote do not work in the rain; diagnosed as a junction box failure caused by rain. • Automatic windows will not reverse if they are closing on an object. • Early failure of the original equipment Michelin Energy tires. **2008**— Rough idle, hesitation when accelerating. **2009**—Transmission replacement due to fluid leakage though weep hole. • Brake pedal goes to the floor without effect; premature wearout of brake pads, calipers, and rotors. • Corroded tire stems caused tire failure. • HID lights give inadequate field of illumination.

Secret Warranties/Internal Bulletins/Service Tips

626: **2002**—Rough idle, hesitation, and stumble. • Grinding, rubbing noise at front of vehicle. • Tips to silence wind noise around doors. *Mazda6:* **2003**—Doors hard to close in cold weather. • Sticking traction-control system switch. • Wind noise around doors. **2003–05**—Procedures to cure an engine camshaft ticking noise. • 1–2 gear shift shock with automatic transmission. **2003–06**—Rough idle and hesitation. • Excessive body vibration. **2003–07**—Pull or drift to the side when driving. **2003–08**—3.0L engine ticking. • Headlight lens condensation or water entry. • Steering shaft clunk. • Various wind noise concerns. • Unstable idle, engine stalling just after stopping. • Troubleshooting tips to correct brake noise, judder, and dragging. **2003–10**—Information relating to windshield flaws, scratches, cracks, etc. and the elimination of seatback creaking. • Front-seat head restraint rattling. • Noisy, wobbly seats. **2004**—Engine surging at 80 km/h. • Hesitation or rough idle at high altitudes. • Remedies for brake judder and moan. • Special Service Program #60 to replace the fan control module. • Special Service Program for evaporative emission-system leak monitoring failures. • Special Service Program for oxygen sensor failure. • Front suspension popping, clunking. **2005**—Surging at 60–90 km/h with the 2.3L 4-cylinder engine. **2005–08**—3.0L engine surging. • AC is inoperative when brakes are applied. **2006–07**—Front axle knocking noises in extreme cold. • Low-speed engine stalling. **2006–08**— No-start; inoperative AC or defroster. • Parking brake lever drops down after engagement in extremely cold climate. **2009**—Poor AC performance; engine runs hot. • Excessive manual transmission noise when shifting. • Transmission servo-cover fluid leaks. • Inaccurate fuel gauge. A Hyundai Campaign (MSP 22) will repair an electrical short that causes the wipers and headlights to work erratically. **2009–10**—Manual transmission hard to shift into Third or Fourth gear. • Rear combination light lens heat deformation. • Rear door locks inoperative in freezing temperatures. • Front door speaker rattling. • An electrical short circuit may cause the horn to intermittently self-activate. • Water in tail lights.

292

MAZDA6, 626 PROFILE

	2001	2002	2003	2004	2005	2006	2007	2008	2009
Cost Price ($)									
626	23,175	23,470	—	—	—	—	—	—	—
Mazda6	—	—	24,295	24,395	23,795	23,795	24,395	24,495	22,695
Mazda6 GT	—	—	—	—	29,795	29,895	30,295	29,895	27,695
Sport Hatchback	—	—	—	25,495	25,495	25,495	26,295	26,395	—
Sport Wagon	—	—	—	26,995	26,995	26,995	27,895	—	—
Used Values ($)									
626 ▲	3,500	4,000	—	—	—	—	—	—	—
626 ▼	3,000	3,500	—	—	—	—	—	—	—
Mazda6 ▲	—	—	5,000	6,500	9,500	11,000	13,000	15,000	17,500
Mazda6 ▼	—	—	4,500	5,500	8,000	10,000	11,500	13,500	16,000
Mazda6 GT ▲	—	—	—	—	9,500	11,500	13,500	17,500	21,000
Mazda6 GT ▼	—	—	—	—	8,000	10,000	12,000	16,000	19,500
Sport Hatchback ▲	—	—	—	7,500	9,000	10,000	13,500	16,500	—
Sport Hatchback ▼	—	—	—	6,500	8,000	9,000	12,000	15,000	—
Sport Wagon ▲	—	—	—	8,500	9,500	11,500	13,500	—	—
Sport Wagon ▼	—	—	—	7,500	8,500	10,000	12,000	—	—
Reliability	3	3	3	4	4	4	4	4	4
Crash Safety (F)	4	4	5	5	5	5	5	5	5
Side (626 4d)	3	3	—	—	—	—	—	—	—
Mazda6	—	—	3	3	3	4	4	4	5
IIHS Side	—	—	1	1	1	1	—	—	5
Offset	5	5	5	5	5	5	5	5	5
Head Restraints	2	2	2	2	2	2	2	2	2
Roof Strength	—	—	—	—	—	—	—	—	3
Rollover Resistance	—	—	5	5	5	5	5	5	5

Note: The 2003–05 Mazda6 models earn a higher score for head-restraint protection if the seats don't have a lumbar adjustment mechanism.

Nissan

ALTIMA, ALTIMA HYBRID   ★★★★/★★★

RATING: Above Average (2008–09); Average (2002–07). *Altima Hybrid:* Average (2007–09). **Ideal model year:** Best choice would be a $10,000 to $11,000 2006 3.5 S or SE version. **"Real" city/highway fuel economy:** *2.5 manual: 10.3/ 7.3 L/100 km. 2.5 automatic: 10.3/7.4 L/100 km. 3.5 manual: 11.3/8.3 L/100 km. 3.5 6-speed manual: 11.5/7.3 L/100 km. 3.5 automatic: 12.3/8.3 L/100 km. 1.8 manual: 8.8/6.2 L/100 km. 1.8 automatic: 9.0/6.5 L/100 km. 2.0 manual: 9.9/7.0 L/100 km.*

All ratings on a numbered scale where ▢ is good and **1** is bad. See page 132 for a more detailed description.

2.0 automatic: 9.8/7.2 L/100 km. *2.4 automatic:* 10.9/7.6 L/100 km. **Maintenance/ repair costs:** Higher than average. Repairs are dealer-dependent. **Parts:** Owners complain of frequent parts shortages. Parts on earlier models are relatively inexpensive. **Extended warranty:** Get an extended warranty to protect you from automatic transmission failures and a host of other problems. **Best alternatives:** Acura Integra; later-model GM Cavalier or Sunfire; Honda Accord; Hyundai Elantra wagon, Sonata, or Tiburon; Mazda6; and 2005 or 2006 Toyota Camry. **Helpful websites:** *www.nissanforums.com.*

Strengths and Weaknesses

Expect only average acceleration and fuel economy with the pre-2002 4-cylinder engine. It has insufficient top-end torque and gets buzzier the more it's pushed. In order to get the automatic to downshift for passing, for example, you have to practically stomp on the accelerator. Manoeuvrability is good around town but twitchy on the highway. There are few reliability problems reported with the 16-valve powerplant; however, the 5-speed manual transmission is sloppy and the automatic transmission's performance has been problematic. The uncluttered under-hood layout makes servicing easy. Body assembly is only so-so, with more than the average number of squeaks and rattles.

The 2002–09 redesigned models are shaped like Passats with Maxima hearts, and provide scintillating V6 acceleration, flawless automatic transmission operation, good braking, well laid-out instruments and controls, and better-than-average interior room and craftsmanship. Too bad their exceptional performance is hobbled by chronic stalling, unreliable brakes, short circuits by the dozen, suspension glitches, and worse than average fit and finish.

Highway handling isn't impressive. The 4-cylinder engine isn't as refined as the competition and is noisy when pushed. The V6's acceleration overpowers this car and causes excessive rear-end instability and steering pull to one side. Brakes tend to lock up on wet roads; dash gauges wash out in sunlight; interior appointments lack panache; the dashboard reflects onto the windshield; rear seating for three adults is snug, there's limited rear headroom, and rear visibility is obstructed; and parts are often back ordered. Quality problems multiply as these cars age.

The car's 180 hp 2.5L 4-cylinder engine is almost as powerful as the competition's V6 powerplants, and the optional 245 hp 3.5L V6 has few equals among cars in this price and size class. And when you consider that the Altima is much lighter than most of its competitors, it's obvious why this car produces sizzling (and sometimes uncontrollable) acceleration.

VEHICLE HISTORY: **2002**—Completely revised with two high-performance engines (a 180 hp 2.5L 4-cylinder or an optional 245 hp 3.5L V6), a larger interior, and a more-supple ride combined with sportier handling. Quality declines. **2005**—The sporty new SE-R model arrives with a 260 hp V6. Other V6 models now use a 5-speed automatic. Interior trim is upgraded throughout the lineup. **2007**—

Restyled, more standard safety features, and the debut of Nissan's first gas/electric hybrid model. **2008**—ABS is a standard feature, and an all-new Coupe model comes on the scene.

The engine, fit and finish, automatic transmission, fuel and electrical systems, and brakes (squealing and premature wearout of pads and rotors) continue to be troublesome on 2009–09 models. Owners report electrical glitches; excessive brake wear, noise, and pulsations; an annoying and hazardous dash reflection onto the windshield; and engine surging, stalling, and hard starting, possibly because of a defective engine crank sensor or throttle switch. Rear shocks are noisy and failure-prone; the ABS warning light stays lit; the clutch pressure plate throw-out bearing and flywheel may fail when downshifting into Fourth gear; and snow builds up in the small wheelwells, making steering difficult and causing excessive shimmy.

 Safety Summary

2001–03—Airbags fail to deploy. **2002–03**—Dealerships said to be aware of redesigned Altima's tendency to catch fire: fire erupted after collision; fire ignited because of a faulty fuel-injection system; fire ignited while vehicle was cruising on the highway. • One vehicle was idling and then suddenly went into Reverse and accelerated as groceries were being unloaded from the trunk (dash indicator showed car in Park). • Driver run over by his own car when it slipped into Reverse. • Sudden acceleration when brakes are applied. • Transmission slips and engine hesitates when accelerating. • Chronic stalling. • Windshield distortion. • Exhaust-pipe hanger pin catches debris that may ignite. • Crankshaft position sensor failure. • Tail lights constantly fail. • Seat belt fails to retract. • Instrument panel gauges wash out in sunlight. **2004**—Sudden stalling and hard starts. • Vehicle starts, but won't move forward. • Brake rotors completely wear out during first year. • Rear windshield shatters as door is closed. • Right front tire falls off vehicle. • Car is a hostage-taker:

> The problem that I face now is that I cannot get out of my car!!!!!! I arrived home one day and found that the driver's side door would not open from the inside. I am 7 months pregnant and was very scared when I found this problem. What if there is ever a car fire or an accident and I cannot get out? You can open the door from the outside but not the inside. Hyannis Nissan claims it's a door latch problem and it had to be replaced. So since my warranty just ran out I have to pay $192.00 to get this repaired. Are you kidding me?

2005—Sudden, unintended acceleration while parking. • Seat belts failed to lock when one Altima was rear-ended. • Rear control bar breaks (see also TSB #NTB05-114b in "Secret Warranties/Internal Bulletins/Service Tips," following):

> Rear passenger control bar (2 rods) broke at the weld while driving and caused my car to spin out of control, causing damage to the tire, and the rear housing. I was told it would not be covered under either warranty that I carry. I was told to turn it over to my insurance company. This same part has a recall in other states, just not Florida?

• Transmission hesitates and then slams into gear. • Excessive steering vibration resolved:

> I have a 2005 Nissan Altima 3.5 SL. Last summer I was having problems with the car's handling at highway speeds. I had the car aligned, replaced all 4 tires, one by one and was still having [problems] with the car—which was shaking at speeds over 60 mph [97 km/h]. I took it to the dealer again and they determined that the shaking was like a turbulence effect. The spoiler under the car was not allowing the wind to flow through properly.

2006—Many complaints that the 2.5L engine stops running without warning due to an overheated crankshaft position sensor (not included in an earlier recall). • Engine surges after vehicle comes to a complete stop. • Early strut and tie-rod failures. • DOT 3 brake fluid breaks down too easily. • Clutch pedal goes to the floor and stays there. • Dry-rotted tire valve stems. • Side wall splits on Bridgestone Turanza EL-42 tires. **2007**—Snapped stabilizer bar:

> 2007 Nissan Altima 3.5SE rear sway bar snapped in two while driving. There was no damage to the surrounding area where the bar snapped. At close inspection, the bar is hollow inside. There are web blogs that I have found where other owners have experienced the same problem. See *wiki.answers.com/q/should_the_2007_Nissan_Altima_rear_sway_bar_be_recalled.*

• Passenger-side airbag is disabled when an average-sized adult is seated. • Sudden steering lockup. • Defective tire-pressure sensor. • The Tire Pressure warning light comes on for no reason. **2007–08**— Unstable driver's seat moves side to side and fore and aft when as the car turns, accelerates, or slows down. **2008**—Airbag shuts off when passenger seat is occupied. • Chronic stalling. • Defective automatic CVT (warranty extension for 10 years). • Sudden brake lock-up. • Leaking brake master cylinder. • Windshield wipers blur the windshield. • Continental ContiPro Contact tires perform poorly on snow-covered, wet highways. • Back doors don't close properly.

Secret Warranties/Internal Bulletins/Service Tips

All years: Diagnostic and correction tips for brake vibration and steering-wheel shimmy. • TSB #NTB99-028 outlines the procedures necessary to fix slow-to-retract seat belts. • TSB #NTB00-037a covers possible causes of the vehicle's pulling to the side. **2002–03**—Hard starting. • Excessive engine, fuel-sloshing, and suspension noise. • Low power, poor running, and MIL stays lit. • Inoperative AC; warm air flows from vents. • Poor heater performance. • AC drain hose may leak into interior. • Sunroof water leaks. • Wind noise from doors and sunroof. • Water leakage on front floor area. • Sunroof won't close at highway speeds. • Automatic transmission slips in Reverse and won't brake when in Drive 1 range. **2002–04**—The control valve assembly may be the culprit responsible for erratic shifting. **2002–05**—Secret 13-year extended warranty on the rear subframe:

CAMPAIGN—REAR SUSPENSION MEMBER, BUSHING REPLACEMENT

BULLETIN NO.: NTB05-114B   DATE: MARCH 24, 2006

VOLUNTARY SERVICE CAMPAIGN REAR SUSPENSION REPLACEMENT/BUSHING REPLACEMENT AND SEALING

On some model year 2002–05 Nissan Altima and 2004–05 Nissan Maxima vehicles, there is a possibility that corrosion of the rear sub-frame may occur. Corrosion is most likely in cold climates where heavy salting of roads is common practice in freezing conditions…. In severe cases, cracking of the rear sub-frame may occur, which may result in a knocking noise coming from the rear of the vehicle…. On most vehicles, Nissan will replace the rear sub-frame assembly. On some 2005 Model Year vehicles, where sub-frame replacement is not necessary, Nissan will replace and seal the front bushings and seal the rear bushings.

WARRANTY EXTENSION: To ensure the highest levels of customer satisfaction, Nissan is also extending the warranty for cracking of the rear sub-frame due to corrosion to a total of 13 years with unlimited mileage on all model year 2002–05 Nissan Altima and 2004–05 Nissan Maxima vehicles. Vehicles included in the Service Campaign (as described above) are also covered by the Warranty Extension.

2002–06—Hard starts or no-starts in cold weather. • Ticking noise from the engine area. • Oil cooler oil leaks do not require the replacement of the complete engine oil cooler assembly, says TSB #NTB06-029. • Pop, thump noise when operating front-door window. **2003–05**—Nissan's bulletin admits that a harsh-shifting condition is factory-related. **2004**—Hard starts or no-starts may signal the need for a new fuel-pump assembly. • Engine won't crank in low temperatures. **2004–08**—Leak from the tire pressure monitor sensor. **2007–08**—Erratic speedometer readings. • ABS and Brake lights lit. • Silencing front brake noise at slow speeds. • Sunroof seals poorly. • Front suspension rattling. • Inoperative "power up" window. **2007–09**—Ignition may not turn to the On position (steering lock unit may need to be replaced under warranty or via "goodwill"). • Sunroof may operate erratically. • Inoperative power window "Auto Up" feature. • Folding door mirror wind noise. • Front brake squealing or squeaking at low speeds; replace brake pads and install brake kit per TSB # NTB08-057B, published August 19, 2009. **2007–10**— Driver's power seat moves side to side. • Troubleshooting tips for correcting fuel gauge malfunctions. **2008–09**—Driver seat may not move forward or backward. **2009**—Nissan has set up a special Campaign (#PCO 44) to prevent the front windshield wipers from scraping the windshield. Parts and labour are Nissan's responsibility. Another Campaign (#PC005) provides free replacement of the rear suspension knuckle.

ALTIMA, ALTIMA HYBRID PROFILE

	2001	2002	2003	2004	2005	2006	2007	2008	2009
Cost Price ($)									
XE/S	19,998	23,498	23,798	23,798	23,798	24,698	24,398	24,499	25,998
GXE/SE	22,698	27,698	24,675	24,298	29,098	29,698	30,198	30,298	29,498
Coupe S	—	—	—	—	—	—	—	27,799	25,998
Coupe SE	—	—	—	—	—	—	—	31,398	29,798
Sedan 3.5 SE-R	—	—	—	—	21,498	29,698	—	—	—
Hybrid	—	—	—	—	—	—	32,998	33,998	32,298

Used Values ($)

XE/S ▲	3,000	4,500	5,000	6,500	8,000	9,500	12,500	15,000	17,500
XE/S ▼	2,000	3,000	4,500	5,500	7,000	8,500	11,000	13,500	16,000
GXE/SE ▲	4,500	5,500	6,500	8,500	10,000	12,500	14,500	16,500	21,500
GXE/SE ▼	4,000	4,500	6,000	8,000	9,000	11,000	13,000	15,000	20,000
Coupe S ▲	—	—	—	—	—	—	—	16,500	19,500
Coupe S ▼	—	—	—	—	—	—	—	15,000	18,000
Coupe SE ▲	—	—	—	—	—	—	—	18,500	21,500
Coupe SE ▼	—	—	—	—	—	—	—	17,500	20,000
Sedan 3.5 SE-R ▲	—	—	—	—	10,000	12,000	—	—	—
Sedan 3.5 SE-R ▼	—	—	—	—	8,500	10,500	—	—	—
Hybrid ▲	—	—	—	—	—	—	14,000	19,000	23,000
Hybrid ▼	—	—	—	—	—	—	12,500	17,500	21,500

Reliability	2	3	3	3	3	4	4	4	4
Crash Safety (F)	4	4	4	4	5	5	5	4	4
4d	—	—	—	—	—	—	—	5	5
Hybrid	—	—	—	—	—	—	—	5	5
Side	3	3	3	3	3	3	5	5	5
4d	—	—	—	—	—	—	4	5	5
Hybrid	—	—	—	—	—	—	—	5	5
IIHS Side	—	1	1	1	1	1	5	5	5
Offset	2	5	5	5	5	5	5	5	5
Head Restraints (F)	1	3	3	3	3	3	2	2	3
Roof Strength	—	—	—	—	—	—	3	3	3
Rollover Resistance	—	4	4	4	4	4	4	5	5
4d	—	—	—	—	—	—	4	4	4

Toyota

CAMRY, HYBRID, SOLARA ★/★★★★

bad buy

RATING: *Camry:* Not Recommended (1996–2009). Toyota's sudden, unintended acceleration, loss of brakes, and airbags that fail to deploy are a triple whammy that may kill you. Sadder still, NHTSA shows these three interconnected problems have carried over to the 2010 and 2011 model years. Despite Toyota's recalls, there is apparently still "a ghost in the machine":

> In order to avoid the collision, I shifted part of my car to the shoulder. Then I discovered a car parked on the shoulder with no signals/lights. I braked the 2011 Toyota Camry really hard to the floor, but the car could not slow down and could not stop completely. The brake system in the 2011 Toyota Camry had obviously failed and the car was even accelerating during the last few seconds prior to the collision. After the severe collision at the front driver side, none of the airbags in the Camry deployed.

The mileage after the collision was 3595 miles [5,800 km] (8-9 Dec 2010). I was hurt severely in the lower back/lumbar spine area.

Interestingly, when the 2007 model Camry was redesigned, quality control and safety took a serious hit with the exception of the Solara and Hybrid models. From falling sun visors to lurching powertrains, the company could have done much better, and knows it, as evidenced by a few contrite apologies issued by top Toyota executives. *Hybrid:* Not recommended (2007–09). Although not as failure-prone as the conventional Camry, the Hybrid's high cost and safety defects make it less affordable and more hazardous than the competition. Camrys have elicited an unusually high number of safety complaints that are carried over from one model year to the next. Safety defects include loss of braking; engine compartment fires; poor headlight illumination; automatic transmission breakdowns; severe wandering at highway speeds; V6 engine failures from sludge buildup; hesitation followed by sudden acceleration; and transmission interlock failures, which allow a parked vehicle to roll away. There's nothing you can do to prevent these failures, and you may have to force Toyota to pay for their correction through CAMVAP arbitration or small claims court. *Solara:* Above Average (2006–08); Average (1999–2005). Almost identical to the Camry, the Solara has had almost no meaningful safety complaints and resale prices are relatively reasonable. **Ideal model year:** The Solara, a two-door Camry clone, was overpriced when bought new; however, the 2006–08 models are good buys because they are more reasonably priced as used cars and are likely to have some of the original factory warranty coverage left. Of all the model years, I'd go for the 2006 Solara to get the maximum depreciation discount and a good array of standard features. **"Real" city/highway fuel economy:** *Camry, Solara 2.4 automatic: 10.1/6.7 L/100 km. Camry, Solara 3.3 6-cylinder: 11.7/7.4 L/100 km. Camry 2.2 manual: 10.0/6.8 L/100 km. Camry 2.2 automatic: 9.0/6.5 L/100 km. Camry 2.4 automatic: 10.4/7.3 L/100 km. Camry 3.0 automatic: 11.9/7.3 L/100 km. Camry Hybrid: 5.7/5.7 L/100 km.* These estimates may be off by as much as 20 percent. **Maintenance/repair costs:** Higher than average, but repairs aren't dealer-dependent. **Parts:** Can be more expensive than for most other cars in this class, making it worth your while to shop at independent suppliers. Parts availability is excellent. **Extended warranty:** Essential for 1997 and later model years. **Best alternatives:** Ford Escape Hybrid; Honda Accord; Hyundai Elantra wagon, Sonata, Tiburon, or Tucson; Mazda6; and Nissan Sentra. **Helpful websites:** *www.toyotanation.com/forum* and *www.toyotaowners.net.*

 ## Strengths and Weaknesses

The Camry is basically a Japanese Oldsmobile (the old rear-drive kind); it drives and coddles you. Safety complaints aside, it's an excellent small family hauler because of its spacious, comfortable interior, good fuel economy, and impressive reliability and durability. Just make sure you change the oil more frequently than Toyota (or Lexus, for that matter) suggests for its V6 engine if you want to prevent engine sludge.

"De-contenting" hit Toyota's 1996–2004 lineup hard, resulting in many changes that cheapened the Camry and precipitated a huge increase in owner complaints over problems that had never appeared on Toyota vehicles before. Many of these defects continue to reappear to this day. Specifically, owners have endured leaky, noisy struts; self-destructing AC; excessive steering-wheel vibrations; warning lights that constantly come on; water leaking into the car after a hard rain; front power windows that often run off their channels; a suspension that bottoms out when carrying four adults; failure-prone engine head gaskets and automatic transmissions; moonroofs that are prone to water leaks and annoyingly loud wind noise; frequent hesitation or stalling out when accelerating or braking; charcoal canisters that need early replacement (covered by the emissions warranty, if you insist on it); and constantly irritating brake pulsations, plus brake components (pads, rotors, calipers, master cylinder, and the ABS valve) that wear out early. Side pillar rattling is also a chronic annoyance.

The 2007 models are particularly failure-prone, leading the pack in sheer number of complaints reported to NHTSA. Engine stalling and surging and transmission failures lead the list. Other problems relate to loose headliners/moulding; chronic water and air leaks; and poor-quality fit and finish, evidenced by poor paint application. Brake problems and electrical shorts continue unabated.

The 2008 and 2009 models may be somewhat less troublesome, inasmuch as it appears that a flurry of internal service bulletins and goodwill warranty extensions have been used to placate owners. Nevertheless, the jury is still out on these models. One distressing note: Toyota's "lag and lurch" powertrain hazard is still in evidence on these more recent models, and safety defects affecting acceleration, brakes, and airbags haven't gone away.

VEHICLE HISTORY: 2002—Car gets larger and now carries a 157 hp 2.4L 4-cylinder engine. **2004**—SE version gets a 225 hp 3.3L V6 hooked to a revised 5-speed automatic, improved fuel injection, and additional soundproofing. The 3.0L V6 available in the LE and XLE also gets the new 5-speed automatic and gains 18 hp, giving it 210 hp. **2005**—Standard ABS, and an upgraded automatic transmission for models equipped with a 4-cylinder engine. Less effective rear drum brakes are kept on the entry-level models, while other Camrys have four-wheel discs. **2007**—Totally redesigned, equipped with an all-new 268 hp 3.5L V6, or a more powerful (four more horses) 158 hp 2.4L 4-cylinder engine (buzzy at high revs). Although the Camry's overall length is the same, this year's version has a longer wheelbase and is a bit wider and lower, with new exterior and interior styling. A hybrid model, equipped with the 2.4L four-banger, makes its debut as well. **2010**–The 2.4L is replaced by a slightly more powerful 2.5L.

Camry Hybrid

The Hybrid combines a 2.4L 4-cylinder gas engine with a battery-powered electric motor (187 hp) and a CVT. Similar to Toyota's other hybrids, the Camry HV runs on one or both of its power sources, depending on driving conditions, and requires no plug-in charging.

Although the car is less fuel-thirsty than the base 4-cylinder Camry, it also costs about $7,000 more. And the kicker: Your first two years' depreciation will be $8,000. You will also become a captive customer of the hybrid-selling dealer. If you don't like its service, prices, or attitude, tough! And God forbid you should get caught with an electrical problem on a driving vacation.

Both the 2007 and 2008 Hybrid models have serious safety-related deficiencies caused by poor design. 2009 Hybrids are relatively trouble-free, with only six safety-related incidents reported. The two most worrisome failures are the afore-mentioned lag and lurch powertrain syndrome and the sudden downshifting/surging associated with the cruise control as the vehicle passes over hilly terrain. Other complaints involve failure of the brakes and electrical system, subpar fit and finish, and poor-quality paint. Reports one angry Hybrid owner to NHTSA:

> Hybrid 2007 black paint is defective design technology. Toyota changed to a water-based paint two years ago, and the product is a manufacturer's defective design and process. Toyota is hiding this fact from its customer base.... Be honest, you paid a lot of money for a defective paint job and they know it.

Solara

Introduced in the summer of 1998 as a '99 model, the Solara is essentially a two-door coupe or convertible Camry that's longer, lower, and more bare-bones, with a more stylish exterior, sportier powertrain and suspension, and fewer quality problems. Most new Toyota model offerings, such as the Sienna, Avalon, and RAV4, are also Camry derivatives.

Year 2000 models returned unchanged, except for the addition of a convertible version and three additional horses. The Solara was redesigned for 2004 and adopted the latest Camry sedan platform and upgrades. Convertibles arrived with seating for four instead of five and resemble the two-seat Lexus SC 430 hardtop convertible. The 2007 Solaras underwent a mild front and rear restyling, got standard side curtain airbags and a coloured rear spoiler, and dropped the SE V6 model. For 2008, the Solara's last model year, only the SLE remained. The 4-cylinder engine was replaced by the 3.3L V6, coupled to a 5-speed automatic transmission.

Relatively rare on the used-car market, you have a choice of either four or six cylinders. Unfortunately, vehicles equipped with a V6 also came with a gimmicky rear spoiler and a headroom-robbing moonroof. The stiff body structure and suspension, as well as tight steering, make for easy, sports-car-like handling with lots of road feel and few surprises. Unfortunately, the 4-cylinder base engine in pre-2007 models is wimpy and constantly reminds you and everyone else that it's a Toyota. Get the V6 instead.

Safety Summary

All models/years: Airbag fails to deploy, or is accidentally deployed. • Sudden acceleration when braking, shifting, or parking. • Stalling, then surging when accelerating or braking. • Car rolls away when parked on an incline. • Owners report that original-equipment Firestone tires fail prematurely. • Vehicle wanders all over the road or drifts into oncoming traffic. **All models: 2001**—Under-hood fire (left side) while vehicle is parked overnight. • Fire ignites from underneath vehicle while driving. • Excessive grinding noise and long stopping distances associated with ABS braking. • Suspension bottoms out too easily, damaging the undercarriage. • Automatic transmission slippage. • In one incident, with engine running and transmission in Park, car rolled down a hill. Two small girls inside the car jumped out, but one was then run over. • Vehicle parked overnight had its rear window suddenly blow out. • Floor-mounted gearshift indicator is hard to read. • Seat belts are too tight on either side and tighten up uncomfortably with the slightest movement. • Shoulder belt twists and won't lie straight. • Leaking suspension struts and strut-rod failure. • Trunk lid may suddenly collapse. • Faulty driver's window track. • Driver-side door latch sticks. • Tire jack collapses during change of tire. **2001–02**—Brake pedal goes to floor with no braking effect. • ABS suddenly locks up when coming to a gradual stop. **2002**—An astounding 620 owner complaints up to May 2007 puts the Camry in Ford Focus territory for safety-related failures. • One vehicle's starter caught on fire while vehicle was parked. • Faulty cruise control causes vehicle to suddenly accelerate. • Sudden acceleration without braking effect. • Defective rear brake drum. • Many owners complain of poor brake pedal design:

> Arm that holds up brake pedal is interfering with the driver's foot. Driver stated if consumer had a large size foot, it could easily get wedged and stuck on brake pedal. Foot gets caught between the floormat and the brake arm, needs to be redesigned.

• Front right axle broke six months after a car was purchased. • High rear end cuts rear visibility. • Turn signal volume is too low. **2003**—Over 400 safety-related complaints were registered by NHTSA, mostly identical to the incidents detailed for the 2002 model. **2004**—Fire ignites in the side wheelwell. • Sudden, unintended acceleration when braking, using the cruise control, shifting from Park to Reverse, or pulling into a parking space:

> Difficulty shifting from Park to Reverse, then upon shifting into Drive the car accelerated uncontrollably, would not stop, collided with a mobile home, airbags did not deploy, resulting in the death of one passenger and injury of driver.

> •

> While parking the car, the steering locked turning the car to the right. The car accelerated and surged despite depressing the brake (same as ODI PE04021), the car broke a metal flag pole, damaged a retaining wall, and fell seven feet [2 m] into a major street. The airbags did not deploy.

> Caller's mother-in-law just got her car washed and when she pulled out of the car wash, the vehicle accelerated without warning. She pumped the brakes and tried to stop the car, and it would not stop. The car went into an 8-lane highway and was hit by an 18-wheeler and a pickup truck. Driver sustained injuries and so did the driver of the pickup truck.

• Steering U-joint bearing falls out. • Steering knuckle defective:

> Problem has been going on for two weeks. Now after taking it to an official Toyota dealer repair shop, problem still not fixed. Now at least two weeks to a month wait on part. Was told we were number 536 on waiting list, and was told it was not a safety issue in short term, but do not believe that. Steering is loose, and a catch occurs in steering. Passenger can even feel when this occurs. Dealer has reported three exact same problems with other Camrys in the same week.

• Brake and gas pedal are mounted too close together. • Sudden brake failure. • Brake pedal goes all the way to the floor, and braking distance is increased. • When in Drive on a hill, the vehicle rolls backward. • When shifted into Reverse, vehicle goes forward. • When accelerating, engine and transmission will hesitate for up to four seconds, then will surge forward. This problem extends over several model years and also includes the Lexus ES 300/330. • Poorly designed, misadjusted headlights cause a blinding glare. • Backup lights are too dim. • Repeat failures of the cruise-control, odometer, and speedometer control modules. • Airbags are disabled even when a heavy adult sits in the seat. • Inside cabin hood release latch not attached to release mechanism. • The bumpers are easily dented. • Premature wearout of Firestone tires. • Original-equipment Goodyear Integrity "all-season" tires perform poorly in snow. • Unstable tire jack. • Electronic gas mileage calculator is off by 2 km/L (4.7 mpg). Dealer says they are all off and no repair is being contemplated. • Are Camrys "rat-prone"? Read the following owner's complaint and decide for yourself:

> O_2 sensors failed due to rodents or rabbits chewing the plastic wiring housing the internal electrical wires. O_2 sensors had to be replaced at a cost of about $600. The outside coatings, or sheaths, for the wiring is made of a soy-based plastic and possibly contains a "fish oil" in the sheath, which attracts rodents and rabbits, and they chew on the plastic wire coverings, thereby destroying the O_2 sensor's wiring mechanism. This problem is prevalent in the Denver and mountain state areas and should be corrected as the problem could lead to engine fires or engine failures. The wiring housing should be changed to a "retardant" type of wiring to prevent other incidents of this problem, and not just for Toyota but for all manufacturers.

2005—Vehicle hesitates and then surges. • Sometimes, the Camry will suddenly lurch forward when easing into a parking space:

I was slowly turning right to park in front of a store with my foot on the brakes preparing to stop when my 2005 Camry accelerated, jumped the curb and crashed into a storefront window.

• V6 has chronic hesitation problems at lower speeds. • Engine surges when slowing for a traffic light, or when applying moderate brake pressure. • Car constantly veers left. • Transmission shifts with a jolt when car slows down and then accelerates. • Brake pedal will sink to the floor intermittently. • Windshield has hash marks that obstruct vision when sun shines through. **2006**—225 safety-related complaints, which is about average for a five-year-old car, with most reports relating to sudden acceleration, brake failures, and airbag malfunctions. • Too much steering play, knocking noise. • Side windows fall down. **2007**—Over 1,166 safety-related complaints posted on NHTSA's website; 200 complaints would be normal for a 2007 model. • Top complaint categories are airbag failures, sudden, unintended acceleration, and loss of brakes or reduced braking. • Many reports that the car hesitates on takeoff; transmission slips. • Steering wheel binds. **2008**—231 safety-related complaint posted on NHTSA's website. • Passenger-side airbag is disabled when the passenger seat is occupied. • Sudden acceleration while parking the car and cruising on the highway. • Throttle response has intermittent delay. • Chronic stalling, hesitation, and surge. • 6-speed automatic transmission slippage. • Poor braking performance. • Excessive vibration once underway. • Rear window glare, and dash reflects onto the front windshield. **2009**—432 safety-related incidents reported; brakes, airbags, and unintended acceleration still appear as troublesome. *Hybrid:* **2007**—Only 79 safety incidents reported to NHTSA. This is less than half what one would normally see on the average three-year-old vehicle. • Sudden acceleration after floor mats were removed. • Chronic stalling. • Sudden loss of steering. • Cruise control malfunctions:

The car's cruise control behavior on level ground is fine, but on rolling hills it's totally egregious, and indicates to me that this feedback control system may be close to instability and therefore potentially dangerous. I think that the control algorithm used is dreadfully sub-optimal, and has such long internal control-loop processing delays that its reactions to changing road conditions are alarming. What I find is the following behavior: The car substantially overshoots (by 10 mph [16 km/h] or more) the set speed on the downhill portion of each hill, but then waits so long before reacting to the beginning of the next uphill portion, that it then undershoots the set speed by such a large amount (5 mph [8 km/h] or more) that it has to "floor" the accelerator in order to catch up. Still on the uphill portion, it then proceeds to overshoot the set speed again, before finally settling down to the desired speed. This cycle of events repeats over and over again as one negotiates rolling hills with the cruise control "on"... The cruise control's behavior could be fixed by a simple firmware update.

•

The speed [decreases] by as much as 5 mph [8 km/h] while descending...a hill, then as it begins to climb it quickly accelerates way over the target speed. This causes a whiplash effect to all passengers and may cause the driver to lose control and collide with vehicles.

• While driving in the snow, the car's traction control feature cuts all power:

There appears to be a lot of similar complaints about this issue...see *www.consumeraffairs.com/news04/2008/01/prius_winter.html*.

• Engine sludge requires an $8,000 rebuild; Toyota had this problem a decade earlier and refunded the repair costs under a secret goodwill warranty they later publicized. • Both sun visors fall at the pivot point. • Sun glares from the dash's stainless steel appliqué. • Oily residue coats interior windows. Dealer says it is the car's plastic trim and fabrics "outgassing":

The contact stated that the vehicle was emitting fumes that made her sick. However, she was unsure of the composition of the fumes. She went to the hospital three different times, and was admitted for a week each of the last two times. Her doctor said that she had chemical pneumonia or statis asthmaticus. Neither speed nor weather conditions were a factor.

• A rock passed through a hole in the grille of one vehicle and destroyed the radiator. • Premature tire wear. • Long wait for replacement parts. **2008**—Only 25 incidents recorded by NHTSA. • Airbag deployment broke driver's finger and acid-like substance from the airbag ate into her leg tissue:

All surface skin & few layers deep gone! Eaten away like acid. I am sure 100% airbag powder soaked in at implosion and ate its way out! I never knew powder in "air" bags. At emergency room no one told me to cleanse legs. Went to wound care doctors & skin continued to disingrate. On April 20 2010, had emergency surgery to remove necrotic area, not healing. Graft July 2010 not healing. Aug 31 took last bandage off, huge ugly scar, chunk of calf missing/deformity now. Airbag powder like caustic acid. Many people say they had blisters, too. Lawyers too said same. Most people cars are gone before anyone can investigate.

• Fire ignited in the engine compartment. • Vehicle lunges forward when shifted into Reverse. • No brakes, or reduced braking capability. • Loss of power as car limped home; no data found in the car's black box. • Loss of steering control as car veered off into oncoming traffic. • When it rains the car leaks water, which soon fouls the cabin air. **2009**—Only six safety-related problems logged by NHTSA, yet sudden acceleration and poor braking make encore appearances (along with one rodent report):

2009 Toyota Camry acceleration problem happened after recall fixes. Was pulling into parking space slowly when Acc. pedal dropped and engine able to stomp hard on brakes and not hit the building since hybrid gas part of engine disengages when the brake pedal is used.

When I am braking and go over a bump, the car feels like it speeds up before braking resumes.

Rodents chewing on biodegradable wire harness in 2009 Camry 4 door sedan hybrid. Complaint given to customer service mgr was inoperative gas gauge. No explanation given for entry points or solution other than replacement of wiring harness. Toyota customer experience center representative Emanual put customer on hold to review internal Toyota documents regarding issue, but refused to give document name, page number or file name.

• Vehicle feels like it speeds up, instead of braking, just after passing over a speed bump. • Acceleration recall repair makes it hard to keep foot on the accelerator pedal. • Vehicle may shift over to gasoline power and runs with reduced power until battery is dead. • Ventilation system air smells mouldy, and dealer counter-measures aren't effective.

Secret Warranties/Internal Bulletins/Service Tips

All models/years: To reduce front brake squeaks on ABS-equipped vehicles, ask the dealer to install new, upgraded rotors (#43517-32020). • Owner feedback over the last decade as well as dealer service managers who wish to remain anonymous tell me that Toyota has a secret warranty that will pay for replacing front disc brake components that wear out before 2 years/40,000 km. If you're denied this coverage, threaten small claims court action. **All models: 2002**—Catalytic converter heat-shield rattle. • Campaigns to repair the washer reservoir tank; remove coil-spring spacers. **2002–06**—Plugging a front-door water leak. **2002–08**—Front power seat grinding and groaning. **2003–06**—Tips for silencing intermediate steering shaft noise. **2003–11**—Remedy for a rear windshield ticking noise. **2004–05**—Correction for drifting or pulling into oncoming traffic involves installing new springs and struts. **2004–06**—Rear suspension thumping. **2004–08**—Front seat squeaking. **2006–09**—No shift from Park; multiple warning lights come on. **2007**—Engine oil leaks from the timing cover. • Rough idle, stalling. • Shift flare. • Noisy rear suspension. **2007–08**—No crank; engine starts and dies. • Premature brake pad wear; squeaking rear brakes. • Excessive steering-wheel vibration, flutter, and noise. • Instrument panel rattle. Frame creaking noise. • Rear suspension squeaking, rubbing. • Engine oil leak from camshaft housing. • Engine ticking noises. • Torque converter shudder. • Floor pan creaking noise. • Moonroof knocking when underway. • Troubleshooting brake pulsation/vibration. • Rattle from trunk area. **2007–09**—Water leaks onto headliner and footwell area. • Silencing engine ticking and floor pan creaking. • Inoperative moonroof. **2007–10**—Limited Service Campaign #90K will cover the full cost of replacement of the V6 engine VV-1 oil hose until March 31, 2013. • Braking vibration, pulsation can be reduced through the use of new brake pads and brake rotor R & R. Work should be paid for by Toyota, whether vehicle was bought new or used:

		VIBRATION/PULSATION WHEN BRAKING		

BULLETIN NO.: T-SB-0169-09

DATE: JUNE 4, 2009

Some 2007–10 Camry vehicles may exhibit a vibration or pulsation condition when braking. New front brake pads are available to address customer concerns. Follow the repair procedure below.

APPLICABLE WARRANTY: This repair is covered under the Toyota Comprehensive Warranty. This warranty is in effect for 36 months or 36,000 miles, whichever occurs first, from the vehicle's in-service date. Warranty application is limited to correction of a problem based upon a customer's specific complaint.

REPAIR PROCEDURE: Machine both front rotors with an on-car lathe to minimize rotor run-out. Make sure that the rotors are within minimum thickness. After machining the maximum allowed rotor run-out is 0.05 mm (0.002 inch). If the rotors are unserviceable or below minimum thickness replace the rotors.

• A rattle or buzz coming from the driver's side dash may require an updated vacuum check valve. • Tips on correcting a roof knocking sound. • Intermittent noxious AC odours. • Loose sun visor mounts. • Dust, powder may blow in through the dash air vents. **2008–09**—TCM update for shift improvements. **2008–10**—Ignition coils may need replacing if the MIL alert is illuminated. *Hybrid:* **2007–09**—No shift from Park; multiple warning lights come on. • Water leaks onto headliner and footwell area. • Inoperative moonroof. **2007–10**—Ways to fix a knocking sound from the roof area. *Solara:* **All years:** Water leaking into the trunk area. • Poor durability of rear-view mirrors. **2002–03**—Harsh automatic transmission shifts. • Excessive brake vibration. • Sliding-roof repair tips (TSB #BO002-03). • Power front seat feels loose (TSB #BO004-03). • Poor AC/heating. **2002–05**—Fuel door hard to open. • Remedy for rotten-egg exhaust smell. **2004–06**—Convertible top hard to close. **2004–08**—Water leaks at headliner and floor areas.

CAMRY, HYBRID, SOLARA PROFILE

	2001	2002	2003	2004	2005	2006	2007	2008	2009
Cost Price ($)									
Base Sedan CE	24,565	—	—	—	—	—	—	—	—
LE	27,695	23,755	24,800	24,800	24,990	24,990	25,800	25,900	23,400
LE V6	—	27,585	27,070	27,070	27,475	27,475	29,400	29,500	28,235
Camry Hybrid	—	—	—	—	—	—	31,900	32,000	30,660
Base Solara	27,580	28,175	28,175	28,800	26,850	27,545	29,200	—	—
V6	33,075	33,990	34,290	27,777	30,950	32,850	33,400	36,975	—
Convertible/SE	39,105	39,505	39,505	39,100	39,100	34,700	36,500	36,500	—
Used Values ($)									
Base Sedan CE ▲	4,000	—	—	—	—	—	—	—	—
Base Sedan CE ▼	3,500	—	—	—	—	—	—	—	—
LE ▲	5,500	6,500	8,000	10,500	11,000	13,500	16,500	19,500	
LE ▼	4,000	5,500	7,000	9,000	9,500	12,500	15,000	18,000	
LE V6 ▲	—	6,500	8,500	10,000	11,500	12,500	15,500	19,000	22,000
LE V6 ▼	—	5,500	7,500	9,000	10,500	12,000	14,000	17,500	21,500

All ratings on a numbered scale where 5 is good and 1 is bad. See page 132 for a more detailed description.

Camry Hybrid ▲	—	—	—	—	—	—	16,000	22,000	24,500
Camry Hybrid ▼	—	—	—	—	—	—	14,500	20,500	23,000
Base Solara ▲	5,000	6,500	7,500	9,000	10,000	11,500	14,000	—	—
Base Solara ▼	4,500	6,000	6,500	8,000	9,000	10,000	13,000	—	—
V6 ▲ 7,000	8,000	9,000	11,000	12,000	13,000	15,500	22,500	—	
V6 ▼ 6,000	7,000	8,000	10,000	11,000	12,000	14,500	21,000	—	
Convertible/SE ▲	8,000	9,500	10,500	12,000	13,500	15,500	19,000	25,500	
Convertible/SE ▼	7,500	8,500	9,500	11,500	12,000	14,500	17,500	24,000	—

Reliability	2	2	3	3	3	2	2	3	3
Crash Safety (F)	4	5	5	4	5	5	5	6	5
Solara	—	—	—	—	—	—	—	5	—
Side	3	3	3	5	5	5	5	5	5
Solara	3	3	3	5	5	5	—	5	—
IIHS Side	—	1	1	5	5	5	5	5	5
Solara Cvt.	—	—	—	3	3	3	3	3	—
Offset	5	5	5	5	5	5	5	5	5
Solara Cvt.	—	—	—	5	5	5	5	5	—
Head Restraints	—	—	—	1	2	2	2	2	2
Solara	3	—	3	1	1	1	1	1	—
Roof Strength	—	—	—	—	—	—	5	5	5
Rollover Resistance	5	4	4	4	4	4	4	4	4

Note: Without head- and torso-protecting side airbags, 2002–06 Camrys receive a side crashworthiness rating of Poor from IIHS. Hybrid NHTSA ratings are identical to the four-door Camry. Incidentally, look at how quickly the 2007 Camry Hybrid has lost almost half its original value.

PRIUS ★★

RATING: Below Average (2001–09). A "runaway" success combining high-tech electronics with impressive fuel economy. Where the car disappoints is in its proclivity to run away (sudden, unintended acceleration), lose steering and braking capability, and burn out headlights at $300 apiece. Servicing is also highly dealer-dependent and expensive. **Ideal model year:** A side airbag-equipped 2007 that sells for about half its original price. Put aside some of your savings from the purchase to buy an anchor you can throw out to brake the car. **"Real" city/ highway fuel economy:** Transport Canada estimates fuel economy to be in the range of 4.5/4.6 L/100 km, though owners say they burn much more fuel than that, especially in cold weather. **Maintenance/repair costs:** Higher than average. **Parts:** Good luck. Parts are hard to find and mainly available only at exorbitant prices from some Toyota dealers. As Toyota accelerator, brakes, steering, and corrosion recalls mount, dealer inventory will be crowded out by recall parts, and mechanics will spend much of their time fixing the recalled vehicles. Get your 12-volt battery from any independent retailer; it'll cost way less. **Extended warranty:** A good idea. **Best alternatives:** Comparable high-mileage models include the Ford Focus, Ford Fusion Hybrid, Honda Civic, Toyota

Echo, and Volkswagen Golf/Jetta diesel. **Helpful websites:** *http://priuschat.com/ forums, www.toyotanation.com/forum* and *www.toyotaowners.net.*

Strengths and Weaknesses

Seating five passengers, the Prius carries both a 4-cylinder gasoline engine and an electric motor, which work together or separately, depending on driving needs. The Prius accelerates from a stop using its electric motor alone. However, once underway, the gas engine becomes the sole power source. For merging or passing power, the electric motor may kick in to add additional power. Conversely, when coasting or braking, the gas engine may shut off, and the electric motor takes over as a generator to recharge the battery pack. While stopped, the gas engine stays off unless the air conditioner is in use. Prius's powertrain system uses a CVT, which has no gears but uses a system of belt and pulleys to deliver power to the wheels. When the wheels are moving, they charge the battery pack, which means the Prius never needs to be plugged into an AC outlet.

VEHICLE HISTORY: 2004—This redesigned model grew in size, features, and weight; ABS and traction control were standard. Optional front torso and curtain side air-bags. **2005**—A standard rear wiper was added. **2006**—A slight restyling. **2007**—Front side airbags and side curtain airbags are standard features; they are a plus. **2008**—An entry-level Standard model is offered.

The 2001–03 models weren't particularly noteworthy and changed very little over the years. They did conserve fuel; however, these early models lacked power and interior room, and handled poorly. The 2004s were redesigned to provide more interior room and better handling. Power, though, was still anemic; rear passenger room remained fairly tight, handling still was not impressive, and worst of all there came a deluge of reports of sudden acceleration, brake and steering loss, and head-light failures that increased exponentially through the 2010 models. The 2006 models were little changed, but the 2007s got a major safety upgrade with new standard airbags. The 2008 models changed little, as steering and handling stayed sub-par, cargo room was Lilliputian, and acceleration remained wimpy and scary:

> Struggles on highways at even 70 mph [113 km/h] (it's much more geared towards urban driving). Engine refined and quiet during cruising, but sounds like a plane taking off when accelerating. Automatic transmission hasn't got a kick down mode, so flooring it does nothing.

The Prius warranty includes 8-year/160,000 kilometre powertrain coverage, plus roadside assistance. The battery pack price has come down, but it is still quite expensive at $2,588 for the 2001 model and $2,299 or more for the second-generation hybrid (2002–09). See the letters about unreasonable battery pack costs in the Prius Chat website link above.

Buyers can expect rear seating that's cramped for three adults, minimal power for passing and merging, a rear windshield that cuts visibility, higher-than-average insurance premiums, 50 percent depreciation after three years, dealer-dependent servicing creating higher servicing costs, and sales and servicing that may not be available outside of large urban areas. The CVT has a mixed reliability record and cannot be easily repaired by independent agencies, and the engine is stall-prone and may suddenly accelerate when the brakes are applied. When the brakes do work as they should, they aren't very precise or responsive. Other safety concerns you may not discover until it's too late: The car is very unstable when hit by crosswinds; highway rescuers are wary of the car's 500-volt electrical system and are taking special courses to prevent electrocution; and rare, toxic battery components offset any positive environmental impact from cleaner and reduced emissions.

Other shortcomings

Toyota says the Prius is engineered to be as fuel-frugal, versatile, and hassle-free as possible. Unfortunately, Toyota has fallen far short of this goal. Some shortcomings: Acceleration is a mixture of yawning and screaming (also known as "lag and lurch"); handling is mediocre; braking is life-threatening; the steering is numb at best, nonexistent at worst; the steering-wheel position takes some getting used to; and seats could use better bolstering and lumbar support. Hatch struts weaken progressively, and there are frequent problems with the multifunction display, a screen in the dash that provides information about fuel consumption and manages some radio and climate-control functions.

Other failings include constant stalling, electrical system glitches, and tire failures. Plus the gas pump shuts off when refuelling, the fuel gauge is inaccurate, and the vehicle runs out of gas despite the gauge showing plenty of fuel in the tank.

A fuel-sipper?

Fuel economy is nowhere near what's advertised. In fact, it may be 30 to 40 percent less, say *Consumer Reports*, the Society of Automotive Engineers, and others, and they all agree gas consumption is higher in colder weather and over hilly terrain.

Consumer tests over the past three years have shown that gas-electric hybrid cars in general are just a little more fuel-efficient (by fuel volume) than manual transmission–equipped diesels. Again, keep in mind that the ratings are all over the map and seldom come anywhere near the government-estimated fuel consumption figures. Diesel fuel has a significantly higher energy density than the gasoline used by the Prius, and in some countries diesel is less expensive than gasoline, so a diesel engine coupled to a manual transmission may be competitive with hybrid technology in some cases.

- In a *Motor Week* and *Cars.com* comparison with the Honda Insight, Audi A3, Volkswagen Jetta TDI, Smart ForTwo, and Ford Fusion Hybrid (September 2009), the Prius returned the highest mileage with 4.8 L/100 km (49.2 mpg). The Insight ranked second-most fuel-efficient, managing 5.8 L/100 km (40.5 mpg).

- A *Popular Mechanics* comparison (September 2008) shows that the 2009 Jetta TDI diesel has slightly better highway fuel economy than the 2008 Prius with 5.2 L/100 km (45.4 mpg) compared to 5.3 L/100 km (44.8 mpg). The Prius did better than the Jetta in city fuel economy, however: 5.3 L/100 km (44.7 mpg) compared to 7.4 L/100 km (32.0 mpg).
- *Consumer Reports* (June 2008) gave a real-world fuel consumption rating of 5.4 L/100 km (44.0 mpg) for the Prius.
- The Prius was the overall winner of the *Edmunds.com* "Gas-Sipper Smackdown" fuel economy test, winning three of the five tests (May 2008), including lowest overall fuel costs. The 2005 Jetta TDI won the remaining two tests, but factoring in the higher cost of diesel, the Jetta ranked third in fuel costs behind both the Prius and the Smart Fortwo.
- UK's *Auto Express* magazine (August 2007) performed independent fuel efficiency tests on public roads on a number of hatchbacks and published its list of the 10 most efficient. The Prius landed 10th on the list. The Citroën C4 Coupe 1.6 HDi took first place.

Safety Summary

All years: Most of the complaints logged by NHTSA from 2005–08 involve the same sudden acceleration accompanied by loss of braking that figured in the recall of the 2005–10 Avalon. So far, Toyota has recalled only the 2009–10 Prius. • Sudden acceleration when slowing down, and loss of braking:

> I have a 2005 and a 2009 Toyota Prius. On both of these vehicles, I have experienced the same [braking] problems which are being described in the news about the 2010 Prius model. I have never had an accident relating to this problem, but the potential is certainly there. The problem occurs when I am moving forward, have the brake slightly depressed, and I hit a pothole or speed bump.

> •

> Driver tapped the brakes to disengage the cruise control, and vehicle suddenly veered out of control to the left.

> •

> My wife and I bought a new Prius in early March of 2005. My wife was coasting to stop (around 5 mph [8 km/h]) for a stop sign and when she put her foot on the brake the car started to accelerate. She came to a stop after hitting another car head on. Before she hit the car (she also sideswiped another car) she was able to look at her feet to confirm that she was indeed pressing on the brake pedal.

• Electric motor or Smart Key can cause pacemakers to fail. • Chronic stalling:

> I have a 2005 Prius that has lost all engine power on two occasions. I believe the "stalling" is intentionally designed into the software to protect the transmission. I think a design decision intended to protect the car is putting my life at risk...the

car was unresponsive to the throttle and the gearshift. In both cases I coasted to a safe spot (try crossing five lanes of 70+ mph [115 km/h] freeway traffic at night).... I called Toyota corporate headquarters and was told they are unaware that this is a recurrent issue. This despite discussions in the press and on *hybridcars.com*. I am contacting you in case I am killed or injured before Toyota figures out that this is a serious and recurrent issue. The first incident was around January or February 2005.

• Extremely vulnerable to side winds. • Steering failure. • Floormat gets stuck between pedals. • Occupant accidentally bumped gearshift knob and put Prius into Dynamic Braking Mode, which almost caused a semi-truck to rear-end the car. • Poor emergency braking:

While test driving a new '05 Toyota Prius, I came to the conclusion that its braking system is inadequate. Emergency braking while turning easily induces understeer because of the regenerative braking. As the aggressive brake-assist takes over there is "snap" oversteer and front wheel lockup. For average drivers this can result in complete loss of control.

• Tail lights don't work. • Headlights fail prematurely. • Difficulty in fastening seat belts. • Goodyear Integrity 185/65R/R15 tires have no traction when roads are wet. **2001**—159 complaints. • Steering failure recall not enough:

Once the recall replacement has been performed, Toyota will no longer perform further replacements at their cost. If the failure should happen again, as it did for me as a third owner of the vehicle, it is an expense replacement (at over $1,300 USD). At this point to my best knowledge any current owner of an '01 Prius or certain models of the '02 Prius are gambling that an essential safety related component of the car such as the electric assist power steering will not fail.

2002—Early transmission replacement. • Car drifts from lane to lane. **2002–03**—Steering lockup and excessive steering shake (see *priuschat.com/forums/care-maintenancetroubleshooting/36358-03-power-steering.html*). **2003**—Floormat jams accelerator pedal. • Frequent tire blowouts and premature wear. • Inaccurate fuel gauge. **2004**—400 complaints logged by NHTSA; most relate to sudden acceleration and the simultaneous loss of brakes. • Malfunctioning computer causes many of the accessories and gauges to shut down or function erratically. **2004–07**—HID headlights go on and off intermittently, then go out for good:

I took the car to the Toyota dealer, where they replaced the headlights for $990. A few weeks later the same thing happened, headlights cut out at night. I took the car back to the dealer, where they kept it for several days. They then returned the car, assuring me that the problem was solved. Since that time the driver's side headlight has gone out several times.

2005—Close to 500 complaints, or twice the average for a six-year-old car. • Loose screws in the steering column cause severe shake. **2005–06**—Airbag fails to deploy. **2006**—Yikes! Almost 900 complaints, when the average vehicle would generate no more than 200. • Cruise control won't disengage unless the driver slams on the brakes. **2007**—Almost 800 safety-related complaints posted to NHTSA's site when 150 incidents would be the average for a vehicle this age. **2008**—NHTSA has logged over 500 safety-related complaints. Normally, one would expect to see an average of 50 complaints a year. • After the HID headlights have been turned on, they will often go off and come on again. Toyota bulb replacement cost is six times what independents charge (lifespan is about two years; cost is about $300 each). Toyota has a "secret warranty"—they will pay half of the bulb's $300 replacement cost. Owners believe the lights are okay, and that the ECU computer is at fault:

> Took car back three additional times for same issue. Finally dealer said there'd been numerous complaints and changed out the headlamp at a cost of $250.00. ($150 for the headlamp and $100 for labor) Later, I got a letter from Toyota acknowledging the faulty headlamp issue, but said Toyota had given us a discount by only charging $150.00 for the headlamp instead of the regular $300.00 cost. $300.00 for a headlamp seems excessive and if it's a common issue, why is Toyota not issuing a recall for this matter?

Secret Warranties/Internal Bulletins/Service Tips

All years: It is surprising that with so many serious defects, most Prius service bulletins are bereft of any reference to major deficiencies. One interesting maintenance tip: The battery can drain its charge and be damaged if the vehicle isn't started and left in idle for a half-hour at least once every two weeks:

> I was shocked and alarmed to read the following on page 8 of the Owners' Manual, which I didn't get until after the Prius was delivered:
>
> "If you do not use the vehicle for a long time (2 weeks or more), the hybrid vehicle battery and auxiliary battery will discharge and their condition is liable to decline. Therefore, in order to make up for discharging, charge them once in every two weeks for about 30 minutes by starting the hybrid system with all electrical components turned off…"
>
> When I mention not being able to take a two-week vacation without hiring a car sitter, people thank me for letting them know and state they would not buy the car under those circumstances.

Read more at *www.consumeraffairs.com/automotive/toyota_prius_battery.html*. **2000–08**—Multiple warning lights on; vehicle won't shift out of Park. • Steering pulls to the right. **2003–08**—Windshield back glass ticking. **2004–08**—Troubleshooting an engine knock and inaccurate fuel gauge readings. • Intermittent instrument display in cold weather. • Noxious AC odours.

PRIUS PROFILE

	2001	2002	2003	2004	2005	2006	2007	2008	2009
Cost Price ($)									
Prius	29,990	29,990	29,990	29,990	30,330	31,280	31,280	29,500	27,400
Used Values ($)									
Prius ▲	4,500	5,000	6,000	8,000	10,000	13,000	15,500	19,000	22,000
Prius ▼	3,500	4,500	5,500	7,000	8,500	11,500	14,000	18,000	19,500
Reliability	2	2	3	4	4	4	4	4	4
Crash Safety (F)	3	3	3	5	5	4	4	4	4
Side	—	3	3	4	4	4	5	5	5
Offset	—	—	—	5	5	5	5	5	5
IIHS Side	—	—	—	5	5	5	5	5	5
Head Restraints	—	—	—	2	2	2	2	2	2
Rollover Resistance	4	4	4	4	4	4	4	4	4

Note: The Prius depreciates more quickly in its later years because buyers are wary of paying for the car plus a $2,500+ battery pack—an amount almost equal to the car's worth.

Volkswagen

NEW BEETLE ★★

RATING: Below Average (2008–09); Not recommended (1999–2007), although a well-maintained 2006 or earlier diesel model will do if you have reliable, inexpensive servicing available. The New Beetle has always been a bad car that's both unreliable and expensive to troubleshoot. Safety-related complaints registered by NHTSA include electrical fires, chronic stalling, and transmission failures. **Ideal model year:** A 2006 GLS TDI for about $10,500. **"Real" city/ highway fuel economy:** *1.8 manual: 9.6/7.2 L/100 km. 1.8 automatic: 10.3/7.3 L/100 km. 2.0 manual: 9.8/7.0 L/100 km. 2.0 automatic: 9.6/7.2 L/100 km. 1.9 diesel manual: 6.2/4.6 L/100 km. 1.9 diesel automatic: 6.5/5.2 L/100 km.* Owners report gasoline fuel savings may undershoot these estimates by at least 10 percent, or 15 percent for diesel fuel. **Maintenance/repair costs:** Average, but only a VW dealer can repair these cars. **Parts:** Usually easily found, since they're taken mostly from the Golf and Jetta parts bin, but body parts are harder to find. **Extended warranty:** A good idea. **Best alternatives:** Acura Integra, CSX, or RSX; Ford Fusion; Honda Accord; Hyundai Elantra wagon, Sonata, Tiburon, or Tucson; Mazda6; and Nissan Sentra. **Helpful websites:** *http://newbeetle.org/ forums/questions-issues-concerns-problems-new-beetle, http://forums.vwvortex.com,* and *http://volkswagenownersclub.com.*

Strengths and Weaknesses

VW resurrected the Beetle as a 2000 model and produced a competent front-engine, front-drive compact car set on the chassis and running gear of the Golf hatchback. It's much safer than its predecessor, but, oddly enough, it's still afflicted with many of the same deficiencies that we learned to hate with the original. Without the turbocharger, the 115 hp 2.0L engine is underwhelming when you get it up to cruising speed (the 90 hp turbodiesel isn't much better), plus there's still not much room for rear passengers, engine noise is disconcerting, front visibility is hindered by the car's quirky design, and storage capacity is at a premium.

On the other hand, the powerful optional 1.8L turbocharged engine makes this Beetle an impressive performer; the heater works fine; steering, handling, and braking are quite good; and the interior is not as spartan or as tacky as it once was.

VEHICLE HISTORY: 2001—Larger exterior mirrors, and a trunk safety release. **2002**—Introduction of the 180 hp Turbo S and a new Electronic Stabilization feature. **2003**—Convertible and turbodiesel arrive. **2004**—Upgraded head-protecting airbags and front head restraints, improved spoiler, and new wheels. The GLX model is axed. **2006**—The 115 hp 2.0L and 150 hp turbocharged 1.8L are replaced by a 150 hp 2.5L 5-cylinder engine. A hatchback TDI model with a 100 hp 1.9L turbodiesel is the only diesel model available. Standard anti-lock four-wheel disc brakes and front side airbags with head and torso protection, and an anti-skid system and traction control. **2007**—No more diesel-engine Beetles; all models come with a 150 hp 5-cylinder gasoline engine.

In a nutshell, here are the New Beetle's strong points: standard side airbags; easy handling; impressive braking; sure-footed and comfortable, though firm, ride; comfy and supportive front seats with plenty of front headroom and legroom; and a cargo area that can be expanded by folding down the rear seats.

On the minus side, owners have reported serious safety defects, powertrain performance is unimpressive, and body construction is second-rate. Some specific owner gripes: Frequent ECM failures; malfunctioning dash gauges; excessive engine and brake noise; faulty window regulators; early brake component replacement; limited rear legroom and headroom; axle oil pan and oil pump failures; difficult rear entry/exit; car is easily buffeted by crosswinds; skimpy interior storage and trunk space; diesel engines lack pep and produce lots of noise and vibration; faulty oxygen sensors cause the Check Engine light to come on; delayed shifts from Park to Drive, or failure to shift into Fourth gear; awkward-to-access radio buttons and door-panel-mounted power switches; coolant leaks onto the wiring harness also causing the Check Engine light to come on; the 2.0L engine runs out of steam around 100 km/h and may overheat; and optional high-mounted side mirrors, large head restraints, and large front roof pillars obstruct front and rear visibility. Also, interior vent louvres loosen and break, the hatchback rattles and sometimes fails to open, the AC disengages when decelerating, the AC fan motor howls and the engine makes a loud humming noise when the AC is turned on, front lights retain water and short out, and the low-slung chassis causes extensive undercarriage damage when going over a curb.

Safety Summary

2000–01—Airbags fail to deploy. • Airbag warning light stays lit constantly. • Many complaints of prolonged hesitation when accelerating. • Steering suddenly locks up. • Low mounted fuel tank is easily punctured. • Mass airflow sensor and secondary air-injection-pump motor failures. • Windows fall into door channel because of defective regulators. • Hard to keep rear window free of rain, snow, or dew. • Rear seat-belted passengers hit their heads on the unpadded side pillars. **2000–03**—Back glass suddenly shatters. **2002**—ABS failure. • Window goes up and down on its own. • Brake fluid leakage. • Harsh downshifts; vehicle loses power (mass airflow sensor is the suspected cause). **2003**—Sudden acceleration, stalling. • Side airbag deploys for no reason. • Driver-side airbag fails to deploy. • Punctured fuel tank leaks fuel. • Steering-wheel locks up; excessive shake; constant pulling to the right (torque steer). • Rear windshield is hard to see through. • Dash warning lights come on constantly for no apparent reason. • Head restraints still sit too high to be comfortable, and obstruct rear visibility. • Open sunroof sucks exhaust into the cabin. • Left front strut slips down through the spindle, causing the spindle to hit the wheelwell. **2004**—Complete transmission failure; replaced transmission also shifts poorly. • Delayed shifting and long hesitation when accelerating. • Sudden stalling and loss of electrical power while underway. • Complete loss of steering. • Electrical shorts cause the odometer and other accessories to malfunction. • Wiper suddenly quits working. • Airbag warning light comes on constantly. • Annoying beep when seat belt isn't buckled. • Driver-side window lowers on its own. • On convertible models, the windows catch on the top when the doors are opened. **2004–05**—Airbags fail to deploy. **2005**—Owners report the worst of both worlds when describing engine performance. For example, there are reports of the car suddenly accelerating when coming to a stop, or, conversely, losing power when accelerating. • Driver's window explodes. **2006**—Rear seat belt unlatches in a rear-end collision. • Sudden stalling in traffic. • Megatronic automatic transmission shifts roughly and binds; long wait for parts. • Rear engine mount failure. • Dual-mass flywheel blows apart in the manual transmission clutch assembly. • Brake pedal goes to the floor with no braking effect. • Right side of the windshield distorts the driver's view. **2007**—Vehicle lags and then surges when accelerating. • Frequent brake and brake master cylinder failures. Hard starting due to electrical failures. • Trunk is hard to open. **2008**—Sudden acceleration when stopped at a traffic light. • Key won't turn in the starter; easy to break off the key in the ignition or damage the starter:

> I was told there were hundreds of backorders nationally for this starter part. When I received the car back with the new part, I immediately began experiencing the same problem. I also noted the same problem in two loaner cards (2009 models of the VW New Beetle) provided by my dealer.

2009—Two incidents reported that a fire ignited in the vehicle's front end while it was parked:

> While parked for 30 minutes the vehicle caught on fire. The fire started in the front under the engine. The fire department stated it could be an electrical fire or a leak in the engine. The vehicle was completely destroyed.

• Sudden, unintended acceleration, vehicle crashed, and airbags failed to deploy. • Snapped motor mount bolts cause severe vibration throughout the vehicle and excessive engine noise:

> Upon returning on Monday morning, the technician informed me that the motor mount bolts (two) were missing and the threads for each was completely stripped. The motor was rocking back and forth creating this dreadful noise. The threads were restored using tap and dye set and new bolts were installed. I was informed that sometimes the bolts snap and this is a manufacturers defect. I was told there were other signs of damage and I kind of feel something will be found once my warranty is up as a result of this mishap.

Secret Warranties/Internal Bulletins/Service Tips

2000–08—Door windows may separate from regulators. **2000–11**—Removing nasty smells emanating from the air vents. **2001–08**—Inoperative or malfunctioning sunroof. **2002**—Transmission appears to leak fluid. • Inoperative fresh-air blower motor. **2003–05**—Corroded rotors may be the cause of excessive brake vibration. • Convertible top may not operate correctly. **2003–10**—Excessive brake vibration troubleshooting tips. **2004**—Hard starting, no-starts, or rough running when wet. **2004–07**—Transmission fluid leakage between case halves. **2005–10**—Poor heating. • Engine cooling fan stays on after the ignition has been shut off. **2006–07**—The 6-speed automatic transmission won't shift out of Park. **2006–08**—AC doesn't get cold enough. **2007**—Insufficient heater output at idle. **2007–08**—Cluster lights flicker with wipers on.

NEW BEETLE PROFILE

	2001	2002	2003	2004	2005	2006	2007	2008	2009
Cost Price ($)									
Base	21,950	21,950	23,210	23,690	23,910	24,490	22,780	21,977	21,976
Cabrio	27,900	28,530	29,250	29,610	30,160	29,880	27,790	26,975	26,975
Used Values ($)									
Base ▲	4,000	5,000	6,000	6,500	8,000	10,500	12,500	15,000	17,000
Base ▼	3,500	4,500	5,000	6,000	6,500	9,000	11,000	13,500	15,500
Cabrio ▲	6,500	7,500	8,500	10,000	11,000	13,000	16,000	19,000	21,000
Cabrio ▼	6,000	6,500	7,500	9,000	10,500	12,000	14,500	17,500	19,500

Reliability	1	1	1	1	1	1	1	3	3
Crash Safety (F)	4	4	4	4	4	4	4	4	4
Cabrio	—	—	5	4	—	—	4	4	4
Side	5	5	5	5	5	5	5	5	5
IIHS Side	—	—	—	1	1	1	1	1	1
Offset	5	5	5	5	5	5	5	5	5
Head Restraints (F)	5	5	5	3	3	3	3	3	3
Rollover Resistance	—	—	4	4	4	4	4	4	4
Cabrio	—	—	4	4	—	—	4	4	4

Note: Used diesel models will cost from $500 to $1,000 more than the gasoline-powered versions. They didn't start out that way, but higher fuel costs have pushed up their resale value. Also, seats with adjustable lumbar support scored 5 consistently.

PASSAT ★★

RATING: Below Average (1999–2009). About as unreliable and expensive to service as the New Beetle. The Passat is loved by car columnists who get the car for free. Word has gotten out that these cars are over-hyped for their performance prowess, that they aren't very dependable, and that they cost a lot to maintain. Consequently, Passats have lost their lustre to Japanese luxury cars, and they now depreciate quickly. But beware; their low price won't cover the extraordinarily high repair bills you'll get from Otto, Hans, and Ingrid. **"Real" city/highway fuel economy:** *1.8 manual: 9.8/6.9 L/100 km. 1.8 automatic: 11.7/7.3 L/100 km. 2.8 6-cylinder automatic: 12.7/8.3 L/100 km. 4.0 8-cylinder 6-speed manual: 14.0/8.9 L/100 km. 4.0 8-cylinder 6-speed automatic: 13.4/8.8 L/100 km.* Owners say the 8-cylinder engines burn at least 20 percent more fuel than the above figures show. **Maintenance/repair costs:** Higher-than-average costs; dealer-dependent. **Parts:** Parts and service are more expensive than average; long waits for parts are commonplace. **Extended warranty:** Yes, principally for the powertrain. **Best alternatives:** Acura Integra, CSX, or RSX; Ford Fusion; and Honda Accord. **Helpful websites:** *http://forums. vwvortex.com* and *http://volkswagenownersclub.com.*

Strengths and Weaknesses

These front-drive compact sedans and wagons use mechanical parts borrowed from the Golf, Jetta, and Corrado. A 2.8L V6 became the standard powerplant beginning with the '99 wagon. Its long wheelbase and squat appearance give the Passat a massive, solid feeling, while its styling makes it look sleek and clean. As with most European imports, it comes fairly well-appointed.

As far as overall performance goes, the Passat is no slouch. The multi-valve 4-cylinder engine is adequate, and its handling is superior to that of most of the competition. The 2.8L V6 provides lots of power when revved and is the engine that works best with an automatic transmission.

VEHICLE HISTORY: 2001—Mid-year changes include a new nose, upgraded tail lights and dash gauges, chassis improvements, and the debut of a 170 hp engine alongside a new W8 270 hp AWD luxury car. **2002**—Given a 134 hp 2.0L turbocharged diesel coupled to either a front-drive or an all-wheel-drive powertrain. Also new is a 5-speed automatic transmission with manual capability. **2003**—W8 is given a 6-speed manual transmission. **2004**—A diesel powerplant joins the lineup, and AWD is offered on more models. **2005**—No more W8 series, GL models come with a turbodiesel only, and the GLX gets 17-inch wheels. **2006**—Redesigned with fresh styling, a larger interior, and more power. The turbocharged 2.0L picks up 30 more horses, while the 280 hp 3.6L V6 adds 90 more horses. V6 models come with an automatic transmission only. **2007**—Return of the popular Passat wagon. **2008**—Not much new, except for a 3.6L engine powering the 4Motion all-wheel drive and a standard 12-way power driver's seat.

Passats are infamous for automatic transmission failures, engine ignition coil/fuel-system stalling and no-starts, and engines gummed up by oil sludge—all costly to repair. Even when they're operating as they should, the Passat's manual and automatic gearboxes leave a lot to be desired; for example, the 5-speed manual transmission's gear ranges are too far apart (there's an enormous gap between Third and Fourth gear), and the 4-speed automatic shifts poorly with the 4-banger. Also, owners report that the transmission won't shift from lower gears, and as the car ages there are problems with MacPherson struts, clutch slave cylinder (leaks), the fuel and electrical systems, and the front brakes (rotor warpage, premature wear, excessive noise, brake booster failures, and master cylinder replacements) . Additionally, engines often leak oil; early replacement of the power-steering assembly is often needed; fuel and computer module problems lead to hard starts and chronic stalling; and defective tie-rod and constant velocity joint seals allow debris to enter into the vehicle's system, effectively causing the premature wearout of internal components.

On the body side, the sunroof rattles; rear door mouldings warp easily; door speakers need frequent replacing; the front spoiler and rear trim fall off; the driver-seat memory feature fails; windshields may be optically distorted; trim and controls are fragile; heated seats are a pain in the...well, you know; water leaks persistently from the pollen filter; the fuel gauge malfunctions, indicating fuel in the tank when it's empty; the rear-view passenger-side mirrors are too small and cause several blind spots; and interior there's a helicopter-type wind noise when cruising with the windows or sunroof open.

Owners report that VW dealer servicing is the pits. Cars have to be brought in constantly to fix the same problems, recall campaign repairs are often slow because parts aren't available, and warranty coverage is spotty because VW headquarters doesn't empower or pay dealers sufficiently to take the initiative. Competent servicing and parts are particularly hard to find away from large cities, and many of the above-mentioned deficiencies can cost you an arm and a leg to repair.

 **Safety Summary**

All years: Sudden, unintended acceleration. • An incredible number of automatic transmission malfunctions, breakdowns, and early replacements. • Airbag light comes on for no reason. • Airbags fail to deploy, or deploy for no reason. One VW employee told U.S. federal investigators he was fired shortly after complaining about the airbag hazard:

> The driver-side head airbag (air curtain) of a 2003 Volkswagen Passat W8 sedan deployed spontaneously while I was driving the car...a few minutes later, when the car was stopped, the steering wheel airbag deployed spontaneously.... I suffered a permanent wrist injury and am suffering from post-traumatic stress syndrome.... The incident, which happened during a test drive, was reported to the management of the VW dealership for which I was working and to the VW of America by the management.

2000–03—Many reports of fires igniting in the engine compartment. • Excess raw fuel flows out of the exhaust system. • Hard starts and chronic stalling. • Check Engine light comes on intermittently, and then engine shuts down. • While cruising, vehicle speeds up; when brakes are applied, it slows down until foot is taken off the brake, then surges again. • Braking doesn't disengage cruise control. • Hesitation and long delays when accelerating. • Automatic transmission suddenly drops out of gear. • Many complaints of windshield distortion (there's an accordion effect, where objects expand and contract as they pass by). • Passenger window suddenly explodes just after being rolled up. • Windshield wipers cut out. • Plastic engine nose shield falls off. • Rear tire failure damages the fuel-filler neck, causing a fuel leak. **2002**—Premature CV joint failure. • Oil pan is easily punctured because of low ground clearance. • Some electrical and fuel-system glitches cause chronic stalling, loss of engine power. • Gas pedal remains stuck to the floor. • Brakes don't grab as well when vehicle is cold; premature brake wear **2003**—Vehicle runs out of fuel despite the fuel gauge showing one-quarter tank of gas. • Super-heated seats. **2004**—Vehicle lurches forward when braking or accelerating. • Transmission control module and clutch failure; hard shifting; gears slam into place with a clunking sound. • Automatic transmission tends to hesitate and then jumps forward. • Loss of power steering; grinding noise. • Prematurely worn rear brake pads. • Electrical short circuits shut off lights. • Seat heater burns through seat:

> The heated drivers seat in my 2004 VW Passat caught on fire and burned through my wife's jeans. This occurred after driving only 1/4 mile [0.4 km]. She felt something on her leg, and when she looked down there was smoke coming out of the seat. She stopped and got the fire out, but it had burned her (left a red mark on her leg), her jeans, and put a hole in the seat.

• Insufficient space between the footrest and clutch pedal; foot gets trapped. • Windshield wiper collects snow and ice in wiper groove. • Water leaking into interior causes serious electrical shorts, primarily affecting the drivetrain:

> Water coming into front passenger seat resulting in damages to the TCM (transmission control module), wet carpeting, and rust under the passenger seat.

• Low-mounted oil pan is easily damaged when passing over uneven terrain. **2005**—Chronic stalling may cause engine failure. • Seat belts fail to retract. **2006**—More safety incidents reported than is normal for a four-year-old vehicle. • Several under-hood fires. • Sudden loss of power while cruising on the highway. • Engine over-revs when the AC is turned on; foot has to be kept on the brake pedal. • The bolt that holds the oil pump in place backs out and shears off, requiring an engine replacement:

> Sheared oil pump bolt at 16,000 miles [25,750 km]. [Engine] lost all power. Dealer replaced oil pump, timing chain and all related hardware. Asked manufacturer (Volkswagen) and dealership for new engine due to [likely] oil starvation after oil pump was inoperative. Request denied.

• Steering-column lock failure (lock control module: $2,400 (U.S.)). • Catalytic converter busted at a flange seam, damaging the brake vacuum tube with hot gases. • Tires wear out prematurely. • Trunk will not latch. • Airbag light is always lit. **2007**—Under-hood electrical harness fire. • Seat-warmer catches fire. • Vehicle recalled for sudden acceleration, but problem reappears after the fix. • Premature failure of the engine piston rings. • Oil pump socket broke, causing complete engine failure. • Engine over-revs when decelerating. • Chronic loss of power and misfiring. • Brakes slip and then grab when applied. • Subframe bolt failure. • Dash gauge cluster behaves erratically. • Original-equipment Pirelli tires develop side wall bulges. **2008**—Severe windshield distortion. • Sudden acceleration when slowing for traffic; problem identical to a recall campaign announced by VW for earlier Passats, but the involved car was excluded. • Chronic stalling cured only after the fuel pump is replaced. • Front axle and automatic transmission failure. • Car shifts into Neutral when stopping. • The 2.0L T engine is an oil-burner:

> I must frequently add oil to the engine and have brought it in to be serviced for this oil consumption issue several times. From research done online, this is not a problem unique to me.

Secret Warranties/Internal Bulletins/Service Tips

All models/years: Failure-prone, malfunctioning automatic transmissions. **All models: 1999–2006**—Condensation inside exterior lights. **1999–2008**—Inoperative heated rear glass lines. **2000–11**—Removing smelly odours from vents. **2003–10**—Excessive vibration when braking. **2005–10**—Cooling fan continues to run after ignition has been turned off. • Poor heater output.

2006–07—Airbag light constantly lit. • Front suspension creak. 2006–08—Front-seat creaking, cracking. • Inoperative AC and seat heater. • Rear brakes squeak in cold weather. • Seatback creaking; inoperative lumbar support. • Front suspension knocking. • Rear cupholder hard to remove. • Back glass sunshade damaged or fails to work properly. 2006–09—Wind noise from the top of the doors. 2006–10—Inoperative front-seat back recliner. 2008—Door mirrors loose or won't fold properly. • Inoperative keyless remote. *Diesels:* 2004–05—Engine hesitation on acceleration.

PASSAT PROFILE

	2001	2002	2003	2004	2005	2006	2007	2008	2009
Cost Price ($)									
Sedan	29,500	29,550	29,550	29,550	30,190	29,950	29,970	27,476	27,476
Wagon	27,900	30,500	30,725	30,725	31,020	31,660	27,780	31,425	28,976
Used Values ($)									
Sedan ▲	4,000	5,000	6,500	7,000	8,500	12,000	14,500	17,000	20,000
Sedan ▼	3,500	4,500	5,500	6,000	7,000	11,500	13,000	15,500	18,500
Wagon ▲	5,000	6,000	7,000	8,500	10,000	11,500	16,500	18,500	21,000
Wagon ▼	4,500	5,000	6,000	7,500	9,000	10,000	15,500	17,000	19,000
Reliability	1	1	1	1	1	1	2	2	2
Crash Safety (F)	5	5	5	5	5	4	4	4	4
Side	4	4	4	4	4	5	5	5	4
IIHS Side	—	—	—	—	—	5	5	5	5
Offset	5	5	5	5	5	5	5	5	5
Head Restraints (F)	1	1	1	1	1	3	2	2	5
Roof Strength	—	—	—	—	—	5	5	5	5
Rollover Resistance	—	—	4	4	4	4	4	4	4

LARGE CARS

Quintessential highway cruisers for law enforcement agencies, travelling salespeople, large families, or retirees, full-sized American cars are icons of a time long passed. They can't compete in a market of rising fuel costs and the availability of more versatile crossover minivans like the Mazda5, small sport-utilities like the Hyundai Tucson, or upscale, sporty coupes and sedans like the Hyundai Azera and Genesis. There are only two rear-drive Detroit choices left: Ford's once-popular, bland-leading-the-bland fleet anchor, the Grand Marquis, which was axed in 2008, and Chrysler's quality-challenged 300 series, Charger, and Magnum: three mediocre cars that should have been axed a long time ago.

It's surprising Chrysler's large cars have stuck around this long. True, they are attractively styled, but their reputation as gas-guzzling, unreliable sedans places them several notches below the Ford and GM competition. Chrysler's desperate

Chrysler's "Tyrannosaurus" cars: a mixture of the bad and the beautiful.

appeal to nostalgia and high performance rear-drive enthusiasts fell flat. These fully featured cars equipped with Hemi V8 engines were done in by high fuel prices and the manufacturer's poor quality control and shortened powertrain warranty. All three Chryslers are now scheduled for radical redesigns by Fiat within the next two years. You can bet that if fuel prices continue to rise, these large cars will be put back on the shelf next to the leftover *polenta* and *piccoli uccelli.*

Station Wagons (Full-Sized)

Once popular, full-sized rear-drive wagons—such as the GM Caprice and Roadmaster (both axed in 1996)—lost out to sport-utilities and minivans over a decade ago and have now been reincarnated as crossover front-drives. If passenger and cargo space and carlike handling are what you want, a used minivan, light truck, downsized SUV, or compact wagon can meet your needs at little cost, and will probably still be around a decade from now.

Some disadvantages of large station wagons include difficulty keeping the interior heated in winter, atrocious gas consumption, sloppy handling, and poor rear visibility. Also, rear hatches and rear brake supporting plates tend to be rust-prone, and the bodies become rattletraps.

LARGE CAR RATINGS

Above Average

Hyundai Azera (2006–09)

Average

Ford Grand Marquis (1999–2008)

Below Average

Chrysler Charger, SRT8 (2006–09)
General Motors Allure/LaCrosse, Lucerne (2006–09)

Not Recommended

Chrysler 300, 300C, 300M, Concorde, Intrepid, LHS,
   Magnum (1999–2009)

Chrysler

300, 300C, 300M, CHARGER, CONCORDE, INTREPID, LHS, MAGNUM, SRT8   ★ / ★ ★

RATING: *300, 300C, 300M, Concorde, Intrepid, LHS, Magnum:* Not Recommended (1999–2009). These models are a lemon grove—if *Lemon-Aid* had a rating lower than one star, these models would earn it. *Charger, SRT8:* Below Average (2006–09). The Mercedes connection didn't mean that Daimler shared its top-quality front- and rear-drive components; the cars actually got worse. Chrysler has gone from subpar front-drive vehicles to sub-par rear-drive 300 and Magnum models that are just as unreliable. Sure, they look good, but that's about all these gas hogs offer. Although all these large cars have large discounts, factory glitches will steal away most of your savings—and endanger your life, too. Parts are rare, and mechanics cringe when these hard-to-service cars arrive in their service bays. **"Real" city/highway fuel economy:** *Chrysler 300:* 12.2/8.1 L/100 km. *300C:* 12.6/8.6 L/100 km. *300C Hemi:* 13.5/8.0 L/100 km. *300C Hemi AWD:* 13.4/8.7 L/100 km. *300C Hemi SRT8:* 16.0/10.6 L/100 km. *Dodge Charger 2.7 6-cylinder:* 11.3/7.7 L/100 km. *Charger 3.5 6-cylinder:* 12.2/8.1 L/100 km. *Charger 3.5 6-cylinder AWD:* 12.6/8.6 L/100 km. *Charger 5.7 Hemi:* 13.5/8.0 L/100 km. *Charger 6.1 Hemi SRT8:* 16.0/10.6 L/100 km. *Concorde 2.7:* 12.6/8.0 L/100 km. *Concorde 3.5:* 12.5/7.9 L/100 km. *Intrepid 2.7:* 11.0/7.4 L/100 km. *Intrepid 3.5:* 12.5/7.9 L/100 km. Owners report fuel savings often undershoot these estimates by at least 20 percent. **Maintenance/repair costs:** Higher than average, but most repairs aren't dealer-dependent. **Parts:** Higher-than-average costs. Hemi engine parts are hard to find and cost an arm and a leg. **Extended warranty:** Look for an extended warranty that offers bumper-to-bumper protection—usually a $2,000–$3,000 extra expense. **Best alternatives:** Ford Crown Victoria or Grand Marquis; GM Allure, LaCross, or Lucerne; and Hyundai Azera. The Lincoln Town Car is a good choice, as well. **Helpful websites:** *www.allpar.com* and *www.chargerforums.com/forums.*

Strengths and Weaknesses

All the cars in Chrysler's full-size lineup share the same chassis and offer most of the same standard and optional features. They provide loads of passenger space and many standard features, such as four-wheel disc brakes and an independent rear suspension. Unfortunately, since their 1998 redesign, base models are equipped with a hard-to-service, failure-prone, and wimpy 200 hp 2.7L V6 aluminum engine. Higher-line variants get a more powerful 225 hp 3.2L V6 powerplant or a 242 hp 3.5L V6. (Earlier models also carried a 153 hp 3.3L 6-banger, but 70 percent of buyers chose the 3.5L for its extra horses.) Both variant engines provide plenty of low-end torque and acceleration, but this advantage is lost somewhat when traversing hilly terrain—the smaller V6 powerplant strains to keep up. The newer 5.7L and 6.1L Hemi engines have plenty of torque and spare power to handle steep inclines and merging; however, there is a tremendous fuel penalty to pay, in addition to serious engine and drivetrain malfunctions.

The early cars have better handling and steering response than the Ford Sable and Taurus or GM mid-sized front-drives, but the difference is marginal when you tote up the Chryslers' $3,000–$10,000 cost for powertrain, brake, and AC repairs.

Owner reports confirm that there are chronic problems with leaking 3.3L engine head gaskets, engine sludge gumming up the works of the 2.7L engine (change your oil more often than recommended), and noisy lifters wearing out prematurely around 60,000 km. Water pumps often self-destruct and take the engine timing chain along with them (a $1,200 repair). Complaints of engine surging and unintended acceleration are also frequent refrains for all model years. However, the one recurring safety problem affecting almost all model years concerns the steering system. As you can read at *www.daimlerchryslervehicleproblems.com* ("The Truth Behind Chrysler"):

> Chrysler has been under investigation by NHTSA for more than 55,000 warranty claims for steering problems with these vehicles and 1,450 reports of steering control problems, some including complete loss of steering control.

The 4-speed LE42 automatic transmission is a spin-off of Chrysler's failure-prone A604 version, and owner reports show it to be just as unreliable. Owners tell of chronic glitches in the computerized transmission's shift timing and other computer malfunctions, which result in early replacement and driveability problems (stalling, hard starts, and surging). AC failures are commonplace and costly to repair.

Rear visibility is quite poor and body problems abound. Expect exposed screw heads; lots of interior noise; power-window motor failures; distorted, poorly mounted windshields; steering-wheel noise when the car is turning; uneven fit and finish with misaligned doors and jagged trunk edges; poor-quality trim items that break or fall off easily; windows that come off their tracks or are misaligned and poorly sealed; and faulty door hinges that make the doors rattle-prone and hard to open.

VEHICLE HISTORY: 2002—The 300M Special performance model comes with a new grille, upgraded ABS, and more user-friendly child safety seat anchors. Concorde gets the LHS's styling and most of the other LHS amenities, including leather trim, ABS, high-tech gauges, traction control, 17-inch alloy wheels, and a 250 hp 3.5L V6. The LXi acquires the 3.2L V6 with a 234 hp variant of the 3.5L V6. **2003**—Intrepid gets a 244 hp 3.5L V6, Concorde horsepower goes to 250, and the 300M's power is boosted to 255 hp. **2005**—Debut of the rear-drive 300, 300C, and Magnum. **2007**—The wheelbase is lengthened and shared with the Dodge Charger sedan and Magnum wagon. **2008**—A slightly restyled exterior and interior. **2009**—Hemi V8 gets 19 more horses (bringing the engine to 359 hp).

300M and LHS

More show than go, these cars are near-luxury and sport clones of the Chrysler Concorde. Although they use the same front-drive platform as the Concorde, their bodies are shorter and they're styled differently. Both cars are powered by a 253 hp 3.5L V6 mated to Chrysler's AutoStick semi-automatic transmission. Mechanical and body deficiencies generally mirror those of the Concorde and Intrepid.

300, 300C, and Magnum

These rear-drive, full-sized, and feature-laden (standard ABS, traction control, and electronic stability control) sedans and wagons were first launched as 2005 models. Their first year on the market was accompanied by a plethora of factory-related problems, as well as limited parts supply and problematic servicing due to the cars' new design and relatively small sales volume. The residual value for these cars is in freefall as more buyers flock to fuel-efficient front-drives.

The top-of-the-line Chrysler 300 shares its platform with the sportier Dodge Magnum wagon and comes in three packages: the base model with a 190 hp V6; a Touring version with a 250 hp V6; and the high-performance 300C with a 340 hp V8 Hemi engine. The V8 employs Chrysler's Multi-Displacement System, which uses eight cylinders under load and then switches to 4-cylinder mode when cruising to save fuel. AWD is available on Touring and 300C models. V6-equipped models have a 4-speed automatic transmission. AWD and V8 versions use a 5-speed automatic with a manual shiftgate.

Charger and SRT8

Charger's rear-drive sedan shares its platform and engines with the Dodge Magnum and Chrysler 300. It seats five and comes in three trim levels: SE with a 3.5L V6, R/T with a 5.7L V8, and SRT8 with a 6.1L V8. The 5.7L V8 has Chrysler's Multi-Displacement System also. All Chargers have 5-speed automatic transmissions. R/T and SRT8 models have firmer suspensions, and the SRT8 adds Brembo brakes and upgraded trim. An AWD joined the lineup for the 2007 model year, while the 2008 models returned relatively unchanged, except for some minor interior upgrades. For 2009, the horsepower for the SRT8's 5.7L engine was increased from 340 to 350. It also upgraded to 20-inch aluminum wheels, power-folding mirrors with automatic tip-down, and a retuned performance suspension.

Safety Summary

All models/years: No airbag deployment in a collision. • 2.7L engine suddenly self-destructs because of excess oil sludge and overheating. Owners describe the failure this way:

> The primary symptom is that the car heater, for no reason, does not blow hot air. If this has been happening it is likely that your car engine has been overheating and causing sludge to build up in the top half of the engine. Ultimately your engine will

fail with very little warning. Some symptoms are: car starts to burn oil, very light traces of white smoke from exhaust, and the engine may seem to run a little rough at idle.

Cost for repairs averages $6,500 (U.S.). Two excellent websites that cover this problem from both a Canadian and an American perspective are *www. intrepidhorrorstories.blogspot.com/2003_11_01_archive.html* ("Dodge Intrepid Owner? Read This!") and *www.autosafety.org/article.php?did=961&scid=122*. Interestingly, Mercedes-Benz settled its own class action lawsuit for $32 million (U.S.) over engine sludge breakdowns affecting its 1998–2001 lineup of luxury cars. See *www.legalnewswatch.com/news_182.html*. • Engine rod bearing failure. • Chronic stalling, engine surging, and sudden, unintended acceleration. • Many reports of sudden transmission failures, often because of cracked transmission casings. • Transmission fluid leakage caused by defective transmission casing bolt. • Gas fumes enter the interior. • Windshields are often distorted and may fall out while vehicle is underway. • High rear windowsill obstructs rear visibility. • Headlights may be too dim for safe motoring, may cut out completely, or may come on by themselves. • Both ABS and non-ABS brakes perform poorly, resulting in excessively long stopping distances or the complete loss of braking ability. • Brake rotors rust prematurely and warp easily, and pads have to be changed every 15,000 km. • Overhead digital panel is distracting and forces you to take your eyes from the road. • Emergency brake pedal catches pant cuffs and shoelaces as you enter and exit the vehicle. **All models: 2002**—Steering drifts, sometimes takes undue effort, or squeaks and clunks. • Seat belt button is too sensitive; belt is easily unlatched inadvertently. **2005**—Seat heater can burn your butt. • Premature tire wear. • Chronic stalling and hard starting in vehicles with the Hemi engine. • Transmission hesitates, then slams into gear. • Steering freezes or breaks in low temperatures. • Stabilizer bar separation. • Persistent electrical shorts. • Lights suddenly shut off. • Horn doesn't work. • Pulling to the right while driving (the camber bolt service bulletin fix doesn't help). • Rear hatch seizes shut so that the owner has to crawl through the back of the vehicle to open it. • Sudden acceleration with the Hemi engine is particularly common among these more recently reported incidents:

> I have a new 2005 Dodge Magnum. The car has the 5.7L Hemi motor. My wife cranked the car and put it in reverse. She then depressed the accelerator and the engine did not respond with any rpm change until the accelerator pedal was depressed in excess of 50%. When the engine did respond, it was violent, causing the car to spin tires and accelerate backward at a high rate of speed, hitting another car in our driveway. This has happened about 6 times and actually happened while the insurance appraiser was in the car.... I have posted this problem on a Dodge talk forum and am finding additional people with very similar problems.

2006—Fire ignites in the wiring harness and in the trunk. • Seat warmer burns driver's back. • Sudden acceleration when taking off from a stop. • Shifter replaced in one vehicle because it wouldn't go into Drive (a "goodwill" repair). • Automatic transmission slams into gear. • Faulty tie rod causes excessive front-end shake. •

Vehicle rolls away when parked with emergency brake applied. • Original-equipment Goodyear tires wore out after only two years of use; Vogue tires have side wall cracks. **2007**—Check Engine light stays on, and emissions officials won't pass the car with light lit. Chrysler says the repair will cost $2,000. • Battery ignites a fire:

> Ground wire melted causing loss of electrical grounding leading to an electrical fire. Vehicle was a total loss. Fire began in front of vehicle even though battery actually located in trunk.

• Transmission stuck in Park:

> I was driving with my two children and we were stranded when our 2007 Chrysler 300 was stuck in Park. We cannot get it out of Park and were left in a very dangerous part of town.

> •

> With only 44,000 miles [71,000 km] on the car, my gear would not shift out of Park. There is an override switch ("pink") that did not work as well. I got online to check to see if there were any recalls on this matter and there was not; however, when I checked online, I noticed several complaints and blogs about these cars with the same problem from 2005 to current. This should be a recall matter. Today, Monday, July 6, 2009, I took my vehicle to the shop and they told me that the entire gear shift assembly was busted. They said that it was a crappy design and Chrysler has since made a little better design shift gear than the one that is in my vehicle now. I believe Chrysler is aware of this problem and they should be responsible for recalling these.

• Hard downshifts. • Air intake is poorly designed and will suck water into the engine. • Excessive torque converter shudder. • Continental tire-tread separation. • Water leaks from the rear windshield area. • Tail light, fuse failures:

> I am a master technician in the state of Calif. I have worked on Chrysler for 16 years. What burns me is this particular manufacturer uses a system called Star to hide defects from becoming full recalls to avoid cost. I am complaining about all Dodge, Chrysler 300, Magnum, Charger 3.5L models. The rear license plate harness retainer clip above the oversize 3.5L muffler comes loose and the two wire harness melts to the muffler and causes parklight/taillamp failure. The consumer will attempt in desperation to install fuses of a larger amp causing a major meltdown of the fusebox (wire domino of one wire in the fusebox melts to other sources). Well, I complained and was told to shut up by Chrysler!!! I've seen six [other] cases.

• ESP/anti-lock brakes fail, causing the vehicle to slide on very little snow or rain. • Doors close without warning. • Limo conversions may be unsafe:

> When is NHTSA going to look into the extra long limousine conversions being completed on the Chrysler 300 and Dodge Charger cars? Chrysler does not offer a

limo conversion chassis like Lincoln and Cadillac. The axles, wheels, tires and brakes are seriously overloaded based on the federal door labels.... Operators are experiencing premature front end component failures and excessive tire wear. Does someone have to die before this industry practice is reviewed?

2008—One car exploded:

My 2008 300 Touring was parked in a parking lot. The alarm started going off by itself. Then a fire started out of nowhere from under the hood. Then my car exploded from the front to the back through the exhaust pipe. I only had 6,100 or so miles [10,000 km] on my car. I just leased it in March of this year.

• Sunroof may also explode. • Another scary ESP/anti-lock brake story:

I rented a Chrysler 300 over this past weekend. I want you to know that it was the scariest ride I've had in a while. Have you ever tested the electronic stability program on ice? It not only does not work, it is extremely dangerous. I had to drive about 600 miles [1,000 km] on icy and windy Wyoming roads which proved to be quite scary in the 300 with ESP. Since I don't have another vehicle of my own with this feature, it took a while to figure out why the car didn't want to drive straight down the road, even at fairly slow speeds. These cars should have a huge red warning sticker on the dash to warn prospective drivers that this feature is not safe to use in the wind and on ice.

• Goodyear Integrity tires are prone to hydroplaning at 9 km/h. • Excessive effort is needed to honk the horn. • Transmission bangs when shifted into gear. • Defective tire pressure sensors and valve stems. • Sudden loss of engine power. • No power for accessory features:

I have found that I have no accessory power while driving. I.e. no heat/AC. No radio. No control of windows. It may actually have no accessory power from the time I start the car, as I often notice it within the first mile when I try to use an accessory. The only way to get the power back is to pull over, turn off the car and restart. Occassionally I have had to repeat this process several times to get the accessory power back. I complained to the dealer within the first 6 months, and they replied that it is too intermittent for them to solve.

• Defective front seat belt buckle. • Hard to keep interior windows free from condensation:

I have tried various settings of the climate control including making sure it is taking in outside air vs recirculating, setting the temp at hot, cold, medium, defrost, AC, etc. I have even purchased a product like damp rid to pull moisture from the air, but it is now a daily problem to try to see especially through the sides of the windshield and front side windows.

2009—Accelerator falls to the floor, and vehicle accelerates. • Defective steering pinion gear. • Horn doesn't sound if the vehicle isn't running. *300M:* **2001**—Unstable driver's seat. • Fuel tank easily overflows. **2002**—Brake failure, then engine surges. • Sunroof explodes. • Right front wheel disconnects from vehicle. **2003**—Surging when stopped. • Rear visibility compromised by narrow rear windows. **2004**—Trunk collects water, interferes with spare-tire access. • Sudden stalling on the highway believed to be caused by a batch of faulty cam sensors. • Transmission failure; the car suddenly downshifts to Second or First gear while the vehicle is underway:

> Car just randomly throws itself into second gear or goes into limp [m]ode and stays locked there. Once you turn the car off and back on again, you can drive with normal gears. However, once you hit 50–60 mph, the transmission automatically goes into limp mode and stays locked in second gear. All signs point to solenoid pack assembly.

• Many complaints that the car always pulls to the right. • Seat belts do not restrain a child safety seat sufficiently. • Passenger-side airbag is disabled when an average-sized passenger sits in the seat. • Driver's seatback suddenly reclined into the backseat while vehicle was underway. • Rear windows won't go down. • Faulty chrome wheels:

> Chromed steel wheels from Chrysler corroding and leaking air every other day 20 PSI or more, extreme safety hazard. Tire store has tried three times to seal the tires with very little success.

Secret Warranties/Internal Bulletins/Service Tips

All models: 1999–2004—Remedy for a 3.5L engine that stumbles or misfires (TSB #09-002-03). • Rear headliner sags or rattles. **2000–04**—Fuel tank slow to fill; this has been a chronic problem affecting five model years. **2001**—Troubleshooting automatic transmission surge and sag and shift bump complaints (TSB #18-007-01). **2002**—Transaxle limp-in; engine misfire; engine no-start. **2002–04**—Vehicles equipped with a 3.5L engine that has a rough idle when cold may need the PCM recalibrated or replaced, a free service under the emissions warranty (TSB #18-042-03). **2003–04**—Harsh downshifts. • Poor transmission shifting. **2005–06**—Hard starts with the V6. • Automatic transmission 1–2 upshift shudder or rough shift. • Transfer case shudder on slow-speed turns. • Transmission shudder or buzz due to water contamination; torque converter may require replacement. • Headliner sags. **2005–07**—Dash squeak, rubbing sound. • Sunroof rattles. • Inoperative window "express up" feature. **2005–08**—Steering pulls to one side. **2006–07**—Water leaks from the A-pillar area. **2005–09**—Difficult fuel fill-up; nozzle shuts off. **2007**—Torque converter shudder. • Oil Pressure light on intermittently. **2007–08**—Inoperative AC. **2007–10**—Harsh 4–3 shift; poor shift quality. • Lower door hinge popping, groaning. **2008–09**—How to reduce engine whistling. **2009**—Poor steering wheel returnability.

300, 300C, 300M, CHARGER, CONCORDE, INTREPID, LHS, MAGNUM, SRT8 PROFILE

	2001	2002	2003	2004	2005	2006	2007	2008	2009
Cost Price ($)									
300	—	—	—	—	29,995	30,225	30,785	32,095	32,095
300C	—	—	—	—	43,095	43,595	44,190	45,595	45,595
300M	40,900	39,900	40,335	40,910	—	—	—	—	—
Charger	—	—	—	—	—	27,635	28,370	29,095	29,095
Concorde	28,485	29,690	30,240	30,775	—	—	—	—	—
Intrepid	25,910	25,765	25,095	25,615	—	—	—	—	—
LHS	41,655	—	—	—	—	—	—	—	—
Magnum	—	—	—	—	27,995	28,135	28,800	29,395	—
SRT8	—	—	—	—	—	44,790	45,690	46,395	46,595
Used Values ($)									
300 ▲	—	—	—	—	5,500	6,500	8,000	12,000	15,000
300 ▼	—	—	—	—	4,500	5,500	6,500	10,500	13,500
300C ▲	—	—	—	—	7,500	9,500	12,500	15,500	21,500
300C ▼	—	—	—	—	6,000	8,000	10,500	14,500	20,000
300M ▲	3,000	3,500	4,000	5,000	—	—	—	—	—
300M ▼	2,500	3,000	3,500	4,500	—	—	—	—	—
Charger ▲	—	—	—	—	—	7,500	8,500	11,000	14,500
Charger ▼	—	—	—	—	—	6,000	7,000	9,500	13,000
Concorde ▲	2,000	2,500	3,000	4,000	—	—	—	—	—
Concorde ▼	1,500	2,000	2,500	3,000	—	—	—	—	—
Intrepid ▲	1,500	2,000	2,500	3,500	—	—	—	—	—
Intrepid ▼	1,000	1,500	2,000	2,500	—	—	—	—	—
LHS ▲	2,000	—	—	—	—	—	—	—	—
LHS ▼	1,500	—	—	—	—	—	—	—	—
Magnum ▲	—	—	—	—	5,000	7,000	8,000	9,500	—
Magnum ▼	—	—	—	—	4,500	5,500	6,500	8,000	—
SRT8 ▲	—	—	—	—	—	13,500	16,500	22,000	26,000
SRT8 ▼	—	—	—	—	—	12,000	14,500	19,500	24,500
Reliability	1	1	1	1	1	1	1	1	1
Crash Safety (F)	4	4	4	4	5	5	5	5	5
300M	3	3	3	4					
Side	4	4	4	4	4	4	4	4	4
IIHS Side	—	—	—	—	1	1	1	1	1
Offset	3	3	3	3	5	5	5	5	5
LHS/300M	3	3	3	3	—	—	—	—	—
Head Restraints									
300/Magnum	—	—	—	—	3	2	2	2	2
300M (F)	2	1	1	1	—	—	—	—	—
Intrepid (F)	4	4	4	4	—	—	—	—	—
Intrepid (R)	—	3	3	3	—	—	—	—	—
LHS	3	—	—	—	—	—	—	—	—

Rollover Resistance									
300/Magnum	—	▦	▦	▦	▦	▦	▦	▦	▦
300M	—	▦	▦	▦	—	—	—	—	—
Concorde	—	—	▦	▦	—	—	—	—	—
Intrepid	—	—	▦	▦	—	—	—	—	—

Note: All these vehicles are practically identical and should have similar crashworthiness scores, even though not every model was tested in each year.

Ford

GRAND MARQUIS ★★★

RATING: Average (1999–2008). Downgraded to Average because powertrain, electrical system, and brake failures are endemic with the Grand Marquis and its Crown Victoria twin. Other minuses include excessive engine noise, poor fuel economy, no electronic stability control, no curtain airbags, and low IIHS side-impact marks without side airbags. Yet these large sedans can be bargain buys as their owners bail out and sell them for next to nothing as fuel prices increase. **Ideal model year:** Get the 2006 high-end and fully-loaded LS Ultimate. It's a $43,000 car that's now worth $10,000. 2008 models are good second choices. They are little-changed, are likely to have some of the original warranty left, and cost about $16,500. **"Real" city/highway fuel economy:** 13.9/8.7 L/100 km. Owners report fuel savings may undershoot this estimate by about 20 percent. **Maintenance/repair costs:** Average, but some electronic repairs can be carried out only by Ford dealers. **Parts:** Average parts costs (independent suppliers sell for much less) and most parts are easy to find. **Extended warranty:** Yes, either buy an extended powertrain warranty or get your transmission repaired by a garage that offers an extensive warranty. **Best alternatives:** The Ford Fusion or Hyundai Azera. Also consider a downsized SUV, like the Honda CR-V or Hyundai Tucson. **Helpful websites:** *www.fordforums.com/f102.*

Strengths and Weaknesses

These rear-drive cars are especially well-suited to seniors, who will appreciate the roomy interiors and convenience features (although entry and exit may require some acrobatics). The high crash protection scores and ease of servicing are also major advantages. Handling, though, is mediocre and can be downright scary on wet roads, where the car can quickly lose traction and fishtail out of control.

Both the 4.6L and 5.0L V8s provide adequate though sometimes sluggish power, with most of their torque found in the lower gear range. The Lincoln Town Car shares the same components and afflictions as the Crown Vic and Grand Marquis.

As is the case with most full-sized sedans, high insurance premiums and fuel costs have walloped the resale value of both models, making these cars incredibly good used buys. The only caveat is to make sure the undercarriage, powertrain, electronics, and brakes are in good shape before you ink a deal.

VEHICLE HISTORY: 2001—A small horsepower boost, minor interior improvements, adjustable pedals, seat belt pretensioners, and improved airbag systems. **2002**—Traction control to offset the car's notoriously poor wet-weather traction. **2003**—A revised frame and upgraded suspension, plus the debut of a high-performance Marauder equipped with a 302 hp V8, sport suspension, and exclusive trim. **2006–08**—Not much new, except for a restyled grille, front fascia, headlights, and different interior trim.

A number of factory-related problems appear year after year. These include chronic front suspension noise when passing over small bumps; failure-prone fuel-pump, sender, fuel-filter, and fuel-hose assemblies; ignition module and fuel cut-off switch malfunctions that cause hard starting and frequent stalling; and brakes (rotors, calipers, and pads), shock absorbers, and springs that wear out more quickly than they should. Inadequate inner fender protection allows road salt to completely cover engine wiring, brake master cylinder, and suspension components; therefore, frequent inspection and cleaning is required. Hubcaps frequently fall off. Finally, such a high number of safety-related complaints concerning brake and fuel lines, the suspension, and steering components means an undercarriage inspection is prerequisite to buying models three years old or older. Other annoying body defects include trunk leaks, poor fit and finish, flimsy plastic trim, subpar interior materials, and paint peeling:

> Paint has cracked and is falling off the hood, top, and back. It is rusted on top where the paint peeled off and now it's starting on the hood.

Safety Summary

All years: Sudden, unintended acceleration. • Cracked intake manifolds cause loss of coolant. • Airbags fail to deploy, or deploy for no reason. • ABS failures. • Premature brake rotor warpage and pad wearout cause excessive brake noise (grinding), vibration, and extended stopping distances. • Brake and accelerator pedals mounted too close together. **2001**—When the car is driven in rainy weather, water gets into the engine compartment, causing the water pump to throw the fan belt and leading to loss of control of the vehicle. • Frequent complaints of little traction on wet roads. • Spongy brakes sink to floor with little braking effect. • Vehicle moves forward when shifted into Reverse. • Vehicle rolls back when stopped on an incline. **2002**—The cruise control doesn't disengage. **2003**—Vehicle struck from behind exploded into flames. • Brake booster fails. • Fan belt comes off in rainy weather, causing overheating and loss of power steering, water pump, and other accessories. • Horn "sweet spot" too small; horn takes too much effort to sound. • Sunlight causes a reflection off the defrost vents onto the windshield and poor dash panel illumination. **2004**—Transmission slips;

shifts into Reverse on its own. **2005**—Stuck accelerator. • Fuel tank punctured by road debris. • Brake pedal travel is excessive before brakes are applied. • Horn does not work. **2006**—Engine surges when vehicle is stopped in gear. • Foot can get caught under the brake pedal. • Floormat can get trapped under the accelerator pedal. • Faulty AC blower motor. • Digital speedometer is unreadable in daylight. **2007**—Many complaints of faulty TR414 tire valve stems that leak air:

> Contact owns a 2007 Mercury Grand Marquis. While driving 60 mph [97 km/h] the passenger front tire lost air. He was able to safely exchange the tires. The vehicle was taken to the dealer and the valve stems were replaced on all four tires at an expense of $63.00. The manufacturer was notified, and he will be reimbursed for the valve stems.

• Michelin Energy tire vibrates and then blows out the side wall. • Inaccurate fuel gauge. **2008**—Frequent reports that the vehicle suddenly accelerates when stopped at a light or once underway; applying the brakes sometimes makes the car accelerate faster. • Vehicle loses all electrical power, disabling the trunk release. • Airbag is disabled when an average-sized adult occupies the front passenger seat:

> Ford claims the system is working as designed and that my wife's weight (110 lbs.) is the problem. Ford confirms that when the passenger side warning light is on the passenger side airbag will not deploy. Ford cannot explain why this malfunction is intermittent and why seat position, bumps, or turns cause a malfunction. WE tried a 2010 Mercury Grand Marquis with same airbag system and could not get the warning system to activate duplicating the condition as noted above. Ford's customer relations dept refuses to do anything more to fix the defect.

Secret Warranties/Internal Bulletins/Service Tips

2000–07—Aluminum body panels may be afflicted with early corrosion. **2001**—Correcting a 3–4 shift flare. **2003**—Defective front coil springs may cause the vehicle to have a harsh ride or the suspension to sit low in the front. Install revised front coil springs: #3W1Z-5310-EA and #3W1Z-5310-HA. • Cracked wheel rims. **2003–04**—Countermeasures for suspension squeaking or rubbing. • Ignition-lock cylinder binding. **2003–06**—Noisy suspension air compressor. **2004**—Vehicle won't shift into Overdrive. **2004–05**—Delayed shifting into Reverse. **2005–06**—Sagging driver's seat cushion. • Steering too light at highway speeds. **2005–10**—Torque converter locks up on 1–2 upshift. **2006–07**—Engine overheating; inoperative cooling fan. **2006–10**—Trunk lid won't latch. **2007–08**—Low idle hesitation; the fix is to reprogram the powertrain control module under the Emissions Warranty. • Free tire valve stem inspection and replacement if stem is cracked. **2007–09**—Cracking sun visors. **2008**—Inoperative keyless entry transmitter. **2008–10**—White flakes may come out of the AC dash vents.

GRAND MARQUIS PROFILE

	2001	2002	2003	2004	2005	2006	2007	2008
Cost Price ($)								
Grand Marquis GS	34,125	35,120	35,800	36,720	36,735	37,099	43,099	44,749
Used Values ($)								
Grand Marquis GS ▲	3,500	4,500	5,000	6,000	7,500	9,500	12,500	16,500
Grand Marquis GS ▼	3,000	4,000	4,500	5,000	6,000	8,000	11,000	15,000
Reliability	3	3	3	3	4	4	4	4
Crash Safety (F)	5	5	5	5	5	5	5	5
Side	5	4	4	4	5	4	4	4
IIHS Side	—	—	1	1	1	1	1	1
Offset	—	—	3	5	5	5	5	5
Head Restraints	1	1	2	2	2	2	2	2
Rollover Resistance	5	5	5	5	5	5	5	5

Note: 2008 was the car's final year in Canada; in the States, it soldiered on for a couple more years.

General Motors

ALLURE/LACROSSE, LUCERNE ★★

RATING: Below Average (2006–09). The Allure/LaCrosse and Lucerne are similarly equipped large front-drive sedans that are hobbled by mediocre road performance and poor quality control. The Lucerne is the larger of the three cars and the model that has accumulated the most performance- and safety-related complaints. **Ideal model year:** *Allure/LaCrosse:* Smart used-car shoppers should look to a 2007 Allure/LaCrosse for the best combination of price and added safety features ($7,000 to $8,500). *Lucerne:* With a list price of $43,095, the 2006 first-year V6 model is barely worth $13,500 today—but it's no bargain when you look at its many first-year quality shortcomings. **"Real" city/highway fuel economy:** *LaCrosse 2.4 4-cylinder.:* 10.8/6.5 L/100 km. *LaCrosse 3.6 V6:* 12.2/7.3 L/100 km. *LaCrosse AWD 3.6 V6:* 12.7/7.7 L/100 km. *Lucerne 3.9 V6:* 12.0/7.4 L/100 km. *Lucerne 4.6 V8:* 13.8/8.7 L/100 km. Owners report fuel savings often undershoot these estimates by at least 20 percent. **Maintenance/repair costs:** Higher than average, but most repairs (Northstar engine and AWD components excepted) aren't dealer-dependent or prohibitively expensive. **Parts:** Higher-than-average costs for emissions, engine, and AWD repairs. **Extended warranty:** A good idea, especially on AWD-equipped cars. **Best alternatives:** Ford's Crown Victoria or Mercury Grand Marquis; Hyundai Azera or Genesis; and a downsized SUV like the Ford Escape or Hyundai Tucson. Lincoln's Town Car is a good second choice. **Helpful websites:** *www.automotiveforums.com/vbulletin/f727.*

Strengths and Weaknesses

Allure/LaCrosse

GM's 2005–09 Allure/LaCrosse (Canada/United States) is a substantially upgraded and stiffened version of the Century and Regal, resulting in improved quality in both ride and handling. The rack-and-pinion steering is revised for a better response, but it has proven to be troublesome, and the four-wheel disc braking system is completely new, though, not very durable. Overall, the Allure/LaCrosse isn't an improvement over the cars it replaces, and sales have been underwhelming. The car has a full complement of standard safety features, along with optional Ultrasonic Rear Parking Assist (of doubtful value) and a factory-installed remote starting system that works when it wants to. Crash test scores have been acceptable.

Lucerne

The Lucerne is a full-size car sold by GM's Buick division that replaced the Park Avenue and LeSabre in 2006. Buick's largest car shares its basic design with the Cadillac DTS. A 197 hp 3.8L V6 engine was standard in the CX, CXL, and CXL Special Edition V6 and then it was replaced by the 227 hp 3.9L V6. The Northstar 4.6L V8 ("hell to troubleshoot" and "parts are on back order") is standard in the CXL Special Edition V8 and CXS. The V8 added 17 horses in 2008 (to 275) and has remained relatively unchanged to this day. To say the Northstar has been a troublesome powerplant is an understatement. The new high-performance Super (2008–11) version is a 292 hp variation of the same V8, along with retuned steering, a sportier suspension, and upgraded interior trim. All Lucernes use a 4-speed automatic transmission and seat six.

VEHICLE HISTORY: *Allure/LaCrosse:* **2006**—Adoption of new safety features, including ABS (CX and CXL models) and side curtain airbags. **2008**—Interior and exterior upgrades along with the LaCrosse Super V8 option and sport suspension. *Lucerne:* **2008**—Adoption of a lane departure warning system. **2009**—A new 3.9L V6 engine, Bluetooth phone connectivity, and XM NavTraffic. Since 2009, the Lucerne has been mostly carried over with few changes.

Safety Summary

All models/years: Sudden, unintended acceleration with or without the cruise control engaged. • Chronic stalling (defective fuel pump or throttle position sensor). • No starts. • No airbag deployment. • Faulty front passenger airbag sensor module. • Airbag light constantly lit. • Chin-to-chest front head restraints. • Premature automatic transmission failure. • Loss of brakes. • Early replacement of the brake rotors and pads. • Light steering that allows the car to wander, pulling to the right when accelerating. • Excessive vibration on the highway. • Front strut bushing failures. • Defective steering-column intermediate shaft produces a screeching, clunking, crunching, or groaning noise. • Power-steering high pressure fitting failures. • Early tie rod replacement. • Rear windshield exploded when the defroster was turned on. • Low-beam headlights suddenly go out. • Dash gauges can't be read in daylight. • Instrument panel lights and headlights are too dim. • Various reflections into the side mirror and rear windshield. • The fuel gauge gives incorrect readings. • Windshield wiper failures. • Heated windshield washer recall is inadequate; it disables the feature, instead of repairing the problem. • Snow and ice collects just below the front windshield wipers. • Weak, cheap plastic door handles. • Sun visor suddenly drops down. • Remote won't open the door locks; passenger had to climb out via the window. • Tires lose air. *Allure/LaCrosse:* **2006**—Engine camshaft failure. **2008**—Early replacement of steering and suspension components:

> Replaced power steering rack and pinion, frame bushing, stabilizer shaft link, front sway bar end links, intermediate steering shaft, left front struts and retorqued suspension bolts.

Lucerne: **2006**—Defective motor mounts:

> These motor mounts are known to be defective and many bulletins have been posted, along with many known customers getting them replaced. I however have had ba[d] luck getting my local Buick dealership to replace them. The problem happens while taking off from a stop. The defective mounts cause the engine to vibrate and shake the car. This to me seems like a very dangerous issue to have to deal with.

• Rear passenger door cannot be locked from the inside or out. • Chrome wheels corrode in valve stem openings causing air loss. • Excessive brake vibration and shimmy. **2007**—Front safety belts may not lock up. • Underside of the interior door handle can cut a hand. • Tire system sensor goes off for no reason. • Aluminum wheels lose air and chrome peels away. • Tire jack bent when lifting vehicle. **2008** Acceleration is hard to modulate:

> I purchased a 2008 Buick Lucerne in Sept. of 08. My concern deals with the accelerator. This model I am told has an all electronically controlled accelerator. I find it almost impossible to hold an even speed on the highway as it is constantly either speeding up or slowing down, and I have no perception of ever moving the pedal. At stop signs/lights it will sometimes leap out with a "jack rabbit" start which was totally unplanned for. This I feel is a major safety issue plus I also think it has a lot to do with the poor mileage I am experiencing. I am only getting 15–23 mpg which is far from the 23–29 I got on my 05 Lasabre with the same engine.

• Steering wheel suddenly locks up. • Gas spews out of the filler pipe when filling up. • Instrument panel lights are dim or go dim while driving. • Ice builds up at the base of the windshield; the wipers become clogged with ice. **2009**—Sudden, unintended acceleration accompanied by loss of brakes and failure of the airbag to deploy:

My wife was stopped waiting for a car to leave the parking lot. She had her foot on the brake ready to put it in Park. The car suddenly surged forward and she could not stop it with both feet on the brake. She hit a building and 3 vehicles before she was stopped by the 3rd vehicle. She was headed for another part of the building when she stopped. The air bags did not deploy. There was less than 600 miles on the car. Fortunately no [one] was injured badly. My wife has driven 31 years without an accident. This was not her fault. Someone could have easily been killed if it happened on the street.

• Premature failure of the front-end struts, lower control arm bushings, brake master cylinder, steering control module, and the StabiliTrak stability control. • Door stoppers don't hold doors open on an incline.

Secret Warranties/Internal Bulletins/Service Tips

Allure/LaCrosse: **2005–07**—Automatic transmission shudder when accelerating. **2005–08**—Countermeasures for harsh shifting and slipping. • Repair for a steering column clunk heard when turning:

STEERING COLUMN CLUNKING WHEN TURNING

BULLETIN NO.: 01-02-32-001P   DATE: NOVEMBER 25, 2009

CLUNK FELT/NOISE HEARD FROM STEERING COLUMN AND STEERING GEAR AND/OR FRONT OF VEHICLE DURING TURNING MANEUVER AND/OR STEERING WHEEL ROTATION (REPLACE INTERMEDIATE SHAFT).

2001–04 Buick Regal; 2005–08 Buick Allure (Canada Only); LaCrosse; 2000–08 Chevrolet Impala; 2000–07 Chevrolet Monte Carlo; 1998-2002 Oldsmobile Intrigue; and the 2004–07 Pontiac Grand Prix.

2005–09—Automatic transmission slips in gear; left-side axle seal leaks (see bulletin on following page). • Wind noise diagnostic tips. • Airbag warning light comes on intermittently. **2005–11**—Reduced power, as MIL alert lights up (see bulletin on following page). **2006–09**—Airbag warning light stays lit. **2007–09**—Steering gear mount to frame may make a pop, creak, or click noise. **2008**—Power steering leak may require the replacement of the steering gear cylinder line. • Tips on reducing tire vibration. **2008–09**—Poor AC performance. • Inaccurate fuel gauge readings. **2008–09**—V8 engine oil leak from the rear cover assembly area. **2009**—V8 engine valve tick noise remedy (replace the valve lifters). *Lucerne:* **2006–08**—Inoperative Park Assist feature. • Frayed headliner (front edge). **2006–09**—Airbag warning light stays lit (replace the right front seat belt buckle). • Vehicle pulls to the right when accelerating. • Bump, clunk on slow speed turns. • Front door won't open or unlock. • Inoperative inside and outside rear door handles. • Hard to view instrument panel cluster in sunlight. • Hard starts, no-starts (repair and re-route transmission wiring harnesses). **2006–11**—Reduced power as MIL alert lights up. **2007–10**—Low-speed automatic transmission moan or whine noise. **2009**—Parking Assist gives erratic visual and audio warnings. **2009–10**—Engine coolant leaks (replace coolant crossover pipe gaskets). • Campaign and service bulletin number: #10142, dated May 12, 2010, provides for the re-securing of the electronic brake control module

SLIPS IN GEAR/AXLE SEAL LEAKS

BULLETIN NO.: 08-07-30-009B   DATE: MAY 01, 2008

SLIPS IN GEAR (REPLACE THIRD CLUTCH HOUSING WITH REVISED SERVICE PART)

2001–08 GM passenger cars with HYDRA-MATIC(R) front wheel drive 4T80-E automatic transmission.

CONDITION: Some customers may comment on a transmission oil leak and/or that the transmission slips in gear.

CAUSE: An oil leak may be caused by bushing wear in the third clutch housing, causing excessive fluid build-up at axe sea.

CORRECTION: DO NOT replace the transmission for above concerns. Instead, replace the third clutch housing with service P/N 8682114, which has revised bushing material to extend life and reduce left front axle seal leaks.

INTERMITTENT MIL/REDUCED POWER

BULLETIN NO.: 07-06-04-019D   DATE: JUNE 28, 2010

INTERMITTENT MALFUNCTION INDICATOR LAMP (MIL) ILLUMINATED, DTC P2138 WITH REDUCED ENGINE POWER (REPAIR INSTRUMENT PANEL (IP) TO BODY HARNESS CONNECTOR)

2005–11 GM Passenger Cars and Light Duty Trucks (Including Saturn); 2005–09 HUMMER H2; 2006–10 HUMMER H3; 2005–09 Saab 9-7X

CAUSE: This condition may be caused by water intrusion into the instrument panel (IP) to body harness connector, which carries the APP sensor signals to the ECM/PCM. This water intrusion results in a voltage difference between APP Sensor 1 and APP Sensor 2 that exceeds a predetermined value for more than a calibrated period of time, setting P2138.

NOTE: Aftermarket equipment can generate DTC P2138 and/or other DTCs, so verify that aftermarket equipment is not electrically connected to any of the APP sensor signal or low reference circuits or to any other ECM/PCM 5V reference or low reference circuits.

at no charge to the vehicle owner. Courtesy transportation will also be provided. This is not a recall. • Oil leak at the front of the engine (replace the front cover seal). • Parking Assist gives a phantom beep when car is shifted into Reverse. **2009–11**—Procedures outlined to reduce front brake rotor noise and pulsation.

ALLURE, LACROSSE, LUCERNE PROFILE

	2005	2006	2007	2008	2009
Cost Price ($)					
Allure/LaCrosse CX	25,200	26,295	26,395	26,495	26,995
Lucerne CX V6	—	43,095	43,595	44,190	45,595
Lucerne CXL V8	39,675	40,900	39,900	40,335	40,910
Used Values ($)					
Allure/LaCrosse CX ▲	—	6,500	8,500	12,000	15,000
Allure/LaCrosse CX ▼	—	5,500	7,000	10,000	13,000
Lucerne CX V6 ▲	—	13,500	16,500	19,000	22,000
Lucerne CX V6 ▼	—	12,000	15,000	17,000	20,000

Lucerne CXL V8 ▲	2,500	3,000	3,500	4,500	6,000
Lucerne CXL V8 ▼	2,000	2,500	3,000	4,000	5,000
Reliability					
Lucerne	1	1	1	1	1
Crash Safety (F)	4	4	4	4	4
Lucerne	—	3	3	3	4
Side (Lucerne)	4	4	4	4	4
Offset	3	3	3	3	3
Lucerne	1	3	3	3	3
Rollover Resistance					
Lucerne	—	—	4	4	4

Hyundai

AZERA ★★★★

RATING: Above Average (2006–09). **Ideal model year:** The 2008 GLS for its 50 percent depreciation (deduct $18,000 from $36,000). **"Real" city/highway fuel economy:** 12.2/7.8 L/100 km. **Maintenance/repair costs:** Average costs; some repairs are dealer-dependent and cost more than average. **Parts:** Most parts are easily found. **Extended warranty:** Not needed. **Best alternatives:** Ford Crown Victoria, Grand Marquis, or Lincoln Town Car and Hyundai Genesis. **Helpful websites:** *www.hyundai-forums.com/f78-azera-forum.htm.*

Strengths and Weaknesses

Hyundai's Azera is a full-size, five-passenger sedan that is roomy, refined, and loaded with standard features that would cost extra on most of the competition. It is a bit larger and more luxurious than the average midsize family sedan and placed just a notch above the Sonata in Hyundai's lineup. Azera has more total interior volume than the Toyota Avalon, Mercedes E-Class sedans, and the BMW 750i. Safety features include eight standard airbags, a high-tensile steel unibody, active front head restraints, electronic stability control, traction control, and a refined braking system.

Powered by a 3.3L V6 that produces 234 horsepower and an optional 3.8L 263 hp V6 engine, the Azera's smooth engines produce plenty of low-end torque and have plenty of reserve power for highway cruising and merging. Both the 5-speed and 6-speed automatic transmissions shift precisely and quietly, while giving fuel economy that is a bit better than average for a vehicle this size.

Other pluses: Strong brakes, a roomy backseat, and a quiet ride.

Some of the Azera's deficiencies are a floaty ride, average handling, and IIHS side-crash-test results that are rated only "Acceptable." A too-high seating position for the driver.

VEHICLE HISTORY: 2006—Azera replaces the XG350. **2009**—Upgraded steering and suspension systems.

Safety Summary

All years: Faulty front passenger airbag sensor. • Stalling caused by defective throttle position sensors; transmission goes into "limp mode":

> Faulty throttle position sensors which causes the car's engine to stumble and then switch into "limp home" mode. This mode only allows a top speed of 20mpg with very little acceleration power. This problem occurs when you are depressing the gas pedal, such as pulling out into traffic or merging into traffic. This is a serious safety issue that could lead to crashes, as the car will not accelerate as it is supposed to. Currently, Hyundai has issued TSB 09-FL-003-2, but will only cover the repair costs if the car is under warranty.

• Unstable driver's seat and seatback. • Airbag dash cover cracks. • Inadequate low-beam headlight illumination:

> The driver's side headlights do not project out properly. There is a very noticeable shadow causing a totally unlit part of the road. I have seen over 23 complaints on this year model and make of car on one site.

2006—Intermittent no-starts. • Inadvertent deployment of the side curtain airbag. • Vehicle hesitates and lurches when downshifting. • Headlight and dash lights dim on and off randomly. • Split airbag covers. • Driver's seatback moves forward when the vehicle is underway. **2006–07**—Sudden, unintended acceleration:

> I was on an interstate in NH and floored the accelerator (kicked-down) to pass....The car accelerated and would not stop accelerating until I shifted to neutral.... Then it went back to normal rpm... I thought my winter floor mat got stuck.... moved it and all appeared fine.... Then yesterday it happened again...however this time it was on a curvy road in VT with a 45mph speed limit...at 70mph...shifted to neutral and applied breaks as a big curve was approaching.... This time I know it was not the floor mat.... During both incidents, cruise control was not activated.

2007—Accelerator pedal sticks to the floor. • Premature brake rotor wearout. • Dashboard airbag cover cracking. • Dashboard reflects onto the windshield. • When the driver-side window is rolled up, the exterior side mirror reflects the AC vent. • Brake and gas pedal are mounted too close together. • Sticking rear sunshade. **2008**—Side airbags failed to deploy. • Vehicle surging followed by transmission going into "limp mode." • Frequent stalling possibly caused by a faulty throttle body. • Driver's seat suddenly goes to its farthest rearward extension; sometimes the seatback moves to its most forward position:

> Driver seat moves by itself pinning the driver to the steering wheel. Seat moves by itself with the key in the Off position.

2009—Sudden, unintended acceleration. • Sudden loss of power on the freeway (throttle position sensor blamed). • Defective Michelin Energy Plus original equipment tires.

Secret Warranties/Internal Bulletins/Service Tips

2006–09 Automatic transmission defaults into "limp mode"; MIL alert is enabled. • Harsh transmission engagement. • Sunroof creaking, ticking. • Power steering pump whine. • Rear brake squeal when the brakes are applied. • Harsh, delayed upshifts and downshifts. **2006–10**—Steering squeaks and rattles when turning. **2007–08**—Corrective measures for hard starts and rough cold idle.

AZERA PROFILE

	2006	2007	2008	2009
Cost Price ($)				
Sedan	34,495	34,995	35,995	36,995
Comfort/Limited	37,495	38,195	39,195	—
Used Values ($)				
Sedan ▲	10,500	13,500	18,000	23,000
Sedan ▼	9,000	12,000	16,500	21,500
Comfort/Limited ▲	11,500	15,000	20,000	—
Comfort/Limited ▼	10,500	13,500	18,500	—
Reliability	4	5	5	5
Crash Safety (F)	4	4	4	4
Side	5	5	5	5
IIHS Side	3	3	3	3
Offset	5	5	5	5
Head Restraints	3	3	3	3
Rollover Resistance	4	4	4	4

All ratings on a numbered scale where 5 is good and **1** is bad. See page 132 for a more detailed description.

LUXURY CARS

"What's the difference between a $30,000 car and one that costs $50,000? A lot of wasted money, according to Steve Sharf, a former Chrysler Corp manufacturing executive.... Sharf says all the amenities like heated steering wheels and leather seats just don't add up to that extra $20,000. He suggests it would be better to buy a pair of gloves and forgo the heated steering wheel. If it's prestige you're looking for, he says, 'it would be cheaper and make more sense to buy $20 cigars.'"

WARDS AUTOMOTIVE REPORTS

Guaranteed to get you from 30 to 50...er, thousand...with the stroke of a pen.

Luxury in a Recession?

You bet.

Cadillac sales increased 35 percent in 2010 with 90 percent of Cadillac dealers declaring a profit. GM is so confident that luxury sales will continue to grow that the automaker plans a replacement next year for the STS and DTS, called the XTS, in addition to a small sedan, the ATS.

Let's not minimize the damage done to the auto industry around the world by a recession that's still being felt. The late-2000s recession was the first time since the Great Depression of the 1930s that the luxury car market lost so many sales in so little time. However, not all automakers suffered equally. For instance, some of the sharpest drops in sales had come at the high end, including Mercedes-Benz, the BMW 7 Series, and Rolls Royce Phantom.

Nevertheless, luxury vehicle sales are rebounding much more quickly than their non-luxury counterparts because they generally have more financially stable dealerships, better leasing and certified pre-owned programs, and a loyal customer base. Moreover, there is a shift in buyer interest from North America to emerging markets such as China, India, and Russia. Also, the entry-level luxury

Not even the Rolls Royce Phantom could ride out this recession.

segment has been very competitive, and there has been some price-overlapping with well-equipped non-luxury cars. For instance, General Motors now sells more vehicles in China than it does in the United States.

Canadian consumers have benefited from lower prices on "luxurified" Detroit-built mid-size and large cars and SUVs, while several luxury import manufacturers set sales records in August 2009, due mostly to aggressive incentives on their own entry-level vehicles. In September 2009, Audi, BMW, Lexus, and Mercedes-Benz all saw their Canadian sales increase by more than 10 percent compared to a year earlier, despite overall Canadian auto sales being down 3.5 percent compared to September 2008. While other competitors were posting losses, BMW managed to remain profitable in 2009 by scaling down production quickly to avoid cash burn from bloated inventories.

Rank	Automaker	January 2011	% Change	Rank	Automaker	January 2011	% Change
#1	Ford	14,022	+25.5	#19	Lexus	728	-23.6
#2	Dodge	10,924	+22.3	#20	Acura	574	-19.8
#3	Chevrolet	8,892	+3.8	#21	Cadillac	490	+10.4
#4	Toyota	8,161	-1%	#22	Chrysler	416	-39.2
#5	Hyundai	6,684	+9.9	#23	Suzuki	413	-20
#6	GMC	4,426	+3.9	#24	Volvo	397	+0.3
#7	Nissan	4,008	-11.9	#25	Infiniti	330	-22.9
#8	Mazda	3,688	-11.6	#26	Lincoln	302	-16.8
#9	Honda	3,467	-38.9	#27	Land Rover	173	-1.1
#10	Kia	3,049	+26.2	#28	Scion	162	—
#11	Volkswagen	2,861	+22.7	#29	Mini	158	+0.6
#12	Jeep	2,247	-3.4	#30	Porsche	143	+52.1
#13	Subaru	1,753	+1.4	#31	Smart	82	-6.8
#14	Mercedes-Benz	1,482	-7.7	#32	Jaguar	32	-8.6
#15	Mitsubishi	1,412	+29.9	#33	Saab	11	—
#16	BMW	1,215	+16.7	#34	Maserati	7	+40
#17	Audi	1,140	+29	#35	Bentley	3	+50
#18	Buick	734	+43.6				

Source: Automakers, DesRosiers Automotive Reports and Automotive News Data Center

Canada sales chart by automaker for January 2011.

Used Luxury

Used luxury cars can be great buys if you ignore most of the hype and remember that many high-end models don't give you much more than the lower-priced, entry-level versions, without all the options. For example, the Lexus ES 300 is a Toyota Camry with a higher sticker price; the Audi A4 isn't much different from the Volkswagen Passat; Lincoln's front-drive Continental uses mostly junky Ford Taurus and Sable powertrains; and the Acura 3.2 TL, Infiniti I35 (formerly called the I30), and Jaguar X-Type are fully loaded, high-tuned versions of the Honda Accord, the Nissan Maxima, and the European Ford Mondeo, respectively.

Both high- and low-end models project a flashy cachet, come loaded with high-tech safety, performance, and comfort features, and can be bought, after three years or so, for half of what they sold for as new. Furthermore, if you can get servicing and parts from independent garages, you'll save even more. On the downside, there are overpriced luxury lemons out there (such as the front-drive Lincoln Continental and the Cadillac Allanté and Catera) that aren't sold anymore and are unreliable, with hard-to-service engines and transmissions and servicing costs that rival the national debt.

Mercedes-Benz owners, for example, can't say they weren't warned. Almost two decades ago, a $5 million study conducted over five years by the Massachusetts Institute of Technology said that the German automaker had begun making lousy cars by committing the same assembly-line mistakes as American automakers: allowing workers to build poor-quality vehicles and then fixing the mistakes at the end. As one reviewer of *The Machine That Changed the World*, by James P. Womack, Daniel T. Jones, and Daniel Roos (HarperCollins, November 1991), wrote:

> This study of the world automotive industry by a group of MIT academics reaches the radical conclusion that the much vaunted Mercedes technicians are actually a throwback to the pre-industrial age, while Toyota is far ahead in costs and quality by building the automobiles correctly the first time.

Readers of *Lemon-Aid* know from the internal service bulletins I quote extensively that Mercedes' C-Class compacts and M-Class sport-utilities have been plagued by serious factory defects, running the gamut from powertrain failures to fit and finish deficiencies.

Traditionally, the luxury-car niche has been dominated by American and German automakers. During the past decade, however, buyers have gravitated toward Japanese and south Korean models. This shift in buyer preference has forced Chrysler out of the market, has made Ford drop its problem-plagued Lincoln Continental, and has GM returning to rear-drive Cadillacs. Audi, BMW, Mini, and Porsche are the only European automakers with respectable sales.

Depreciation helps

Okay, so you're well advised to choose an Asian model, but doesn't that mean you'll have to dig deep in your wallet, wiping out most of your expected savings from buying used? Not necessarily. Smart buyers can pick up a $40,000 2008 G35 Infiniti sedan for $18,500 to $20,000. Similar savings are realized by purchasing a fully-loaded Honda Accord, Nissan Maxima, or Mazda6, all of which offer similar equipment, reliability, and performance to their higher-end brethren sold by Acura, Infiniti, and Lexus, but for much, much less.

Detroit does make some good luxury cars, like the 2008 Lincoln Town Car Signature pictured above—just not that many.

But if you want to buy a reliable and inexpensive Detroit-built luxury car, you can't do better than a 2008 Lincoln Town Car Signature for $2,000 with some of the original warranty left. That's for a car that sold for $58,599 just 36 months ago.

Worthwhile choices

I am not a big fan of luxury cars. If I was, however, I would limit my choice to reliable vehicles that look good and are relatively easy to maintain. For me, that would be the BMW 3 Series and Hyundai's Genesis 3.8

DEPRECIATION: A EUROPEAN LUXURY CAR NIGHTMARE

MODEL	NEW 2006	NEW 2008	USED 2006	USED 2008
Audi A3 2.0T	$32,950	$31,800	$11,000	$19,000
Audi A6 Quattro	$62,510	$63,600	$21,500	$36,500
BMW 323i	$35,200	$35,900	$12,000	$21,000
BMW 525i, 528i	$58,600	$59,900	$17,500	$33,000
BMW X3	$44,900	$45,300	$17,500	$27,000
BMW X5	$59,500	$61,900	$22,000	$35,500
Jaguar S-Type	$64,295	$62,000	$15,000	$28,500
Jaguar XJ	$88,500	$85,000	$19,000	$36,000
Mercedes B-Class	$30,950	$29,900	$9,500	$17,000
Mercedes E-Class	$74,300	$65,800	$20,000	$35,000
Mercedes ML350	$55,750	$59,900	$22,000	$35,000
Land Rover LR3	$53,900	$44.900	$18,000	$26,000
Land Rover Range Rover	$99,900	$100,900	$29,000	$44,000
Porsche Boxster	$64,100	$58,100	$25,500	$40,000
Porsche Cayenne	$60,100	$55,200	$23,500	$34,500
VW Passat AWD	$44,990	$44,675	$16,500	$20,500
Volvo S80	$54,995	$54,995	$18,500	$33,000
Volvo XC70 AWD	$47,121	$46,495	$18,000	$30,500

sedan 430. The quality of these cars, the durability of their powertrains, and their overall performance cannot be faulted.

Older BMWs are almost all good buys, but the 3 Series stands out because it comes as a two-door, a four-door, a wagon, and a convertible, and has gradually evolved over the years. Unlike Mercedes and Audi, BMW models are consistently well built. A 2006 323i in good condition can be found for less than $12,000. Better yet, a 2008 won't cost you more than $21,000. Drive it for four years, and then sell it for about $4,000 less—you will pay a little more than $1,000 a year to own a BMW that others paid $36,000 to buy new.

Future Luxury Cars: Asia and Europe

Let's face it: There aren't any American luxury cars that can match an equivalent Japanese model for overall reliability, durability, and value. And this isn't because Japanese products are that well made; far from it, as anyone who's purchased an engine-sludged Lexus will attest. No, it's simply because GM, Ford, and Chrysler vehicles are so poorly made that they make everyone else's look better. This fact has been reflected in the head-spinningly high depreciation rates and plummeting market share seen with most large-*cum*-luxury cars put out by the Detroit automakers. GM's rear-drive Cadillacs and Lincoln's Town Car come closest to meeting the imports in overall reliability and durability, yet they still come nowhere near the quality and performance level of many entry-level imports.

LUXURY CAR RATINGS

Recommended

Acura RL (2009)
Acura TL (1999–2009)
Ford/Lincoln Town Car (1999–2009)

Hyundai Genesis sedan (2009–10)
Infiniti G35 (2007–08)
Infiniti G37 (2009)

Above Average

Acura RL (1999–2008)
BMW 3 Series, 5 Series, M Series,
    Z4 (1999–2009)
Ford/Lincoln MKZ (2007–09)
Hyundai Genesis Coupe (2010)

Infiniti G37 (2008)
Infiniti I30 (2000–03)
Infiniti M35, M45 (2006–07)
Kia Magentis (2007)
Toyota Avalon (1999–2004)

Average

BMW Z3 (1999–2002)
Ford/Lincoln LS (2000–06)
Ford/Lincoln Zephyr (2006)
General Motors DeVille (2001–05)

Kia Amanti (2007)
Kia Magentis (2005–06)
Lexus ES 300/330/350, GS
    300/350/430/450h/460, IS 250/300/350,
    LS 400/430/460/600h, SC 300, SC 400/430 (1999–2009)

Infiniti I35 (2002–04)
Infiniti M35, M45 (2003–05)
Infiniti Q45 (2002–05)

Mercedes-Benz B-Class (2006–09)
Nissan Maxima (2007–09)
Toyota Avalon (2005–09)

Below Average

General Motors CTS, CTS-V, DTS,
    STS, STS-V (1999–2009)
Infiniti G35 (2003–06)
Infiniti Q45 (1997–2001)

Kia Amanti (2004–06)
Kia Magentis (2001–04)
Mercedes-Benz 300 Series, 400 Series,
    500 Series, E-Class (1999–2009)
Nissan Maxima (1999–06)

Not Recommended

Audi A3, A4, A4 S-Line, A6, A8,
    S4, S6, TT Coupe (2000–09)
Ford/Lincoln Continental (1999–2002)
Infiniti G20 (1999–2002)

Mercedes-Benz C-Class (1999–2009)
Volvo C30, C70, S40, S60, S70, S80, V40, V50,
    V70, XC70, XC90 (all years)

Acura

RL ★★★★★

RATING: Recommended (2009); Above Average (1999–2008). Basically, this is a fully loaded, longer, wider, and heavier TL, equipped with a larger engine that produces less horsepower than its smaller brother. Watch out for the failure-prone, notchy, 6-speed manual transmission. **Ideal model year:** A $69,500 2006 can be had for around $18,500 and the much improved 2009 $63,900 3.5L V6 version will cost $40,000, or $24,000 less than its original price and still have some original warranty coverage. **"Real" city/highway fuel economy:** There's not much difference in gas consumption between the old and new V6 engines. *2004 and earlier V6 models:* 13.0/9.1 L/100 km. *2005–2006 V6 models:* 12.9/8.4 L/100 km. *3.7 AWD:* 13.1/9.0 L/100 km. These estimates are fairly accurate, according to owners' experiences. **Maintenance/Repair costs:** Average; most repairs are dealer-dependent. **Parts:** Most mechanical and electronic components are easily found and moderately priced. Body parts may be hard to come by and can be expensive. **Extended warranty:** No, save your $2,000. **Best alternatives:** Consider the departed Acura Legend or Integra, BMW's 5 Series, Infiniti's I30 or I35, and Lexus's GS 300/400. Also, you may want to take a look at the TL sedan: It's not as expensive, and it's a better performer, though passenger room is more limited. **Helpful websites:** *http://acuraforum.net*; *www.cbel.com/acura_cars*; and *www.acurasucks.com*.

Strengths and Weaknesses

The RL has a comfortable ride, exceptional steering and handling, top-quality body and mechanical components, good (though not impressive) acceleration that's smooth and quiet in all gear ranges, and it's loaded with goodies. The steering can be numb, however, and manual and automatic transmissions are sometimes problematic.

The 3.5 RL is loaded with the innovative high-tech safety and convenience features one would expect to find in a luxury car. These include ABS, traction control, heated front seats, "smart" side airbags, an anti-skid system, a rear-seat trunk pass-through, front and rear climate controls, and xenon headlights (get used to oncoming drivers flashing you with their headlights). The 3.5L 210–225 hp V6 mated with a 4-speed automatic transmission provides good acceleration that's a bit slower and more fuel-thirsty than the TL, partly because of the RL's extra pounds. The 2005's 300 hp V6 coupled to a 5-speed automatic (a manual shifter isn't available) resolves this problem. The car handles nicely, with a less firm ride than the TL, although steering response doesn't feel as crisp. Interior accommodations, which fit four occupants, are excellent up front and in the rear because the RL's platform is larger than the TL's. Headroom is a bit tight, though, and the 2005's smaller dimensions may irk some buyers who don't mind sacrificing performance for extra room. Be wary of the poor-performing Collision Mitigation System and run-flat tires on the 2006–08 models. Also, the 2007–08 models continue to offer limited rear seating and an awkward keyless locking/starting system.

VEHICLE HISTORY: 2002— Wider tires, larger brakes, OnStar assistance, more sound deadening, and small horsepower boost (15 hp). **2005**—A major redesign reduces the car's size but it now comes with more features: standard all-wheel drive, a 300 hp V6 hooked to a 5-speed automatic, more safety and convenience features, and refreshed styling. Safety features include standard anti-skid control, front side airbags and side curtain airbags, anti-lock four-wheel disc brakes, steering-linked xenon headlights, and a navigation system. **2006**—Horsepower is cut by 10 to total 290 hp. Introduction of run-flat tires and the Collision Mitigation Braking System. **2007**—Upgraded braking. Steering-linked xenon headlights and a voice-activated navigation system are now optional features. **2008**—A couple new colours. **2009**—Returns repowered and with refreshed styling. Car carries a 300 hp 3.7L V6 hooked to a 5-speed automatic transmission.

Owner-reported problems on more recent models include frequent stalling; electrical shorts; front-wheel liner cracking; malfunctioning accessories; noisy transmission engagement and steering; a failure-prone, misshifting manual transmission; and premature brake wear, and a loud, metallic-sounding squeal when braking (see *www.cbel.com/acura_cars* and *www.acurasucks.com*).

Safety Summary

All years: Early automatic transmission replacements. • Chronic stalling when accelerating. • Premature wearout of the front and rear brake pads. • Dash display is unreadable in daylight. **2005**—Inadequate headlight illumination:

> The vertical self adjusting headlights pose serious safety concerns on unlit road-ways.... On hilly terrain, the headlights will adjust down as the vehicle starts uphill, illuminating [only] approximately 40 feet [12 m] in front of the vehicle. This also occurs when the vehicle travels over bumps and any minor changes in vehicle altitude. It is very easy to overdrive the headlights, often at speeds less than 20 mph [32 km/h]. You simply cannot see road hazards or pedestrians.

• Suspension bottoms out with a full load and damages the undercarriage. • Loose steering high-pressure hose may detach. • Faulty AC compressor. **2006**—Sudden, unintended acceleration. • Airbags failed to deploy. • Fire ignited in the overhead door channel. • Headlights don't sufficiently illuminate the road. • Vehicle accelerates when the cruise control is engaged. **2007**—Car accelerates suddenly when the brakes are applied. • Sudden stall-out on the freeway (fuel pump is suspected). • Collision Mitigation System does not perform as advertised. • Headlights flicker when car is underway. **2008**—Gas fumes infiltrate the cabin. **2009**—Sudden acceleration when pulling away from a light, accompanied by one airbag deploying and the doors refusing to open. • Gas pedal and brake pedal engage at the same time because they are mounted too close together.

Secret Warranties/Internal Bulletins/Service Tips

All years: Acura guidelines for submitting paint claims. **1999–2006**—Diagnosis and correction of drift/pull problem. **2003**—Airbag light comes on for no reason. • Troubleshooting automatic transmission malfunctions. **2004**—Sticking fuel-filler cap. **2005**—Hot weather may cause stalling, hard starts caused by vapour lock. **2005–06**—Front brake rattle, squeal. • Defective automatic door locks. **2005–07**—Low, soft brake pedal. **2005–09**—High mount stop light cover is loose, or falls off. • Door handle sensor does not unlock the doors. **2005–10**—Loose windshield side trim retainer. **2009**—Long crank, hard start. **2009–10**—Moisture in the tail lights.

RL PROFILE

	2001	2002	2003	2004	2005	2006	2007	2008	2009
Cost Price ($)									
Base	53,000	54,000	55,000	55,800	69,500	69,500	63,900	63,900	63,900
Used Values ($)									
Base ▲	7,000	9,000	11,500	13,500	16,000	19,000	24,500	30,000	40,000
Base ▼	5,500	8,000	10,000	12,000	14,500	17,500	23,000	28,000	38,000

All ratings on a numbered scale where ▩ is good and **1** is bad. See page 132 for a more detailed description.

Reliability	5	5	5	5	5	4	4	4	5
Crash Safety (F)	4	4	4	4	5	5	5	5	5
Side	—	—	—	4	5	5	5	5	5
IIHS Side	—	—	—	—	5	5	5	5	5
Offset	3	3	3	3	5	5	5	5	5
Head Restraints	**1**	**1**	**1**	**1**	2	2	2	2	5
Roof Strength					2	2	2	2	**2**
Rollover Resistance	—	—	4	4	5	5	5	5	5

TL ★★★★★

RATING: Recommended (1999–2009). **Ideal model year:** Take a look at the redesigned and slightly enlarged 2009 models. A $40,000 TL sedan now costs $27,000 and gives you a year of factory warranty to boot. **"Real" city/highway fuel economy:** 11.7/7.7 L/100 km. Owners report fuel savings may undershoot this estimate by about 10 percent. **Maintenance/Repair costs:** Average costs for the most part, but many repairs are dealer-dependent, which drives up servicing costs if you can't find a competent technician. **Parts:** Higher-than-average costs, but parts aren't hard to find. **Extended warranty:** Not needed. **Best alternatives:** Consider the Acura Integra; BMW 3 Series; redesigned Infiniti I30 or I35; Hyundai Genesis; Mazda Millenia; and Lexus ES 300, ES 330, or ES 350. Also, take a look at Acura's CL coupe: It isn't as expensive, and it's as close as you can get to the Accord, with lots of standard bells and whistles thrown in. **Helpful websites:** *http://tl.acurazine.com*.

Strengths and Weaknesses

The TL handles well, rides comfortably, boasts impressive acceleration, and is well put together, with quality mechanical and body components. However, the suspension may be too firm for some, and the vehicle creates excessive road noise and has uncomfortable rear seating, limited cargo room, and problematic navigation system controls (see *www.vtec.net* [The Temple of VTEC], *www.acuraworld.com/forums*, *www.cbel.com/acura_cars*, and *www.autosafety.org/autodefects.html*).

Filling the void left by the discontinued Vigor, the TL combines luxury and performance in a nicely styled front-drive, five-passenger sedan that uses the same chassis as the Accord and CL coupe. A 235 hp 3.2L V6 engine came on board with 1999 models. A 5-speed automatic transmission replaced the 4-speed unit in 2000. The 2002 Type-S carried a 260 hp version of the same V6. From 2004 to the present, the sole engine remained the 3.2L V6, putting out 270 horses, versus 225 or 260 hp on previous TLs.

Performance enthusiasts will opt for versions equipped with the more-refined 3.2L 225/270 hp V6 mated to a 6-speed manual transmission and a firmer suspension introduced with the 2004 model. It provides impressive acceleration (0–100 km/h in just over eight seconds) in a smooth and quiet manner, without any fuel penalty. Handling is exceptional with the firm suspension but can be a bit tricky when pushed. Bumps are a bit jarring, and the ride is somewhat busier than with other cars in this class.

VEHICLE HISTORY: **2002**—A new performance version based on the CL Type S, a minor facelift, new wheels and headlights, and more-comfortable seat belts. **2004**—New styling, 10 more horses, and more standard safety features like head-protecting side curtain airbags. Other improvements include a 6-speed manual tranny, a sportier suspension, high-performance tires, Brembo front brakes, and a limited-slip differential. **2007**—The return of the Type-S, last seen in 2003. Base models have a 258 hp V6 engine teamed with 5-speed automatic transmission. The Type-S has a 286 hp V6 mated to either a 6-speed manual or 5-speed automatic. Type-S also includes firmer suspension, Brembo front brakes, an upgraded interior, and better soundproofing. Other new features include an optional rearview camera, a revised instrument panel, and one-touch starting on vehicles equipped with an automatic transmission. **2008**—A very slight exterior restyling.

Interior accommodations are better than average up front, but rear occupants may discover that legroom is a bit tight and the seat cushions lack sufficient thigh support. The cockpit layout is very user-friendly, due in part to the easy-to-read gauges and accessible controls (far-away climate controls are the only exception).

Common complaints involve poor body fits, electrical shorts, engine surging and stalling, premature brake and tire wear, malfunctioning airbags and accessories, the 6-speed manual transmission shifting roughly into Third gear and sometimes popping out of gear, and chronic automatic and manual transmission failures (covered by a "goodwill" warranty up to eight years). Owners point out that the window regulator may need replacing, the ignition switch buzzes, the trunk lock jams, and the rear bumper is often loose.

Safety Summary

All years: Horn is difficult to locate in emergency situations. • Airbags fail to deploy in a collision. • Sudden, unintended acceleration. • Automatic transmission failures at high speeds; grinds when shifting from First to Second gear; and sometimes fails to downshift or upshift. • Front brake rotors warp early. • Door locks operate erratically. • Frequent tire failures. • Instrument panel is washed out in daylight. • It's easy for drivers to confuse the brake and gas pedals. **2004**—Stability control activates right front brake, causing the vehicle to swerve suddenly. • Excessive steering-wheel shake and chassis vibration often blamed on tires, but it can be caused by a defective transmission torque converter. • Cracked alloy wheel rim caused tire failure. • Headlight low beam creates a dark/blind spot. • Multiple malfunctions with the hands-free phone system. • Windshield easily broken. •

Many complaints of hydroplaning and excessive vibration from the Bridgestone Turanza EL42 tires. • Power mirrors, auto-dimming mirror, windshield wiper washer, and power-seat position memory often malfunction due to the system's fuse constantly blowing. **2004–06**—Low, soft brake pedal. **2005**—Car pulls to either side when underway. • Severe rear brake corrosion and grooving extends stopping distances. • Premature failure of Bridgestone and Michelin tires. • Early replacement of side window motor and regulator. **2006**—Sudden brake and steering failures. • ABS and vehicle stabilization system fail in icy conditions. • Keys stuck in ignition and doors won't unlock after vehicle stopped. **2007**—Under-hood fire. • Sudden loss of power and lights. • Vehicle suddenly shifts from Third to Neutral. • Airbag alert constantly lit. • Premature clutch failure ($2,000):

> I know how to drive manual. The clutch gave out around 28,000. Acura of Riverside has looked at it and said the clutch is no good and needs to be replaced. He also said a few weeks ago another Acura TL Type S has replaced the clutch. The service tech has quoted me over $2,000 to get the car working. I believe that Acura has a problem with the manual transmission in the past. My other cars lasted between 120K to 150K with the factory clutch. I have research[ed] online and other [people] are having this problem.

• Manual transmission frequently pops out of Third gear. • Brake and steering failure when coming to a sudden stop. • False alerts from the Fuel System light. • Driver's side window crushed driver's finger. **2008**—Premature engine timing belt failure. • Piston rod broke and destroyed the engine. • Bridgestone tire side wall blowouts. • Door stoppers don't hold the doors open when exiting the vehicle:

> As a passenger, I often find the big heavy door will not stay in the open position while I am trying to exit from the car. There are several "locking" positions, but none of them hold firmly. This is especially true if the car is on even a slight incline. I find myself kicking the door out of the way so I can safely exit.

Secret Warranties/Internal Bulletins/Service Tips

All years: Seat belts that fail to function properly during normal use will be replaced for free under the company's lifetime seat belt warranty. • Diagnostic procedures and correction for off-centre steering wheels. • Acura guidelines for submitting paint claims. **1999–2002**—Front, middle, or rear engine oil leaks likely caused by a too-porous cast aluminum engine block (TSB #01-041). **1999–2006**—Diagnosing and fixing a drift/pull to one side. **2000–03**—Honda extends its warranties to 7 years/160,000 km (100,000 mi.) on automatic transmissions. **2004**—A Fifth-gear vibration or drone may require the installation of a dynamic damper (Part #50207-SEP-305). • A lit ABS light may indicate moisture in the sensor. **2004–05**—TSB #05-033 says you should install a #10A fuse if the windshield wiper washer, power-seat position memory, power mirrors, or auto-dimming mirror don't work. • A faulty outside temperature gauge probably needs a new gauge control module. • A clicking or popping brake pedal may have a misaligned brake-pedal position switch plunger. Turn it around so the connector lock faces the 5 o'clock position. **2004–06**—Tips on silencing front brake squeal. • Inoperative, noisy side window regulators. **2004–07**—Manual transmission pops out of gear; hard to shift into Third gear; makes a grinding noise. **2004–08**—Power steering moans, whines upon cold startup. • Front door glass reverses, shudders, or is noisy. • Cracked roof console bezel. • Interior rearview mirror loose, vibrates. • Front seatback panel loose or detaches. • Headliner sagging. • Rear shelf rattles. **2005–08**—Timing belt chirping. • Loose driver's seat cushion. **2006–08**—Door mirror doesn't operate properly. **2009**— Steering column makes a popping or clicking sound. • Audio speaker rattling. • AC blower changes speed. • Front door panel fabric pulls out.

TL PROFILE

	2001	2002	2003	2004	2005	2006	2007	2008	2009
Cost Price ($)									
Base	36,000	37,000	37,800	40,800	41,000	42,000	42,500	42,700	39,900
Used Values ($)									
Base ▲	5,000	6,000	7,500	9,000	11,500	14,000	17,500	20,500	27,500
Base ▼	4,000	5,000	6,500	8,000	10,000	12,500	16,000	21,000	26,000
Reliability	3	3	3	4	5	5	4	4	4
Crash Safety (F)	4	4	4	5	5	5	5	5	5
Side	4	4	4	4	4	5	5	5	5
IIHS Side	—	—	—	5	5	5	5	5	5
Offset	5	5	5	5	5	5	5	5	5
Head Restraints	1	1	1	2	2	2	2	2	5
Rollover Resistance	—	5	4	4	4	5	4	4	5

Audi

A3, A4, A4 S-LINE, A6, A8, S4, S6, TT COUPE ★

RATING: Not Recommended (2000–09). Beautiful to behold; deadly to drive, and hell to repair. *Lemon-Aid* has dropped Audi's rating as low as we can because of these vehicles' failure-prone electronics, chronic electrical shorts, unreliable headlights, and terrifying DSG transmission and engine failures that can stop you dead on the highway and then shoot you forward like a NASA rocket. One owner filmed the entire sequence: *www.autoinsane.com/2009/08/21/news/recalls-tsbs/flash-of-death-volkswagen-audi-dsg-recall-issues-caught-on-video.*

These cars, like Mercedes and Volkswagen models, seem to quickly go downhill quality-wise after the five-year mark. **Ideal model year:** "Do you feel lucky, Punk?" (as Dirty Harry would say). If yes, then take a chance on a 2008 A3 2.0T for

From the entry-level A3 to the higher-end TT Roadster, an Audi transmission failure can be deadly (see video cited on the preceding page).

about $18,500. It hasn't been as plagued by the factory-related quality demons we've seen with other Audis. Which begs the question: Is the A3 that improved, or are we too early on the scene? The 2008 A4 is another risky but doable buy. It originally sold for $41,200 and dealers sell the car used for $22,000 retail. Your best strategy: Buy the A4 from a private owner for about 20 percent less than dealer retail ($18,000) and make sure the vehicle has some of the original warranty left. Then have your A4 serviced top to bottom by a Audi dealer. Ask for warranty coverage on all the defects that pop up. Get the warranty work done and keep your work orders that mention problems or symptoms that were never corrected, particularly powertrain glitches. Then go to a cheaper independent service centre for the rest of your servicing and get estimates for the correction of those problems that were never fixed by the dealer. File a small claims court action against the Audi dealer and Audi Canada for the cost of those repairs estimated by your independent garage. **"Real" city/highway fuel economy:** *A3 2.0 6-speed manual:* 10.2/7.1 L/100 km. *A4 1.8 manual:* 11.2/7.2 L/100 km. *Quattro 3.0 manual:* 13.5/8.7 L/100 km (this version burns a lot more fuel than the A4!). *S4 manual:* 15.8/10.2 L/100 km. *A6 3.0:* 11.5/8.1 L/100 km. *TT Coupe 1.8 Selectronic:* 11.3/7.5 L/100 km. *TT Coupe 3.2:* 10.9/8.1 L/100 km. Owners report fuel savings are fairly accurate for those models equipped with a manual transmission. Estimates for vehicles with an automatic tranny may be off by about 10 percent. **Maintenance/Repair costs:** Higher than average, and almost all repairs have to be done by an Audi dealer. Expect long delays for routine repairs. **Parts:** Very expensive, and independent suppliers have a hard time finding parts. **Extended warranty:** A good idea, considering how often the engines and transmissions need work. **Best alternatives:** Acura Integra, TL, or RL; BMW 3 Series; Infiniti I30 or I35; and Lexus ES300. TT Coupe shoppers may also want to look at the BMW Z3 or Z4, Ford Mustang (2011), Honda S2000, Hyundai Genesis Coupe, and Mazda Miata. **Helpful websites:** *www.audiworld.com, www.vwvortex.com,* and *MyAudiTTsucks.com.*

Strengths and Weaknesses

A3

Launched as a 2006 model, the A3 is Audi's entry-level ($32,950 in 2006; $32,300 in 2011) small car. It's a conservatively styled compact hatchback with a small interior, too-light steering (be prepared to make lots of steering corrections at highway speeds), and average reliability. The base model is quite manoeuvrable and quick, thanks to the turbocharged 200 hp 2.0L 4-cylinder engine hooked to a 6-speed manumatic transmission. The AWD variant comes with a powerful 250 hp 3.2L V6 (borrowed from Volkswagen) that quiets the ride and improves handling a touch while sucking up premium fuel.

Sales of the 2006 model were quite good, prompting Audi to boost 2007 prices by almost $1,000. Fortunately, resale prices between the two model years haven't been that different. Nevertheless, 2008 models are favoured over the 2006 versions because of the fewer factory-related defects evidenced after the cars got through their first-year teething period, when product quality is at its lowest.

A4

Audi's best-selling line, these cars handle well, and are attractively styled, comfortable to drive, and provide a fairly comfortable interior. But you'd better know how to separate the wheat from the chaff, since some model years can be wallet-busters due to their rapid depreciation, poor quality, and high servicing costs.

Replacements for the Audi 90 for the 1996 model year, these alphabetically named cars are conservatively styled, often slow off the mark (in spite of the V6 addition when hooked to an automatic), and plagued by electrical glitches, mechanical breakdowns, and outrageously expensive servicing and repair costs—when you can find a competent Audi mechanic. The 4-speed automatic shifts erratically (delayed and abrupt engagement), and the 2.8L V6 engine needs full throttle for adequate performance. Handling is acceptable, on a par with the BMW 3 Series, but the ride is a bit firm and the car still exhibits considerable body roll, brake dive, and acceleration squat when pushed, although acceleration times beat out those of Mercedes.

Overall quality control has improved very little over the last two decades. To this day, owners continue to report an inordinate number of safety- and performance-related defects. The automatic transmission and electrical system are the cars' weakest links and have plagued Audi's entire lineup. Normally this wouldn't be catastrophic; however, as the cars become more electronically complex, with more functions handled by computer modules, you're looking at some annoying glitches, to say the least (failure to go into gear, false obstacle warnings, etc.). Here are some other "annoyances": steering grinds, distorted windshields, brakes that fail in rainy weather, body glitches that would shame Lada, early lower control arm replacement, defective mirror memory settings, premature brake wear and then loud grinding when in Reverse, fuel-system malfunctions leading to surging and stalling, and the transmission suddenly downshifts or jerks into Forward gear. Furthermore, servicing is still spotty because of the small number of dealers in Canada and the fact that these cars are extremely dealer-dependent (see *www.audiworld.com*, *www.vwvortex.com*, *MyAudiTTsucks.com*, and *www.thetruthaboutcars.com*).

TT Coupe

The best of the Audi lineup, but still plagued by failure-prone electrical and mechanical components, the TT Coupe is a sporty front-drive hatchback with 2+2 seating set on the same platform used by the A4, Golf, Jetta, and New Beetle. A two-seat convertible version, the Roadster, was launched in the spring of 2000. The base 180 hp 1.8L engine (lifted from the A4) is coupled with a manual 5-speed, while the optional engine uses a 6-speed manual transaxle. Shorter and more firmly sprung than the A4, the TT's engines are turbocharged.

More beautifully styled and with better handling than the discontinued Chrysler Prowler, the TT comes with lots of high-tech standard features that include four-wheel disc brakes, airbags everywhere, traction control (front-drive models), a power top (Quattro), a heated-glass rear window, and a power-retractable glass windbreak between the roll bars (convertible). An alarm system employs a pulse radar system to catch prying hands invading the cockpit area.

Problem areas reported by owners include steering-wheel clunks, excessive brake noise, early tie-rod wearout, premature wheel bearing failures, poorly performing window regulators, electrical shorts causing dash gauges and instruments to fail, premature transmission failures and grinding of the Second gear synchronizers, and loose bolts that cause the subframe to move while driving over bumps and while braking.

VEHICLE HISTORY: *A4:* **2001**—The base 1.8L engine gets 20 extra horses; an all-new 2001 S4 sedan and Avant, featuring a 250 hp 2.7L twin-turbocharged V6, also join the lineup. Standard side curtain airbags. **2002**—A4 is totally revamped, getting a roomier interior, a 10 hp boost to the base engine, and a 3.0L all-aluminum, 5-valve-per-cylinder, 220 hp V6 engine hooked to a new 6-speed manual transmission. Other features: brake assist, a more-rigid body, and an upgraded independent rear suspension. **2003**—Addition of a convertible. **2004**—S4 returns using the A4's new design. More high-performance models and greater all-wheel-drive availability. Quattro models drop the old 5-speed for a 6-speed manual transmission. **2005**—A mid-year redesign. **2007**—S4 is restyled. **2009**—Redesigned and given more power. *A6:* **2001**—2.7T and the 4.2 A6 models get Audi's electronic stabilization program, which prevents fishtailing and enhances traction control. **2002**—Debut of all-wheel drive, a 2.7L engine, and adjustable air suspension. **2003**—The new RS6 debuts, equipped with a 450 hp 4.2L V8; the sporty S6 Avant adds a more-powerful V8 and sport suspension. On the downside, front-passenger seat memory is no more, and steering-wheel shift buttons are gone. **2004**—A V8 for the all-road Quattro, and a new sports model, the 2.7T S-Line sedan. **2005**—Refreshed styling and additional room and power.

Wheelbase is increased and models are equipped with either a 255 hp V6 or a 335 hp V8, coupled to a 6-speed automatic transmission with manual-shift capability and all-wheel drive. Audi's MMI operating system, like BMW's iDrive, uses a centre console knob to control many of the car's accessories. All A6s now have front side airbags, side curtain airbags, and optional rear side airbags. Anti-lock four-wheel disc brakes and an anti-skid system are both standard. **2006**—A new Avant wagon and front-drive sedan spin-off. **2007**—Debut of the 435 hp V10 S6 Quattro sedan. **2009**—Restyled and equipped with a new 300 hp supercharged 3.0L V6 found on the 3.0T Quattro. Troublesome air suspension feature dropped. *TT:* **2001**—A two-passenger softtop Roadster debuts; addition of a rear spoiler, Electronic Stability Program, and a 225 hp turbocharged 4-cylinder engine. **2003**—All-wheel drive now found only on uplevel models; a revised grille. **2004**—A 250 hp V6, a manumatic transmission, and standard xenon headlights (thieves will love you). **2008**—Fresh styling and a new powertrain: 2.0T models get a 200 hp turbocharged 2.0L four-banger and the AWD gets a 250 hp 3.2L V6 hooked to a six-speed manu-matic transmission. **2009**—A new TTS coupe and convertible. The TTS uses a 265 hp 2.0T supercharged 4-cylinder (15 more horses than the V6 and 65 more than the basic turbo four).

Other 1996 and later Audi models are just as poorly designed and built as the A4 and its many spin-offs. For example, the A6, a reincarnation of the 100 Series, is packed with standard convenience and safety features and is a comfortable, spacious front-drive or all-wheel-drive luxury sedan. It uses the same V6 powerplant as the A4, its smaller sibling, but has 47 additional horses. Unfortunately, the engine is no match for the car's size (0–100 km/h in 13 seconds), and steering and handling are decidedly truck-like.

The A8 competes with the BMW 7 Series and the Mercedes S-Class and loses. Equipped with a 174 hp 2.8L V6 or a 300 hp V8, the A8 is a decently performing—though equally defect-ridden—buy. Its drawbacks: a high price, subpar reliability, imprecise steering, and an aluminum body that only an Audi dealer can repair.

Launched in 1994 and powered by a turbocharged 227 hp 2.2L 5-cylinder engine, the S6 is a high-performance spin-off of the A6. Its reliability is mediocre at best, though its sporty performance leaves the A6 in the dust.

Safety Summary

All models/years: Airbag failures. • Chronic stalling. • Sudden acceleration. • Extremely poor wet braking on later models, caused by water contaminating the brake rotor and disc; brakes delay by almost two seconds. • Many cases of distorted windshields. **All models: 2001**—Brakes fail to stop vehicle. • Headlights blind oncoming drivers. • Hood latch breaks, allowing hood to smash into windshield. **2003**—Stuck accelerator pedal. • No-starts believed to be caused by instrument cluster or steering lock/ignition cylinder failures. • Stalling believed to be caused by a defective fuel pump. • CVT hesitates before engaging. • Parking brake fails to hold. • Outside mirrors don't automatically readjust. • Ice glazes the brake rotors.

• Frequent failure of the windshield wiper motor and washer. • Doors fill with water when it rains. **2004**—Stuck accelerator causes sudden acceleration. • Tire jack stand collapses. • Convertible top fails. **2005**—Car constantly drifts to the right side of the roadway. • Car is a rodent magnet:

> At 2,200 miles [3,540 km], a headlight warning light came on, and I took my car to the dealership. I was told that a mouse had climbed into my engine, built a nest out of the hood insulation, and chewed through wires. Audi refused to cover any damages. This incident cost me $1,400.

• Vehicle hesitates for two to three seconds when accelerating from a complete stop:

> I have almost been T-boned while trying to make a left hand turn, 3 times. The car is dangerous!! I took it in to the dealer on July the 1st. They told me then that that is the way the car is designed to operate.

A3: **2006**—Engine coolant line flange failure allows coolant to drain out:

> Engine coolant line flange failure causes engine coolant to drain from vehicle. The dealer indicates that this is common on the 2.0 engines. Part unavailable in the US (on back order). The car was parked, luckily. Could have been a major expense if on the highway. Drained within several hours while parked. If this is an issue, why isn't Audi replacing this with a metal flange instead of a plastic one?

• Premature automatic transmission failure. • Wheels passed over a manhole cover, and the airbags deployed. • In warm weather, the car's fuel pump will shut off, causing the vehicle to stall in traffic. • Weak sun shade latch. • Horn may not work. **2007**—Chronic loss of power, stalling, and transmission drops into Neutral:

> On my way to work in my 2007 Audi A3—All of a sudden I lose power and my car stops accelerating and shifts into Neutral. I see that the P D N S lights are flashing so I attempt to restart my car. It starts to go again and then sputters forward without me doing anything. Luckily I wasn't far from home and was able to restart my car again and get it home while the car revved like crazy going less than 20 mph. After some research I have found that many Audi/VW's experience this in their vehicles. These are all characteristic of a faulty mechatronic unit associated with the car's DSG.

• More DSG automatic transmission malfunctions:

> My DSG transmission started acting funny. When I would let off of the brake, the car would sit for a split second and then jump forward quickly as if I had blurped the throttle. Sometimes it does it twice before rolling smoothly. I[t] feels like the clutch is engaging too strongly and then letting off. Also, when coming to a stop, the transmission seems like it holds on to the gear a little too long and makes my car jump forward right before a stop. It does this in reverse also. It has caused me to go

too far into the crosswalk at a stop light. It does this all of the time, not just when the engine/transmission is cold.

•

2007 Audi A3 DSG transmission. Vehicle hesitates on acceleration from stop, 2–3 sec. delay in accelerating. Upon decelerating to stop and restarting, transmission delays shifting into 1st for approx. 1 sec causing a severe clunk as the transmission shifts into 1st while engine revs are higher than idle. This problem has increased in frequency in the last 5000 miles. These issues cause near misses merging into traffic and increase the odds of rear end collisions when cars following don't hesitate.

• Faulty Pirelli tires howl and hum; uneven, premature wear. **2008**—Increase in the number of DSG manumatic transmission failures; there is no simple fix:

My 2008 Audi A3 and its DSG transmission have exhibited irregular and dangerous shifting behavior. The transmission surges unpredictably at low speeds, particularly in 1st or Reverse with brakes off and little/no gas. This low speed surging behavior is dangerous in stop-and-go traffic as the car often unpredictably jumps towards other vehicles. Also on several occasions the transmission has completely dropped out of gear and failed to re-engage for approximately 1–2 months, however the problems have since reappeared. It seems clear that this line of transmissions have persistent and possibly dangerous problems.

2009—More DSG transmission failures:

I am travelling on the highway in the middle lane at around 60/65 mph, the transmission (DSG) started making chunk noises and the car started to jerk, then the engine completely shut down in the middle of the highway!! Not to mention my youngest sister (10 years old) was with me. I couldn't restart the engine and I couldn't steer and/or shift without pressing on the break. I ended up in a complete stop in the middle of the highway hoped no one would hit me and thank God it didn't. I then quickly shift the gear back to "P" and fortunately the engine started again so I could get out of this hell zone. This is truly unbelievable for a new vehicle with 200 miles.

• Blinking headlights and interior lights when braking. *A4:* **2006**—HID headlights flicker and often go out; vehicle has to be re-started to put them back on:

Numerous other individuals are having the same problem as evidenced by postings on user forums. *www.fixya.com/cars/t593349.*

• Dealer says the fix will cost $400:

Audi A4 B7 bi-xenon headlights fail during driving at night. Error message "headlight dipped" is shown on the display. No fault code is generated. Had the chance to shoot a video of the failed light on the 1st of March 2010…A problem is occurring since

October 2009. Was reported to Audi, but Audi did not address the issue at that time since there was no fault code saved in the system. Some owners have solved the problem by replacing the headlight igniter or ballasts.

• Delayed acceleration. • Power steering pump pulley separates from the vehicle. Vehicle locks all the doors if the car is exited while the engine is running. **2007**—"Lag and lurch" when accelerating:

I have two Audi A4's, one a 2007 sedan and one a 2008 station wagon. Both exhibit the same problem. Both have done it a number of times, mostly the sedan. When you need to scoot across opposing traffic making a left, sporadically, the car initially responds like you'd expect the gas pedal, but half a second later bogs out with basically no acceleration, so you're rolling leisurely across oncoming traffic, and then about a second later it wakes up and resumes accelerating. I'm serious. Both cars do it, largely turning left.

• Frequent stalling on the highway. • "Cam follower" inside the high pressure fuel pump may be cause of some of the stalling, loss of power incidents; it is a $1,1000+ repair:

2007 Audi A4 Avant. Vehicle loses power when accelerating. The failure occurred each time I would accelerate in excess of 55 mph. To correct this failure a new camshaft, cam follower, and fuel pump were installed in the vehicle for a total of $1,749.97.

•

Fuel cut-off/surging when accelerating. Engine is not throwing any engine codes; however, a loss of power is present when accelerating. This occurs every time I try to accelerate. This is a known issue with the cam follower and high pressure fuel pump on all 2.0T FSI motors from Audi and VW. My cam follower has a hole in it (have the part) and the HPFP is worn down because it has made contact with the cam lobe, which has been scarred. Replacement requires a new cam, HPFP and cam follower. The design however will require constant inspection of the cam follower to avoid major engine failure. All 2.0T FSI engines will experience this problem. Audi has a TSB #2013147/4 Dated June 18, 2007 that warns of this problem upon CEL light being shown. My car never showed the CEL light; however, had the other symptoms described and upon further inspection had a hole in the cam follower, with severe damage to the cam and HPFP.

• Frequent replacement of expensive coil packs and diverter valves. • Many reports that the 2.0L engine is an oil-burner. • Headlight failures caused by faulty xenon bulb or ballast. • Carpet can jam the accelerator pedal. • Driver-side seatbelt easily unlatches if an object is placed near the buckle. • Premature wearout and side bubbling of Continental tires. **2008**—Engine burns oil even after rings were replaced. • Chronic stalling due to a defective fuel pressure regulator. • Pirelli tires constantly lose air. • Sunroof exploded (glass pushed outward). **2009**—More fuel pump failures, causing the vehicle to shut down anywhere. • Original-equipment windshield wipers work poorly:

> OEM wipers provided by Audi on 2008.5 A4 model year onwards fill with water/slush and freeze solid in the winter rendering them useless and creating significant driving hazard. Audi has no replacement and is non-responsive. Further, there are no third-party replacement winter-style blades because it is a proprietary blade-arm connector.

• Severe steering shake. • Suspension noise caused by cracked front upper control arm bushings. • Early replacement of expensive headlight bulbs. *A6 Sedan:* **2003**—Numerous complaints of delayed braking; no brakes in rainy weather; parking brake failure; and premature replacement of the front brake rotors. • Sudden headlight failure. • Blue-white headlights blind oncoming drivers. **2005**—Acceleration is still plagued by engine hesitation. • Right outside mirror tilts down in Reverse gear for parking but does not go back to normal until the vehicle is up to speed in Second gear. Result: No mirror while entering traffic. *TT Coupe:* **2001**—Defective fuel gauge gives false reading (A6 models recalled for the same defect). • All windshields have some kind of visual distortion (anything viewed, especially straight lines, is distorted). • Central computer failure causes door locks to jam, trapping occupants. **2002**—Serious drivetrain failures. • Owners report a multitude of electrical shorts affect the radio, horn, lights, dash gauges, and controls. • Ignition coil failures. • xenon headlights don't adequately light the roadway. **2003**—Dash panel continues to operate erratically, and gauges show false readings. **2004**—DSG transmission disengages from the engine:

> Ultimately I had to have the mechatronic unit in the transmission replaced to fix the problem, at a cost of about $3,200.

• Car jerked violently and would not change gears. • Fuel gauge failures. • Instrument cluster inoperative. • Original tires may have weak side walls. **2005**—Airbag light stays on constantly. **2006**—Brake failure when making a right turn. **2008**—One vehicle burned up from a fire that ignited from the front seat wiring. • Oil pan can be easily damaged: road debris can drive the screws that secure the oil pan into the oil pan itself. • Side-view mirrors do not go out far enough to safely see the road. • DSG transmission continues to jerk and buck when shifting:

> It is difficult to smoothly start the car moving from a stop. The transmission seems to slip while the engine speed increases, and then suddenly grab.

2009—DSG manumatic transmission still locks up the gearbox. • Sudden loss of power, brakes, and steering ability.

Secret Warranties/Internal Bulletins/Service Tips

All models: 1996–2010—Silencing squealing brakes. **2000–08**—Hesitation on acceleration. **2000–10**—Low power, won't move after stopping. • Inoperative keyless entry. • Excessive oil consumption. **2005–10**—Noxious AC odours.

2006–10—Flickering interior lighting. **2007–10**—Multiple electrical malfunctions. **2009–11**—Steering squeak when turning. *A3:* **2005–10**—Headlights go on and off. **2005–11**—Sunroof noises. • Inoperative windshield wipers. **2006–07**—Inoperative windows, locks, and sunroof. **2006–09**—No acceleration when shifted into gear. • Inoperative low beams. **2006–10**—Cluster lights dim, flicker. **2006–07**—Inoperative daytime running lights and One Touch window feature. • Tips on eliminating brake squeal. • Dash ticking noises. **2006–08**—Rear suspension rumble, rattle. **2006–09**—Xenon headlights flicker and fail. **2006–10**—Door electrical malfunctions. **2006–11**—Front suspension cracking, rubbing noise. **2006–11**—Front, rear brake squealing. **2007–09**—AC doesn't cool. **2009**—Stiff steering. **2009–10**—Airbag light stays on. • Hard start; timing chain noise. • Automatic transmission control module update. • Inoperative headlight washer system. *A4, A6, S6:* **2002–05**—Vehicles equipped with the Multitronic automatic transmission buck when accelerating. **2002–08**—Noisy power steering. • Inoperative daytime running lights. **2004–07**—AC compressor rattling. **2005**—Cold engine stumble; warm engine stall. **2005–06**—Oil leak from oil filter housing. **2005–08**—Eliminating brake moan on low-speed turns. • Front window reverses direction when closing. • Inoperative sunroof switch. • Inoperative One Touch window feature. **2005–09**—Long warm-engine crank time. **2005–10**—Headlights go on and off. **2006–08**—Brake squealing. **2007–08**—Eliminating paint spots or stains on upper surfaces. **2009**—Hard start; timing chain noise. **2009–10**—Airbag light stays on. *A4:* **2002–04**—Oil leak at camshaft adjuster. **2002–04**—Hard jerking in Reverse at idle. **2002–06**—Faulty glove compartment door. • Noisy power steering. **2003–04**—Service campaign to replace the engine wire harness. **2005–06**—Remote won't lock/unlock doors. **2005–07**—Xenon headlights flicker and fail. **2005–08**—Remedy for a vehicle that pulls to one side. • Dash clicking noises. • Headlights vibrate. **2006–07**—Inoperative low beams. **2006–08**—Front, rear brake squealing. • Brakes moan when accelerating or turning. **2007**—Multiple electrical failures. **2009–11**—Sunroof noises, concerns. *A6:* **1998–2004**—Noisy power steering. **2001**—Inoperative self-levelling system. **2005**—AC whining, howling. • Fuel gauge reads empty with a full tank. **2005–06**—Rough-running cold engine. • Inoperative sunroof. **2005–07**—Cooling fan runs continuously. **2005–09**—Long warm-engine crank time. **2005–11**—Sunroof noises. • Brakes moan when accelerating or turning. **2006–11**—Front, rear brake squealing. **2007**—AC doesn't cool. • Loose, broken control knobs. **2008–09**—Erratic operating radio and door locks. *TT Coupe:* **2000–10**—Excessive oil consumption. **2002–11**—Front, rear brake squealing. **2004**—Front stabilizer bar upgrade to reduce noise. **2004–05**—Xenon headlight failure. **2004–06**—Momentary delay when accelerating. • Vehicle won't go into gear. **2005–11**—Sunroof noises, concerns. **2006–09**—No acceleration when shifted into gear. **2006–10**—Cluster lights dim, flicker. **2007**—Inoperative windows, locks, and sunroof. **2007–08**—Inoperative One Touch window feature. **2007–11**—Interior buzzing vibrating noises. **2008–09**—Erratic operating radio and door locks. • Inoperative low beams. • Xenon headlights flicker and go out.

2007—Loose, noisy air intake duct. • Rear suspension rumble, rattle. 2007–10—Headlights go on and off. • Inoperative headlight washer system. 2008–11—Front suspension cracking, rubbing noise. 2009—Hard start; timing chain noise. • Stiff steering.

A3, A4, A6, A8, S4, S6, TT COUPE PROFILE

	2001	2002	2003	2004	2005	2006	2007	2008	2009
Cost Price ($)									
A3	—	—	—	—	—	32,950	33,800	31,800	31,800
A4	33,785	37,225	37,310	34,435	34,985	35,270	35,310	41,200	41,200
A6	49,835	54,235	51,710	51,950	59,500	62,500	62,700	52,900	52,900
A8	86,500	86,500	86,500	97,750	93,90	96,250	97,190	95,000	95,000
S4	57,200	57,200	—	67,950	68,250	68,950	70,390	70,400	75,500
S6	—	88,500	88,500	109,000	—	—	101,900	101,900	99,500
TT	50,400	50,400	48,650	49,975	55,475	55,980	—	46,900	46,900
Used Values ($)									
A3 ▲	—	—	—	—	—	11,500	15,000	19,500	22,000
A3 ▼	—	—	—	—	—	10,000	13,500	18,000	20,000
A4 ▲	4,500	5,000	5,500	6,500	7,500	9,500	16,500	21,000	26,500
A4 ▼	4,000	4,500	5,000	6,000	7,000	8,000	15,000	19,500	24,500
A6 ▲	5,500	6,500	7,000	8,000	14,500	17,000	25,000	32,000	37,000
A6 ▼	4,000	6,000	6,500	7,000	13,000	15,500	23,000	30,000	35,500
A8 ▲	10,000	12,000	13,000	15,000	18,000	22,000	31,000	43,000	58,000
A8 ▼	9,000	10,500	12,000	13,500	16,000	20,000	29,000	41,000	56,000
S4 ▲	6,000	8,000	—	14,000	16,000	19,000	28,000	37,000	53,000
S4 ▼	5,000	7,000	—	12,500	14,500	17,500	26,500	35,000	51,000
S6 ▲	—	14,000	17,000	20,000	—	—	32,000	49,000	62,000
S6 ▼	—	12,500	15,500	18,500	—	—	30,000	47,000	60,000
TT ▲	8,000	9,000	10,500	12,500	15,500	16,500	—	29,000	33,000
TT ▼	6,500	8,000	9,500	11,500	14,000	15,000	—	27,500	31,000
Reliability	2	2	2	2	2	2	3	3	3
A4	2	2	2	2	2	3	4	4	4
A6	2	2	2	2	2	3	4	4	4
A8	2	2	2	2	2	3	4	4	4
Crash Safety (F)									
A4/S4	—	4	4	4	4	4	4	4	5
A6	—	—	—	—	5	—	—	—	—
A8	5	5	5	—	—	—	—	—	—
Side (TT)	—	5	5	5	5	5	—	—	—
A4/S4	—	5	5	5	5	5	4	5	5
IIHS Side (A3)	—	—	—	—	—	5	5	5	5
A4	—	—	—	—	5	5	5	5	5
A6	—	—	—	—	5	5	5	5	5

Offset (A6)	3	3	3	3	5	5	5	5	5
A3	—	—	—	—	—	5	5	5	5
A4/S4	—	5	5	5	5	5	5	5	5
Head Restraints									
A3	—	—	—	—	—	3	3	5	5
A4/S4 (F)	5	5	5	**1**	**2**	3	5	5	5
A6	5	5	5	5	3	3	5	5	5
A8	3	2	2	5	—	—	—	—	—
TT Coupe	—	3	3	3	—	—	—	—	—
TT Roadster	5	5	5	5	—	—	—	—	—
Roof Strength (A3)	—	—	—	—	—	5	5	5	5
A4	—	—	—	—	—	—	—	—	5
A6	—	—	—	—	5	5	5	5	5
Rollover Resistance									
A4/S4	—	4	4	4	4	4	4	4	5
TT	—	—	5	5	5	5	—	—	—

Note: A convertible TT Coupe AWD will cost between $3,000 and $6,000 more than the hardtop front-drive Coupe listed above. The A3 has not yet been crash tested by NHTSA.

BMW

3 SERIES, 5 SERIES, M SERIES, Z SERIES ★★★★/★★★

RATING: *3 Series, 5 Series, M Series, Z4:* Above Average (1999–2009). *Z3:* Average (1999–2002). These cars are the best performing and most reliable vehicles Europe has to offer, but that's faint praise when one considers the overall poor quality, dangerous safety-related malfunctions, needlessly complex engineering, and exorbitant retail prices of most European models. There's no reason why Bimmers should cost so much, particularly in view of their high rate of depreciation with the higher-end models. Owner feedback and internal service bulletins show these cars come with a performance and quality reputation that far exceeds what they actually deliver. Safety defects that are carried over year after year confirm BMW's arrogant "What, me worry?" attitude. Some notable examples: sudden unintended acceleration, airbag malfunctions, hesitation upon acceleration, surging gear changes, jammed door latches that "kidnap" occupants, Turanza tires that self-destruct, and costly, poor-quality halogen headlights. Buyers of older Bimmers should be on the lookout for hidden rust damage. Door and fender seams, rocker panels, and rear-wheel openings are likely to be rust-cankered with a dash of paint used to hide the damage. **Ideal model year:** If you want the best price with good overall reliability and performance, the 2008 328i will give you all that for about $24,000, which isn't bad for a high-end car that sold new for $41,000. The 2007 5 Series is also a good bet. It builds upon the redesigned and repowered 2006 model and prices are mouth-watering. For example: a 2007 525i that sold for $58,600 can be had today for about $24,000. Or, a top-of-the-line new 2007 550i that went for $78,600 now costs only (sigh) $31,000. Granted, the 2009 5 Series underwent another redesign with the 2009 models, and *Lemon-Aid* is watching to see what impact those changes will have. What would be the best Z-car? Try a 2007 Z4. Its original $53,900 price has been cut to about $25,500, plus the car had an extra year to smooth out its 2006 redesign. The 2009 revamped model could be a good choice in the future, if its design change-glitches have been "debugged." **"Real" city/highway fuel economy:** *2.2 manual:* 11.3/7.2 L/100 km. *2.2 automatic:* 11.6/7.4 L/100 km. *2.5 manual:* 11.7/7.4 L/100 km. *2.5 automatic:* 12.3/8.0 L/100 km. *3.0 manual:* 11.7/7.2 L/100 km. *3.0 automatic:* 12.2/8.0 L/100 km. *5 Series 2.5 manual:* 11.7/7.4 L/100 km. *5 Series 2.5 automatic:* 12.5/7.6 L/100 km. *3.0 manual:* 11.7/7.2 L/100 km. *3.0 automatic:* 12.9/7.8 L/100 km. *4.4 manual:* 14.4/8.6 L/100 km. *4.4 automatic:* 13.0/8.2 L/100 km. BMW owners report fuel savings estimates are relatively accurate for vehicles equipped with manual transmissions. Other models burn about 10 percent more fuel than estimated. **Maintenance/Repair costs:** Higher than average, but many repairs can be done by independent garages who specialize in BMWs. Unfortunately, these experts are usually concentrated around large urban areas. **Parts:** Higher-than-average costs, and parts are often back ordered. **Extended warranty:** A good idea. **Best alternatives:** There are a number of credible alternatives to the Z Series, such as the AWD 3 Series and the Mazda6. Also look at the Acura TL or RL, and the Hyundai Genesis. **Helpful websites:** *www.roadfly.com/bmw/forums* and *www.bimmerfest.com.*

 ## Strengths and Weaknesses

3 Series

The 3 Series vehicles exhibit great 6-cylinder performance with the manual gearbox, and ride and handling are commendable. The 318's small engine is seriously compromised, however, by an automatic transmission.

Although the 1997 models come with traction control, it is not very effective in giving these vehicles acceptable wet pavement traction. A problem since the early '90s, the rear end tends to slip sideways when the roadway is wet (much like Ford's rear-drive Mustang). The 325e is more pleasant to drive and delivers lots of low-end torque. Through 1998, rear passenger and cargo room is limited. After a redesign of the '99 models, passenger and cargo space was increased. Smart shoppers who opt for the improved 2000 models will keep in mind that rear interior room is still a joke—unless you happen to be sitting there. Various upgrades make the 2001 and later models better choices, although safety- and performance-related failures are legion.

VEHICLE HISTORY: 2001—An engine upgrade, larger brakes and wheels, and optional 44 capability. High-performance M3 Coupe returns with a 330 hp engine. **2002**—Entire lineup gets recalibrated steering, reshaped headrests, and an in-dash CD player. **2003**—Coupes and convertibles are restyled, along with a transmission upgrade. **2004**—Expanded availability of the sequential manual transmission. **2005**—Coupes get a sunroof (except the M3) and run-flat tires along with a tire-pressure monitor (all three items are of doubtful value). **2006**—New styling (vehicles are longer and wider than before) and more power; the much-hated, complicated iDrive is offered as an option. Debut of a premium sedan and wagon. 325i and 325xi models are powered by 215 hp engines, up from 184 hp produced by the previous model's 2.5L 6-cylinder. Wagons get a 30 hp boost. All cars come with a 6-speed manual transmission. Coupes and convertibles are carried over unchanged. **2007**—Coupes are revamped with more power (45 more horses with the turbocharged 6-cylinder), a standard 6-speed manual tranny, a larger platform, steering-linked xenon headlights that bring joy to thieves and parts suppliers, and 90 kg (200 lb.) of extra weight. Rear-drive coupes get a firmer suspension and more-comfortable seats. The new convertible has a retractable hardtop that uses a complex electronic mechanical system to open and close the roof. **2008**—Carried over with few changes except for the addition of the high-performance M3.

Handling with all model years is still tricky on wet roads, despite the ASC+T traction control; rear-seat access is problematic; rear passenger space continues disappoint; and styling is the essence of bland. The brakes, tires, engine, transmission, suspension, electrical system, and some body trim and accessories are the most failure-prone components. Paint peeling and delamination has afflicted BMW for the past several decades up through 2009. Owners who complain "energetically" are usually offered compensation:

> Paint defects on new 2009 BMW, purchased on March 2010. The paint is peeling in 4 places. Car manufacturer claims peeling is from an "external service". This is not plausible, as peeling is in 4 spots, two different locations. BMW's own warranty vendor for body work indicated that it was "apparently a paint defect". The BMW regional inspector said no, it was an external problem, denying what is obviously a manufacturing (painting) defect. BMW offered a "good faith" adjustment of 50% of repair cost, but if it is a defect, it should be covered in full as part of the warranty. Clearly, a new car's paint on a BMW should not be peeling in a few months in 4 places and BMW should acknowledge and cover this paint defect.

Incidentally, BMW paint peeling and subsequent repairs was the principal reason for the well-known U.S. class-action judgment, *BMW vs. Gore*, rendered on May 20, 1996 by the U. S. Supreme Court (*http://en.wikipedia.org/wiki/BMW_of_North_America,_Inc._v._Gore*). BMW was ordered to pay $2 million, but the award was reduced to $50,000 in lieu of having the case retried.

Engine overheating is also a serious and common failure (see *www.straight-six.com*, *www.mwerks.com*, *www.bmwnation.com*, *www.roadfly.com*, *yoy.com/yoy/auto/m3_failure_index.html* (2002 BMW M3 Engine Failures Page), *www.bmwboard.com*, and *www.bmwlemon.com*).

5 Series

Essentially a larger, more-powerful 3 Series, the 5 Series has made its reputation by delivering more performance in a larger, more-versatile interior. The 6-cylinder and V8 engines are somewhat fuel-thirsty and occasionally a bit noisy, but they are quite remarkable, durable performers. There is no problem with rear seatroom or cargo room with the 5 Series Bimmer. Handling and ride are superb, although these weighty upscale models do strain when going over hilly terrain if they have the automatic gearbox.

5 Series owners report starter failures, faulty turn signal indicators, numerous electrical and fuel glitches, and excessive steering-wheel or brake vibrations.

Overall Bimmer reliability has been very poor over the past decade. Electronic failures are the chief culprit, but brake, powertrain, and electrical problems lead the list of other persistent failings. Also, whenever a problem arises, repair costs are particularly high because of the small number of dealers, the relative scarcity of parts, and the difficulty of getting a correct, unbiased diagnosis as to the cause of a breakdown.

In fact, it appears that manufacturers of European makes all too often blame drivers (abusive driving and poor maintenance) rather than their own poor design and inadequate quality control.

Owners say that premature brake wear causes excessive vibration, noise, and severe pulling to one side when the brakes are applied. The 4.0L engines are known to sometimes click, rattle, and knock due to faulty crankshaft main bearing shells or poor oil viscosity. The 3.0L 6-cylinder engines are also noted for producing an irregular clicking noise. There are some reports of water leaks through the doors and from the AC.

Year 2000–07 models are plagued by airbag malfunctions; front-door water leaks; automatic transmission failures; steering degradation when braking at slow speeds; cooling fan malfunctions, leading to engine overheating and fires; and a manual transmission that's hard to shift into Second gear, pops out of gear, and grinds when shifting.

The 5 Series 2004 and later models seem to have hit a quality plateau, and the addition of features from the 7 Series' iDrive is an accident waiting to happen. iDrive uses a console "joystick" knob to control entertainment, navigation, communication, and climate functions, which annoys and distracts drivers who aren't so techno-savvy.

VEHICLE HISTORY: 2001—525i Sedan and Wagon debut. **2002**—540i's V8 gets an extra 8 hp. **2003**—A sunroof for all 6-cylinders, and a new Sport Package with the manual 540i Sedan. **2004**—Redesigned with new styling, new features, and a more-powerful V8. The 545i 6-speed is given a sport suspension teamed with run-flat tires, plus Active Steering and Active Roll Stabilization to counteract body lean. All models still come with BMW's controversial iDrive console joystick. Critics say that the iDrive takes a University of Waterloo degree in engineering to operate, plus it's a safety hazard. The 545i and 545i 6-speed models use a 4.4L V8 with 325 hp, up from 290 hp in last year's 540i. The wagon is gone. **2005**—Coupes get a sunroof, and coupes and convertibles join the M3 in getting a standard tire-pressure monitor. **2006**—Return of wagons, a redesigned M5, and an overall power increase. **2007**—The M3 is dropped for one year and the sedans and wagons get a power increase and new "325" monikers. **2008**—New 6-cylinder engines and a slightly restyled exterior.

M Series

Launched in 1996 as a four-door model, the M3 is a high-performance vehicle originally equipped with a potent 240 hp 3.0L engine (later bumped up to 3.2L), a manual shifter, a firm suspension, and 17-inch tires.

VEHICLE HISTORY: 2001—Arrival of a new 315 hp inline-six, Dynamic Stability Control, and a tighter suspension (watch those kidneys), while the M3 returns in convertible and coupe formats, equipped with a high-performance 333 hp engine. **2002**—M3 gets a new 6-speed sequential manual transmission. All models are given a modified aluminum suspension, wider 18-inch tires and wheels, a new limited-slip differential, and a refreshed interior. **2007–08**—The new M3 is now available as a coupe, sedan, and convertible and is powered by a 414 hp 4.0L V8.

Owning any M3-powered BMW is a breathtaking driving experience, but at too high a cost. Servicing must be done by the book, and it's expensive, as is maintenance on all BMWs (use dealers only as a last resort). Insurance premiums are way beyond what would normally be reasonable. Another serious problem is that M-car and Z-car reliability isn't very good; owners say most of the failures that have become legendary during the past decade are related to the fuel system (frequent stalling when decelerating), electrical and climate control systems, accessories (sound system, AC, etc.), premature brake and tire wear, and poor-quality fit and finish characterized by paint delamination and poor paint application. And don't forget that the 2001s and 2002s have a serious wallet-busting, life-endangering flaw: Their engine self-destructs and has been dubbed by owners "The Engine of Damocles."

Z Series

BMW's first sports car, the two-seater Z3 debuted in early 1996 and was based on the 3 Series platform. Its 138 hp 1.9L 4-banger is outclassed by the competition (such as the Porsche non-S Boxster, the Mercedes-Benz 3.2L V6 SLK, and the Honda S2000), and you have to get the revs up past 3000 rpm to get adequate passing torque. The 2001 model, with its 2.5L 184 hp 6-cylinder engine, is an all-around better performer and offers more features at a fairly depreciated price.

Dynamic Stability Control, large 17-inch wheels, and Dunlop SP Sport performance tires don't enhance handling as much as BMW pretends they do: Get used to lots of steering corrections.

The Z4 is a more feature-laden convertible, equipped with an inline 6-cylinder engine and a standard manual softtop. It still carries a base 184 hp 2.5L engine coupled with a 5-speed manual transmission; the higher-end Z4 3.0i has a 225 hp 3.0L mated to a 6-speed manual gearbox. ABS, an anti-skid system, and run-flat tires (a dubious advantage, considering cost, failures, scarcity) are standard features.

In 2000, BMW launched its $190,000 super-luxury Z8: a limited-production, fully equipped model with a power softtop, a removable hardtop, a body made largely of aluminum, and a 4.9L V8 hooked to a mandatory 6-speed manual transmission. The car lasted four model years; a 2000 Z8 is now worth about $40,000 in Canada, if you can find one.

VEHICLE HISTORY: 2001—Debut of the Z8. Roadsters and coupes adopt a 3.0L powerplant (instead of the 2.8L), and bigger brakes and wheels are added. Also, the 2.5L engine is tweaked to unleash 14 additional horses. **2003**—Launch of the Z4, a longer, wider variant of the Z3. The Z8's last model year. **2005**—The Sequential Manual Gearbox is dropped from the 2.5i. **2006**—More power, restyled, and the addition of a new hatchback coupe. The new 215 hp 3.0i boosts horses by 31 on the base convertible. Debut of the 255 hp 3.0si convertible and coupe. **2009**—After two years of no changes, the 2009 returns with a new design and powertrains. The two-seater now comes as a convertible with a power-retractable roof. The fixed-roof coupe is no more. The 3.0L 6-cylinder 30i has 255 horses and a manual 6-speed, though, an optional automatic is available. A turbocharged 35i augments power up to the 300 horsepower range, and offers an optional 7-speed automatic transmission.

Safety Summary

All models/years: Sudden acceleration. • Airbag malfunctions include the bag deploying inadvertently or failing to go off in an accident. • Seat belt doesn't retract properly. • Premature failure of the magnesium alloy control arms and steering damper. • Severe suspension hop when passing over small bumps. • Transmission pops out of gear. • Multiple electrical failures. • Inoperative door latches that will make you exit through the window (if you're lucky). **All models: 2001–02**—Cooling fan failure causes engine to overheat or a fire to ignite (see *www.roadfly.com/bmw*). *318:* **2001**—Defective gas pedal assembly causes jerky acceleration. *320:* **2002**—Distorted windshield. *323:* **2002**—Poor steering when braking at slow speeds. • In rainy weather, brakes stiffen as they are applied, leading to extended stopping distances. • Faulty sunroof. *325i:* Transmission failure within five days of purchase. • Electrical system fire. • Steering column is kinked to the left. • In one case, right-door airbag deployed even though vehicle was hit on the left. • Sunroof glass suddenly explodes (several incidents reported). • Doors lock without prior warning. **2005**—On one vehicle, three Continental ContiSport tires blew out within a year. **2005–06**—When parking in an indoor garage, one vehicle suddenly accelerated as the brakes failed. **2006**—When accelerating, car delays, then surges. • Fire ignited under the hood while one vehicle was underway. • More Turanza tire failures. • Jammed door latch forces you to open the lock with the key from the outside:

> I was at the store when the car locks jammed. The only way to get into the car was by manually using the key. The key fob would not unlock the door. The real issue was that the only door that could be opened was the drivers side all the others were jammed shut.... This is a very common problem with this make. It['s] attributed to a faulty design. See thread...*www.e90post.com/forums/showthread.php?p=3080752*.... [T]he consequences are that if there is an accident, there is no way to get to passengers, also, fire situations would be deadly, submerging in water could also prove to be... disastrous. The only repair is replacement with the same actuator, but the problem is only a temporary fix. Over time it will reoccur. It is a design flaw. Employee: Kennedy Space Center Space Shuttle Program (United Space Alliance) safety, quality, and mission assurance engineer.

328i: **2007**—Sudden acceleration as the car was turning into a garage. • When accelerating to merge with freeway traffic, vehicle hesitates and then surges. • Steering wheel locked when vehicle was underway. • Cracked tie rod. • Chronic electrical short circuits make most gauges and controls go haywire. • Key sticks in the ignition. • A blown fuse could deactivate the electronic door latches and force occupants to exit through a broken window; automatic locks operate erratically. • Convertible roof tries to put itself in the trunk when the trunk is closed. • Windshield cracks easily. • Excessive road noise and premature wear of the Bridgestone Turanza tires. Tires will be replaced free of charge on a case-by-case basis.

> I found out that these tires are not wearing properly. In my searches on the Internet, I have found that this problem has been ongoing for at least 2 years. BMW refuses to pay for replacing all the tires if you are over 10K miles [32,190 km]. My tires are wearing horribly and causing a safety risk. BMW knew of this problem in January 2007 when they issued a service info bulletin to all the dealers.

2008—Chronic stalling. One fix for the stalling is to replace the fuel pump and retune the engine. However, one 3 Series owner has found that this correction creates a "turbo lag" that wasn't there before. BMW has advertised widely that its turbo-equipped cars have no turbo lag. • Electric door locks operate erratically. • Driver was locked in his car; horn could not be activated to alert passersby. • Battery loses its charge if car isn't driven frequently on trips of more than five kilometers. Fog lights may ignite, causing a front-end fire. • Beware of cracked wheels and prematurely worn Continental run-flat tires:

Upon mounting new tires on my 2008 BMW 328i convertible, the technicians informed me that both of my rear wheels were cracked, and they could not mount the new tires on the vehicle. Upon inspection at BMW of San Francisco, my service advisor told me that it was in their opinion that an "impact" from a pothole or other irregular road surface caused the cracks in both rear wheels and that warranty coverage would be denied. Upon my own investigation, I found several other BMW customers having a similar concern on *www.bimmerfest.com*, as well as an investigation performed by the BBC in October of 2009.

•

Continental run flat tires new with new 328i BMW sedan purchased in 2008 had tread worn down after 8100 miles, as noticed when vehicle was brought in for servicing. Tires were replaced by dealer. Research on the web showed a large number of individuals reporting similar problem: *www.bmwrunflattire.com*.

2009—More complaints of chronic stalling, run-flat tire defects, and sudden, unintended acceleration. • Owners claim Bridgestone Turanza tires are cupping so badly that the car is dangerous to drive. One owner says there is ample legal precedent to force BMW and Bridgestone to take back these defective tires:

The BMW Bridgestone run flat tire RFT class action lawsuit reportedly concerns BMW 2006 and 2007 3 series vehicles originally equipped with Bridgestone Turanza EL42 RFT 205/55R16 or 225/45R17 run-flat tires. The lawsuit (*Chandran v. BMW of North America, LLC*, et al., Case No. 2:08-CV-02619-KSH-PS) reportedly alleges that defendants should have known that the tires were defective and prone to excessive noise and/or irregular wear, resulting in the tires needing frequent replacement and causing the vehicles to ride roughly.

330i, 330Ci: **2002**—Side airbag deploys when vehicle hits a pothole. • Vehicle overheats in low gear; tires lose air. • Vehicle slips out of Second gear when accelerating. **2003**—Chronic stalling, rough idle. • Transmission slipping. **2004**—Airbags fail to deploy. • Constant stalling • Engine bearing failures:

The issue is the dual VANOS unit they put into the M54 engine using [D]elrin bushings and they are failing. There is a company called Dr. Vanos that fixes this issue by rebuilding the OEM VANOS with upgraded bushings. This unit cost $500.

• Automatic transmission failure. • After a cold start, transmission delays going into gear for up to 30 seconds. • Distorted windshields. • Door locks operate erratically. **2005**—More delayed gear shifts. **2006**—Water enters through the door sills and causes the doors to freeze shut. • Turanza tire blowouts. *525i:* **2006–07**—Loss of engine power. • Valve lash adjuster noise. • Oil leak from the right-hand side of the engine crankcase. • Intermittent engine vibration, drone at idle. • Automatic transmission won't go into Drive or Reverse. • AC poor performance at start up or when idling. • AC stops cooling after a long drive. •

Sunroof wind noises and water leaks. • Steering column noises. • Halogen low-beam headlight failure. • Electrical issues due to water intrusion. • Rear door locking issues and diagnostics. • Dunlop run-flat tires that are noisy, have worn out prematurely, or create excessive on-road vibration will be replaced, free of charge, if they have no more than 20,000 miles, says TSB #SI B36 02 05, published September 2008. This service bulletin opens the door for compensation from small claims court to owners who have "problem" run-flat tires and feel the extended warranty is too limited. **2007**—Front seat noise. *528i:* **2008**—Loss of engine power. **2008–09**—Brake squeak and squeal. **2009**— Loss of engine power. *M3:* **2001**—Rear-end clunking, leading to failure of the driveshaft attachment at the differential (confirmed by other complaints on *www.roadfly.com/bmw*). *Z3:* **2001**—Engine stalls when decelerating. • Exterior and interior lights dim and engine loses power when AC is engaged. • Driver's seat rocks to and fro.

Secret Warranties/Internal Bulletins/Service Tips

All models: Many of the service bulletins listed in this BMW section apply to other cars in the BMW lineup. If you want to check if there is an overlap that includes your car, ask a BMW dealer. If that doesn't work, go to *www.safercar.gov* and look up the service bulletins applicable to your car. As a last resort, pay $26.95 (U.S.) to Alldata (*www.alldatadiy.com/buy/index.html*) to get a digital copy of every bulletin applicable to your vehicle. *3 Series:* **2002**—Incorrect fuel gauge readings. • Rattling, tapping engine noise. • Troubleshooting navigation system malfunctions. • No 1–2 upshifts. **2003**—Harsh 3–2 and 2–1 downshifts. **2004**—Delayed Park–Drive shift. • Numerous malfunctions of telematics components. **2005–06**—Reduced engine power. **2008**—Instrument cluster displays go blank. • Intermittent engine valve lash adjuster noise. **2008–09**—Water leaks into footwell area. **2009**—Airbag warning light stays on. • Front seatbelt doesn't retract smoothly. • Heated steering wheel malfunction. • No start, or reduced engine power. • Poor AC performance. • Rattling noise from the radio area. • No Reverse or Forward gear. • An oil leak at the right-hand side of the V6 engine crankcase may require that the crankcase be replaced. • Excessive engine vibration. • Silencing brake squeak and squeal. • No start, or false fuel reading. • Steering column noises. • Front suspension creaking and groaning. *5 Series:* **All years:** Water inside of headlight. • Erratic performance of the navigation system. *525i:* **2006–07**—Troubleshooting AC compressor noise. *528i:* **2007–09**—Automatic transmission jolt or delay when accelerating from a stop. • You won't believe this, but BMW admits it made a batch of crappy halogen headlight bulbs that burn out prematurely (see TSB on following page). **2009**—Reduced engine power. • Automatic transmission jumps out of Drive or Reverse into Neutral (requires a software adjustment). • Troubleshooting front seat noise. • Front brake squeak or squeal upon light brake application. • An oil leak at the right-hand side of the V6 engine crankcase may require that the crankcase be replaced. • Intermittent engine valve lash adjuster noise. • Exhaust system vibration or drone at idle. • Poor AC performance. • Steering column noises. • Halogen headlight bulb failure. *530i:* **2005–07**—Front brake squeak or squeal upon light brake application. • Sunroof wind noise and water leaks.

HALOGEN LOW-BEAM HEADLAMP BULB FAILURE

BULLETIN NO.: SI B 63 08 09

DATE: SEPTEMBER 2009

REPLACE BOTH HALOGEN LOW-BEAM HEADLAMP BULBS

E60 (5 Series) produced from February 28, 2007 to September 28, 2009.

SITUATION: Low-beam headlamp bulb failure.

CAUSE: The halogen headlamp bulb (standard life) has reached the end of its design life. Later produced vehicles have been equipped with long life bulbs.

CORRECTION: In the event that one halogen low-beam headlamp bulb is found to be defective, replace the bulb on both the left and right sides of the vehicle with a long life bulb.

3 SERIES, M SERIES, Z SERIES PROFILE

	2001	2002	2003	2004	2005	2006	2007	2008	2009
Cost Price ($)									
320i 4d	34,500	34,900	34,950	34,950	—	—	—	—	—
323i 4d	—	—	—	—	—	35,200	35,600	35,900	34,900
325i, 328i	44,900	37,950	41,200	39,300	39,450	39,900	41,000	41,000	39,900
Convertible	—	52,500	52,800	53,400	54,400	55,800	56,300	56,600	56,600
330Ci Convertible	—	62,800	62,900	63,500	63,950	64,400	—	—	—
335Ci Convertible	—	—	—	—	—	—	66,300	66,600	65,600
M/M3 2d	62,900	69,800	73,500	73,800	73,950	68,900	68,900	68,900	69,900
M Performance	—	—	—	—	54,300	54,200	—	—	—
M5 4d	102,650	104,250	105,500	105,500	—	115,500	113,300	113,300	106,900
M6 2d Coupe	—	—	—	—	—	130,500	130,500	128,300	121,300
M6 2d Convertible	—	—	—	—	—	—	140,500	138,300	131,300
Z3 1.9L/2.3L	45,901	46,900	—	—	—	—	—	—	—
Z3 2.8L	55,900	56,200	—	—	—	—	—	—	—
Z4 2.5L	—	—	51,500	51,800	51,900	—	—	—	—
Z4 3.0L	—	—	59,500	59,900	59,900	53,900	53,900	55,400	53,900
Z8	190,000	190,000	195,000	195,000	—	—	—	—	—
Used Values ($)									
320i 4d ▲	6,500	8,000	9,000	10,500	—	—	—	—	—
320i 4d ▼	5,500	7,000	8,000	9,000	—	—	—	—	—
323i 4d ▲	—	—	—	—	—	12,000	17,500	21,000	25,000
323i 4d ▼	—	—	—	—	—	10,500	16,000	19,500	23,000
325i, 328i ▲	8,000	9,000	10,500	11,500	12,500	15,000	18,500	23,000	28,000
325i, 328i ▼	7,000	8,500	9,500	10,500	11,500	13,500	17,000	21,000	26,000
Convertible ▲	—	12,500	13,500	15,000	18,000	21,000	25,000	34,000	40,000
Convertible ▼	—	12,000	13,000	13,500	16,500	19,500	23,500	32,000	38,000
330Ci Convertible ▲	—	13,500	15,000	17,000	19,000	22,000	—	—	—
330Ci Convertible ▼	—	13,000	13,500	15,500	17,500	20,500	—	—	—
335Ci Convertible ▲	—	—	—	—	—	—	29,000	38,000	46,000
335Ci Convertible ▼	—	—	—	—	—	—	27,500	36,000	44,000
M/M3 2d ▲	9,000	11,500	13,500	16,000	19,000	23,000	28,000	40,000	49,000
M/M3 2d ▼	8,000	10,500	12,000	14,500	18,000	21,000	26,500	37,000	45,000

All ratings on a numbered scale where 5 is good and 1 is bad. See page 132 for a more detailed description.

M Performance ▲	—	—	—	—	15,500	17,500	—	—	—
M Performance ▼	—	—	—	—	14,000	16,000	—	—	—
M5 4d ▲	15,000	17,000	19,000	22,000	—	27,000	38,000	57,000	70,000
M5 4d ▼	13,500	15,500	17,500	20,000	—	25,000	35,000	54,000	65,000
Z3 1.9L/2.3L ▲	14,000	16,500	—	—	—	—	—	—	—
Z3 1.9L/2.3L ▼	12,500	15,000	—	—	—	—	—	—	—
Z3 2.8L ▲	17,000	18,500	—	—	—	—	—	—	—
Z3 2.8L ▼	15,500	17,000	—	—	—	—	—	—	—
Z4 2.5L ▲	—	—	14,000	16,000	—	—	—	—	—
Z4 2.5L ▼	—	—	12,500	15,000	—	—	—	—	—
Z4 3.0L ▲	—	—	16,000	17,500	19,000	22,500	26,000	34,000	37,000
Z4 3.0L ▼	—	—	15,000	16,500	17,000	21,000	24,000	31,000	35,000
Z8 ▲	40,000	56,000	64,000	85,000	—	—	—	—	—
Z8 ▼	35,000	50,000	60,000	75,000	—	—	—	—	—
Reliability	3	4	4	4	4	4	4	4	4
Crash Safety (F)	—	4	4	4	4	4	4	4	4
Side	3	3	3	3	3	5	5	5	5
IIHS Side	—	—	—	—	—	5	5	5	5
Offset	5	5	5	5	5	5	5	5	5
Head Restraints	3	1	1	1	1	3	3	3	5
M3	2	2	2	2	—	—	—	—	—
Convertible	—	—	—	—	—	—	1	1	—
Z3	3	3	—	—	—	—	—	—	—
Z4 —	—	5	5	—	—	—	—	—	—
Rollover Resistance	—	4	4	4	4	4	4	4	4

Note: The huge price difference between entry-level models and their top-of-the-line variations narrows to almost nothing after seven years.

5 SERIES PROFILE

	2001	2002	2003	2004	2005	2006	2007	2008	2009
Cost Price ($)									
525i, 528i, 530i	54,700	55,200	55,500	66,500	66,500	58,600	58,600	59,900	56,200
Used Values ($)									
525i, 528i, 530i ▲	7,500	8,500	11,000	13,000	15,000	17,500	24,000	33,000	39,000
525i, 528i, 530i ▼	6,500	7,500	10,000	11,500	13,500	16,000	22,000	31,000	37,000
Reliability	5	5	5	4	4	4	4	4	4
Crash Safety									
Frontal (NHTSA)	5	5	5	5	5	5	5	3	5
Side	5	5	5	5	5	5	5	5	5
Offset	5	5	5	5	5	5	5	5	5
Side (IIHS)	—	—	—	—	—	—	—	2	2
Head Restraints (F)	3	—	5	3	3	3	3	5	5
Rollover Resistance	—	4	4	4	4	4	4	4	4

Ford/Lincoln

CONTINENTAL, LS, TOWN CAR, ZEPHYR, MKZ ★/★★★/★★★★/★★★★

RATING: *Continental:* Not Recommended (1999–2002). A front-drive luxury lemon cobbled together from leftovers fallen out of the Taurus and Sable parts bin. *LS:* Average (2000–06). *Town Car:* Recommended (1999–2009). *Zephyr:* Average (2006). 2006 was the Zephyr's first and last year in Canada; it became the 2007 MKZ. *MKZ:* Above Average (2007–09). In a nutshell: Rear-drives are generally more reliable buys than front-drive versions. For example, the discontinued 1988–2002 front-drive Continentals are dirt-cheap, mediocre performers. Servicing has become more problematic as parts dry up and knowledgeable mechanics die off, leaving you with a garaged car that's more of a sculpture than a conveyance. The rear-drive Town Car and LS are the best choices for quality and performance. The MKZ and its Zephyr twin are also quite competent performers that are good second choices. A smart move would be to buy a fully equipped Grand Marquis, thereby escaping the luxury price penalty altogether. Then, after a few years, consider buying a used Zephyr/MKZ, or the less-expensive Fusion/Milan. **Ideal model year:** Town Cars haven't changed much over the years. Look for a $16,500 2007 Signature L model, with 60,000 to 80,000 km on the clock. Interestingly, there's now only about $500 difference between the entry-level Signature Limited and the higher-end Signature L. When both were new the difference was $7,000. So, treat yourself and go whole hog. **"Real" city/highway fuel economy:** *Town Car:* 13.9/8.7 L/100 km. *LS 3.9:* 14.0/9.4 L/100 km. *Zephyr 3.0:* 11.9/7.8 L/100 km. *MKZ 3.5:* 12.6/8.0 L/100 km. *MKZ 3.5 AWD:* 13.2/8.4 L/100 km. Owners report fuel savings may undershoot these estimates by at least 20 percent. **Maintenance/Repair costs:** Higher than average if done by a Ford or Lincoln dealer. **Parts:** Higher-than-average costs, but parts aren't hard to find (except electronic components and body panels). **Extended warranty:** Yes, for the front-drive Continental; no, for any of the rear-drives. **Best alternatives:** Hyundai Genesis and Infiniti G35. **Helpful websites:** *www.lincolnforums.com/forums.*

Strengths and Weaknesses

These large luxury cruisers are proof that quality isn't always proportional to the money you spend. Several designer series offer all the luxury options anyone could wish for, but the two ingredients most owners would expect to find—high quality and consistent reliability—are sadly lacking, especially with the front-drive versions. The front drives use poor-quality brakes, automatic transmissions, electrical systems, body hardware, and fit and finish. NHTSA-recorded safety complaints also target more front-drive than rear-drive Lincolns, with engine, transmission, airbag, and brake failures cropping up repeatedly over the years. What about the trade-off in better fuel economy with the front drives?

Fuhgeddaboudit. What little fuel savings you'll enjoy will be eaten up in brake and suspension repairs.

Continental (front-drive)

When the Continental converted to front-drive in 1988, what was merely a mediocre luxury car became an automotive affliction with serious safety- and performance-related failings. The frequency and cost of repairs increased considerably, and parts became more complex, complicating easy diagnosis and repair. The automatic transmission tends to self-destruct; engine head gaskets blow; electrical components are unreliable, with intermittent loss of all electrical power; stopping performance is compromised by premature brake wear and wheel lock-up; and body hardware is an embarrassment. The redesigned 1995 Continental featured a new V8 powerplant, more-aerodynamic styling, and fibreglass panels. That redesign engendered an upsurge in complaints relative to brake, engine, transmission, and electrical system deficiencies until the Continental was finally ditched after the 2002 model-year run.

No, the Continental is not worth keeping with the hope it will be designated a "classic" some day and be worth some real money. The car is junk. Its only value resides with junkyard "collectors" of hard-to-find Lincoln electrical, suspension, and powertrain parts.

These cars don't offer the kind of trouble-free driving one would expect in a luxury vehicle. The failure-prone and expensive-to-repair automatic levelling air-spring suspension system makes for a stiff ride (especially on early models) while still allowing the Continental to "porpoise" because of its heavy front end. The Continental's anemic V6 powertrain is poorly suited to a car of this heft. The engine hesitates in cold weather, and the automatic transmission shifts roughly.

Mechanical defects include frequent engine flywheel and transmission forward clutch piston replacements; failure-prone ABS, electrical, suspension, and steering systems; and glitch-ridden electronic modules, causing hard starts and sudden stalling. The mass of electrical gadgets increases the likelihood of problems as the cars age. For example, automatic headlight doors fail frequently, and the electronic antenna and power windows often won't go up or down. The computerized dashboard is particularly glitch-ridden.

Other reliability complaints concern transmission fluid leakage, rough upshifting caused by a defective valve body, and inadequate air conditioning and heating.

Town Car

The rear-drive Town Car shares most of its parts with the fairly reliable Crown Victoria and Grand Marquis, and is easily found with little mileage and at bargain prices. Cheaper high-mileage units are frequently sold by airport limousine companies and taxi services that run the airport shuttle service.

Toronto Pearson Airport is a hotspot for frugal shoppers. That's where fleet owners sell used Town Cars dirt cheap because federal government regulations force the companies to update their fleet every few years, creating a flow of perfectly suitable luxury cars sold at next-to-nothing prices.

The car's rear-drive configuration is relatively inexpensive to repair, and parts aren't hard to find. Nevertheless, the Town Car is still afflicted with many generic problems that appear year after year. Some of the more common problems are engine head gaskets that warp because a plastic part in the intake manifold has failed; transmission, AC, and electrical system failures; disintegrating tie-rod ends; and body hardware fit and finish deficiencies.

VEHICLE HISTORY: 2001—25 horses are added to the engine. Gains adjustable pedals and seat belt pretensioners. **2003**—Restyled, with revised frame, suspension, and steering system, and 17-inch tires. Also new are four-wheel, fully assisted ABS disc brakes, front side airbags, an upgraded navigation system, and a 14 hp boost. **2004**—Standard rear obstacle detection system, and additional rear legroom. Executive model is dropped. **2008**—Standard navigation system dropped.

LS

The LS rear-drive sedan comes with a high-performance 200 hp variant of the Taurus 3.0L V6, mated with an optional manual or standard automatic gearbox. A better engine is the 250 hp 3.9L V8 (based on the Jaguar XK8 coupe's engine) coupled with a semi-automatic transmission. There is very little difference between the 2000 and 2001 models, except that the 2001 carries standard traction control. The 2002 models came back unchanged.

Lincoln's return to rear-drive opened up a Pandora's box of AC, body, powertrain, and electrical system glitches. Owners report jerky transmission shifting, excessive drivetrain and body noise and vibrations, inconsistent braking response, and erratic AC performance. The LS was dropped in mid 2006.

VEHICLE HISTORY: 2001—Standard traction control. **2002**—The V6 got 10 more horses. Debut of an LSE version with a rear spoiler, special wheels, and new lower-body trim. **2003**—More-powerful engines. Restyled and quieter-running. The manual transmission is dropped. **2004**—Suspension tweaked to reduce vibration, harshness, and noise.

Zephyr/MKZ

Ford's smallest Lincoln ever, the mid-size, entry-level 2006 Zephyr was sized and priced below the rear-drive Lincoln LS that it replaced. It's essentially a luxury-equipped spin-off of the front-drive Ford Fusion and Mercury Milan mid-size sedans, vehicles that are quite similar to the Mazda6. Zephyr carries a 221 hp V6 engine hooked to a 6-speed automatic transmission, plus all of the most important safety features. Zephyr and MKZ's competitors are the Acura TL, Cadillac CTS, Infiniti G35, and Lexus ES 330 or ES 350.

VEHICLE HISTORY: 2007—Zephyr's name is changed to MKZ—no one knows why. All-wheel drive is added, styling is revamped, and a larger V6 engine corrals 42 more horses, for a total of 263 hp (the Ford Fusion and Mercury Milan keep their anemic 221 hp V6). **2008**—Addition of a standard rear obstacle detection feature and heated front seats. **2009**—Anti–skid system becomes a standard feature.

Safety Summary

All models/years: Sudden, unintended acceleration; gas pedal sticks. • Sudden forward acceleration when shifter is placed into Reverse—a common theme that has affected the entire model lineup over several decades. • Loss of braking. • Airbags deploy inadvertently, or don't deploy when they should. • Gas and brake pedal are mounted too close together. • Sudden loss of electrical power. • Severe pull and vibration when braking. • Brake failures caused by premature wear of rear drums and rotor warpage. • Steering control degrades or locks up when car passes through puddles. • Annoying reflections onto the front windshield. • Horn is hard to activate. • Mirrors vibrate excessively and don't adjust easily. *Continental:* **2001**—Car suddenly accelerates while in Reverse; brake/transmission interlock not connected. • Driver's foot can be snared by two console cables when going from the gas pedal to the brakes. • Instrument panel washes out in bright sunlight. **2002**—Car speeds up while going downhill with cruise control engaged. • In one incident, while in Park with the brakes applied, vehicle rolled back into another car. *LS:* **2000–01**—Lurching, hesitating automatic transmission shifting. • Brakes fail during the first five minutes after a cold start. • Brake pedal becomes hard and resists application, or turns mushy and goes to the floor. • Warning lights come on for no reason. • Defective steering causes violent swerving from side to side. • Automatic door locks engage by themselves, locking out driver. **2002**—Sudden shutdown while on the highway. **2003**—Transmission suddenly seizes. • Loss of steering due to computer malfunction. • Head restraints obstruct visibility **2004**—Hard starts. • Harsh upshifts and gear hunting. • When accelerating, vehicle hesitates and then surges. **2005**—Fuel leak from a cracked fuel tank. • Sudden loss of power. • Broken wheel lug nuts. • Defective side wall (Continental tires). **2006**—Vehicle rolled backwards down an incline even though the transmission was in Park. *Town Car:* **2001**—Sudden acceleration when brakes are applied. • Wheel lug studs break off at the hub. • Ignition locks up when key is inserted. • Brake and accelerator pedal set too close together. • Dash reflects onto windshield. **2002**—Repeated brake master cylinder failures. • Head restraints set too low. **2002–03**—While car was underway, one vehicle's sunroof blew off; another vehicle's hood latch snapped. **2003**—Brake light causes an annoying reflection onto the rear windshield. **2004**—When key was turned in the ignition, fire ignited immediately. • Many reports that the vehicle accelerates when brakes are tapped. • Cruise control doesn't hold the car's speed when descending a hill. • Poor braking. • Sunshine reflects on dashboard metal strip, creating an annoying glare. • Tires leak air due to faulty chrome wheels. **2005**—Engine surges as brakes are applied. • Vehicle suddenly accelerated when put into Reverse. Dealer saw no computer error code present, so ignored the problem. • Vehicle hesitates a few seconds before going into passing gear. • Due to the front seat belt's location, the buckle cuts off circulation, causing right leg numbness. • It can take up to 15 minutes to put in a few gallons of gas due to a faulty fuel-tank valve. • Trunk slams shut due to a dislodged torque rod in the closure assembly. **2006**—Brake pedal depresses below the level of the accelerator; both are too close together:

> The gas pedal is located too close to the brake pedal. It is very easy to press on both pedals at the same time. This has happened to me 4 times in the six months I have been driving this car. The problem is alleviated somewhat by positioning the adjustable brake pedal at the most extended extreme, but it is still far too easy to depress both pedals simultaneously.

• Car rolls backward down an incline when in Park. • Seat belt warning alarm/ light comes on for no reason. • Front tie rod failures. • Rear passengers cannot get out of the vehicle unless a front seat occupant unlocks the doors. **2007**—Chrome peels from the wheels and the tires lose air. • Windshield distortion. **2008**— Vehicle rolled backwards in Park as driver was exiting. **2009**—Airbag deactivation light comes on when an average-sized passenger sits up front. *Zephyr/MKZ:* **2006**—Windows and sunroof can be opened by the remote fob, without the vehicle being started. • Inadequate heater output. **2007**—Seat belt and airbag failure during a collision. • The accelerator pedal can be inadvertently depressed when braking. • Michelin tire valve stem failures. **2008**—Brake and gas pedals are too close together:

> The brake and gas pedals on my Lincoln MKZ are located so close to each other and at the same height that I have twice experienced acceleration instead of braking when putting on the brakes because I did not move my foot enough to clear the gas pedal. I have inquired to my dealer about making an adjustment to the brakes pedal height or spacing but was advised that this could not be done. This design is an "accident waiting to happen" and I am lucky that in both instances I was able to react in time to avoid one.

2008–09—Sunlight washes out the instrument control panel gauges.

Secret Warranties/Internal Bulletins/Service Tips

All models: 1993–2006—Paint delamination, peeling, or fading. *LS:* **2000–01**—Hard starts or no-starts. • Frequent bulletin references to automatic transmission defects producing delayed engagement (PCM module seen as likely culprit), driveline vibration and buzz/clunk/drone, and fluid leakage. • Trunk may suddenly open. • Inoperative AC dual zone heater. • ABS, Airbag, and Service Engine lights come on for no apparent reason. • 3.9L oil leak from the bell housing area. • Poor braking on V6-equipped models. • V6 engine noise on acceleration; highway drone noise. • Instrument panel squeaks and rattles. **2000–02**— Inoperative power windows. • Oil pan drain plug leaks. • Correction for a noisy suspension. **2000–05**—Troubleshooting engine misfires. • Inoperative defroster. **2000–06**—AC heater core leakage or electrolysis. **2003–04**—Harsh upshifts require the reprogramming of the PCM. • An engine stumble or backfire may also be corrected in the same way. • Moisture in the Reverse tail light. • Steering gear noise, vibration. **2004**—Harsh upshifts. • The water pump hose is prone to bursting on 3.0L models. *Town Car:* **1995–2006**—Ford will install for free a fuel-tank fire shield on all limos. **1997–2006**—AC heater core leakage or electrolysis. **1998–2005**—Troubleshooting tips for engine misfiring. **2000–06**—Aluminum body panel corrosion "goodwill" warranty (see bulletin on following page). **2001–04**—Engine ticking countermeasures. **2002–05**—Rear axle shudder or chatter. **2003**—Erratic AC blower motor operation. • Blower motor whistling. • Inaccurate fuel gauge. • Power-steering-assist calibration; excessive power-steering pump noise. • Front wheel area click or rattle. • Rear parking-brake clicking. **2003–04**—Cold-start engine knocking. • Suspension squeaking and rubbing. • Erratic operation of the AC blower. **2003–05**—Inoperative parking assist. **2004**—Exhaust manifold–converter leak. **2004–05**—Delayed Reverse engagement. **2004–09**—Dash popping or clicking noise from the centre of the dash when the AC is working, or just after it is shut off. **2005–06**—Horn is hard to activate. **2005–07**—Hard starts and engine hesitation (repair covered by the Emissions Warranty). **2005–10**—Uncommanded TCC lock-up on 1–2 shift:

A/T-TCC LOCK UP ON 1–2 UPSHIFT

BULLETIN NO.: TSB 09-20-14   DATE: OCTOBER 19, 2009

UN-COMMANDED TCC APPLY ON THE 1–2 SHIFT CAUSING PERCEPTION OF HESITATION AND/OR LACK OF POWER DURING SHIFT

2005–10 Crown Victoria; 2005–06 Expedition; 2005–10 E-150, E-250, E-350, F-150; 2005–10 Town Car; 2006–08 Mark LT; and 2005–10 Grand Marquis

ISSUE: Some 2005–10 vehicles equipped with a 4R70/75E-W transmission may experience an un-commanded torque converter clutch (TCC) apply or TCC partial apply immediately after the 1–2 shift. This may result in the perception that the vehicle lacks power or that the transmission is up-shifting too early. Additional symptoms of uncommanded TCC apply when coming to a stop (before the 2–1 downshift is commanded), are engine stalling or lugging when engaging manual 2nd while at a stop and code P1742 may be present in continuous memory. However, the vehicle should operate normally in park, reverse, neutral and manual 1st gear.

2006–07—Engine overheating, cooling fan inoperative (change the cooling fan). Changing the thermostat will not resolve the problem. **2007–08**—Low idle speed and hesitation may be corrected by reflashing the powertrain control module (PCM) and charging the work to the Emissions Warranty. **2007–09**—Cracking camel-coloured sun visors. **2008–10**—Poor audio reception when rear defroster is on. **2009**—Inoperative front door locks. • Automatic transmission malfunctions (improper gear selection, erratic converter clutch operation, or unusual shift feel). • Fluid leak from the right rear axle wheel bearing oil seal. *Zephyr/MKZ:* **2006–07**—Front axle clicking, ratcheting noise. • Water leak from the roof-opening panel area. • Front-seat squeak, rattle. • Underbody rattle, vibration from the heat shield. • Wind noise from the B-pillar. • Erratic AC blower motor operation. **2006–08**—Power-steering fluid leaks. • Slow glass movement. **2006–10**—Poor AM/FM reception with the rear defroster on. **2007**—Hesitation on acceleration. • Poor heater output at idle. **2007–09**—Front suspension (strut) grunt, rub, pop noises. • Front door glass scratched, noisy, and moves slowly. • Trunk lid won't latch. **2007–10**—Rough idle and idle speed drop. **2008–09**—Excessive engine vibration at 1800–2200 rpm. **2008–10**—Sunroof water leak. **2009**—Reduced heater temperature output at idle.

ALUMINUM BODY PANELS—CORROSION

BULLETIN NO.: 06-25-15   DATE: DECEMBER 11, 2006

Ford: 2000–07 Crown Victoria, Taurus; 2005–06 Ford GT; 2005–07 Mustang; 2000–03 Ranger; 2000–07 Expedition; 2002–07 Explorer; 2004–07 F-150; 2007 Explorer Sport Trac Lincoln: 2000–06 Lincoln LS; 2000–07 Town Car, Navigator Mercury: 2000–07 Grand Marquis and Sable

ISSUE: Some vehicles may exhibit a bubbling or blistering under the paint on aluminum body parts. This is due to iron contamination of the aluminum panel.

ACTION: This TSB provides service tips and procedures, outlining methods to properly prepare and protect aluminum body parts from cross contamination.

BACKGROUND: Ford's Scientific Research Laboratory has performed a number of tests on vehicle body parts returned for corrosion related concerns. Testing has revealed that the aluminum corrosion was caused by iron particles working their way into the aluminum body part, prior to it being painted.

CONTINENTAL, LS, TOWN CAR, ZEPHYR/MKZ PROFILE

	2001	2002	2003	2004	2005	2006	2007	2008	2009
Cost Price ($)									
Continental Ex.	51,920	52,900	—	—	—	—	—	—	—
LS	40,870	42,300	42,500	43,750	43,865	50,599	—	—	—
Town Car	53,970	53,445	55,205	57,645	58,865	58,199	58,499	58,599	58,699
Zephyr	—	—	—	—	—	36,999			
MKZ	—	—	—	—	—	—	37,499	39,499	36,499
Used Values ($)									
Continental Ex. ▲	3,000	4,000	—	—	—	—	—	—	—
Continental Ex. ▼	2,500	3,000	—	—	—	—	—	—	—
LS ▲	3,000	3,500	4,000	5,500	7,000	9,000	—	—	—
LS ▼	2,500	3,500	3,500	4,500	5,500	7,500	—	—	—
Town Car ▲	5,000	7,000	8,000	9,000	10,500	12,500	16,500	22,000	27,000
Town Car ▼	4,000	6,000	7,000	8,000	9,000	11,500	15,000	20,000	25,000
Zephyr ▲	—	—	—	—	—	7,500	—	—	—
Zephyr ▼	—	—	—	—	—	6,000	—	—	—
MKZ ▲	—	—	—	—	—	—	13,000	16,500	22,000
MKZ ▼	—	—	—	—	—	—	11,500	15,000	20,000

Reliability

	2001	2002	2003	2004	2005	2006	2007	2008	2009
Continental Ex.	1	1	—	—	—	—	—	—	—
LS, Zephyr/MKZ	3	3	3	4	4	4	4	4	4
Town Car	4	4	4	4	4	5	5	5	5

All ratings on a numbered scale where   is good and **1** is bad. See page 132 for a more detailed description.

Crash Safety (F)

LS	—	—	—	—	—	—	—	—	—
Town Car	—	—	—	—	—	—	—	—	—
Zephyr/MKZ	—	—	—	—	—	—	4	—	—

Side

LS	4	4	4	4	4	4	—	—	—
Town Car	4	4	—	—	—	—	—	—	—
Zephyr/MKZ	—	—	—	—	—	—	—	—	—

IIHS Side

Zephyr/MKZ	—	—	—	—	—	3	—	—	—

Offset

Continental Ex.	3	3	—	—	—	—	—	—	—
LS	—	—	—	—	—	—	—	—	—
Town Car	—	—	—	—	—	—	—	—	—
Zephyr/MKZ	—	—	—	—	—	3	—	—	—

Head Restraints

Continental Ex.	2	2	—	—	—	—	—	—	—
LS	2	2	3	3	3	3	—	—	—
Town Car	1	1	2	2	2	2	2	2	—
Zephyr/MKZ	—	—	—	—	—	2	2	2	—

Roof Strength

(Zephyr/MKZ)	—	—	—	—	—	3	—	—	—

Rollover Resistance

LS	—	—	—	—	—	—	—	—	—
Town Car	—	—	—	—	—	—	—	—	—
Zephyr/MKZ	—	—	—	—	—	4	—	4	4

General Motors

CTS, CTS-V, DEVILLE, DTS, STS, STS-V ★★✦★★

RATING: Below Average (1999–2009). *DeVille:* Average (2001–05). These cars (except for the DeVille) put the "lack" in Cadillac. **Ideal model year:** A 2005 DeVille for about $9,500. **"Real" city/highway fuel economy:** 13.3/8.2 L/100 km. Owners report the vehicle may use at least 20 percent more fuel than this estimate suggests. **Maintenance/Repair costs:** Higher than average; repairs are very dealer-dependent. **Parts:** Higher-than-average costs, and parts are hard to find. **Extended warranty:** Your best protection is to not buy a Cadillac in the first place. For those who do, an extended warranty is essential. **Best alternatives:** Acura RL or TL, Hyundai Genesis, and Infiniti G35. **Helpful websites:** *www.cadillacforums.com/forums/forum.php.*

Strengths and Weaknesses

CTS

Cadillac's entry-level CTS replaced the Catera in 2003 and has quickly distinguished itself as a particularly unreliable, heavy rear-drive luxury car that purports to performs like a European sports sedan. Its extra weight destroys any pretense of fuel economy, with an estimated city/highway rating of only 13.4/7.8 L/100 km. Suggested alternatives are the Acura TL, Infiniti G35, and Lincoln Town Car.

The CTS's problematic powertrain has constantly evolved during its few years on the market because it was never made right in the first place. First-year models offered only a puny 220 hp 3.2L V6 coupled to a standard 5-speed manual gearbox or an optional 5-speed automatic transmission. The smoother and more-powerful 255 hp 3.6L V6 engine and automatic transmission powers the 2004 models. That same year, the 2004 CTS-V was launched, carrying a Corvette-derived 400 hp 5.7L V8 that is even *more* unreliable than the V6. The 2005 CTS changed over to a 2.8L V6 with 10 fewer horses and a better-performing 6-speed manual gearbox. 2006 models were given revised sport/performances packages.

Nevertheless, the above-noted powertrain changes haven't improved differential reliability, which has been a chronic problem since the CTS was launched:

> The Cadillac CTS-V rear differential is weak and may break causing this car to skid or suddenly stop, causing an accident, injury, or death. Cadillac knows of the problem and has provided some customers with warranty repair, offered 100,000 mile [160,000 km] extended warranties for others and yet denied repair for customers with similar problems. This rear differential is under rated for this car's horse power and was designed for use in the standard CTS version of this car the rear tires have also been a problem showing early signs of wear. I had to replace my first set [of] front and rear [tires] at 8,500 miles [13,500 km] these tires are worst rated tire by consumers at *www.tirerack.com* and *www.cadillacfaq.com*.

Other problems include stability control and ABS failures; constant rear-end whine (a warning that total failure is just around the corner); early replacement of the fuel/water pump, radiator, and power windows; electrical system shorts causing lights, gauges, instruments, and power seats to malfunction; and poor fit and finish, highlighted by loud wind noise from the windshield, clunks and rattles, paint blistering and premature corrosion, and door handle, dash, and radio button plastic peeling.

Although they have better handling and are almost as comfortable as older, traditional Caddies, these front-drive luxury coupes and sedans aren't worth considering because of their dismal reliability, overly complex servicing, and dependence on parts that are impossible to find and not very durable. Poor reliability remains a problem, and the term "Cadillac fuel economy" is an oxymoron. Also, the dash controls and gauges are confusing and not easily accessible, and the high trunk lid and large side pillars obstruct the rear view.

The 4.3L V6, 4.1L V8, and 4.5L V8 engines and 4-speed automatic transmission suffer from a variety of terminal maladies, including oil leaks, premature wear, poor fuel economy, and excessive noise. The electrical system and related components are temperamental. Steering is noisy, the suspension goes soft quickly, and the front brakes often wear out after only 18 months/20,000 km. Problems with the digital fuel injection and engine control systems are very difficult to diagnose and repair. Premature paint peeling and rusting, excessive wind noise in the interior, and fragile trim items characterize poor body assembly.

VEHICLE HISTORY: 2005—Redesigned and sold as the 2006 DTS.

DTS

About the same size as it replaced the DeVille, Cadillac's front-drive 2006 DTS carries a 4.6L V8, 4-speed automatic transmission, and self-levelling rear suspension. A 275 hp Northstar V8 with optional performance packages targets premium full-size sedans like the Buick Lucerne, Lexus LS 430, and Lincoln Town Car (Lexus and Lincoln are the better choices). Every DTS includes anti-lock braking, traction control, front torso side airbags, and head-protecting side curtain airbags. Also standard are Magnetic Ride Control, a tire-pressure monitor, a remote engine start feature, and xenon headlights. The vehicle has changed little since it was introduced.

Cadillac continued its not-so-proud history of making luxury lemons with the advent of the DTS. Owners decry hard starts and no-starts; excessive Continental Tire noise; a key that sticks in the ignition; a gas tank cap that's difficult to open; a plastic undercarriage cover that drags on the ground; a Stability-Control Service light that remains lit; the failure of the Collision Avoidance feature's sensors; a knocking, clicking sound that comes from the steering assembly; a driver-side mirror that fails to correct for a blind spot; and distracting (to other drivers) "strobe" LED tail lights.

STS

Whopping depreciation aside, this rear-drive/AWD Seville replacement has plenty of power and versatility. The V6 engine is more powerful than the BMW 5 Series' and Mercedes E-Class's 6-cylinders, while the V8 produces slightly less horsepower than the comparable BMW but more than the Mercedes or Lexus. Without question, Cadillac's switch to rear-drive or all-wheel drive considerably improves the STS's balance, handling, and overall performance. Shoppers will have to decide if the car's elegant interior and vastly superior performance make up for the loss of a little rear seatroom (it still has at least a couple centimetres more than its closest competitors, and it's close to 7.5 cm larger than the problematic Mercedes E-Class) and for its unproven mechanical components, mediocre fit and finish, and untested crashworthiness.

Although complaints relative to STS reliability have been fewer than average, owners do report a number of serious safety-related failures. For example, the passenger-side airbag sensor fails to detect if the seat is occupied, and leaves the system disabled:

> The dealership tried for over a week to solve the problem, but would only say that the procedure to activate the sensor requires the passenger to enter and sit in the vehicle in a certain convoluted way that is basically unnatural and impossible for certain passengers to achieve.

Acceleration is erratic, the car suddenly loses power when passing another vehicle, the rear differential may suddenly lock up, and the car has poor traction in snow:

> The contact stated that the 2006 STS fails to operate properly while driving in snow. The vehicle slides and causes crashes because there is no traction. The contact was involved in a crash, but no police report was filed. The manufacturer stated that nothing could be done and suggested the contact purchase new tires to accommodate the weather conditions.

Owners report that eye-watering, throat-burning emissions emanate from the interior, principally the trunk area; the sunroof may blow out from excessive interior air pressure; the voice recognition feature executes different commands than what it is given, and prior commands can't be countermanded; the wiring harness and module under the front seat may melt; and electrical shorts play havoc with lights, gauges, and accessory systems. There have also been many complaints that the differential leaks fluid, brake pads quickly wear out and brake rotors warp prematurely, the air dam shield falls down and drags on the pavement, windshields shatter for no reason, headlights have stress cracks, and the battery dies if the car isn't started for several days.

And if all of the above-listed failures aren't embarrassing enough, owners also report that their front seat makes a "noxious" noise:

> Front car seats are making a farting noise. I have had [the] car in the dealership three times and each time they said they fixed the problem. They have not.

Safety Summary

All models/years—Sudden, unintended acceleration; in one incident, vehicle suddenly accelerated, killing one person and injuring others. • Inadvertent airbag deployment, or airbags fail to deploy:

> It was December. I was 5 months pregnant. I was sitting in my 2003 Cadillac CTS warming up the car and putting eyeliner on. All of a sudden boom airbags went off first the steering wheel then driver door it made marks on my face and neck.

• Excessive vibration and chronic stalling while underway:

While traveling at moderate speed vehicle began shaking violently and losing power. The engine was missing on one or more cylinders. This seems to have been caused by a defect mentioned in TSB ID # 1609265 dated 2005. This TSB states that the crankcase vapors and engine oil will vent through the cam/valve cover seals when the crankcase ventilation system becomes blocked. The oil on this vehicle evidently vented and leaked several places including into the ignition coils causing a short.

• Leaking engine oil coolant. • Wheels fall off. • Total brake failure:

I was turning into a parking lot at a slow speed when the brakes did not engage. We took the car directly to the dealership. They recommended that we replace the tires (which we did) and then recommended that we replace the left front wheel bearing/ speed sensor/hub again for the 5th time.

• Many complaints of front and rear brake rotor warpage and premature pad and caliper failure. • Sudden loss of power steering, or excessive steering vibration. • Vehicle tends to wander all over the road. • Can't read speedometer in daylight. • Sun visor obstructs visibility. • Gas-tank sensor failure causes inaccurate fuel readings. • Interior lights frequently malfunction. *CTS:* **2003**—Engine serpentine belt and coil failures. • Badly corroded fuel and brake line, hoses, and fittings:

Recall did not apply to our vehicle. Being skeptical of that assertion because this vehicle had spent its first two years in Connecticut on lease, I had the brake system inspected at a local shop. They found (and I witnessed) the badly corroded brake hose fittings. As the mechanic pushed on the L.H. rubber sleeve covering the hose to metal tube junction to see the extent of the rust, the hose separated from the tube !! This with only the pressure applied with one finger !! We were one hard braking application from a possible accident !! But there are other areas of concern, and those are the metal tubing lines in the front of the chassis that are part of the hydraulic braking (and anti-skid) systems. Many of these lines are heavily rusted, making them as much a contributor to brake failure as the hoses.

• When the stability control system engages, it suddenly pulls the car to the left. • Rear brake lights and plate cover fall off ($550 to replace). • Brake lights frequently burn out. • Trunk lid continually slams down. **2004**—Lower front ball joint separates from the control arm. • Back plastic piece that covers license plate fell off (cost $1,200 to replace). • Transmission cooling line broke away from the radiator. **2005**—Many complaints of a rear differential axle shaft seal failure not covered by warranty. • Rear windshield suddenly shattered. **2006**—Airbag warning light is constantly lit (not part of the airbag sensor recall). • Defective middle rear brake light. • ABS light comes on and car won't brake while turning at slow speeds. • Cars fail mandatory inspection and drivers must pay up to $600 for the needed parts. • Engine timing chain breaks at 66,000 km, requiring a $8,500 3.6L V6 engine replacement. • Rear differential axle shaft seal failures continue (not covered by previous recall. **2007**—Passenger-side airbag is disabled even though an average-sized occupant is seated (not part of a previous recall). •

Sudden tie rod breakage while vehicle was on the highway. • Ball joint fractured, causing the front driver's side of the vehicle to collapse. • Door latches freeze and door will swing open. **2008**—Rear window suddenly shattered:

> I was driving my CTS Cadillac when with no warning I heard a loud noise, I pulled over to see what it was a[nd] I saw that my rear window had shattered. [N]othing had hit my window. I drove straight to the Cadillac dealer and they informed me they cannot repair it without having me pay for the cost. I went online and searched and found that this type of incident had happened before on GM models and was listed on the TSB and is should b[e] replaced.

• Broken driver's seat frame: $800 to repair. • Driver's side mirror creeps upwards. • Electronic key sometimes fails to lock the vehicle. • Gas and brake pedals are mounted too close together. • Water leaks into the interior. **2009**—Key could not be removed from the ignition:

> Placed the car in "Park" and tried to turn the ignition off. Key would not turn to "Off" position. Engine kept running. Key could not be removed from the ignition. The service technician said that he has encountered similar occurrence with many 2009, 2010 CTS vehicles. My father disabled the engine by removing the fuel pump fuse located in the rear trunk of the vehicle. The car was towed to a Cadillac dealer for repair. This is a dangerous circumstance. If there were an engine fire, one could not "turn-off" the motor and fuel would feed an engine fire.

• Owners feel the heater washer recall is unfair because it offers owners only $100 and disables the system. • Water leaks into the interior (a sunroof problem?). • GM's "foam" spare tire is all froth. *DeVille:* **2001**—Transmission pops out of gear and allows vehicle to roll down an incline. • Side mirror creates a huge blind spot. **2002**—Seat belts are too short for some occupants. • Shoulder belt fits short drivers poorly. • Distorted windshield. **2003**—Chronic stalling caused by electrical failure. • Instrument panel shuts down. **2004**—Vehicle caught fire while parked. • Transmission fluid leakage is a fire hazard. • Hesitation when accelerating. • Early tie rod replacement. • Hood latch isn't secured tightly. **2005**—Headlights shut off when turning signals are enabled. • Tail lights have a "strobe effect" that blurs drivers' vision in following cars. • Door won't stay open when the car is parked on an incline. • Lengthy delay when transmission is shifted into Reverse. *DTS:* **2006**—Adaptive cruise control operates abnormally. • Cruise control fails to maintain speed when going downhill. • Steering suddenly pulls the vehicle to one side. • Total failure of the lower control arm sent the car careening out of control. • A fleet manager reports that all of their vehicles' high-intensity headlights go out due to defective ballast assemblies. • Sun reflects off the clock into driver's eyes. • The front windshield has lines flowing across it. **2007**—Car stalled in traffic and then proceeded at a snail's pace. • One driver stepped on the gas to avoid hitting a truck, and the car failed to respond. • Wind can blow doors shut on occupants' legs. • Many reports that the driver's right foot gets stuck between the gas pedal and the centre console. • Twilight sensors come on too early and go off too late (see *www.cadillacforums.com/forums/cadillac-forum/t-92975. html*). • Centre door post and driver-seat head restraint block the driver's view when turning or looking rearward. • Sun visor falls down on its own; fails to block the sunlight. *STS:* **2006**—Long wait for recall parts for the axle shaft seal repair. • Passenger-side airbag is disabled even though a 100 lb. adult is seated. • Seat bezel breaks constantly.

Secret Warranties/Internal Bulletins/Service Tips

All models/years: Reverse servo cover seal leak. • Paint delamination, peeling, or fading. **All models: 1996–2003**—Excessive oil consumption can be corrected with new piston rings if a ring-cleaning process doesn't work (TSB #02-06-01-009C). *CTS:* **2005–11**—Loss of engine power may be caused by water intrusion into the instrument panel:

REDUCED POWER

BULLETIN NO.: 07-06-04-019D   DATE: JUNE 28, 2010

INTERMITTENT MALFUNCTION INDICATOR LAMP (MIL) ILLUMINATED, DTC P2138 WITH REDUCED ENGINE POWER (REPAIR INSTRUMENT PANEL (IP) TO BODY HARNESS CONNECTOR).

2005–11 GM Passenger Cars and Light Duty Trucks (Including Saturn); 2005–09 HUMMER H2; 2006–10 HUMMER H3; 2005–09 Saab 9-7X.

CONDITION: Some customers may comment on an intermittent malfunction indicator lamp (MIL) being Illuminated with a message or an indicator that displays Reduced Engine Power.

CAUSE: This condition may be caused by water intrusion into the instrument panel (IP) to body harness connector, which carries the APP sensor signals to the ECM/PCM.

2008–09—Clunk noise while turning, or automatic transmission extension housing leaks. • Front brakes squeal when braking. GM suggests owners replace the brake pads with Kit #PN 25958115). Owners should ask for a partial reimbursement. • Front seat lateral movement, clunking. • Front door window drops incrementally. • Rear door windows may go down by themselves. • Front door latch freezing "Customer Satisfaction" policy: At no charge, dealers are to seal the latch housing on both front doors to prevent water intrusion:

CAMPAIGN—FRONT DOOR LATCH FREEZING

BULLETIN NO.: 09104A   DATE: JANUARY 5, 2010

2008–09 Cadillac CTS; 2009 Cadillac CTS-V. Condition: Certain 2008 and 2009 model year Cadillac CTS vehicles and 2009 model year Cadillac CTS-V vehicles registered in Canada, may have a condition where water may enter the front door latch housing and potentially freeze. If water enters the latch housing and freezes, the customer may not be able to open the front doors using the outside door handle, or the door may not latch when the door is closed. If the door does not latch, the interior lamps will illuminate, a message will display on the driver information center warning that the door is not closed, and a chime will sound for 4 seconds.

2008–10—Front door window is slow or noisy when activated. 2008–11—Noise heard when shifting between Reverse and Drive. • Inoperative low-beam headlights. *DeVille:* 2000–02—Loss of power when accelerating. • 1–2 shift concerns. 2000–04—Remedies for excessive vibration, shaking while cruising. • Troubleshooting rear suspension noise. 2000–05—Silencing a front-end clunk. • Hood blistering, premature corrosion. 2001—Intermittent inoperative instrument panel (requires replacement of the I/P cluster assembly). • Delayed Reverse engagement. 2001–03—Loss of engine coolant. 2001–05—Harsh upshifts. 2003—Intermittent no-starts; no electrical power (align engine wiring junction block, says TSB #06-03-009). • Erratic transmission shifting. 2003–04—Right rear-door air leak. 2005—Difficult to move shifter out of Park. • Moan, squawk during low-speed turns. *DTS:* 2006–07—Automatic transmission slips, overheats, or won't shift. • Inoperative power seats. • Brake pulsation when travelling down steep grades (get improved brake pads). *STS:* 2005–07—Front or rear axle pinion seal leak. • Torque converter clutch surge, shudder, exhaust moan, and chuggle. • Inaccurate fuel gauge. 2007–08—Sunroof rattling.

CTS, CTS-V, DEVILLE, DTS, STS, STS-V PROFILE

	2001	2002	2003	2004	2005	2006	2007	2008	2009
Cost Price ($)									
CTS	—	—	39,900	39,200	37,800	35,555	35,780	38,900	40,485
CTS-V	—	—	—	70,000	70,700	68,755	70,670	—	68,995
DeVille	51,895	52,555	54,925	56,235	57,050	—	—	—	—
DTS	—	—	—	—	—	52,680	52,935	53,415	55,590
STS V6	—	—	—	—	—	56,600	57,750	57,910	60,920
STS V8	—	—	—	—	—	69,470	71,275	68,880	70,230
STS-V	—	—	—	—	—	97,995	98,265	102,955	105,075
Used Values ($)									
CTS ▲	—	—	5,000	7,500	9,500	11,500	14,500	19,500	25,000
CTS ▼	—	—	4,000	6,000	8,000	10,000	13,000	18,000	23,000
CTS-V ▲	—	—	8,000	9,500	12,000	15,000	19,500	—	38,000
CTS-V ▼	—	—	7,500	8,000	10,000	13,500	18,000	—	36,000
DeVille ▲	3,500	4,500	6,000	8,000	10,500	—	—	—	—
DeVille ▼	3,500	4,000	5,000	6,500	9,000	—	—	—	—
DTS ▲	—	—	—	—	—	11,500	14,500	22,000	27,000
DTS ▼	—	—	—	—	—	10,000	13,000	20,000	25,000
STS V6 ▲	—	—	—	—	—	13,500	18,500	24,500	30,000
STS V6 ▼	—	—	—	—	—	12,000	17,000	23,000	28,000
STS V8 ▲	—	—	—	—	—	15,500	20,000	29,000	37,000
STS V8 ▼	—	—	—	—	—	14,000	18,500	27,000	35,000
STS-V ▲	—	—	—	—	—	18,500	23,000	37,000	55,000
STS-V ▼	—	—	—	—	—	17,000	21,500	35,500	53,000

Reliability	1	1	1	1	1	1	1	1	1
Crash Safety (F)									
CTS	—	—	4	4	4	4	4	4	4
DeVille	3	1	1	4	4	—	—	—	—
DTS	—	—	—	—	—	5	5	5	5
STS	—	—	—	—	—	—	5	5	4
Side									
DeVille	4	4	4	4	4	—	—	—	—
DTS	—	—	—	—	—	4	4	4	4
STS	—	—	—	—	5	5	5	5	4
IIHS Side									
CTS	—	—	—	—	—	—	—	5	5
DTS	—	—	—	—	—	3	3	3	3
STS	—	—	—	—	—	3	3	3	3
Offset									
CTS	—	—	5	5	5	5	5	5	5
DTS	—	—	—	—	—	5	5	5	5
STS	—	—	—	—	5	5	5	5	
Head Restraints									
CTS	—	—	1	1	1	1	1	5	5
DTS	—	—	—	—	—	1	1	2	2
STS	—	—	—	—	1	1	1	1	1
Rollover Resistance									
CTS	—	—	4	4	4	4	4	4	4
DeVille	—	5	5	5	5	—	—	—	—
DTS	—	—	—	—	—	4	4	4	4
STS	—	—	—	—	—	—	5	5	5

Note: New Cadillacs that are far apart in their prices have almost equal worth after a few years. For example: A 2007 STS V6 sold originally for $57,750, while the V8 version went for $71,275. Today, a 2007 V6 sells for about $18,000. The V8? It will cost you about $2,000 more.

Hyundai

GENESIS SEDAN/COUPE ★★★★★/★★★★

RATING: *Sedan*: Recommended (2009–10); *Coupe*: Above Average (2010). **Ideal model year:** *Sedan*: A 2009 is your best used choice; it can be found for around $25,000. *Coupe*: Costs almost as much as the sedan but is a year newer. A high-performance 3.8L model that sold for $32,995 now can be bought used for $25,000. **"Real" city/highway fuel economy:** *Sedan V6*: 11.4/7.2 L/100 km. *3.8L V8*: 12.6/81 L/100 km. *Coupe V6 manual*: 10.1/6.6 L/100 km. *V6 automatic*: 10.4/6.6 L/100 km. *V8 automatic*: 11.9/7.3 L/100 km. Owners say these estimates are fairly accurate. **Maintenance/Repair costs:** Below average costs; most repairs are reasonably priced, and some routine tasks can be carried out by independent shops. **Parts:** Parts are easily found and moderately priced. V8 engine components, emissions modules, and body parts are the exception. **Extended warranty:** Not needed, save your $2,000. **Best alternatives:** *Sedan:* The BMW 3 Series, Cadillac CTS, Ford Taurus, Lincoln MKS, Mercedes-Benz E-Class, and Toyota Avalon (only with the brake override feature). *Coupe:* The Chevrolet Camaro, Ford Mustang, and—for sheer sportster thrills without the bills—Mazda MX-5. **Helpful websites:** *www.hyundai-forums.com/f92-genesis.htm*, *www.genesisowners.com*, and *www.carcomplaints.com/Hyundai/Genesis*.

Strengths and Weaknesses

Hyundai's Genesis targets BMW and Mercedes-Benz big spenders with its own luxury rear-drive until the Equus gets its footing later this year.

These luxury cars are loaded with high-tech safety gear that includes ABS, traction control, an anti-skid system, side curtain airbags, front side airbags, and rear side airbags. There's also a heated and cooled driver's seat, wireless cell phone link, a navigation system with hard drive for storing digital music files, a rear-view camera, and front- and rear-obstacle detection. A knob in the centre console governs audio, navigation, and other functions.

Sedan: The Genesis is almost a perfect upscale luxury sedan that's fully equipped with features found on more expensive competitors. It features two performance-focused engines: a 2.0L turbocharged 4-cylinder and a range-topping, all-aluminum 3.8L V6. If you want more power, the 3.8L V6 is available. The basic version comes standard with a 6-speed manual; shoppers looking for a 5-speed Shiftronic automatic with manual mode will pay a few thousand dollars more. In any case, you get quick and smooth acceleration with the refined V6 (a V8 is optional); excellent, no-surprise handling; and good fuel economy. The interior is tastefully done with most features and instruments well within reach. Not only is the cabin roomy, but it accommodates 6-foot-plus passengers quite well, especially in the rear seating area, where the seats are both comfortable and supportive. The Genesis features first-class interior fit and finish; a quiet, vibration-free, and spacious cabin; clear and easy-to-read gauges; and impressive crashworthiness rankings. Controls are simple to use, as long as you stay away from the optional navigation feature, which takes some study to operate correctly.

On the downside, both the V6 and V8 engines produce less torque at higher rpm than do the Chrysler 300 or Pontiac G8, the ride can be twitchy at times, and there's excessive body roll during hard cornering. Hyundai mechanics say the suspension is tuned for a full load, so anything less makes the vehicle wander. Long-term reliability has still to be determined.

Coupe: The smaller 2010 Genesis Coupe was launched a year after the sedan and targets the Chevrolet Camaro and Ford Mustang. The coupe is a different animal that maximizes the vehicle's highway performance through a high level of driver input. Original-equipment Dunlop tires may be too sensitive to the crown of the road. Navigation and audio system controls are cumbersome. Hyundai recommends premium fuel for extra horsepower from the V8, but it's not worth the higher fuel cost for just eight more horses.

Safety Summary

All models: 2009—Many reports of sudden loss of power on the highway, due to a faulty throttle sensor. • Stuck throttle. • Jerky acceleration as transmission "hunts" for the proper gear. • Premature wearout of Dunlop original-equipment tires. • Intermittent short circuits that would cut out interior lights. • Steering has a severe pull to the left, say owners:

> Research this problem by *Google.com*—"Hyundai Genesis steering issue and left or right pull" and you will get more than hundred similar complaints from new owners since 2008/2009 model release. I have been to the dealer 3 times to fix this issue within 3000 miles—but Hyundai dealers are just performing alignments...butdoesn't fix the problem.

Coupe: 2010—Sudden, unintended acceleration. • Acceleration "flat spot" causes vehicle to almost "die out" when accelerating. • Premature transmission failure. • Lurching when put into gear. • Traction control doesn't work on occasion. • Many Coupe owners irate over the severe steering pull to the right and car's inability to track in a straight line. • Hood bolts came off (*www.rwdcoupe.com/general-discussion/2331-hood-problem-bolts-came-off-traffic.html*). • Hood is often misaligned, causing lots of hood buffeting. • Excessive raw fuel smell pervades the cabin. • Brakes lock up for no reason.

Secret Warranties/Internal Bulletins/Service Tips

2009—No start in Park, Neutral. • Self-activating anti-theft alarm. • Brake lights flash for no reason. • Troubleshooting tips to eliminate sunroof creaking, ticking. • Engine rpms slowly drop to idle. • Front bumper gaps. • Quarter panel creak, tick when passing over rough roads. • Sunroof sun shade slides open when car accelerates. • The anti-theft alarm self-activates.

GENESIS PROFILE

	2009	2010
Cost Price ($)		
Genesis Sedan	37,995	38,999
Genesis Coupe	—	24,495

Used Values ($)

Sedan ▲	25,000	29,000
Sedan ▼	23,000	27,000
Coupe ▲	—	19,500
Coupe ▼	—	18,000

Reliability	4	4
Crash Safety	5	5
Side	5	5
Side (IIHS)	5	5
Head Restraints (F)	3	3
Rear	2	2
Roof Strength	5	5
Rollover Resistance	5	5

Infiniti

G20, G35, I30, I35, M35, M45, Q45   ★/★★★/★★★★/★★★

RATING: *G20:* Not Recommended (1999–2002). *G35:* Recommended (2007–08); Below Average (2003–06). *G37:* Recommended (2009); Above Average (2008). *I30:* Above Average (2000–03). *I35:* Average (2002–04). *M35, M45:* Above Average (2006–07); Average (2003–05). *Q45:* Average (2002–05); Below Average (1997–2001). **Ideal model year:** If you want the performance thrills for a lot less money and only 20-some fewer horses than the higher-priced G37, opt for a 2008 G35 sedan. It costs about $20,000, which is pretty good for a car that sold new for double that figure. Sure, the 2009 G37s have 7-speed automatic trannies and 6-speed manual gearboxes, but you will pay lots more for powertrains that haven't yet been time-tested, especially in the AWD versions. Plus, there are more G35s on the market. **"Real" city/highway fuel economy:** *G20:* 10.0/6.9 L/100 km. *G35 coupe* 10.0/6.9 L/100 km. *G35 sedan:* 12.2/8.4 L/100 km. *G35 AWD:* 12.6/8.6 L/100 km. *G37 coupe:* 11.7/7.6 L/100 km. *G37 convertible:* 12.0/7.8 L/100 km. *I30 3.0:* 12.1/8.1 L/100 km. *I35:* 12.1/8.3 L/100 km. *Q45 4.1:* 13.4/9.2 L/100 km. *Q45 4.5:* 13.6/8.8 L/100 km. Owners report these vehicles use about 10 percent more fuel than these estimates would suggest. **Maintenance/Repair costs:** Higher-than-average costs, and repairs must be done by either an Infiniti or a Nissan dealer, especially for the higher-end models that have been off the market for a few years. **Parts:** Higher-than-average costs, and hard to find:

> They found the problem...but told me that it couldn't be repaired and that the part wasn't sold separately. Instead the entire headlight assembly needed to be replaced with the light assembly costing $1,500.00 and with taxes and labour the cost would exceed $1,800.00.

All ratings on a numbered scale where 5 is good and **1** is bad. See page 132 for a more detailed description.

Extended warranty: Not necessary. **Best alternatives:** A fully equipped Honda Accord is a better buy from a price and quality standpoint, but Accords don't have the same luxury cachet. Also consider the Acura RL or TL and the Hyundai Genesis. **Helpful websites:** *www.nicoclub.com/infiniti-technical-articles* and *http://forums.nicoclub.com.*

Strengths and Weaknesses

With its emphasis on sporty handling (diluted somewhat with the '97 and later model years), the Infiniti series takes the opposite tack from the Lexus, which focuses on comfort and luxury. Infiniti models do come fully equipped and offer owners the prestige of driving a comfortable and nicely styled luxury car, but the lineup isn't as refined or as reliable as the Toyota competition.

G20

The least expensive Infiniti, 1999 and later G20s aren't as refined as their entry-level Lexus counterparts in interior space, drivetrain, or convenience features. The 140 hp engine's lack of low-speed torque means that it has to work hard above 4000 rpm—while protesting noisily. The automatic transmission shifts roughly, particularly when passing; the power steering needs more assist during parking manoeuvres; and the dealer-installed fog lights cost an exorbitant $500 to replace. Tall drivers will find the legroom insufficient, and rear passengers will feel cramped. Trunk space is limited by the angle of the rear window.

Owner complaints target automatic transmission failures, engine coolant leaks, prematurely worn brake rotors and brake pads, excessive noise when braking, malfunctioning power seats, and clunky springs and shock absorbers.

G35

Infiniti's rear-drive, sporty luxury car was introduced in the spring of 2002. The sedan is equipped with a 260 hp engine, versus 280 hp for the coupe. Coupes are feature-laden, stretched versions of Nissan's problem-prone 2003 350Z sports car, with less power and a small fold-down back seat added. Sedans are quite long and provide sportier performance than Infiniti's front-drive I35 does. Initially, both G35s offered a 5-speed automatic transmission with manual shiftgate, but a 6-speed manual was phased in within a year. Both body styles offer four-wheel ABS disc brakes, front side airbags, and side curtain airbags (only for the front seats in the coupe). Manual transmission coupes come with more performance-oriented upgraded brakes. Alternative choices would be the Acura TL, Audi A4, BMW 3 Series, and Cadillac CTS.

Owner complaints primarily concern chronic engine noise, excessive brake squealing, very poor fuel economy, a noisy manual 6-speed transmission, automatic transmission failures and erratic shifting, metal flakes in the paint (bird droppings will eat through the finish), early replacement of brake pads and rotors ($600), and excessive engine oil consumption requiring a rebuilt engine. The low-tire-pressure monitoring system must be reprogrammed by the dealer if wheels are rotated or a full-size spare tire is installed.

G37

While leaving the 2008 G35 unchanged, Infiniti launched a G37 coupe, equipped with a 330 hp 3.7L V6. In 2009 all Infiniti "G" cars became G37s equipped with the 3.7L powerplant coupled to a 6-speed manual, or a 7-speed automatic transmission. An AWD option and convertible, with a retractable hard top, were added to the lineup.

VEHICLE HISTORY: 2004—Debut of an all-wheel-drive sedan with Snow Mode that provides a 50/50 front/rear torque split. The base sedan gets 17-inch wheels; manual-shift coupes receive upgraded brakes and 18-inch wheels; the sedan variant gets a limited-slip differential. **2005**—Automatic transmission–equipped sedans share the coupe's 280 hp V6, while manual-equipped models have 18 more horses (298 hp). The all-wheel-drive G35x comes with an automatic transmission only. Models using a manual tranny use a standard limited-slip differential and sport suspension. **2006**—Very little new, except for a keyless entry/engine-start system. **2007**—Sedan gets a bit more power and new styling, while the coupe stands pat. **2008**—Debut of the G37 Coupe. **2009**—All "G-cars" are now G37s. They have upgraded transmissions, a bit more horsepower, and an AWD option.

I30/I35

Introduced as an early '96 model, the I30 is a sport sedan spin-off of the Nissan Maxima with additional sound-deadening material and a plusher interior. The car's interior is also roomier, but its ride is unimpressive and handling is compromised by excessive body lean when cornering. Engine and road noises are omnipresent. The redesigned 2000 model adds rear seatroom and reduces body lean considerably. I35s have a quieter and better-performing engine, a much improved ride, and more responsive handling.

VEHICLE HISTORY: 2002—Renamed the I35 and given a larger V6 engine, new styling, and more standard features.

The more-recently minted I35 models elicited more performance-related complaints than the earlier I30, which was no paragon of quality control. I30 owners report chronic suspension failures, drivetrain vibration and clunking, faulty steering, and defective transverse links, springs, and struts. I35s are known for vibration, loose steering, drivetrain noise, rattling noises, electrical shorts, excessive front-end play, incorrect fuel gauge readings, inoperative seat memory buttons, and hesitation and surging when accelerating.

Q45

Faster and glitzier than other cars in its category, this luxury sedan provides performance, while its chief rival, the Lexus LS 400, provides luxury and quiet. Up to the '96 model, the Q45 used a 32-valve 278 hp 4.5L V8 tire-burner not frequently found on a Japanese luxury compact. It accelerates faster than the Lexus, going 0–100 km/h in 7.1 seconds without a hint of noise or abrupt shifting. Unlike the base engine of the G20, though, the Q45's engine supplies plenty of upper-range torque as well. That potent powerhouse was dropped with the less-than-dazzling 1997–2001 models' 266 hp 4.1L V8. High-performance power was rediscovered, however, when the 2002–06 models returned to a more-powerful 340 hp 4.5L V8. The suspension was softened in 1994, but the car still rides much more firmly than its Lexus counterpart. The four-wheel steering is precise, but the standard limited-slip differential is no help in preventing the car's rear end from sliding out on slippery roads, mainly because of the original-equipment "sport" tires, which were designed for 190 km/h autobahn cruising. ABS is standard. There's not much footroom for passengers, and cargo room is disappointing. Fuel economy is nonexistent.

VEHICLE HISTORY: 2002—A new 4.5L V8 produces 340 hp (up from 266 hp). The transmission is a 5-speed automatic with a manual shift mode. High-end electronics are standard, including traction control, Vehicle Dynamic Control, Electronic Brake Force Distribution, tire-pressure monitors, and high-intensity xenon headlights. **2003**—A rear-axle upgrade for faster and smoother acceleration. **2004**—A rear-view camera. **2005**—A minor facelift and a recalibrated transmission for smoother shifts.

The Q45 has been exceptionally reliable throughout its model run, despite some reports of electronic computer module malfunctions and crashes, premature AC failures, power-steering problems, excessive wind noise around the A-pillars, sunroof wind leaks, and tire thumping. Paint is easily scratched and flakes off. Now that the car has been off the market for six years, parts are harder to find and independent repairers are reluctant to fool with the electronics, hence its Average rating.

M35, M45

The 2003 M45 replaced the I30/I35 as Infiniti's mid-size, rear-drive luxury car. Powered by a 340 hp V8 engine and coupled to a 5-speed automatic transmission, the first three model years sold poorly primarily due to the car's bland design and cramped interior. The redesigned 2006 and 2007 models offer more interior room and high-tech features, like four-wheel steering, upgraded brakes, a performance-tuned suspension/transmission, and a V8 with more pep despite 15 fewer horses. M35 sedans use a 275 hp V6 that's available with rear-drive or all-wheel drive.

Owners complain of excessive oil consumption, poor tire performance with the Michelin Pilots, and a host of other problems:

> [p]erforated leather seats had mesh coming out, CD changer jammed, AC compressor busted, belts on the motor had to be replaced, glove box had to be readjusted, hood had to be readjusted to stop the squeaking when closing the doors, front window guides and stabilizer-inner door had to be replaced to stop all the squealing when

letting the windows up/down…. [I had to] schedule another visit to see if the engine/ exhaust problem could be repaired. The dealership had my car for 3 weeks…and cleaned out the combustion chamber at their cost and the day I got it back, it was still smoking out the pipes. The dealership says they know nothing else to do but to replace the motor if it's consuming oil.

Safety Summary

G20: **2001**—Brake failure. • Brake rotors glaze over and need turning. • Airbags fail to deploy. *G35:* **2003**—When the AC is engaged and the brakes applied, the vehicle accelerates. • Early automatic transmission replacement. • Poor upshifting from First gear. • Loss of front braking capability. • Premature wearout of brake pads and rotors. • Rear window shatters suddenly. • Seat belt cuts across the neck of small-statured drivers. • Driver's seat rocks back and forth. • Rear defroster takes forever to work. **2004**—Sudden acceleration due to pedal sticking, or when the speed control is engaged. • Transmission failures and premature brake replacement still dominate owner complaints. • Parking brake won't secure vehicle on an incline. • In one incident, ABS system locked up, flipping the car and killing the driver and two passengers. • Michelin Pilot tires perform poorly in winter conditions. • Heated air is constantly drawn in from the engine compartment. **2005**—Speed control causes the car to suddenly accelerate. Car also accelerates when brakes are applied. • Brake failure. • Car pulls to the right (service bulletins were issued for this problem, affecting 2003 and 2004 models). **2006**—Fire believed to have been caused by a defective seat heater. • Cruise control causes car to suddenly accelerate. • Stuck fuel-filler door. • Tail/brake lights are too bright; blind following drivers. **2007**—Passenger-side airbag is disabled when average-sized adult is seated. • Vehicle often hesitates when accelerating. • Dynamic Control system suddenly engages, causing the car to speed up and veer to the right. • Car seems to be constantly braking when going downhill with the cruise control engaged. • Manual transmission clutch sticks to the floor due to insufficient pressure in the line. • Sunroof explodes. • Defective Goodyear Eagle RS-A tires. • Driver-side automatic window won't go up, or operates very slowly. • Intelligent Key failures. *G37:* **2008–09**—Vehicle suddenly accelerates when brakes applied while parking:

> Experienced over six weeks five incidents of engine speed increase when braking as described by Infiniti in their bulletin ITB07-048. Reprogramming the 2008 G37 per this bulletin was unsuccessful. Dealer claims no problem because they cannot verify.

2008—Sidewall tears on the original-equipment Bridgestone tires. **2009**—Faulty electronic control module leads to engine suddenly losing power. • Severe brake judder:

> Technical Service Bulletin ITB09-037 from Infiniti states overheating of the brakes can cause judder. They recommend installing a brake backing plate, resurfacing, or replacing the rotors. I took my car to my Infiniti dealer and the plate was installed. The front rotors were resurfaced, brake pads replaced, and I still had the brake judder.

I took it back and they resurfaced the rear rotors and recommended balancing and rotating tires. I did this (at my own cost) and the brake judder is still present. The car had 15,000 miles when the problem occurred. I feel a mandatory replacement of the rotors and the pads at the same time is required. The warped rotors continue to cause vibration after resurfacing and my dealer will not replace them at cost.

• Owner says rodents are snacking on his car's wiring:

2009 Infiniti G37 has electrical wiring insulation made of soy-based polymer. Soy based polymer is apparently biodegradable. The problem is that it is also attractive to rodents, who eat the wiring, creating electrical safety hazards. In addition to the safety hazards, it also creates an economic stressor on consumers and insurers who have to pay for repairs done to these automobiles, which Infiniti claims is not covered under any existing warranty.

I30/I35: **2000–01**—Sudden, unintended acceleration. **2001**—Rear suspension fails. • Cruise control won't disengage when brakes are applied. **2002**—Airbags fail to deploy. • Steering wheel pulls sharply to one side when accelerating. • Poor braking. • Stalling. *M35:* **2006**—Brake failure. • Steering is hard to control; car wanders all over the road. • Emergency spare tire makes the car undrivable. • Driver seat frame stress crack. • Tire tread separates. • Leaky sunroof. *Q45:* **2001**—Sudden acceleration when vehicle is shifted into Reverse gear. **2002**—Excessive vibration caused by bent original-equipment wheels. **2004**—Laser-controlled cruise control abruptly cuts power when passing another vehicle and doesn't work in rain or when driving into the sun at sunset.

Secret Warranties/Internal Bulletins/Service Tips

All models/years: Troubleshooting tips to correct brake pedal judder and hard starts. • Windshield cracking. • Sunroof wind noise. • Erratic operation of the power antenna. *G20:* **1999–2001**—Power seat won't move, or makes a grinding noise. **2001–02**—Rear brake caliper clunk, rattle, or knock. *G35:* **2003–06**—No-starts in cold weather. **2005**—Dash squeak and rattle repair. **2005–06**—Gap between glove compartment and dash. *I30/I35:* **2000–01**—No-starts may be caused by a faulty engine wire harness. • Transmission slippage. • Troubleshooting tips to correct self-locking doors. **2000–04**—Poor transmission performance. **2001–02**—Rear brake caliper clunk, rattle, or knock. **2002**—Faulty sunroof. **2002–03**—Upgraded brake pads to reduce brake judder or other anomalies. *M45:* **2003–04**—A ticking or thumping noise coming from the engine area may signal that fuel damper assembly should be replaced. • Diagnosing and correcting an engine knocking or tapping noise. *Q45:* **2002**—Engine hesitation. • Steering pull to the right; excessive vibration. • Difficult to move shift lever. • Front suspension noise. • Trunk lid hard to close. • Poor AC performance. **2002–03**—Incorrect shifting. **2002–04**—Remedy for engine knocking after a cold start. **2002–06**—Ticking, thumping noise at idle. **2004–06**—Tire-pressure monitoring system sensor seal leaks.

G20/G35, I30/I35, M35/M45, Q45 PROFILE

	2001	2002	2003	2004	2005	2006	2007	2008	2009
Cost Price ($)									
G20	29,900	29,900	—	—	—	—	—	—	—
G35 Sedan	—	—	38,900	39,600	39,900	39,990	39,990	39,990	—
G35 Coupe	—	—	45,000	45,200	46,100	47,000	47,200	—	—
G37 Sedan	—	—	—	—	—	—	—	—	37,090
G37 Coupe	—	—	—	—	—	—	—	47,350	45,200
I30/I35	39,900	39,500	39,700	41,200	—	—	—	—	—
M35	—	—	—	—	54,800	56,100	56,400	49,400	53,700
M45	—	—	62,000	62,000	64,400	65,700	66,000	66,950	67,750
Q45	70,000	73,000	74,900	75,500	88,000	—	—	—	—
Used Values ($)									
G20 ▲	4,000	4,500	—	—	—	—	—	—	—
G20 ▼	3,000	4,000	—	—	—	—	—	—	—
G35 Sedan ▲	—	—	7,500	9,000	10,500	12,500	15,000	20,000	—
G35 Sedan ▼	—	—	6,000	8,000	9,500	11,000	13,500	18,500	—
G35 Coupe ▲	—	—	9,500	11,500	12,500	14,000	17,000	—	—
G35 Coupe ▼	—	—	8,000	10,500	11,500	12,500	15,500	—	—
G37 Sedan ▲	—	—	—	—	—	—	—	—	25,000
G37 Sedan ▼	—	—	—	—	—	—	—	—	23,500
G37 Coupe ▲	—	—	—	—	—	—	—	22,500	28,000
G37 Coupe ▼	—	—	—	—	—	—	—	21,000	26,500
I30/I35 ▲	3,000	4,000	5,000	7,000	—	—	—	—	—
I30/I35 ▼	3,000	3,500	4,000	6,000	—	—	—	—	—
M35 ▲	—	—	—	—	13,000	15,000	18,500	23,500	31,000
M35 ▼	—	—	—	—	11,500	13,500	17,000	22,000	29,500
M45 ▲	—	—	11,000	13,000	15,000	16,500	21,000	30,000	40,000
M45 ▼	—	—	9,500	11,500	13,500	15,000	19,500	28,000	38,000
Q45 ▲	9,000	11,000	13,000	14,500	17,000	—	—	—	—
Q45 ▼	7,500	9,500	11,500	13,500	15,500	—	—	—	—
Reliability	2	2	2	2	3	3	3	4	4
Crash Safety (F)									
G37 4d	—	—	—	—	—	—	—	—	5
I30/I35	—	4	4	4	—	—	—	—	—
Side									
G37 4d	—	—	—	—	—	—	—	—	5
I30/I35	4	4	4	4	—	—	—	—	—

All ratings on a numbered scale where 5 is good and **1** is bad. See page 132 for a more detailed description.

IIHS Side									
G35	—	—	—	—	—	3	5	5	5
Offset									
G35	—	—	5	5	5	5	5	5	—
G37	—	—	—	—	—	—	—	5	5
I30/I35	3	3	3	3	—	—	—	—	—
Q45	2	—	6	6	6	—	—	—	—
Head Restraints									
G20	1	1	—	—	—	—	—	—	—
G35	—	—	—	—	1	1	2	2	—
G37	—	—	—	—	—	—	2	2	2
Q45	—	—	—	—	2	—	—	—	—
Rollover Resistance									
G37 4d	—	—	—	—	—	—	—	—	5
I35	—	4	4	4	—	—	—	—	—

Kia

AMANTI, MAGENTIS ★★★/★★★★

RATING: *Amanti:* Average (2007); Below Average (2004–06). *Magentis:* Above Average (2007); Average (2005–06); Below Average (2001–04). With these two vehicles, you want to avoid the early models and go for a V6-powered Magentis; the 4-cylinder version is a dog. **Ideal model year:** A 2009 Magentis LX V6 that originally sold for $24,295 is the best buy for $14,000. The low price, added features, better performance, and likelihood of some non-expired warranty all work in your favour. **"Real" city/highway fuel economy:** *2.4:* 10.9/7.2 L/100 km. *V6:* 11.7/7.9 L/100 km. Owners say they use about 10 percent more fuel than these estimates indicate. **Maintenance/Repair costs:** Average. **Parts:** Average costs, but parts aren't widely available yet. **Extended warranty:** A good idea only if you plan to keep the car more than five years. **Best alternatives:** A loaded Honda Accord, Nissan Maxima, and Toyota Camry. **Helpful websites:** *www.8thcivic.com/forums/mechanical-problems-technical-chat.*

Strengths and Weaknesses

Amanti

Carrying the Hyundai XG350's 3.5L V6 and 5-speed manumatic transmission, the 2004 Amanti is Kia's first large sedan. Amanti's styling is different from the XG350's, though, and it sits on a 5 cm longer wheelbase and a 10 cm longer body, giving it about 180 additional kilograms that erode overall handling, on-road performance, and fuel economy. The car comes with a modicum of safety and convenience features, like anti-lock four-wheel disc brakes, front and rear side airbags, side curtain airbags, dual-zone climate control, keyless entry, and power front seats. Unfortunately, the much-recommended traction/anti-skid control is offered only as an option.

2006 models got additional standard features that included power front seats, leather upholstery, heated front seats, and a sunroof. The following year, the car's 200 hp V6 was replaced by a more-powerful 264 hp 3.8L V6, the suspension firmed up, and the interior and exterior styling were updated. On the downside, Kia dropped the standard leather upholstery, heated front seats, and sunroof. 2008 models returned unchanged and 2009 models got a new audio system.

Amanti reliability has been worse than average, characterized by rapid brake and tire wear, electrical short circuits (Airbag light is constantly lit), chronic front-end noise, and fuel problems that cause the engine to start poorly, suddenly shut down, jerk when accelerating, or hesitate and then surge. Fit and finish is also problematic, with owners complaining of multiple water and air leaks.

Amanti highway performance is very disappointing. Engine power is unreliable, steering is imprecise, handling is clumsy, and body roll is excessive.

Magentis

Sold in the States as the Optima, this front-drive, five-passenger sedan is basically a Hyundai Sonata without traction control. The Magentis comes with a twin-cam 138 hp 2.4L 4-cylinder or an optional 170 hp 2.7L V6 hooked to a 4-speed automatic transmission (V6s have the Sonata's separate gate for manual shifting and four-wheel ABS). Other standard features include tinted glass, a tilt steering column, front seat belt pretensioners, a 60/40 split-folding rear seat, and independent double wishbone front suspension and independent multi-link rear suspension.

The Magentis is nicely appointed, provides good V6 performance with the 5-speed automatic, handles competently, and rides comfortably. There's also plenty of front headroom and better-than-average fuel economy with regular fuel. The car is a bit better built than Kia's other models, but fit and finish is still inferior to other Asian makes.

Unfortunately, this car has some major weaknesses that include mediocre braking; limited rear headroom; a small trunk opening; faulty door locks that trap occupants; considerable body lean when turning; excessive tire, wind, and suspension noise; a poorly performing 4-speed automatic transmission; a wimpy 2.4L 162 hp 4-cylinder engine; and a weak dealer network. Owner complaints deal primarily with harsh shifts, stalling, brake failures, faulty door locks, poor servicing, electrical shorts, AC overheating, subpar fit and finish, premature brake pad and rotor wear, and sudden acceleration (maybe wimpy is good).

VEHICLE HISTORY: *Magentis:* **2002**—A larger V6 engine with a gain of 8 horses and 15-inch wheels; SE sedans adopt standard automatic headlights. **2003**—Refreshed interior and exterior styling that includes new audio and climate controls, a new grille and hood, larger body mouldings, and restyled tail lights. **2004**—Larger wheels and a newly designed grille. **2009**—Restyled and more power. Entry-level models come with a 175 hp 2.4L 4-cylinder engine. A 194 hp 2.7L V6 is available on the EX and SX. Horsepower gains are minimal.

Safety Summary

All models/years: Airbags fail to deploy; warning light stays lit. • Poor engine, fuel system, and transmission performance. • Hesitation and surging. • Sudden acceleration. *Amanti:* **2004**—Fuel leaks when fuelling gas tank. • Engine hesitates and then surges when foot is taken off the gas pedal. • Car tends to surge just after a fill-up. • Car jerks when accelerating. • Engine sludge leads to chronic stalling. • Hard starts. • Accelerator and brake pedals are mounted too close together. • Power steering goes from insensitive to oversensitive. • Headlights blow out frequently. • Driver-side mirror wobbles in the wind. **2005**—Many complaints that the car still "lags and lurches." • Premature rear tire wear. **2006**—Repeated failure of the front suspension control arm. • Driver's power seat moves forward by itself. **2007**—Bright dashboard trim reflects onto driver-side mirror. • Sunroof shatters. **2008**—Driver's mirror adjustment memory setting works erratically. • Throttle is too aggressive and results in car jumping forward with just a light pressure on the gas pedal. *Magentis:* **2001**—Chronic hesitation, stalling, and surging. • Transmission failures. • Excessive AC condensation in the interior. • Inaccurate fuel gauge. • Faulty door locks. **2002**—Delayed acceleration. • Sudden stalling while cruising on the highway. • Complete brake failure. • Windows won't go down. • Faulty door locks. **2003**—Accelerator sticks. • Sudden loss of power. • Brake failures. • Vehicle starts on its own. • Rainy weather causes the car to run roughly. • Large rear-view mirror blocks visibility. • Inoperative headlight high beams. • Doors lock and unlock on their own. • Sticking door locks trap occupants. **2004**—Fire ignites in the dashboard area. • Suspension pulls vehicle into oncoming traffic. • Engine surges when manual transmission is shifted from Second to Third gear. • Vehicle suddenly loses power. • Power-steering leaks. • Delayed acceleration. • Leaking fuel regulator. • Mud compromises EGR valve performance. • Inoperative cruise control. **2005**—Defective steering assembly causes the vehicle to suddenly veer right. • Faulty high-beam headlights. **2006**—Passenger-side airbag won't work if a small adult occupies the seat. • Headlights frequently burn out. • Sometimes the transmission won't downshift. **2007**—Broken engine crankshaft pulley and drive belt. • Vehicle won't shift into Park. • Parking brake cable failure costs $750. • Premature wearout of brake pads and rotor. • Rear brakes make a grinding sound. • Cannot take key out of ignition. • When refuelling, fuel spurts out of the filler pipe. • Sun visors fall down. **2007–08**—Passenger-side airbag is disabled when an average-sized adult is seated in the front passenger seat. **2008**—Chronic stalling when underway. • Insufficient low-beam illumination and headlights dim at low speeds, or when applying the brakes. **2009**—When the automatic transmission downshifts it slams into gear:

> Bought a 2009 Kia Optima a few months ago and recently it has developed a dangerous shifting pattern when down shifting from 2nd to 1st about 20mph it jerks the !@#$%¿ out of you and if you happen to be braking at the time you meet a snap from the seat belt as you fly towards windshield causing severe neck and back pain. [T]his is getting worse, dealers willing to fix but Kia is ignoring the issue as I have heard of others having same problem.

• Oil pump failure; took two weeks to get a replacement. • Instrument panel gauges wash out in daylight.

Secret Warranties/Internal Bulletins/Service Tips

Amanti: **2004**—Suspension noise when passing over uneven surfaces. **2004–09**—Front door armrest trim peeling, wrinkled. **2005–06**—Computer module upgrade to correct engine's poor performance. **2006–07**—Reducing suspension noise, especially when braking. **2007**—Engine hesitation and surging fix. • Measures to reduce engine and exhaust noise. *Magentis:* **2001–06**—Correcting engine hesitation by changing the throttle position sensor values. **2003–04**—Hesitation when accelerating can also be corrected by recalibrating the engine control module. **2009–10**—Troubleshooting passenger-side airbag malfunction that disables the airbag for no reason. **2009**—Rattling fuel caps will be replaced free of charge under Campaign SA006.

AMANTI, MAGENTIS PROFILE

	2001	2002	2003	2004	2005	2006	2007	2008	2009
Cost Price ($)									
Amanti	—	—	—	34,995	35,995	30,995	31,995	37,195	29,995
Magentis LX	20,995	21,295	22,250	22,250	22,450	22,450	21,895	21,895	21,195
LX V6	23,995	24,295	25,750	25,750	25,850	25,850	23,995	24,195	24,295
SE/EX V6	27,995	29,095	28,750	28,750	28,850	28,850	—	—	—
Used Values ($)									
Amanti ▲	—	—	—	5,000	6,500	9,000	12,500	16,000	17,500
Amanti ▼	—	—	—	4,000	5,500	7,500	11,000	14,500	16,000
Magentis LX ▲	2,500	3,000	3,500	4,000	5,000	7,000	9,000	11,500	14,000
Magentis LX ▼	2,000	2,500	3,000	3,500	4,500	6,000	7,500	10,000	12,500
LX V6 ▲	3,500	4,000	4,500	5,500	6,500	8,000	9,500	12,000	14,500
LX V6 ▼	3,000	3,500	4,000	5,000	6,000	7,000	8,500	10,500	13,000
SE/EX V6 ▲	7,000	8,500	10,500	13,000	15,500	12,000	—	—	—
SE/EX V6 ▼	6,000	7,000	9,000	11,500	14,000	10,500	—	—	—

Reliability	2	2	2	2	2	3	3	4	4
Crash Safety (F)									
Magentis	—	—	4	4	4	4	5	5	5
Side (Magentis)	—	—	—	4	4	4	5	5	5
Amanti	—	—	—	—	—	4	5	—	—
IIHS Side (Amanti)	1	1	1	1	1	3	5	5	5
Offset (Amanti)	—	—	—	5	5	5	5	5	5
Magentis	3	3	3	3	3	5	5	5	5
Head Restraints									
(Amanti)	—	—	—	—	3	3	2	2	2
Megantis	1	1	1	1	1	5	5	5	5
Rollover Resistance									
Magentis	—	—	5	5	5	—	5	5	5

Lexus

ES 300/330/350, GS 300/350/430/450H/460, IS 250/300/350, LS 400/430/460/600H, SC 300, SC 400/430 ★★★

RATING: Average (1999–2009). A bit more refined than the Infinitis, Lexus' lineup offers first-class performance but only average reliability. The powertrain is prone to dangerous stalling and surging, and the Lexus' rating has been downgraded because of serious design deficiencies relating to sudden acceleration, poor braking, and a chronic engine/transmission stumble, shudder, and surge. **Ideal model year:** Get a 2007 ES 350 for about $18,000. It comes with lots of powertrain improvements, but a fix for sudden unintended acceleration was not one of them. Ask the seller to throw in a rabbit's foot (or maybe the whole rabbit). **"Real" city/highway fuel economy:** *ES 300:* 12.3/8.2 L/100 km. *ES 330:* 11.6/7.5 L/100 km. *GS 300:* 13.1/8.6 L/100 km. *GS 400:* 13.4/9.4 L/100 km. *GS 430:* 13.3/9.3 L/100 km. *IS 300 manual:* 13.2/8.8 L/100 km. *IS 300 automatic:* 13.1/8.9 L/100 km. *LS 430:* 13.2/8.6 L/100 km. *LX 470:* 17.9/12.9 L/100 km. Real-world fuel savings may be lower by about 10–15 percent. The ES 330 burns less fuel than its ES 300 predecessor, even though the ES 300 is equipped with a smaller, 3.0L engine. **Maintenance/Repair costs:** Higher-than-average costs, and repairs are highly dealer-dependent. **Parts:** Expensive, but parts aren't hard to find (except body panels). **Extended warranty:** Not necessary. **Best alternatives:** Look at the fully equipped Acura Legend, Honda Accord, Hyundai Genesis, Infiniti G35, and early Nissan Maxima, to provide airbags, comparable highway performance, and reliability at far less initial cost—but without the Lexus cachet. **Helpful websites:** *www.clublexus.com/forums/es350-180.*

Strengths and Weaknesses

These are benchmark cars known for their comfort, convenience features, and good looks. Sports cars, they're not. But if you're looking for your father's Oldsmobile from a Japanese automaker, these luxury cars fit the bill. Like Acuras and Infinitis, Lexus models all suffer from some automatic transmission failures; engine sludge buildup (see *www.consumeraffairs.com/news04/2007/01/toyota_sludge_settlement.html*); early rear main engine seal and front strut replacements (front struts are often replaced under a "goodwill" warranty); and front brake, electrical, body, trim, and accessory deficiencies.

ES 300/330/350

Resembling an LS 400 dressed in sporty attire, the entry-level ES 300 was launched in 1992 to fill the gap between the discontinued ES 250 and the LS 400. In fact, the ES 300 has many of the attributes of the LS 400 sedan but sells for much less money. A five-passenger sedan based on the Camry, but 90 kg (200 lb.) heavier and with a different suspension and tires, it comes equipped with a standard 3.0L 24-valve engine that produces 181–210 horses coupled to either a 5-speed manual or a 4-speed electronically controlled automatic transmission. Like some Infiniti models, however, the ES 300 hesitates and surges when accelerating. Headroom is also surprisingly limited for a car this expensive.

ES 330s came on the scene as 2004 models and offered buyers a more-powerful 3.3L V6 that produced more horses and a bit more torque. 2005 models got very little that was new, except for power front seats with a memory feature and power door mirrors that tilt down when in Reverse.

The 2007 ES 350 arrived with new styling, more power, and additional features, but it remained an upscale Toyota Camry. It has a slightly larger wheelbase and a new 6-speed transmission, and is powered by a 272 hp 3.5L V6 instead of the ES 330's 218 hp 3.3L V6. Standard features include anti-lock braking, traction/anti-skid control, front side airbags, side curtain airbags, and front knee airbags. ES 350 competes against the Acura TL, BMW 3 Series, Cadillac CTS, and Infiniti G35.

VEHICLE HISTORY: *ES 300/330/350:* **2002**—A longer, taller body; new 5-speed automatic transmission; improved brakes, steering, and suspension; and more standard luxury features. No more standard traction control. **2004**—ES 330 (designating a 3.3L engine) debuts with 15 extra horses and larger head-protecting side airbags. **2007**—ES 350 debuts. **2008**—Modified mirrors; no big deal.

Government-reported safety-related defects are surprisingly omnipresent. These reports include airbag-induced injuries; sudden acceleration; an unreliable powertrain that surges, stumbles, stalls, and shifts erratically; ABS and Goodyear tire failures; excessive vibration when underway; interior window fogging; unreadable dash gauges; poor AC performance; and a frequently disconnecting Bluetooth.

GS 300/350/430/450h

The rear-drive GS 300 is a step up from the front-drive ES 300 and just a rung below Lexus' top-of-the-line LS 400. It carries the same V6 engine as the ES 300, except that it has 20 more horses. This produces sparkling performance at higher speeds, though the car is disappointingly sluggish from a start. Fuel economy is sacrificed for performance, however, and the base suspension and tires pass noisily over small bumps and ruts. Visibility is also less than impressive, with large rear pillars and a narrow rear window restricting the view. There's not much usable trunk space, and the liftover is unreasonably high.

VEHICLE HISTORY: 2001—Substantially upgraded with a 300 hp 4.3L V8, upgraded transmission controls, standard side curtain airbags, smart airbags, an emergency trunk release, and a host of other convenience features. **2006**—More power, fresh styling, a larger interior, and all-wheel drive. The rear-drive and all-wheel-drive GS 300s get a 245 hp V6 engine. The rear-drive GS 430 keeps its 300 hp V8. All models use a 6-speed automatic manumatic transmission, anti-skid/traction control, and anti-lock brakes. The GS 430 adds driver-adjustable shock absorbers and 18-inch wheels. Run-flat tires (more a boondoggle than a boon) are standard with AWD. All models have front knee airbags, front torso side airbags, and head-protecting side curtain airbags. **2007**—Entry-level models get a new 3.5L V6 that produces 303 hp, up from 245 hp with the prior 3.0L. In fact, the added horsepower beats the V8 by 13 horses, though the V8 is torquier. The lineup now: GS 350, GS 430, and GS 450h hybrid. **2008**—A slight restyling and a more powerful engine. The new engine powering the GS 460 is a 342 hp 4.6L V8 hooked to an 8-speed automatic transmission.

Owner complaints have centered on brake failures, electrical shutdowns, prematurely worn wheel bearings, excessive front-end vibrations, fragile wheel rims, run-flat tire problems (cost, availability, performance, and durability), and electrical and fuel system malfunctions resulting in hesitation followed by sudden, unintended acceleration ("lag and lurch").

IS 250/300/350

Targeting BMW's 3 Series, this rear-drive sports-compact sedan comes with similar power and features to the BMW 325i—for a few thousand dollars less, in the case of the IS 250. Moreover, there is practically no difference in fuel economy between the manual and automatic transmission modes. The only engine is a 215 hp 3.0L inline-six (borrowed from the GS 300) mated to a 5-speed automatic transmission and incorporating Lexus' E-shift feature for manual shifting. Other important features are four-wheel ABS-equipped disc brakes, 17-inch wheels, performance tires, front seat belt pretensioners, and traction control. Just a bit narrower than the BMW 3 Series, the IS 300 is a competent performer both for routine tasks and in emergency situations. Look for models equipped with a limited-slip differential, but don't pay more for models featuring a sunroof, heated seats, or leather upholstery.

VEHICLE HISTORY: 2002—A SportCross wagon is added, which comes with an automatic transmission only. Manual-shift sedans have a firmer suspension; ABS is upgraded; side curtain/front side airbags and traction control are standard. **2006**—After dropping the slow-selling wagon, Lexus revamps its sporty small sedan along the lines of the larger GS sedans, creating two rear-drive models and an all-wheel-drive version: the IS 250 and IS 250 AWD, equipped with a 204 hp V6, and the IS 350, powered by a 306 hp V6. All IS models come loaded with the latest high-tech safety and performance features to compete primarily against the Acura TSX, BMW 3 Series, and Infiniti G35. **2008**—Debut of the IS F, featuring a 416 hp 5.0L V8. **2009**—A modest restyling and a retuned suspension.

In a nutshell, these cars stand out with a comfortable ride; a nice array of standard features; quality-looking gauges; good acceleration, handling, and braking; a low beltline for a great view; and first-class workmanship. On the other hand, rear seating is a bit cramped; the car requires premium fuel; owners report excessive road noise and tire thump; the instrument panel reflects in the windshield; seat cushions don't provide adequate thigh support; no crashworthiness data is available; trunk hinges eat up trunk space and may damage luggage; the interior doesn't feel as plush as the competition's; and the automatic transmission's manual E-shift is awkward to use and isn't as sporty as a BMW's. Other cars worth considering are the Acura TL and BMW's 3 Series.

LS 400/430/460

The Lexus flagship, the LS 400 rear-drive arrived in 1990 with a 250 hp 4.0L V8. It outclasses all other luxury sedans in reliability, styling, and function. Its powerful engine provides smooth, impressive acceleration and a superior highway passing ability at all speeds. Its transmission is smooth and efficient. The suspension gives an easy ride without body roll or front-end plow during emergency stops, delivering a major comfort advantage over other luxury compacts. Other amenities include anti-lock brakes, a driver-side airbag, and automatic temperature control.

VEHICLE HISTORY: 2001—Totally redesigned with a sleeker body, a 4.3L V8, an upgraded suspension, and a more-spacious, reworked interior. Additional safety and comfort features are also added. **2003**—A firmer suspension and 17-inch wheels. **2004**—A 6-speed manumatic transmission, driver's knee-protecting airbags, steering-linked headlights, a power rear sunshade, and a tire-pressure monitor are added. Suspension, steering, and ABS systems are also upgraded. **2007**—A redesigned LS 460 gains a long-wheelbase body style, more power, and the industry's first 8-speed automatic transmission, plus a basketful of high-tech safety, performance, and convenience features. Two models are offered: the regular-sized LS 460, which is slightly longer and wider than the 2001–06 models, and the LS 460 L, which is even larger. The 278 hp 4.3L V8 is replaced by a 380 hp 4.6L V8, hence the name change from the LS 430 to the LS 460. The additional power and larger dimensions clearly target the car's main rivals: the Audi A8, BMW 7 Series, and Mercedes-Benz S-Class. **2008**—Debut of the LS 600h a hybrid variant, equipped with a 389 hp 5.0L V8 and two motor generators that boost output to 438 horses.

Here's an important downside: the brakes don't inspire confidence, owing to their mushy feel and average performance. Furthermore, there's limited rear footroom under the front seats, and the rear middle passenger has to sit on the transmission hump. Plus, this car is a gas-guzzler that thirsts for premium fuel.

Owner complaints over the years deal mainly with spongy brakes; main computer failures; electrical glitches; door locks that stick shut, trapping occupants; sudden, unintended acceleration; stalling caused by a faulty throttle sensor; failure of the Vehicle Stability Control to activate; and traction control that causes the vehicle to swerve unexpectedly (usually to the left).

SC 300, SC 400/430

These two coupes are practically identical, except for their engines and luxury features. The cheaper SC 300 gives you the same high-performance 6-cylinder engine used by the GS 300 and Toyota Supra, while the SC 400 uses the 4.0L V8 engine found in the LS 400. You're likely to find fewer luxury features with the SC 300 because they were sold as options. Nevertheless, look for an SC with traction control for additional safety during poor driving conditions. On the downside, V8 fuel consumption is horrendous, rear seating is cramped, and trunk space is unimpressive. Also, invest in a good anti-theft device, or your Lexus relationship will be over almost before it begins.

VEHICLE HISTORY: 2005—Upgraded shock absorbers and navigation system. **2006**—Addition of a 6-speed automatic transmission. **2007**—Convertibles get front-knee airbags.

Safety Summary

ES 300/330/350: **All years:** Sudden, unintended acceleration. **2001**—In one incident, engine fire ignited from what investigator said was fuel leaking from a rubber hose that had disconnected from the fuel filter. • Car suddenly accelerates as driver slows coming to a stop sign or when pulling into a parking space. • Traction control engages much too easily when merging into traffic. • One vehicle started up and began moving down the street in Reverse, despite the fact that there was no key in the ignition cylinder and the vehicle was left in Park. • Vehicle hesitates when applying accelerator after decelerating. **2002**—Airbags fail to deploy. • Impossible to read speedometer and other gauges in sunlight. • Won't go into gear properly. • Warped brake rotors. **2002–03**—Chronic engine/transmission surging and stalling not fixed by computer module recalibration, switching to premium fuel, etc. **2004**—Sudden acceleration; brake failure. • Stuck accelerator. • Delayed shift and surging when accelerating still occurs frequently, despite Toyota's special campaign "fix" that involves changing the electronic module:

> This car is extremely dangerous. It's either a defective transmission or bad drive-by-wire design. The car hesitates extremely badly on acceleration. For example, when you are entering a limited access highway, if you slow down and then step on the gas, there is a long lag before the car begins to pick up speed. This lag is often a second or more. I have nearly been hit numerous times while the car makes up its mind whether it wants to move or not. The dealer has refused to fix the problem.

• Transmission goes into Reverse when shifted into Drive. • Vehicle lunges forward when transmission is shifted into Reverse. • Steering pulls vehicle into oncoming traffic. • Passenger-side airbag is disabled when adult of any weight sits in the front passenger seat. • Serious blind spots caused by side rear-view mirrors. **2005**—Hesitation and then surging continues to be a major complaint category. • Sudden loss of braking capability. **2006**—Car suddenly accelerated and killed a pedestrian. • Vehicle lags and lurches. • Headlight range is too short; HID lights may ignite on impact. **2007**—Airbag on passenger side is disabled when a small adult occupies the seat. • Sudden acceleration when cruise control is engaged. • Automatic transmission flares even though foot is taken off the accelerator (car suddenly accelerates). **2008**—Car suddenly accelerated as it was being parked:

> I had almost finished parking my '08 Lexus ES 350 in a parking place at a business park when it surged forward very fast. I had not touched the accelerator. I braked hard, but the car went up over a cement divider and crashed into the car parked facing me. I had had the car one and a half years, and this was the first time it happened. I had it towed to the Lexus dealership. An inspector found nothing wrong externally, but the EDR showed I had not stepped on the accelerator before the crash, only the brake, and yet it had surged forward. I had taken the car in earlier for the recall, and had removed the mat and had something added to the software. I sold the car back to Lexus immediately as I never wanted to step foot in it again. This is a very dangerous car, and something is wrong with the electronics to cause this.

• Airbags fail to deploy. • Lost steering control while underway. • Door locks open by themselves. **2009**—More sudden acceleration complaints:

> When I was going to park my car in the box in front of the hotel room, I touched the accelerator slightly to advance the two meters distant to be properly parked, then the accelerator run in high speed the brakes did not respond. To reduce the impact, I turned the wheel to the right and crashed into the hotel wall.

• A fuel smell permeates the interior. • Headlights are too dim. • Windows and sunroof open by themselves. • Frequent security system false alarms. • Fuel in gas tank makes a thumping noise when the car accelerates. *GS 300:* **2002**—Fire ignites from fuel filter leak. • Sticking accelerator. • Vehicle starts without key. • Traction control engages too easily. • Inadequate headlight illumination. • Digital dash indicator washes out in sunlight. **2003**—Sudden, unintended acceleration and hesitation when accelerating. *GS 350:* **2007**—Vehicle crashed into a brick wall after suddenly accelerating. • Floormat caused accelerator pedal to stick. *GS*

450h: **2007**—Vehicle emits high levels of electromagnetic radiation emanating from the motor and/or generator (causes tingling in the hands and feet, numbness in the face, and dull headaches).

Secret Warranties/Internal Bulletins/Service Tips

All models: 1997–2002—The engine warranty that was extended to eight years to cover engine oil sludge claims (see *www.autosafety.org*) has run out. Nevertheless, a case can be made in small claims court that compensation should still be given because a luxury car of this caliber should have a more durable engine. **2002**—Harsh 2–3 shift. • Troubleshooting steering pull and interior squeaks and rattles. **2002–03**—TSB #TC004-03, issued August 4, 2003, gives recalibration instructions for correcting erratic shifting. This free repair is in effect for 96 months/128,000 km (80,000 mi.). • Unreadable dash gauges. • Body creak or snap from top of front windshield. **2002–04**—Inoperative AC. **2002–05**—Countermeasures for poor shift quality. **2002–06**—Troubleshooting tips for vehicles that pull to one side when underway. • Inoperative rear power window. **2003–05**—Steering clunk, pop. **2003–06**—Windshield ticking noise. **2004**—Troubleshooting tips for a malfunctioning front-seat occupant seat belt sensor. • Vehicle pulls into oncoming traffic. *ES 350:* **2007–09**—Engine ticking noise. • Upgraded front brake pads will reduce brake pulsation. Toyota TSB #L-SB-0070-09 (June 4, 2009) says the brake pads are covered under the Lexus Comprehensive Warranty. • Sunroof popping or creaking. • Vehicle won't shift out of Park:

MULTIPLE WARNING LAMP/CAN'T SHIFT FROM PARK	
BULLETIN NO.: L-SB-0057-09	DATE: MAY 13, 2009

INTRODUCTION: Some customers may experience multiple warning lights illuminated vehicle not shifting from park to drive and other accessories becoming inoperative after the vehicle has cold soaked in sub-freezing (below 14 F [-10 C]) ambient air temperatures. A new relay and wire harness has been made available to improve this condition.

2007–10—Rubbing noises from rear of vehicle. *GS 300/350:* **2006–10**—Front sway bar thumping noise. *LS 460/600h:* **2007–09**—Side window wind noise at highway speeds. • Rear suspension rattle, knock. • Uncomfortable lower seat cushion. • Squawk from the brake actuator.

ES 300/330/350, GS 300/350/430/450H/460, IS 250/300/350, LS 400/430/460/600H, SC 400/430 PROFILE

	2001	2002	2003	2004	2005	2006	2007	2008	2009
Cost Price ($)									
ES 300/330/350	44,000	43,400	43,800	43,800	43,900	42,900	42,900	42,900	39,950
GS 300/350	60,700	60,700	61,700	61,700	61,700	64,300	59,750	59,900	51,900
GS 430/460	71,300	68,800	69,500	69,500	69,500	74,700	71,300	73,000	63,300

GS 450h	—	—	—	—	—	—	76,900	71,100	62,500
IS 250	—	—	—	—	—	36,300	36,400	31,900	32,350
IS 300/350	40,830	37,820	37,775	37,775	37,990	48,900	49,000	43,350	43,850
IS F	—	—	—	—	—	—	—	64,400	65,300
LS 400/430/460	80,000	81,900	82,800	83,200	84,900	85,700	86,440	86,500	75,900
LS 600h	—	—	—	—	—	—	—	132,000	118,700
SC 400/430	—	84,000	85,500	86,800	89,770	86,800	93,250	93,250	79,900
Used Values ($)									
ES 300/330/350 ▲	6,000	7,000	9,000	11,000	12,500	14,500	19,000	24,000	27,500
ES 300/330/350 ▼	5,500	6,000	7,500	9,500	11,000	13,000	17,500	22,000	26,000
GS 300/350 ▲	8,000	9,000	11,500	13,000	15,000	18,000	23,000	29,000	37,000
GS 300/350 ▼	7,500	8,500	10,000	11,500	13,500	16,500	21,000	27,000	34,000
GS 430/460 ▲	11,500	13,000	15,000	17,000	20,000	22,000	27,000	37,000	45,000
GS 430/460 ▼	10,500	12,000	13,500	15,500	19,500	20,500	24,000	34,000	42,000
GS 450h ▲	—	—	—	—	—	—	26,000	35,000	45,000
GS 450h ▼	—	—	—	—	—	—	24,000	33,000	43,000
IS 250 ▲	—	—	—	—	—	12,500	16,000	20,000	24,000
IS 250 ▼	—	—	—	—	—	11,000	14,500	18,500	22,000
IS 300/350 ▲	8,500	10,000	12,000	14,000	16,000	18,000	19,500	28,000	33,000
IS 300/350 ▼	7,500	9,000	10,500	12,500	15,000	16,500	18,500	26,000	31,000
IS F ▲	—	—	—	—	—	—	—	41,000	49,000
IS F ▼	—	—	—	—	—	—	—	38,000	45,000
LS 400/430/460 ▲	10,000	12,500	14,000	16,000	19,000	23,000	29,000	40,000	51,000
LS 400/430/460 ▼	9,000	11,500	12,500	14,500	17,500	20,500	27,000	36,000	47,000
LS 600h ▲	—	—	—	—	—	—	—	132,000	118,700
LS 600h ▼	—	—	—	—	—	—	—	128,000	114,000
SC 400/430 ▲	—	15,500	18,000	21,000	25,000	30,000	38,000	48,000	56,000
SC 400/430 ▼	—	14,000	16,000	19,000	23,000	27,000	35,000	45,000	50,000

Reliability	4	4	4	4	4	4	4	4	4
Crash Safety (F)									
ES 300/330/350	4	—	—	—	5	5	5	5	5
IS 250/350	—	—	—	—	—	—	—	4	4
Side									
ES 300/330/350	5	—	5	—	5	5	5	5	5
IS 250/350	—	—	—	—	—	—	—	5	5
IIHS Side									
ES 330/350	—	—	—	—	—	5	5	5	5
LS 400/430/460	—	—	—	—	—	5	5	5	5
Offset									
ES 300/330/350	—	—	—	5	5	5	5	5	5
GS 300/350	5	5	5	5	5	5	5	5	5
LS 400/430/460	**5**	**5**	**5**	**5**	**5**	**5**	**5**	**5**	**5**
Head Restraints									
ES 300/350	3	—	3	**1**	**1**	**1**	**2**	**2**	**2**
GS 300/350	—	—	**2**	**2**	**2**	**2**	**2**	**2**	**2**

All ratings on a numbered scale where 5 is good and **1** is bad. See page 132 for a more detailed description.

IS 250/300/350	2	2	2	2	2	3	3	3	3
LS 430/460	2	2	2	2	2	2	2	2	2
Roof Strength									
LS 430/460	—	—	—	—	—	3	3	3	3
Rollover Resistance									
ES 300/330/350	—	—	—	—	4	4	5	5	5
IS 250/350	—	—	—	—	—	—	5	5	5

Mercedes-Benz

B-CLASS, C-CLASS ★★★/★

RATING: *B-Class:* Average (2006–09). *C-Class:* Not Recommended (1999–2009). These luxury lemons are outclassed by most Asian luxury models, which offer more safety, reliability, and comfort for much less money. **Ideal model year:** Go for the 2007 B200 for about $12,000; the 2008's few insignificant upgrades don't merit $4,500 more. **"Real" city/highway fuel economy:** *B200 manual: 9.2/6.7 L/100 km. B200 automatic: 9.2/7.2 L/100 km. B200 Turbo manual: 10.3/6.9 L/100 km. B200 Turbo automatic: 9.5/7.4 L/100 km. C230 manual: 9.5/7.2 L/100 km. C230 automatic: 10.2/7.1 L/100 km. C240 manual: 12.9/8.4 L/100 km. C240 automatic: 12.4/8.9 L/100 km. C32 AMG: 14.6/10.3 L/100 km. C320 manual: 12.7/8.3 L/100 km. C320 automatic: 11.8/8.2 L/100 km. CL500: 14.7/9.1 L/100 km. CL600: 18.4/11.6 L/100 km. CL55 AMG: 16.6/10.3 L/100 km.* Owners report fuel use is higher than these estimates by about 15 percent. **Maintenance/Repair costs:** Higher-than-average costs, and most repairs must be done by a Mercedes dealer. Look out for electronic glitches, engine oil sludging, and fuel-system malfunctions. **Parts:** Highly dealer-dependent and expensive. **Extended warranty:** A smart idea. **Best alternatives:** Acura Integra, RL, or TL; BMW 3 Series; Hyundai Genesis; and Infiniti G35. **Helpful websites:** *www.benzworld.org* and *www.carsurvey.org/reviews/mercedes-benz/c-class.*

Strengths and Weaknesses

B-Class

Mercedes' B-Class, launched as a 2006 model spun off of the smaller A-Class, answers a question that few serious-minded motorists have asked: "Can Mercedes make a classy compact car?" The B-Class answers the question with a yes and a no. Can they make it small? Yes. Can they make it classy? No.

The car looks like a mini-minivan, without any of the stylistic lines that would identify the B200 as a Mercedes product. But it does have a roomy interior and smooth-running drivetrain. A 136 hp 2.0L engine is standard, and a torquier, turbocharged 193 hp variant is optional. Although the car is quite vulnerable to crosswinds due to its extra height, overall highway performance is above average.

Crashworthiness testing has not yet been done by NHTSA. The bottom line: there are half a dozen other cars that perform as well or better, with classier lines, more-extensive dealership networks, proven reliability, and good crashworthiness scores.

VEHICLE HISTORY: 2007—The B200 receives upgraded alloy wheels, leather-covered steering wheel and shifter knob, telescopic steering column, removable ashtray/storage cup, and heated windshield washers. The Turbo variant gets telescopic steering column adjustment, auto-dimming mirrors, an exterior "light and sight" package, rain-sensing wipers, a removable ashtray/storage cup, heated washers, and an interior lighting package. **2008**—B200 gets a standard storage net on front seatbacks, cruise control, an interior light package, and more-comfortable seats.

C-Class

Replacing the low-quality, unreliable, power-challenged, bland 190 series, the 1994 C-Class gained interior room and two new engines: a base 147 hp 2.2L and a 194 hp 2.8L 6-cylinder—a real powerhouse in this small car when coupled to the manual 5-speed transmission. The 4-speed automatic is a big disappointment—it requires a lot of throttle effort to downshift and prefers to start out in Second gear. Although this series got small, incremental power increases and additional features over the years, you don't see a major redesign until 2001. Unfortunately, the new engines and other features added at that time only add to the car's poor reliability. Engine and road noise are still bothersome, and interior space is still inadequate. Since then, these cars have coasted on the Mercedes name and been touted mainly as fuel-sippers with a high-end cachet. That's poor recompense for what little the car actually offers.

VEHICLE HISTORY: 2001—Completely revamped, gaining two new engines, additional safety features, and more-aerodynamic styling. **2002**—Additional rear room and storage space, more high-performance features. Variants include a wagon, and an AWD sedan and wagon. **2003**—All-wheel drive and another wagon (C240) are added, and the C230 hatchback coupe gets a new supercharged 4-cylinder engine, losing 3 horses in the process. **2004**—Sports coupes adopt a standard three-spoke steering wheel, enlarged chrome exhaust tip, and other pseudo-sporty paraphernalia. **2005**—Restyled and joined by a high-performance 362 hp V8-equipped C55 AMG sedan. The C320 gets a 3.5L V6. **2006**—New engines and model designations, fewer body styles, and the wagons and coupes are gone. Sedans come with rear-drive and all-wheel drive. The C230 Sport gets a 201 hp V6 in place of a 189 hp supercharged 4-cylinder. The C280 Luxury has a 228 hp V6 instead of its predecessor's 168 hp engine. The C350 Sport and Luxury have a 268 hp V6 that replaces the 215 hp powerplant used by the C320. The C55 returns for its last year. **2008**—Redesigned, with a longer wheelbase and added length. **2009**—A 10-way driver's memory seat and steering column.

Owner surveys give the entry-level C-Class cars a worse-than-average rating. C-Class owners report frequent problems with sudden, unintended acceleration; slipping, or soft-then-hard shifts; drivetrain noise and vibration; and windshield squeaks. Brakes, engines (oil sludge), the AC electrical system, and computer-controlled electronic components (telematics) are glitch-prone, hell to diagnose, and expensive to repair:

> Check valve on my 2005 C230 has a defect allowing the supercharged air to enter into the crankcase of the engine pushing oil into it. It caused a misfire reading, loss of power and the Check Engine light to go on. The campaign I found identical to my problem is number...2008020002. However it[s] repair coverage is only associated with a range of VIN #'s throughout 2003–2005. My car is a 2005, but the campaign is not listed under my VIN#.

Fit and finish is also subpar (gearshift "chrome" shreds easily, for example), and original-equipment tires may have weak side walls.

Safety Summary

All models/years: Airbags fail to deploy. • Sudden, unintended acceleration and brake failure. • Faulty gas gauge sensor. • Rear suspension bouncing makes it difficult to maintain directional control. • Car is very vulnerable to side-wind buffeting. • Window failures. • Brakes fail on incline. • When the vehicle is cold, the automatic transmission slips, sticks in gear, and shifts abruptly. • Many reports of a sudden loss of power and stalling. • Multiple electrical short circuits. • Differential failure. • Vehicle wanders over highway. **All models: 2004**—Fire ignites in the electrical wires housed in the dashboard. • Transmission fails to shift into Reverse. • Loose driver's seat. • Front windshield is easily cracked by road debris. • Auto-dimming rear-view mirror sometimes turns pitch-black. • AC corrosion produces a noxious odour in the cabin. **2005**—Engine compartment fire. • Airbag suddenly deployed when it was not needed. • Vehicle hesitates and then slams into gear. • Instrument panel is hard to read in daylight. • Tire side wall failures. **2007**—Several incidents reported that the airbag deployed for no reason. • Sudden brake failure. • No-starts due to faulty fuel pump. *C240:* Wide rear quarter panel blind spot.

Secret Warranties/Internal Bulletins/Service Tips

All models/years: Seat noises can be eliminated by installing a seat-noise kit. **All models: 1997–2004**—Engine oil sludge refund guidelines. **2001**—Troubleshooting hard starts and poor engine performance. **2002**—Lack of power, engine hesitation. • Inoperative cruise control. • Power-window motor locks up when closing. • Inoperative central locking system. • Tail/brake lights stay on. **2002–04**—Engine rattling. • Inoperative cruise control. • Harsh transmission shifts. • Transmission fluid leaks at the electrical connection. • Scraping noise comes from the transmission tunnel area. • Inoperative trunk/cargo light. • Free corrosion repairs along the door bottoms. **2003–04**—Troubleshooting tips for fixing a rough-running engine. • Windshield blistering near rain/light sensor. **2004**—Engine oil leaks through the cylinder head bolt threads. • Steering leaks. • Suspension rumbling. • Exhaust rattling, hissing, and humming. **2004–05**—Campaign to check and replace, if necessary, the automatic transmission pilot bushing. **2005**—The following items may also apply to previous model years. If you have identical problems, ask your dealer service manager to check the files. • Engine won't start. • Engine oil leaks from the oil-level sensor. • Rough idle. • Harsh shifts with the automatic transmission. • Transmission fluid leaks at the electrical connector. • Inoperative central locking system and AC heater blower motor. • Steering assembly leaks fluid. • Sliding roof water leaks, rattling. • Moisture in the turn signal lights and mirrors. • Tail lights won't turn off; trunk light won't turn on. • Door frames will get free rustproofing under a special Service Campaign (read: "secret warranty"). • Another Service Campaign calls for the free modification of the lower door seal. **2006–07**—Countermeasures to rid the interior of an oily, vinegary smell. **2007**—Rough shifting. • Automatic transmission shift chatter. • Steering rack leaks. • Inoperative AC blower motor. • Remedy for brake squealing. • Front-end/dash noise. • Front axle knocking when parking. • Torsion bar front-end creaking. • Inoperative turn signals. • Rear seatback rattle. • Loose head restraint. • Horn may not work due to premature corrosion of the assembly. • Front centre armrest may fall off. *350:* **2009**—Oil leaks at the rear of the engine may be fixed by changing the camshaft cover plugs. • Hard 1–2 shifts. • Harsh engagement when shifting from Park to Drive. • Delayed Reverse engagement. • What to do if the automatic transmission goes into "limp home" mode. • Front axle noise when maneuvering. • Front axle dull, thumping noise when going over bumps. • Front-end suspension or steering grinding noise. • Front seat backrest noise. • Interior lights flickering. • Four-way lumbar support fails. • Internal steering gear leakage. • AC is inoperative or supplies insufficient cooling.

B-CLASS, C-CLASS PROFILE

	2001	2002	2003	2004	2005	2006	2007	2008	2009
Cost Price ($)									
B200	—	—	—	—	—	30,950	31,400	29,900	29,900
C230	—	33,950	34,450	35,290	36,450	36,450	38,400	35,800	35,800
C240	37,450	37,950	38,450	41,290	42,250	—	—	—	—
C280	—	—	—	—	—	42,850	42,800	—	—
C300	—	—	—	—	—	—	—	41,000	41,200
C320/C350	49,950	50,600	49,750	40,700	40,600	54,950	51,000	47,900	48,200
Used Values ($)									
B200 ▲	—	—	—	—	—	10,000	13,000	17,500	20,000
B200 ▼	—	—	—	—	—	9,000	11,500	16,000	18,500
C230 ▲	—	5,000	6,000	7,500	10,000	13,000	16,000	20,500	25,000
C230 ▼	—	4,500	5,500	6,500	8,500	11,500	15,500	18,500	23,000
C240 ▲	4,500	5,500	6,500	8,000	10,500	—	—	—	—
C240 ▼	3,500	5,000	6,000	7,000	9,000	—	—	—	—

All ratings on a numbered scale where **5** is good and **1** is bad. See page 132 for a more detailed description.

C280 ▲	—	—	—	—	—	13,500	17,000	—	—
C280 ▼	—	—	—	—	—	12,000	15,500	—	—
C300 ▲	—	—	—	—	—	—	—	22,000	27,500
C300 ▼	—	—	—	—	—	—	—	21,500	25,500
C320/C350 ▲	6,500	7,500	9,000	11,000	12,500	16,500	18,500	27,000	32,000
C320/C350 ▼	6,000	6,500	8,000	10,000	11,500	15,000	17,000	25,500	30,000
Reliability	1	1	1	1	2	2	2	3	3
B200	—	—	—	—	—	2	3	3	3
Crash Safety (F)	—	—	4	4	4	4	4	4	4
Side	—	—	5	5	5	5	5	5	5
IIHS Side	—	—	—	—	3	3	3	—	5
Offset	5	5	5	5	5	5	5	5	5
Head Restraints (F)	—	—	—	2	2	3	3	5	5
Roof Strength	—	—	—	—	—	—	—	5	5
Rollover Resistance	—	—	4	4	4	4	4	4	4

300 SERIES, 400 SERIES, 500 SERIES, E-CLASS ★★

RATING: Below Average (1999–2009). Mercedes' quality has deteriorated over the past decade because of the increased complexity of mechanical, emissions, and electronic components. Beware of engine oil sludge. **Ideal model year:** It's a toss-up as to the best 350E model to choose. The 2006 rear-drive gives you lots of new features and added horsepower for about $18,000 (for a car that sold originally for $74,300), while the 2007 version will cost you about $7,000 more, throws in AWD and adds more standard safety features. **"Real" city/highway fuel economy:** E320: 13.2/8.1 L/100 km. E500: 14.4/9.1 L/100 km. E55 AMG: 16.6/10.3 L/100 km. Owners report these vehicles use about 20 percent more fuel than these estimates suggest. **Maintenance/Repair costs:** Higher-than-average costs, but many repairs can now be done by independent garages. **Parts:** Higher-than-average costs, and limited availability. **Extended warranty:** A good idea. **Best alternatives:** The natural inclination is to seriously consider one of the BMW variants. Don't. They are just as poorly made and unreliable. Equivalent 2001 and later 5 Series, 6 Series, 7 Series, and X5 models come with standard iDrive—a complicated cockpit electronic controller that will drive you batty. Says *Electronic Design* magazine (*www.elecdesign.com/Articles/Index.cfm?AD=1&AD=1&ArticleID=8246*):

> BMW's 2001 introduction of iDrive, its pioneering driver information/entertainment system, was arguably the biggest corporate disaster since Coca-Cola Co. decided to tinker with the formula for its eponymous beverage.

Granted, by the time the 5 Series adopted iDrive a few years later, the system was redesigned so the driver could use it without looking at the small LCD panel. The

2007 X5 incorporates iDrive's third redesign in seven years. All this effort does make for a more user-friendly operation, but the learning curve is still rather steep. Instead, consider the Acura Integra, RL, or TL; Infiniti G35 series; Hyundai Genesis; and Lincoln Town Car or Mercury Grand Marquis. **Helpful websites:** *www.benzworld.org, www.troublebenz.com, www.carsurvey.org/reviews/mercedes-benz, and www.oil-tech.com/32million.htm*).

Strengths and Weaknesses

These cars were once ideal mid-sized family sedans, until Mercedes started churning out feeble downsized models and installing failure-prone electronic components and sludge-prone engines. Nevertheless, the E-Class sedans are edible lemons that are a bit less sour because they have been around so long, are full of nifty safety and comfort/convenience features, and provide all the interior space that the C-Class leaves out. Their major shortcoming is a weak dealer network that limits parts distribution and drives up parts and servicing costs and brain-numbing, complex electronic glitches that confirm the automotive industry adage: There's a right way, a wrong way, and a German way to build cars.

VEHICLE HISTORY: *E-Class:* **2004**—Increased availability of all-wheel drive, a revamped wagon body style, and a new 7-speed automatic transmission. **2005**—A turbocharged diesel, the E320 CDI, debuts as an early 2005 model. **2006**—The E350 gets a more-powerful 268 hp 3.5L engine (47 additional horses). **2007**—New styling, more power, and additional safety features. **2009**—An improved audio system… yawn.

Quality control has traditionally been below average with the E-Class cars, although not a bad as with the C-Class models. Owners point out recurring problems with the fuel and electrical systems, causing lights, instruments, and gauges to shut off and the trunk lid to open when the engine is shut down. Other common problems include engine oil leaks; oil sludging, stalling and engine surging; premature rusting and paint delamination; engine problems caused by a stretched timing chain; computer module failures (in both the engine and transmission); and erratically performing, leaky, and noisy transmissions.

The 2002–07 models haven't improved much. Problem areas are similar to what's been reported with Mercedes' entire lineup, including the C-Class, CLK, M-Class, R-Class, S-Class, and SLK models. Foremost are transmission malfunctions, electrical short circuits, suspension problems, brake failures, premature wearout of key brake components, unreliable climate and audio systems, and pathetically substandard fit and finish, best exemplified by complaints that the paint peels away on the lower doors.

Safety Summary

All models/years: The following safety failures exclude the B200 because that model isn't sold in the States where the safety logs for NHTSA are kept. • Frequent transmission breakdowns. • Serious, often total, electrical failures. • Chronic stalling. • Sudden, unintended acceleration. • Vehicle lags and lurches when accelerating. • Steering locks up. • No child safety locks for the rear doors. • Airbag warning light stays lit or doesn't light, and airbag deploys inadvertently:

> While driving down the highway, my passenger side curtain and rear side door airbags deployed for no reason at all.... It scared the hell out of me and nearly caused me to crash the car.

• Water enters the automatic transmission control module, preventing the transmission from changing gears. • Vehicle hesitates when accelerating with gas pedal halfway depressed, then it lurches forward. • Steering locks up while turning. • Total electrical failure in traffic, leading to vehicle shutdown. • Windows don't stay up. **All models: 2003**—Faulty gateway module and software cause failure in the braking system and tire-pressure feedback. • Electrical failures can leave the vehicle with no rear brakes and limited use of the front brakes. **2004**—Sudden loss of power while underway or merging. • Total brake failure. • Intermittent failure of the radar-controlled cruise control. • Mirrors tilt down when backing up but don't tilt up until car goes forward at 14 km/h. **2005**—Seat belt chime goes off when the seat is unoccupied. • Distracting reflections on the driver-side mirror; dash reflects onto the front windshield. • Diesel engine acceleration is unacceptably slow. • Excessive black soot and a tar-like residue generated by the diesel engine. • Faulty AC/defrost blower motor. • Erroneous navigation/GPS directions will get you into serious trouble:

> The problem, as I see it, is that a fair percentage of drivers will blindly follow the verbal instructions with serious consequences. Incidentally, talking with the salesman about this problem, he told me that they already had a woman drive into a lake.

320: **2005**—Failure of many brake components, some of which cannot be easily repaired. • HID headlight glare angers and blinds oncoming cars. *320 Blue:* Diesel engine surges when shifting gears, causing car to lurch forward and skid on ice. • Sudden brake failure when parking. • Electrical short circuits caused by a dried-up, cracked wiring harness. *350:* **2006**—7-speed automatic transmission failures disable steering and brake boost, ABS, and Electronic Stability Control system. • Other incidents where the tranny suddenly locks up in high gear and requires that the car be restarted to return to normal. • Automatic transmission behaves like the clutch is slipping, slowing car to a snail's pace. • Vehicle will often not start because electrical shorts have disabled the electronics. • Electronic key fob doesn't work. • Sunroof explodes while vehicle underway. • All four original-equipment tires blow out during their first year of use. • If the back seats are lowered to carry more cargo, the front seats cannot be pushed back. **2007**—Vehicle will suddenly stall while on the highway. • Child opened the rear door while car was idling at a red light. • All four wheels replaced because they were bent at the rim. • Rubber ring inside the fuel tank failed, allowing fuel to leak out of the tank. **2008**—Sunroof shattered spontaneously. • Excessive driver-side mirror vibrations. **2009**—Vehicle surged when the accelerator was barely pressed.

Secret Warranties/Internal Bulletins/Service Tips

All models: 1998–2004—Free engine repairs or replacement if afflicted by engine oil sludge, following the O'Keefe class action settlement in April 2003. Order No. S-B-18.00/16a, published December 2003, gives all the details on the problem and Mercedes' payout rules. **2002–05**—Free replacement of the alternator voltage regulator. **2003**—Piston-slap engine noise. **2004**—No-starts. • Harsh transmission shifts. • Steering leaks. • Sliding roof-rack cover cracks. • Wheelhouse water drain modification. • Rear axle rumbling. **2005**—Oil leaks from the oil-level sensor. • Rough automatic transmission engagement, droning, buzzing noises. • Transmission leaks fluid at the electrical connector. • Campaign to check and repair possible automatic transmission pilot bushing leakage; another campaign concerns the free cleaning of the front axle carrier sleeve and bolt replacement; a third campaign will reprogram the battery control module; and a fourth campaign will inspect or replace the alternator/regulator. • Foul interior odours. • Steering fluid leaks and steering squeal when turning. • Front-seat noise. • Sliding roof water leaks, rattling. • Moisture in the turn signal lights and mirrors. • Rear seatback rattle. • Loose passenger head restraints. • Fanfare horns may not work due to premature wiring corrosion. *350:* **2006–07**—Rough transmission shifts. • Upshift/downshift chatter or shudder. • Front axle creaking, grinding, knocking noise when parking, and other front-end noises. • Brake squeal. • Steering-rack leaks. • Rivet replacement to prevent water leakage. • Inoperative AC, faulty blower motor, or compressor failure. • False oil readings. • Inoperative turn signals. • Loose front centre armrest falls off. • Noisy seats.

300 SERIES, 400 SERIES, 500 SERIES, E-CLASS PROFILE

	2001	2002	2003	2004	2005	2006	2007	2008	2009
Cost Price ($)									
280/300 AWD	—	—	—	—	—	—	45,400	65,800	65,800
320 Blue	67,900	68,350	69,950	72,050	73,000	75,450	67,801	68,100	68,100
350 AWD	—	—	—	—	—	57,200	53,600	74,500	74,500
420E, 430	75,750	76,150	—	—	—	—	—	—	—
500E/S/AWD	114,650	116,950	81,500	83,500	84,600	84,600		—	—
550 AWD	—	—	—	—	—	—	85,000	85,300	85,300
55/63 AMG	100,550	101,600	113,000	101,150	115,650	117,745	118,900	121,000	121,000
Used Values ($)									
280/300 AWD ▲	—	—	—	—	—	—	27,000	31,000	37,000
280/300 AWD ▼	—	—	—	—	—	—	24,000	29,000	34,000
320 Blue ▲	9,000	10,500	12,000	13,000	14,500	18,000	26,000	34,000	38,000
320 Blue ▼	8,000	9,000	10,500	12,000	13,000	16,500	24,000	32,000	35,000
350 AWD ▲	—	—	—	—	—	18,500	24,000	35,000	38,000
350 AWD ▼	—	—	—	—	—	17,000	22,500	33,500	36,000
420E, 430 ▲	11,500	13,000	—	—	—	—	—	—	—
420E, 430 ▼	10,500	12,000	—	—	—	—	—	—	—
500E/S/AWD ▲	9,000	10,000	11,500	13,000	15,500	20,000	—	—	—
500E/S/AWD ▼	8,500	9,000	10,500	12,000	14,000	18,000	—	—	—

550 AWD ▲	—	—	—	—	—	—	29,000	41,000	48,000
550 AWD ▼	—	—	—	—	—	—	27,000	38,000	44,000
55/63 AMG ▲	10,000	11,000	13,500	16,000	18,000	22,000	32,000	55,000	65,000
55/63 AMG ▼	9,000	10,000	12,000	14,000	16,500	19,000	30,000	50,000	60,000
Reliability	1	1	2	2	2	2	2	3	3
Crash Safety (F)	—	—	4	4	4	4	4	4	4
Side	—	—	5	5	5	5	5	5	5
IIHS Side	—	—	—	—	—	—	3	3	3
Offset	5	5	5	5	5	5	5	5	5
Head Restraints (4d)	5	5	5	3	3	5	5	5	5
Wagon	3	3	—	—	—	—	—	—	—
Rollover Resistance	—	—	5	5	5	5	5	5	5

Nissan

MAXIMA ★★★

RATING: Average (2007–09); Below Average (1999–06). The 1999 models were problem-prone, but the 2002 and 2004 model redesigns made matters worse and heralded a dramatic decline in quality that continued until 2007. **Ideal model year:** Upgraded powertrains, better quality control, and fresh styling make the 2007 the best choice at $13,500 (the car originally sold for $37,000). **"Real" city/highway fuel economy:** *3.0 manual: 10.8/7.9 L/100 km. 3.0 automatic: 12.1/8.1 L/100 km. 3.5 manual: 11.5/7.3 L/100 km. 3.5 automatic: 11.6/7.9 L/100 km.* Owners report fuel savings are less than these estimates by about 10 percent. **Maintenance/Repair costs:** Higher than average. **Parts:** Higher-than-average costs, but parts are easy to find. Xenon headlights are frequently stolen from the car because they are easily accessed, and can cost $800 each to replace. **Extended warranty:** A must-have. **Best alternatives:** Acura Integra, RL, or TL, Hyundai Genesis, and the Infiniti G35. **Helpful websites:** *www.nicoclub.com.*

Strengths and Weaknesses

Early models (2001 and earlier)

These front-drive sedans are very well equipped and nicely finished, but they're cramped for their size. Although the trunk is spacious, only five passengers can travel in a pinch (in the literal sense). The 6-cylinder 190 hp engine, borrowed from the 300ZX in 1992, offers sparkling performance; the fuel injectors, however, are problematic. The '93 models got standard driver-side airbags, and the Maxima remained unchanged until the 1995 model's redesign. There was a second redesign for the year 2000 version.

Electrical and front suspension problems afflict early Maximas. Brakes and engine timing belts need frequent attention in all model years as well. Weak automatic transmissions and ignition systems fail frequently. There have also been many reports of cooked transmissions caused by the poorly designed transmission cooler. The cruise control unit is problematic: When it's engaged at moderate speeds, it hesitates or drifts to a lower speed, acting as if the fuel line was clogged.

Nissan has had problems with weak window regulators for some time. If the window is frozen, don't open it. Also, the rubber weather stripping around the window cuts easily and causes the window to go off track, which in turn causes stress on the weak regulators. Driver-side window breakage is common and can cost up to $300 to repair. Costly aluminum wheels corrode quickly and are easily damaged by road hazards. Maximas usually suffer from rust perforation on the sunroof, door bottoms, rear wheelwells, front hood edges, and bumper supports. The underbody should also be checked carefully for corrosion damage.

2002–06: More of the same

Each Maxima redesign has been followed by an increase in owner complaints, a normal occurrence with most revamped vehicles. Usually (but not always), after a couple of years, quality rebounds and complaints diminish. But not with Nissan. Factory-related goofs, poor designs, and low-quality suppliers have kept Nissan quality in the basement for the better part of a decade, as confirmed by the post-redesign glitches emblematic of the Quest minivan.

Recent redesigns have hobbled the powertrain. Owners have difficulty controlling the engine speed with the gas pedal. There's engine popping and knocking when accelerating, surging or stalling when braking or decelerating, and transmission malfunctions galore. Premature front brake pad wear and rotor warpage; a choppy, jarring suspension; excessive front-end shaking and shimmy; faulty ignition coils; and inadequate headlight illumination continue to be major problems.

The 2004–06 revamped Maximas continue to have the following major quality problems: seat shifting; broken struts; transmission failures; harsh automatic shifting; a gear grind from First to Second; windows that are slow to roll down; paint that's easily chipped or scratched; side mirrors that won't reposition; a screeching sound that's caused by a loose heat shield; water leaks by right floorboard and through sunroof; inoperative steering-wheel stereo buttons; no-starts caused by a loose fuel-pump connector or ignition switch failure; HID lights with high beams that won't return to low and bulbs that burn out prematurely; and brake shimmy or judder (dealers lean toward all the usual suspects before they resort to the steering-rack friction adjustment that has cured the shimmy for some of the most persistent cases).

2007–09 improvements

The number of safety-related complaints posted on NHTSA's webpage (*www.safercar.gov*) has slowed to a trickle, indicating that Nissan is making more reliable and better-performing vehicles, but it has been a slow road to travel and there's still much more they need to do. Recent models still have some brake, powertrain,

AC compressor, electronics, and suspension problems along with sub-par fit and finish like warped dashboards and a symphony of clicks, rattles, pops, and clunks. Hopefully, the chronic engine and transmission failures of the past are long-gone.

VEHICLE HISTORY: 2002—Completely revamped, featuring a 260 hp 3.5L V6 coupled to a 6-speed manual or 4-speed automatic transmission; revised interior trim; larger front brakes; new front-end styling; and xenon headlights (a thief's Holy Grail). **2003**—GLE gets standard front side airbags. **2004**—Another redesign adds to the size and weight, along with 5 more horses. Once again, quality takes a big hit. **2005**—Improved 6-speed manual transmission. **2007**—Revised interior and exterior styling, keyless starting, and a new transmission. Sporty 3.5 SE and 3.5 SL models are offered with a 255 hp V6 coupled to a new, fuel-saving CVT automatic transmission with a manual shiftgate and six pre-selected gears. **2009**—Fresh styling and additional power. All models come with a 290 hp 3.5L V6 hooked to a CVT automatic transmission, resulting in 35 more horses.

Safety Summary

All years: Airbag failed to deploy. • Sudden loss of power, resulting in inoperative brakes and steering. • Chronic stalling. • Erratic transmission performance. • ABS failures. **2001**—Engine compartment fire. • Steering lock-ups and loss of brakes. **2002**—Vehicle suddenly swings to the right. • Steering wheel overheats. • Sudden acceleration in Reverse with gearshift lever indicating Drive. • ABS and traction control malfunction every time car is washed. • Front wheels lock up or get no power; ABS light remains lit. • Hesitation on acceleration. • Vehicle accelerates when foot is taken off accelerator. • Defective mass air sensor or crank sensor causes sudden loss of power and transmission bucking and jerking. • Vehicle rolls backward when parked on an incline. • Right front wheel buckles when brakes are applied. • In one incident, vehicle surged when brakes were applied while parking, and car hit a brick wall. • Faulty air control valve causes sudden acceleration. • Suspension transverse link failed, causing loss of control; owners report that cars not in the recall have the same defect. • Lower control-arm failure as in recall notice, but car isn't among those recalled. • Chronic brake failures. • Back window suddenly shatters. • Rear quarter window air leaks. • Trunk water leaks. **2002–03**—Xenon headlights are easily stolen and expensive to replace:

> Headlights easily stolen on Nissan Maxima 2002, 2003. I have a 2002 Maxima SE and the other day, my headlights were stolen while the car was parked outside my mother-in-law's house. I found out this has been an ongoing problem with this vehicle and Nissan isn't telling anyone about this problem when purchasing this vehicle...the way the lights are connected they are easily stolen and will be an ongoing problem.... Nissan will retrofit new lights at the owner's expense, about $300.00.

2003—Passenger-side airbag deploys on its own. • O_2 sensor failure. • Hard-to-read instrument panel lights. **2004**—Vehicle was underway at 100 km/h when the steering wheel suddenly locked up and the brakes failed. • In another instance, the front wheels locked up while the vehicle was in motion, causing extensive undercarriage damage. • Vehicle suddenly swerves out of control. • Vehicle suddenly accelerates in Reverse when put into Drive. • Sudden acceleration upon start-up (a faulty air control valve is suspected). • Unable to control engine speed with the accelerator pedal. • Vehicle stalls without warning in cold weather (suspect the computer module). • Many complaints that the headlights are poorly designed, placing the high beams too high for adequate visibility; drivers complain they can't see between the high and low beams. • Trunk lid and latch are hazardous when raised. • Several incidents of the SkyView roof shattering. • Sunroof opens and closes on its own. • Steering wheel overheats in direct sunlight. • The driver-side windshield washer may not work in cold weather. **2005**—Stalling and hard starts. • Engine surges when downshifting. • There is a one-second delay from when the accelerator pedal is released to when the car begins to slow down. • Engine threw a rod and had to be replaced. • Erratic transmission shifts. • Strong vibration and shimmy, probably related to faulty suspension strut assemblies that often wear out within a year. • Sudden total brake loss. • Accelerator and brake pedals are mounted too close together. • Rack-and-pinion steering assembly wears out early. • Broken axle. • Headlights don't work properly and are a thief magnet. **2006**—Airbag deployed for no reason; airbag deployed inadvertently. • Sudden, unintended acceleration. • Automatic transmission jerks and jumps. • Goodyear Eagle RS-A tires fly apart; side walls cave in. • Corroded ABS sensors produce a brake grinding sound. • Car shakes, jerks, and veers to the right or left when brakes are applied. • Car is very difficult to steer. • Excessive steering-wheel vibration. • Crack in the rear suspension subframe. • Doors lock and unlock on their own. • Battery exploded when ignition was turned on. • Excessive windshield reflection impairs visibility. **2007**—Sudden, unintended acceleration with no brakes at the car wash:

> I have a 2007 Nissan Maxima and my car shot out of a car wash and across 4 lanes of traffic and crashed into federal property. After the car was pushed from the dry option I put my foot on the brake took the car out of Neutral, put it into Drive and the car took off like a rocket. I had both feet on the brakes and had to use two hands to steer the car away from traffic. I had the choice of a light pole or a fence on federal property. I decided on the fence to be the least damaging. My grandson was in the car and it all happened within two minutes. I made eye contact with the drivers to my left and right and honked my horn and everyone around saw I was having a problem and they stopped. I had no brakes.

• Poor ABS brake design leads to huge repair bills:

> 2007 Nissan Maxima ABS activates with normal braking. There was a service bulletin NTB07-016B for this problem which is clearly a design defect from Nissan. As I was driving and catching speed I noticed my car slipped into a lower gear I would hear ABS engaging and if I stepped on the brake pedal ABS would be activated. Took it to the dealer even though I had no warranty they told me it would cost me $1,200 to replace the bearings and the sensors as they were corroded due to water and dirt

trapped where the sensors rest. The service bulletin clearly states that a piece has to be grinded off on knuckle in order to allow proper drainage of water and dirt.

• Brake master cylinder and ABS sensor failures. • Automatic transmission electronic malfunctions won't permit shifting out of First or into Second gear. • Frequent stalling on the highway. • Car jerks and transmission slips. • Incorrect fuel gauge readings (vehicle not part of the recall campaign, but has the problem). • Driver noticed the Service Engine light was lit and dealer says it was because gas cap wasn't screwed on tightly and charged him $100 to reset the computer. Driver says dealer's head was not screwed on tightly and wants his $100 back. • Continental and Goodyear original-equipment tires can cause excessive vibration and may fail prematurely. **2008**—Airbag alert flashes for no reason and driver must fork over $914 to get it put out. • Tire pressure warning system gives false alarms. • A four-month-old car needed its automatic transmission replaced. • CV axle broke while car was being parked. • Suspension rattles when passing over small bumps. Steering column has a similar rattle and Nissan is replacing the steering assembly free of charge. Rattling noise is heard from the rear of the car as it accelerates. This is caused by fuel in the tank sloshing around. • Uncomfortable front head restraints. • Goodyear Eagle tires fail prematurely. **2009**—Sudden, unintended acceleration. • Passenger-side airbag disabled for no reason whenever anyone occupies the seat. • Brake failures. • Wheels bend easily and cause vehicle to vibrate. • Driver's seat isn't stable when car speeds up or stops. • Doors lock and unlock on their own.

Secret Warranties/Internal Bulletins/Service Tips

2000–01—Automatic transmission gear slippage. **2000–02**—Doors may intermittently lock by themselves. **2000–03**—Driver's seat won't go forward or backward. • Abnormal shifting (the control valve assembly is the likely culprit, says TSB #NTB04-035). **2000–06**—Oil leaks from oil-cooler oil seal. **2001–02**—Rear brake caliper clunk, rattle, or knock. • Rear suspension bottoms out (also an Infiniti problem). **2002**—Erratic sunroof operation. • Driver's power seat won't move forward or backward. **2002–03**—Hesitation on acceleration. • Lack of engine power. • Sunroof operates on its own. **2002–06**—How to silence an engine ticking noise. **2003**—Troubleshooting brake noise and judder. **2003–04**—Harsh 1–2 shifts. **2004**—Cold upshift shock; abnormal shifting. • Fuel system misfires. • Hard start after a cold soak. • Engine won't crank in cold weather. • Front brake noise. • Water leaks from roof. • Headlight fogging. • Loose headliner. **2004–05**—Exhaust rattle/buzz when accelerating. • Voluntary service campaign entails the free replacement of the rear suspension and bushing sealing for 13 years (see bulletin on page 260). **2004–06**—No-cranks in cold weather. • Erratic gauge, AC operation. • Front power-seat malfunction. • Hard-to-move shifter. **2004–07**—Engine noise coming from the timing chain area. • ABS activates when it shouldn't. • Noisy driver's power seat. **2004–08**—Tire-pressure-monitor sensor may leak fluid. • Inoperative power-door mirrors. • Heat shield rattles. **2007–08**—Front suspension rattling. • Inoperative lumbar support.

2007–09—Sunroof is inoperative or operates erratically. **2009**—Sunroof glass chatter, creaking, or popping. • Sunroof wind noise. • Power window "Up" and steering column adjustment may both be inoperative. • Loose headliner. • Front passenger seat shakes at highway speeds. • Voluntary Service Campaign #PC005 to replace the steering knuckle for free:

CAMPAIGN PC005—L/H REAR SUSPENSION KNUCKLE

BULLETIN NO.: NTB09-031   DATE: APRIL 23, 2009

2009 Maxima and 2009 Altima Sedan, Coupe, and Hybrid

INTRODUCTION: On some 2009 Altima and Maxima vehicles, the left hand rear suspension knuckle may not be manufactured to specification, which may result in noise or vibration under certain circumstances. Although no safety issue is presented, Nissan is conducting this service campaign to identify and replace those affected units. This service will be performed at no cost for parts or labor. **DEALER RESPONSIBILITY:** Dealers are to inspect each vehicle falling within range of this campaign that enters the service department, and if necessary, perform the indicated knuckle replacement. This includes vehicles purchased from private parties or presented by transient (tourist) owners and vehicles in a dealer's inventory.

2009–10—Transmission "booming" countermeasures. • Front power seats won't move. • Driver's seat is wobbly. • Can't turn ignition to the On position. • Fuel gauge issues.

MAXIMA PROFILE

	2001	2002	2003	2004	2005	2006	2007	2008	2009
Cost Price ($)									
Base	29,000	32,900	32,900	34,500	34,600	35,098	36,998	36,998	37,900
Used Values ($)									
Base ▲	4,500	5,000	6,500	8,000	9,500	12,000	14,500	20,000	24,000
Base ▼	4,000	4,500	5,500	7,000	8,000	10,500	13,000	18,000	22,000
Reliability	3	2	2	2	3	3	4	4	4
Crash Safety (F)	4	4	4	5	5	5	5	5	5
Side	4	4	4	4	4	4	4	4	5
IIHS Side	—	—	—	2	2	2	2	2	5
Offset	3	3	3	5	5	5	5	5	5
Head Restraints (F)	5	5	5	1	1	1	2	2	2
Roof Strength	—	—	—	—	—	—	—	—	3
Rollover Resistance	—	4	4	4	4	4	4	4	5

All ratings on a numbered scale where 5 is good and **1** is bad. See page 132 for a more detailed description.

Toyota

RATING: Average (2005–09); Above Average (1999–2004). A *Lemon-Aid* Recommended car for decades, the Avalon now suffers from the same "less for more" philosophy we have seen since 1997 with most of Toyota's lineup. Surprisingly, post-1996 Avalons fare better than most other Toyotas, but during the 2005–06 period, following the car's last major redesign, quality declined markedly. Hopefully, the 2007 model Avalon has fixed those glitches. **Ideal model year:** If you must buy an Avalon, go for the 2007 XLS for about $17,000 (pretty good price for a car that first sold for $41,135). Make sure the sudden acceleration recall fix has been performed and the powertrain works as it should. **"Real" city/highway fuel economy:** 11.0/7.4 L/100 km. Owners report fuel savings match this estimate. **Maintenance/repair costs:** Higher than average: Some owners feel that Toyota and its dealers are acting like "warranty weasels" by charging them to repair defects related to the automaker's own negligence:

In my opinion and based on my recent interaction with Toyota, they are not being honest about their safety issues with [the] public. Two weeks ago, I took my Toyota Avalon 2007 with only 33452 miles to Bob Smith Toyota because brake fluid was leaking out from brake master cylinder. They told me the car is not safe to drive and master cylinder needs to be replaced. I left the car to be repaired. I did some research online and notice that Toyota has a recall for 2005 and 2006 Avalon for the same exact issues *www.toyota.com/recall/avalon-highlander.html*. Further research and based on data from dealership, Toyota Avalon made prior to 7/2007 use the same brake master cylinder as the ones being recalled, part ID # 47028-0710. When I asked Toyota dealer about this, they told me that Toyota has only recalled 2005 and 2006 and can not offer any evidence that part used in 2007 was any different. They suggested that I contact Toyota which I did. In return, they told me to contact the dealership. After multiple follow up, which I have documented and will be more than happy to forward to you, no one is giving me any evidence that master cylinder in Avalons built before 7/2007 are any different than the ones they recalled. The car was in the shop for 12 days, I just paid for repair and asked for the old part. However, if it is the case that Toyota has decided to ignore this issue with 2007 Avalon, they are putting a lot of lives at risk.

•

A pool of washer fluid was on my garage floor. I immediately took the car to the Toyota dealer for service on 2/14/2009. I was told leaking was a common problem because the OE line used to carry fluid through the system was the wrong size. The dealer removed the incorrect line and replaced it with the recommended correct sized one. I was charged $78.26 for parts and service. When I complained that this was a safety issue and the OE was not the right size, I was advised to contact Toyota corporate for relief. My complaint elicited a $47.50 "goodwill reimbursement" (which was the cost of the parts).

Parts: Higher-than-average costs, and limited availability. **Extended warranty:** Not needed. **Best alternatives:** A fully loaded Camry, but if you want a more driver-involved experience in a Toyota, consider a Lexus ES 300 series or something in the GS 300 lineup. Other good choices are the Acura Integra, RL, or TL and the Infiniti G35 series. **Helpful websites:** *www.toyotanation.com/forum.*

Strengths and Weaknesses

This near-luxury four-door offers more interior space and performance than do other cars in its class that cost thousands of dollars more. Basically a front-engine, front-drive, mid-sized sedan based on a stretched Camry platform, the six-passenger (up to the 2004 model) Avalon is similar in size to the Ford Taurus. Sure, there's a fair amount of Camry in the Avalon, but it's quicker on its feet, better attuned to abrupt manoeuvres, and 5 cm longer.

VEHICLE HISTORY: 2005—The third-generation Avalon is restyled and is larger and more powerful. It seats five instead of six, due to new front bucket seats, and offers 2.5 cm more legroom. Toyota's 280 hp 3.5L V6 coupled to a 5-speed automatic, instead of the previous year's 4-speed, replaces the 210 hp 3.0L V6 transmission. All models come with four-wheel ABS disc brakes, front side airbags, side curtain airbags, and a driver's knee airbag. Traction/anti-skid control is available for most models, except the Touring. Other features added to the 2005 models: reclining backrests for a split-folding rear seat, a steering wheel with telescopic as well as tilt adjustment, heated/cooled front seats, keyless starting, and xenon headlights (Touring and Limited). **2008**—A 6-speed automatic replaces the 5-speed; a restyled grille and bumper. **2009**—Standard traction control and anti-skid system.

Quality control up through 2004 is better than average, though steering, suspension, and fuel-system components are failure-prone, and many owners have complained of engine sludge forcing them to spend thousands of dollars on engine repairs.

Owners of 2005–07 Avalons report their cars continue to have serious safety, performance, and reliability problems. And word is getting around. Says *LemonLawClaims.com* (*www.lemonlawclaims.com/toyota_avalon__problems_ lemon.htm*):

> For the [2005] Avalon, [Toyota] has provided service bulletins, which alerts dealers to problems [that include] bad U-joint welds, faulty catalytic converters and a leak in the oil supply line for variable valve timing.... Transmission hesitation problems, which have plagued the automaker in the past, also have resurfaced with the five-speed automatic transmission installed in the Avalon. While the earlier transmission problems were experienced by consumers in a variety of situations, this round of trouble surfaces particularly when the driver presses the acceleration pedal for greater speed.

Other performance gripes posted by *Lemon-Aid* readers include hydroplaning, excessive body lean, highway wandering, major engine oil leaks, suspension strut failures, poor transmission performance, premature front brake repairs, faulty navigation systems, under-steering when cornering, a rotten-egg smell in the cabin, numerous electrical system glitches, a malfunctioning laser-guided cruise control, clunky steering that vibrates and pulls to either side, and a problematic Vehicle Stability Control and Traction Control system:

> The problem with the 2005 Avalon is that there is no way of disengaging the Vehicle Stability Control (VSC) and the traction control (TRAC) feature to allow you to spin the tires if you become stuck in snow or mud.... So, what happens is when you get in snow, the tires refuse to spin and the vehicle just sits there and won't move.... Both the less costly Toyota Camry and 4Runner models have buttons to disengage the Vehicle Stability Control (VSC) and the traction control (TRAC) feature for this purpose or other emergency.

Body construction and assembly are no longer first class, with poor fit and finish, rattles, and water/air leaks the most common complaints. Trunk leaks have been reported on late '90s models, and paint spotting/flaking has afflicted all models. Except for some engine sludge complaints, premature brake wear, and body and accessory glitches (wind noise, AC, and audio system malfunctions), the 2002 and 2003 models have had fewer problems.

Safety Summary

All years: Airbags failed to deploy in an accident. • Sudden, unintended acceleration. • Excessive highway wandering. • Automatic transmission slippage. • Brake pedal goes to the floor with no braking effect. • Driver's seat rocks back and forth. • Steering wheel is off-centre. • Dash lights and gauges reflect onto windshield. • Bridgestone/Firestone, Dunlop, and Michelin tire failures. **2001**—Engine surging at idle. • Front and rear suspension bottoms out when carrying four adults. • Insufficient steering feedback. • Jerky acceleration. • Sudden failure of the instrument and information panel lighting and headlights. • Driver's side-view mirror has a small viewing area. **2002**—Cruise control doesn't slow car when going downhill. • Vehicle veers to the left at high speeds. **2003**—Extended braking distances. • Front brakes appear to apply themselves. **2004**—Rear wheel seizes while vehicle is underway. • Stalling when AC is activated. • Key won't turn in the ignition. **2005**—Throttle stuck to the floor. • Hesitation and surging when accelerating. • Engine surges and then shuts off and can't be restarted. • Cruise control speed drop is hazardous:

> When my car slows down suddenly because of the car in front, there is no warning for the car behind me. Toyota was notified of this problem and told me not to use the sonar in heavy travelled roads. That is no solution. There should be a fix to make the brake lights go on when the car is slowed down by the sonar.

• Brakes suddenly fail due to a faulty master cylinder. • Loose motor mounts cause noise and instability when accelerating from a stop. • Wheel bearing axle grease leaks onto front disc pad, causing poor braking. • Rear windshield distortion causes road to appear wavy and cars to appear to be swerving. • Electrical shorts:

> Three different electrical shorts in a 2005 Toyota Avalon Limited with less [than] 5000 miles [8,000 km]. The shorts were in the brake light switch, the engine control unit, and the fuse box. The first and third short prevented the car from starting. The second short caused the engine to stall while traveling at 55 mph [90 km/h] on a major highway. It is a miracle that there was not an accident. The switch, engine control unit, and fuse box have all been replaced.

2006—Fire ignited in the rear middle seat from the seat heater overheating. • Sudden acceleration while cruising. • Engine hesitates on acceleration to merge with traffic. • WTI oil line corroded and ruptured, resulting in all of the oil leaking out of the engine. • Transmission hunts for the proper gear, lurches, and slips, and it shifts erratically at low speeds. • Navigation system doesn't function as intended. • Leaking brake master cylinder and booster may lead to loss of braking. • Sudden application of the brakes may cause the telescopic steering wheel to collapse inward. • Faulty "intermediate steering shaft" results in clunks when turning. • Laser cruise control fails intermittently. • Rough-riding Cooper Lifeliner tires. **2007**—Sudden acceleration when cruising. • Airbags fail to deploy. • Knee airbag deployment is alleged to have caused massive leg injuries to the driver. • When the laser cruise control is activated, rear brake lights don't come on to warn following drivers that the car is braking. • Excessive steering vibrations and pulling to the left and right. • Automatic transmission "bumps" into gear. • Inoperative push-button starter. • Ignition switch can cause keys to bend. • Smart Key ignition system can cause heart pacemakers and defibrillators to malfunction:

> The owner's manual of my 2007 Toyota Avalon warns that persons with implanted pacemakers or defibrillator[s] should not go near the antennae on the Smart Key system. My 91-year-old dad has an implanted defibrillator. Is there any way to get in, start the car, and disable the Smart Key so he can then approach the car and get in? What is the radio frequency and effective radiated power of the system so I can pass the information along to his cardiologist? What is the liability if I have the car parked on a public street and someone with an implanted defibrillator or pacemaker should happen to walk past the car without knowing the danger? Please help, as the dealer has not been able to find anything out about this. Also, the owner's manual warns about getting the Smart Key too close to electromagnetic devices such as credit cards and cell phones, cordless phone rechargers, fluorescent lights, etc. How can my wife carry the Smart Key in her purse with credit cards and cell phone?... Do I have to rearrange my life to avoid problems with the Smart Key? Also, the owner's manual warns the Smart Key might not work near broadcast operations. Several times a week, I have to go to a cable television head end.... I haven't taken the car there yet for fear of what might happen. Will I have to have it towed some distance away before the Smart Key technology will work?

• A $100 gas cap?

> Service Engine and many other trouble indicators at the same time. Trouble found for $80.00 loose gas cap. Days later found gas cap strap missing. Return to dealer who said the strap is what caused the poor seal so the tech removed it (as this happens all the time). Ask to purchase a replacement strap – not available. Purchased new gas cap which comes with strap (a 2 cent tiem) cost $25.00. Total cost for a known problem $100. Toyota knows about the little problem for most or all of its vehicles and has done nothing to correct it. It is a money maker for the dealers who never suggest looking at your gas cap. They connect it to anylizer for $80.00. Remove the strap and send you on your way. Shame shame shame.

2008—Headlights suddenly go out:

> Driving down a dark road, the high beams would not come on. Took it to Toyota dealership and they said high beams burned out and the repair would cost $2600. The dealership stated if they were replaced, they may burn out again.

•

> I just heard on the radio this morning there is a recall on the headlamps intermittently working/not working on the Prius. Please add the 2008 Toyota Avalon to this recall. On December 24, 2010, as my wife and I were leaving my daughter and son in-law's house at approx. 8:30 p.m., I used my remote start and started my car. My son-in-law looked outside and said, "You have a headlight out." It was the right front headlamp. I got in the car and turned the light switch off and turned it back on to "Auto" and both headlights came on once again. However, I had to turn them off and turn them back on to get them both working.

• Headlight transformer failed; dealer estimated it would cost $2,096 to fix. 2009—Sudden, unintended acceleration. • More headlight failures:

> 2009 Toyota Avalon; mileage at failure unknown, but less than 42,000. Both high beam bulbs exploded on the vehicle. Based on Internet research, this seems to be a known problem. Toyota issued a TSB 0044-10 on this failure 1/27/2010, yet they refuse to take ownership of the issue.

• Brake failures. • Steering column telescopic lock won't stay locked.

Secret Warranties/Internal Bulletins/Service Tips

1997–2002—Extended warranty will pay for engine sludge damage up to eight years, without any mileage limitation. 2000–01—Measures to reduce instrument panel luminosity. • Wheel bearing ticking noise. • Door popping and creaking. 2000–04—Fuel door hard to open. 2003–07—Windshield ticking noise. 2004—Correction for vehicle tendency to pull to the left. • Front suspension knocking. 2004–07—Front-seat squeak. 2005–06—Engine oil leaks. • Water leaks onto the front floor area. • Pull/drift to one side while driving. • Diagnosis and correction of steering-column noise. • Creaking and ticking noise heard from base of rear windshield. • Rear suspension thump, clunk. • Inoperative horn. **2005–07**—Rear vents blow warm air with AC on. • Front-door window won't roll up. • Windshield wiper fluid leaks. **2005–08**—Knocking noise from front of sunroof. **2005–09**—Leaks at headliner and floor areas. • Front power seat grinding, groaning. **2006–07**—Harsh shifting. **2006–08**—Excessive dust from vents. **2007**—Rough idle, stalling. **2007–08**—Steering-wheel flutter; body vibration.

AVALON PROFILE

	2001	2002	2003	2004	2005	2006	2007	2008	2009
Cost Price ($)									
XL	36,370	38,365	—	—	—	—	—	—	—
XLS	44,710	45,135	45,560	45,830	39,900	39,900	41,135	37,755	41,840
Used Values ($)									
XL ▲	4,500	5,000	—	—	—	—	—	—	—
XL ▼	3,500	4,000	—	—	—	—	—	—	—
XLS ▲	5,000	6,000	7,000	8,500	10,500	14,000	17,500	22,000	26,000
XLS ▼	4,500	5,500	6,000	7,500	9,000	12,500	16,000	20,000	24,000
Reliability	5	5	5	5	3	4	4	4	4
Crash Safety (F)	3	4	4	5	5	5	5	5	5
Side	4	4	4	4	5	5	5	5	5
IIHS Side	—	—	—	—	5	5	5	5	5
Offset	5	5	5	5	5	5	5	5	5
Head Restraints (F)	1	1	1	1	1	1	1	1	5
Rollover Resistance	—	4	4	4	4	4	4	4	4

Volvo

C30, C70, S40, S60, S70, S80, V40, V50, V70, XC70, XC90   ★

RATING: Not Recommended. All Volvos for all years (C30, C70, S40, S60, S70, S80, V40, V50, V70, XC70, and XC90). The C70, S70, and V70 are recent high-tech Volvos that are particularly dealer-dependent and will suffer most in servicing and value now that Volvo has been sold to the Chinese. Surprisingly, for a car company that emphasizes its commitment to safe cars and quality components, Volvo's entire lineup during the past decade has deteriorated from both quality and safety perspectives. There are two reasons for this decline: the use of more-complex, failure-prone electronics and Ford's poor stewardship of Volvo, which has led both firms to the point of bankruptcy. As a result, good dealers and technicians have left Volvo in droves to sell used cars or to work in independent garages; parts suppliers are in hiding, afraid of their own suppliers who haven't been paid; and customers are reluctant to buy a car from a company soon to be on the skids. Horrendous reports of safety- and performance-related problems abound, including engine and seat fires, loss of steering, sudden acceleration, transmission failures, electrical shorts, light failures, and tire blowouts. As if this weren't bad enough, Ford's Marquis de Sade–trained customer relations staff has left many new- and used-Volvo buyers so angry they could spit nails. **"Real" city/highway fuel economy:** *Turbo manual: 12.8/8.4 L/100 km. Turbo automatic: 12.3/8.4 L/100 km. C70 manual: 11.7/8.0 L/100 km. C70 automatic: 11.4/7.6 L/100 km. XC70 2.5: 12.6/8.8 L/100 km. XC90 2.5: 13.3/9.1 L/100 km. XC90 T6 2.9: 15.6/10.6 L/100 km. S40, V40 manual: 10.8/7.3 L/100 km. S40, V40 automatic: 10.7/7.0 L/100 km. S60 manual: 10.8/7.3 L/100 km. S60 automatic: 10.7/7.0 L/100 km. S60 2.4T AWD: 11.7/7.9 L/100 km. S60 R manual: 13.1/8.6 L/100 km. S60 R automatic: 13.2/8.6 L/100 km. S60 T5: 11.5/8.0 L/100 km. S70 manual: 11.2/7.6 L/100 km. S70 automatic: 10.6/7.7 L/100 km. S80 2.9: 11.9/7.8 L/100 km. S80 2.5L AWD: 11.7/7.9 L/100 km. S80 T6: 12.6/8.3 L/100 km. V70 2.4 manual: 10.8/7.3 L/100 km. V70 2.4 automatic: 10.9/7.1 L/100 km. V70 2.5LT AWD: 11.7/7.9 L/100 km. V70 2.5LT R AWD manual: 13.1/8.6 L/100 km. V70 2.5LT R AWD automatic: 13.2/8.6 L/100 km.* Actual fuel consumption may be higher than these figures by 10–20 percent. **Maintenance/Repair costs:** Higher-than-average costs, and repairs must be done by a Volvo dealer. **Parts:** Higher-than-average costs, and limited availability. **Extended warranty:** A good idea, considering that even some of the most mundane repairs can be costly to perform. **Best alternatives:** Acura RL or TL; Hyundai Genesis; Infiniti G35; and early Nissan Maxima. If you have to scratch that itch for a European car, pick up an Above Average BMW. **Helpful websites:** *www.volvoforums.com/forum* and *www.volvoforum.com.*

Strengths and Weaknesses

70 Series

Bland and failure-prone but practical to the extreme, the 1998 model 850s were renamed the C70, S70, and V70; they all have a disappointingly high number of safety- and performance-related deficiencies reported by owners taken in by Volvo's safety and quality hype. The letters S, V, and C preceding the numerical designation stand for sedans, wagons, and coupes.

With the front-drive 70 Series, all-wheel drive is offered with the wagons, and the base 2.4L 5-cylinder engine comes with three horsepower ratings: 168, 190, and 236 hp. Only two transmissions are available: a manual 5-speed (relatively rare) and an automatic 4-speed. Handling is superb, with the suspension dampened somewhat for a more-comfortable ride than what many European imports offer. AWD performs flawlessly, road and body noise are muted, and the cars are well appointed with a full array of standard safety features, with the exception of traction control, which is optional.

VEHICLE HISTORY: 2001—Station wagons get more interior room. The S70 sedans, base and GLT wagons, and the high-performance R-type are gone, but the C70 coupe and convertible remain. Traction control is standard on the T5 only; all models have anti-lock all-disc brakes, front head/chest side-impact airbags, curtain window airbags, and more-protective head restraints. **2002**—An all-wheel-drive 2.4T comes on board, Volvo's anti-skid system is standard on the T5, and traction control is standard on all front-drives. **2003**—The V70 2.5T AWD and XC70 get a power boost of 11 extra horses, and the T5's power is cranked up to 247 horses. **2004**—Debut of the high-performance 300 hp V70R, equipped with AWD and a 6-speed manual or 5-speed automatic transmission. **2005**—Refreshed styling, optional run-flat tires (a bad idea), and a firmer suspension for the T5. The AWD V70 2.5T is gone.

On the downside, rear seating is cramped for three adults, and the instrument panel appears overly busy, with a confusing array of gauges, instruments, and controls on the centre console. Plus, the three rear head restraints induce claustrophobia while severely restricting rear visibility.

As far as quality control and dealer servicing are concerned, Volvo technical service bulletins and owner complaints indicate that factory defects on all models have been on the rise over the past 10 years. For example, the car's electrical system may go berserk or shut down entirely in rainy weather or when the car is passing over puddles; headlights, turn signal lights, and other bulbs burn out monthly; power window switches and locks fail constantly; wheels are easily bent; the turn signal lever doesn't return; airbags deploy for no reason; and springs are noisy.

The above defects clearly show that quality control is less stringent at the factory level since Ford acquired the company almost a decade ago. Volvo blames Ford for its poor-quality cars, while Ford targets Volvo factories and dealers' service personnel for failing to prevent and repair factory mistakes. They both are arguing a moot point: Volvo sales have fallen so far that Ford has secretly put Volvo on the auction block (no takers so far), and many dealers are shutting their doors before Ford's mismanagement bankrupts them.

C70

The C70's strong points: good acceleration with lots of torque, exceptional steering and handling, first-class body construction and finish, and predicted better-than-average reliability. Its weak points: difficult rear-seat entry/exit, some engine turbo lag, excessive engine noise, a jarring suspension, and an uncertain future.

Seating four comfortably, the luxury coupe and convertible are based on the 850 (pardon, S70) platform and marketed as high-performance Volvos. C70 comes with two turbocharged engines: a base 190 hp 2.4L inline 5-cylinder and a 236 hp 2.3L variant. Either engine can be hooked to a 5-speed manual or 4-speed automatic transmission. Of the two engines, the 2.4L appears to offer the best response and smoothest performance, although servicing and durability remain problematic. Acceleration is impressive, despite the fact that the car feels underpowered until the turbo kicks in at around 1500 rpm—a feature that drivers will find more frustrating with a manual shifter than with an automatic. Steering and handling are first class; build quality leaves much to desire.

Other things not to like are turbo lag, tire thumping caused by the high-performance tires, excessive engine and wind noise, and power-sliding rear seats that require lots of skill and patience to operate.

C30

The C30 two-door hatchback is Volvo's smallest car, and a mini version of the S40 sedan and V50 wagon. This $27,500 (new in 2007) midget performer is powered by a 227 hp 2.5L turbocharged 5-cylinder engine coupled to a 6-speed manual transmission (a 5-speed automatic is optional). Available safety features include ABS, traction control, anti-skid system, front side airbags, and side curtain airbags. All models have four bucket-style seats.

Drivers looking for a small car they can throw into corners and quickly merge with fast traffic will love this peppy, nice-handling, sporty luxury car. On the other hand, interior room in the rear is quite limited, and there's not much trunk space either. Quality is a crapshoot, if you use as your guide the poor ratings garnered by the V50 (fuel, electrical, audio, and climate systems as well as fit and finish). Of more immediate concern is the imminent sale of Volvo by Ford to another automaker. This move will guarantee a low resale value, decimate the dealer network, and make parts and servicing a nightmare for this relatively new model.

S40 and V40

Volvo's small sedan and wagon come with a 150 hp 1.9L turbocharged 4-cylinder engine coupled with an automatic transmission. Two side airbags, anti-lock brakes, air conditioning, cruise control, and power windows are also standard. The 2001 model got a minor facelift, an upgraded engine and 5-speed automatic transmission, side curtain airbags, and some handling improvements.

These models have also generated an unacceptably high number of complaints concerning chronic brake repairs, automatic transmission failures, fuel-system malfunctions leading to poor driveability, and myriad electrical shorts and body defects.

S60

This sporty, mid-range sedan uses the same large-car platform as the V70 and S80 but has proven to be more reliable, beginning with the 2004 models. A 197 hp 5-cylinder engine teamed with an all-wheel-drive powertrain has been added to the lineup. Drivers will have the choice of three inline 5-cylinder engines: a 168 hp naturally aspirated version, a 197 hp low-pressure turbo, and a 247 hp high-pressure turbo.

Some of the S60's pluses are fair acceleration; exceptional handling and braking; a good array of user-friendly instruments and controls; comfortable front seating; and very good front, side, offset, and head-restraint crashworthiness scores. Some of the car's deficiencies include an imprecise manual shifter; lots of turbo throttle hesitation and torque steer pulling when accelerating; a jarring ride with some tire thump (worse with the T5) when passing over uneven pavement; rear visibility that's obstructed by a high parcel shelf, obtrusive head restraints, and a descending roofline; cramped rear seating, made worse by rear legroom that disappears when the front seats are pushed back only halfway; a narrow trunk with a small opening; and turbo engines that require premium fuel. Other cars worth considering are the Acura TL and Infiniti I35.

S80

The S80 is a redesign of the S90 (dropped after the 1998 model year) and offers several interesting new features, such as a powerful 268 hp transverse inline 6-cylinder engine and a sophisticated automatic transmission called the "Geartronic"—a 4-speed automatic with a feature for manually changing gears if one so desires. Additionally, the car is chock full of safety features, has the largest interior of any Volvo, gives impressive performance and handling, and is attractively styled.

VEHICLE HISTORY: 2001—Dual-stage airbags and 16-inch wheels. **2002**—Engine tweaks give more power at a lower rpm, and the base engine drops a few horses. Addition of an in-trunk emergency release and new alloy wheels. **2004**—Refreshed styling, new gauges, and all-wheel drive added. **2005**—Wood interior trim, optional run-flat tires, and larger wheels on the high-performance models.

Unfortunately, the S80's numerous defects closely resemble the problems reported in prior years' models and seriously undermine Volvo's much-touted safety claims.

XC70, XC90

Essentially a renamed V70 station wagon, the XC70 is an SUV wannabe that offers five-passenger seating, high ground clearance, sleek styling, and AWD versatility. Its mechanical components are practically identical to those of Volvo's other sedans. The base engine is a 168 hp (non-turbo) 2.4L 5-cylinder. The turbo version has been replaced by a 208 hp 2.5L turbocharged 5-cylinder hooked to a 5-speed automatic gearbox. It is followed by the 247 hp 2.5L turbocharged T5 and a 300 hp variant found on the V70R.

XC90 models are based on Volvo's S80 car platform and aren't intended for off-road use. They offer seven-passenger seating along with a base turbocharged 208 hp 2.5L 5-cylinder and an optional 268 hp 2.9L V6 on the T6 version. All transmissions have a manual shiftgate. However, the AWD system lacks low-range gearing. Anti-lock four-wheel disc brakes, anti-skid/traction control, and Roll Stability Control are standard. Also included are front torso side airbags and head-protecting side curtain airbags that cover all seating rows.

Problem areas are limited to frequent brake maintenance (rotors and pads), chronic stalling, and electrical system and body faults (inoperative moonroof, door locks, and gauges), notably excessive windshield/dash glare and side windows that won't close until the control button is pressed three times. Poor fuel economy is also a recurring complaint.

Safety Summary

All models/years: Sudden acceleration when applying brakes. • Vehicle shuts down when making a left turn. • Airbags fail to deploy. • While underway, driver seat suddenly moves backward. • Fuel fumes leak into interior. • Brake pedal locks up. • Chronic light failures. • Automatic door locks, and trunk lock fails to open. • Automatic gas-tank door jams shut. • Tailpipe extends beyond bumper, burning anyone who brushes up against the back of the car. • Inside door handles pinch fingers. *C70:* **2006**—Many complaints that tires lose air due to cracked rims. • Airbag light is always on. **2007**—Xenon headlights fail to illuminate the road sufficiently; they produce a black "curtain" extending halfway down the windshield. • Window rattling and various air and water leaks. • Defective driver-side seat heater, and the AC blows super-heated air from the driver-side air vent. *S40:* **2006**—Sudden stall-out in traffic; doors automatically lock, wipers self-activate, lights go off, and vehicle will not restart. • Many complaints that the heater blower won't defrost the front windshield or side mirrors. • AC blows hot air. • Many owners report serious electrical malfunctions when it rains (2004 models were recalled for the same problem). • Brake and gas pedals are mounted too close together. • Michelin Energy tire side wall blowout. **2007**—Fire ignites in the rear brakes while vehicle underway. • Manual 5-speed clutch pedal operation is compromised by a protruding panel. *V70:* **2001**—Excessive reflection of beige dash onto windshield. • Engine mounts break. • Vehicle can roll away when parked on an incline. • Brake pedal is too close to gas pedal. • Front door indent doesn't hold door open. • Sunroof blows in while going through a car wash. • Rear tailgate door won't lock. • Coffee spilled from cupholder shorts the airbag computer. • Frequent bulb failures. **2002**—Shoulder belt crosses at neck. • Sunroof breaks and falls into roof liner. **2003**—Emergency brake bracket comes apart. **2004**—Car easily damaged when going over a bump at low speed:

> Car was damaged going over a speed bump (on public road) at about 5 mph [8 km/h]. There is a recall in Europe to fix this problem (by removing a bracket that...can be forced upwards, damaging the exhaust and driveshaft).

• Fuel gushes out when refuelling. • Vehicle pulls to the right. • Loose steering caused by a prematurely worn-out tie rod. • One driver suffered a concussion in an accident when the driver's head hit the interior handholds, which are often bumped into. • Poor headlight illumination. **2005**—Car frequently stalls out. • Unexpected and intermittent brake failure (see *forums.swedespeed.com/zerothread?id=32551*). • Passenger-side airbag is disabled if the occupant moves. *S80:* **2001–02**—Lights continually burn out. **2003**—Sudden, unintended acceleration. • Front wheel falls off after the ball joint separates. **2004**—Excessive steering shake causes car to go out of control. **2005**—Cracked oil pump. *V40*: The brake pedal won't depress, causing total brake loss or extended stopping distances and premature wearout of the front brake pads (around 20,000 km). **2001**—Under-hood electrical fire. • Cracked fuel regulator pump spilled fuel onto hot engine, and fumes spread into the interior. • Sudden, unintended acceleration when vehicle put into Drive. • Chronic stalling attributed to faulty idle control valve and air mass meter. • Complete loss of braking. • Brakes don't stop vehicle within a reasonable distance. • Brake pedal is too close to the gas pedal. • In one vehicle, the brake pedal snapped, went to the floor while the car was going downhill. • When applying the brakes in cold weather, pedal won't depress, causing extended stopping distances. • Premature replacement of the front and rear rotors and pads. • Vehicle pulls to the left when accelerating or coming to a stop. • Repeated automatic transmission failures. **2002**—Sudden, unintended acceleration. • Annoying reflection of the dash onto the windshield. • ABS failure. • Rear brake pads wear out prematurely and ruin the rotors. • Horn is hard to activate. **2003**— Faulty engine fuel line. • Transmission slips from Second to Third and shifts harshly:

> This transmission slipping usually lasts for 2 to 3 seconds and this loss of power can easily put me into a major accident.

2004—Sudden, unintended acceleration. • Total loss of braking capability. • Brake and accelerator are mounted too close to each other. • Sun glare washes out dashboard instrument readings. • Gas gauge gives inaccurate readings. • Power windows and doors malfunction. • Tail lights, parking lights, and side marker lights won't come on, and sometimes all of the dash gauges go out. • Radio and climate controls turn off by themselves. **2005**—Parking brake won't hold the car on an incline. • Original-equipment scissor jack won't hold up the car. *XC70*: **2003**—Loose fuel lines. **2004**—While cruising on the highway, engine suddenly started racing, steering wheel and brakes locked, and all gauges went dead. • Rear-view mirror auto-dim feature doesn't work. *XC90*: **2003**—Unable to turn key in the ignition. **2004**—Airbags fail to deploy when car hit from the side. • Vehicle's all-wheel-drive feature causes the car to handle erratically and go out of control. • When shifting into Park, shifter inadvertently goes into Reverse. • Engine seizure due to a buildup of engine sludge. • Transmission interlock becomes disengaged when remote door-lock key fob is activated; one incident caused the car to roll down a hill. • Transmission replacement during car's second year on the road. • Gearshift indicator either goes blank or shows the wrong gear. • Doors suddenly unlock themselves and open while vehicle is underway.

Secret Warranties/Internal Bulletins/Service Tips

All models/years: Check the valve-cover nuts at every servicing interval to prevent oil leakage. • Free front seat belt extenders available. • Rear suspension popping or "boing" noise. **All models: 1999–2004**—Knocking noise when turning. **1999–2005**—Manual transmission may not shift easily into First or Reverse gear. **2002–04**—Engine knock, rattle, and low power. **2003–04**—Xenon headlights may be inoperative due to a faulty ballast. **2003–06**—Eliminating musty odours from the air vents. **2004**—Reasons why engine may run roughly. • Electrically powered seats rock back and forth. • Rear suspension noise. **2004–05**—Wheel bolt corrosion. **2005**—Engine may have a rough idle, misfire, run roughly, or lack power. • AC stops working intermittently. **2005–06**—Seat backrest play/noise. • Vent air temperatures cycle from hot to cold. *C70, V70, S60, S70, S80:* **1999–2001** Defective throttles cause the vehicles to stall and fail air emissions tests, sticking owners with costly repairs. Volvo has "quietly" agreed with U.S. Environmental Protection Agency and California authorities to extend the warranty up to 10 years/320,000 km (200,000 mi.). As part of the agreement, Volvo will also reimburse owners who have already had the defective throttles replaced. The cost to replace the throttle can reach up to $1,000. The faulty throttles are also the subject of a class action lawsuit charging that Volvo violated California law by issuing a "secret warranty" to assist some, but not all, owners of vehicles with defective throttles. *850, S70, V70:* **1998–2004**—Manual transmission doesn't easily shift into Reverse or First gear. *S60, S80, V70:* **1999–2004**—Brake, exhaust system resonance, vibration. *S60, V70:* **2001**—Uneven idle. • Front-seat noise, rocking. **2002–04**—Engine knock and rattle with reduced power. *C70:* **1998–2002**—Uneven idle. **2003–05**—Wheel bolt corrosion. *S80:* **1999–2001**—Defective electronic throttle module covered by a secret 10-year warranty. **1999–2003**—Suspension resonance, vibration. **2001**—Body squeak or crunch noise brought on by wet or cold weather. **2002–04**—Engine knock and rattle with low power. **2003–06**—Eliminating musty odours coming from the air vents. **2004–05**—Park assist relay free replacement campaign. **2005–06**—Vent temperature cycles from hot to cold.

C30, C70, S40, S60, S80, V40, V50, V70, XC70, XC90 PROFILE

	2001	2002	2003	2004	2005	2006	2007	2008	2009
Cost Price ($)									
C30	—	—	—	—	—	—	27,495	27,495	27,695
C70	52,995	49,995	59,595	59,595	—	55,995	56,495	56,795	52,095
S40	31,400	31,495	31,495	31,495	29,995	31,120	31,495	31,695	31,495
S60	35,995	36,495	36,495	36,495	36,995	40,620	40,995	31,495	36,395
S80	54,395	54,395	54,895	54,895	54,995	54,995	54,995	54,995	49,995
V40/50	32,400	32,495	32,495	32,495	31,495	32,620	32,995	32,995	33,195
V70	37,495	37,995	37,995	37,995	38,495	39,120	39,495	41,995	43,995
XC70 AWD	—	—	49,495	49,495	46,495	47,121	47,496	46,495	44,095
XC90 AWD	—	—	—	—	49,995	49,995	50,995	50,995	48,595
Used Values ($)									
C30 ▲	—	—	—	—	—	—	12,500	16,000	18,000
C30 ▼	—	—	—	—	—	—	11,000	14,500	16,000
C70 ▲	7,500	9,000	11,000	13,000	—	18,000	22,000	31,000	35,000
C70 ▼	6,000	8,000	9,500	12,000	—	16,000	20,000	28,000	33,000
S40 ▲	4,000	4,500	5,500	6,500	8,000	9,500	12,500	16,000	20,000
S40 ▼	3,500	4,000	5,000	5,500	7,000	8,000	11,000	14,000	18,500

S60 ▲	4,500	5,500	7,000	8,500	10,000	13,000	17,000	22,000	26,000
S60 ▼	4,500	5,000	6,000	7,500	8,500	11,500	15,000	20,000	24,000
S80 ▲	5,500	7.000	8,500	10,000	12,000	14,500	20,000	28,000	31,000
S80 ▼	5,000	6,000	7,500	9,000	10,500	13,000	18,000	25,000	19,000
V40/50 ▲	3,500	4,000	5,000	6,000	8,000	9,500	12,500	17,000	21,000
V40/50 ▼	3,000	3,500	4,000	5,000	6,500	8,000	11,000	15,500	19,000
V70 ▲	4,500	5,000	6,000	8,500	10,500	14,000	17,000	22,000	29,000
V70 ▼	4,000	4,500	5,000	7,000	9,000	13,000	15,000	20,000	27,000
XC70 AWD ▲	—	—	6,500	8,500	11,000	14,000	18,000	23,500	30,000
XC70 AWD ▼	—	—	5,500	7,000	9,500	12,500	16,000	21,500	28,000
XC90 AWD ▲	—	—	—	—	13,000	16,500	20,000	24,000	31,000
XC90 AWD ▼	—	—	—	—	11,500	15,000	18,000	22,000	29,000
Reliability	2	2	2	2	2	2	2	2	2
S60	2	3	4	4	4	4	4	4	4
Crash Safety (F)									
S40	—	—	—	4	4	4	4	4	4
S60	4	4	4	4	4	4	4	4	4
S80	5	5	5	5	5	5	—	—	—
V70	—	—	—	—	5	5	5	—	—
XC70 AWD	—	—	—	—	5	5	5	—	—
XC90 AWD	—	—	4	5	5	5	5	5	5
Side									
S40	—	—	—	—	5	5	5	5	5
S60	5	5	5	5	5	5	5	5	5
S80	5	5	5	5	5	5	—	—	—
V70	—	—	—	—	5	5	5	—	—
XC70 AWD	—	—	—	—	5	5	5	—	—
XC90 AWD	—	—	5	5	5	5	5	5	5
IIHS Side									
C30	—	—	—	—	—	—	—	5	5
C70	—	—	—	—	—	5	5	5	5
S40	—	—	—	—	3	3	3	3	3
S60	—	—	—	—	3	3	3	3	3
XC90 AWD	—	—	—	—	5	5	5	5	5
Offset									
C30	—	—	—	—	—	—	—	5	5
S40	—	5	5	5	5	5	5	5	5
S60	5	5	5	5	5	5	5	5	5
S80	5	5	5	5	5	5	5	5	5
XC90 AWD	—	—	5	5	5	5	5	5	5
Head Restraints									
C30	—	—	—	—	—	—	—	5	5
C70	—	—	—	—	—	5	5	5	5

All ratings on a numbered scale where ▒ is good and **1** is bad. See page 132 for a more detailed description.

S40/V40	—	—	—	5	5	5	5	5	5
S60	—	—	5	5	5	5	5	5	5
S80	—	—	5	5	5	5	5	5	5
XC90 AWD	—	—	—	—	5	5	5	5	5

Roof Strength

C30	—	—	—	—	—	—	—	5	5
S40	—	—	—	3	3	3	3	3	3
XC90 AWD	—	—	5	5	5	5	5	5	5

Rollover Resistance

S40	—	—	—	—	4	4	4	4	4
S60	—	—	5	5	5	5	5	5	5
S80	5	5	5	5	5	—	—	—	
V70	—	—	—	—	4	4	4	—	—
XC70 AWD	—	—	—	—	4	4	4	—	—
XC90 AWD	—	—	—	4	4	4	4	4	4

SPORTS CARS

Sudden, "Intended" Acceleration

I hooked up my accelerator pedal in my car to my brake lights. I hit the gas, people behind me stop, and I'm gone.

STEVEN WRIGHT

Four-Wheeled Fun

Yes, we all know that these small, low cars with high-powered, fuel-thirsty engines and seating for only two are a dangerous choice for young drivers, and scream "Mid-life crisis!" when driven by pony-tailed, open-shirted middle-aged men. They're also usually way overpriced and astronomically expensive to insure and service as they top off Helmut and Luigi's Canada Pension Plan. Most sports cars beg to be driven too fast and attract more traffic tickets than chicks.

But they're so much fun to drive, especially for those of us who missed our chance to own one in our youth because we were too poor, practical, or preoccupied with our Cavaliers, Corollas, or Beetles to give in to our primal instincts.

If real driving performance is important to you, though, remember that big isn't always better. Consider getting an agile, fun-to-drive small car, such as a used Acura Integra, Honda Civic Si, Mazda Miata, or Nissan Sentra SE-R. If you want to be a little more "in your face," however, it's hard to lose money with a Detroit muscle-car sportster built through 1974.

Look at the list below for some of the more popular sports cars sold over the last three decades. If you have a limited budget, or little experience driving a performance car, start out with one of the "sporty" makes, then move through the two-seaters, muscle cars, and then the ultimate: the luxury sports cars. Remember, though, there are some real dogs on this list, so check their ratings carefully.

Affordable Sports Cars

TWO-SEATER SPORTS CARS

BMW Z3 3.0 Roadster (2002: $56,200; used: $12,000)
BMW Z4 3.0 Roadster (2006: $53,900; used: $21,000)
Chevrolet Corvette (2006: $67,805; used: $23,000)
*Mazda MX-5 Miata (2006: $27,995; used: $12,500)
Mercedes-Benz SLK350 (2006: $59,950; used: $23,500)
Nissan 370Z Touring (2009: $38,998; used: $26,500)
Nissan 350Z Grand Touring (2006: $45,998; used: $13,500)
Porsche Boxster (2006: $64,100; used: $23,000)

SPORTY CARS

*BMW 135i (2008: $41,600; used: $26,000)
Chevrolet Cobalt S/C (2006: $24,195; used: $11,000)
Dodge Caliber SRT4 (2008: $24,995; used: $8,000)
*Honda Civic Si (2006: $25,880; used: $10,500)
*Honda Prelude (2001: $28,300; used: $5,000)
*Hyundai Tiburon GT (2007: $24,495; used: $10,000)
*Mazda3 GT (2006: $21,545; used: $8,500)
*Mazda6 GT (2006: $33,795; used: $11,500)
Mazda RX-8 GT (2006: $40,295; used: $13,500)
Mini Cooper S (2006: $30,600; used: $11,500)
*Mitsubishi Eclipse GT (2006: $32,998; used: $9,500)
Mitsubishi Lancer Ralliart (2006: $22,778; used:
    $6,500)
*Nissan Sentra SE-R (2006: $21,698; used: $8,000)
Subaru Impreza WRX STi (2006: $48,995; used:
    $12,000)
*Toyota Celica (2005: $24,900; used: $10,500)
Volkswagen GTi (2006: $27,630; used: $10,500)
Volvo C30 (2007: $27,495; used: $12,500)

MUSCLE CARS

Chevrolet Camaro (2002: $26,995,000; used: $4,000)
Dodge Challenger SRT8 (2009: $45,995; used: $31,000)
*Ford Mustang GT (2006: $32,999; used: $12,500)
*Hyundai Genesis V8 (2009: $43,995; used: $29,000)
*Pontiac Firebird (2002: $27,695; used: $5,000)

LUXURY SPORTS CARS

BMW 650i (2006: $101,400; used: $41,000)
Chevrolet Corvette Z06 (2006: $89,900; used: $32,000)
Dodge Viper (2006: $127,000; used: $37,000)Lexus SC 430 (2006: $92,650,000; used: $30,000)
Mercedes-Benz SL550 (2007: $133,500; used: $55,000)
*Nissan GT-R (2009: $89,900; used: $68,000)
Porsche 911 Carrera S (2006: $119,000; used: $40,000)

* *Lemon-Aid* rates this car a good buy.

If you want a cheap and fairly reliable Mustang, consider a 2007 GT convertible for about $18,000, or almost $20,000 off its original price. The car had two model years to digest its redesign glitches and is a good performer.

Varieties of Sports Cars

There are different kinds of sports cars to consider: traditional two-seater roadsters, styled much like the MGB of the early '70s or Mazda's Miata; sporty coupes and hatchbacks, such as the Japanese Acura Integra, Honda Civic Si, Mazda MX-3, and Toyota Celica, which offer sportier styling, performance, and handling than their entry-level versions and are cheaper and more versatile to maintain than traditional sports cars; and muscle cars, which feature large engines and a few more creature comforts. The best deal in the latter category is the V8-equipped Ford Mustang with the GM Camaro or Firebird a distant second. Interestingly, that lead has increased with Ford's reworked 2011 iteration giving its V6 the power of the previous year's V8 powerplant, with better fuel economy.

There's a comprehensive forum at *www.sportscarforums.com* that goes into mind-numbing detail as to what makes a good sports car. Different cars are rated, service tips are given, and the age-old feud between domestics and imports is omnipresent and unresolved.

The biggest irony of all is that Japanese high-performance sports cars and pickups have won favour in the Deep South and throughout Canada because they deliver high-performance thrills without the service bay bills. No longer do you hear contemptuous references to Asian "rice-burners" now that Toyota and other Asian automakers are successfully racing their cars and trucks at NASCAR-sanctioned tracks.

The Downside

We all know the drawbacks. Most sports cars—or "high-performance vehicles," as they're euphemistically named—don't offer the comfort or reliability of a Honda Civic, a Toyota Celica, or even a Hyundai Tiburon. Instead, they sacrifice reliability, interior space, and a comfortable suspension for speed, superior road handling, and attractive styling. They also need a whole slew of expensive and quick-to-depreciate high-performance packages, because many entry-level sports cars aren't very sporty in their basic form. Remember, too, that used sports cars often have serious accident damage that may not have been repaired properly, resulting in serious tracking problems if the chassis is bent.

Forget how quickly the Z06 goes from 0 to 100 km/h; check instead how fast its value drops from $90,000 to $32,000!

Beware of false bargains. Although a 2008 Dodge Charger or 2009 Challenger is a steal at $10,500 and $17,500, respectively, the money saved will be quickly spent in high maintenance costs and frequent repairs.

Fully loaded used sports cars usually sell at a fraction of their original cost, and very few end up as collectibles. Most models that have been taken off the market—such as the Toyota Supra, Nissan 300ZX, and Chevrolet Corvette ZR1—aren't likely to become collectors' cars with soaring resale values. In fact, a 2006 Corvette 7.0L Z06 that sold originally for $90,000 in Canada can now be picked up for about $32,000! A 2011 version goes for $95,705. Even discontinued popular Japanese sports cars haven't done nearly as well as some of the British roadsters that were taken off the market in the '70s.

Like early Mustangs, GM Camaros and Firebirds can be fun cars to drive and can make you a tidy profit as a trade-in, once tricked out with some relatively inexpensive options. Not only are they reasonably reliable and cheap cars to maintain, but their resale prices are fairly stable and there's plenty of used stock to choose from. But don't expect them to appreciate in value any time soon, especially, with much-improved models waiting in the wings.

When buying a sports car, keep in mind that the more features you add, the less reliable the car becomes, and that there are some modifications that are more important than others. For example, good-quality high-performance tires are the first investment you should make (check the owner-polled recommendations at *www.tirerack.com/tires/reviews/MenuServlet?search=surveyComments*). Other improvements that should have a high priority are an upgraded set of brakes and suspension. And, if you have a few dollars left, consider getting a more-responsive rear end and a high-performance transmission.

SPORTS CAR RATINGS

Recommended

Mazda MX-5 (Miata) (1999–2009)

Above Average

Ford Mustang (2006–09)

Average

Ford Mustang (2001–04)   General Motors Corvette (2005–09)

Below Average

Ford Mustang (2005)   General Motors Corvette (1999–2004)

Not Recommended

Ford Cobra (1999–2004)

Ford

MUSTANG, COBRA	★★★★/★

RATING: *Mustang:* Above Average (2006–09); Below Average (2005); Average (2001–04). The 2006 version worked out many of the 2005 redesign glitches, and incremental improvements reduced factory-related defects found on the pre-2005 models. *Cobra:* Not Recommended (1999–2004). Here's the problem: A decade ago, Ford alienated its parts suppliers and reduced reliability through unrealistic price-cutting and last-minute, poorly thought-out component changes. During the past several years, though, supplier relations have improved dramatically and quality has improved as well. Keep in mind, however, that Mustangs that aren't equipped with traction control are treacherous on wet roads, and they have had a frighteningly high number of safety-related mechanical failures (especially chronic stalling). Additionally, new crash data indicates the vehicles may be fire-prone following collisions at moderate speeds. GM's Camaro and Firebird are the Mustang's traditional competition as far as performance is concerned, and they're good buys even though they haven't been built since 2002. Ford has the pricing and servicing advantage, with a base Mustang costing a bit less than the cheapest Camaro, but it lags from a performance standpoint. In that area, the equivalent model-year Camaro and Firebird offer more sure-footed acceleration, crisper handling, standard ABS, a 6-speed transmission, and more-comfortable rear seats. Fuel-savers beware: All 4-cylinder Mustangs should be shunned because they provide insufficient power, they aren't very durable, and the fuel savings are much less than you'd think. **Ideal model year:** You won't want to hear this, but here it goes anyway: The best Mustang you can buy that gives you first-class performance, great fuel economy, optimum safety features, quality craftsmanship, and a base price your gardener can afford is the…2011 Mustang V6. Anything less, and you're buying third-rate. Still, if you want a 'stang right now, you should consider a 2007 LX for about $10,500. That gives the car two model years to digest its redesign anomalies and keeps you mobile for a few years until you can buy a much better-performing used 2011 version. **"Real" city/highway fuel economy:** *Mustang 3.8 manual: 11.8/7.4 L/100 km. Mustang 3.8 automatic: 12.0/8.0 L/100 km. Mustang 3.9 manual: 11.7/7.4 L/100 km. Mustang 3.9 automatic: 12.3/8.2 L/100 km. Mustang 4.6 manual: 14.0/8.7 L/100 km. Mustang 4.6 automatic: 13.2/9.4 L/100 km. Mustang Mach 1 manual: 13.9/8.5 L/100 km. Mustang Mach 1 automatic: 13.8/9.5 L/100 km. Cobra: 14.1/9.1 L/100 km.* Fuel savings may be lower by about 20 percent on 4-cylinder models, 15 percent with 6-cylinders, and almost 25 percent with 8-cylinders. **Maintenance/Repair costs:** Average, particularly because repairs can be done anywhere. **Parts:** Average costs, and parts are often sold for much less through independent suppliers. Some parts are continually back ordered, particularly if involved in recall repairs. **Extended warranty:** A good idea for the powertrain. **Best alternatives:** GM Camaro, Honda Civic Si, Hyundai Genesis, Hyundai G35, and Mazda MX-5 (Miata) or Mazda3. **Helpful websites:** *www.mustangforums.com/forum/2005-2011-mustangs-43*; *www.allfordmustangs.com*; and *www.flatratetech.com/community*.

 ## Strengths and Weaknesses

This is definitely not a family car. A light rear end makes the car dangerously unstable on wet roads or when cornering at high speeds, unless equipped with traction control (optional on most models). But for those who want a sturdy and stylish second car, or who don't need room in the back or standard ABS, 2001–04 and 2006–09 Mustangs are reasonably good sports car buys, thanks to their maxed-out depreciation, powertrain improvements, and fewer factory defects.

1994–2004 Mustang

Through the years, these models got four-wheel disc brakes, more-powerful engines, additional airbags, manumatic gearboxes with more gears, and a more-rigid chassis meant to reduce rattles and water leaks (which didn't work). Even more disappointing, Ford's performance- and safety-related problems were carried over year after year (see "Safety Summary"). Engines and transmissions continue to be glitch-prone: Both the V6 and V8 have a propensity for chronic surging and stalling, and they experience failed motor mounts; engine stalls when decelerating; prematurely worn clutch pressure plates; faulty differential carrier bearings; blown engine intake manifold and head gaskets; differential howling or whining (ring and pinion failures); fuel-system malfunctions, highlighted by frequent fuel-injector replacement; poorly shifting automatic transmissions, especially from First to Second gear; and ticking and rattling at 3000 rpm until the car shifts into Second gear. Owners also frequently complain of electrical short circuits causing instrument panel shutdown; the early replacement of brake rotors, pads, and calipers; and unbelievably poor fit and finish highlighted by wind noise, water leaks, premature rusting, an easily pitted windshield, paint delamination and peeling, and various clunks and rattles. Other noises include engine ticking caused by bad lifters, steering creaks when turning, a clunking front suspension, tie-rod ends that "pop," and rear-end pinion gear whine. The Shaker 1000 stereo system constantly malfunctions, and fuel gauge readings are erratic, especially when the tank is less than half full.

2005–09 Mustang

The redesigned 2005 models gain about 15 cm in wheelbase and overall length over their 1999–2004 predecessors, plus about 45 kg on coupes and 125 kg on convertibles. A 210 hp 4.0L V6 replaces the previous 193 hp 3.8L. GTs carry a 4.6L V8, but with 300 hp instead of the 2004's 260 hp. The optional automatic is a 5-speed, versus the previous 4-speed. All 2005 Mustangs come with AC and four-wheel disc brakes, but ABS and traction control are standard only on the GT version. No anti-skid system is available, and full-body front side airbags are optional. All Mustangs come with air conditioning and a CD player.

Ford's reworking of the 2005 gave the Mustang a bit more muscle and slightly better performance, but the absence of ABS, an anti-skid system, independent rear suspension, and side airbags are four notable deficiencies when compared with the competition. Reliability actually went downhill during the first year of the redesign, only to improve with later models.

Nevertheless, a new subset of failures appeared with the 2006–09 cars, including tire-air leakage from faulty tire stems, rear-end howling, transmission fluid leakage, premature transmission failure, lag-and-lurch acceleration, transmission clutch slippage, sudden control-arm breakage, difficult refuelling, front end noise with low-speed turns, excessive brake noise, and electrical, fuel delivery, and fit and finish deficiencies (particularly, damage to the driver's side window from scratches caused by the hard plastic gasket on the window assembly's inner seal).

Cobra

Launched as a limited-production, high-performance 1993 sports car, the Cobra has garnered a reputation for mind-spinning depreciation, wallet-busting powertrain defects, and mediocre performance and handling. The first models came with a 240 hp V8, a firm suspension, all-disc ABS, and unique styling. In subsequent years (there were no 2000 or 2002 models), Cobras got more-powerful (yet unreliable) engines, a fully independent suspension, and hood and side scoops. The car's road performance remained seriously compromised by its loose rear end, which swings out when cornering under speed or on wet highways.

VEHICLE HISTORY: 2001—GT models receive hood and side scoops and larger wheels. All models get spoilers, an upgraded centre console, and blacked-out headlights. **2002**—New 16-inch alloy wheels; sporty Cobra stays home again this year. **2003**—Three 4.6L V8 models: the 260 hp GT, the new 305 hp Mach 1, and the 390 hp supercharged SVT Cobra. **2005**—Restyled, with more power, more features, and a 15 cm larger wheelbase. **2007**—Debut of the high-performance Shelby GT and GT500. All models get a digital audio jack. **2008**—Debut of the Bullitt and the Shelby GT500KR, Ford's most powerful pony car ever. The Bullitt uses a 315 hp 4.6L V8 coupled to a 5-speed manual transmission, while the Shelby GT500KR carries a 540 hp 5.4L supercharged V8 engine paired with a 6-speed manual transmission. **2009**—Ho-hum minor changes.

Safety Summary

All models/years: Get high-performance tires and "feather" the accelerator. Regularly equipped Mustangs, like most rear-drive Fords, don't handle sharp curves or wet pavement very well. The rear end swings out suddenly, and the car tends to spin uncontrollably. Traction is easily lost, and braking is hardly reassuring. • Serious concerns have been raised about the Mustang's fuel system failing safety integrity standards and about the tendency of the convertible's doors to jam shut in a 57 km/h frontal collision. • Sudden acceleration because of a stuck throttle. • Transmission allows vehicle to roll away when parked on an incline; emergency brake disengages. • Airbag fails to deploy; inadvertent airbag deployment. • Seat belt becomes twisted, continually tightens up when worn, or fails to retract. • Brake failure, and premature replacement of the brake master cylinder. • Side windows fall off their tracks. **All models: 2001**—Lower control arm comes off. • Sudden brake lock-up. • ABS control module failures. • Foot hits fuse box when engaging clutch pedal. **2002**—Fire ignites in the wiring harness under dash area. • Chronic stalling when coasting or braking, or when clutch is depressed. • Serpentine belt comes off, causing loss of power steering and brakes. • Wheel lug nuts fall off. • Sudden acceleration. • Sudden loss of steering when making a left-hand turn. • In one incident, a car left on an incline with transmission in Park and motor shut off rolled down after 10 minutes and hit a tree. • Emergency brake ratchet assembly breaks, making mechanism inoperable. • Gas spills out of fuel tank because clamps not sufficiently tightened. • Left front wheel falls off when the lower control arm and ball joint become loose. **2003**—Gas pedal can be caught by the carpet ("Oh, what a feeling."). • Sudden acceleration tied to the cruise-control mechanism. • Chronic stalling when decelerating; computer reflash doesn't fix the problem. • Automatic transmission failures. • Loss of brakes. • Spark plug blows out of the passenger-side cylinder head:

> This left me with a $4,463 repair cost to fix my car that I only owned for three months. While doing research on the Internet and asking questions in mechanic shops, it has been apparent that Ford engines have defective cylinder heads.

• Serpentine belt often shreds, causing the brakes to fail and engine to overheat and stall. • Water leaks through side windows. • AC condensation drips onto the exhaust pipe, rusting it out prematurely. **2004**—Throttle sticks under the carpet. • Faulty rear differential; it whines and is wobbly when making turns. • Seatback collapsed from a rear-ender; seatback bolt broke while driving. • Head restraints don't adjust enough. • Steering locks up:

> Power steering unit was excessively noisy and distracting ... Locks up on hard turn. Dealer says nature of the beast, won't replace it. Complained 3 times, car just went out of warranty.... Several hundred local police cruisers have had their power steering replaced by dealer after "negative publicity on TV...." Dealers attempt to make you out as stupid, and keep obfuscating [until] you just go away.

• Sharp tailpipe sticks out and can severely cut anyone brushing against it. • Rear window explodes for no reason:

> When driver notified his insurance carrier, he was informed that their glass installer was aware of the spontaneous rear window explosions occurring in the 2002–2004 model year of Mustangs.

2005—Following Ford's redesign, almost 200 safety-related incidents were reported to NHTSA—about a third more complaints than normal and equal to what the 2001 models have registered over seven model years. • Stuck accelerator pedal. • When slowing for a stop, engine hesitates then surges, and the automatic transmission slams into gear. • When parking, car suddenly accelerates in Drive or in Reverse. • Faulty fuel pumps blamed for frequent stalling. • The manual transmission clutch engages abruptly. • Brake fluid leaks from the master cylinder. • Brakes suddenly lock up, and in some cases, catch fire:

> The parking brake calipers and pads freeze and will not release when temperature drops below 32 degrees [Fahrenheit] [0°C]—while the handle is fully released inside the vehicle. When in neutral and pushed, car will not roll, and when in gear and given gas car barely budges. Taken twice to dealership—by tow truck—but when arrived temperature had risen above 32 degrees and pads etc. had released.

• Parking brake cable seizes or breaks. • The powertrain "tunnel" located down the centre of the car gets extremely hot while driving. • Steering locks while turning left. • Rear strut/shock absorber support brackets rust out. • Fuel spews out the filler pipe, and gas station pumps shut off before the fuel tank is full—a problem that's carried over to the 2006 models:

Intermittently, will not allow a full fill-up on gas. Several different gas stations tested. Only allows for half tank fill-up. Seems to worsen when the weather is cold.

• Fuses may not be seated properly, resulting in dash gauges going dark. • When underway, flimsy hood vibrates and twists violently. • Dash panel cannot be read on a sunny day while wearing sunglasses. • Airbag warning light remains lit. • Newly designed tail lights look lit in daylight, confusing following drivers. • Complete lighting failure; reprogrammed computer fixed the problem. • Convertible-top lifting mechanism froze halfway up; will cost $6,000 to fix. • Original-equipment tires pit and bulge. **2006**—So far, only 66 safety-related complaints have been posted; about half of what one would expect. • When accelerating, vehicle hesitates then surges. • Car continues to be hard to refuel (nozzle shuts off when tank is a quarter to half full). • Faulty fuel pumps. • Dim headlights due to interior condensation. • Manual transmission clutch slippage. • Manual transmission failure. • Side window shattered for no reason. • Windshield distortion causes wavy white lines to appear, or following car headlights "flash" in the mirror. • Broken seatback levers and side mirrors. **2007**—Mustang GT throttle stuck. • Car hesitates and then surges when accelerating. • Frequent complaints that the right control arm broke at the weld. • Fuel tank takes a long time to fill. • Clutch slippage. • Erratic shifting with the automatic transmission. • A faulty Second-gear clutch causes a whining noise and then transmission failure. • Parking brakes seize in cold weather. • Convertible top leaks and floods vehicle. • Many complaints of tires failing due to loss of tire pressure (cracked valve stems); have to be inflated three times weekly to maintain the proper pressure. • Saleen model rear visibility obstructed by the spoiler. • Some rear windshield defroster/defogger embedded wires don't work. **2008**—Airbags failed to deploy, or deployed for no reason (side). • Sudden, unintended acceleration:

Parking car into parking bay between building support and other car. With my foot on brake and at a stop I reached to place car in Park when for no reason the car accelerated over a concrete parking stop, through a ditch, out of the ditch before striking another truck head on in the parking area across the ditch. My foot was on the brake the entire time and I did not touch the shifter at all!

• False tire pressure alerts. • Multiple automatic transmission replacements. • Excessive steering wheel shake. • Primary hood latch failure. • Cracked tire valve stem (a common Ford failure). **2009**—Sudden, unintended acceleration. • Frontal and side airbags failed to deploy. • Check Engine light continuously lit. • Clutch failure on the GT500:

Ford has issued a TSB on the clutch and its flywheel indicating that heavy stop and go traffic will warp the flywheel and in turn ruin the clutch and tran[s]mission. Ford did nothing to fix the problem (identified in the TSB, NHTSA 10032615 - TSB-09-19-11).

• Brake and accelerator pedals mounted too close together. • Premature ball joint wear.

Secret Warranties/Internal Bulletins/Service Tips

All models/years: Paint delamination, peeling, or fading. • Ford's seven-year "goodwill" warranty extensions usually cover engine and transmission components. • Stalling, rough idle, long crank times, or cold hesitation when accelerating may signal the need to clean out excessive intake valve deposits. • Excessive oil consumption likely caused by leaking gaskets, worn piston rings, poor sealing of the lower intake manifold, or defective intake and exhaust valve stem seals; install new guide-mounted valve-stem seals for a better fit as well as new piston rings with improved oil control. • A thumping or clacking heard from the front brakes signals the need to machine the front disc brake rotors. **All models: 1998–2002**—Guidelines for replacing defective ignition lock cylinders. **1998–2006**—Troubleshooting tips for correcting a rough-running engine. **1999–2004**—Manual transmission is hard to shift into Reverse or First. **2001–03**—Wind noise from the A-pillar area. **2001–04**—4.6L engine rattle. **2002**—Air leaks in the intake manifold or engine. • In 4.6L engines, oil leaks from the head gasket area. • Manual transmission clashes or grinds. • Rear whine heard during coastdown from 100 km/h. • Vehicles equipped with a 5-speed manual transmission may stumble or hesitate when cold. • Electrical problems include hard starting, erratic operation of turn signals, and illuminated ABS warning light. • Inoperative door window because of faulty window regulator. • Defective ignition-switch lock cylinder. **2003–04**—Hard to shift, rattling manual transmission. • Ford will install four revised hood scoop insulators (#2L7Z-9P686-AA) to eliminate a hood rattle. **2003–06**—Leaking, inoperative AC compressor. **2005–06**—Hesitation on acceleration. • AC compressor clutch failure. • Erratic fuel gauge. • Parking brake cable freezes; rear brakes drag. • Rattling from the gearshift, dash area. • Rear axle hum, whine. **2005–07**—Fourth gear rattle with the 4.0L engine. • Front-end noise on bumps. • Ford finally admits it has a fuel-tank fill-up problem and offers to change the tank under warranty, according to TSB #07-21-12. • Power window malfunctions. • Paint blistering and early corrosion on aluminum body panels. • Abnormal, premature convertible-top wear, malfunction. **2005–08**—Water leaks onto front floor. • Exhaust system buzz, rattle. • Manual transmission ticking. • Door handle not flush, rattles. **2005–09**—Shudder on acceleration. • Loss of key gears in the automatic transmission shift sequence (see TSB on following page). • Excessive rear axle whine. • Dash/pillar rattle. • Water leak onto the front floor area:

WATER LEAK ONTO FRONT FLOOR AREA

BULLETIN NO.: 08-26-7   DATE: JANUARY 5, 2009

2005–09 Mustang
ISSUE: Some 2005–09 Mustang vehicles may exhibit a difficult to diagnose water leak in the front floor area. This may be caused by loose grommets and/or sealer skips around the cowl area, loose A-pillar window weatherstrip retainer, misaligned body harness grommet through the firewall, or a misaligned body harness grommet from the passenger door.

2005–10—4.0L V6 engine buzzing. • Rear axle vent fluid leaks and axle whine. **2006–10**—Trunk lid won't latch. **2007–09**—Airbag light stays on. **2009**—Rough-running 4.0L V6 engine. • Engine squeal, chirp on cold start-up (4.0L V6). *Cobra:* **2001–05**—Rear axle shudder, chatter. **2003**—Defective engine cylinder heads or valve guides (replacement cylinder head Part #3R2Z-6049-GA). **2004**—Intermittent loss of power, no-starts. • Engine overheating. • Manual transmission gear whine and grind, and loss of Second gear. • Driveline clunk during gear changes or quick acceleration. • Squealing noise from the steering assembly. • Front suspension squeaking noise when vehicle passes over bumps. • Inoperative rear window defroster. • Thump noise when AC clutch engages. **2005–06**—Paint blistering and early corrosion on aluminum body panels.

MUSTANG, COBRA PROFILE

	2001	2002	2003	2004	2005	2006	2007	2008	2009
Cost Price ($)									
LX/Coupe	22,275	22,795	22,990	23,495	23,795	23,999	23,999	24,799	24,799
Coupe GT	30,525	31,055	31,505	31,795	32,795	32,999	33,499	33,999	33,999
Cobra	38,495	—	41,995	46,855	—	—	—	—	—
Cvt.	42,495	—	45,995	50,655	—	—	—	—	—
Shelby GT500	—	—	—	—	—	—	51,999	54,299	54,229
Shelby Cvt.	—	—	—	—	—	—	56,099	58,399	58,399
Convertible	26,945	27,465	27,760	28,095	27,995	27,999	27,999	28,899	28,899
Convertible GT	34,490	35,020	31,505	35,795	36,795	36,999	37,599	38,099	38,099
Used Values ($)									
LX/Coupe ▲	4,500	5,000	6,000	7,500	9,000	10,000	11,500	14,500	16,500
LX/Coupe ▼	4,000	4,500	5,000	6,500	7,500	9,000	10,000	13,000	15,000
Coupe GT ▲	6,000	7,000	8,000	9,000	11,500	12,500	15,500	19,000	23,000
Coupe GT ▼	5,000	6,000	7,000	8,000	9,500	11,000	14,000	17,500	21,500
Cobra ▲	6,000	—	8,000	10,000	—	—	—	—	—
Cobra ▼	5,500	—	6,500	8,500	—	—	—	—	—
Cvt. ▲	8,000	—	10,500	12,000	—	—	—	—	—
Cvt. ▼	7,000	—	9,500	11,000	—	—	—	—	—

Shelby GT500 ▲	—	—	—	—	—	—	23,000	29,000	35,000
Shelby GT500 ▼	—	—	—	—	—	—	21,000	27,000	32,000
Shelby Cvt. ▲	—	—	—	—	—	—	27,000	33,000	39,000
Shelby Cvt. ▼	—	—	—	—	—	—	25,000	31,000	35,000
Convertible ▲	6,000	6,500	7,500	9,000	10,500	13,500	15,000	17,000	20,000
Convertible ▼	5,500	6,000	7,000	8,000	9,000	12,000	13,500	15,500	18,500
Convertible GT ▲	8,500	9,000	11,000	12,500	14,000	16,000	19,000	22,000	27,000
Convertible GT ▼	7,500	8,000	9,500	11,000	12,500	14,500	17,500	20,500	24,000

Reliability	2	2	3	3	3	4	4	4	4
Crash Safety (F)	5	5	5	5	5	5	5	5	5
Convertible	—	—	—	—	—	—	—	5	5
Side	3	3	3	3	4	4	4	5	5
Convertible	2	2	2	2	—	—	—	5	5
IIHS Side (Convertible)	—	—	—	—	—	—	5	5	5
Offset (Convertible)	—	—	—	—	3	3	3	3	3
Head Restraints (F)									
Convertible	—	—	—	—	1	1	1	1	1
Rollover Resistance	—	5	5	5	5	5	5	5	5

General Motors

CORVETTE ★★★

RATING: Average (2005–09); Below Average (1999–2004). Keep in mind that premium fuel and astronomical insurance rates will drive up your operating costs. And don't discount the serious safety-related problems you're likely to experience on all models. They run the gamut of sudden steering lock-ups when underway, electrical shorts causing vehicle shutdowns, nonfunctioning parking brakes, brake failures caused by premature rotor warpage (around 16,000 km), seat belts that jam in the retractor, and, on the 2005, the top suddenly flying off (a 2002 Ford Mustang trait as well). The locked-up steering is particularly scary because it apparently has carried over to many model years, and traffic accident investigators may simply conclude that a resulting accident was because of driver inexperience or unsafe driving. **Ideal model year:** Shh! Don't tell anyone, but anything after 1962 is too big and the 1953–57 versions were handling nightmares. So that leaves my favourites: the 1958–1962 models, of which, I feel the 1958 Vette is the best. Among the more recently minted models, I vote for the 2006 entry-level model for about $23,000, or almost one-third the car's original selling price. It had a year to fix the 2005 design changes and came with an upgraded 6-speed automatic transmission. **"Real" city/highway fuel economy:** *Manual:* 12.3/7.7 L/100 km. *Automatic:* 13.2/7.9 L/100 km. Fuel consumption may actually be greater by more than 20 percent. **Maintenance/Repair costs:** Much higher than average, although most repairs can be done by any independent garage. Long waits for recall repairs. **Parts:** Pricey, but easy to find. Surprisingly, it is often easier to find parts for older Corvettes through collectors' clubs than it is to find many of the high-tech components used today. **Extended warranty:** Get a GM-backed supplementary warranty, or look for a recent model that has some of its original warranty left. The frequency of repairs and the high repair costs make maintenance outrageously expensive. **Best alternatives:** Ford Mustang, GM Camaro or Firebird, Hyundai Genesis Coupe, Mazda Miata, and Toyota Celica or Supra. **Helpful websites:** *www.corvetteforum.com* and *http://forums.corvetteforum.com.*

Strengths and Weaknesses

Corvettes made in the late '60s and early '70s are acceptable buys, mainly because of their value as collector cars and their uncomplicated repairs (though parts may be rare). Unfortunately, the Corvette's overall reliability and safety have declined over the past 40 years as its price and complexity have increased. GM has chosen to update its antiquated design with complicated high-tech add-ons rather than come up with something original. Consequently, the car has been gutted and then retuned using failure-prone electronic circuitry. Complicated emissions plumbing, braking, and suspension systems have also been added in an attempt to make the Corvette a fuel-efficient, user-friendly, high-performance vehicle—a goal that General Motors has missed by a wide margin.

The electronically controlled suspension systems have always been plagued by glitches. The noisy 5.7L engine frequently hesitates and stalls, there's lots of transmission buzz and whine, the rear tires produce excessive noise, and wind whistles through the A- and C-pillars; these, and the all-too-familiar fibreglass body squeaks and paint delamination (yes, fibreglass delaminates), continue as unwanted standard features throughout all model years. Also, the electronic dash never works quite right (speedometer lag is one example).

Ownership of more-recent Corvette models does have its positive side. For example, the ABS vented disc brakes, available since 1986, are fade-free and easy to modulate. The standard European-made Bilstein FX3 Selective Ride Control suspension can be pre-set for touring, sport, or performance. Under speed, an electronic module automatically varies the suspension setting, finally curing these cars of their earlier endemic oversteering, wheel spinning, breakaway rear ends, and other nasty surprises.

Owners admit the redesigned '97 models offer improved performance, better handling, and additional safety features, but they find fault with the stiff ride, poor fuel economy, and excessive interior noise. From a reliability standpoint, these models are much more refined than earlier versions, but they are hell to diagnose and are knuckle-busters to service. And you can expect chronic engine stalling and surging, excessive engine oil consumption, an oily black buildup on the exhaust tips, and catalytic converter failures within the first five years. A real hair-raiser is the tendency of steering columns on 1977–2001 models to suddenly lock while the vehicle is underway or parked. This continues to be a widespread hazard, despite a recall to fix the defect. Says the following Corvette owner:

> This item has failed on an estimated 3,000 Corvettes throughout the U.S. Please see Internet site *www.corvetteforum.com*. As a safety professional, I see this as a hazard that Chevrolet needs to address with more severity. The loss of steering control because the steering wheel locks can lead to property loss, as well as death.

Some performance deficiencies make these cars unsafe: The active handling system often malfunctions and makes the vehicle veer into traffic or spin out of control; faulty electronic and electrical systems cause it to abruptly shut down; the brake, AC, and suspension systems are unreliable; and body accessories and electronics suddenly short out.

Factory-related defects on the post-2000 models are commonplace: The engine is excessively noisy; the cabins overheat; the driver's seat moves while driving; the trunk door warps; seat belts twist easily and tend to pull down uncomfortably against the shoulder; the passenger seat belt jams and won't extend or retract; smelly exhaust fumes enter the cabin, causing watery eyes and dizziness; excessive heat buildup from catalytic converters deforms the rear bumper assembly and heats up the interior even more; the glass rear window limits vision; and front and rear wheel weights sometimes fly off the wheels.

Servicing the different sophisticated fuel-injection systems isn't easy, and this may be the primary reason why so many owners complain of having to take their Corvettes back to the shop repeatedly to correct poor engine and transmission performance.

The 2005–09 redesigned models have produced their own subset of problems, although not as extensive a list as prior models: engine stalling and transmission jerking, electrical short circuits, lousy fit and finish, and squeaky, squealing brakes (see *www.corvetteforum.com* and *www.carreview.com*).

VEHICLE HISTORY: 2001—A horsepower boost and an Active Handling performance upgrade, plus the addition of a high-performance Z06 variant. **2002**—The Z06 gets a 20 hp boost to 405 hp, and enhanced rear shocks, aluminum front stabilizer-bar links, high-performance brake pads, and new aluminum wheels. **2005**—Revised styling, more power, and new features. The new power top is an instant success. The car's wheelbase is stretched by 3 cm over the 1997–2004 C5, and overall length shrinks by 12.7 cm. The 400 hp 6.0L V8 replaces the C5's 5.7L V8 and adds 50 more horses for good measure. Standard performance safety features still include ABS and traction/anti-skid control. Cars sold with the Z51 package may fetch $1,000 more on the used market due to their firmer, nonadjustable suspension, larger brakes, and automatic transmission that's built for sporty handling. Wheel diameter grows an inch to 18/19. Front side airbags remain standard on the convertible. Thief-magnet xenon headlights are newly standard, along with keyless access and ignition. **2006**—A new 6-speed automatic transmission and the return of the high-performance Z06 model mark. **2007**—The two-seat V8-powered sports cars come as a coupe and a convertible. **2008**—The base engine gets a new 430 hp 6.2L V8 that replaces a 400 hp 6.0L V8 that can be hooked to the 6-speed manual or a 6-speed automatic transmission An available "dual-mode" exhaust system gives you six more horses. Corvette Z06 and 427 Limited models offered as coupes only, equipped with a 505 hp 7.0L V8 and mandatory 6-speed manual transmission with sporty suspension tuning, tires, and brakes. **2009**—The return of the ultra-high-performance ZR1 coupe with a 638 hp supercharged 6.2L V8.

Safety Summary

1999–2001—Engine serpentine belt and tensioner failures. **2000–01**—Catalytic converter catches fire. • More reports that when the fuel tank is full, fuel leaks from the top of the vent. • More fuel leaks; this time, owners report leaks from the fuel lines near the firewall inside the engine compartment. • Chronic stalling; fuel-injector failures cause vehicle to shudder and stall. • Engine dies while driving in the rain, and brakes don't work. • If one wheel loses traction, the throttle closes, starving the engine. • Brakes drag and lock up; brake pedal doesn't spring back; overheated rotors are common. • Car is nearly uncontrollable at time of brake lock-up. • Seat belt doesn't retract properly when reeling it out and tightens up progressively when driving. • Driver's seat rocks. • Foot easily slips off clutch and brake pedals. **2002**—Sudden stalling on the highway accompanied by brake failure. • Erratic transmission performance (shifts to Fourth before entering Second gear; won't shift into Second when going uphill). • Horn is hard to access since it's just a small indentation on the steering wheel. **2003**—Very low number of complaints reported. • Sudden engine surge while underway. • When accelerating from a stop, vehicle fails to shift from First to Second gear and then stalls out. • Constant leaking, and failure of rear differential and suspension system. • Leaking oil pan gasket. • Annoying dash reflection onto the windshield. • Inaccurate fuel gauge. • Driver's seat belt locks up. **2004**—Defective steering, despite recall:

> The so-called "fix" GM has for the 1997–2004 Corvette column lock problem does not fix the problem. It merely puts a band-aid on the problem to protect them from lawsuits. I do not understand how this can be allowed by law. I have had to resort to an aftermarket part to fix the problem and chose to ignore the recall.

• Fuel leaks found outside of the car at the fuel-tank, fuel-pump seal, and interconnecting hoses. • Fuel leakage from the crossover pipe and other fuel lines:

> I smelled gas in my garage for approximately 1 week but found no leaks. While filling up at gas station I noticed a large puddle forming under the car and saw gas leaking from the tank. Dealer said gas leak was found in gas tank, crossover fuel line and two other fuel lines. Very dangerous situation. Dealer blamed a manufacturer defect in parts. Took 10 days to repair, as the first time tank was replaced there was no fuel pressure, and it had to be redone.

• Sudden stalling caused by faulty fuel pump. • Steering linkage failure at the steering knuckle. • Power seat pinned driver against the steering wheel. • Clutch won't disengage. • Shifter pops out of Reverse. • Parking brake won't hold car in Neutral on a hill. • Inoperative passenger window regulator. **2005**—Car often throws or shreds the serpentine belt, leading to steering/brake loss and engine overheating. Some owners have experienced the problem several times after it was first repaired. **2005–06**—Corvette also "throws" its top:

> The contact stated the vehicle's roof had separated and flew off while driving 40 mph [65 km/h]. This was the second time the vehicle had problems with the roof. A NHTSA recall #06V181000 was performed in 05/06 regarding structure body: roof and pillars, however the recall did not remedy the problem.

2007—Roof panel separated while underway. • Metal pedals become very slippery in the rain. • Traction control and stability features come on when they shouldn't, causing loss of vehicle control. • Seat belt locks when driving and won't release. • Steering is unsafe:

> When driving home from the GM dealer, the vehicle skipped sideways on rough roads at a moderate speed (20–40 mph). I got online to the Corvette forum and was immediately referred to the Sep 07 Car and Driver magazine article specifically addressing this steering issue. The professional drivers in the article rate the 2007 Corvette steering as unsatisfactory.

• Rear window view is distorted. • Goodyear Eagle tires have bulges on the interior sidewalls. **2008**—Corvettes continue to "lose their tops":

> Brand new 2008 convertible Corvette. Roof tore off driving on highway from dealership. GM currently stating not a warranty item because cables cannot break simply from the wind.

• Cracked headlight lenses. • Chronic stalling. • Transmission fails to accelerate when slowing for a stoplight or when turning. • Rear axle nut works itself loose. • Keyless start would not work and doors would not unlock:

> It was over 125 degrees in the car. Kept trying until car started. Did not panic cause I knew there is a way out. Can you imagine if I let somebody else drive and they don't know what to do? GM should fix this problem cause after looking it up on the Web it look like this has been happening for a long time!

•

> The contact and passengers were locked inside of the vehicle. He attempted to activate the OnStar feature, but it also would not work. Several dealers were notified, but none could provide assistance with exiting the vehicle. The contact and passengers were locked in the vehicle for 15 minutes.

2009—Headliner droops and obscures rear vision. • Owner was locked in his Corvette because the power shut off once he entered the car. He had to remove the convertible top and climb out. Comments one owner who was trapped with his wife:

> This vehicle is a death trap if the battery or electrical system fails or if the driver side door release cable snaps or jams in an accident. Emergency escape requires climbing through roof or into back hatch—elderly people could not do what we had to do to exit the car. There should be manual release for both doors on the doors. The batteries used by GM for these cars are notorious for quick drawdown & should be replaced at GM's expense with quality batteries such as Odyssey PC1200.

• The "Service ABS System," "Service Active Handling System," and "Service Traction Control System" alerts come on and the car runs sluggish.

> My understanding is that this is a known issue for earlier years Corvettes: TSB 06.02.35.002A and TSB 06.02.35.002B. But my Corvette is a 2009 and I have the same exact problem.

Secret Warranties/Internal Bulletins/Service Tips

All years: A rotten-egg odour coming from the exhaust is probably caused by a defective catalytic converter, which should be covered by the emissions warranty on 2002 and later models. • Clearcoat paint degradation, whitening, and chalking, long a problem with GM's other cars, is a serious problem with the fibreglass-bodied Corvette, says TSB #331708. It too is covered by a secret warranty for up to six years. • Reverse servo cover seal leak. **1993–2002**—GM has a special kit to prevent AC odours in warm weather. **1997–2001**—Sound system speakers make the door panel rattle or buzz. **1997–2002**—Tips on correcting water leaks in various areas. • Loose driver's seat. **1997–2003**—Inoperative AC. **1997–2004**—Remedy for a leaking rear differential. **1998–2002**—Remedy for engine spark, knock. **1999–2001**—Wind noise around the B-pillar. **1999–2002**—Poor transmission performance; SES light lit. • Excessive oil consumption. **2000–06**—Delayed automatic transmission shifts. **2001**—Incomplete brake pedal return can be fixed by replacing the vacuum brake booster. **2001–02**—Slipping or missing Second, Third, or Fourth gear. **2001–03**—Engine knock or lifter noise. **2001–05**—Harsh upshifts. **2002**—Engine knock. • Erratic fuel gauge or radio operation. • False Service Engine light illumination. • Harsh transmission shifts; 2–4 band and 3–4 clutch damage; transmission pump leaks. • Light brake drag; brake light remains lit. • B-pillar wind noise. **2001–08**—Transmission oil leak; slips in gear. **2002–04**—Exhaust system jingle noise. **2003–11**—Oil leaks from engine's rear cover assembly. Should be covered by GM's 8-year emissions warranty or small claims court intervention. **2004**—Erratic idle, idle surge, rough running, and stalling. • Coolant leak from head cup plugs. • Transmission fluid leaks; inoperative Second, Third, and Fourth gears. • Rear axle side cover oil leak. • Poor automatic transmission shifting, slipping. • Transmission squawk, grunt, rattle, growl, or buzz noise. • Intermittent or inoperative fuel gauge addressed in

TSB #01659, January 2004. • Wind noise or water leak at top of door glass. • Tire wander. • Seat belt won't release from retractor. • Blotches in all glass. • Inoperative Twilight Sentinel automatic headlight control. **2004–05**—Erratic fuel gauge readings. **2005–06**—Vibration or shudder at idle (replace power-steering inlet pressure hose). • Vehicle's top flies off. **2005–07**—Creak or popping noise from the windshield near the front pillar. • Power-steering shudder, vibration at idle. **2005–08**—Axle nuts appear loose. • Rear axle chatter, clunk when turning. **2005–09**—Tapping or scraping noise from the rear wheel area (replace wheel driveshaft nut). **2005–11**—Intermittent reduced power (repair instrument panel to body harness connector). • Crazing/cracks in transparent removable roof panel:

CRACKS IN TRANSPARENT REMOVABLE ROOF PANEL

BULLETIN NO.: 08-08-67-001A   DATE: OCTOBER 28, 2010

CRAZING/CRACKS IN TRANSPARENT REMOVABLE ROOF PANEL (REPLACE ROOF)

2005–11 Chevrolet Corvette

CONDITION: Some customers may comment that the removable top has stress cracks developing on the right side and/or has crazing across the tint.

CAUSE: The cracking may be caused by an unsealed edge from a machining operation. The crazing may be the result of UV load. Correction: Replace the existing roof with a new one that doesn't have all the hardware attached. At time of repair, the weatherstrip retainers, weatherstrips and rear latch handles will have to be transferred from the old roof.

WARRANTY INFORMATION:

Labor Operation	Description	Labor Time
2298	Roof Lift Off Panel Replacement	Use Published Labor Operation Time

---

Don't pay for this repair. It normally falls under the warranty. If the dealer rejects your claim, file a small claims court lawsuit. There's no way in heck that stress cracks and crazing can be blamed on the car owner. A sad commentary on GM quality for the past (count 'em) *7 years*.

• The roof is also quite a noise-maker. Another confidential service bulletin (#08-08-67-031E) covers fixes to eliminate the snap, pop, crackle, or rattle noise coming from the roof. **2006–11**—Tips on reducing front tire chatter and rear differential "hop." **2007–08**—No-shifts, multiple electrical malfunctions. • Erratic power-window operation. **2007–09**—Premature headliner wear. Loose rear glass moulding. **2008–09**—GM agrees to pay for torn roofs and also refund money spent renting other transportation until May 31, 2011 (see TSB on following page). I'm betting any small claims court judge would find that warranty extension as cheapskate as they come. Expect the courts to extend the body warranty for this defect up to 8 years just like the existing Emissions Warranty and 8- to 10-year hybrid battery pack warranty. **2009**—Clutch spring fractures are another GM secret warranty-covered failure (pardon, I mean "Customer Satisfaction Program") that's valid until July 31, 2011. After that, a small claims court judge may extend the expiry date. • Okay, you're not going to believe this, but it's absolutely true: GM put the wrong piston rings in its half year's production of 6.2L V8 Corvette

---

CONVERTIBLE TOP COVER SEPARATION

BULLETIN NO.: 08312A   DATE: JULY 1, 2010

CUSTOMER SATISFACTION, CONVERTIBLE ROOF COVER SEPARATION—INSTALL NEW RETAINER BRACKET

2008–09 Chevrolet Corvette With Manual or Power Roof Convertible

CONDITION: Certain 2008 and 2009 model year Chevrolet Corvette manual or power roof convertible vehicles may have a condition in which the fabric roof cover may begin to separate from its retainer bracket near the top edge of the windshield. When the vehicle reaches speeds of approximately 100 mph (160 km/h) or greater, the roof cover could begin to pull away from the retainer bracket and, depending on the speed of the vehicle and duration at that speed, could tear to the rear glass. If this were to occur, the headliner would remain intact and the roof cover would not separate from the vehicle.

CORRECTION: Dealers are to install a new design retainer bracket.

---

engines. (And it took them eight months to discover this?) They have to replace the engines. Here's the proof:

CAMPAIGN—ENGINE REPLACEMENT

BULLETIN No.: 09043   DATE: MARCH 9, 2009

EXCESSIVE OIL CONSUMPTION—INCORRECT PISTON—EXPIRES SEPTEMBER 30, 2009

2009 Corvette, Equipped with a 6.2L V8 Engine

PURPOSE: This bulletin provides a service procedure to replace the engine on certain 2009 model year Corvette vehicles equipped with a 6.2L V8 engine. Some of these vehicles may have one or more incorrect oil control rings installed in the engine. This could result in high oil consumption. This service procedure should be completed on involved vehicles currently in dealership inventory as soon as possible but no later than September 30, 2009, at which time this bulletin will expire.

This warranty extension has expired. See a small claims court judge to get your money if GM refuses your claim. On the other hand, don't we and the labour unions own GM? Ask the federal government and the CAW to cut you a check.

CORVETTE PROFILE

	2001	2002	2003	2004	2005	2006	2007	2008	2009
Cost Price ($)									
Base	61,400	62,400	68,120	69,940	67,395	67,805	68,565	69,500	66,145
Convertible	68,315	69,665	74,120	75,940	79,495	79,905	80,665	81,610	76,955
Used Values ($)									
Base ▲	10,000	12,000	15,000	17,500	20,000	23,000	27,000	33,000	39,000
Base ▼`	8,500	10,500	13,000	16,000	18,500	21,000	25,000	31,000	36,000
Convertible ▲	13,000	15,000	18,000	20,000	24,000	26,000	29,000	38,000	46,000
Convertible ▼	11,500	13,000	15,500	17,000	22,000	24,000	27,000	35,000	44,000
Reliability	3	3	3	3	3	3	3	3	3

NOTE: Although U.S. testing agencies haven't crash-tested the Corvette, European agencies give the car a "Good" crashworthiness rating.

All ratings on a numbered scale where **5** is good and **1** is bad. See page 132 for a more detailed description.

Mazda

MX-5 (MIATA)   ★ ★ ★ ★ ★

RATING: Recommended (1999–2009). This is the only sports car *Lemon-Aid* has ever rated Recommended every year from its first model year (1990). For over 20 years this has been an almost-perfect sports car, except for its poor braking performance on rain-slicked roadways and spotty fit and finish. The redesigned 2006–08 models are the best choices for power and performance. **Ideal model year:** A 2007 Miata GT is your best choice. It is full of newer features and costs about $15,000, or less than half the car's original price. **"Real" city/highway fuel economy:** *5-speed manual:* 10.1/7.6 L/100 km. *6-speed manual:* 10.2/7.7 L/100 km. *6-speed automatic:* 10.6/7.8 L/100 km. Owners say fuel savings may be lower than these estimates by about 10 percent. **Maintenance/Repair costs:** Below-average costs, and most repairs aren't dealer-dependent. **Parts:** Average costs, with good availability. **Extended warranty:** A waste of money. **Best alternatives:** Honda S2000, Hyundai Tiburon, Ford Mustang, Mazda3, Mini Cooper Clubman, Pontiac Solstice, Saturn Sky, Scion tC, and Toyota Celica. **Helpful websites:** *www.miata.net* and *www.miataforum.com*.

Strengths and Weaknesses

The base engine delivers adequate power and accelerates smoothly. Acceleration from 0–100 km/h is in the high eight-second range. The 5-speed manual transmission shifts easily and has well-spaced gears; the 6-speed adds 27 kg (60 lb.) and isn't that impressive. The vehicle's lightness, precise steering, and 50/50 weight distribution make this an easy car for novice drivers to toss around corners.

VEHICLE HISTORY: 2001—A slight horsepower boost, a restyled interior and exterior, 15-inch wheels, seat belt pretensioners, improved ABS, and an emergency trunk release. **2003**—16-inch V-rated tires and strut-tower braces. **2004**—Debut of the MazdaSpeed, equipped with a 178 hp turbocharged engine, 6-speed manual transmission, sport suspension, and 17-inch wheels. **2006**—Name is changed to MX-5. Given about 6.25 cm in wheelbase, 4.25 cm more width, and 4 cm more length while gaining only about 23 kg. Base engine is a 170 hp 2.0L (166 hp with an automatic transmission), in place of the 142 hp 1.8L engine that powered the previous model. An optional 6-speed automatic transmission with steering-wheel shift paddles replaces the 4-speed automatic. Full-torso side airbags, anti-lock four-wheel disc brakes, and a manual-folding soft top with a heated glass rear window are standard features. **2007**—A retractable hardtop adds 35 kg to the car's weight. Mazda continues to offer a removable hardtop for softtop models.

Owners' top performance gripes target the same characteristics that make other sports car enthusiasts swoon: inadequate cargo space, cramped interior for large adults, excessive interior noise, and limited low-end torque that makes for frequent shifting.

Mechanics report that it is wise to change the engine timing chain every 100,000 km. Other reported problems include crankshaft failures, leaky rear-end seals and valve cover gaskets, rear differential seal failures, leaking or squeaky clutches, hard starts and stalling, torn drive boots, transmission whining in upper gear ranges, engine and exhaust system rattles, electrical system glitches, brake pulsation, valvetrain clatter on start-up (changing oil may help), prematurely worn-out shock absorbers and catalytic converters, softtop covers that come off or break, and minor body and trim deficiencies. Redesigned 2006s have a few more fit and finish deficiencies due to their redesign. Most of the problems were fixed on the 2007s; however, there are still some reports of later models rattling and an interior leak that soaks the carpet from the driver's front area to underneath the seat.

Safety Summary

All years: Used Miatas will likely have some collision damage; make sure you run a *Carproof.com* check online or by fax. **2001**—Vehicle rolled downhill despite being parked with emergency brake engaged. **2002**—Interior can heat up to 54°C (130°F) because exhaust system is mounted too close to the centre console. **2003**—When accelerating from a cold start, car lurches and then stalls. • Hard starts. • Wheel rims are easily bent. • Poor headlight illumination. **2004**—Hard starts despite changing the fuel pump. • Seat belt locks up during normal driving. **2006**—While complaints for other years have been nonexistent or in the single digits, the 2006 models logged 10 reports of safety-related failures (still about 40 less than normal). • Constant steering corrections are necessary due to the vehicle wandering all over the road. • In moderately cold temperatures, the power windows won't work. • It is easy to accidentally engage First gear when Reverse is required, or Reverse when First is needed. **2007**—Sudden, unintended acceleration. • "Fix-a-Flat" kit doesn't fix flats caused by a cut tire. • The point where the manual transmission clutch catches keeps moving upward. • Anchorage pins for some floor mats may be missing.

Secret Warranties/Internal Bulletins/Service Tips

All years: TSB #006/94 gives all of the possible causes and remedies for brake vibration. • TSB #N00198 addresses complaints that the steering wheel is off-centre. • Other bulletins address the issue of musty AC odours. **1999–2003**—Clutch chatter on cold start-up. **2000–06**—Troubleshooting body vibration and steering-wheel shimmy. **2002**—Fuelling difficulty caused by gas pump shutting off early. • The 6-speed manual transmission won't shift into Fifth gear or Reverse. **2004**—Door rattling. **2005**—Free replacement of the keyless entry fob. **2006**—Rough idle, hesitation. • Clutch pedal squeaking when depressed. • Abnormal heater performance. • Water leaks from top of door windows and at the front of the convertible top. • Excessive gaps between the header weather stripping and the body above the windshield; windshield adhesive oozes out onto the paint. • Console lid won't stay closed; squeaking noise. • Tire valve stem breaks when removing valve cap. **2006–07**—Manual transmission clutch hard to disengage, excessive pedal free play. • Front brakes produce a low-speed creaking noise. • Convertible-top latch rattling. • Gap in plastic door-trim panel. • Special Program MSP13 allows for the free replacement of the fuel-filler cap. • Poor AM band reception. • Water accumulation in footwells. **2006–08**—Seat belt buckle rattles, squeaks. • Audio system rattle. **2006–09**—Unstable engine idling, stalling. • Water accumulation in the footwell area. **2006–10**—Troubleshooting tips on eliminating brake noise, judder, or dragging. • Seat and seatback squeaking noises. • Upper surface dash board may have a poor appearance. **2007**—Retractable hard top difficult to open, makes crunch noise, contacts deck panel. **2007–08**—Hard top rattles at the windshield header.

MX-5 (MIATA) PROFILE

	2001	2002	2003	2004	2005	2006	2007	2008	2009
Cost Price ($)									
Base GX	27,605	27,695	27,695	27,895	27,995	27,995	28,095	28,195	28,495
GS	—	—	—	30,100	30,200	30,995	34,500	31,350	32,795
GT	—	—	—	33,165	34,265	33,995	34,195	34,500	39,295
Used Values ($)									
Base GX ▲	5,500	6,000	7,500	9,000	10,500	12,500	15,000	17,500	20,000
Base GX ▼	5,000	5,500	6,500	7,500	9,000	11,000	13,500	16,000	18,000
GS ▲	—	—	—	9,000	11,000	13,000	15,500	18,000	22,200
GS ▼	—	—	—	7,500	10,000	11,500	14,000	16,000	20,000
GT ▲	—	—	—	9,000	11,500	13,500	16,500	19,500	26,000
GT ▼	—	—	—	8,000	10,000	12,000	15,000	17,000	24,000
Reliability									
Crash Safety	—	4	4	4	4	—	—	—	—
Side	—	3	3	3	3	—	—	—	—
Head Restraints (F)	3	3	3	3	—	—	—	—	—
Rear	2	2	2	—	—	—	—	—	—
Rollover Resistance	—	—				—	—	—	—

MINIVANS

How About a 5-Speed Tranny That Works?

Chrysler-Fiat maestro Sergio Marchionne admitted to dealers this week that the company had "historically ignored" quality complaints, but vowed that the new Chrysler would banish its ghosts with better technology, such as 9-speed automatic transmissions.

One of your best bets, the Mazda5, is actually a mini-minivan.

Minivans and Maxi-troubles

Poor Mr. Marchionne. He still doesn't get it. Chrysler minivan buyers haven't fled the automaker because their vehicles had too few gears; they left because too few gears worked. And to add insult to poor engineering, Chrysler Caravan owners et al. got tired of being given the gears when their trannies were repaired.

After embracing Chrysler's minivans in the early '80s and saving Chrysler from bankruptcy, disenchanted car buyers turned against Detroit's failure-prone minivans a decade later. They still loved the concept, but they wanted better quality. So they waited in line for a Honda Odyssey or Toyota Sienna minivan they knew was more reliable and held its value longer. Detroit, Mazda, and Nissan never recovered their lost market share. Smart buyers now steer away from minivans sold by these companies, regardless of the thrift shop bargain prices.

Gone and best forgotten are Ford's godawful Windstar/Freestar, Mazda's lacklustre MPV, and GM's failure-prone Venture, Montana, Relay, Transport, Terraza, Silhouette, and Outlander. You might get by with a recent-model Chrysler, if you can find a garage willing to do cheap transmission, brake, and AC repairs—year after year.

Your only real choice is Asian: Honda's Odyssey or Mazda's Mazda5 mini-minivan (for the Mazda5, refer to Small Cars), followed by the nicely appointed Hyundai/Kia Entourage and Sedona. These latter two minivans sell for much less than what used Hondas and Toyotas are fetching due to their rapid depreciation: good news for buyers, bad news for sellers.

A fully loaded 2008 Entourage LTD that sold new for $39,495 is now worth only $17,500; a comparable Sedona EX Luxury sells for $13,000, or $4,500 less than the Entourage.

Most minivans are upsized front-drive cars that are mainly "people-movers," meaning they handle like cars and get great fuel economy. The Honda Odyssey and Toyota Sienna are the best examples of this kind of minivan. Following Honda's 2005 Odyssey improvements, its road performance, reliability, and retained value surpasses that of the front- and rear-drive minivans built by Detroit. Toyota's 2004 Sienna upgrades produced the opposite results: the Sienna became less reliable and less safe and its resale values began dropping like a stone as new Sienna prices softened.

GM's Astro and Safari minivans are "bland leading the bland" downsized trucks that are dirt-cheap minivan choices, but they haven't held up very well since they were dropped after the 2005 model year. Using rear-drive, 6-cylinder engines, and heavier mechanical components, they handle cargo and passengers equally well. On the negative side, their fuel economy is no match for the front-drives, highway handling is ponderous, with lots of wind buffeting and quirky braking, and their overall reliability is below average. Generally, GM's rear-drive, full-sized Express and Savana vans are much more reliable performers than the rear-drive GM Astro and Safari and Ford Aerostar, or the front-drive Ford Windstar/Freestar but this doesn't mean much, because the benchmark is set so low for Detroit's progeny. Steer clear of any minivan equipped with an AWD powertrain. These systems are notoriously failure-prone, expensive to repair, and will keep you walking for weeks while the parts stay back ordered.

Rear-drive vans are better suited for towing trailers in the 1,600–2,950 kg (3,500–6,500 lb.) range. Most automakers say their front-drive minivans can pull up to 1,600 kg (3,500 lb.) with an optional towing package (often costing almost $1,000 extra), but don't you believe it. Owners report white-knuckle driving and premature powertrain failures caused by the extra load. It just stands to reason that Ford, Chrysler, and GM front-drives equipped with engines and transmissions that blow out at 60,000–100,000 km under normal driving conditions are going to meet their demise much earlier under a full load.

Chrysler

Chrysler has churned out millions of minivans since 1984, paying scant attention to chronic ABS, 4-cylinder engine, automatic transmission, airbag control module, electrical system, and fit and finish deficiencies, or to rust-damaged steering and suspension systems.

Indeed, Chrysler minivans caught on from their debut in 1984, when they were seen as fairly reliable and efficient people-haulers; that is, until the comprehensive warranty expired, or was cut back post-2000. Nevertheless, these minivans have continued to dominate the market despite their well-known mechanical and body problems. In fact, it's amazing how little Chrysler's defect patterns have changed during the past two decades (see *www.autosafety.org/autodefects.html*, *http://terpconnect.umd.edu/~gluckman/Chrysler/index.html* (The Chrysler Products' Problem Web Page), and *www.daimlerchryslervehicleproblems.com* (The Truth Behind Chrysler).

Ford

Ford's minivans went from bad to worse over two decades. Its first minivan, the 1985–97 Aerostar, had recurring brake, tranny, electrical system, and coil-spring problems. Collapsing coil springs have caused tire blowouts on all model years.

Ford's quality decline continued with the mediocre front-drive Mercury Villager, a co-venture that also produced the Nissan Quest. Both vehicles were only so-so highway performers that often resided in dealer repair bays awaiting major engine, transmission, or electrical repairs. The Villager/Quest duo lasted through the 2000 model year. The Quest continued on its own with minimal changes to its 2001–03 models. The 2004 Quest's redesign was both a conceptual and engineering disaster. First-year models were so glitch-prone and stylistically beyond the pale that Nissan sent over 200 engineers to North America to correct the defects and change the interior design. Sales have never recovered.

Then Ford brought out the 1995 Windstar—one of the poorest quality, most dangerous minivans ever built; the year 2000 model logged 736 safety-related complaints at NHTSA. Renamed the Freestar in 2004, the vehicle's failure-prone fuel, braking, electrical, powertrain, and suspension (broken coil springs) systems put owners' wallets and lives at risk.

Ford compounded the Windstar's failings with its hard-nosed attitude toward customer complaints and by refusing warranty coverage for what were clearly factory-induced defects. Fortunately, there was a flood of Canadian small claims court decisions that came to the owners' aid when Ford wouldn't. These Canadian courts ruled Ford and its dealers must pay for engine and transmission repairs, even if the original warranty has expired or the minivan was bought used (see page 63).

General Motors

GM's minivans are even less reliable than Ford's. To begin with, they have more-serious powertrain problems than either Ford or Chrysler, other mechanical components such as fuel gauges and brakes aren't dependable, and fit and finish is so bad that not even the roof can escape developing rust holes, as GM service bulletins confirm.

Asian automakers

Asian competitors don't make perfect machines either, as a perusal of NHTSA-registered safety complaints, service bulletins, and online complaint forums will quickly confirm. Asian companies, looking to keep costs down, have also been bedeviled during the past decade by chronic engine and automatic transmission failures, sliding door malfunctions, catastrophic tire blowouts, and electrical glitches.

A word of warning about Nissan and Toyota: Yes, these importers have made fairly dependable vehicles—including minivans—for the past four decades. However, the newly redesigned Nissan Quest and Toyota Sienna minivans also have some serious factory glitches and both automakers have learned from Detroit the art of obfuscation. Presently, Toyota's sudden, unintended acceleration, brake failures and rust-cankered trucks have tarnished the company's reputation to the point that it no longer has the public trust. Resale values are soft and the automaker has thrown millions of dollars into dealer sales incentives and customer rebates.

Volkswagen

And, finally, we come back to where we started—Volkswagen. Its vans, including the 1979 Vanagon and 1993 EuroVan/Camper, have never been taken seriously since they came to North America in 1950 with the Transporter cargo van and the nine-seater, 21-window Microbus. A reputation for poor overall quality, puny engines, and insufficient parts and servicing support continues to drive buyers away.

As part of an agreement with Chrysler, Volkswagen has sold 2009 through 2011 minivans cloned from the 2008 Chrysler Town & Country. VW says it has added Euro touch steering and suspension, but most drivers will only notice a firmer ride...not always a good thing on rough roads. Another surprise that will hit families hard is that the VW version has dropped the useful Stow 'n Go and Swivel 'n Go seats. Instead, you get second-row seats on rollers.

VW's new minivan is called the Routan, which some say is German for "biodegradable." Says *Truth About Cars* columnist Martin Martineck (*www.thetruthaboutcars.com/2008/10/2009-volkswagen-routan-review*):

> There's no disguising the Routan's modern roots: a non-Germanic vehicle made for people comfortable living inside a box. If you can't see the problem, blinded as you

are by the steering wheel's big-ass logo, you can feel it. The switchgear and cabinetry respond with Chrysler-esque imprecision.

Long-term prospects for this slow-seller are sombre. A 2009 Routan that sold for $27,975 can now be picked up for half that price.

Larger and Smaller Alternatives

Most minivans are overpriced for what is essentially an upgraded car or downsized truck. Motorists needing a vehicle with large cargo- and passenger-carrying capacities should consider a Chrysler, Ford, or GM full-sized van, even if it means sacrificing some fuel economy. You just can't beat the excellent forward vision and easy-to-customize interiors that these large vans provide. Furthermore, parts are easily found and are competitively priced because of the great number of independent suppliers.

On the other hand, a minivan may be too large for some shoppers who want the same versatility in a smaller package capable of carrying six passengers. For them, a 2008 Mazda5 minivan/wagon is a good place to start. Although it originally sold for $20,795, the used value has dropped to about $12,000.

MINIVAN RATINGS

Above Average

Honda Odyssey (1999–2004)   Mazda5 (2006–09; see Small Cars)

Average

Chrysler Caravan, Voyager, Grand   Honda Odyssey (2005–09)
   Caravan, Grand Voyager,   Hyundai Entourage (2007–09)
   Town & Country (2008–09)   Kia Sedona (2007–09)
Chrysler PT Cruiser (2001–09)   Toyota Sienna (2005–09)

Below Average

Chrysler Caravan, Voyager,   Kia Sedona (2002–06)
   Grand Caravan, Grand Voyager,   Nissan Quest (2004–09)
   Town & Country (2002–07)   Toyota Sienna (1999–2004)

Not Recommended

Chrysler Caravan, Voyager,   General Motors Montana, Montana SV6, Relay,
   Grand Caravan, Grand Voyager,   Silhouette, Terraza, Uplander, Venture
   Town & Country (1999–2001)   (1999–2009)
Ford Freestar, Windstar (1999–2007)   Nissan Quest/Ford Villager (1999–2003)

Chrysler

RATING: Average (2008–09); Below Average (2002–07); Not Recommended (1999–2001). If Chrysler goes bankrupt again, all warranties will be worthless and the minivan and Jeep division will likely be sold off separately. Do you feel lucky? **Ideal model year:** A 2008 Grand Caravan SXT for about $10,000 is your best choice. It is full of new features and costs much less than the $30,495 original price. **"Real" city/highway fuel economy:** *Caravan 2.4 4-cylinder:* 11.8/8.2 L/100 km. *Caravan 3.0 V6:* 12.7/8.3 L/100 km. *Caravan 3.3 V6:* 12.2/8.2 L/100 km. *Grand Caravan 3.3 V6:* 12.9/8.5 L/100 km. *Grand Caravan 3.8 V6:* 13.2/8.7 L/100 km. *Town & Country 2.7:* 15.5/10.0 L/100 km. *Town & Country 4.0:* 12.2/7.9 L/100 km. *Town & Country AWD:* 13.6/9.1 L/100 km. Owners report fuel savings may undershoot these estimates by 20 percent or more. **Maintenance/Repair costs:** Higher than average. **Parts:** Easy to find and reasonably priced when bought from and installed by independent suppliers. **Extended warranty:** Yes, mainly for the powertrain. Buy the warranty from an insured third party. Why not from Chrysler? With Chrysler pinching pennies for its Fiat overlord, how generous do you think it will be in approving your warranty repairs? **Best alternatives:** Honda's Odyssey should be your first choice, followed by Mazda's Mazda5 and Toyota's Sienna (but not the 2004 model). GM and Ford front- and rear-drive minivans aren't credible alternatives because of their failure-prone powertrains; brake, suspension, and steering problems; electrical short circuits; and subpar bodywork. Full-sized GM and Chrysler rear-drive cargo vans are more affordable and practical buys if you intend to haul a full passenger load or do some regular heavy hauling, if you have physical challenges entering and exiting most vehicles, if you use lots of accessories, or if you take frequent motoring excursions. Chrysler's German-built Sprinter van is a poor alternative due to its shoddy reliability, weak parts network, and dealer-dependent servicing. **Helpful websites:** *http://dodgeforum.com/forum/ dodge-caravan-23* and *www.carcomplaints.com/Chrysler.*

Strengths and Weaknesses

Chrysler's minivans continue to dominate the new- and used-minivan markets, though they're quickly losing steam because of the popularity of crossover wagons and better-quality products from Japanese and South Korean automakers. Nevertheless, they offer pleasing styling and lots of convenience features at used prices that can be very attractive. They can carry up to seven passengers in comfort, and ride and handle better than most truck-based minivans. The shorter-wheelbase minivans also offer better rear visibility and good ride quality, and are more nimble and easy to park. Cargo hauling capability is more than adequate.

Nevertheless, these minivans can pose serious safety risks. Owners report bizarre defects such as seat belts that may strangle children, airbags that deploy when the ignition is turned on, transmissions that jump out of gear, and sudden stalling and electrical short circuits when within radar range of airports or military installations.

Other common problems include the premature wearout of engine tensioner pulleys, automatic transmission speed sensors, engine head gaskets, motor mounts, starter motors, steering columns, front brake discs and pads (the brake pad material crumbles in your hands), front rotors and rear drums, brake master cylinders, suspension components, exhaust system components, ball joints, wheel bearings, water pumps, fuel pumps and pump wiring harnesses, radiators, heater cores, and AC compressors. Fuel injectors on all engines have been troublesome, the differential pin breaks through the automatic transmission casing, sliding doors malfunction, door locks often won't lock, engine supports may be missing or not connected, tie rods may suddenly break, oil pans crack, and the power-steering pump frequently leaks. Factory-installed Goodyear and Bridgestone Turanza tires frequently fail at 40,000–65,000 km.

Chrysler's A604, 41TE, and 42LE automatic transmissions, phased in with the 1991 models, are reliability nightmares that can have serious safety consequences. Imagine having to count to three in traffic before Drive or Reverse will engage, "limping" home in Second gear at 50 km/h, or suddenly losing all forward motion in traffic.

Fit and finish has gotten worse over the past two decades. Body hardware and interior trim are fragile and tend to break, warp, or fall off (door handles are an example). The premature rust-out of major suspension and steering components is a critical safety and performance concern. Paint delamination often turns these solid-coloured minivans into two-tones.

And as the minivan takes on its albino appearance, you can listen to a concerto of clicks, clunks, rattles, squeaks, and squeals as you drive (you'll love the reed section). Giving new meaning to the phrase "surround sound," these noises usually emanate from the brakes, poorly anchored bench seats, misaligned body panels, and suspension and steering assemblies.

VEHICLE HISTORY: 2001—A small horsepower boost for the V6s; front side airbags, adjustable pedals, upgraded headlights, and a power-operated rear liftgate across the rest of the lineup. **2002**—Fuel-tank assembly is redesigned to prevent post-collision fuel leakage; a tire air-pressure monitor is added. **2005**—Side curtain airbags and second- and third-row seats that fold flush with the floor; AWD dropped (owners gain; repair bays lose). **2008**—Redesigned with fresh styling, a more powerful engine, and new seating features. The '08 model is 5 cm (2 inches) longer in wheelbase and overall length than the 2007. The shorter wheelbase Caravan model is discontinued, as is the 4-cylinder engine. All Caravans now have a V6. The 3.3L and 3.8L engines carry over from 2007, but new for 2008 is a 253 hp 4.0L engine. The 3.3L V6 teams with a 4-speed automatic transmission, while the 3.8L and 4.0L engines are hooked to a 6-speed automatic.

Don't buy any Chrysler minivan with a 4-cylinder engine—it has no place in a vehicle this large, especially when hooked to the inadequate 3-speed automatic transmission. It lacks an Overdrive and will shift back and forth as speed varies, and it's slower and noisier than the other choices. The 3.3L V6 is a better choice for most city-driving situations, but don't hesitate to get the 3.8L or 4.0L V6 if you're planning lots of highway travel or carrying four or more passengers. The sliding side doors are a costly, failure-prone gizmo. Child safety seats integrated into the rear seatbacks are convenient and reasonably priced, but Chrysler's versions have had a history of either tightening up excessively or not tightening enough, allowing the child to slip out. Try the seat with your child before buying it. You may wish to pass on the tinted windshields as well; they seriously reduce visibility. Be wary of models featuring all-wheel drive and ABS: The powertrain isn't reliable and is horrendously expensive to repair, and Chrysler's large number of ABS failures is worrisome. Ditch the failure-prone Goodyear original-equipment tires, and remember that a night drive is a prerequisite, in order to check out headlight illumination, which many call inadequate.

Safety Summary

All years: Sudden, unintended acceleration; owners report that cruise-control units often malfunction, accelerating or decelerating the vehicle without any warning. • Airbag malfunctions: Get used to the term "clockspring." It's an expensive little component that controls some parts within the steering wheel and, when defective, can result in the Airbag warning light coming on or the airbag, cruise control, or horn failing. It has been a pain in the butt for Chrysler minivan owners since the 1996 model year. Chrysler has extended its warranty for 1996–2000 minivans in two separate recalls and replaced the clockspring at no charge. Apparently, the automaker has found that the part fails because it was wound too tight or short-circuited from corrosion. • Defective engine head gaskets, rocker arm gaskets, and engine mounts. • Engine sag, hesitation, stumble, hard starts, or stalling. • No steering/lock-up. • Carbon monoxide comes through air vents. • Brakes wear out prematurely or fail completely. • Transmission fails, suddenly drops into low gear, won't go into Reverse, delays engagement, or jumps out of gear when running or parked. • One can move the automatic transmission shift lever without applying brakes. • Several incidents where ignition was turned and vehicle went into Reverse at full throttle, although transmission was set in Park. • ABS failure. • Many complaints of front suspension-strut towers rusting then cracking at the weld seams; jig-positioning hole wasn't sealed at the factory. • Brakes activate by themselves while vehicle is underway. • Seatbacks fall backward. • Rear windows fall out or shatter. • Power window and door lock failures. • Sliding door often opens while vehicle is underway, or jams, trapping occupants. • Weak headlights. • Horn often doesn't work. • Several incidents where side windows exploded for no apparent reason. • Adults cannot sit in third-row seat without their heads smashing into the roof as the vehicle passes over bumps. **2006**—Turn signals function erratically, and headlights flicker and dim. **2007**—Automatic transmission "bumps" into gear. • Ruptured front brake hoses. • Complete loss of steering because the "roll pin" on the steering shaft was improperly installed at the factory. • Sudden veering to the right. **2008**—Airbags failed to deploy. • Side airbag deactivated due to pinched driver side door wiring harness. • Defective (broken) tire valve stems:

> I was about to add air to the front tire and was removing the cap when the valve blew apart about halfway down the stem. The tire went flat immediately. We had the dealer replace the TPM valve stem but they had to order it and it took a week to get the part. I asked them to change the other 3, but they said they will only replace one valve at a time as they fail. Sure enough, two weeks later a second valve stem failed and the tire went flat very fast. Again, I'm told they will just order one valve and replace them as they fail. This is obviously a problem they know about but don't want to deal with. Hopefully no one is injured or killed in an accident from one of these failing.

• Many complaints that brake pads still wear out at 15,000 miles; rotors last barely double that. • Sliding passenger door will not stop if it catches an arm or a leg. **2009**—Sudden, unintended acceleration. • Vehicle may suddenly lose power. • Front wheel bearing failures. • More cracked tire valves. • Erratic operation of the sliding side door. • Brake pads and rotors continue to wear out prematurely. • Faulty gear shift assembly:

> The handle fell to the floor, as did the button and the internal spring.... I now have a pointed piece of metal sticking out of my dash.

Secret Warranties/Internal Bulletins/Service Tips

1996–2006—Rusted, frozen rear brake drums. **2001–02**—Wind or water leaks at the rear quarter window. **2001–03**—Oil filter leaks with 3.3L and 3.8L engines (confirmed in TSB #09-001-03). **2001–04**—AC water leaks. **2001–06**—Water leaks under passenger-side carpet. **2002–07**—Power liftgate malfunctions. **2003**—Troubleshooting water leaks. • Three bulletins relating to automatic transmission malfunctions: delayed gear engagement, harsh 4–3 downshift, and excessive vibration and transfer gear whine. **2003–05**—Crack, split and/or water leak in the upper body-seam sealer at the B- or C-pillar. **2005**—Engine squeak under light throttle. • Campaign for the free replacement of the rear AC heater tube if it is corroded; another campaign will replace at no charge the underbody heater hose. **2005–06**—AC condenser road debris damage can be prevented by installing a condenser guard supplied by Chrysler (under warranty, of course). **2006–07**—Silencing moonroof noises. **2007**—Troubleshooting body noises. **2008**—Harsh shifting. • Abnormal front brake pad wear. • Outside sliding door handle is inoperative in freezing temperatures. • Roof rack howling sound. • Howl, honk from the front windshield. • Front door rattle or window won't roll down. • Exhaust system rattle, clunk. • Slow fuel tank fill; pump shuts off prematurely. **2008–09**—Roof rack cross bar adjuster corroded/seized. • Coolant leak around the radiator cap. **2008–10**—Power steering fluid leaks. • An inoperative power sliding door may only require a reflashing of the sliding door computer module. **2009**—Front brake squeal, pulsation.

CARAVAN, GRAND CARAVAN, TOWN & COUNTRY PROFILE

	2001	2002	2003	2004	2005	2006	2007	2008	2009
Cost Price ($)									
Caravan	24,885	25,430	25,430	27,620	28,205	27,065	27,445	—	—
Grand Caravan	29,505	28,875	29,295	30,190	30,740	31,070	29,305	26,495	26,595
Town & Country	41,150	40,815	42,705	44,095	44,595	44,920	42,255	35,995	36,995
Used Values ($)									
Caravan ▲	2,500	2,500	3,000	3,500	4,000	5,000	6,500	—	—
Caravan ▼	2,000	2,000	2,500	3,000	3,500	4,000	5,000	—	—
Grand Caravan ▲	3,000	3,500	4,000	4,500	5,000	6,500	8,000	10,500	13,000
Grand Caravan ▼	2,500	3,000	3,500	4,000	4,500	5,500	6,500	9,000	11,500
Town & Country ▲	4,000	4,500	5,000	6,000	7,500	9,000	11,500	17,000	21,500
Town & Country ▼	3,500	4,000	4,500	5,000	6,500	8,000	10,000	15,500	20,000
Reliability	2	2	2	2	2	3	3	3	3
Crash Safety (F)									
Caravan	4	4	4	4	4	—		—	—
Grand Caravan	4	4	4	4	—				
Town & Country	—	—	4	4	4				
Town & Country LX	4	4	4	4	—		—		
Side									
Caravan	4	4	4	—	—	—	4	—	—
Grand Caravan				—	—				
Town & Country LX	4			4	4		—		
IIHS Side									
Grand Caravan	—	—	—	—	—	3	3		
Town & Country	—	—	—	—	—	1	1		
Offset									
Grand Caravan	1	3	3	3	3	3	3		
Town & Country	1	3	3	3	3	3	3		
Head Restraints (F)									
Grand Caravan	—	—	—	1	1	1	1	2	2
Town & Country	3	3	3	1	1	1	1	2	2
Town & Country LX	2	2	2	1	1	1	1	—	—
Rollover Resistance	3	3	3	—	—	4	4	4	4

PT CRUISER ★★★

RATING: Average (2001–09). This mini-minivan has defied all of the odds and shown Chrysler can make a versatile and fairly reliable small van out of Neon parts. Despite its hot-rod flair, the Cruiser's popularity is waning. **Ideal model year:** Consider the 2007 wagon for $7,500; it's cheap and has a full allotment of features that weren't augmented over the ensuing years. **"Real" city/highway fuel economy:** *Manual: 9.8/7.5* L/100 km. *Automatic: 11.0/8.1* L/100 km. *Turbo* *manual:* 10.4/7.9 L/100 km. *Turbo automatic:* 11.4/8.1 L/100 km. **Maintenance/ Repair costs:** Average. **Parts:** Reasonably priced and easily found, except for body parts. **Extended warranty:** A toss-up. **Best alternatives:** Try the Mazda5 or the Subaru Legacy Outback Limited. Sport-utilities worth considering are the Ford Escape, Honda CR-V EX, Hyundai Tucson, Jeep Liberty, Mazda Tribute, and Subaru Forester. **Helpful websites:** *www.ptcruiserlinks.com/forum.*

Strengths and Weaknesses

The PT Cruiser is essentially a fuel- and space-efficient small hatchback minivan. It's noted for excellent fuel economy (regular fuel), nimble handling around town, good braking, lots of interior space, easy access, a versatile cargo area, many thoughtful interior amenities, slow depreciation, and unforgettable hot-rod styling.

Forget about hot-rod power with the base engine, though. The 150 hp 2.4L 4-cylinder powerplant is not very smooth-running and, when matched with the automatic transmission, it struggles when going uphill or merging with highway traffic. This requires frequent downshifting and lots of patience. Costlier turbocharged models will give you plenty of power, but you risk some steep repair bills. The automatic transmission has little low-end torque, forcing early kickdown shifting and deft manipulation of the accelerator pedal. High-speed handling isn't impressive; hard cornering produces an unsteady, wobbly ride because of the car's height. The ride is firm, with lots of interior engine, wind, and road noise.

VEHICLE HISTORY: 2002—A CD player and underseat storage bin. **2003**—A 215 hp turbocharged GT and 17-inch wheels. **2004**—A 180 hp 2.4L turbocharged 4-cylinder joins the 220 hp turbocharged and the 150 hp non-turbo powerplants. **2006**—Revised front ends and dash. **2008**—The high-performance 230 hp GT model is gone. **2009**—The convertible is also gone.

Reliability is problematic for all model years, with frequent drivetrain complaints that include faulty valve cover gaskets, causing oil burning, and automatic transmission control modules, forcing the drivetrain to gear down to "limp home" mode. Power-steering pump units and steering units are also frequently replaced. Fit and finish deficiencies read like an anthology of common Chrysler defects: drivetrain whine, water leaking through the passenger-side window, annoying wind noise when driving with the rear window or sunroof open, and moisture between the clearcoat and paint turning the hood a chalky colour. (See *www-odi. nhtsa.dot.gov/complaints*, *www.ptcruiserlinks.com*, *http://terpconnect.umd. edu/~gluckman/Chrysler/index.html* (The Chrysler Products' Problem Web Page), *www.daimlerchryslervehicleproblems.com* (The Truth Behind Chrysler), and *www. autosafety.org/autodefects.html*).

Safety Summary

All years: Airbag malfunctions. • Sudden, unintended acceleration; chronic stalling. • Steering clockspring failure. • Side-wind instability. • Front axle breaks while vehicle is underway. • Instrument pods are difficult to read in the daylight. • Tall drivers beware: The windshield is uncomfortably close, and overhead traffic lights will disappear. • Wide pillars obstruct one's view. • Headrests are too high, block vision, and are unstable. • Constant short circuits; no lights, gauges. • Lights flicker and dim. • Doors lock and unlock on their own. **2001**—When parked, transmission slipped out of gear and vehicle rolled down driveway. • Engine suddenly shuts down when vehicle passes through a large puddle. • Steering wheel loosens on its shaft. • Headlight failures; low beams may cut out, and only part of the headlight beam illuminates the roadway. **2002**—Gas pedal goes to the floor with no acceleration. • Suddenly shifts into First gear while cruising. • Brake lock-up. **2003**—Chronic engine overheating. • Sudden front axle/bearing seizure threw car out of control and caused $7,000 damage to the drivetrain. • Automatic transmission failures while car is underway. • Self-activating door locks and seat heater. **2004**—Electrical fires. • Steering locks up. **2005**—Power windows can strangle a child due to the location of the button:

> We were parked in a parking lot with the car running talking to another group when my 6 year old stuck her head out the window to join the discussion. When she did, she accidentally kicked the power window button with her foot. The button was located near the floor in the backseat on the middle console. She rolled the window up on her own head and was stuck in the window. She only lived through the event because 1) her head was tilted at the time so the window rolled up on the side of her neck and not on her trachea; and 2) her 8 year old sister in the back seat with her heard her screams and got her foot off the button and rolled the window back down.

• Sunlight reflects off the silver-painted airbag, blinding the driver. **2006**—Cracked engine head gasket. • Early transmission failure. • Side window shattered. • Driver must "pound" the horn. • Driver's power seat has no forward stop; jams driver against the steering wheel. • Light assemblies collect water. **2006–07**—Goodyear Eagle LS side-wall blowouts. **2007**—Engine camshaft, crankshaft bearing, and seal failures; head gaskets warp. • Automatic transmission slips in and out of gear. • Brakes fail on wet pavement. • Power-steering fluid leakage. • Exploding rear window. • Driver's seat adjusts when it isn't necessary. • Hazard lights flick on and off. • Horn sticks. **2008**—Sudden, unintended acceleration. • Airbags failed to deploy and seatbelt stretched allowing driver's spine to be crushed. • Windows stick, or go down on their own. • Headlights come on when no one is in the car. • Radio volume goes up or down on its own. • Foglights turn on or off by themselves, draining the battery while parked. **2009**—Only 10 safety-related complaints posted on NHTSA's website, when 100 incidents would be the norm. • Return of sudden, unintended acceleration. • Side airbags failed to deploy. • Prematurely worn control arm bushings; the car wobbles at all speeds and pulls to the right. • Tire aluminum valve stems continue to fail. • The seat adjustment mechanism plastic part fails and suddenly readjusts whenever the vehicle goes over a bump. Cost to fix: $300. • Repeated loss of brakes. • Driver side rear window suddenly shattered. • Driver must punch centre of steering wheel several times to shut off horn.

Secret Warranties/Internal Bulletins/Service Tips

2001—A faulty transmission control module (TCM) may cause harsh shifting. • MIL comes on because of a faulty TCM harness connector or a defective evaporator purge flow monitor. • Poor acceleration, spark knock. • Left or right floor latch on rear seat won't release. • Fuel gauge won't indicate full. • Airbag pads fall off. • Wind buffeting with the windows and/or sunroof open or partially open. **2001–02**—Highway speed surge. **2001–03**—Transmission slips in Reverse or First gears. • High-speed engine surging. **2001–06**—Moisture accumulation in headlights. **2003**—Turbo engine hesitation, loss of boost, and screeching. • Delayed gear engagement. • Harsh 4–3 downshifts. • Warning lights come on for no reason. • Warped rear bumper. **2004–09**—Fuel nozzle shuts off. **2005–07**—Driveability improvements related to engine surging. **2006–07**—Windshield crack diagnosis (warranty or no warranty). **2006–08**—Starter won't crank; engine doesn't crank. • Harsh shifts. **2007**—Automatic transmission shudder; harsh shifting.

PT CRUISER PROFILE

	2001	2002	2003	2004	2005	2006	2007	2008	2009
Cost Price ($)									
Base	23,665	23,850	22,500	24,360	21,270	21,670	19,840	20,895	21,995
Limited	27,180	27,305	27,420	28,800	—	—	—	—	—
Turbo	—	—	27,700	31,350	31,665	31,665	30,350	27,545	—
Convertible	—	—	—	—	26,995	27,790	28,220	29,695	—
Used Values ($)									
Base ▲	3,000	3,500	4,000	4,500	5,500	6,500	8,000	10,000	12,500
Base ▼	2,500	3,000	3,500	4,000	5,000	5,500	7,000	8,500	11,000
Limited ▲	3,500	4,000	5,000	5,000	—	—	—	—	—
Limited ▼	3,000	3,500	4,500	5,000	—	—	—	—	—
Turbo ▲	—	—	5,500	6,000	7,000	7,500	9,500	11,500	—
Turbo ▼	—	—	4,500	5,500	6,000	7,000	8,000	10,000	—
Convertible ▲	—	—	—	—	8,000	9,000	11,000	12,500	—
Convertible ▼	—	—	—	—	7,000	8,000	9,500	11,500	—
Reliability	3	3	3	3	3	3	3	3	3
Crash Safety (F)	2	4	4	4	4	4	—	4	4
Side	4	4	4	—	—	4	—	4	4
Side (IIHS)	—	—	—	—	—	—	—	1	1
Offset	—	—	—	—	—	4	4	—	—
Head Restraints	4	4	4	4	—	1	1	1	1
Rollover Resistance	4	4	4	—	—	4	—	4	4

Ford

FREESTAR, WINDSTAR ★

RATING: Not Recommended (1999–2007). The Freestar is a Windstar in disguise, with the same poor-quality components and lousy fit and finish that made driving hell for Windstar owners. The Windstar is infamous for atrocious quality control (particularly, with such vital powertrain components as the engine and automatic transmission), stonewalled owner complaints, and life-threatening defects. **"Real" city/highway fuel economy:** 11.0/7.1 L/100 km. Owners report fuel savings may undershoot this estimate by at least 15 percent. **Maintenance/ Repair costs:** Average while under warranty; outrageously higher than average thereafter. **Parts:** Reasonably priced parts are easy to find. Digital speedometers can cost almost $1,000 to replace at the dealer. Scrounge around. **Extended warranty:** Definitely; a Saint Christopher medallion would also help. **Best alternatives:** The Honda Odyssey and Toyota Sienna (but not the 2004) are the best choices. Some full-sized Chrysler (Ram Van), Ford (Econoline), and GM (Chevy Van, Vandura, Express, or Savana) rear-drive cargo/passenger vans are more affordable and more practical buys. **Helpful websites:** *www.carcomplaints. com/Ford.*

Strengths and Weaknesses

Ford can call it the Windstar or the Freestar; the fact remains that owners call it a "death trap." Sure, the Windstar combines an impressive five-star crash safety rating, plenty of raw power, an exceptional ride, and impressive cargo capacity. But these minivans have failure-prone engines, self-destructing automatic transmissions, collapsing rear axles, "Do I feel lucky?" brakes, and unreliable electrical systems.

More than half a million 1998–2003 Windstars were recalled in August 2010 to replace rust-damaged rear axles that could separate and cause the vehicle to career out of control. Because the minivan hasn't been built since 2003, Ford doesn't know when replacement parts will be available. Drivers have been told to drive carefully (omigod!).

The Windstar's suspension includes rust-prone coil springs that frequently break, blow out the front tire, and make the minivan uncontrollable. As solace, Ford says it will pay for coil breakage up to 10 years on vehicles registered in rust-prone regions.

Another counterpoint to Ford's Windstar crashworthiness boasting is the frightening archive of Windstar safety-related failures compiled by NHTSA. Besides the many coil-spring failures already noted (these have affected almost all of Ford's vehicles for practically a decade), owners report sudden stalling, acceleration, steering loss, exploding windows, horn failures, wheels falling off, sliding doors that open and close on their own, and vehicles rolling away while parked.

Other safety-related deficiencies include the lack of head restraints for all seats on early Windstars and a digital dash that's often confusing, failure-prone, and expensive to replace. Optional adjustable pedals help protect drivers from airbag injuries. Be careful, though; some drivers have found that these pedals are set too close together and seem loose. Drivers must also contend with mediocre handling, restricted side and rear visibility, and an abundance of clunks, rattles, and wind and road noise (see *www.tgrigsby.com/views/ford.htm* (The Anti-Ford Page) and *www.autosafety.org/autodefects.html*).

VEHICLE HISTORY: 2001—The base 3.0L V6 is gone; the Windstar gets an upgraded automatic transmission (still unreliable), a low-tire-pressure warning system, "smart" airbags, and a slight restyling. **2002**—Dual sliding doors. **2003**—An optional anti-skid system. **2004**—Freestar arrives and flops; a two-passenger cargo van arrives.

Freestar: Too little, too late

Built on a modified Taurus platform, the Freestar gives you the same uninspired, though predictable, carlike handling characteristics of Ford's mid-size family sedans. You'll also encounter to a lesser extent many of the horrific engine, automatic transmission, electrical, suspension, and brake system problems experienced by Taurus and Sable owners.

Ford's denial of owner claims has been blasted in small-claims court judgments across Canada. Judges have ruled that engines and transmissions (and power-sliding doors) must be reasonably durable long after the warranty expires, whether the vehicle was bought new or used, notwithstanding that it was repaired by an independent or that it had the same problem repaired earlier for free. The three best engine judgments supporting Ford owners are *Dufour v. Ford Canada Ltd*, *Schaffler v. Ford Motor Company Limited and Embrun Ford Sales Ltd.*, and *John R. Reid and Laurie M. McCall v. Ford Motor Company of Canada* (see Part Two).

Dangerous doors

We noted previously that the courts have slammed Ford for allowing dangerously defective sliding doors to go uncorrected year after year. Typical scenarios reported by owners include the following: a sliding door slammed shut on a child's head while the vehicle was parked on an incline; passengers are often pinned by the door; the door reopens as it is closing; the door often pops open while the vehicle is underway; a driver's finger was broken when closing a manual sliding door; and the handle is too close to the door jam, which is a hazard that has been reported on the Internet since 1999. Owners also report that the 2003 Windstar's automatic sliding door opens by itself or the door will not power open, and the door lock assembly freezes.

In *Sharman v. Formula Ford Sales Limited, Ford Credit Limited, and Ford Motor Company of Canada Limited* (Ontario Superior Court of Justice (Oakville), No. 17419/02SR, 2003/10/07), Justice Shepard awarded the owner of a 2000 Windstar $7,500 for mental distress resulting from the breach of the implied warranty of fitness plus $7,207 for breach of contract and breach of warranty. The problem—the Windstar's sliding door wasn't secure and leaked air and water after many attempts to repair it. Interestingly, the judge cited the *Wharton* decision, among other decisions, as support for his award for mental distress (see page 116).

Safety Summary

All models/years: Severe injuries caused by airbag malfunctions. • Vehicle suddenly accelerates while parked, cruising, when brakes are applied, or when the ignition is turned. • Chronic stalling caused by fuel-vapour lock or faulty fuel pump; engine shuts down when turning. • Control arm and inner tie-rod failures cause the wheel to fall off. • Sudden steering lock-up or loss of steering ability. • Engine head gasket failures. • Frequent transmission failures, including noisy engagement, inability to engage Forward or Reverse, and slipping or jerking into gear. • Many reports that the vehicle jumps out of Park and rolls away when on an incline, or slips into Reverse with the engine idling. • Transmission and axle separation. • Automatic transmission suddenly seizes. • Steering wheel locks up. • Loose or missing front brake bolts could cause the wheels to lock up or the vehicle to lose control. • Chronic ABS failures. • Faulty fuel pump, sensor, and gauge. • Built-in child safety seat is too easy to get out of; sometimes the securing seat belts are too tight; in one incident, a child was almost strangled. • Faulty rear liftgate latches; trunk lid can fall on one's head. • Rear side windows, liftgate window, and windshield often explode suddenly. • Sliding door opens and closes on its own, sticks open or closed, or suddenly slams shut on a downgrade. • Door locks don't stay locked. • Horn button "sweet spot" is too small. • Interior windows are always fogged up because of inadequate defrosting. • Body seams not sealed; water intrudes into floor seat anchors. • Driver's seat poorly anchored. • Dashboard glare onto windshield. • Check Tire warning light comes on for no reason. • Tire jack collapses. *Freestar:* **2004**—Sudden, unintended acceleration. • Loss of steering. • Airbag warning light stays on; airbags may not deploy. • A-frame drops out of the tie-rod collar. • Front axle suddenly breaks while underway. • Automatic transmission failure. • Left inner brake pad falls apart and locks up brake. • Sliding door closed on a child in one incident, causing slight injuries; in another incident it crushed an adult's leg. • Plastic running board broke, blocking sliding door operation and locking occupants inside the vehicle. **2005**—A shameful litany of self-destructing automatic transmissions. NHTSA is investigating reports that 2004–05 Ford Freestar and Mercury Monterey minivans have defective transmissions that fail without warning. While underway at highway speeds, the engine suddenly surges and then loses all power. The vehicle is forced to coast powerlessly, with no power steering, to a safe spot out of the flow of traffic. Owners are usually stranded and stuck with $3,500 repair bills. There have been 654 customer complaints and 2,791 warranty claims, but as many as 205,000 vehicles may be affected. The investigation, expected to take a year, will focus on the torque converter output shaft which drives the wheels. • Biodegradable brake rotors and pads. • Tire blowouts caused by defective valve stems. • Premature wheel bearing failures preceded by an annoying whine. **2006**—Fire ignited under the hood. • Highway stall-outs. • Transmission here today, gone tomorrow…sigh. • Automatic transmission torque converter is failure prone:

> The spines in the transmission torque converter fail because they were not hardened. When this happens the vehicle stops and cannot move. This is very dangerous, and at some point (if it hasn't already) will cause an accident, and possible death.

• Vehicle suddenly loses power. • Traction control system activates for no reason. • Wheel hub assembly failures. • Rear turn signal lights often burn out. • Gasoline odour comes in through the air vents. • Premature failure of the Goodyear Integrity tires. **2007**—Van suddenly went out of gear. • Vehicle suddenly lost all power.

Secret Warranties/Internal Bulletins/Service Tips

All models/years: An exhaust buzz or rattle may be caused by a loose catalyst or heat shield. • Sliding-door malfunctions. • Buzzing noise in speakers caused by fuel pump. • A MIL lit for no reason may simply mean that the gas cap is loose. • If the power-sliding door won't close, replace the door controller; if it pops or disengages when fully closed, adjust the door and rear striker to reduce closing resistance. • Front wipers that operate when switched off need a revised multi-function switch (covered under a service program and recall). • Engine oil mixed with coolant or loss of coolant signals the need for revised engine lower intake manifold side gaskets and/or front cover gaskets. Ford's benchmark for refunding repair costs for this problem: 7 years/160,000 km. **All models: 2000–07**—Erratic fluid level readings on the transaxle dipstick; transmission fluid leaks. **2001**—In Special Service Instruction #01T01 Ford admits automatic transmission defects (slippage, delayed shifts). **2001–02**—Service tips for reports of premature engine failures. • Concerns with oil in the cooling system. • Hard starts; rough-running engines. • Shudder while in Reverse or during 3–4 shift. • Transmission fluid leakage. • Power-steering fluid leaks. • Brake roughness and pulsation. • Rear brake drum drag in cold weather. • Fogging of the front and side windows. • False low-tire-pressure warning. **2001–03**—Remedy for a slow-to-fill fuel tank. **2002**—MIL comes on; vehicle shifts poorly or won't start. • Buzz, groan, or vibration when gear selector lever is in Park. • Some vehicles may run roughly on the highway or just after stopping. • Defective ignition-switch lock cylinders. • Sliding doors rattle and squeak. **2003**—Airbag warning light stays lit. *Freestar:* **2004**—Transmission has no 1–2 upshift (TSB #04-15-12). • False activation of parking assist. • TSB #04-2-3, published September 2, 2004, lists ways to find and fix the sliding doors' many failures. **2004–05**—Accelerated rear brake pad wear. • Front brake squeal or squawk. • Excessive vibration. • Faulty, inoperative power door and liftgate. **2004–06**—Seat belts are slow to retract. • Inoperative AC compressor; seal leaks. **2004–07**—Poor engine/transmission response due to water entering the powertrain control module. • Spark knock under light load. •

Power-steering hose leak in extreme cold. • Erratic fluid level readings. **2006–07**—Engine intake popping noise. **2007–08**—Ford dealer will inspect at no charge and replace defective tire valve stems under its warranty. A case could be made that Ford is bound by the reasonable durability doctrine which is for much longer than the written warranty.

FREESTAR, WINDSTAR PROFILE

	2001	2002	2003	2004	2005	2006	2007
Cost Price ($)							
Freestar (Base)	—	—	—	27,295	27,995	22,999	23,299
SE	—	—	—	29,695	29,695	25,699	26,000
SEL	—	—	—	37,695	37,020	32,800	33,099
Windstar (Base)	—	24,900	24,901	—	—	—	—
LX	26,750	25,995	26,195	—	—	—	—
SEL	33,190	33,685	37,015	—	—	—	—
Used Values ($)							
Freestar (Base) ▲	—	—	—	3,000	4,500	5,500	7,500
Freestar (Base) ▼	—	—	—	2,500	4,000	5,000	6,000
SE ▲	—	—	—	3,500	5,000	6,000	8,000
SE ▼	—	—	—	3,000	4,500	5,500	6,500
SEL ▲	—	—	—	4,000	5,500	6,500	8,500
SEL ▼	—	—	—	3,500	5,000	6,000	7,500
Windstar (Base) ▲	—	2,000	2,500	—	—	—	—
Windstar (Base) ▼	—	1,500	2,000	—	—	—	—
LX ▲	2,500	3,000	3,500	—	—	—	—
LX ▼	2,000	2,500	3,000	—	—	—	—
SEL ▲	2,500	3,000	3,500	—	—	—	—
SEL ▼	2,000	2,500	3,000	—	—	—	—
Reliability	1	1	1	2	2	2	2
Crash Safety (F)	5	5	5	5	5	5	5
Side	5	4	4	4	4	4	4
IIHS Side	—	—	—	—	—	1	1
Offset	3	3	3	5	5	5	5
Head Restraints (F)	5	5	5	5	5	5	5
Rear	3	3	3	5	—	—	—
Rollover Resistance	4	4	4	4	4	4	4

General Motors

MONTANA, MONTANA SV6, RELAY, SILHOUETTE, TERRAZA, UPLANDER, VENTURE ★

bad buy

RATING: Not Recommended (1999–2009). These minivan orphans should have never left the factory. They are unreliable and dangerous, as evidenced by their automatic transmission and engine head gasket/intake manifold gasket failures and sliding doors that may crush children. **"Real" city/highway fuel economy:** *3.4:* 12.0/7.8 L/100 km. *3.4 AWD:* 13.7/9.6 L/100 km. Owners report fuel savings may undershoot these estimates by at least 15 percent. **Maintenance/Repair costs:** Average costs, except for engine and tranny glitches that cost $3,000 each to repair. **Parts:** Reasonably priced and not hard to find. **Extended warranty:** Definitely needed for both the engine and automatic transmission. **Best alternatives:** Honda Odyssey and Toyota Sienna (but not the 2004 Sienna). **Helpful websites:** *www.topix.com/forum/autos/chevrolet-uplander* and *www.carcomplaints.com/Chevrolet/Uplander*.

Strengths and Weaknesses

These minivans have more carlike handling than GM's truck-based Astro and Safari. Seating is limited to five adults in the standard models (two up front, and three on a removable bench seat), but this is increased to seven if you find a vehicle equipped with the additional seats. Seats can be folded down flat, creating additional storage space.

Passengers who require mobility assistance may use an optional Sit-N-Lift power seat system that provides convenient access to the right-hand second-row seating area and is capable of lifting 300 pounds. Operated via remote control, the power bucket seat rotates and then extends out of the vehicle before lowering for easy entry and exit. This enables a person with limited mobility to enter and exit the vehicle without needing someone to lift them. For added safety, the seat only operates when the vehicle is in Park and the door is open.

Thousands of these minivans were fitted with this unique invention from GM since they were first offered with the 2003 minivan models. If you can't find a minivan with this feature already installed, selected GM dealerships can install it as a $5,000 U.S. aftermarket option (see *www.gm.com/vehicles/services/gm_ mobility*).

As with most minivans, be wary of vehicles equipped with a power-assisted passenger-side sliding door—it's both convenient and dangerous. Despite an override circuit that should prevent the door from closing when it's blocked, a number of injuries have been reported. Furthermore, the doors frequently open when they shouldn't and can be difficult to close securely.

All models and years have had serious reliability problems—notably, faulty rear-seat latches; abysmal fit and finish; side-door glass that pops open; chronic sliding-door malfunctions; a badly mounted sliding door; automatic transmission breakdowns; AC evaporator core failures; wind buffeting noise around the front doors; engine head gasket and intake manifold defects; premature wearout of the inner and outer tie rods; electronic module (PROM) and starter failures; a fuel-thirsty and poorly performing automatic transmission; premature front brake component wear, brake fluid leakage, and noisy braking; squeaks, rattles, and clunks in the instrument panel cluster area and suspension; and short circuits that burn out alternators, batteries, power door lock activators, and the blower motor.

VEHICLE HISTORY: 2001—Slightly restyled with a fold-flat third-row seat and a driver-side power door. **2003**—Optional ABS and front side airbags. **2005**—Venture drops the regular-length model and AWD in a shortened model-year run. Uplander arrives, along with the identical Montana SV6, Relay, and Terraza. **2006**—Optional second-row side airbags, a shorter-length model, and an upgraded automatic transmission are introduced. *Uplander et al:* **2007**—A 240 hp 3.9L V6 replaces the 201 hp 3.5L V6; all-wheel-drive and the load-levelling suspension option are gone. **2008**—Only the Uplander is left in its final year, although production continued for export to Canada and Mexico through the 2009 model year. It was replaced by the Chevrolet Traverse crossover SUV.

Fit and finish deficiencies: body panels corrode easily, paint is prone to blistering or delaminating, and the front windshield is particularly prone to leak water from the top portion into the dash instrument cluster (a problem also affecting rear-drive vans and covered by a secret warranty). Sliding side doors are hexed; a priest would be more effective than most GM mechanics, who simply throw up their hands.

Other trouble spots include eccentric wipers, blurry front windshield; EGR valve failures; a noisy suspension; electrical glitches; failure-prone AC condensers; flickering lights and dimming headlights; the radio losing its settings; a grinding, shaking steering assembly; air constantly blowing through the centre vent; early bearing, front strut, sway bar, wheel hub, and tie-rod failures; a constantly lit Check Engine light (which causes vehicle to fail provincial emissions tests).

Safety Summary

All years: Fire may ignite around the fuel-filler nozzle or within the ignition switch. • Tie-rod failures may cause loss of steering control. • Sudden steering loss in rainy weather or when passing through a puddle (serpentine belt slippage). • Chronic brake failures or excessive brake fade. • Airbags malfunction. • Sliding doors suddenly open or close, come off their tracks, jam shut, stick open, injure children, and rattle during highway driving. • Transmission failures; slips from Drive into Neutral; won't hold gear on a grade. • Some front door-mounted seat belts cross uncomfortably at the neck, and there's a nasty blind spot on the driver's side that requires a small stick-on convex mirror to correct. • Headlight assembly collects moisture, burns bulb, or falls out. • Seatback suddenly collapses. •

Accelerator and brake pedals are too close together. • Fuel slosh/clunk when vehicle stops or accelerates (replacement tank is useless). • Self-activating door locks lock people out or trap them inside. • Faulty fuel pump causes chronic stalling, no-starts, surging, and sudden acceleration. • Rear control arm snaps. • Steering idler arm falls off because of missing bolt. • Brakes activate on their own, making it feel as if the van is pulling a load. • Electrical harness failures result in complete electrical shutdown. • Headlights, interior lights, gauges, and instruments fail intermittently. • Excess padding around horn makes it difficult to depress horn button in an emergency. • Poorly performing rear AC. • Flickering interior and exterior lights. • Airbag warning light stays lit. • Windshield glass distortion. **2004**—Engine surging, stalling. • Loss of coolant, engine overheating. • Broken rear sway bar. • Frequent brake failures blamed on faulty brake master cylinder. • Tail lights fail intermittently. • Power-sliding door opens and closes on its own while vehicle is underway. • Two children's wrists were fractured after their elbows and hands were caught between the seat and the sliding-door handle. • Door doesn't lock into position; slides shut and crushes objects in its path. **2005**—Sudden transmission failure. • When underway, vehicle suddenly veers to one side. • Traction control comes on at the wrong time, forcing vehicle to "limp home." • Early failure of the sliding-door motor. • Vehicle stalls if gas tank is half full. • Dash lights are too dim for bright days. • Windshield chips easily. **2006**—Early replacement of the front sway bar links and struts. • Steering feels as if it has lost power. • Incorrect fuel gauge readings; vehicle runs out of fuel when going downhill. • Sliding doors open on their own. • Headlight failures. • Flickering interior and exterior lights. **2007**—Fire ignited near the sliding door motor. • Rear window wiper harness caught fire. • Stability control failures. • Service ABS light stays on all the time. • Excessive steering wheel vibrations. • Interior, exterior lights flicker. • Continental tires crack between the tread. • GM maintains its "Open Door" Policy by ignoring customer sliding door complaints. **2008**—Brakes and tires quickly go bad:

> These are state fleet vehicles we have purchased over 98 of these Uplanders and have had problems with the front brakes and the driver's tire going flat on over 33 of these vehicles.

• Stability control malfunctions and suddenly applies the brakes for no reason. • Wiper water pump failures. • Sliding door crushes hands. • "Door Open" light stays lit when there is no problem and hides view to other information. • Broken fan blade flew into radiator core. • Faulty traction control system cuts engine power dramatically:

> While driving our 08 Chevy Uplander at highway speeds, for no reason, the DIC shows reduced engine power and service traction control. When this happens the van slows, almost to a stop and cannot get back to speed until it is shut off for at least 5 minutes. This happens several times in a 20 mile trip (at least 5). Our mechanic has put it on his diagnostic computer and shows no problem. This even happens while the DIC is showing service traction control and reduced engine power. After reading all the posts online about this specific vehicle (Chevy Uplander) I am very afraid to

drive it. It has occurred while on the Interstate at the speed of 70mph. Had to pull over to avoid getting rear-ended, re-start the van, only to get a few miles down the road and it do the same thing, over and over again.

Secret Warranties/Internal Bulletins/Service Tips

1993–2005—GM says that a chronic driveline clunk can't be silenced and is a normal characteristic of its vehicles • Paint delamination, peeling, or fading. **1995–2004**—Engine intake manifold/head gasket failures. GM Canada has settled out of court for about $40 million in claims relating to intake manifold gasket failures, and owners of 1995–2004 V6-equipped models are eligible for refunds of $200–$800. Simply Google "GM Canada" and "intake manifold settlement" to find out how to make your claim. (An excellent law article relative to successfully framing any engine claim for small claims court, John W. Hanson's "New Guidance for *Consumers Legal Remedies Act* Claims," *Trial Bar News*, February 2006, pages 7–8, can be found on California lawyers Rosner and Mansfield's website at *www.rosnerandmansfield.com/pdf/hanson2.pdf*.) **1996–2001**—Poor heat distribution in driver's area of vehicle (install new heat ducts). **1997–2003**—Rust holes in the roof. **1994–2009**—Rust spots in the paint. **1999–2003**—Incorrect fuel gauge readings caused by a contaminated fuel-tank sensor/sender. If a fuel cleaner doesn't work, GM says it will adjust or replace the sensor/sender for free on a case-by-case basis. This failure afflicts GM's entire lineup and could cost up to $800 to repair. **2000–04**—Tail light/brake light and circuit board burn out from water intrusion. Repair cost covered by a "goodwill" policy (TSB #03-08-42-007A) up to five years. **2000–06**—Delayed shifts. **2001–08**—Harsh shifts, slippage. **2003–04**—Power-sliding door binding. **2004–06**—Noisy steering can be silenced by replacing the inner tie-rod boot, says TSB #06-02-32-005. **2005–06**—A defective harmonic balancer may cause severe engine damage. • Hard start/no-start, stalling, inoperative gauges. • Silencing sliding-door rattles. • Inaccurate temperature and fuel readings. • Poor AC performance. **2005–07**—Remedy for rear brake squeal or squeak. **2005–09**—Inoperative horn; difficult to use. **2005–09**—TSB #07-05-23-003BA says a brake pulsation, vibration fix requires rotor variation and new front brake shields and pads (GM should pay for this work). • **2005–11**—Intermittent reduced engine power. **2006–08**—Guess what? More head gasket leaks to add to the 1995–2004 GM Canada class action settlement (TSB #08-06-01-012, dated June 18, 2008, also includes the 2006–08 Saturn Aura and Chevrolet Monte Carlo, Impala, and Malibu). **2006**—Harsh shifts. **2007–08**—Engine squealing, vibration on start-up. • Harsh shifts.

MONTANA, MONTANA SV6, RELAY, SILHOUETTE, TERRAZA, UPLANDER, VENTURE PROFILE

	2001	2002	2003	2004	2005	2006	2007	2008	2009
Cost Price ($)									
Montana	26,755	27,870	28,520	29,380	32,840	—	—	—	—
Montana SV6	—	—	—	—	26,620	24,525	24,550	25,060	25,060
Relay	—	—	—	—	27,995	26,995	27,770	—	—
Silhouette	31,105	33,060	35,695	36,290	—	—	—	—	—

Terraza	—	—	—	—	33,745	32,210	33,025	—	—
Uplander	—	—	—	—	25,405	23,240	23,880	24,390	24,390
Venture	25,230	25,195	25,865	26,680	30,590	—	—	—	—
Used Values ($)									
Montana ▲	1,500	2,000	2,500	3,000	3.500	—	—	—	—
Montana ▼	1,000	1,500	2,000	2,500	3,000	—	—	—	—
Montana SV6 ▲	—	—	—	—	6,500	8,000	10,000	14,000	11,500
Montana SV6 ▼	—	—	—	—	5,500	6,500	8,500	13,50	10,000
Relay ▲	—	—	—	—	5,000	6,500	8,500	—	—
Relay ▼	—	—	—	—	3,500	5,500	7,000	—	—
Silhouette ▲	2,500	3,000	4,000	6,000	—	—	—	—	—
Silhouette ▼	2,000	2,500	3,500	4,500	—	—	—	—	—
Terraza ▲	—	—	—	—	7,000	10,500	14,500	—	—
Terraza ▼	—	—	—	—	5,500	9,000	13,000	—	—
Uplander ▲	—	—	—	—	5,500	8,000	10,000	12,000	—
Uplander ▼	—	—	—	—	4,500	7,000	8,500	11,500	—
Venture ▲	2,000	2,500	3,500	4,500	5,000	—	—	—	—
Venture ▼	1,500	2,000	3,000	4,000	4,500	—	—	—	—
Reliability	1	1	1	1	1	1	2	2	2
Crash Safety (F)	4	4	4	4	4	5	5	5	5
Side	5	5	5	5	5	4	4	4	4
IIHS Side	—	—	—	—	—	1	1	1	1
Offset (Venture)	1	1	1	1	1	—	—	—	—
Montana SV6	—	—	—	—	5	5	5	5	5
Relay	—	—	—	—	5	5	5	—	—
Terraza	—	—	—	—	5	5	5	—	—
Uplander	—	—	—	—	5	5	5	5	5
Head Restraints (F)	5	5	3	3	1	1	1	1	1
Rear	3	3	2	2	—	—	—	—	—
Rollover Resistance	3	3	3	—	—	3	3	3	3

Honda

ODYSSEY ★★★

RATING: Average (2005–09); Above Average (1999–2004). Odyssey's redesigns didn't engender as steep a decline in quality as we have seen with Mazda, Nissan, and Toyota makeovers. The upgraded 2005 Odyssey generated an increase of reports concerning safety- and performance-related failures, hence *Lemon-Aid*'s downgrade of formerly Recommended recent-model Odysseys. Of particular concern are run-flat Pax tire problems, airbag malfunctions, automatic sliding-door failures, damaged AC condensers, and transmission breakdowns with erratic shifting (2000–03 models). **Ideal model year:** A 2008 LX sells for about half

All ratings on a numbered scale where ☐ is good and **1** is bad. See page 132 for a more detailed description.

what the car originally cost ($33,590) and comes slightly restyled. **"Real" city/ highway fuel economy:** *2.2:* 11.9/9.2 L/100 km. *2.3:* 10.9/8.3 L/100 km. *3.5:* 13.2/8.5 L/100 km. Owners report fuel savings may undershoot these estimates by about 10 percent. Fuel economy drops dramatically if the rear AC is engaged. **Maintenance/Repair costs:** Average; any garage can repair these minivans. **Parts:** Moderately priced, and availability is better than average because the Odyssey uses many generic Accord parts. **Extended warranty:** Not needed; save your money. **Best alternatives:** If you want something cheaper and reasonably reliable, consider a three-year-old Chrysler minivan or a Hyundai Entourage. If you want handling and dependability, look to Toyota's Sienna (but not the 2004 model). Sadly, GM's front-drive minivans aren't in the running because of their self-destructing engines and malfunctioning automatic transmissions. GM's Astro, Safari, or full-sized van are much more reliable and provide additional towing muscle. **Helpful websites:** *www.carcomplaints.com/Honda/Odyssey*; *www. odysseyownersclub.com/forums*; and *www.odyclub.com/forums*.

Strengths and Weaknesses

When it was first launched in 1995, the Odyssey was a sales dud. Canadians and *Lemon-Aid* saw through Honda's attempt to pass off as a minivan an underpowered, mid-sized four-door station wagon with a raised roof. In 1999, however, the Odyssey was redesigned, and it now represents one of the better minivans on the Canadian market.

It's easy to see what makes the Odyssey so popular: strong engine performance, carlike ride and handling, easy entry/exit, a second driver-side door, and a quiet interior. Most controls and displays are easy to reach and read, there's a lot of passenger and cargo room and an extensive list of standard equipment, and Honda is willing to compensate owners for production snafus.

This minivan does have its drawbacks, though. A high resale price makes bargains rare, front-seat passenger legroom is marginal because of the restricted seat travel, and third-row seating is suitable only for children. Additionally, power-sliding doors are slow to retract, there's some tire rumbling and rattling and body drumming at highway speeds, premium fuel is required for optimum performance, and rear-seat head restraints impede side and rear visibility.

VEHICLE HISTORY: 2001—User-friendly child safety seat tether anchors, upgraded stereo speakers, and an intermittent rear-window wiper. **2002**—A slight restyling, 30 additional horses, disc brakes on all four wheels, standard side airbags, and additional support for front seats. **2003**—Changes include an auto up/down driver-side window, plus new-style keys that Honda says are harder to duplicate. **2005**—Honda updates its minivan for 2005, revising the styling and adding additional safety features. The '05 Odyssey continues with a 255 hp 3.5L V6 and a 5-speed automatic transmission. EX-L and Touring models come with a Variable Cylinder Management system. Standard safety features include anti-lock four-wheel disc brakes, traction control, an anti-skid system, front side airbags, and side curtain airbags for all three seating rows. Most models (except the LX) have power-sliding side doors. 2005 models also have a storage compartment in the floor and side windows that power partly down into the sliding doors. **2006—** Horsepower rating cut by 11 (to 244 hp). **2007—**Two added features are a tilt and telescopic steering wheel and a tire pressure monitoring system. **2008—** Addition of a cheaper DX trim line, and restyled wheels, taillights, hood, bumper, and front grille. Also, revised Variable Cylinder Management deactivates two or three cylinders. Also new: an MP3/auxiliary input jack and upgraded front seat head restraints.

Reliability is better than average, but Honda still has a few serious safety- and performance-related problems to work out. Four examples: failure-prone sliding doors; troublesome, expensive-to-replace Pax run-flat tires; easily damaged AC condensers; and "soft," spongy brakes that extend stopping distance. The sliding doors open when they shouldn't, won't close when they should, catch fingers and arms, get stuck open or closed, are noisy, and frequently require expensive servicing. The Check Engine light may stay lit because of a defective fuel-filler neck. There's a fuel sloshing noise when accelerating or coming to a stop and an engine pinging when driving up steep hills, and the transmission clunks or bangs when backing uphill or when shifting into Reverse. There are also reports of rattling and chattering when the minivan is in Forward gear. Owners note a loud wind noise and vibration from the left side of the front windshield, along with a constant vibration felt through the steering assembly and front wheels. Passenger doors may also require excessive force to open.

Other problems include noisy steering and suspension; exhaust that rattles or buzzes; leather seats that split, crack, or discolour; the vehicle pulling to the right when underway; front-end clunking caused by welding breaks in the front subframe; accessory items that come loose, break away, or won't work; buckling of the airbag cover on the passenger-side dashboard; electrical glitches and defective remote audio controls; excessive wind noise at the pillars separating the front and middle seats; wheel bearings and front brakes that wear prematurely and are excessively noisy, as are the original-equipment tires; and transmission breakdowns, transmission seal leaks, and transmission gear whine at 90 km/h or when in Fourth gear (the transmission can be replaced under a "goodwill" warranty).

Plastic interior panels have rough edges and are often misaligned and have dirt in the paint.

Safety Summary

All years: Passenger seatbacks collapsed when vehicle was rear-ended. • Airbag malfunctions. • Sudden, unintended acceleration when slowing for a stop sign or when in Drive with AC turned on. • Stuck accelerator. • Automatic transmission failures. • Transmission doesn't hold when stopped or parked on an incline; gas or brakes have to be constantly applied. • Entire vehicle shakes excessively at highway speeds and pulls to the left or right. • The rear head restraints seriously hamper rear and forward visibility, and it's difficult to see vehicles coming from the right side. • Power-sliding doors are a constant danger. • Static-electricity shocks. **2001**—In a frontal collision, van caught fire because of a cracked brake-fluid reservoir. • Cracked wheel rims. • Passenger-side door window suddenly exploded while driving on the highway. **2002**—Owners say many engines have faulty timing chains. • Loose strut bolt almost caused wheel to fall off. • Axle-bearing wheel failure caused driver-side wheel to fall off. • Head restraints are set too low for tall occupants. • Rear windshield shatters from area where the wiper is mounted. • Rear seat belt unlatches during emergency braking. • Brake line freezes up in cold weather. • Abrupt downshift on deceleration. • Driver-side door came off while using remote control. • Passenger window exploded. • Airbag light comes on for no reason. **2003**—Fire ignited in the CD player. • Fuel spits out when refuelling. • Inaccurate fuel gauge readings. **2004**—Chronic stalling even after recall; repairs to the fuel-pump relay to correct the problem. • Gas pedal will not work due to a broken throttle cable. • Sliding door crushes arms and legs. • Right-hand fingers can get caught in the gap on the steering wheel between the cruise-control buttons and the airbag area. • If vehicle is started and left in idle, the doors lock automatically. This could lock the driver out after a 10-second delay. **2005**—Sudden acceleration while cruising. • Defective power-steering pump and fuel pump. • Front and rear AC temperature varies. • Snow and ice accumulated under the spoiler, causing it to fall off along with the brake light. • Child's hand was crushed in one incident by rear power-sliding door. • Run-flat tire problems:

> My wife and I purchased a new Honda Odyssey van in 2005 which was equipped with Pax run-flat tires. At the time, we were told that the tires would wear like regular non run-flat tires, and would be 10–15% more expensive to replace. We were also told that all Honda dealers would have the necessary equipment to service these special tires. None of these statements has proven to be true. The tires are all worn out at 31K miles [50,000 km], and we were quoted a price of $1300 plus tax to have them replaced. Worse yet, our nearest dealer (Flagstaff Honda) does not have the necessary equipment to service them 2 years after their release. To make things worse, we now have a flat and getting it fixed will require us to drive 50 mph [80 km/h] on a busy interstate.

2006—Engine crankshaft and motor mount failures. • Power-steering flywheel fell off. • Loss of power steering and alternator due to belt slipping when driving on rain-soaked roads. • Binding steering shaft. • AC condenser damaged by road debris. • Premature brake and sway bar replacement. • Sliding passenger-side doors still fly open and closed when the moon is in Venus. **2007**—Engine surges while brakes feel "soft"—they can be depressed halfway down before any braking effect is felt. • Automatic transmission skips from First to Third gear; sometimes it also jerks into gear. • Brake and gas pedals still mounted too close together. • Vehicle constantly pulls to the left when underway. • Sliding door flew open on the highway; crushed a child's hand in another incident. • Rear window exploded. • AC condensers continue to be destroyed by road debris. • Third-row glove box gets extremely hot. • Tire-pressure monitor alerts driver intermittently as the outside temperature changes. **2008**—Sudden, unintended acceleration believed caused by the computer module. • Floor mat may jam the accelerator pedal. • Engine surging. • No-starts:

> If the vehicle is parked facing downhill, fuel cannot flow back to the vehicle for it to start. The manufacturer stated that the vehicle could not be repaired because it was designed in that manner.

• Rear-view camera has no alarm and distorts the true depth and sense of distance between objects. • A child safety seat cannot be installed safely in the middle-row centre. • Dangerous third-row seat:

> My child folded down the third row seat in my 2008 Honda Odyssey and the seat collapsed and fell on his hand, breaking three of his fingers. I contacted Honda and nothing was done.

• Automatic transmission makes a loud grunting when shifting. • Excessive vibration when downshifting. • Vehicle will not drive straight after making a turn. • Rear glass window exploded as vehicle was backing out of the driveway. • Tailgate liftgate hydraulic failure allowing the liftgate to crash down. • Sliding door craziness. • Spongy, soft, ineffective brakes:

> Brake pedal goes almost to the floor before the vehicle stops. Pedal continues to get softer and softer. It feels like there is air in the brake system, you can pump them up if you have time before you stop. It now requires you to push the brake pedal lower than the gas pedal to stop.

2009—Sudden, unintended acceleration. • Airbags fail to deploy. • Seat belts are too short. • Rough downshifts. • Spongy brake pedal results in the vehicle rolling past stop signs, etc. • VSA (stability control) warning light came on, and brakes suddenly were gone. • Premature replacement of the brake pads and rotors. • Liftgate hatch fell on owner's head. • Power windows open on their own. • Rear window shattered for no reason. • Sticking fuel-filler door and power-sliding door.

Secret Warranties/Internal Bulletins/Service Tips

All years: Most of Honda's TSBs allow for special warranty consideration on a "goodwill" basis by the company's District Service Manager or Zone Office. • There's an incredibly large number of sliding-door problems covered by a recall, and a plethora of service bulletins too numerous to print here. Ask Honda politely for the bulletins or "goodwill" assistance. If refused, subpoena the documents through small claims court, using NHTSA's complaint and service bulletin summaries as your shopping list. **1999–2003**—Engine oil leaks. • Deformed windshield moulding. **1999–2006**—Troubleshooting vehicle pull or drift to one side. **2002–03**—Free replacement of the engine timing belt auto-tensioner and water pump under both a recall and "product update" campaign. **2002–04**—Free tranny repair or replacement for insufficient lubrication that can lead to heat buildup and broken gears. **2002–06**—Warranty mileage limitation extended by 5 percent to compensate for defective odometers. • Rear brake noise. **2003**—Engine cranks but won't start. • ABS problems. • Faulty charging system; electrical shorts. • Front door howls in strong crosswind. • Squealing from rear quarter windows and motors. • Fuel-tank leak. **2003–07**—Honda has a secret warranty extension that covers paint defects up to 7 years (no mileage or prior ownership limitation), says TSB #08-031, issued January 8, 2010. Although this service bulletin is specifically for blue metallic paint defects, the coverage can be easily extrapolated to cover any other Honda or colour, as indicated in TSB #10-002 "Paint Defect Claim Information," issued January 20, 2010. **2005**—Windshield noise remedy. • Front and rear AC temperature varies. • Correction for middle-row seat that won't unlatch. **2005–06**—Noise remedy for the power steering, front brakes, front wheel bearings, windshield, sliding door, and exhaust system. **2005–07**—Headphones inoperative in DVD mode. • Drivetrain ping, squeal, or rattle. • Power steering pump whine or buzz. • Power seat won't move forward or backward. **2005–09**—Engine timing belt chirp. • Sliding door doesn't open all the way. • Power door locks continually lock while driving. **2007**—Delayed First gear engagement. • Insufficient AC cooling at idle. **2007–08**—If the brake pedal feels low and spongy, the dealer should replace the ABS/TCS or VSA modulator control unit under warranty, says Honda TSB #07-045 issued March 5, 2009. **2008**—Engine knocking or ticking at idle. **2008–09**—Water accumulates in the inner tail lights in the tailgate. **2008–10**—Gap between the front passenger's airbag lid and the dashboard. • Front door glass opens/closes slowly or sticks.

ODYSSEY PROFILE

	2001	2002	2003	2004	2005	2006	2007	2008	2009
Cost Price ($)									
LX	30,800	31,900	32,200	32,400	32,700	33,200	33,300	33,590	33,590
EX	33,800	34,900	35,200	35,400	35,900	36,400	36,900	36,990	36,990
Used Values ($)									
LX ▲	4,500	5,500	7,000	8,000	10,000	12,000	14,500	18,000	21,500
LX ▼	4,000	5,000	6,000	7,000	9,000	10,500	13,000	16,500	20,000
EX ▲	6,000	7,000	8,500	10,500	12,000	15,500	16,500	20,000	25,000
EX ▼	5,000	6,000	8,000	9,500	11,000	14,500	15,500	18,500	23,500
Reliability	4	4	4	4	4	4	4	4	4
Crash Safety (F)	5	5	5	5	5	5	5	5	5
Side	5	5	5	5	5	5	5	5	5
IIHS Side	—	—	—	—	5	5	5	5	5
Offset	5	5	5	5	5	5	5	5	5
Head Restraints (F)	—	—	—	—	**2**	**2**	**2**	5	5
Rollover Resistance	—	4	4	4	—	4	4	4	4

Kia/Hyundai

RATING: *Sedona:* Average (2007–09); Below Average (2002–06). *Entourage:* Average (2007–09). The Sedona is a very user-friendly, roomy, versatile, and comfortable mid-sized minivan that comes with a comprehensive base warranty and a spotty reliability record, just like its Entourage cousin. Think of Hyundai's first seven-seat minivan as a Sedona twin with styling borrowed from the Hyundai Santa Fe SUV. Even though it survived only three model years, its depressed price and easily available Kia servicing and parts make it a good buy that flies well under the radar. **Ideal model year:** A 2007 Kia Sedona EX for about $8,500 is the best choice. It has six more horses than the previous model. The Entourage costs a few thousand dollars more for what is essentially a Sedona clone. **"Real" city/highway fuel economy:** 15.4/10.9 L/100 km. Owners report fuel consumption may be even worse than this estimate by about 20 percent. **Maintenance/Repair costs:** Average. **Parts:** Average cost and availability. **Extended warranty:** Yes, for the powertrain. **Best alternatives:** Honda Odyssey, Toyota Sienna (excluding the 2004 model), and a bargain-priced Chrysler minivan with a checked-out powertrain. The smaller Mazda5 will also do in a pinch. **Helpful websites:** *www.hyundaikiaforums.com* and *www. carcomplaints.com/Kia.*

Strengths and Weaknesses

Used Sedonas cost several thousand dollars less than comparable Detroit-built minivans. Embodying typically bland minivan styling, the front-drive, seven-passenger Sedona is 18 cm shorter than the Honda Odyssey and 11 cm longer than the Dodge Caravan. It comes with a good selection of standard features, including a 195 hp 3.5L V6 engine hooked to an automatic 5-speed transmission, a low step-in height, and a commanding view of the road.

Poor fuel economy and mediocre handling are the nemesis of these two minivans. Engine power is drained by the Sedona's heft, giving it a 10–20 percent higher fuel-consumption rate than the V6-equipped Dodge Caravan or Toyota Sienna. The upgraded 2006 V6 engine, however, provides much more power while posting fuel economy numbers that are similar to those of the competition. Handling is compromised by vague steering and a wallowing suspension, owners' ears are assailed by excessive engine and wind noise, braking is mediocre, and overall quality control, especially fit and finish, is embarrassingly bad.

Poor reliability that improved with the 2007 and 2008 versions has traditionally been the Sedona's weakest link. Areas of most concern have been seat belts, brake pads and rotors, AC compressor, transmission (failures and lock-ups), fuel and electrical systems, overall body construction, especially sliding door glitches and sub-par side window mouldings, and the engine (misfiring, head gasket leaks, and a rattling timing chain), (see *www.kia-forums.com* and *www.autosafety.org/autodefects.html*).

VEHICLE HISTORY: 2003—New tail lights. The LX adds a standard AM/FM/CD player, central door-lock button, and remote fuel-door release, while the EX version gets additional stereo speakers and a second remote for the keyless entry. **2004**—A new grille, and the LX's centre tray table becomes a standard feature. **2006**—Larger dimensions, more power, and standard side curtain airbags. A more-powerful 244 hp 3.8L V6 hooked to a 5-speed manumatic provides an important 50 hp boost. Comfort and convenience are enhanced through seven-passenger seating, second-row removable bucket seats that slide fore and aft, a third-row bench that splits 60/40 and folds into the floor, and sliding side-door power windows. Standard anti-lock four-wheel disc brakes and traction/anti-skid control are two new standard safety features that distinguish these models from the rest of the pack. Additionally, all Sedonas have front side airbags and side curtain airbags that cover all three seating rows. **2007**—The 2006 redesign goofs have been mostly fixed, the V6 engine gains 6 hp, and a short-wheelbase model arrives. Kia's owner, Hyundai, launches an identical Entourage minivan. **2008**—Additional trim items, and electronic stability and traction control for the EX. *Entourage:* **2007**—Identical to the Sedona, the Entourage arrives and sells for a few dollars more. **2008**—The mid-level SE model is gone. **2009**—The Entourage is axed.

Safety Summary

Sedona: Airbags fail to deploy. • Sudden, unintended acceleration. • Intermittent stalling. • Poor braking performance due to warped brake rotors and prematurely worn brake calipers and pads. • Parking brake doesn't hold vehicle on an incline. • Defective wheel bearings. • Multiple electrical shorts; electrical system continually blows fuses. • Dash lights fail repeatedly; replacing the instrument-cluster board is only a temporary solution. • Weak rear hatch struts. • Power-sliding door doesn't close properly; opens when vehicle is underway. • AC condenser is vulnerable to puncture from road debris. **2002**—Fuel-tank design could cause fuel to spray onto hot muffler in a collision. • Oil leaks onto the hot catalytic converter. • Fuel leaks from the bottom of the vehicle. • Loose fuel-line-to-fuel-pump clamp. • Fuel-tank filler hose vulnerable to road debris. • Fuel spits back out when refuelling. • Vehicle continues to accelerate when brakes are applied. • Brake failure; pedal simply sinks to the floor. • ABS brake light comes on randomly. • Power-steering pulley breaks. • Windshield may suddenly shatter for no apparent reason. • Windshields distorted at eye level. • Electrical shorts cause lights, windows, and door locks to fail. • Child safety seat can't be belted in securely. • Child-door safety lock failure. • Inoperative rear seat belts. • Seat belt holding child in booster seat tightened progressively, trapping child. **2003**—Brakes fail because of air in the brake lines. • Broken window regulator. • While reclined, passenger seatback releases upright and slams occupant forward. • Electrical shorts cause door lock malfunctions. **2004**—Fire ignites in the under-hood wiring. • Transmission and TCM replaced because vehicle loses power and gears down constantly. • Loose left rear wheel and suspension struts. • Rear brake assembly and wheel fall off. • Seat belts fail to lock upon impact. • Low-beam headlights burn out repeatedly. **2005**—Engine hesitates for almost five seconds when accelerating. • Rear passenger-side wheel fell off the vehicle due to defective wheel bearings; original recall needs to be extended. • Early replacement of the windshield wiper motor. • Driver left the vehicle running and then found himself locked out. • Toxic mould can grow in the ventilation system because filters were installed beginning only with the 2006 models. **2006**—Engine failure due to sludge buildup. • Transmission suddenly drops out of Drive. • Hole in the fuel tank. **2007**—Front windshield wiper linkage comes loose. • Cruise control doesn't work properly on long hills. **2008**—Chronic stalling or loss of power. • Accelerator pedal falls off its mount. • Cruise control cannot be disabled. • Loss of power steering. • Vehicle rolls away when parked on an incline with the handbrake engaged. • Premature replacement of the brake pads and rotors. Airbag, sliding door, and front door sensors go bad. • IP computer (fuse box) burns out. *Entourage:* **2007**—No-starts due to a faulty ignition module. • Multiple sliding-door defects similar in nature to the Sedona's. • Water leaks from the roof. • Windshield cracks when driver adjusts the rear-view mirror. • Seat belts lock up and choke passengers. • Many complaints of veering to the left and a serious front-end vibration. • Bent wheel rims cause excessive vibration and a poor ride. • Original tires wear out quickly; don't hold their air. • Faulty tire valve stems. • Battery doesn't hold its charge. • Frequent brake light switch failures. **2008**—Sliding doors don't work properly:

> The left passenger door opened while the vehicle was in motion at approx 60 miles per hour. As a result, the driver had to perform an emergency stop on the highway to close the door. Until the vehicle was brought to a complete stop, the adult passenger in the front passenger seat had to hold onto the child seated at the open door.

2009—Sudden, unintended acceleration. • Engine leaks oil. • Anti-lock brakes and engine stability control problems include brake pedal thumping and gas pedal rumbling. • Sticking passenger-side sliding door.

Secret Warranties/Internal Bulletins/Service Tips

Sedona: **2001–05**—Heater pipe corrosion. **2002**—Correction for engine hesitation after cold starts. • Free replacement of seat belt buckle anchor bolts. **2002–03**—Changes to improve alternator output to prevent hard starts or battery drain. **2002–05**—Harsh, delayed shifts. • Insufficient AC cooling, and excessive AC noise. • Sliding door is hard to open. **2004**—Engine head gasket leak. **2006**—Free replacement of the power-sliding door cable (Campaign #SC062); the power-sliding door switch (Campaign #SC063); and the rear-door pinch strip attachment (Campaign #SC066). • Inoperative driver-seat lumbar support. • Fuel-tank humming noise. **2006–07**—Intermittent no-start condition. • Engine runs rough, hesitates. • Tips on silencing various engine noises. **2006–08**—Loose assist handles and headliner. **2007–08**—Engine knocking noise at idle with the AC on. • AC knocking noise. • Remedy for a noisy exhaust.

Entourage: **2007**—Intermittent no-crank; no-start. • Engine misfire; defective oxygen sensor. • Harsh, delayed shifts, especially when going into Reverse or Drive. • Cannot shift into or out of Park. • Oil leaks from differential seals. • Fuel-pump buzzing, humming. • Front suspension clicking, ratcheting. • Front strut noise. • Tapping noise when AC is activated. • Electromagnetic interference with the Tire Monitor System. • Inoperative driver-seat lumbar support. • Loose roof-assist handles. **2007–08**—Erratic idle. • Sliding door reopens after closing. **2008**—Troubleshooting 3.8L engine hesitation and misfires.

SEDONA/ENTOURAGE PROFILE

	2002	2003	2004	2005	2006	2007	2008	2009
Cost Price ($)								
Sedona LX	24,595	24,995	25,595	26,995	29,495	29,495	29,745	26,745
EX	27,595	28,295	28,995	29,495	31,895	32,495	32,795	32,495
Entourage GL	—	—	—	—	—	29,995	30,995	33,395
Used Values ($)								
Sedona LX ▲	3,500	4,000	4,500	5,500	6,500	8,500	12,000	14,500
Sedona LX ▼	3,000	3,500	4,000	5,000	5,500	7,000	10,500	13,000
EX ▲	3,500	4,500	5,000	6,000	7,000	9,000	12,500	15,000
EX ▼	3,000	4,000	4,500	5,500	6,000	7,500	11,000	13,500
Entourage GL ▲	—	—	—	—	—	12,000	15,500	—
Entourage GL ▼	—	—	—	—	—	11,000	14,000	—
Reliability	2	2	2	2	3	3	3	3
Crash Safety (F)	5	5	5	5	5	5	5	5
Side	5	5	5	5	5	5	5	5
IIHS Side	—	—	—	—	5	5	5	5
Entourage	—	—	—	—	—	5	4	—
Offset	3	3	3	3	5	5	5	5
Entourage	—	—	—	—	—	5	5	—
Head Restraints (F)	5	3	3	—	5	5	5	5
Entourage	—	—	—	—	—	5	5	—
Rear	3	3	3	—	—	—	—	—
Rollover Resistance	4	4	—	4	4	4	4	4

Nissan/Ford

RATING: *Quest:* Below Average (2004–09). Even though it's larger, more powerful, and better appointed than the old Quest/Villager, the 2004 Quest's redesign was badly done and the model has never recovered from those mistakes. Engineering goofs and poor-quality body and electrical components still plague the Quest.

When the model is dropped next year, Quest resale prices will plummet and servicing will become more problematic. *Quest/Villager:* Not recommended (1999–2003). **"Real" city/highway fuel economy:** *3.0:* 13.4/9.3 L/100 km. *3.3:* 13.9/9.0 L/100 km. *3.5:* 12.4/8.2 L/100 km. Owners report fuel savings may undershoot these estimates by at least 20 percent if the vehicle is equipped with poorly performing Goodyear LS2 tires. **Maintenance/Repair costs:** Higher than average. **Parts:** Best found at Nissan dealers or with independent suppliers. **Extended warranty:** A good idea. **Best alternatives:** Honda's Odyssey and Toyota's Sienna (except the reworked 2004 model, which has quality bugs similar to the Quest's). A smaller Mazda5 mini-minivan might also fill the bill. **Helpful websites:** *http://questdriver.com*; *www.carcomplaints.com/Nissan*; and *www. carcomplaints.com/Ford*

Strengths and Weaknesses

1993–2003 Quest/Villager

Smaller and more carlike than most minivans, the pre-2004 Villager and Quest are sized comfortably between the regular and extended Chrysler minivans. These minivans' strongest assets are a 170 hp 3.3L V6 engine plus carlike ride, handling, and cornering achieved by borrowing Nissan Maxima parts.

These fuel-thirsty minivans are quite heavy, though, and the 3.0L and 3.3L engines have to go all out to carry the extra weight. GM's 2.8L engines produce more torque, and the Quest/Villager powertrain set-up trails the Odyssey in acceleration and passing. Other minuses: the interior looks cheap, suspension is too soft, rear-seat access can be difficult, and the control layout can be a bit confusing.

Most owner-reported problems involve excessive brake noise and premature brake wear, door lock malfunctions, interior noise, and driveline vibrations. There have also been many reports of engine exhaust manifold and crankshaft failures that cost up to $7,000 to repair. Other problems include electrical shorts; brake failures because of vibration, binding, or overheating; premature front disc, rotor, and pad wear; chronic stalling, possibly because of faulty fuel pumps or a shorted electrical system; and loose steering with veering at highway speeds.

Fit and finish is subpar. Owners complain of doors opening and closing on their own and poorly fitted panels that produce a cacophony of wind noise, squeaks, and rattles, as well as water leaks, paint defects, and premature rusting.

2004–09 Quest

A totally different minivan than its predecessor, the 2004–08 Quest is an Altima/Murano spin-off that is larger, more powerful, and better equipped than before. It's also less reliable. Skyroof leaks and dangerous sliding doors are quite common. Owners also complain of malfunctioning engines, prematurely worn out engine timing chains on 2007 models (replacement cost: $3,300 U.S.), and early replacement of transmissions, brake pads and rotors, and Pax run-flat tires:

I own a 2007 Nissan Quest with the Michelin Pax Run-Flat tire system. The Pax Run-Flat Tire System is a defective product. I purchased the car in November 2007. By 13 months, at 18,000 miles, 2 of the tires had worn to the point where the dealer said they needed to be replaced. At 20,600 miles we had all 4 tires replaced.

•

The shop has had the vehicle for more than 35 days and he does not know when it can be retrieved. The shop does not have the tires and the liner that are needed to repair the tire.

Goodyear tires are notorious for premature wear and poor performance on these minivans (see *www.tirerack.com*).

VEHICLE HISTORY: *Quest:* **2001**—A slightly restyled exterior and upgraded dashboard. **2004**—Totally redesigned—and made even less reliable. **2005**—A new base model called the 3.5 arrives. **2007**—Restyled interior and exterior.

Safety Summary

1993–2003—Airbags malfunction. • Steering wander and excessive vibration. • Chronic ABS failures; brake pads and rotors need replacing every 5,000 km. • Brake failures (extended stopping distances, noisy when applied). • Brake and accelerator pedals are the same height, so driver's foot can easily slip and step on both at the same time. • Cycling or self-activating front-door lock failures; occupants have been trapped in their vehicles. • Weak tailgate hydraulic cylinders. • Instrument panel's white face is hard to read during daylight hours. • Seat belts don't retract properly. • Rear window on liftgate door shattered for unknown reason. • Leaking front and rear struts degrade handling. • Steering wheel may be off-centre to the left. **1993–2004**—Sudden, unintended acceleration. **2004**—Sliding door traps occupants, or continually pops open. • Reflection of dash onto windshield. • Automatic transmission won't downshift. • Faulty tire valve stems. **2005**—Fire ignited in the tail light housing. • Transmission slippage. • Loss of all electrical power due to alternator failure. • Power windows and locks often malfunction. • Chronic stalling caused by water leaking onto the engine control module. • Defective tire stems leak air. • Sliding door suddenly opened while van was underway; 2004 recall should be extended to the 2005s. • Headlights often blow out. **2006**—Premature brake caliper, rotor wearout. • Sliding door inoperative; closes with such force it can seriously injure a child. • Door hinges make opening and closing difficult. • Doors unlock and windows roll down by themselves. • Driver's sun visor falls down. • Gas tank vulnerable to road debris. **2007**—Fire ignites in the wiring. • Engine surging while vehicle stopped at a traffic light. • "Soft" brakes. • Windshield is easily cracked. • Sliding door won't open or shut properly; worse on cold days. • Speedometer may be 20 km/h slower than indicated. • Premature wearout of Michelin PAX tires. • Second-row driver-side seat recliner lever breaks easily. **2008**—Hatchback crashed down as driver was removing items from the trunk. **2009**—Power sliding doors won't close automatically, or may suddenly close without warning or a fail-safe mechanism:

Last week the van owner was putting the kids in the back of the van and asked the three year old to get in the car while she was helping the other 2 year old get in as well. The sliding door was opened, moved to the end but not latched in the open position. It was a windy day and the door started to slide down to the close position. The 3 year old child was getting in and had his hand by the door lock helping himself up. At that time, the door closed very hard with the wind, pinched his hand and latched closed with the child's hand in between. He was taken to the emergency room to check his hand. I worked as a design controls quality engineer. I am required to ensure we minimize any potential risk by building risk mitigation features into the design to avoid any hazardous situations due to any product failure or user handling. Thus, I am writing to inquire how you can use this feedback to eliminate this safety concern? The Quest is most likely used by families with children. If the door slides itself to the close position and latches closed with a kid's hands in between and there is no sensor to prevent the door from closing, or some indication to the user that the door is not locked in the open position, or a way to ensure the door is only closed by human handling, I am concerned about what they could do in the product development to eliminate this potential hazard from happening?

• Brakes are too spongy; driver has to constantly "pump" them. • Excessive steering wheel shake (suspect prematurely worn brake rotors).

Secret Warranties/Internal Bulletins/Service Tips

All models: 1993–2006—Paint delamination, peeling, or fading. **1996–2002**—Power door locks that intermittently self-activate are a common occurrence that's covered in TSB #98-22-5. **1999–2004**—Troubleshooting abnormal shifting. • Cooling system leaks/overheating. • Side windows pop open. **2002–07**—How to silence engine ticking. **2004**—No-start, hard start remedies. • Tips on correcting an abnormal shifting of the automatic transmission. • Harsh 1–2 shifts. • AC blows out warm air from floor vents. • Guidelines on troubleshooting brake complaints. **2004–05**—Low power, stays in Third gear. • Insufficient AC cooling. • Sliding door squeaks and rattles and is hard to latch. **2004–06**—Skyroof water leaks. **2004–07**—Front brake judder. • Noisy power driver-seat lifter. **2004–08**—Inoperative driver's side "power up" window. • Overhead vents come loose, fall from the headliner. • Tire monitor seal leaks. **2004–09**—Exhaust system buzz, rattle (heat shield). • Engine buzz, whine from the engine timing chain area. • Front axle clicking upon acceleration. • Power liftgate won't open/close and may be noisy. **2007–09**—Inoperative, erratic sunroof.

	2001	2002	2004	2005	2006	2007	2008	2009
Cost Price ($)								
Quest GXE/3.5	30,498	30,698	32,900	31,698	31,898	32,498	32,598	29,998
Quest GXE/SL	35,198	35,198	36,600	36,100	36,198	36,998	37,398	37,398
Used Values ($)								
Quest GXE/3.5 ▲	4,500	5,500	6,500	7,000	9,000	11,000	14,000	17,000
Quest GXE/3.5 ▼	4,000	5,000	6,000	6,500	7,500	9,500	12,500	15,500
Quest GXE/SL ▲	5,000	5,500	6,500	8,000	9,000	11,000	13,500	20,500
Quest GXE/SL ▼	4,500	5,000	6,000	7,000	8,000	9,500	12,000	19,000
Reliability	3	3	2	2	3	3	3	3
Crash Safety (F)	4	5	5	5	5	5	5	5
Side	5	5	5	5	5	5	5	5
IIHS Side	—	—	—	—	5	5	5	5
Offset	1	—	5	5	5	5	5	5
Head Restraints (F)	—	—	1	1	1	1	1	1
Rear	—	1	1	—	—	—	—	—
Rollover Resistance	—	4	4	4	4	4	4	4

Toyota

SIENNA ★★★

RATING: Average (2005–09); Below Average (1999–2004). A resurgence of safety-related defects carried over to the 2005 model following the 2004 Sienna's redesign. Although the Sienna was excluded from Toyota's initial sudden acceleration recall, it is apparent the 2004 and later models have had the problem (see "Safety Summary"). **Ideal model year:** A 2007 Sienna CE for about $14,000; it's well-appointed, has a more powerful engine than the previous year's model, and costs less than half what it sold for originally ($31,200). **"Real" city/highway fuel economy:** 3.0: 12.4/8.8 L/100 km. 3.3: 12.2/8.1 L/100 km. 3.5: 11.7/8.1 L/100 km. *AWD:* 13.1/9.0 L/100 km. *3.5L AWD:* 13.3/9.5 L/100 km. Owners report fuel savings may undershoot these estimates by at least 15 percent. In fact, poor fuel economy is a recurring theme. **Maintenance/Repair costs:** Average; very dealer-dependent. **Parts:** There's an excellent supply of reasonably priced Sienna parts found in the Camry parts bin. **Extended warranty:** Only for the problematic 2004 and 2005 powertrains. **Best alternatives:** Honda CR-V, Mazda5, and a heavily discounted, well-checked-over (AC, brakes, and powertrain especially) Chrysler minivan. **Helpful websites:** *www.carcomplaints.com/Toyota/Sienna* and *www.toyotanation.com.*

Strengths and Weaknesses

The Sienna is Toyota's Camry-based front-drive minivan. It replaced the Previa for the 1998 model year and abandoned the Previa's futuristic look in favour of more-conservative styling.

Some of the Sienna's strong points are standard ABS and side airbags (LE, XLE); a smooth-running V6 engine, and a more-refined transmission; a stable ride and quiet interior; a fourth door and easy entry/exit; and better-than-average reliability. Its weak areas: V6 performance is compromised by the AC and the automatic transmission powertrain; it lacks the trailer-towing brawn of rear-drive minivans; and sliding doors won't close, won't open, and are child-crushers.

The redesigned 2004 Sienna has more interior room than previous models (accommodating up to eight passengers), is better-handling, rides more comfortably, and uses a more-powerful, fuel-efficient 230 hp 3.3L V6 engine. However, the 2007 Sienna's 3.5L V6 is the most powerful of all. There's less vulnerability to wind buffeting, and minimal road noise. Sienna's interior and exterior have been gently restyled. The third-row seats split and fold away, head restraints don't have to be removed when the seats are stored, and second-row bucket seats are easily converted to bench seats.

Although the rear seats fold flat to accommodate the width of a 4×8' board, the tailgate won't close, the heavy seats are difficult to reinstall (it's a two-person job, and the centre seat barely fits through the door), and the middle roof pillars and rear head restraints obstruct rear visibility. Also, there's no traction control, the rear drum brakes are less efficient, fuel economy is mediocre (using premium fuel), the low-mounted radio is hard to reach, and third-row seats lack a fore/aft adjustment to increase cargo space.

Reliability can be problematic, with a large cluster of redesign-related deficiencies appearing around the 2004–05 model years. The most serious concerns are self-destructing, sludge-prone engines (1998–2002 models) and defective automatic transmissions that "lag and lurch" (1998–2009). Many other failure-prone mechanical and body components continue to compromise the Sienna's safety and performance through the 2008 models, including electrical shorts; stalling when the AC engages; collapsing rear hatch struts and faulty power-sliding doors; premature brake wear and excessive brake noise (mostly screeching); 3.5L engine "piston-slap" (noise means excessive wear and early failure) and a clunk or banging in the driveline; the vehicle jolts or creeps forward when at a stop, forcing you to keep your foot firmly on the brake; and expensive, hard-to-find, run-flat tires:

> The dealer could not mount the tire on the rim and had to send it to a special tire place, because th[ese] are special rims, I have been told. The price for this one tire was $269.56 including mounting, balancing and sales tax. Since this type of a van

with Run-Flat tires, does not come with a spare tire. They told me, it is not necessary to have on. What will happen when you are in the middle of the wilderness in the country. Yes you can drive over 100 miles on the flat tire, but when you get to the next town and they have to order this tire and it can take days before they get one.

Also, owners report distracting windshield reflections and distorted windshields; sliding-door defects; the window suddenly shattering; easily chipped paint; and various other body glitches, like a hard-to-pull-out rear seat, water leaks, and excessive creaks and rattles.

VEHICLE HISTORY: 2001—A rear defroster, some additional horsepower and torque, and a driver-side sliding door. **2004**—New styling, larger dimensions, more power, more safety options, and about 90 extra kilograms. The not recommended optional AWD adds even more weight and includes problematic run-flat tires. A 230 hp 3.3L V6 and 5-speed automatic transmission add 20 more horses. Power windows for the sliding rear side doors are newly standard, and the CE and LE can carry eight with a removable second-row bench seat. A hideaway third-row bench seat folds into the floorwell, *à la* Honda's Odyssey, but the Sienna's 60/40 split adds to its functionality. **2005**—Dual front power seats. **2006**—Standard front-side and curtain-side airbags. **2007**—A 266 hp 3.5L V6 replaces the 215 hp 3.3L V6 as Sienna's sole engine.

Safety Summary

All years: When accelerating from a stop, vehicle lags than lurches forward. • Airbag malfunctions. • A multiplicity of sliding-door defects covered by internal bulletins. • Windshield distortion; shatters spontaneously. • Reflection of the dashboard onto the windshield impairs visibility. • Wheel lug nuts shear off. • Chronic transmission failures. • Vehicle rolls down the driveway while in Park. • When proceeding from a rolling stop, acceleration is delayed for about two seconds. • Child can knock gearshift lever into Drive from Park without key in the ignition. • Sluggish transmission downshift; vehicle sometimes seems to slip out of gear when decelerating. • Skid-control system lock-up. • Slope of the windshield makes it hard to gauge where the front end stops. **2004**—Sudden, unintended acceleration:

Additional research into my 2004 Sienna van led to the discovery that Toyota implemented a relatively new technology in 2003 vehicles called the electronic throttle th[at] uses a "drive-by-wire" sensor to control the throttle position. This system uses a series of rheostats, voltage comparators and sensors to determine the position of the accelerator pedal. The electronic control unit (computer) receives these signals, processes the information and sends a signal from the sensors to the throttle butterfly valve to indicate how much to increase/decrease engine speed.

These vehicles no longer use the traditional mechanical cable between the pedal and throttle, it is all controlled electronically.

I honestly believe that Toyota has a serious problem in this drive-by-wire electrical circuit that enables a faulty signal to be sent to the throttle valve that will enable it to go wide open. There have been so many cases that there is even a book by Clarence Ditlow called *Sudden Acceleration: The Myth of Driver Error* written to refute NHSTA findings that most incidents of sudden acceleration are caused by driver error. It accuses auto manufacturers of withholding evidence that would prove that there is a serious problem in this technology.

Toyota acknowledged that they have a problem but they are blaming it on car mats. In the case of my van, there is no way that car mats caused the sudden acceleration, it was clear that it was electronically-driven. Car mats causing all the documented Toyota vehicle sudden acceleration cases is highly unlikely.

On May 1, 2008 my 2004 Toyota Sienna was declared a total loss by the insurance company. Hard to imagine that in 3–4 seconds, and traveling less than 25 yards in front of an elementary school that I could completely total a large van like my 2004 Toyota Sienna. By the Grace of God, there were no children present when this happened.

• Fuel-tank leakage after recall repairs; leaking fuel line. • Complete loss of brakes. • Rapid brake degradation (glazed and warped rotors). • Sliding door catches passenger's arm or leg; manual door doesn't latch properly (particularly when windows are open); door opens when turning, jams or closes when vehicle is parked on an incline:

Our two-year-old son pulled on the sliding door handle, and the door began to open (we thought the child locks were on, but this was not the case). He was surprised and was afraid of falling out of the van, so he just held onto the handle. As the door was opening, his head then was dragged between the sliding door and the side of the van. But the van door did not stop opening. It just continued opening, exerting even more force on our son's head. Fortunately we were able to grab the door and forcefully pull it back closed before our son was horribly injured.

• Small brake lights inadequate. • Daytime running lights blind oncoming drivers (2004 Highlander has the same problem). **2005**—Airbag deployed for no reason while vehicle was underway. • Airbag is disabled when passenger seat is occupied. • Hesitation when accelerating, then sudden acceleration. • Laser-controlled cruise control jerks back to former speed when the way seems clear. • Gearshift lever can be accidently knocked from Fourth gear to Reverse. • Vehicle Stability Control engages when it shouldn't. • Brake pedal stiffens intermittently. • Premature brake rotor wear leads to longer stopping distances and increased braking noise. • Run-flat tires don't signal driver when they are damaged; may catch fire:

2005 Toyota Sienna has Bridgestone run flat tires and the back right passenger tire went flat, then smoked and caught fire.

• When the rear windows are down, the door will not stay open. • Sliding doors fail to latch when they are opened. • Power-sliding door continues closing even if something is in its way (similar to complaints on previous model-year Siennas). • Rear hatch may fall:

> The liftgate on a power liftgate 2005 Toyota Sienna will not stay open. It has come down and wacked my wife and I on the head many times. I found out the replacement is $450.

• Automatic interior light shut-off fails intermittently, draining the battery. • Rear heater core leaks coolant. • Front heater airflow is inadequate. **2006**—Seat belt unbuckled during a collision. • Head restraints cannot accommodate tall people. • Power steering cuts out intermittently. • Increased engine speed when stopped. • Vehicle pulls to the right. • Rear disc clip rust causes the caliper piston to stay extended and keep the disc brake pad in contact with the disc. • Dunlop tires leak air and wear out prematurely. • Windshield optical distortion causes eye strain, headaches, dizziness. • Second-row passengers have no armrests for support and are thrown into the side windows when the vehicle turns. **2006–07**—Tire-pressure monitoring system gives false alerts. **2007**—Hesitation and then sudden acceleration ("lag and lurch") continues. • Engine surges while stopped at a traffic light. • Power-sliding doors still failing, trapping, and injuring passengers. • Tires often have side wall bulges. **2008**—Airbags did not deploy in a side collision. • Seatbelt tightened around child's stomach; he had to be cut free. • If battery power is cut from a collision or power drain, front seat passengers may be locked in. One young mother had this to say:

> There should be an override where if the battery power is lost everything automatically unlocks—and there should be a way to open the trunk from the inside! I am freaked out to think of getting in an accident and no one being able to get in to help out my kid(s). This is a huge safety concern!

• More cases of sudden acceleration. • When making a left-hand turn it is easy to hit the cruise control "Resume" button and suddenly accelerate. • After a rolling stop, vehicle hesitates when accelerating. • Faulty passenger-side sliding-doors. • Hood suddenly flew up and broke the windshield when vehicle was underway. • Tire inflation warning light stays on constantly. • Michelin Energy tires blow out at the sidewall. • Faulty HomeLink garage opener transmitter. **2009**—Sudden, unintended acceleration. • Sticking cruise control. • Power sliding doors are still dangerous:

> I have a 2009 Toyota Sienna mini-van with automatic sliding doors. These doors are an accident waiting to happen. Unlike an elevator door that will immediately reverse if someone or something is in its path. The Sienna's doors continue to close unless forcibly pushed back to retract with a serious amount of strength. My arm has been bruised and I could only imagine a child's hand being caught. It's inconceivable to me how these doors do not operate on the same premise as an elevator. Very dangerous!

Our automatic sliding door was opened but would not close. No amount of tugging, finessing, or cursing would make it shut. Children were stranded in Phoenix heat in August because the vehicle was unsafe to drive with a door that could not be closed. There are many mentions of this exact problem on various blogs and all report difficulty in getting Toyota to offer a solution that didn't cost $1–2K. Almost all owners reported the "fixed" doors to have failed in some way again with dealers refusing to cover the cost of the second (or third) fix. The failure had to do with the actuator that unlocks the "U" shaped striker assembly. It seems evident that the cable is either breaking, stretching, or that some solenoid is not doing its job. The outcome of our problem was that a second vehicle had to be obtained, children and their seats moved to the new vehicle and the van driven in an unsafe condition back to our house 10 miles away because the dealership was closed. To complicate this, the Sienna was down to no gasoline and it was the driverside door that was stuck in open position which made it impossible to put fuel in the vehicle. What if the same scenario happened in the middle of the desert here at the rest stop in 120-degree heat with no tow truck in 100 miles and no way to drive the van with children inside? This is not only possible, but likely. Our van has two (2) automatic doors and this problem has been reported by many people. Lastly, no one who reported the problem reported the problem permanently fixed by anything the dealerships were able to do. For us, the first incident is probably covered by warranty, but how about future problems? The actuator issue is a design flaw. The fuel door behind sliding door makes it an inconvenient design flaw. That this is on a vehicle that transports children makes the design flaw a serious safety concern. And that Toyota is not addressing the problem in any substantial way just plain sucks!

• Rear sliding doors won't stay open if vehicle is parked on the slightest incline. • Total brake failure. • Power rear hatch struts fail, allowing the hatch to come crashing down.

Secret Warranties/Internal Bulletins/Service Tips

All years: Sliding door hazards, malfunctions, and noise are a veritable plague affecting all model years and generating a ton of service bulletins. • Owner feedback confirms that front brake pads and discs will be replaced under Toyota's "goodwill" policy if they wear out before 2 years/40,000 km (in spite of Toyota's pretensions that brakes aren't a warrantable item). • Rusting at the base of the two front doors will be repaired at no cost, usually with a courtesy car included. **2001**—Special service campaign to inspect or replace the front subframe assembly. **2003–05**—No-start in extreme cold. **2003–09**—Upper, lower windshield ticking noise. **2004**—VSC activates intermittently when it is not needed. • New ECM calibration for a poorly shifting transmission (TSB #TC007-03). • Rear disc brake groan (TSB #BR002-04). • Intermediate steering shaft noise on turns. • Front-door area wind noise (TSB #NV009-03). • Power-sliding door inoperative, rattles (the saga continues). • Backdoor shudder and water leaks. •

Seat heaters operate only on high. **2004–05**—Remedy for hard starts in cold weather. • Transmission lag, gear hunting. • Premature brake pad wear. • Fuel-injector ticking. • Inoperative AC light flashing. • AC blower or compressor noise; seized compressor. **2004–06**—Silencing engine ping, knock. • Power-hatch door shudder and leakage. • Power-sliding door rattles. • Excessive steering effort in high road-salt areas. • **2004–07**—Back power-sliding doors are hard to close. • Back power-door shudder. **2004–08**—Front power-seat grinding, groaning. • Remedy for front brake pads that wear out prematurely:

FRONT BRAKE PADS WEAR PREMATURELY

BULLETIN NO.: BT-SB-0044-08   DATE: APRIL 21, 2008

2004–08 Sienna

INTRODUCTION: A new brake pad kit has been developed to address brake pad wear complaints on vehicles operated under severe conditions. Continue to use the original service part for normal maintenance.

NOTE: Use of this pad kit may increase brake noise under certain conditions.

PREVIOUS PART NUMBER	CURRENT PART NUMBER	PART NAME	QTY
N/A	04465-45030	Pad Kit, Disc Brake, Front	1

Toyota says this isn't a warranty item, but when they use the term "prematurely" Toyota is admitting to manufacturing negligence. So they can either give you a prorata refund for new brakes and the brake kit or pay you when a small claims court says they must. Remember, both the dealer and Toyota are part of the chain of liability. Incidentally, his is a common problem with Toyota's other models, and the same liability applies.

2004–10—Front seat squeaking. • Sliding doors don't operate smoothly (change the lock assembly). • Sliding door rattling. • Brake rattle, buzz from driver's side of the dash. **2007**—Inoperative front, sliding-door windows. • Front-seat squeak. **2006–09**—No shift from Park. **2007–08**—Engine compartment squeaking.

SIENNA PROFILE

	2001	2002	2003	2004	2005	2006	2007	2008	2009
Cost Price ($)									
Sienna CE 4d	29,535	29,335	29,060	30,000	30,000	30,800	31,200	31,750	28,990
Sienna LE 4d	31,900	32,985	31,925	35,000	35,420	36,255	36,860	37,225	37,225
Used Values ($)									
Sienna CE 4d ▲	4,500	5,500	6,500	7,000	8,500	11,500	14,000	16,500	20,000
Sienna CE 4d ▼	3,500	5,000	5,500	6,500	7,500	10,000	12,500	15,000	18,500
Sienna LE 4d ▲	5,500	6,500	8,000	9,500	11,000	13,000	16,000	19,500	23,500
Sienna LE 4d ▼	5,000	6,000	7,000	8,500	10,000	12,000	14,500	18,000	22,000

Reliability	3	4	4	4	3	3	3	3	3
Crash Safety (F)	5	5	5	5	4	4	4	4	4
Side	—	4	4	4	5	5	5	5	5
Offset	5	5	5	5	5	5	5	5	5
Side (IIHS)	—	—	—	—	3	5	5	5	5
Head Restraints (F)	—	—	—	—	1	1	1	1	1
Rear	—	—	—	—	3	—	—	—	—
Rollover Resistance	—	4	4	4	4	4	4	4	4

All ratings on a numbered scale where 5 is good and **1** is bad. See page 132 for a more detailed description.

VANS

The North American full-sized van is an endangered species. If it weren't for commercial users like contractors, electricians, and plumbers, who need these rolling tool boxes, vans would have disappeared long ago.

I have owned two GM full-sized vans (a 1985 Chevy Van and a 1996 GMC Vandura). Each van was bought used for under $3,000, kept for five years, and resold privately for a couple grand.

Full-sized vans are particularly popular with seniors because of the comfort and outward visibility these large haulers provide. Two much-appreciated advantages our tired bodies and slowed reaction times require. And speaking of *slow*: Fewer motorists blare their horns at us for driving too slow, because that's what's expected of vans, and seniors driving vans.

There's also the camping advantage. Campers customize vans to travel the country in comfort—canoe or bikes on top and trailer in tow. And, despite high fuel costs, retirees are still cruising Canada's highways with large vans chock-full of every safety and convenience feature imaginable, turning their vehicles into mobile condos.

Canadian drivers are leaning more and more towards versatile, full-sized trucks over vans, even though vans have the advantage of an enclosed, secure rear storage area. In fact, one of my friends puts three dirt bikes in the back of his van and never worries about prying eyes or theft when he stops to eat or walk around a bit.

Full-Sized Advantages

What's the attraction of full-sized vans? Simple: they're cheap used and easier to handle and maintain than a "recreational vehicle" (RV). Sure, they may not be sleek, fuel-efficient, or sexy, their styling is likely decades old, and their popularity has certainly waned, but large vans are versatile carriers that have more grunt than front-drives and are much more reliable as well. Okay, they *are* fuel-thirsty. But I'll bet that'll be the last thought on your mind when you pass more fuel-efficient front-drive minivans stuck on the side of the road with cooked engines or burned-out transmissions.

There are also some safety reasons for choosing a large van, including excellent outward visibility, plenty of room to sit away from a deploying airbag and housing, and the inclusion of electronic stability control as a standard feature. SUVs and other vehicles are also less likely to run up over the frame and crash into the van's passenger compartment.

Handling, though, is definitely not carlike (regardless of hype to the contrary); expensive suspension modifications may be needed to produce a reasonable ride and manoeuvrability. Rear visibility is also problematic, so be sure to invest in the biggest and best rear-view and side-view mirrors available. Vans will require some additional driving skills due to their large size and truck platforms that make for ponderous handling. They are very susceptible to crosswinds, they wander at highway speeds, and they demand greater driver attention simply to corner safely and to park in the city.

The 15-passenger vans are particularly hazardous. Often used to shuttle sports teams, church groups, and airport passengers, they are three times more likely than regular vans to roll over when carrying 10 or more passengers, according to NHTSA. This is because the van's centre of gravity shifts up and to the back unexpectedly, and excess baggage adds to this instability. Ford paid $37.5 million in a 2004 Kentucky van crash case after a Scott County jury found the automaker's 15-passenger van responsible for two deaths.

Chrysler Vans

Chrysler's full-sized, American-built rear-drive vans (the Tradesman and Ram Van or Ram Wagon series) are Above Average buys that have always been more reliable than Chrysler's front-drive minivans, like the Grand Caravan. But rear-drives in

A 2009 Sprinter Cargo Van originally sold in Canada for $45,600 is now worth about $29,000. Ouch!

good condition are hard to find, as 2003 was their last model year. Don't forget that these full-sized vans may also need expensive repairs generated by blown transmissions, collapsed ball joints, and premature wearout of brake components. On the other hand, the problems are well known and easily fixed by independent garages. Ram Van prices are also quite reasonable, with fully equipped 2000 to 2003 models selling from $2,000 to $3,000. Crashworthiness is fairly good, as well: 2001 through 2003 models scored four stars out of five in frontal collision occupant protection and three stars for rollover resistance.

When Chrysler dumped its full-sized vans, the company chose the overpriced and under-performing Mercedes/Freightliner Sprinter to fill the gap in its van lineup. Not Recommended by *Lemon-Aid*, the Sprinter was a sales flop from the start. North American sales were repatriated from Chrysler and are now overseen by Mercedes and Freightliner.

The Sprinter is an expensive van, retailing for almost $20,000 more than the discontinued Van Wagon. Crashworthiness is also problematic. NHTSA-tested rollover resistance for the 2008 and 2009 models was rated one star out of five. Other disadvantages: Service is provided by only a few select dealers, parts are hard to find, and depreciation is brutally fast. A second-year 2005 now sells for $9,000; its original price was $45,000.

Ford and GM Vans

Both automakers are struggling with their vans due to a stalled economy and high fuel prices. GM has hedged its bets by shoehorning the Duramax 6600 diesel engine into its large vans, making them less fuel-thirsty and more attractive to frugal buyers. However, this is too little, too late. Many remember the Duramax's poor past performance and are angry that the old GM warranty is worthless now that the automaker has come out of bankruptcy.

Ford's Econoline joins GM in the middle of the pack in terms of value for dollar. Servicing this Ford van is a breeze due to the large number of generic parts in Ford's truck parts bin and the few changes made to the E-150 series over the years. As with all full-sized vans, depreciation is your friend, allowing you to pick up a 2008 Econoline XL for about $14,500.

GM has substantially redesigned its full-sized vans within the past few years to improve both their handling and the ride, and to add important safety features like stability control, ABS, and additional airbags. Following this redesign, GM has led the Detroit pack with better-handling and smoother-riding models than those available from Ford or Chrysler.

Some of the more-common problems shared by all three automakers: engine and drivetrain breakdowns, brake failures, premature brake and suspension/steering wearout, AC failures, electrical and computer module glitches, and defects in both manual and sliding doors.

The reason why there's such similarity in the defect trending among Asian and Detroit van builders is that they all get their key components from a small band of suppliers. And, as they cut supplier profits, quality goes down the drain. Hence, as Toyota and Honda become more skinflint in their supplier payouts, they, too, see a corresponding quality decline, evidenced by engine and transmission defects and sliding-door failures.

VAN RATINGS

Above Average

Chrysler Ram Van/Wagon (1999–2003)
General Motors Express, Savana (2003–09)

Average

Ford Econoline Cargo Van, Club Wagon (2004–09)
General Motors Express, Savana (1999–2002)

Below Average

Ford Econoline Cargo Van, Club Wagon (1999–2003)

Not Recommended

Chrysler Sprinter Van/Wagon (2003–09)

Ford

ECONOLINE CARGO VAN, CLUB WAGON	★ ★ ★

RATING: Average (2004–09); Below Average (1999–2003). Easily found at reasonable prices, Econolines don't possess any glaring virtues or vices; they all perform in a manner similar to that of the Chrysler and GM large, rear-drive vans. Overall reliability is on par with similar Chrysler and GM full-sized vans. **Ideal model year:** A 2008 Econoline Wagon is your best choice. Its new features are important additions, and the $14,500 cost is far less than the van's original price ($32,599). **"Real" city/highway fuel economy:** *E-150 4.2:* 16.6/11.7 L/100 km. *E-150 4.6:* 17.6/12.2 L/100 km. *E-150 5.4:* 17.4/12.3 L/100 km. **Maintenance/ Repair costs:** Lower than average. **Parts:** Inexpensive and not hard to find. **Extended warranty:** Not needed; invest, instead, in a thorough pre-purchase inspection. **Best alternatives:** Any GM rear-drive, full-sized van, or Dodge Ram Van. Both models are cheaper and more-easily serviced than Chrysler's 2004 and the later, German-bred Sprinter, a narrow, overpriced, and under-serviced Mercedes-Benz van with a 152 hp turbodiesel used mainly for commercial deliveries. Remember, Chrysler's 2003 and earlier Ram Vans have an edge over Ford and GM vans from a price, performance, and quality standpoint. It's just that they are so old. **Helpful websites:** *www.carcomplaints.com/Ford.*

Strengths and Weaknesses

First launched in 1961 on the Falcon platform, the rear-drive Econoline has long been a fixture in the commercial delivery market, primarily because of its 4,536 kg (10,000 lb.) carrying capacity. Like Chrysler, Ford has made few changes over the last several decades, figuring that a good thing is best left alone.

The Ford Club Wagon, which is an Econoline dressed up for passenger duty, offers lots of room with capacity to spare for luggage. Nevertheless, full-sized vans have a very high floor, long panelled windows, and seats that are bolted to the floor—unlike most minivans, which feature powered middle windows and seats that stow into the floor or fold to the side.

There are a number of sound reasons for buying a used Ford Econoline: It's more reliable than any Detroit front-drive; all models are reasonably well equipped; it carries a more-refined powertrain and brakes that were phased in with the 2004s;

and it has a good control and instrument layout, adequate interior room, and an acceptable ride. Negatives: It's huge and heavy with sloppy handling, similar to the Ram lineup. With earlier vehicles, excessive braking distances and harsh transmission shifting and hunting are the norm. Get used to limited second-row legroom and lots of engine, wind, and road noise. Quality control isn't the best, especially in regards to the failure-prone 6.0L diesel engine, alternators, and AC compressor.

VEHICLE HISTORY: 2004—A 4.6L V8 base engine; the 7.3L diesel is ditched for a problematic 6.0L turbocharged variant; and a new 5-speed automatic transmission is added (turbo models only) along with rear disc brakes on larger wheels. **2006**—Much-needed standard electronic stability control. **2007**—An upgraded stabilizer bar for the E-150; an engine oil cooler for all models, and a power driver's seat comes with the E-150 Chateau. **2008**—A restyled front-end that increases engine airflow; more responsive steering and front and rear suspensions; additional load-carrying capability; and improved seats in passenger wagons. Chassis improvements include a better-tuned suspension, larger sway bars, revised rear shock absorbers; better road feedback and reduced steering effort plus an upgraded braking system with larger rotors and calipers. *Commercial Van:* Similar improvements plus a cargo protection system for added security.

Econoline quality is on the decline. Perhaps Ford has put all of its resources into making better small cars and crossovers and has adopted a benign neglect policy for the Econolines, since the van is expected to be replace next year by the Transit Connect.

Ford engine defects are legion, with turbocharger, high-pressure pump, oil pump, and injector malfunctions, and with EGR valve coking, when unburned deposits coat the valve and cause power loss, surging, and stalling. Electrical, fuel, and ignition systems are constantly on the fritz. The 3- and 4-speed automatic transmissions, steering and suspension components (lower steering shaft/tie rods), and brakes (calipers, pads, rotors, and torn rear caliper boots) have also come under considerable criticism.

Body fit and finish are typically below average, and have been that way for the past several decades. Premature rusting hasn't been a serious problem since the mid-1980s (except for rusted-out oil pans), but water does leak into the cabin, principally through the windshield, doors, and third-brake light. Paint delamination and peeling are also quite common.

Safety Summary

All models/years: Airbag malfunctions. • Sudden acceleration when idling or when cruise control is activated. • Van rolled away while parked with emergency brake engaged. • Chronic stalling. • Electrical shorts cause fuses to blow and make brakes, turn signals, and transmissions malfunction. • Lots of complaints of road wander, vibration, and premature brake rotor warpage and pad wearout, leading to extended stopping distances and front brake lock-up. • Loss of power steering. • Exhaust fumes enter the vehicle. • Steering tie-rod end failures. • Sticking or binding ignition lock cylinder. • Tire-tread separation; faulty valve stems cause tires to lose their air. • Windshield stress crack at base of wiper arm. • Horn doesn't work. • Wheel rubs against the torsion bar when turning left. **All models: 2001**—Flat mirrors create a large blind spot. **2002**—Engine damaged because water entered through the air intake. • Loss of power steering. • Fuel tank won't fill up completely. **2003**—Engine stalled and then exploded. • Transmission slipped out of Park into Reverse. **2004**—5.4L slow throttle response. *E-150:* **2005**—When the vehicle stalls going uphill, there are no brakes or steering to maintain control as it backs down. **2006**—Under-hood fire while vehicle was parked. • Throttle sticks. • Brake and gas pedal are mounted too close together. • Sudden stalling while cruising in traffic. • Side door fails to latch properly. **2007**—Passenger-side rear-door lock failure. **2008**—A child safety seat cannot be installed to function safely; the tether is too short. **2009**—Vehicle caught fire while parked. Wires leading into the fuel tank shorted. • Sudden unintended acceleration. • Front passenger-side airbag is disabled whenever that seat is occupied. • Loss of brakes. • Rearview camera failed to alert driver he was backing into another vehicle. • Automatic 6-speed transmission allows vehicle to roll back when stopped on a grade if the gear selector is in either 2 or 3; Ford says this is "normal." • Another owner warns that the Park gear allows the vehicle to roll away on an incline. • A slight turn of the steering wheel to the right and the vehicle veered sharply in that direction. • Automatic transmission slips, slams into gear, sticks in gear, or defaults to Neutral. • When starting or stopping, there is a thump and a slight surge forward; dealer says it is a common problem with the 2-speed rear axle. Ford says it is "normal." • Water accumulates in the right-side cab kickplate:

> At around 3500 miles on my 2009 Ford F150 Supercrew, I noticed a mildew smell and condensation forming on the inside of my windows. I did some research and found it is due to liquid in the cab somewhere. I pulled up each kickplate and found the problem to be under my right rear cab kickplate. Water was accumulating down there with all the electrical wires. I took it to the dealer and they stated it was due to the third brake light. It was replaced. At 5000, I noticed the smell again and knew right where to look. I did and had the same problem. Took it back to the dealer and they replaced the same third brake light only they said this one had a stronger seal. I just hit 6500 miles and noticed the same problem and smell, and popped the kickplate and had the water again.

•

> While driving in a rainstorm a passenger in the right rear seat noticed water pouring in from the headline onto her shoulder. First glance we thought maybe the window seal was leaking. Called the dealership and started explaining the situation and before I could complete my sentence they replied "…Oh yes its the third brake light seal, bring it in and we'll replace it." Wow a known issue and I was never informed of the problem.

• Ford's tire pressure monitoring system sends false alerts. • Head restraints are angled for chin-to-chest driving. • Deep grooves in front brake rotors after barely a year in service. • Intermittent headlight failure due to a faulty smart junction box. • Right rear window suddenly dropped into the door housing (bad regulator). • Sunroof shattered while vehicle was parked in the garage. • Steel wheel rims crack and must be taken out of service. • Hankook Dynapro tires are failure-prone. E-350: **2005**—Assorted electrical wiring and alternator problems affect powertrain performance and dash warning lights. • Brake vacuum pump failure caused loss of brakes. • Ambulance firm complained their diesel-equipped ambulance was constantly stalling when sent out on emergency calls:

> 2005 Ford E-350 ambulance had a total engine failure while driving to a 911 call. The Ford dealership service center diagnosed an oil pump failure as the cause and replaced it under warranty. This is compliant #2 of 6. All of the 2005 Ford ambulances we purchased have suffered total engine failures from either the oil pumps or the wiring harness systems, and several have had AC problems as well. Ford is unwilling to replace these parts on the other units until they fail.

E-450: **2005**—Engine surging when foot taken off of the accelerator pedal. • Sticking throttle. • Chronic stalling. • Faulty transmission torque converter. **2008**—Premature replacement of the automatic transmission. • Loose steering causes the vehicle to float over the road. • The rattle clips on the front pads/calipers vibrate out of position while the vehicle is underway.

Secret Warranties/Internal Bulletins/Service Tips

1993–2005—Paint delamination, peeling, or fading. **1997–2005**—Tips for correcting a rough idle. **1997–2006**—A driveline clunk may signal that the slip yoke needs lubrication. **1997–2007**—Remedy for a brake pedal that kicks back or grabs. **1998–2003**—7.3L diesel engine turbocharger pedestal may leak oil around the exhaust back-pressure actuator; high-pressure oil pump may leak. **1998–2006**—Troubleshooting a no-crank condition. **1999–2003**—Models with the 7.3L diesel engine may have premature oil pan corrosion, or a high-pressure oil pump leak (TSB #04-4-4). **1999–2010**—Troubleshooting broken intake manifold studs. **2000–03**—Poor engine performance. **2001**—Front shaft seal leakage. • Water-pump shaft seal leakage. **2003–04**—6.0L diesel engine runs rough, loses power, or has fuel in the oil (TSB #04-9-3, issued November 5, 2004. **2004–06**—TSB #06-9-7, issued May 15, 2006, gives more diagnostic and repair tips for poorly performing diesel engines. • Reasons why the AC may not cool properly. **2004–07**—Full tank slow to fill. **2005**—Engine stalls when shifting into Drive or Reverse, or when coming to a stop. **2005–10**—Inadvertent transmission lockup during 1–2 shifts. **2007–08**—Extension housing seal fluid leak. **2008**—Front-end brake rattle when passing over bumps. **2008–09**—Automatic transmission cold weather failures. **2008–10**—Repair tips to cure steering wander:

STEERING/SUSPENSION—STEERING WANDER	
BULLETIN NO.: TSB 10-9-8	DATE: JULY 24, 2010

2008–10 E-150, E-250, E-350.

ISSUE: Some 2008–10 E-Series 150-350 vehicles built on or before 11/30/2009 may exhibit steering wander or free play.

SERVICE PROCEDURE: Several factors may contribute to steering wander or free play condition and are addressed below:

• Steering gear mesh load adjustment. Steering free play is normally attributed to low mesh load torque. But in some vehicles high mesh load torque may result in a condition called sticky on-center feel that may be misinterpreted as wander.

• Front end alignment may be adjusted to improve the wander/free play condition

• Sticky on-center feel may also be due to ball joint tightness and/or high friction/rubbing of the intermediate shaft boot.

1. Lubricate the intermediate shaft boot seal with Motorcraft(R) Silicone Spray Lubricant.

2. Install grease/zerk fittings (obtain locally) in the lower ball joints and lubricate with Motorcraft(R) Premium Long-Life Grease.

WARRANTY STATUS: Eligible Under Provisions Of New Vehicle Limited Warranty Coverage

2009—Automatic transmission erratic shifting.

ECONOLINE CARGO VAN, CLUB WAGON PROFILE

	2001	2002	2003	2004	2005	2006	2007	2008	2009
Cost Price ($)									
Cargo Van	25,970	27,273	28,960	28,485	28,740	29,199	29,799	29,999	30,099
Club Wagon	28,195	30,045	30,046	31,120	31,375	31,899	32,400	32,599	34,999
Used Values ($)									
Cargo Van ▲	3,000	3,500	4,000	4,500	6,000	7,500	10,000	13,000	16,500
Cargo Van ▼	2,500	3,000	3,500	4,000	5,000	6,000	8,500	11,500	15,000
Club Wagon ▲	4,000	4,500	5,000	6,000	7,000	8,500	11,500	14,500	18,500
Club Wagon ▼	3,500	4,000	4,500	5,500	6,000	7,000	10,000	13,000	17,000
Reliability	2	3	3	3	3	3	3	3	3
Crash Safety (F)	4	4	4	—	—	—	—	—	—
Rollover Resistance	2	2	2	—	—	—	—	—	—

All ratings on a numbered scale where ☐ is good and **1** is bad. See page 132 for a more detailed description.

General Motors

RATING: Above Average (2003–09); Average (1999–2002). These rear-drive full sized vans are better buys than the Ford Econoline and cheaper and more easily serviced than Chrysler's 2004 and later German-bred Sprinter. **Ideal model year:** A 2009 Cargo Express for about $16,000. **"Real" city/highway fuel economy:** *Express 4.3 automatic:* 16.0/11.4 L/100 km. *Express 5.0 automatic:* 16.9/12.5 L/100 km. *Express 5.7 automatic:* 17.3/11.9 L/100 km. **Maintenance/ Repair costs:** Lower than average. **Parts:** Inexpensive and found everywhere. **Extended warranty:** A waste of money. **Best alternatives:** Ford Econolines and Dodge Ram Vans. **Helpful websites:** *www.carcomplaints.com/Chevrolet/ Express_Van* and *www.carcomplaints.com/GMC/Savana.*

Strengths and Weaknesses

These vans are low-priced bargains because the recent increase in fuel costs drove so many buyers away. Surprisingly, even though gasoline is cheap again, used van prices have stayed in the basement. Passenger versions are usually heavily customized and can mean great savings if you don't pay top dollar for accessories you are unlikely to use.

GM's full-sized vans come with a large array of powerful engines; multiple wheelbase configurations; a comfortable, soft ride; reasonably good transmission and brakes; plenty of interior room; and dual side-access doors. They are also quite easy to convert to the needs of drivers or passengers who use wheelchairs. On the other hand, base models are poorly equipped, and their interior is cheap-looking and rather spartan. The automatic transmission has always been a bit clunky, brakes wear out early, and body fit and finish is bottom-drawer. As with all large vans, handling is ponderous and fuel-economy is nonexistent. Little crashworthiness data is available.

The products of GM's 1996 redesign of the Chevy Van and GMC Vandura, the Express and Savana are full-sized cargo-haulers and people-movers that are only a bit better than the vans they replaced. Powered by Vortec engines and a turbocharged diesel, they are built on longer wheelbases and use a ladder-type frame, as opposed to the unit-body construction of their predecessors. This has improved ride quality somewhat, but overall performance remains unchanged. Both vans are a better choice than the average full-size van for hauling capacity, especially if you often need to carry a lot of cargo or large animals. They also out-pull the average full-sized van by a big margin.

VEHICLE HISTORY: 2001—A powerful 8.1L V8 replaces the 7.4L. **2003**—Optional all-wheel drive, four-wheel disc brakes, a stiffer box frame, enhanced ride and handling, dual side doors that open outward, and a minor facelift. Engines and transmissions are revised, and the suspension retuned. Although the engine-gasket-challenged 200 hp engine remains the base, GM adds the GEN III V8 engines used in full-sized trucks since 1999. **2004**—Standard stability control on 15-passenger models following U.S. government charges that these vans easily roll over. **2005**—Upgraded automatic transmission components. **2006**—Addition of a Duramax 6.6L turbo diesel. **2007**—A 5.3L V8 engine becomes a standard feature on 1500 models. **2008**—A standard tire pressure monitoring system, curtain side air bags, and a restyled interior, with an expanded information console. **2009**—An engine-oil cooler, a transmission-oil cooler, a 125-amp alternator on the 195 hp 4.3L V6, and a fast-idle option on the 323 hp 6.0L V8.

Owner complaints target diesel injectors and oil cooler lines, turbochargers, and other diesel maladies. Other problem areas: doors; tires; AC; ABS sensors; brake pads and rotors; paint (delamination, peeling); suspension, catalytic converter, steering gearbox, and power-steering pump; and the starter, EMC fuses, electrical system, fuel sending unit, and fuel pump (black and grey wires fuse together inside the fuel tank).

Safety Summary

All years: Front wheel flies off. • PCM/VCM computer module shorts from water intrusion. • Vehicle won't decelerate when gas pedal is released. • Power-steering and ABS brake failures. • Premature brake pad/rotor wear. • Broken power-seat anchor/brackets (repairs: $900). • Broken or weak side-door hinges. • Faulty tire valve stems leak air. • Rear shoulder belts cross too high on the torso. **2001**—Under-hood fire caused by electrical short under dash on passenger side. • Delayed 2–3 transmission shifts. • Brake pedal goes to floor without stopping vehicle. • Vehicle wanders all over the road at 100 km/h. **2002**—Fire ignited at the bottom of driver's door. • Fuel leak. • 5.7L engine loses power when AC is engaged. • Cruise control won't decelerate vehicle when going downhill. • Leaking axle tube seals. • Leaking front grease seals contaminate the front inner disc brake pads, causing loss of braking effectiveness. • Door opened while vehicle was underway. **2003**—Extended stopping distance when brakes are applied; sometimes they fail to hold. • Fire ignited from a short in the right rear door-lock motor. • Horn and wiper failures. **2005**—Seatbelt on a 15-passenger van malfunctioned, and passenger had to be cut free. • Unsafe rear-view mirror design cuts peripheral vision. **2006**—Seat belt design creates a strangulation hazard for 10 of the 15 passengers. • Sudden steering loss. **2007**—Airbags fail to deploy. • Automatic transmission failure. Early ball joint replacement. • Van needs a larger, wide-angle rear-view mirror. **2008**—Brake and gas pedals are mounted too close together. Instrument cluster panel goes blank; no speedometer reading. **2009**—Frequent tire valve stem failures. • Diesel fuel oil heater exhausts into the cab:

Chevy Express 4500 Diesel Cutaway. Fuel oil heater (FOH) is an auxiliary heater located under the cab of the vehicle and exhausts in the same area. Odor of partially burned fuel and a strong exhaust smell would enter the cab of the vehicle during low speed operation in cold weather. Due to the intermittent character of the odor a home CO monitor was placed in the cab of the vehicle which did alarm, prompting the vehicle to be removed from service and sent for repair. The FOH required replacement.

Secret Warranties/Internal Bulletins/Service Tips

All years: GM bulletins say automatic transmission clunks are "normal." • Many diesel engine failures. • Paint delamination, peeling, or fading. **1996–2002**—Cargo door binding requires new hinge pins and bushings. **1997–2008**—Automatic transmission slips, harsh shifts, and delayed shifts. **2001**—Automatic transmission harsh shifting. • Reports of automatic transmission 2–4 band or 3–4 clutch damage. • Inaccurate fuel gauge. **2001–09**—Side cargo door binding. **2002**—Check Engine light comes on, followed by poor engine and automatic transmission performance; transmission feels like it has slipped into Neutral. • Leaking engine oil cooler lines. **2003**—Hard starts, rough idle, and intermittent engine misfiring. • Driveshaft may fracture. • Vehicle difficult to fill with fuel. **2003–04**—Suspension clunk and slap. Install a new spring insert and insulator. **2003–05**—Lack of power when the 4.3L engine is hot. **2003–06**—ABS activation at 3 km/h. • Ignition key cylinder won't turn. **2006–08**—No movement in Drive or Third gear. **2004–09**—4.6L and 6.0L engines may produce a rattle or knocking noise (replace the flywheel/flexplate). **2006–09**—Silencing a front end rattle noise. **2008–09**—Inoperative power rear-view mirrors. **2008–11**—Oil leak at oil cooler/hose pipe assembly.

EXPRESS, SAVANA PROFILE

	2001	2002	2003	2004	2005	2006	2007	2008	2009
Cost Price ($)									
Savana Cargo	24,905	25,025	25,125	26,465	26,835	27,080	27,435	29,590	31,125
Express	30,885	29,105	29,215	30,000	26,780	27,080	27,670	29,590	31,125
Used Values ($)									
Savana Cargo ▲	2,500	3,000	3,500	4,000	5,000	7,000	9,000	12,000	16,000
Savana Cargo ▼	2,000	2,500	3,000	3,500	4,000	5,500	7,500	11,500	14,500
Express ▲	3,000	3,500	4,000	4,500	5,500	7,500	9,500	12,500	16,500
Express ▼	2,500	3,000	3,500	4,000	4,500	6,000	8,000	11,000	15,000
Reliability	4	4	4	4	4	4	4	4	4
Crash Safety (F)	—	—	—	—	—	—	—	5	5
Rollover Resistance	—	—	—	—	—	—	—	3	3

SPORT-UTILITY VEHICLES

Love Thy Neighbour?

My wife, Pamela, whom I cherish, spends many hours a week at the wheel of our Grand Cherokee, and frankly it gives me an added feeling of confidence when she leaves the driveway in that rugged package. Neither she nor I fret over the possibility of her rolling some hapless victim in a Geo Metro into a wad of metal.

BROCK YATES, CHIEF EDITOR FOR *CAR AND DRIVER MAGAZINE*, WROTE THE ABOVE
IN AN OP-ED PIECE FOR *THE WALL STREET JOURNAL* OVER A DECADE AGO

Large SUVs—Low Prices

Times have changed, Brock. The Geo Metro has been turned into "a wad of metal" by junkyard recyclers, the Cherokee is now a Fiat, and Pamela is working the night shift at Tim Hortons.

Middle East liberation movements and China's insatiable quest for fuel—at any price—have sent gas prices soaring and savaged full- and mid-sized SUV sales, forcing Detroit's automakers to drop negotiated prices by thousands of dollars and creating a market shift to downsized and "crossover" models.

Automakers say reduced prices are only temporary, but that's what you'd expect them to say. Independent industry sources believe lower new and used prices will continue well into 2012. They believe buyers can expect deep discounting led by Chrysler's excess capacity of big haulers and Jeeps, followed by Toyota cutting prices thousands of dollars in its desperate drive to put sudden acceleration and brake failures behind it. As Toyota's quality woes slash that automaker's prices, Honda and Nissan won't be far behind with fistfuls of loonies, viz. customer rebates and dealer incentives. And when new vehicles sell for less, used models sell for a *lot* less.

Used SUVs, like the Ford Expedition and Excursion, the Jeep Grand Cherokee, and the GM Suburban, Yukon, and Tahoe, are selling for a song. Imagine: Three-year-old large SUVs are worth less than half their original suggested retail price. Of course, poor fuel economy and high insurance costs need to be figured into your overall cost estimate. Still, a $25,000 savings can buy a whole lot of gas, not counting the reduced GST or HST, insurance premiums, and dropped $1,500 "freight charge."

Dealers are offering $10,000 discounts on leftover models, while used prices spiral downward to match the incentives. But some behemoths, like the Ford Excursion and full-sized Hummer, can't even be given away and therefore have been discontinued. Furthermore, the Ford Expedition, Lincoln Navigator and Aviator, and Mercedes M-Class are at the top of the hit list—even though Mercedes is in denial that its SUVs are in peril. In fact, no SUV larger than Honda's CR-V or Toyota's RAV4 has a secure future.

Small sport wagons, like the Ford Escape, Honda CR-V, Hyundai Tucson, and Mazda Tribute, are selling fairly well despite the recent economic recession; buyers are attracted by the more-reasonable used prices, better fuel economy, and easier handling than larger SUVs. Plus, there are plenty of used downsized SUVs available, as five- and three-year leases from the 2006 and 2007 "boom years" start expiring.

Safety

One of the main reasons buyers choose sport-utility vehicles is the safety advantages they offer their drivers, at the expense of others on the road. The large windshield and high seating give the driver a commanding view of the road ahead, though rear vision may be obstructed by side pillars, rear head restraints, or the spare tire hanging off the back end. As we react more slowly with age, increased visibility comes in handy (a few extra seconds of warning can make a big difference). Improvements have also been made with three-point seat belts in the front and rear, seat belt pretensioners, optional adjustable brake and accelerator pedals, four-wheel anti-lock brakes, electronic stability control, a high centre brake light, adjustable head restraints on all seatbacks, side head-protecting airbags, side-door beams, and reinforced roofs to protect occupants in rollovers.

Reliability and Quality

In the last decade, many domestic and imported SUVs were rushed to market with serious quality and performance deficiencies. How much you spent was irrelevant: SUVs have their own luxury lemons. Mercedes' 1997–2006 M-Class luxury sport-utilities, for example, are nowhere near as reliable as entry-level Hyundais.

During the past couple decades, the Detroit Three haven't closed the quality gap with Asian automakers, or not by much. Yes, much has been written about how Chrysler, GM, and Ford were raising their quality standards, but the benchmark was already in the sub-basement. Dodge's Durango has a barely acceptable reliability score. Jeep's Cherokee and Grand Cherokee have been afflicted by serious brake, body, AC, and powertrain defects, and the Jeep Commander is mediocre at best. The Jeep Wrangler's been around forever, yet its quality is barely acceptable. And don't forget another oldie, the Ford Explorer: The most popular SUV ever produced was probably the least reliable, most dangerous vehicle Ford ever built (yes, even worse than the automaker's "You light up my life" Pinto).

GM's post-2000 SUVs are the best of Detroit's worst. Their relatively recent redesigns (the Acadia, Enclave, and Outlook) have improved overall safety and performance, but reliability is still the pits, with serious engine, transmission, and fit-and-finish defects. After three to five years of use (about when the warranty ends), buyers would be wise to get an extended warranty or dump these vehicles.

"Crossovers"

Advertising hype for a tall wagon, the term describes most family-sized vehicles that incorporate unibody construction, a relatively high seating position, four-wheel drive (usually), a good amount of cargo space, and seating for at least four. Crossover models embrace a wide range of sizes and configurations, from the compact quality- and performance-challenged Dodge Caliber to the seven-passenger Buick Enclave. Some models are styled like traditional SUVs, others may look like downsized SUVs or upsized wagons (Pontiac Vibe and Toyota Matrix), and an emerging type resembles a mini-minivan (Mazda5).

SPORT-UTILITY RATINGS

Recommended

Honda CR-V (2002–09)   Hyundai Tucson (2005–09)

Above Average

Ford Escape Hybrid (2005–09)   Honda CR-V (1999–2001)
General Motors Escalade, ESV, EXT, Denali,
    Suburban, Tahoe, Yukon, XL (1999–2009)

Average

Chrysler TJ Wrangler (1999–2009)   Lexus RX 300, RX 330, RX 350 (2000–06)
Ford Escape/Mazda Tribute (2002–09)

Below Average

Ford Escape/Mazda Tribute (2001)   Toyota RAV4 (1999–2009)
Lexus RX 300, RX 330, RX 350 (2007–09)

Not Recommended

Lexus RX 400h (2006–09)

Chrysler

TJ WRANGLER ★★★

RATING: Average (1999–2009). **Ideal model year:** A 2007 Wrangler Sahara is a good choice. It has lots of extra safety, performance, and convenience features, and costs only $9,500, far less than its $26,450 original. **"Real" city/highway fuel economy:** The 5-speed manual and 6-cylinder engine give you the best fuel economy. *2.4 4-cylinder automatic: 15.7/12.1 L/100 km. 3.8 6-cylinder manual: 14.1/10.8 L/100 km. 3.8 6-cylinder automatic: 14.1/10.3 L/100 km. 4.0 6-cylinder automatic: 16.8/11.7 L/100 km.* **Maintenance/Repair costs:** Average. **Parts:** Inexpensive and not hard to find. **Extended warranty:** Only for the transmission. **Best alternatives:** Honda CR-V or Element, Hyundai Tucson, and Subaru Forester. But remember, none of these other models can follow the Wrangler off-road. **Helpful websites:** *www.carcomplaints.com/Jeep/Wrangler* and *www.wranglerforum.com/f33.*

Strengths and Weaknesses

A direct descendent of the original Jeep, the 1941 Willys MB, the Wrangler should be every off-roader's first car. It's primitive, capable, and fun to drive. Plus, the Wrangler's not a bad looker for Saturday night cruising along Yonge or Burrard, and short commutes with the 4-speed automatic are a breeze (for 2003 and later models).

Best choice: an improved, second-series 2007–09 model for both on- and off-roading capability. The 2007 model's complete redesign gave it more power, more interior room, better off-road capability, and more on-road refinement. It has more standard features and handles much better than earlier versions.

You will have to take some bad with the good, however: a wobbly, noisy, rough and tumble ride; vague, imprecise steering; mediocre braking; cramped rear seating; little storage space; a canvas top that is a chore to open and leaks like a sieve; plastic windows that don't stay clean for long; a high step-in; some powertrain and body shortcomings; and mediocre fuel economy.

VEHICLE HISTORY: 2003—An optional 4-speed automatic is introduced. SE models use the Liberty's 147 hp 2.4L 4-cylinder engine, and the X, Sport, Sahara, and Rubicon versions now carry a 190 hp 4.0L inline-six powerplant. **2004**—Unlimited gets larger and longer. **2005**—A 6-speed manual transmission replaces the 5-speed. **2007**—A new 205 hp 3.8L V6 with 15 more horses than the 4.0L V6, Electronic Stability Program, electronic roll mitigation, dual-stage airbags, seat-mounted side airbags and Occupant Classification System, increased ground clearance, larger wheels and tires, enhanced Dana front and rear solid axles, Command-Trac and Rock-Trac transfer cases, new electric axle lockers, and a revamped front sway bar. Also, a stiffer frame, a 5 cm (2 in.) longer wheelbase, 9 cm (3.5 in.) wider track, lower spring rates, better brakes, and a retuned suspension. The larger interior gives about 12 cm (4.75 in.) more hip room and 13 cm (5 in.) more shoulder room, combined with additional legroom of 5 cm in front and 2.5 cm (1 in.) in the rear. The three-piece hardtop is also new. **2008**—A tire-pressure monitor becomes a standard feature. **2009**—Trailer Sway Control added.

Factory-related defects have always plagued these vehicles, although the cars have gotten marginally better after their 2007 redesign. Premature front brake wear is a frequent complaint. Owners say that the 5-speed and 6-speed manual transmissions don't shift smoothly. The 6-speed grinds when going into Reverse, or pops out of Reverse. The 5-speed constantly grinds when shifting or when in Neutral with the clutch depressed; the shifter won't come out of or go into gear, may suddenly pop out of gear, and sticks in Second gear when hot or when accelerating in First or Second; and the Fifth gear suddenly disengages. One dissatisfied owner says:

> There have now been four transmissions in my Jeep, and all have had problems with noise, shifting into and out of gear, and getting stuck in gear.

Another owner had to replace the transmission at 600 km. Clutches aren't very durable (and squeal a lot). Watch out for transfer-case malfunctions, engine overheating, engine and transfer-case oil leaks, worn-out steering components and suspensions (ball joints, especially), and ignition-component malfunctions.

Windshield cracks going up the middle are a common failure. Body welds and seams are susceptible to premature rusting, and there have been frequent complaints about peeling paint and water leaks. The worst leaks occur at the bottom of the windshield frame. An easy way to check for this is to examine the underside of the frame to see if there's excessive rust. This has consistently been a problem area for Jeeps; hence, all the ads for aftermarket windshield frames. The good news is that you can replace the windshield frame and all of the seals relatively cheaply.

Safety Summary

All years: Insurance industry figures show a much higher-than-average number of accident injury claims, aggravated by a high incidence of sudden rollovers when drivers exceed the Jeep's very low tolerance for sporty driving. • Failures that crop up repeatedly are malfunctioning airbags; fuel-tank leaks; fuel-pump failures; malfunctioning fuel gauges; sudden, unintended acceleration; chronic engine stalling when accelerating or decelerating; clutch master and slave cylinder leaks; premature brake wear; and brake failure—there have been several incidents of sudden brake loss where the pedal goes all the way to the floor with no braking effect (corrected by replacing the master cylinder). Other brake complaints include a seal leak in the power-brake booster that might cause a brake failure; the brake drum not keeping its shape; the vehicle pulling to the left when braking; the rear brakes suddenly locking up while driving in the rain and approaching a stop sign; and the vehicle going into open throttle position when brakes are applied. **1995–2003**—Manual and automatic transmission failures. **2001**—Many engine-related steering column fires. • Sudden steering lock-up. • Camshaft sensor binding and breaking, causing vehicle to stall. • Broken rear axle seal. • Manual tranny pops out of Third gear and grinds as the clutch is let out. • Premature wearout of the rear brake pads. **2003**—Driveshaft fell out while vehicle was underway. • Vehicle slips into Neutral from Drive. • Sudden axle and steering failure. • Seat belts unlatch too easily. **2004**—Sudden stalling caused by defective crankshaft position sensor. • Left-front axle seal leak. • Gas-line leaks. • Seized front brakes. • Defective steering stabilizer responsible for steering shudder. **2004–05**—Partial loss of control when passing over bumps or railroad tracks. **2005**—Defective steering stabilizer responsible for steering shudder. • Carpet causes accelerator pedal to stick. **2006**— Excessive front shimmy. • Inoperative instrument cluster. • Windshield cracks. • Faulty 6-speed manual transmission:

> The clutch rod comes out of the floor board and attaches to the clutch pedal with a clip/attachment that bolts into the clutch pedal. The problem here is, as part of their new design, the clip or attachment piece can break very easily and disable your Jeep.

2007—ABS may suddenly lock up while underway. **2008**—Fire ignites in the engine compartment. • Chronic stalling and no-starts linked to a faulty C-Bus module. • No-start due to the WCM computer module failure (a $400 repair). • Overheated transmission spilled fluid onto the exhaust, which caused a fire. • Transmission failure: 6-speed transmission violently jumps out of gear when accelerating in First gear. • Early clutch failures. • Prematurely worn-out front end torsion bar. • Severe front end "wobble" and "wheel hop" when passing over small changes in the road surface like an expansion joint, rippling of the road, or a small pothole):

> My brand new 2008 Jeep Wrangler X 4×4 began the dreaded "death wobble" (loss of steering control) around 550 miles. Thought I was about to "die". Happened 4 more times until I got it to the dealer. After searching Jeep forums and such, I found that 1000s of Jeep owners have experienced this problem, with many Jeep models. And, I learned that Chrysler does not consider the death wobble an issue.

• Fuel overflows whenever refuelling. • Hood rises up several inches with headwinds, or when a large truck passes. • Defective turn signal switch. • Gas tank replaced due to a faulty emissions valve. • Driver's head poorly protected:

> There is a poorly designed bracket right behind the drivers and passengers head. The bracket has a sharp metal corner right behind the front drivers and passengers heads. If there [was] even a small accident, there would be significant trauma to the head if they were to hit the bracket.

2009—Manual transmission popped out of gear. • Clock spring module fails, causing loss of stability control. • When refuelling, the tank often overflows:

> I own a 2009 Jeep Wrangler 2 door model that has been having issues when I fill up my gas tank. I have seen on numerous online forums that I am not alone in this matter. When I use the pump to fill my tank it will auto shut off the pump then spew at least 2–3 cups of gasoline out of the gas intake onto the side of the my vehicle, ground and on occasion myself. I have read that many have also filed a complaint so that Chrysler will perform a recall while others have paid out of pocket to fix this defect.

• Driver's side brake lines worn through. Vehicle not part of the recall in place to fix this problem. • Hood shakes violently when trucks pass from the other direction. Jeep is aware of the hood latch problem and has a Customer Satisfaction Program in place to assist owners, or so they say. • Front suspension suddenly collapsed:

> While driving 65 mph, the entire front suspension broke, almost causing a crash. The contact pulled over and look[ed] under the vehicle and noticed that the axles were split in two places. The contact had the vehicle towed to a local repair shop and it was then towed to a local dealer who stated that the contact would be responsible for repair costs.

Secret Warranties/Internal Bulletins/Service Tips

1997–2005—Tips on repairing a leak in the engine rear main oil seal. 1997–2006—Tips on plugging door leaks. 1999–2001—Tips for correcting windshield/cowl water leaks. 1999–2004—A rough idle may require the installation of a fuel-injector insulator sleeve. 2001–05—If the vehicle tends to drift, install upgraded ball joints. 2003—Manual transmission may have defective Third gear weld. 2005—Manual 6-speed won't stay in gear. 2007–08—Oil seepage at front of engine. • No-crank, no-start due to a defective wireless control module. • Water leaks onto dash and console areas. • A squeaking clutch calls for a clutch disc replacement. • Steering rubbing sound when cornering. • Body tapping or knocking sound. 2007–09—Excessive steering vibration when passing over rough surfaces. • Difficult fuel fill. • Wind noise and water leaks from the windshield/soft top header. 2007–10—Manual transmission pops out of First gear when upshifting. • Hard starts, no-start, or dead battery. • Special Campaign #J34 for free replacement of the steering damper hardware. 2009–10—Transmission fluid may overheat; a chime will be installed to alert the driver when this happens. This is a Customer Satisfaction Program, not a safety recall.

TJ WRANGLER PROFILE

	2001	2002	2003	2004	2005	2006	2007	2008	2009
Cost Price ($)									
TJ, SE	20,355	21,000	21,340	21,995	22,910	23,230	19,995	19,995	19,995
Sahara	29,285	28,120	28,715	29,950	—	—	26,450	26,995	27,195

TJ Rubicon	—	—	29,425	30,420	31,790	32,210	28,150	28,595	30,195
Unl. Rubicon	—	—	—	—	33,250	33,160	29,895	30,595	32,195
Used Values ($)									
TJ, SE▲	3,000	3,500	4,000	4,500	5,000	7,000	8,000	10,500	13,500
TJ, SE ▼	2,500	3,000	3,500	4,000	4,500	6,000	7,500	9,000	12,000
Sahara ▲	4,000	4,500	5,000	6,000	—	—	10,000	14,000	18,000
Sahara ▼	3,500	4,000	4,500	5,000	—	—	8,500	12,500	17,000
TJ Rubicon ▲	—	—	5,000	7,000	9,000	11,000	13,000	15,000	19,500
TJ Rubicon ▼	—	—	4,000	5,500	7,500	9,500	11,500	13,500	18,000
Unl. Rubicon ▲	—	—	—	—	11,000	13,000	14,500	16,000	20,500
Unl. Rubicon ▼	—	—	—	—	9,500	11,500	13,000	14,500	19,000
Reliability	2	2	2	2	2	3	3	3	3
Crash Safety (F)	4	4	4	4	4	4	5	5	5
IIHS Side	2	2	2	2	2	2	—	—	—
Offset	3	3	3	3	3	3	—	—	—
Head Restraints	1	1	1	1	1	1	2	2	2
Rollover Resistance	3	3	3	—	4	4	4	4	3

Ford/Mazda

ESCAPE, TRIBUTE, ESCAPE HYBRID ★★★/★★★★

RATING: *Escape, Tribute:* Average (2002–09); Below Average (2001). The Escape and Tribute's safety-related problems involving the brakes, steering, and electrical system is the main reason *Lemon-Aid* has lowered the cars' ratings this year. *Escape Hybrid:* Above Average (2005–09). **Ideal model year:** For $15,500, a 2009 Escape XLT V6-equipped front-drive will cost just a little over half the car's original price of $26,699. Plus you get lots of extra power and other standard features. **"Real" city/highway fuel economy:** *2.3 4-cylinder:* 9.7/7.3 L/100 km. *2.3 Hybrid:* 6.6/7.0 L/100 km (hybrids are more economical in the city). *3.0 V6:* 13.3/9.9 L/100 km. **Maintenance/Repair costs:** Average. **Parts:** Reasonably priced and usually not hard to find, although, the coolant pump's high failure rate keeps it on back order. **Extended warranty:** Only for the transmission. **Best alternatives:** The Honda CR-V, Hyundai Tucson, Jeep Wrangler, Mitsubishi Outlander, and Nissan Xterra. **Helpful websites:** *www.carcomplaints.com/Ford/Escape* and *www.carcomplaints.com/Mazda/Tribute.*

Strengths and Weaknesses

Launched as 2001 models, both the Escape and Tribute combine a carlike ride and handling—thanks to an independent rear suspension and front MacPherson struts—with the ability to drive in the snow and carry up to five passengers and their luggage. Neither vehicle is an upsized car or a downsized truck—they're four-doors that sip fuel, look like sport-utilities, and drive like sedans.

Improvements on 2005 model-year vehicles correct the quality, power, and performance deficiencies of previous models. Before then, the Escape/Tribute promised a lot but delivered a low-quality SUV that would frequently stall or suddenly accelerate at any time.

VEHICLE HISTORY: *Escape, Tribute:* **2005**—A quieter engine and 26 more horses with the 2.3L Duratec 4-banger. The V6 engine uses upgraded engine mounts and computers to smooth out the idle and improve throttle response. Safety is also enhanced with dual-stage airbags, side curtain airbags, head restraints and three-point safety belts for all seats, "smart" seat sensors, and larger-diameter four-wheel disc and anti-lock brakes. The front structure is reinforced to better protect occupants in offset frontal crashes. Other enhancements include a fully automatic 4A system; front shocks that are larger in diameter; a new stabilizer system; a floor-mounted shifter; new headlights, fog lights, grille, and front and rear ends; different gauges; upgraded seat cushions; more storage space; additional sound-absorbing materials (though it still lets in excessive wind noise); and alloy wheels. **2007**—A slight restyling of the exterior and interior. *Escape Hybrid:* **2005**—This gasoline-electric hybrid is equipped with a 2.3L 4-cylinder engine, a 65 kW electric motor, and a 28 kW generator. It has off-road and towing capability, plus acceleration comparable to the Escape's 200 hp V6 engine. **2007**—A minor restyling. **2008**—Restyled inside and out and with additional features. No change in size or power. **2009**—A 171 hp 2.5L 4-cylinder engine replaces the 153 hp 2.3L four; the optional 3.0L V6 gained 40 hp for a total of 240.

Most owner complaints target powertrain reliability, like chronic stalling and hard starts; engine oil leaks (engine crankshaft out of spec); automatic transmission gear-hunting; loss of Reverse gear; transmission fluid leaks; frequent short circuits; a cruise control that turns itself off; faulty side windows; front wheels that let ice form, causing excessive vibrations; lots of squeaks, rattles, and wind noise; poor fit and finish; and engine hesitation when the AC is engaged.

Safety Summary

Escape, Tribute: **2001**—Fuel leakage around fuel injectors. • Fuel line clip fails, causing loss of power, and fuel sprays onto hot engine. • Vehicle may roll over while driving 25–40 km/h. • CV joints and front axle fall off vehicle. • Automatic transmission pops out of Drive into Neutral while underway. • When going downhill, vehicle often suddenly loses all electrical power and shuts down on the highway with loss of steering and brake assist (faulty EGR valve suspected as the cause of the problem). • Chronic electrical problems. • Left rear wheel suddenly locks up, pulling vehicle into traffic. • Vehicle pulls randomly to the right or left when steering wheel is let go. • Steering is too tight. • Sometimes steering tugs a bit to one side and then freezes. • Rear seats don't lock properly. • Car seatback collapses in collision. • Left rear seat belt frequently jams. **2001–04**—Stalling; sudden, unintended acceleration; airbag and brake malfunctions; and frequent transmission replacements are major problems. **2002**—Gas-tank filler pipe allows

fuel to spill out when refueling. **2002–04**—Cruise control won't deactivate. •
Rear window explodes. • Nauseating mildew smell from AC. **2003**—Fire ignites
due to faulty fuel injectors. • Throttle cable jams. • Poor starting. • Rainwater leaks
at the driver window pillar area, shorting out the electrical system. **2004**—
Headlights go on and off. **2005**—Accelerator sticks. • Faulty transmission pump
shaft causes vehicle to jump out of gear and not shift. • Excessive steering play. •
Constant pulling to the left when underway. • Vehicle nosedives when stopping,
due to poorly calibrated suspension. • Passenger-door latch failure causes door to
fly open. • Airbag disables when an average-sized passenger occupies the front
seat. • Sunroof explodes. • Foglights afflicted with stress cracks. **2006**—Driver's
window suddenly shatters. • Brakes fail. **2006–07**—Liftgate fails:

> I was knocked out and pinned by the rear hatch door of our 2006 Ford Escape. I
> opened the rear hatch and leaned in to remove some items from rear of the Ford
> Escape and the hatch came slamming down, hitting me in the back of the head and
> rendering me unconscious (I am not sure as to how long). I came to face-first inside
> the Ford Escape with the door pinning me down and my feet hanging out the rear.

2007—Fire ignites in the trunk area. • In one incident, driver-side airbag and seat
belt failed in a head-on collision. • Passenger-side airbag is disabled even though a
small adult occupies the seat. • All four wheels suddenly lock up while the vehicle
is underway. • Gas smell permeates the interior. • Excessive Continental tire
vibration. **2008–09**—Airbags failed to deploy. **2008**—Throttle binds. •
Automatic transmission cooler leaks fluid and then the transmission self-
destructs; fluid is flammable:

> I went to this website: *www.carcomplaints.com/Ford/Escape/2008/transmission/
> transmission_cooler_failure-TSB_exists.shtml* and found many people are having
> transmission issues.

• Car hesitates when accelerating; gas pedal has to be pumped, which causes
vehicle to accelerate faster than desired. • Many complaints of no power steering,
or steering lockup; repair cost can range from $1,000 to $1,700. • Brake pedal
went to the floor without braking (broken throttle cable suspected). • Rear hatch
window shatters for no reason. **2009**—Engine timing chain cover frequently
cracks. • Window exploded as hatch door was closed:

> It was like the window exploded sending glass all over the driveway behind the vehicle.
> The window cost almost $60 to replace and the Ford body shop estimated almost
> $1,300 damage to the hatch finish for the nicks and scratches from the broken glass.
> We contacted Ford but they refused to cover any of the damage. Our insurance covered
> the cost of the repairs except for our $250 deductible. We found a web site where
> there [are] 31 incidents of Escape rear windows shattering [reported]. We believe
> there must be a defect in the glass or window design and want to go on record that
> this is a problem with the Ford Escape.

• Jerky acceleration. • Automatic transmission often slips into Neutral. • Broken left front axle. • Transmission fluid leakage. • Seat belt retractor locks and won't release the passenger. • Passenger side airbag disables itself for no reason. White flakes blow from the AC (see TSB #09-21-6). • Tire pressure monitoring system sends out false alerts. *Escape Hybrid:* **2005**—Sudden shutdown while underway, allegedly due to a defective water pump. • Shifter gets stuck in Park. **2005–06**—Loss of power:

> As fleet manager, I have experienced engine failure on all three 2006 Ford Escape Hybrid vehicles. During each failure, the main engine shuts down and the vehicle goes to straight electrical power, which could cause a wreck in situations where a rapid drop in speed could cause an accident. The failure has happened on all three hybrids at about 15,000 miles [24,000 km] and now again at 36,000 miles [58,000 km]. The dealership replaces the water pump that supplies coolant to the electric motor after each failure. I feel that this situation should be reported due to the fact that I researched *Edmunds.com* and this problem is well documented in their CarSpace automotive [forums]. Ford needs to re-engineer this system.

2005–07—Loss of brakes and steering. **2006**—Fuel tank slow to fill; frequent pump shut-offs. **2007**—Occupants are trapped by their seat belts that must be cut away due to over-ratcheting. • Vehicle will suddenly lose power at any time:

> One of the times it stopped, I was stopped at a red light, the light turns green, I am accelerating to get on the highway and it cuts off again at about 30–40 mph. Cars are behind me and honk and I have nowhere to go but to the side of the road slightly, wait a few seconds and turn it back on. Very scary.

• Erratic braking; ABS failures; Stop Safely Now and Service Brake System alerts are often lit; plus, the master brake cylinder travel sensor and ABS control assembly and tone ring don't last very long:

> Intermittent brake/system issues. Including grabbing during transition from regenerative to normal braking during wet/frozen conditions (causing poor control/sliding on slippery roads). First dealer: no trouble found, second dealer replaced front tone ring, did not correct, told to wait maybe a bulletin will be issued. Dealer retained part. Intermittent Brake ABS/Traction Control/4×4 warning messages (vehicle may fail to accelerate during failure and/or unexpectedly jump side to side during normal acceleration). Dealer replaced rear rotation sensor. Dealer retained part clunking, lurching and loss of braking during transition from regenerative to normal braking (causes driver to depress pedal harder then when braking restores vehicle stops abruptly).

2008—Sudden, unintended acceleration. • Dashboard electrical system goes out while driving, setting off a concerto of alarms and an instrument and gauge light show. • Steering may lock up until brakes are applied. • Escape continues to suddenly shut down, as dealers keep ordering new motor coolant pumps to mitigate, but not resolve, the problem. • Cracked tire valve stems cause the original equipment to lose air. **2009**—Vehicle destroyed following an under-hood fire that originated in an electrical wire cable located on the passenger side of the engine wire harness near the ABS unit. • Owners report the steering continues to lock up and braking capability may be cut by 90 percent as all kinds of chimes and lights come on.

Secret Warranties/Internal Bulletins/Service Tips

All models/years: Engine hydromount insulator and rear driveshaft replacement. • No forward transmission engagement (yes, the forward clutch piston, the cause of so many Windstar and Taurus/Sable failures, once again rears its ugly head). • Rear axle pinion seal leak. • Driveline grinding and clicking. • Possible leak in the transmission converter housing near the cooler line. • Intermittent loss of First and Second gears. • Manual transmission gear shifter buzz or rattle in Third or Fourth gear is being investigated by Ford technicians. • Possible causes for a lit malfunction indicator light. • EGR valve failures. • Fuel-pump whine heard through speakers (a Ford problem since 1990). • Vehicles with 3.0L engines may show a false Low Coolant condition. • ABS light may stay lit. • AC temperature-control knob may be hard to turn or adjust. **All models: 2001–02**—Harsh, delayed upshifts • Defective door latches. • Power-steering leaks. **2001–03**—3.0L engine stalling remedy. **2001–04**—Engine misfire troubleshooting tips. • Correction for a sagging rear headliner. **2001–05**—Diagnostic and repair tips for an unstable idle, transmission shuddering, and steering pull and drifting. • Poor shifting in cold weather; install a Cooler Bypass Kit. • Slow-to-retract seat belts. **2001–06**—3.0L engine ticking noise. • Driveline whine. **2001–07**—Heater core leakage. **2001–09**—Suspension noise when turning. **2002**—Coolant, oil leakage from engine cylinder head area. • Defective Duratec engines. • Brake squealing. • Wheels make a clicking sound. **2001–10**—Underbody creak, squeak noise. **2003**—Automatic transmission shudder and whine. • Powertrain throttle body service replacement. • Front wheel bearing noise. • Rear shock leak and noise. **2003–04**—False activation of Parking Assist. ("Stop, there's something behind you! Just kidding.") You know what's most worrisome? Ford says this device may be operating as it should. **2003–06**—Inoperative AC; compressor leakage. **2003–08**—Remedy for excessive wheel/tire vibration. **2005**—Engine overheating. • Troubleshooting engine hesitation, miss. • An engine oil leak from the oil dipstick or front/rear crankshaft seals can be fixed by installing a Heated PCV Kit. • Rear brake noise. **2005–06**—Hard starts may require a recalibrated PCM; the half-hour labour charge is covered by the emissions warranty, says TSB #05-26-1. • Excessive steering vibration likely caused by faulty Continental tires, which will be replaced under an extended warranty. • Stalling when vehicle is put in gear, likely caused by excessive torque converter wear. **2005–08**—Engine stalling when accelerating or stopping. • Slow fuel fill. **2005–09**—Drivetrain fluid leak from the PTU vent. **2005–10**—A front end click or pop noise may come from the front stabilizer bar. **2006–08**—Engine camshaft ticking noise. **2007–08**—Free tire valve stem inspection, replacement. **2008**—

Engine drive belt idler pulley bearing noise. • Engine grinding, rattle noise. • 3.0L engine oil leak from the dipstick or crankshaft seal. • Transmission cooler fluid leak. • Wind noise, whistle at cruising speed. **2008–09**—Steering column pop, clunk when turning. • All instrument cluster warning lights come on intermittently. • Uncommanded liftgate opening or closing. • Exterior heated mirror glass cracking. • Front grille chrome peeling. **2008–10**—Steering wheel vibration can be remedied by installing a special damper Ford has devised. • Special Ford fix for steering column pop or clunk. • Windows squeak, grind when operated. • Ignition key binds in ignition cylinder. • Washer nozzles leak fluid onto the hood. • Poor radio reception. • White flakes blowing from dash vents. **2009–10**—Automatic transmission sticks in Fifth gear (reprogram the power control module). A harsh-shifting automatic transmission requires the same remedy. • Harsh engagements, shifts, or starts in Fifth gear from a start signal there's an open signal in the output shaft speed sensor or the main control lead frame connector. • Automatic transmission axle shaft seal fluid leak. • AWD models may produce a vibration, rumble, and/or excessive exhaust noise in cold temperatures. • The rear axle may also produce a "hoot" noise on light acceleration just before the 1–2 shift. Ford says this noise is normal; all of its Escapes are hooters. **2009**—Ford Customer Satisfaction Program #10B15100419-001 (secret warranty) was set up April 19, 2010, to cover the cost of reprogramming the Power Control Module to reposition the solenoid regulator valve and eliminate bore wear. Mechanics are also empowered to replace the valve body, overdrive, and forward clutch. Ford says these measures are needed to increase the transmissions durability. • Automatic transmission fluid leaks from the dipstick tube. • Exterior door handles may be hard to open and may not be flush.

ESCAPE, TRIBUTE, ESCAPE HYBRID PROFILE

	2001	2002	2003	2004	2005	2006	2007	2008	2009
Cost Price ($)									
XLS/XLT 4×2	22,895	21,510	21,595	21,895	22,795	23,000	23,000	23,999	23,999
XLS/XLT 4×4	24,795	24,190	30,300	27,825	28,125	28,399	28,399	27,800	27,499
Tribute 4×2	22,150	22,415	22,790	22,790	24,495	24,595	—	22,295	22,560
Tribute 4×4	24,800	25,065	25,575	25,445	27,295	27,395	—	26,990	26,245
Hybrid 4×2	—	—	—	—	33,195	33,599	33,600	31,499	32,399
Hybrid 4×4	—	—	—	—	35,925	36,399	36,399	33,899	34,799
Used Values ($)									
XLS/XLT 4×2 ▲	3,000	3,500	4,000	4,500	5,000	5,500	7,000	10,500	14,000
XLS/XLT 4×2 ▼	2,500	3,000	3,500	4,000	4,500	5,000	5,500	9,000	12,500
XLS/XLT 4×4 ▲	4,000	4,500	5,000	5,500	6,000	7,000	9,000	13,000	15,500
XLS/XLT 4×4 ▼	3,500	4,000	4,500	5,000	5,500	6,000	7,500	11,500	14,000
Tribute 4×2 ▲	3,000	3,500	4,000	4,500	5,500	7,000	—	12,500	12,500
Tribute 4×2 ▼	2,500	3,000	3,500	4,000	4,500	6,000	—	11,500	11,000
Tribute 4×4 ▲	4,500	5,000	5,500	6,000	7,000	8,000	—	10,500	14,000
Tribute 4×4 ▼	4,000	4,500	5,000	5,000	6,000	7,000	—	9,500	13,000

Hybrid 4×2 ▲	—	—	—	—	5,000	5,500	7,000	14,500	19,500
Hybrid 4×2 ▼	—	—	—	—	4,000	4,500	5,500	13,000	18,500
Hybrid 4×4 ▲	—	—	—	—	6,000	7,000	9,000	15,500	21,000
Hybrid 4×4 ▼	—	—	—	—	5,000	6,000	7,500	14,000	19,500

Reliability	2	2	2	2	2	3	4	4	4
Crash Safety (F)	5	5	5	5	4	4	4	3	5
Side	5	5	5	5	5	5	5	5	5
Side IIHS	1	1	1	1	1	1	1	5	5
Offset	2	2	2	2	3	3	3	3	5
Head Restraints	—	—	—	—	3	3	3	3	5
Roof Strength	—	—	—	—	—	—	—	2	2
Rollover Resistance	3	3	3	—	3	3	3	3	3

General Motors

ESCALADE, ESV, EXT, DENALI, SUBURBAN, TAHOE, YUKON, XL ★★★★

RATING: Above Average (1999–2009). These are brawny, large SUVs for actors, rock stars, and politicians with money to burn (unfortunately, with politicians, it's *our* money). This year ratings have been raised a notch because Tahoe et al. safety and reliable problems have been fewer during the past few years. Other SUVs like the Ford Escape and Mazda Tribute have been downgraded as their numbers of reliability and safety deficiencies have risen. **Ideal model year:** A 2007 V8-equipped model like a Chevrolet Tahoe LTZ 4×4 (original list price $61,075) will give you a more powerful engine, lots of safety and performance features, and a cut-to-the-bone price ($19,000). A 2009 version will throw in a 6-speed automatic transmission and cost you a whopping $20,000 more (get used to driving a 5-speed). **"Real" city/highway fuel economy:** *Tahoe and Yukon 4.8, with or without 4×4:* 16.9/12.7 L/100 km. *Tahoe, Suburban, Yukon, Yukon Denali, and Yukon XL 5.3 4×4:* 17.1/12.6 L/100 km; *6.0:* 17.3/12.5 L/100 km. **Maintenance/ Repair costs:** Higher than average. The early Suburban's many mechanical and body deficiencies boost its upkeep costs. One saving grace, however, is that it can be serviced practically anywhere. **Parts:** Good supply of inexpensive parts. **Extended warranty:** An extended warranty is a good idea, but it isn't critical. **Best alternatives:** Choose a 2007 GMC Acadia or Saturn Outlook, or an identical 2008 Buick Enclave. If you want to stay with the Tahoe trio, go for the 2007 models, which offer substantial interior and performance upgrades. If you're looking for a cheaper version, opt for the 2005s, which sell for about $7,000 (original price: $45,615). Try to find a Suburban with the 7.4L V8 engine— the 5.7L is barely adequate for this behemoth. Don't become mesmerized by a luxury nameplate on a practically identical model. For example, a 2002 Cadillac Escalade originally retailed for $72,700, or $8,000 more than a Yukon Denali

4×4, but today there's only a few thousand dollars separating the two vehicles' resale values. Alternatively, a full-sized van or extended minivan may be a better choice if off-road capability isn't a priority. If size isn't your primary concern, look to more-reliable Asian SUVs that are less costly to operate. **Helpful websites:** Go to *www.carcomplaints.com/Chevrolet/Tahoe* and then key in Escalade, Suburban, Yukon, or the hybrid variants.

Strengths and Weaknesses

The GMC Yukon and Denali and the Cadillac Escalade share the basic Tahoe/ Suburban design but differ in styling, options, and price. Although these models are some of GM's best-performing large SUVs, they can't match the Japanese competition in overall reliability and quality control. Plus, spending over $47,650 (2009 Tahoe 4×2) for the cheapest model in this series is way too much. Used models at about half that price, perhaps. New? You've gotta be kidding.

Don't sell these models short, however. They have a lot to offer, like standard stability control, a fuel-saving cylinder-deactivation feature, a lavishly appointed interior, a good selection of instruments and controls, a good variety of competent engines that are great for trailering, a large and comfortable cabin that adds passenger and cargo space (with the redesigned 2007s), high ground clearance, a rattle-resistant body, and slow depreciation. The Suburban and Yukon XL are the largest heavy-hitters of this group, and they actually acquit themselves quite well, with reasonably predictable handling and more than enough power for most driving needs.

But there are important disadvantages: These vehicles lose value quickly, and the 4-speed automatic transmission wastes fuel and hinders powertrain performance. A high step-up takes some acrobatics, the wide turning circle complicates parking, and braking is barely acceptable. Furthermore, get ready for bizarre electrical short circuits that require an exorcist's intervention, and seats that are lint-catchers:

> Excessive lint build up on ebony cloth seats in 2008 Tahoe. GM knows there is a problem—GM bulletin #07-08-50-018A, 10/02/2007. Model year 2007 and 2008 Tahoes and many other models built with cloth seats prior to 8/01/07. Supposed to recover the seats but after many phone calls back and forth with GM they are not willing to do anything for us. Fabric seats pull cloth fibers from any type of clothing you are wearing and the seats look filthy all the time. The fibers are difficult to remove with a lint brush or a vacuum. It only takes getting in and out once and your seats look terrible.

Other complaints include biodegradable fuel pumps, premature brake wear, excessive suspension and steering vibrations, vague steering, a suspension that provides a too-compliant, wandering ride, and excessive road and engine noise.

VEHICLE HISTORY: The GMC Yukon 4×4 (and its twin, the Tahoe) came on the scene in 1992 when GMC gave the Jimmy name to its smaller sport-utility wagon line and rebadged the big one as the Tahoe/Yukon. **2001**—The 6.0L V8 gains 20 hp. A 340 hp 8.1L V8 for the Suburban 2500. The upscale Yukon Denali (the Cadillac Escalade's big brother) moves to GM's new full-sized platform. **2002**—More standard features, such as AC, power windows, power front seats, heated power mirrors, and rear climate controls. **2003**—An anti-skid system, four-wheel steering, and adjustable pedals. **2005**—The StabiliTrak anti-skid system becomes standard for all Tahoe and 1500 models, and swing-out rear cargo doors are gone. **2006**—No more Quadrasteer; Yukons get a 5.3L V8 that uses gasoline and ethanol. Standard stability control. An Active Fuel Management cylinder shutoff system saves gas while cruising. **2007**—More power (the 5.3L V8 comes with 320 hp versus 295 hp), new styling, a larger interior, and additional features like improved second-row seats, a revised navigation system, a power liftgate, and a rear obstacle-detection feature. These models provide more-agile handling, much better steering and braking responses, and a more-comfortable and controlled ride. **2008**—A gas/electric hybrid and a 380 hp 6.2L V8 for the Tahoe LTZ and Yukon Denali rear-drives. Pre-2000 models are set on GM's C/K truck platform and have been available with a variety of V8s over the years. The best choice, though, is the 5.7L gas engine mated to an electronic 4-speed automatic. This matchup provides gobs of torque at low rpm, making these part-time 4×4s great for towing, stump pulling, or mountain climbing.

Except for the Denali's 6-speed automatic, transmission alternatives are limited to your choice of 4-speeds: the manual or the automatic. On early models, standard-equipment hubs must be locked manually before shifting into 4×4. The diesel provides a good compromise between power and economy, although it has been plagued by malfunctions for decades and has never been the equal of the Cummins used by Chrysler.

As far as highway performance is concerned, these are the best SUVs sold by the Detroit automakers...ho-hum. Overall reliability improved with the 2007 redesign—then it nosedived, with the drivetrain, brakes, electrical system, and fit and finish cited as the worst offenders. There have been lots of complaints relative to poor driveability and factory-related defects that include excessive wander and vibration, hesitation when accelerating, transmission failures, wheel bearings wearing out after only a year's use, and incredibly loud squeaking brakes. Other complaints pertain to the premature replacement of brake rotors, AC squealing, and electrical, fuel, and exhaust system malfunctions. Body assembly and paint application is below standard.

Suburban, Yukon XL

Although it's classed as a full-sized SUV, the Suburban is really a combination of a station wagon, a van, and a pickup. It can carry nine passengers, tow just about anything, and go anywhere with optional 4×4.

These vehicles didn't change much until the launch of the 2000 models. Chevrolet restyled the Suburban by setting it on the Silverado/Tahoe/Yukon platform and using generic parts from the same parts bin. With the changeover, GMC's Suburban name was swapped for the Yukon XL, while the Chevrolet division soldiered on, keeping the Suburban name alive.

The Suburban and Yukon XL are GM's largest sport-utilities: 37.3 cm (14.7 in.) longer than the Ford Expedition but 18.8 cm (7.4 in.) shorter than the Excursion. Handling improves considerably, but fuel economy remains atrocious. Improvements include a wider and taller body; new 5.3L and 6.0L V8 engines that replace the 5.7L and 7.4L engines, and a turbocharged diesel V8; an automatic transmission with tow/haul mode for smoother shifting; standard front side airbags; and four-wheel disc brakes. Rear leaf springs have been replaced by rear coil springs.

Cadillac Escalade

This is GM's pop culture party wagon, favoured by rappers and politicos. Cadillac's first truck, the 1999 Escalade 4×4, was nothing more than a warmed-over GMC Yukon Denali covered with ugly, poorly designed side cladding in an effort to disguise its parentage. The redesigned 2002 Escalade got many improvements, including an EXT version (a Suburban/Avalanche clone with additional luxury features), a 6.0L V8, and a more-refined AWD system.

VEHICLE HISTORY: 2003—A longer ESV and Escalade EXT, an all-dressed version of the Chevrolet Avalanche SUV/pickup truck. Other changes include standard power-adjustable gas and brake pedals and second-row bucket seats for the wagons. **2004**—A tire-pressure monitor, trailering package, and satellite radio are added. A new Platinum Edition offers a standard navigation system and 20-inch wheels. **2005**—An improved cooling system and upgraded interior trim and gauges. **2006**—Standard electronic stability control. **2007**—More power and fresh styling. The only engine is a 403 hp 6.2L V8; it replaces the 345 hp 6.0L V8. A 6-speed manumatic is the sole transmission available. New standard features include curtain side airbags, power-adjustable pedals, and leather upholstery. Wagons get a standard power liftgate with opening glass and heated first- and second-row seats. **2008**—A new Tahoe Hybrid debuts, equipped with a 332 hp 6.0L V8. The ESV is available for the first time with rear-wheel drive; EXTs are AWD only. **2009**—6-speed transmission and heated seats.

Safety Summary

All models/years: This SUV will wander and will require constant steering corrections, particularly when buffeted by crosswinds. • Airbags frequently fail to deploy, or deploy when they shouldn't, causing severe trauma. • Braking is terrible—one of the worst in the sport-utility class (100–0 km/h: 50 m). • Sudden, unintended acceleration. • Tire, steering, door lock, transmission, ABS and brake rotor and pad, and engine head gasket and exhaust manifold failures. • Vehicle vibrates excessively and jerks to one side when braking. • Seat belt tightens progressively; in one incident, a child had to be cut free from a locked-up seat belt. • Gas tank leaks fuel. • Fuel pumps often need replacing. • Gas fumes permeate the interior. • Rear liftgate window explodes. • Chronic electrical failures. **All models: 2003–07**—Airbags fail to deploy in rollovers or in high-speed frontal collisions, and OnStar fails to activate. *Tahoe, Yukon:* **2001**—Erratic shifting, slipping, jerking, and clunking. **2002**—Loose steering feels unstable, causes vehicle to wander. • Faulty transmission, delayed shifts. **2003**—Faulty steering linkage. • Vehicle can be shifted out of Park without pressing the brake pedal. • Rear passenger doors don't lock properly. **2005**—Overheated fuel-pump wiring. • Wheels intermittently lock up while driving. • Transmission slips from Drive to Neutral. **2006**—Driver's seatback suddenly collapses. • Tread of Goodyear Eagle LS tire splits. **2007**—Automatic transmission failure. • Transmission slips when accelerating after morning start-up. • Brake rotors quickly become deeply grooved. • Auto Start feature doesn't work properly. • Incorrect speedometer. • Instrument panel cannot be read during the day. • Faulty wheel bearings. • Heated seats don't work. • Wipers start on their own (defective wiper module). • Car locks itself, and liftgate opens on its own:

> The electric rear liftgate opens while driving 50 mph [80 km/h]. The failure also occurs while the vehicle is parked. The liftgate opens just enough so that all of the doors continuously lock and unlock and the interior lights illuminate.

• Premature tire wear ("feathering"). **2008**—Fire ignited in the cigarette lighter area. • Airbag warning light is constantly lit. • When accelerating, there is a transmission delay and then the engine surges. • Persistent vibration problems:

> Chevy dealers have replaced my tires 3 times, rims twice, new drive shaft, new driver side rear axle, new steering shaft, and balanced my tires 7 times. I still have the vibration.

• Automatic rear load leveling suspension is pressured up so high that passing over small potholes produces a dangerous rear-end bounce that can easily throw the vehicle out of control. • Back brake grinding indicative of prematurely worn out brake rotors. Owners say this happens on all four wheels, but rear wheels tend to go first. • Excessive side-to-side movements in lateral winds, or when following high-profile vehicles. • The automatic door locks don't work with the key fob; estimated repair cost is $180 per door. • Parasitic power draw on the battery means no-starts, or the car shuts down. • Electrical short circuits cause instrument panel lights, gauges, and controls to go haywire. Then doors lock and unlock on their own as the windshield wipers suddenly come on. Car acts as if were possessed by Detroit demons. **2009**—Frequent stalling. • Loss of braking capability as Service Brakes and Service StabiliTrak alerts come on. • Door locks continue to lock and unlock at will; intermittent failure of instrument panel gauges. • Frequent steering rack and pinion gear failures. • Rear window and top hinges suddenly break off. *Tahoe Hybrid:* **2008**—In a sudden stop, the Stow 'n Go seat slams against the driver and passenger seats. • Keyless entry malfunctions. •

Door locks quit locking; dealer says the fix will cost $350 per door. GM insiders blame the wiring harness. • Early transmission replacement. • Power brake failure after the hybrid battery pack loses power:

> The warning indicators illuminated on the instrument panel. Suddenly, there was no response when the brake pedal was depressed. The driver experienced extreme difficulty stopping the vehicle and had to slam on the brakes. The vehicle was able to slow down upon reaching its destination. The OnStar device was engaged and recommended that the engine be turned off and restarted. Immediately, the computer system reset itself; however, the failure recurred the following day.

2009—Multiple incidents of uncontrolled acceleration when driving on cruise control. *Yukon:* **2005**—Instrument panel gives bizarre readings or simply goes out when vehicle is started. • Chronic stalling. • Headlight fuse burns out constantly. • Spare-tire security device doesn't work as described in manual. *Suburban, Yukon XL:* **2001**—Total electrical shutdown. • Simultaneous failure of steering and brakes. **2002**—Dash lights reflect into mirror and are too bright. • Gas tank hard to refuel, causes premature shutoff. **2003**—Vehicle lunges forward when stopped. • Sudden brake loss. • Premature tie-rod wearout. • Steering shaft failure and differential leaking. • Vehicle registers no gas when the tank is full. • Cab reverberation causes ear pain (not a problem with later models). **2004**—Vehicle fails to accelerate when merging into traffic. • Sharp pull to the right when accelerating, and then vehicle snaps to the left when foot is taken off the accelerator. • Excessive on-road vibration at 110 km/h; vehicle becomes very unstable. • Defroster doesn't clear entire windshield and stops working intermittently. • When using the turn signal, the flashers are activated. • When accelerating from a stop, transmission jumps into gear after a long delay. • Complete transmission replacement followed by chronic electrical system failures. • While driving, tailgate window falls inward. • Inoperative emergency brake. *Suburban:* **2005**—Vehicle rolls backward when parked on a hill. • Sudden brake loss. *Yukon XL:* **2005**—Frequent no-starts. • Transmission shifts harshly when put in Reverse, or is slow to engage Drive. • StabiliTrak fails to activate. • Driver's seat moves on its own; inoperative seat memory. • Rear heater inoperative. *Escalade:* **2006–07**—LED tail lights are distracting. **2007**—Inadvertent side airbag deployment. • Hesitation when accelerating. • Retractable steps don't work.

Secret Warranties/Internal Bulletins/Service Tips

All models: 2000–04—Remedies for inoperative power windows. **2000–06**—If the steering column makes a clunking noise, it may signal the need to change the upper intermediate steering-shaft assembly. **2001**—Fuel-tank leakage. • Harsh shifts. • 2–4 band or 3–4 clutch damage. • Rear heater puts out insufficient heat. • Carpet may be wet or have a musty odour. **2004–06**—Automatic transmission shudder due to water intrusion. *Tahoe, Yukon, Escalade:* **1999–2004**—Transmission failure caused by debris in the 2–3 shift solenoid bleed orifice. **2000–03**—Excessive engine noise. **2002–09**—Front axle whine or click.

2003–04—Inoperative AWD. • Noisy, inoperative power windows. **2004–10**—
V8 engines may leak oil at the rear of the cylinder block:

OIL LEAKS AT REAR OF CYLINDER BLOCK

BULLETIN NO.: 05-06-01-034I   DATE: SEPTEMBER 23, 2009

5.3L, 5.7L, 6.0L, 6.2L, 7.0L—ENGINE OIL LEAK AT REAR COVER ASSEMBLY AREA (ENGINE BLOCK POROSITY RTV REPAIR PROCEDURE)

2004–07 Buick Rainier; 2008–09 Buick LaCrosse Super, Allure Super (Canada Only); 2005–10 Cadillac CTS-V; 2007–10 Cadillac Escalade, Escalade ESV, Escalade EXT; 2003–09 Chevrolet TrailBlazer; 2003–10 Chevrolet Corvette; 2004–06 Chevrolet SSR; 2005–10 Chevrolet Silverado, Silverado SS; 2006–07 Chevrolet Monte Carlo SS; 2006–09 Chevrolet TrailBlazer SS; 2006–09 Chevrolet Impala SS; 2007–10 Chevrolet Avalanche, Suburban, Tahoe; 2009–10 Chevrolet Colorado Pickup; 2010 Chevrolet Camaro; 2003–09 GMC Envoy; 2003–10 GMC Sierra; 2004–05 GMC Envoy XUV; 2007–10 GMC Yukon XL, Yukon Denali, Yukon XL Denali; 2009–10 GMC Canyon; 2004–06 Pontiac GTO; 2005–08 Pontiac Grand Prix GXP; 2008–09 Pontiac G8 GT; 2009 Pontiac G8 GXP; 2005–09 Saab 9-7X 5.3i; 2008–09 Saab 9-7X Aero; 2003–10 HUMMER H2; 2006–10 HUMMER H3 with 5.3L, 5.7L, 6.0L, 6.2L, 7.0L VORTEC(TM) GEN III or GEN IV V8 Engine (All Aluminum Block Gen III and Gen IV V8 Engines).

CAUSE: Upon initial diagnosis, it may be determined that the leak is coming from the rear cover gasket. This condition may be caused by engine block porosity on the sealing surface. This issue pertains to aluminum block applications only.

CORRECTION: Follow the steps for Oil Leak Diagnosis in SI to determine the source of the leak. If the leak has been diagnosed as coming from the engine rear cover assembly, refer to Engine Rear Cover Replacement in SI and remove the engine rear cover assembly. Inspect the engine block and engine rear cover for porosity on the mating surfaces. If porosity is found on the engine rear cover replace the engine rear cover assembly. If porosity is found on the engine block, use the following procedure to apply RTV to repair the engine block porosity.

2007–09—Side airbag deploys if door is slammed. • Engine oil leak from oil cooler hose connection. • Power liftgate opens partly, then reverses. • Door wind noise and water leaks. • Second-row seat rattles; hard to latch or unlatch. • Troubleshooting various electrical problems. **2008–09**—Tire low pressure alert stays on. *Tahoe, Yukon:* **1999–2004**—Paint delamination, peeling, or fading. **1999–2005**—No Reverse, Second, or Fourth gear may be caused by a defective reaction sun gear. **2007–09**—Steering squawk and binding. • Outside door handle pulls out of base. • Clunk noise at stop or when accelerating:

CLUNK NOISE AT STOP OR FROM LAUNCH

BULLETIN NO.: 09-04-21-003B   DATE: AUGUST 11, 2009

CLUNK NOISE AT STOP OR FROM LAUNCH (CLEAN/LUBRICATE REAR PROPSHAFT SPLINES)

2007–09 Chevrolet Silverado 1500 Series; 2008–09 Chevrolet Avalanche, Suburban, Tahoe 1500 Series; 2007–09 GMC Sierra 1500 Series; 2008–09 GMC Yukon, Yukon XL 1500 Series, equipped with 4WD.

ATTENTION: This bulletin contains a procedure to clean/lubricate the rear propshaft slip yoke splines and replace, if necessary. Check the history on this vehicle. If the lubrication procedure has been performed previously, then continue on and replace the transfer case rear output shaft.

• Remedy for noise coming from the front windshield. • Inoperative keyless entry. • Wavy, warped wheelhouse fender liners. **2007–10**—Sunvisor falls down. **2008–09**—Side window problems. *Suburban, Yukon XL:* **2000–05**—Tips on silencing a differential whine are found in TSB #03-04-17-001E. **2002–03**—Second-row footwell carpet may be wet with dirty water. (TSB #03-08-57-001; May 2003). **2002–04**—Suspension clunk, slap. Replace the spring insert and insulator. **2002–06**—Discoloured cargo covers or body cladding (seen as a chalky colour). **2002–09**—Front axle whine or click. **2003**—Harsh automatic transmission 1–2 shifting, slipping caused by a faulty pressure control solenoid (TSB #03-07-30-020; May 2003). **2003–05**—Faulty AC and audio (replace RSA module). • Front suspension rattle, squeak. **2007–09**—Clunk noise when stopping or accelerating (see bulletin on previous page). • Power liftgate opens partly, then reverses. **2007–10**—Sunvisor falls down. **2008–09**—Multiple side window problems. *Escalade:* **2006–07**—A Low Oil level indicator light or a visible oil leak may signal the need to reseal the oil-pressure sensor. **2007**—Liftgate malfunctions. • Wind noise from the rear liftgate area. • Inoperative power-assisted running boards. • Steering gear fluid leaks. • Water leak guide. • Silencing buzz, rattles from the instrument panel. • High-pitched whistle heard while driving. • Driver-seat squeak or creak. • Squeak, scratching noise heard from the upper door area (replace the roof-drip weather stripping). • Rear suspension rubbing, clunking noise. • Inoperative keyless entry feature. • Front-bumper paint peeling. **2007–08**—A noisy AC compressor or serpentine belt can be silenced by reprogramming the PCM computer module. An AC that defaults to full Hot or full Cold requires the same reprogramming. • Third-row seat won't fold flat or requires great effort to release seatback. • Great effort to close hood. • Outside door handle may loosen or crack. • Buzz, rattle heard from the front fender area when accelerating. **2007–09**—Power liftgate opens partly, then reverses. • Side door wind noise and water leaks. • Fixing various electrical malfunctions. **2008–09**—No-crank, no-start, dead battery, and no audio output from the radio (replace the amplifier). • AC not cold enough. • Power steering fluid leakage. • Multiple side window problems.

ESCALADE, SUBURBAN, TAHOE, YUKON PROFILE

	2001	2002	2003	2004	2005	2006	2007	2008	2009
Cost Price ($)									
Escalade	63,805	72,700	74,970	70,675	71,405	71,805	71,730	72,175	78,535
Suburban	37,905	45,875	46,670	46,680	49,820	47,000	46,935	48,455	50,795
Tahoe, Yukon	31,715	42,680	42,530	44,105	45,615	42,795	45,455	45,895	47,650
4×4	46,895	50,385	42,530	48,870	47,785	47,175	49,255	47,155	51,635
Tahoe Hybrid	—	—	—	—	—	—	—	66,125	67,415
Tahoe Hybrid 4×4	—	—	—	—	—	—	—	69,125	70,415
Yukon XL/SLE	35,760	46,895	47,290	44,720	50,415	47,665	47,595	48,855	51,205
Yukon Hybrid	—	—	—	—	—	—	—	66,885	68,255
Yukon Hybrid 4×4	—	—	—	—	—	—	—	69,885	71,235

Used Values ($)

Escalade ▲	6,500	8,500	12,000	14,000	16,000	19,000	27,000	35,000	41,000
Escalade ▼	5,500	7,000	10,500	12,500	14,500	17,500	25,000	33,000	38,000
Suburban ▲	5,000	6,000	7,000	8,500	10,500	15,000	18,000	23,500	28,500
Suburban ▼	4,500	5,000	6,000	7,500	9,000	13,500	17,000	22,000	27,000
Tahoe, Yukon ▲	3,500	4,000	5,500	6,000	8,000	11,500	16,000	20,000	24,000
Tahoe, Yukon ▼	3,000	3,500	4,500	5,500	6,500	10,000	14,500	18,500	23,000
4×4 ▲	5,000	6,000	7,000	8,500	10,000	13,500	18,000	22,000	25,500
4×4 ▼	4,500	5,000	6,000	7,500	8,500	12,000	16,500	21,500	24,500
Tahoe Hybrid ▲	—	—	—	—	—	—	—	—	36,000
Tahoe Hybrid ▼	—	—	—	—	—	—	—	—	34,000
Tahoe Hybrid 4×4 ▲	—	—	—	—	—	—	—	28,000	38,000
Tahoe Hybrid 4×4 ▼	—	—	—	—	—	—	—	26,000	36,000
Yukon XL/SLE ▲	6,000	7,000	8,500	9,500	11,000	15,000	18,500	23,500	28,000
Yukon XL/SLE ▼	5,000	6,500	7,500	8,500	9,500	13,500	16,500	22,000	26,500
Yukon Hybrid ▲	—	—	—	—	—	—	—	28,000	36,000
Yukon Hybrid ▼	—	—	—	—	—	—	—	26,000	34,000
Yukon Hybrid 4×4 ▲	—	—	—	—	—	—	—	30,000	38,000
Yukon Hybrid 4×4 ▼	—	—	—	—	—	—	—	28,000	36,000

Reliability

Tahoe, Yukon Suburban, Yukon XL	3	3	3	3	3	3	3	3	3

Crash Safety (F)

Suburban, Yukon XL	4	4	4	4	4	4	5	5	5
Tahoe/Yukon	3	3	4	4	4	4	5	5	5
Escalade	—	3	—	—	—	—	4	5	5
Side	—	—	4	4	4	4	5	5	5

Rollover Resistance

Escalade	—	3	3	—	3	3	3	3	3
Suburban	—	3	3	—	3	3	3	3	3

Note: IIHS has not tested these vehicles.

Honda

CR-V ★★★★★

RATING: Recommended (2002–09); Above Average (1999–2001). Take solace in knowing that, even if you pay too much, you can drive this bantam 4×4 a decade or longer without paying huge repair bills. **Ideal model year:** Get a 2006 for about $11,000; it will have had a year to iron out the 2005 upgrade snafus. A 2007 version for $13,500 is another *crème de la crème* CR-V to consider. It gives you all of the earlier upgrades, plus a bit better handling. **"Real" city/highway fuel**

economy: 10.9/8.9 L/100 km. **Maintenance/Repair costs:** Average, except for AC compressors and electronic components; easily repaired at independent garages. **Parts:** Easily found and reasonably priced (they come mostly from the Civic parts bin). **Extended warranty:** Extended warranty is unnecessary. **Best alternatives:** Good second choices are the Hyundai Tucson or Santa Fe, Mazda5, and Subaru Forester. **Helpful websites:** *www.carcomplaints.com/Honda/CR-V* and *www.crvownersclub.com.*

Strengths and Weaknesses

Combining sport-utility styling with minivan versatility, this SUV is essentially a restyled Civic with 4×4 capability added. After its '97 launch, the car changed little until the revamped 2002 came out. The small power boost and improved chassis added in 2002 give additional interior space and provide improved functionality. The CR-V's Civic-based platform incorporates a four-wheel independent suspension that shortens the nose and frees up more rear cargo room. The base 160 hp 2.4L i-VTEC 4-cylinder engine is offered with either a 5-speed manual or a 4-speed automatic transmission (through the 2004 models). The 2002–05 versions don't look that different from their predecessors, though they are a bit longer, wider, and higher. The interior, however, underwent a major change, with more space for both passengers and cargo, and more user-friendly features and controls.

Owners laud the CR-V's many standard features; impressive steering and handling, particularly around town; easy front entry and exit; top-quality fit and finish; comfortable seating with lots of passenger room; innovative use of storage space; easily storable flip-folding seats; plastic cargo floor panel *cum* picnic table; fair fuel economy; and superior reliability.

Some negatives: The 1999–2001 CR-Vs have a history of engine failures caused by defective cylinder heads. Other reported problems include minor body trim defects, premature front brake wear and vibrations, driveshaft popping noises, accessories that malfunction (particularly the sound system and AC), and electrical glitches.

There are some performance deficiencies, as well: Acceleration is somewhat compromised on vehicles equipped with an automatic transmission, though the 2005 4-beater rivals many V6 competitors; no low-range gearing for off-roading; a long history of severe steering pull to the right when accelerating ("torque steer"); jittery ride on less-than-perfect roadways; excessive engine and road noise; 2005 redesign reduces front legroom slightly; on some models, the rear cargo door opens to the street, rather than the curb; and 1999–2001 models may be tippy in a side impact, according to NHTSA crash results. Earlier models have a Marginal IIHS offset crash rating, and head restraints scored poorly. Unlike the Toyota RAV4, there's no third-row seat. Fuel economy is okay, but nowhere near Honda's or Transport Canada's overly optimistic figures.

VEHICLE HISTORY: 2001—Standard-issue ABS and user-friendly child-seat tether anchors added to the EX and SE. **2002**—Restyled and given more power, interior room, and features, like a side-hinged tailgate and new interior panels. **2004**—A front-passenger power door lock switch. **2005**—Standard side curtain airbags, skid control, and ABS; an upgraded 5-speed automatic transmission; and minor styling changes. **2007**—A new platform borrowed from the Civic, and a restyled interior and exterior that includes a new swing-up tailgate and a hiding spot underneath the cargo floor for the spare tire. These changes make the car wider and shorter than the previous year's model and enhance ride and handling, especially in turns. Cargo is also easier to load and unload; however, the spare tire is more difficult to access with a full load. **2008**—The EX-L gains a power driver seat and upgraded climate control features.

Safety Summary

All years: Sudden acceleration. • Chronic stalling. • ABS lock-up. • Bridgestone tire blowouts. **2001**—Short drivers find airbags point toward the driver's face. • Rear wheel lock-up while turning caused head-on collision (clutch failure suspected). • Driver's seatback collapsed in rear-ender. • Seat belt tightens uncomfortably. **2002**—Vehicle hesitates when accelerating, or surges and then stalls. **2002–03**—Hood suddenly flies open while cruising. **2003**—Driver-side and rear centre seat belts unbuckled when car was rear-ended. **2003–07**—Airbags fail to deploy, or deploy for no reason. **2004**—Wheel freezes while making a turn. • Stress fractures in windshield. • Wheel lug bolt breaks off. • Removable picnic table caused serious head injuries in a rollover accident. • Gas spews out of filler tube when refuelling. • Water can enter the fuel tank from gas-cap vent. • No seat belt extender available. **2004–05**—Many reports of engine fires after oil has been changed. **2004–06**—Gas pedal sticks. **2005–06**—Dozens of complaints that the vehicle pulls sharply to the right when accelerating:

> Purchased 2005 Honda CR-V for teenaged daughter in December 2004. Her mother drove the car for the first time on March 5, 2005, and was unfamiliar with the severe torque steer present in the vehicle. After making a right turn onto a major highway under hard acceleration, the steering wheel slipped from my wife's hands and the car struck the curb on the right side of the road. This blew both tires on the right side. At my own expense, I had all four tires replaced and a four-wheel alignment done at an independent dealer. Torque steer is still very prevalent.

2006—Vehicle won't hold its alignment settings. • Excessive tire wear. • Seat belt fails to retract. **2007**—Poor acceleration, followed by surging. • Sudden stalling while underway. • Vehicle is unstable when passing over a grooved highway. • Automatic transmission failures. • Defective engine oil seal. • Visibility impaired by windshield lamination. • Frequent AC failures blamed on road debris, but poor quality is suspected. • Hard starts. • False alerts displayed by the tire-pressure warning system. **2008**—Airbag failed to deploy. • Sudden, unintended acceleration. • Broken motor mount bolts. • Premature brake wear. • Windshield wipers fail to clean the windshield of snow; instead, they trap the ice and become frozen. • Low-beam headlights give inadequate illumination. • Premature failure of the AC compressor ($1,200 for a rebuilt unit). • AC condenser is vulnerable to damage caused by road rocks and other debris. Other vehicles have a protective screen in place. • Vehicle sporadically locks the occupants out of the car. • CR-V cannot be driven at 40 km or more with the rear window open. The noise inside the cabin is painfully loud. • Head restraints are angled too far forward, resulting in "chin-to-chest" driving. • Bent or broken wheel studs. • Continental tires continually lose air and perform miserably on wet, snowy roadways. • Bridgestone tires aren't much better. Rear tires can't be aligned due to cambers lacking adjustment mechanism; this leads to tire "cupping" and tire replacement every 20,000 km. • Vehicle steering shimmies and vibrates; plus, it won't track straight on the highway at any speed, despite the replacement of the steering rack. • Vehicle tends to pull to the right:

> Many other owners in U.S. have the same problem. *www.topix.com/forum/autos/honda-cr-v/TCU5MEVBRLJO6CTIK* the car always pull to the right even with 4 brand new tires, both front and back alignment done with correct reading. I visited 3 times to Honda dealer regarding this problem and they could not fix it.

2009—Sudden, unintended acceleration, especially when the vehicle is in cruise control mode. • Airbag fails to deploy. • Loss of braking ability. • Rear brake pads worn out at 30,000 km. • Bridgestone Dueler tires replaced due to tread separation and road noise. • Owner was sitting in car with the engine off, and the doors locked on their own. • Sharp pull to the left or right when accelerating. • AC condensers regularly destroyed by road debris. • Rodents love snacking on Honda's soy-coated wiring:

> The contact owns a 2009 Honda CR-V. The contact stated that mice were able to gain entry into the interior of the vehicle through the heating system and began nesting within the heating system and the glove box. The mice were chewing on different components of the vehicle which is a potential safety hazard. He called the dealer who advised him to put moth balls in the vehicle.

Secret Warranties/Internal Bulletins/Service Tips

All years: Keep in mind that Honda service bulletins almost always mention that "goodwill" extended warranties may be applied to any malfunction. **1999–2007**—Vehicle pulls/drifts to one side. **2001**—Rear differential noise. • Water leaks into the interior. **2002**—Rattling from the passenger grab handle area and above the doors. **2002–03**—Front brake clicking noise caused by faulty lower retaining clips on the front brake pad that may be replaced for free under a "goodwill" program. • Engine stumbles or stalls after a stop. **2002–04**—Troubleshooting a rear brake grinding noise. • Correcting harsh or noisy automatic transmission downshifts when slowing down. **2002–05**—Remedy for a rattle, grind, or growl coming from the A-pillar of the front-right side of the vehicle when turning left. **2002–06**—Water leaks into the interior from behind the dash. • Rear seat won't fold up. **2002–07**—Moan or groan from the rear differential. **2003**—Coolant in the oil pan. **2005–06**—Front suspension clicks while driving over bumps or turning. **2007**—Power steering pump seizure. Honda will cover the cost of this repair under Campaign #08-070. • Inoperative power windows. • Low Tire Pressure light stays on. • Distorted image in driver's outside mirror. • Wiper won't park or turn off. **2007–08**—Poor AC performance on acceleration; AC hoots or whistles. • Headliner rattles or buzzes when driving. • Tailgate rusting near licence trim. • Exhaust system squeaks. • False low tire pressure alert. **2007–09**—Inoperative windshield washer pump. • Roof rack whistling at high speeds. **2007–10**—Rear brakes grind or thump:

REAR BRAKE GRINDING/THUMPING/GROANING NOISES

BULLETIN NO.:10-020　　　　　　　　　　　　　　　　　　　　　　　DATE: MAY 1, 2010

2007–10 CR-V—ALL

SYMPTOM: There is a grinding, thumping, or groaning noise coming from the rear brakes. This occurs during the first several stops after the vehicle has been parked overnight.

PROBABLE CAUSE: Under normal braking, corrosion from the disc surface is not quickly removed, allowing for a temporary grinding or thumping noise. A new brake pad is now available which has improved corrosion removal characteristics.

CORRECTIVE ACTION: Replace the brake pads and refinish the brake discs.

NOTE: Because these brake pads clean the brake discs more efficiently, some minor noise may occur.

PARTS INFORMATION: Rear brake pad Set: P/N 43022-TP6-A00; brake caliper: piston compressor: T/N 07AAE-SEPA101.

WARRANTY CLAIM INFORMATION:

Operation Number: 411842
Flat Rate Time:　　0.9 hour
Failed Part:　　　　P/N 43022-SXS-000
Defect Code:　　　00801
Symptom Code:　　04201

Lemon-Aid believes this repair should be free for the first three years of ownership. After that period, partial compensation should be given. If the claim is refused, appeal to small claims court using this confidential bulletin. Point out that Honda's references to "Failed Part" and "Defect Code" is an admission of their negligence.

2008—Cold engine whine may be corrected by replacing the engine oil pump. **2008–09**—Headliner sagging near the liftgate.

CR-V PROFILE

	2001	2002	2003	2004	2005	2006	2007	2008	2009
Cost Price ($)									
SE/LX	26,300	26,900	27,300	27,200	28,200	29,300	27,700	27,790	27,790
4X4	—	—	—	—	—	—	29,700	29,790	29,790
Used Values ($)									
SE/LX ▲	5,500	6,500	7,500	8,500	10,500	12,500	14,500	16,500	18,500
SE/LX ▼	5,000	5,500	6,500	7,500	9,000	11,000	13,000	15,000	17,000
4X4 ▲	—	—	—	—	—	—	14,000	17,000	20,000
4X4 ▼	—	—	—	—	—	—	12,500	15,500	18,500
Reliability	5	5	5	5	5	5	5	5	5
Crash Safety (F)	4	5	5	5	5	5	5	5	5
Side	5	5	5	5	—	—	5	5	5
IIHS Side	—	2	2	2	5	5	5	5	5
Offset	2	5	5	5	5	5	5	5	5
Rollover Resistance	3	3	3	—	4	4	4	4	4

Hyundai

TUCSON ★★★★★

RATING: Recommended (2005–09). With this better-made Kia Sportage twin, you get a lot of features for your money, but a peppy 4-cylinder engine isn't one of them. **Ideal model year:** A 2007 Tucson GL V6 front-drive is your best choice. Originally retailed for $28,695, it now sells for about $11,000 and there are plenty to choose from, as many are just now coming off-lease. **"Real" city/highway fuel economy:** *2.0 4-cylinder:* 10.6/7.9 L/100 km. *V6:* 11.9/8.4 L/100 km. **Maintenance/Repair costs:** Much lower than average. **Parts:** Easily found and reasonably priced. **Extended warranty:** Not necessary. **Best alternatives:** Honda CR-V and Nissan Xterra. **Helpful websites:** *www.hyundaiforum.com* and *www.hyundaikiaforums.com*.

Strengths and Weaknesses

Hyundai's smallest sport-utility is built on a strengthened and stretched Elantra platform powered by the Elantra's engine, and offers the addition of four-wheel drive. The interior looks fairly low-tech and uses cheap-looking plastics everywhere. The optional 2.7L V6 is harnessed to a manumatic 4-speed automatic transmission, a set-up that leads to excessive gear-hunting, imprecise automatic-to-manual shifting, and compromised fuel economy. What's really needed is a conventional 5-speed, or for the Santa Fe's 242 hp 3.3L V6 to handle the Tucson's heft.

While we're on the subject of weight, the Tucson is heavier than either the Honda CR-V or the Toyota RAV4, so true handling enthusiasts will want to throw their lot in with the RAV4 or Ford/Mazda Escape/Tribute to get their performance thrills. Still, the vehicle is fairly cheap, comes well equipped with standard side airbags and stability control, and has earned NHTSA five-star front and side crashworthiness ratings. The Tucson also brakes well, gives a comfortable ride, has a roomy interior, and comes with fewer factory defects than either the RAV4 or Escape/Tribute. Another advantage is that the Tucson has changed very little over the years, so one model year is about as good as another.

Some minuses: It's underpowered and "under-geared," and has a bland interior, mediocre handling, sluggish steering, limited rear visibility, numerous first-year factory-related deficiencies, a noisy suspension, and only average fuel economy. Owners have reported failures related to the cruise control, automatic transmission, manual transmission shift-lever cable assembly, and stability-control module. There's also poor fit and finish; water pours in from behind the glove box:

> Upon removing the glove box and pulling out the cabin filter, I noticed the water coming down through the AC system...similar complaint filed on service bulletins. Car was parked on a 10 degree angle nose end down. Water leak through and near electrical components and near passenger side airbag.

Safety Summary

All years: Airbags fail to deploy. **2005**—A faulty Electronic Stability Program module can cause the vehicle to stall and the ABS to suddenly engage, and can result in the vehicle going out of control. This has happened to vehicles that have been recalled and "fixed" for the problem and to cars that aren't included in the recall. • Manual and automatic transmissions suddenly fail to go into gear. • Power steering fails while passing through small pools of water on the road. **2005–06**— The passenger-side airbag is disabled even though an adult occupies the seat. **2007**—Head restraints cause neck stiffness and headaches. • Rear window explodes for no reason. **2008**—Firewall insulation ignited. • Sudden, unintended acceleration. • Rear of the vehicle slides as if it were on ice. • Excessive shaking when underway. • Electronic stability control activates when it is not needed. • Wiper inoperative in snow storm. • Horn doesn't always work. **2009**—Sudden, unintended acceleration. • Airbag failed to deploy. • Horn failure even after the clock spring was replaced. • Windshield wiper fluid leaks out of reservoir filler neck.

Secret Warranties/Internal Bulletins/Service Tips

2005—Harsh automatic transmission shifting. **2005–08**—A humming noise may come the 4×4 coupler. **2005–09**—No movement in Drive or Reverse. • Fluid may leak from the area around the automatic transmission torque converter or between the transaxle and the transfer case. • Correcting harsh gear engagement. • Tips on silencing a rattling sunroof. **2006–07**—Troubleshooting complaints relative to a cloudy paint condition. **2006–08**—Harsh, delayed shifting. **2008**—Free TCM software update. • Self-activating antitheft alarm. • Sunroof creaking, ticking.

TUCSON PROFILE

	2005	2006	2007	2008	2009
Cost Price ($)					
GL	19,995	20,596	21,195	22,995	22,995
V6	24,865	25,695	26,395	26,495	26,495
GLS	28,725	29,995	30,795	26,795	26,795
Used Values ($)					
GL ▲	6,000	7,500	9,500	12,500	16,000
GL ▼	4,500	6,000	8,000	11,000	14,500
V6 ▲	7,000	8,000	11,000	13,500	17,500
V6 ▼	5,500	7,000	9,500	12,000	16,000
GLS ▲	8,000	10,500	13,000	15,000	18,000
GLS ▼	7,000	9,000	12,000	13,500	16,500
Reliability	4	4	4	4	4
Crash Safety (F)	5	5	5	5	5
Side	—	4	4	4	4
IIHS Side	3	3	3	3	3
Offset	3	3	3	3	3
Head Restraints (F)	—	**1**	**1**	**1**	5
Roof Strength	**1**	**1**	**1**	**1**	**1**
Rollover Resistance	—	4	4	4	4

Lexus

RX 300, RX 330, RX 350/RX 400H ★★/★

RATING: *RX 300, RX 330, RX 350:* Below Average (2007–09); Average (2000–06). What, Lexus cars aren't the best there is? No, they aren't. Lexus has followed Toyota's example of cutting content to keep prices low, except that they started the process a decade later. Unfortunately, when there's less content, then quality, safety, and reliability suffer, owner dissatisfaction increases, and resale values plummet. *Lemon-Aid* alerted readers to Lexus safety hazards almost a decade ago. Our ratings has been lowered progressively since we noted that many models had engine sludge problems, dangerous automatic transmission delayed shifts, sudden acceleration, unreliable brakes, inadequate and theft-prone headlights, and weak rear hatches that kept falling on people's heads. *RX 400h:* Not Recommended

Japan's earthquake and tsunami may cut RX hybrid supply lines.

(2006–09). Essentially a more fuel-frugal RX model with plenty of horsepower and full-time AWD, but these Japan-built SUVs are ridiculously expensive and dangerous to drive. They are brake-challenged whenever passing over bumpy terrain, and their frequently delayed shifts and engine surges can be deadly either from a rear-ender when you stall, or from a T-boner collision that cuts your car in half as it darts out into traffic. If you must go "green," get a cheaper used Ford Escape Hybrid. **Ideal model year:** The 2000 to 2006 models are good buys, except for the 2004s. Of that group, your best bet is the 2006 AWD RX 330 for $18,000, a far cry from the car's original $50,500 selling price. True, the 2007s got a horsepower boost and a 6-speed automatic transmission, but their redesign glitches spell trouble through 2009, judging from owner complaints and internal service bulletins. **"Real" city/highway fuel economy:** *RX 300:* 9.7/13.0 L/100 km. *RX 330:* 9.0/12.8 L/100 km. *RX 350:* 9.0/12.4 L/100 km. *RX 400h:* 8.1/7.5 L/100 km. **Maintenance/Repair costs:** Higher than average; most repairs are dealer-dependent and expected to cost more for hybrid repairs. **Parts:** Dealers have a quasi-monopoly on parts and can blame high charges on supply lines disrupted by Japan's recent earthquake and tsunami. **Extended warranty:** Not needed. **Best alternatives:** *RX 330 and 350:* The Ford Edge, GM Acadian or Traverse, Honda Pilot, Hyundai Santa Fe Limited or Veracruz SE, Nissan Murano SL or Xterra 5, and Toyota Highlander Limited. **Helpful websites:** *http://us.lexusownersclub. com*; *www.lemonlaw.com/wordpress/toyota-sudden-acceleration*; and *www. germancarforum.com/pit-general-discussion/3318-lexus-makes-reliable-cars-well-not-anymore.html.*

 ## Strengths and Weaknesses

Here are some of the RX series pluses. *RX 300:* Strong powertrain performance; handles well; fully equipped; top-quality mechanical components and fit and finish; pleasant riding (better than the Acura MDX and the Mercedes M series); plenty of passenger room; very comfortable seating; lots of small storage areas; and easy entry and exit. *RX 330:* Quieter, longer, wider, slightly taller, a bit more powerful, and with a longer wheelbase than its predecessor. Comfortable rear seats are adjustable and are easily folded out of the way. Better interior ergonomics, and ride comfort doesn't deteriorate with a full load. Much better emergency handling than with the RX 300. Improved fuel economy; can take regular unleaded fuel. *RX 400h:* Mind-spinning depreciation, which is good news for hybrid buyers.

Now, for some of the RX series faults, and there are many. *RX 300:* Pricey, and it's too big and heavy for sporty handling. No low-range gearing for off-roading, and traction control is optional. Thick roof pillars obstruct outward visibility. Instrument displays wash out in direct sunlight. Tilt steering wheel may not tilt sufficiently for some drivers. Expect lots of wind noise, squeaks, and rattles in addition to wind roar from the moonroof. Limited rear storage area, with a high liftover and excessive wind noise. Takes premium fuel. *RX 330:* Additional power is undermined by the added kilos. Dangerous shift delay when downshifting with the automatic transmission. There's considerable body lean when cornering, the suspension bottoms out easily, steering could be more sensitive, and there's excessive bouncing and body roll with original-equipment shocks. Front and rear seat cushions lack thigh support. Thick rear roof panels continue to obstruct visibility. No third-row seating, and the sloping rear end cuts into cargo space. The power rear door is slow to open, and the moonroof takes up too much headroom. Reduced ground clearance. The optional navigation system screen washes out in sunlight. *RX 400h:* Makes you a captive customer of Toyota/Lexus and limits where you can go for servicing. The $3,000 (U.S.) battery replacement may require a bank loan to pay off. The vehicle takes an unusually long time to start; slow and vague steering; and the instrument panel power gauge is too small. The 18-inch wheels and beefy P235/55R18 tires don't enhance fuel efficiency.

VEHICLE HISTORY: First launched in Canada as a 1999 model, the RX 300 is a compact luxury sport-utility based partly on Toyota's passenger-car platform. It's a bit longer and wider than a Jeep Grand Cherokee, and it's sold as either a front-drive or permanent all-wheel drive. Available only with a 4-speed automatic transmission and a Camry/Lexus ES 300–derived, upgraded 220 hp V6, the RX 300 handles competently on the highway but isn't suitable for off-roading because of its lack of low-range gearing and its tall, four-door wagon body.

RX 330 and 350

The RX 330 eclipses the old model with its many luxury features and extra-cost gadgets, extra interior room, and an upgraded powertrain. On the other hand, competing minivans have more utility, more room inside, more seats, and even, as in the Toyota Sienna, four-wheel drive.

The RX 330 and 350 offer all-wheel drive, a good ride, a plush and innovative interior, great all-around visibility, plenty of power, better-than-average quality, and acceptable reliability. Not bad for a bestselling SUV cobbled together from ES 350, Camry, and Sienna parts. On the downside, these cars have a history of sudden, unintended acceleration and "lag and lurch" drivetrains, cold engine piston "slap," and premature, costly brake pad and rotor replacements.

VEHICLE HISTORY: 2005—Roll-sensing side curtain airbags, rain-sensing wipers, and an eight-way power passenger seat. **2007**—The RX 350 carries a 3.5L V6 that boosts horsepower from 223 to 270; a 6-speed automatic transmission is also new.

RX 400h

The RX 400h Lexus hybrid debuted as a 2006 model, joining other hybrid models like Honda's Insight and Civic, Ford's Escape, and Toyota's Prius and Highlander. Toyota hopes that by putting the hybrid system in a luxury Lexus, it will get back the high costs of hybrid technology—clearly, an impossible dream.

The 230 hp 3.3L engine has been detuned to just 208 horses; however, when coupled with the 68 hp electric motor, there's a net gain in horsepower. Like the Prius, the RX 400h operates by allowing the gasoline and electric motors to kick in when the engine load varies. For example, the electric motor is used when accelerating from a stop or in city traffic, while the gasoline engine is useful for highway cruising. If you floor the accelerator, both motors work in unison to give you the extra horsepower needed (posting 0–100 km/h acceleration scores of about 7 seconds). Nevertheless, Lexus hybrid technology isn't as refined as that of the Honda Accord hybrid, which shuts down half the engine's cylinders when carrying a light load to save even more gas.

Fortunately, there's no need to recharge the battery pack. That's done by the gasoline-engine generator. Toyota guarantees the battery for eight years. A new pack will cost about $3,000 (U.S.)—about what the vehicle will be worth eight years from now.

Other reasons to be wary of a hybrid-equipped vehicle: Fuel economy is hyped by 15–40 percent; cold weather performance isn't as fuel-efficient; repairs and servicing are dealer-dependent; highway rescuers are wary of cutting through the high-voltage electrical system to save occupants; there's no long-term reliability data; the vehicles have a faster-than-average rate of depreciation; and you have to drive several hundred thousand kilometres to amortize the hybrid's start-up costs.

RX Series models and hybrids have declined in quality and safety for most of this decade. In particular, 2004 was a watershed year for brake, transmission, and headlight failures. The automatic transmission lurches between gears and lags in shifting at low speeds, making the car vulnerable to rear-enders. The fuel gauge gives inaccurate readings, and there have been some minor electrical shorts, prematurely worn brake calipers and warped rotors, excessive brake noise, and a variety of interior squeaks and rattles. Also, there are some body trim defects, and the instrument panel display may be too dim. The continuously variable transmission on the RX 400h has had a checkered past, with early failures reported by other automakers (like Saturn) who used a similar CVT design; independent repairers are unable to service it. Sudden, unintended acceleration and engine surging make for risky winter driving. If your Lexus has some of its warranty left, don't let Toyota/Lexus give you the run-around by claiming a problem is "normal." Any car that suddenly accelerates, or hesitates, then surges is *not* operating normally

Safety Summary

All models/years: Many reports of sudden, unintended acceleration while in Drive, when shifted into Reverse, or when applying the brakes to cancel cruise control:

> Accelerator sticks. I had a 2002 Lexus RX300 and the accelerator kept sticking. I took it to the Austin TX Lexus dealer in Spring 2008 and reported it. They said there was nothing wrong. I sold the car and bought a new 2008 RX350 and it does the same thing.

• Drivetrain lags and lurches when accelerating or decelerating. • Airbags fail to deploy. • Cruise control won't release. • Rear hatch closes on driver's neck. • Side windows shatter for no reason. **2001**—Transmission jumps from Park to Reverse. • Defective jack. **2002**—Vehicle rolls backward when stopped on a hill. **2003**—Major rear blind spot. **2004**—Many complaints that brakes fail because of a faulty brake booster. • Suspension defect causes car to pull into oncoming traffic. • Poor headlight illumination. • Dash reflects onto the windshield. • Wipers don't clean effectively. • Suspension bottoms out with a 320 kg (700 lb.) load. • **2004–09**—A physician/Lexus owner says the vehicle emits a dangerously powerful electromagnetic field in the cabin:

> Our two 2007 Lexus RX-350 (and all models 2004–2009) have electromagnetic field near the dashboard of approximately 100 milliguass. This is causing our knees and hand cells to degenerate as Lexus has not done an adequate job of providing Faraday cage or shielding from EMF. This reading of 100 Milliguass is what you find under high voltage transmission lines and studies have linked 2 to 3 milliguass to childhood Leukemia, cancer, headaches or cell de[ge]neration. I contacted Lexus customer service but they brushed off our safety concern, saying most household appliances produce EMF. For reference, 2010 Lexus RX-350 or current model ES-350S have 15 to 20 milliguass. Therefore Lexus has technology to shield but has done an inadequate job of shielding 2004–2009 Lexus RX-350 by [not] issuing a recall.

2005—Xenon headlights are often stolen. • Headlight low beam falls short. • Exhaust fumes are sucked into the cabin if the rear hatch is left ajar. **2006**—Engine destroyed by sludge. • Extended stopping distance caused by brake fluid leaking from the brake booster, making the master cylinder inoperative. • Blue-tinted headlights blind oncoming drivers. **2007**—No brakes. • Oil line burst. • Inhalation of white dust emitted from the AC heat vent caused severe respiratory distress:

> We searched the Internet and found out this is not an isolated event. Lots of people have the same problem with the white dust. Some of them (even a three-year-old child) also developed health problems. Lexus admitted the white dust was from corrosion of the coating material inside the AC/heat vent system. This is a health safety issue. As a physician, myself, I believe Lexus has the responsibility to inform the public. Lexus knew of this problem as early as June of 2007. Lexus has already replaced evaporators in many cars in 2007–2008.

• Backup lights are too dim. • Airbag warning light comes on for no reason. **2008**—Airbag is disabled when the front passenger seat is occupied. • Again, rear backup lights don't seem bright enough. • Driver needs to floor brake pedal before brakes catch. • Engine surges when vehicle goes downhill. **2009**—Cruise control doesn't disengage when brakes are applied. • Loss of brakes and steering. • Brakes work erratically on bumpy roads. • Brake and gas pedal mounted too close together. • Accumulated snow may cause the rear hatch struts to fail, sending the hatch crashing down. *RX 400h:* **2006**—Sudden acceleration. • Surging when brakes are applied makes for risky winter driving. • Sudden brake loss; brake slippage after passing over bumpy terrain. • Erratic cruise-control operation. • Vehicle constantly pulls to the left. • Complete loss of power steering. • While driving on the highway, car will stall out. • Goodyear Eagle RS-A tires wear out at 20,000 km. **2007**—Intermittent loss of braking capability. • Airbag light stays on. • More reports that the white "dust" that blows into the cabin through the AC air vents could be hazardous. **2008**—Sudden acceleration when the brakes are applied. **2008–09**— Brakes disengage for a few seconds when passing over a rough surface.

> It appears to be precisely the same problem now being reported with the Prius braking system. Toyota/Lexus basically ignored us when we complained and the problem is not fixed.

2009—When turning at an intersection, there was no acceleration and then a sudden engine surge ("lag and lurch").

Secret Warranties/Internal Bulletins/Service Tips

All models/years: Free engine sludge repairs. • There are dozens of bulletins that address the correction of various squeaks and rattles found throughout the vehicle. **All models: 2002**—Drivetrain vibration. **2002–03**—Troubleshooting front brake vibration. **2002–06**—Diagnosis and repair of vehicles that pull excessively to one side. **2003–10**—Windshield ticking. **2004**—Under "Special Service Campaign" #3LE, free replacement of the exhaust manifold converter assemblies to curb excessive exhaust noise. • A brake booster upgrade. • Front brake vibration remedy. • Coolant may leak from a crack in the base of the radiator. • Drone, vibration upon acceleration. • AC groaning, moaning; diminished blower speed. • Deceleration thump. • Front suspension creaking and knocking. • Hatch area creak or tick. • Glove box and instrument panel rattles. • Rear wiper upgrade. **2004–05**—No-start in cold weather. • Front-door window noise. • Free headlight theft-prevention kit. **2004–06**—Rear door–stay improvement. • Unacceptable power backdoor operation. • Fuel tank shield rattle. **2004–07**—Troubleshooting dash rattles. • Front seat squeak. **2004–08**—Front power seat grinding, groaning. **2004–09**—Transmission fluid or gear oil leaks from the transfer case vent. • Plugging water leaks at the liftgate area. **2004–10**—Remedy for brake rattle, buzz heard near the driver's side dash. • Power back door noise. **2006–09**—Countermeasures to reduce the white dust emitted through the AC air vents. • Multiple warning lights; can't shift out of Park. • Moonroof auto-close function inoperative. **2007**—Engine timing cover oil leaks. • Engine squealing. • Loose shift lever. • Moonroof rattle. **2007–08**—Oil leak from the engine camshaft housing. • Replace engine VVTI oil hose free of charge. • Engine compartment squeaking. **2007–09**—Driver's door rattle. **2007–10**—Engine ticking noises. **2008–09**—Transfer case fluid leak.

RX 300 SERIES, 400H PROFILE

	2001	2002	2003	2004	2005	2006	2007	2008	2009
Cost Price ($)									
RX	53,000	51,250	51,600	49,900	50,200	50,500	51,550	51,550	42,950
400h	—	—	—	—	—	62,200	62,250	62,250	53,650
Used Values ($)									
RX ▲	8,000	10,000	11,500	14,000	16,500	18,000	22,000	27,000	33,000
RX ▼	6,500	8,500	10,500	12,500	15,000	16,500	20,500	25,000	31,000
400h ▲	—	—	—	—	—	20,000	25,000	32,000	40,000
400h ▼	—	—	—	—	—	18,500	23,000	30,000	38,000
Reliability	4	4	4	3	3	3	2	2	3
Crash Safety (F)	4	4	4	3	—	—	2	2	3
Side	5	5	5	5	—	—	—	5	5
Offset	5	5	5	5	5	5	5	5	5
Head Restraints	—	—	—	1	1	1	1	1	1
Rollover	3	3	3	—	—	—	—	4	4

Toyota

RAV4 ★★

RATING: Below Average (1999–2009) This small SUV is an impressive performer that carries a remarkable array of standard features suitable for limited off-road tasks. But there is a serious downside: The car's faulty powertrain, bad brakes, and erratically functioning cruise control can put your life in danger. **Ideal model year:** A 2008 V6-equipped, front-drive RAV4 is your best choice. It got upgraded airbags, had two years to work out 2006 redesign errors, has fewer safety-related complaints recorded by NHTSA, and now costs only about $17,500, much less than its original price of $31,900. A comparable 2009 sells for $20,000, provides 13 more horses for the extra $2,500, has racked up eight fewer safety-related complaints, and is a bit harder to find. **"Real" city/highway fuel economy:** *Pre-2006 models:* 10.7/8.1 L/100 km. *2006–07 models:* 10.1/7.8 L/100 km. *V6:* 11.1/7.7 L/100 km. **Maintenance/Repair costs:** Below average. **Parts:** Moderately priced and fairly easy to find from independent suppliers. **Extended warranty:** A good idea as the RAV4 quality decline continues. **Best alternatives:** Honda CR-V and Hyundai Tucson or Santa Fe. Other choices worth looking at are the Nissan Xterra or X-Trail and Subaru's Forester. **Helpful websites:** *www.toyotaownersclub.com*; *www.toyotanation.com*; *www.arfc.org/complaints/2009/toyota/rav4*; and *www.carcomplaints.com/Toyota/RAV4*.

Strengths and Weaknesses

A cross between a small car and an off-road wagon with a tall roof, the RAV4 is Toyota's entry into the mini-sport-utility market. It has attractive lines, a high profile, and two drivetrains: permanent 4×4 or front-drive (which doesn't include low-range gearing but has a locking centre differential). The car is based on the Camry platform and features a four-wheel independent suspension and unibody construction. The 2005 and earlier models ride and handle like stiffly sprung, small-wheelbase cars; later models are a bit smoother. Like Honda's CR-V, the RAV4 is an upsized car that has been made more rugged with the addition of AWD, larger wheels, more ground clearance, and a boxy body.

Following the car's 2006 redesign, two engines are now offered: a 166 hp 4-cylinder and a 269 hp V6—RAV4's first V6. Both engines come only with an automatic transmission. ABS and traction/anti-skid control are standard. Front-drive RAV4s have a limited-slip differential. Hill ascent/descent control is standard on V6 models and on seven-passenger 4-cylinder models. RAV4s have a side-hinged rear gate that makes for difficult curbside loading. The second-row seat is a split-folding bench that moves fore and aft and has a reclining seatback. The optional third-row seat folds into the floorwell.

VEHICLE HISTORY: 2001—Restyled and redesigned, growing in size and getting a more-powerful engine, an upgraded suspension, and a more-rigid body. **2004**—Given the Camry's 2.4L engine, rear disc brakes, vehicle skid control, a revised suspension and steering, a tire-pressure monitor, and optional side curtain airbags. **2006**—A major redesign gives the 2006 a V6 and a small horsepower boost for the 4-cylinder engine as well as new styling, a longer wheelbase, additional length, more width, more cargo room, and third-row seating to carry a total of seven passengers. **2007**—Standard front seat-mounted side airbags and roll-sensing front and rear head/side curtain airbags. **2009**—The 2008's 166 hp 2.4L 4-cylinder engine is replaced by a 179 hp 2.5L four.

The peppy 6-cylinder engine provides excellent acceleration while sipping fuel; it gets about the same fuel economy as the 4-cylinder-equipped competition, which puts out 100 fewer horses. The car has adequate 4-cylinder acceleration, good handling, and a smooth ride (the four-door model has a handling advantage over the two-door version); more than enough headroom and legroom for all passengers; more cargo space than most passenger cars with the four-door (but the two-door version reduces that cargo capacity by half); a split rear bench seat that folds for extra cargo space; easy access and a low liftover; a nicely equipped four-door version (the two-door is spartan, though adequate); and an incredibly high resale value.

But owners aren't all happy, and they report the following problem areas: Serious throttle delay followed by engine surging; the automatic gearbox reduces engine performance (simpler front-drive is faster); excessive road and engine noise; and seriously compromised rearward visibility caused by the RAV4's convertible top, high headrests, and spare-tire placement.

The V6 throttle is super-sensitive and tough to modulate, leading to jerky acceleration and rough low-speed shifts; speed control constantly shifts in and out of gear; tall drivers will find the cockpit cramped; wide rear roof pillars obstruct rearward view; second-row seats give insufficient legroom; third-row seats are hard to access; there is no manual transmission available; the globe box lid and headliner is cheap-looking; and there is no separately opening hatch glass.

Quality control has declined over the past five years, with countless reports of "lag and lurch" when accelerating. A faulty speed control causes the transmission to shift constantly in a jerky manner, making the engine race:

> The response has been the same—that's just what Toyotas do. The problem—when accelerating from a stop when my 2008 RAV4 has been idling, the car hesitates. There is a second or 2 during which there is no power. Then, the power kicks in and the car jumps forward, not because the pedal is sticking but because the car suddenly "catches up" with the gas pedal.

The explanation given by two dealers is this: in the Toyota, there is a delay between when the pedal is pressed down and when the car's computer sends the information to the carborator, or whatever passes for it in the new engines. That causes the sequence—press the gas pedal, hesitation, then surge. This is most dangerous when trying to merge into heavy, fast moving traffic. Openings in the traffic are usually small but adequate if the car responds. However, when the car hesitates, then surges, the opening can be missed and the car and driver are at risk for a significant accident. The problem is also intermittent so that the driver can be caught off guard, even when experienced with the car. I'm filing this because I see that your department has gone past the sticking pedal to look at possible problems with the electronics and computer systems in the cars.

"Torque steer" makes the car unstable when merging or accelerating to pass. Rodents munch on the soy-based electrical wiring. The suspension clunks when making slow-speed turns. The brakes screech, squeal, or grind even after the pads have been replaced. Other noises: dash and windshield cowl rattling (worse in low temperatures) and rear suspension creaking when accelerating from a stop. To a lesser degree, owners tell of rear-view mirror and windshield cowling vibrations as well as minor electrical shorts. The AC and heating display is nearly impossible to read in daylight.

Safety Summary

It's important to note that the RAV4's 2006 redesign coincided with a dramatic uptick in safety-related failures reported to NHTSA. From 2005 to 2009 the complaint tally is as follows: 2005—42; 2006—351; 2007—275; 2008—138; and 2009—130 complaints posted at *www.safercar.gov*.

All years: Airbag malfunctions. • Sudden, unintended acceleration • Intermittent hesitation when accelerating or making a slow turn ("lag and lurch"). • Loss of brakes and frequent brake pad replacement. • Windshield is easily chipped. • Vehicle pulls to one side when accelerating; alignment and tires are not the cause. • Rear window suddenly shatters. **2002**—Brake pedal is too small. **2002–04**—Fire ignites in the engine compartment. **2004–05**—Fuel-hose leakage. **2006**—Passenger-side airbag shuts off even though an adult occupies the seat. • More complaints of engine hesitation and surging when accelerating or when coming to a stop:

> My 2006 Toyota RAV4 has a non-responsive throttle. On many occasions, when you give it gas it does nothing, then it takes off like a rocket. I have nearly been in accidents because I pull out from a stop and the throttle is unresponsive while traffic is bearing down on me.

2007—Sudden loss of steering. • Faulty cruise control and engine hesitation when accelerating (a common Toyota problem over the past decade). • Yokohama tire tread disintegrates after only two months of use. **2008**—Stuck accelerator:

It happened only once and hasn't repeated. It was while approaching an intersection red light fortunately with no cars in front of me. I was able to overcome the acceleration by standing on the brake and shifting into neutral. When Toyota came out with the recall for floor mats my car was not one of the models with those type of floor mats and the mats in the car are fastened down. Toyota's current recall does not include this model and a check of the accelerator pedal confirms that this is not one of the current pedal replacements. My vehicle was produced in Japan not the USA. I suspect that this was more of an electronic problem than a pedal problem. I'm concerned that it could happen again. Since my year and model is not on the recall.

•

Driving into a parking space, doing a little under 5 mph. The car suddenly surged forward. I applied the brake even harder and the ABS engaged. Fortunately I missed the BMW parked in front.

•

I own a 2008 Toyota RAV4, with a VIN that begins with a 'J', but I have experienced a problem with acceleration when I depress the brake pedal. It has happened about 3 times in the last 4 months.

• Many reports of sudden brake loss. • Weak defroster:

Under certain weather conditions (wet snow, ice & freezing temps) the defrost system will not keep ice from forming over about 3/4 of the windwhield. After 10 to 12 minutes of driving it is necessary to stop and scrape ice from the windshield and wipers. It's not a good idea to stop on narrow mountain roads in a blizzard.

• Driving with the rear windows open creates intolerable air pressure. • Rear tire cover blows off the car. • Car is a "mouse mansion":

The contact owns a 2008 Toyota RAV4. The contact noticed mice entering the vehicle when it was parked. The vehicle was taken to an authorized dealer for diagnostic testing. The mechanic stated that the failure was due to the air filter not having a screen to prevent the mice from entering the vehicle. The technician recommended that traps be set to catch the mice.

2009—Sudden, unintended acceleration accounts for almost all of the 130 complaints. • Airbag failed to deploy. • Engine camshaft secret warranty applied on a case-by-case basis. • Brake pedal too close to the accelerator. • Brake pads and rotors wear out prematurely. • Loose driver's seat. • All four tires had to be replaced because they were bald. • Under-hood fire. • Windshield wiper inverted like an umbrella strikes the left wiper blade, causing both blades to fail, after damaging the windshield. • Flimsy hood. • Fuel gauge gives incorrect readings.

Secret Warranties/Internal Bulletins/Service Tips

All years: Remedy for front brake clicking found in TSB #BR004-00. • Loose, poorly fitted trim panels. **2001**—Windshield creak noise. • Diagnosing noises in passenger-side dash and the A- and C-pillar areas. • Headlight retainer tab broken. • Improvement to the rear wiper washer nozzle. • Exhaust fumes enter into the interior. • Roof rack rattle or buzz. **2001–02**—Troubleshooting rear brake squeal. • Back door rattles. • Noise from top of instrument panel. **2001–03**—Cowl noise troubleshooting tips. **2001–04**—Fix for a squealing accessory drivebelt and a rattling belt tensioner. **2001–05**—Key sticks in the ignition, lock. **2002**—Service campaign to inspect or repair the cruise-control switch. • Wind whistle from front edge of hood. **2002–06**—Correction for vehicles that pull to the right when accelerating. **2003–11**—Windshield ticking noise considered a factory-related problem (T-SB-0142-08, published July 29, 2008). **2004–05**—Tire Pressure warning light may come on for no reason. **2004–10**—Front-seat squeaking. **2006**—Engine timing cover oil leaks. **2006–07**—Automatic transmission shift lever doesn't move smoothly. • Water leaks onto the passenger floorboard. • Fuel pump droning noise and vibration at highway speeds (TSB #TC006-07). • Front-door locks may be inoperative in cold weather. **2006–08**—Engine compartment squeaks. • Steering clunk, pop, knock. **2006–09**—Engine ticking noise. • Multiple warning lamps lit; no shift from Park. • Brake rattle, buzz heard from the driver's-side dash area. • Inoperative moonroof. **2006–10**—No-crank, no-start requires the installation of a revised neutral switch assembly. • Rough idle. • Loose sun visor mount. • Automatic transmission whining noise. **2007**—Paint stains on horizontal surfaces. **2008**—Water drips from the headliner near the A-pillar.

RAV4 PROFILE

	2001	2002	2003	2004	2005	2006	2007	2008	2009
Cost Price ($)									
4×4	23,260	24,420	24,485	24,485	24,585	28,700	29,300	29,400	26,500
V6	—	—	—	—	—	31,200	31,800	31,900	29,100
Used Values ($)									
4×4 ▲	3,500	4,500	5,500	7,000	9,500	11,500	13,500	16,000	18,500
4×4 ▼	3,000	4,000	5,000	6,000	8,000	10,000	12,000	14,500	17,000
V6 ▲	—	—	—	—	—	12,500	14,500	17,500	20,000
V6 ▼	—	—	—	—	—	11,000	13,000	16,000	18,500
Reliability	4	4	4	3	3	3	3	3	3
Crash Safety (F)	4	4	4	4	4	5	5	5	5
Side		5	5	5	5	5	5	5	5
IIHS Side	**1**	**1**	**1**	**1**	**1**	5	5	5	5
Offset	3	3	3	3	5	5	5	5	5
Head Restraints (F)	—	—	**2**	**2**	**2**	**2**	**2**	**2**	5
Roof Strength	—	—	—	—	—	3	3	3	3
Rollover Resistance	—	3	3	3	—	4	4	4	4

TRUCKS

High Cost, Low Quality

What have they done to our ever-lovin', hay-haulin', run forever, easy-to-repair pickups?

They've been "Lexus-ized." More sizzle, less steak. Served with generous helpings of greed and arrogance.

Remember, Toyota's sudden, unintended acceleration nightmare started with hundreds of complaints of runaway trucks that targeted the automaker's Tacoma small pickup over a decade ago. The ensuing cover-up prompted Toyota's former president Jim Press, a top Toyota executive for 36 years and only American member of the company's 30-member Board of Directors, to do something auto executives rarely do: He told the truth.

Press told *The Detroit News* on February 24, 2010:

> Toyota doesn't want me to speak out, but I can't stand it anymore and somebody has to tell it like it is. The root cause of their problems is that the company was hijacked, some years ago, by anti-family, financially oriented pirates.

This is not news to auto insiders. Over the past decade, American automakers have churned out millions of new pickups equipped with more complicated and hard-to-service safety, performance, and convenience features. At the same time, quality suffered as manufacturers squeezed equipment suppliers to give them more for less, and constantly changed part specifications, confounding suppliers even more. Faced with fewer sales and lower profits, automakers "decontented" their vehicles more than ever; quality took a back seat to cost and styling.

Industry critics agree that these actions have contributed largely to a dramatic decline in pickup quality over the past decade—a conclusion also reached by J.D. Power and Associates and *Consumer Reports*. *CR* says their poll results show that American trucks become less reliable as they age and don't match the Asian automakers' trucks for overall quality.

For example, J.D. Power's 2004 Vehicle Dependability Study found that the most fuel-efficient vehicles—diesels and gas-electric hybrids—have more engine problems than similar gasoline-powered vehicles, a conclusion backed by automaker service bulletins and complaints sent to NHTSA. Ford and Chevrolet diesel pickups were worse than similar gas models, while Dodge and GMC trucks were better overall.

GM's diesel engine failures primarily affect the 6.6L Duramax engine, which has been plagued by persistent oil leaks, excessive oil burning, and defective turbochargers, fuel-injection pumps, and injectors, causing seized engines, chronic stalling, loss of power, hard starts, and excessive gas consumption. To its credit, GM has a Special Policy that extends the warranty to 11 years/193,000 km (120,000 mi.) on injection pumps installed in 1994–2002 models.

Pickup Picks

When choosing a pickup, consider cost, safety, reliability, performance, and style—in that order. Start small with reliable entry-level Honda, Mazda, or Nissan offerings. If you need more brawn and performance and must buy something Detroit-made, go for a Chrysler Ram or a Ford pickup. GM's Sierra and Silverado aren't in the running due to their larger number of failures involving more components.

But be prepared for subpar reliability, high maintenance costs, rapid depreciation, and abysmally poor fit and finish on all Detroit-bred models. This includes Chrysler's much-vaunted Cummins diesel engine. Recent iterations of the Cummins have proven to be almost as quality-challenged as the Ford Power Stroke and GM Duramax (*www.mycarlady.com/2009/01/28/2009-cummins-diesel-problems-continue*).

Cummins diesel problems are primarily related to the 2006–10 models and mostly concern the turbocharger and emissions component failures that stop the truck dead in its track. Says one owner:

> I have had constant problems with this emission system where the particulate filter plugs up constantly causing more fuel to be injected into the particulate and causing very poor fuel mileage, along with carbon soot residue on the bed of the truck from the exhaust. The last 3 visits to the dealership would get the warning light turned off just to have it come back on a few days later. I have a 2002 Dodge with the 5.9 liter, and have never had a problem like this.

What about Toyota's Tacoma and Tundra? Steer clear of both models. Too many owner complaints of sudden acceleration, poor braking, suspension deficiencies, steering failures, and rust-damage undercarriages.

TRUCK RATINGS

Recommended

Honda Ridgeline (2007–09)   Nissan Frontier (2005–09)

Above Average

Ford F-Series (2007–09)
Ford/Mazda Ranger, B-Series (2008–09)

Honda Ridgeline (2006)
Nissan Frontier (1999–2004)

Average

Chrysler Ram (2002–05)
Ford F-Series (1999–2006)

Ford/Mazda Ranger, B-Series (1999–2007)
General Motors C/K, Sierra, Silverado (2006–09)

Below Average

Chrysler Ram (1999–2001; 2006–09)
General Motors C/K, Sierra,
   Silverado (1999–2005)

Toyota Tacoma (1987–2001)

Not Recommended

Toyota Tacoma (2002–09)

Toyota Tundra (2000–09)

Chrysler

RAM ★★★

RATING: Average (2002–05); Below Average (1999–2001; 2006–09). Rams are mediocre buys; however, when equipped with a manual tranny and a diesel powertrain, 2002–05 models are among the best of the Detroit Three, which isn't much of a recommendation. If Chrysler goes bankrupt for the final time, the trucks, Jeep, and minivan divisions will live on, as they are sold separately to other automotive concerns. No matter who ends up buying them, there are enough parts and independent repair agencies in the pipeline to ensure adequate servicing for years to come. **Ideal model year:** Get a 2005 front-drive Ram ST for about $6,500. **"Real" city/highway fuel economy:** *3.9 42:* 15.9/11.0 L/100 km. *5.2 44:* 18.9/13.1 L/100 km. *Hemi V8 with Multi-Displacement System:* 13.9/8.8 L/100 km. *V6:* 12.2/8.1 L/100 km. Pre-2006 models' average real-world fuel consumption has been reported at 21.0 L/100 km. **Maintenance/Repair costs:** Higher than average. **Parts:** Parts distribution has hit the skids since Chrysler's bankruptcy. Prices are unreasonably high and often back ordered. **Extended warranty:** Don't waste your money. If Chrysler goes belly-up, no warranty will cover you. **Best alternatives:** Ford Ranger, Honda Ridgeline, Mazda B Series, and Nissan Frontier V6. **Helpful websites:** *www.carcomplaints.com/Dodge/Ram_1500*; *www.ramforumz.com*; and *www.mycarlady.com/2009/01/28/2009-cummins-diesel-problems-continue.*

Strengths and Weaknesses

Not a spectacular performer with its weak standard powertrain hookup, the Dodge Ram is a full-sized pickup that mirrors Ford's and GM's truck lineups. The 2004 and later 1500 series models come with a 3.7L V6 base engine and optional 4.7L and 5.7L V8s. The latter engine is called the Hemi, and it's sold only with a 5-speed automatic transmission. The V6 and 4.7L V8 offer a manual transmission or a 4- or 5-speed automatic, respectively. Automatics include a tow/haul mode for heavy loads. Chrysler plays the nostalgia card with its 345 hp 5.7L Hemi high-performance engine, last seen as an allegedly 425 hp powerhouse offered from 1965 to 1971. It is sold with the 1500 series heavy-duty Ram pickups and the Dodge 300C/Magnum wagon. Drivers can expect to shave about three seconds off the 1500's time of 0–100km/h in 10.5 seconds, all the while praying that the engine doesn't kill the tranny.

The Ram's strong points are: bargain resale prices, cylinder deactivation for better fuel economy and more power, and plenty of interior room and convenience features. The 4.7L V8 is a good alternative to the larger, fuel-thirstier Hemi version.

Some of the sore points with the 2006–09 models: You won't get the fuel economy, safety features, or manoeuvrability of other full-sized pickups. The ride is jiggly over rough terrain, the steering is vague, the interior is Kmart kitsch, and the climb up to the lofty cab is a chore. The Mexican plant where these vehicles are made isn't one of Chrysler's best facilities in terms of quality control.

Pre-2006 models are even cheaper to buy, and they offer average quality combined with assertive styling, a high-tech engine, full-time 4×4, adequately sized cabs with good stowage utility, one of the longest and roomiest cargo boxes available, and a comfortable and well-designed interior with easily accessed and understood instruments and controls. The 1500 series models have better handling, improved steering, and fewer rattles. Other pluses: powerful Hemi, V8, and V10 engines; a bit more reliable Cummins diesel; good trailering capability; a smooth-shifting automatic transmission (when it's working right); and four-door versatility.

But there are minuses with pre-2006 models, as well: The 1500 series engines may be outclassed by Ford and GM powerplants. The Hemi V8 is quite fuel-thirsty and has had a few quality problems during the short time it has been on the road. Considering Chrysler's inability to make reliable and safe ball joints, ABS brakes, and automatic transmissions, the 2005's engine cylinder deactivation feature may become a problem as these trucks reach their critical fifth year of use. The 2500 and 3500 models were left in the Jurassic Age until the 2006 redesigned models came on board. Outdated mechanical components, like an inconvenient transfer case and a solid front axle, make for a jittery ride (on 2500s and 3500s only); 4×4 must be disengaged on dry pavement; V6 acceleration is poor; steering response is slow; the ride is bouncy over rough spots; controls aren't easy to calibrate; the 1.8 m (6 ft.) bed looks stubby; and the high hood hides obstacles from view. Chrysler ties with Ford for very poor fuel economy at a real-world average of about 21.0 L/100 km (11 mpg). And as with Ford and GM trucks, Rams have also had a disturbingly large number of safety- and performance-related defects reported to NHTSA.

VEHICLE HISTORY: 2001—Improved steering and an upgraded rear-suspension system. **2002**—Revamped handling and ride comfort. The 1500 models get more-aggressive styling, two new engines, roomier cabs, and optional side airbags. The two-door extended Club Cab is axed, Quad Cabs are given four front-hinged doors, and short-box models gain 7.6 cm (3 in.) of cabin length at the expense of bed length. The 44-equipped Rams get an independent front suspension. **2003**—2500 and 3500 series are revised and given the Hemi 345 hp 5.7L V8 and rack-and-pinion steering. **2004**—An expanded model lineup that includes a Hemi-powered Power Wagon off-roader and the SRT-10 Quad Cab, equipped with the Dodge Viper's 500 hp 8.3L V10 engine. **2005**—More models available with manual transmissions (hmm…word must be spreading that the automatics are "fertilizer"). **2006**—The 1500 gets weather seals, a stiffer frame, a softer front suspension, reduced-drag brake calipers, high-intensity headlights, an electrically operated front-axle disconnect system, a revised interior and body style (Mega Cab), and constrained layer (quiet steel) technology in the dash panel area—improvements that should reduce clunks, rattles, and wind noise. There's also a cylinder cut-off system to boost fuel economy—if it functions properly (feeling lucky?). The Mega Cab option can seat six passengers in comfort, which wasn't possible with earlier models. Comfort is enhanced through reclining rear seats that split, fold down, and move forward. Hauling capacity is more than adequate with the Mega's "mega" engine, a 345 hp 5.7L Hemi V8 mated to a heavy-duty 5-speed automatic transmission. **2007**—A new 350 hp 6.7L inline-six Cummins Turbo Diesel (25 more horses than the 2006 version), and the debut of the Class 3 Chassis Cab, equipped with either a 330 hp 5.7L Hemi V8 or a torquier Cummins Turbo Diesel V8. **2008**—The 310 hp V8 replaces the 235 hp 4.7L. **2009**—Redesigned and restyled with added power, comfort, and convenience features. Ram 1500s are available with three engines: A 215 hp 3.7L V6; a 310 hp 4.7L V8; and a 390 hp 5.7L Hemi V8. The 390 hp engine replaces 2008's 345 hp 5.7L Hemi. The V6 comes only with a 4-speed automatic transmission, V8s get a 5-speed automatic. The V6 is only available on rear-wheel-drive models. A new Crew Cab replaces the previous Mega Cab. The 2500 and 3500 models also use the 5.7L V8 with 5-speed automatic, along with an available 6.7L inline 6-cylinder Cummins turbodiesel with 6-speed automatic or 6-speed manual transmission.

The Ram 2500, 2500 Heavy Duty, SRT-10, and Mega Cab were all built in Saltillo, Mexico—not a stellar plant. Fit and finish and powertrain, suspension, steering, brake, electrical, and fuel-system components are still not top quality. Hemi engines have had problems with broken valve springs and rear main seal leaks. The Cummins diesel engine has performed acceptably well, except for frequent engine emissions hardware problems shutting the truck down, or making it "limp" home.

Other owner-reported problems: Electrical fire at the power disbursement box under the hood; sudden transmission and differential failures; and the accelerator pedal jams while backing up. Be wary of front differential damage caused by road debris striking the unprotected housing. Poorly performing brakes must be adjusted at almost every oil change; the rear brake hubs and front brake pads wearout prematurely (5,000 km); and the ABS fails completely. The weak stabilizer bar is easily bent when passing over potholes; the lack of an anti-sway bar on the rear axle in the trailer towing package means excessive swaying, causing steering instability; and some trailer hitches are cracked. Very loose steering allows the vehicle to wander all over the roadway, and a defective steering pump causes loss of steering control. Owners complain of constant pulling to the right on the highway; excessive vibration when approaching 100 km/h; excessive shimmy after hitting a bump or pothole; clunk or rattle felt in the steering wheel after running over a rough surface; and a faulty steering gearbox. Expect inadequate cooling because of AC freeze-up and a strange odour coming from the AC ducts. There's a clunking or rattling noise from the front suspension, a ringing noise from the rear of the vehicle, and a shudder when the truck pulls away from a stop while near maximum gross vehicle weight rating (GVWR), and on the 3500 series, front disc brake noise. The absence of a fuel tank baffle allows gas to slam forward and back in the tank, subjecting connections to stress and causing early failure. The ignition fuse link blows intermittently, shutting down the vehicle. The Ram suffers from fragile front ball joints; transmission seal leakage; and oil-filter adaptor plate and speed-sensor oil seepage. The obstructive rear door latching mechanism prevents easy access to the rear seat and the lap belt rides too high on the abdomen, while the shoulder belt lies too close to the neck and jaw.

Safety Summary

All models/years: Sudden acceleration. • Chronic stalling. • Airbag malfunctions. • Brake pedal goes to floor without any braking effect. • Severe pull to the side when braking. • Warped rotors and worn-out brake pads. • When parked, vehicle rolls down an incline. • Frequent transmission failures and fluid leaks. • Overdrive engages poorly in cold weather. • Vehicle wanders excessively at highway speeds. **All models: 2001**—Many reports of electrical shorts causing under-hood fires. • Power-steering line blows out. • Front suspension bottoms out on speed bumps. • Rear window shatters. • Hood flies up and shatters windshield. **2002**—Front end jumps from side to side when vehicle passes over uneven pavement, or it easily hydroplanes when passing over wet roads. • Premature brake master cylinder failure. • Differential and rear axle bearing fail prematurely. **2003**—Accelerator pedal falls off. • Front suspension collapse. **2004**—Fire ignites in the driver-side rear wheelwell. • Stalling Hemi engine (EGR valve on national back order). • Wheel bearing failure. • Rear axle breaks. **2005**—Electrical fire ignites in the engine compartment. • Vehicle speeds up when going downhill. • Early ball joint failure. **2006**—Tie-rod failures. • Gas and brake pedals are mounted too close together. **2006–07**—Automatic transmission slips out of Reverse and grinds. **2007**—Front control arm (suspension/steering) breaks:

This caused the tire to dislocate from the vehicle. The tire, ball joint, brake system and hoses stayed attached to the rim of the tire. This caused the vehicle to drop and surge to the right, then collide with another vehicle.

• Engine oil sensor failures. • Dashboard cracks may impair airbag deployment. • Michelin tire failures. **2008**—Sudden acceleration. • Airbag malfunctioned, but could not be repaired due to a lack of the required part. • Gas spills out of the filler tube. • Windshield wipers fall off:

I expressed my frustration and concern that the failures were a design flaw. The service manager indicated that the new windshield wipers do not have a retention bolt as do older models. I expressed my opinion that 2 failures in one day indicates the need for investigation.

• Floor mat may jam the accelerator. • Electronic transfer case computer module failures lock up the transmission. • Steering wheel lockup when turning left. • Wheel lug nuts may fail:

Upon hitting a slight dip in the road, my left front wheel sheared from the lug nuts and rolled away, while my truck wheel hub and rotor slammed into the asphalt and grinded 15 feet to a stop.

• Sudden failure of the outer tie-rod ends. • "Wheel-hop" when passing over bumps. • At 70 km/h excessive shake and severe pull to the right (after recall repairs were performed to prevent this problem):

The two front struts on our 2008 Dodge are leaking. This part [is] covered under the extended warranty. The issue is that this part is on a national back order with Chrysler. This is an issue that for whatever reason is not considered a recall item. This item also causes the front tires to deteriorate and go flat regularly. Tires are not covered under warranty so this becomes an expense and/or burden on the owners. This is also a safety issue because the vehicle is not able to properly maintain a lane in traffic when there are changes in road texture, pot holes, or if there are road deterioration issues. These changes cause the vehicle to bounce out of control and it makes it difficult to safely maneuver the vehicle in traffic.

• Premature front shock and tire tread wear. • There is no way to lower the headlights:

A truck is made to carry weight in the back end or pull a trailer, both of which makes the front of the truck raise in height. While pulling my trailer I receive about 100 cars per hour that flash their high beams just as they approach me causing me to be blind for a second or two…While driving through Sacramento in a rain storm at night I could not see the reflectors that mark the lanes and came close to having an accident because my headlights were so high.

2009—Sudden, unintended acceleration:

The contact owns a 2009 Dodge Ram 1500. The contact stated that while driving 60 mph, the vehicle abnormally accelerated to 115 mph. The contact noticed that the accelerator had become stuck in the open throttle position and he then attempted to dislodge the accelerator pedal in order to stop the unintended acceleration. The vehicle was taken to the dealer for diagnosis and repairs. The dealer replaced the accelerator pedal and removed the floor mat however, the failure recurred after repairs.

• Airbag failed to deploy. • No defrosting. • Excessive accelerator pedal vibration. • Spare tire jack won't support the Ram 1500's weight:

We own a 2009 1500 Dodge truck and were stranded in the high desert for well over ten hours up off of Highway 377 in northern Arizona. We had a flat. We proceeded to take the jack that was brand new. We were jacking the truck up when the first extension end tore like it was soft metal so we discarded the first extension and proceeded to use the second which also tore so I used the last extension and then the hook that was connected to the jack became twisted and could no longer be used.

• No brakes. • Warped rear brake rotors. • Drivers find the rearview mirror too small. • Horn intermittently doesn't work. • Chrome trim around the shifter reflects the sun into the driver's eyes.

Secret Warranties/Internal Bulletins/Service Tips

All models: 1999–2008—Paint delamination, peeling, or fading. • An erratically shifting automatic transmission may require only a recalibrated PCM or TCM. Check out this solution before spending big bucks. **2001**—Engine may not crank because of a blown starter-relay circuit fuse. • Low fuel output from the transfer pump may be the cause of hard starts or no-starts. • Troubleshooting tips for complaints of poor diesel engine performance. • Remedy for steering wander. • Rear may sit too high to attach a fifth wheel. **2001–04**—Water leaks on passenger-side floor (Dakota also affected). **2002–04**—Water leaks at grab handle. **2002–05**—PCV system freezes up in cold temperatures. **2003**—Low start-up oil pressure with the Hemi engine requires the replacement of the oil-pump pick-up tube. • Brake vibration or shudder requires the replacement of many major brake components, says TSB #05-008-03, published November 28, 2003. • Poor idle and coasting. • Lack of air from floor vents. **2004**—Brake kit should be installed to eliminate brake shudder, vibration. • Power-window binding or slow operation. **2004–05**—Water leaks at the roof marker lamps. **2004–08**—Sunroof makes a ratcheting sound. **2004–09**—Remedy for fuel overflow or fuel nozzle shutting off. **2005–06**—Delayed shifting. **2005–10**—Lower door hinge popping, groaning noise. **2006**—Electrical malfunctions; no-crank. • Sunroof glass not flush with roof; won't close. • Lack of airflow from rear seat heater duct. **2006–07**—Steering pull or shudder when brakes are applied. • Water leaks onto the rear floor area. **2006–08**—Horizontal paint etching. **2007**—Automatic transmission torque converter shuddering. • Transmission defaults to neutral. **2009**—Steering wander may require installation of a steering shaft kit. • Under a special warranty extension campaign, Dodge will replace free of charge torn seat cushion covers or seat cushions. • Hood squeaking, creaking sound on turns or when passing over bumps. • AC hissing noise. **2009–10**—Quad rear doors won't lock or unlock. • Water leaks diagnostic tips. • Under Customer Satisfaction Notification K23, Dodge will replace a corroded front bumper for free. No mileage or time limitations have been imposed. • Another Campaign will tackle poor AC performance by replacing defective air door actuators free of charge. **2009–11**—Fuel filler housing pops out of opening.

RAM PROFILE

	2001	2002	2003	2004	2005	2006	2007	2008	2009
Cost Price ($)									
D-150, 1500	18,750	23,255	23,865	24,910	26,975	26,020	26,395	26,995	23,795
Quad Cab	—	27,280	26,900	—	—	—	—	—	—
SRT-10	—	—	—	61,000	58,465	61,555	—	—	—
Used Values ($)									
D-150, 1500 ▲	3,000	4,000	5,000	5,500	7,000	10,000	11,500	14,500	16,500
D-150, 1500 ▼	2,500	3,000	4,000	5,000	5,500	9,000	10,000	13,000	15,000
Quad Cab ▲	—	5,000	6,000	—	—	—	—	—	—
Quad Cab ▼	—	4,000	5,000	—	—	—	—	—	—
SRT-10 ▲	—	—	—	10,000	13,500	18,500	—	—	—
SRT-10 ▼	—	—	—	9,000	12,000	17,000	—	—	—
Reliability	2	3	3	3	3	2	2	2	2
Crash Safety (F)	5	4	4	5	5	5	5	5	5
Ext. cab	4	—	—	—	—	5	5	—	—
Quad cab	4	—	—	—	—	5	5	—	—
Side	—	—	—	3	—	—	—	—	—
Quad Cab	—	4	5	3	—	—	—	—	—
Side (IIHS)	—	—	—	—	—	—	—	—	2
Offset	1	5	5	5	5	5	5	5	5
Head Restraints (F)	—	—	1	1	1	1	1	1	5
Rollover Resistance	3	3	3	—	4	4	4	4	4

Ford

F-SERIES ★★★★

RATING: Above Average (2007–09); Average (1999–2006). Without question, the F-Series trucks are versatile and brawny haulers, with much-improved handling, a quieter ride, and a more-comfortable interior incorporated into the 2005 model's redesign. Quality control, however, is mediocre at best and life-threatening at its worst, especially on pre-2007 models. Over the past two decades, owners have had to put up with poor-quality powertrain components and serious safety-related defects like sudden tie-rod separation, torsion bar failures, unintended acceleration, and complete loss of braking. **Ideal model year:** Get a 2007 front-drive Fireside STX Regular Cab for about $11,000; it will have had two years to fix the redesigned 2005 factory-related defects. That said, expect some engine, transmission glitches. **"Real" city/highway fuel economy:** Very poor; average real-world fuel economy hovers around 21.0 L/100 km—equal to the Dodge Ram's. 4.2 4x2: 15.1/11.1 L/100 km. 4.6 4x2: 16.2/11.3 L/100 km. 5.4 4x2: 17.4/12.3 L/100 km. 4.2 4x4: 15.9/12.2 L/100 km. 4.6 4x4: 17.4/12.9 L/100 km. 5.4 4x4: 18.6/13.6 L/100 km. **Maintenance/Repair costs:** Higher than average, but easily repaired by independent garages. **Parts:** With the exception of Power Stroke diesels, parts are generally widely available from independent suppliers and are of average cost. **Extended warranty:** An extended powertrain warranty is a must to counter Ford's well-known powertrain glitches. **Best alternatives:** Honda, Mazda, and Nissan pickups are a lot safer and more reliable. Even a Ranger/Mazda B Series are worth considering. Be wary of Toyota's Tacoma and Tundra rust-prone and "runaway" pickups and GM's quality-challenged trucks. **Helpful websites:** *www.carcomplaints.com/Ford/F-150* and *www.fordf150.net/forums*.

Strengths and Weaknesses

In Ford's glory days, it and GM were the only pickup games in town and relations with parts suppliers were cordial. Now, Chrysler, Honda, Nissan, and Toyota are gobbling up Ford's market share and supplier relations are testy at best. Buyers are clamouring for more versatile and reliable trucks that mix high-tech features with dependability and are covered by stronger warranties. Unfortunately, Ford's F-Series revamp in 2005 was too little, too late, and wasn't corrected until the latest redesign of the 2009 models, which gave these pickups more power, passenger room, and features.

The most obvious changes on the 2005s are a new angular styling, a four-door configuration (a first for entry-level trucks), a deeper bed box, an upgraded interior, and a bigger, quieter cab. Ride comfort was improved by creating a roomier interior and adding a new rear suspension. SuperCab models gained 15 cm (6 in.) in cab length plus larger rear doors and entry and exit handles. Other nice touches include a power-sliding rear window controlled by a button on the overhead console, power rear side windows, and an easier-to-lift tailgate that houses a built-in torsion-bar-assist mechanism.

The Ford 4.2L V6 is rated better in fuel economy than the 4.6L V8, but the V8 gets better mileage in the real world. The V6 also was known for oil pump problems, so it has been dropped from the reworked F-150. An engine Ford should have dropped, but didn't—the 300 hp 5.4L V8, known for chronic production glitches—was added a few years ago. It features three valves per cylinder, variable-cam timing, and an electronic throttle control that dealer mechanics are still trying to master.

Safety features on the 2005 and later F-150s were augmented to include multi-stage front airbags; a sensor to determine if the front passenger seat is empty; five three-point seat belts, with the front shoulder belts integrated into the seats; and a LATCH (lower anchors and tethers for children) system to facilitate the installation of child safety seats.

2007 and later F-150s have easy and predictable handling; a pleasant ride on bad roads; well-thought-out ergonomics, instruments, and controls; and fourth-door access. With a few exceptions (like tacky cloth seats), base models are nicely appointed, with lots of handy convenience features and a classy interior. The F-Series offers a commanding view of the road, lots of cab space, and excellent interior ergonomics. The front bench holds three in relative comfort, though there's insufficient footroom for the front centre passenger. They're some of the quietest pickups available.

The 2006 and earlier F-150s' underpowered base V6 engine and 4.6L V8 don't have sufficient passing power. Other pre-2007 problems: questionable engine, transmission, suspension/steering, and brake performance and reliability; poor braking performance with four-wheel ABS; and an uncomfortable rear seat. The climate-control system is a bit slow in warming up the cabin. There's no left footrest on some models, and the cramped and upright rear seats can't match GM's for comfort. Cargo flexibility is compromised by the second-row layout. An inordinate number of serious safety-related complaints have been collected by NHTSA, with cruise-control switch fires, tie-rod end and front torsion bar failures, and steering vibration and drivetrain shudder heading the list. Watch out for violent body shaking when passing over a bumpy highway and for severe dash glare onto the front windshield. Warranty payouts have been unacceptably Scrooge-like in the past, and fuel economy is astoundingly poor.

Apparently, Ford's '97 and '05 redesigns created more bugs than they fixed. In fact, the company's flagship 6.0L diesel engines, introduced in December 2003, were so badly flawed that Ford had to initiate a service program to fix them and buy back over 500 trucks. Their problems included a rough idle, loss of power, stalling, excessive exhaust smoke, leaky fuel injectors, high fuel consumption, and engine seizures. Ford says the engines are fine now, but there are many skeptics.

Another serious defect, afflicting many recent models, is the collapsing tie rods/torsion bars in the steering/suspension system that throw the truck out of control when they fail. Ford has sent a letter to owners asking them to *please* have their vehicles inspected and repaired—at their own cost, of course. That's just another example of Ford's crappy customer relations attitude. Engine and automatic transmission breakdowns top the list of owners' complaints, which extends to failure-prone engine gaskets, timing belt tensioners, oil pumps, fuel injectors, fuel and ignition systems, and drivelines (principally clutches). If that weren't enough, owners have also been burdened with poor-quality front and rear brake components that include premature pad and caliper replacement and chronic rotor warping; faulty powertrain control modules that cause sudden stalling at full throttle; excessive vibration felt throughout the vehicle; front suspension and steering problems; inadequate AC cooling; and early replacement of the AC compressor. There are also body defects up the wazoo, including door cracks on 1997–2000 models; a vibrating sun roof; cracked door hinges and blistering paint on more recent versions.

VEHICLE HISTORY: 2001—The F-150 Crew Cab debuts with four full-sized doors and a full rear-passenger compartment; the 4.6L V8 gains 20 additional horses; the F-250 and F-350 get a horsepower upgrade for the 7.3L Power Stroke turbodiesel engine; the Trailer Tow package becomes standard on all models, as does four-wheel ABS; and the Lightning gets a slight increase in power and a shorter final drive ratio. **2002**—The mid-year return of the Harley-Davidson Edition; SuperCrew models receive 20-inch wheels and special trim; and the 260 hp 5.4L V8 is joined by a 340 hp supercharged variant. **2003**—Lightning models receive a stiffer rear suspension to support a 635 kg (1,400 lb.) payload. **2004**—The entry-level Heritage debuts. **2005**—All models redesigned. **2007**—F-250 and F-350 pickups offer a new 350 hp 6.4L V8 diesel engine to replace the quality-plagued 6.0L diesel. **2008**—A new flexible-fuel 5.4L V8 equips most models. Ford readies the big changes for its 2009 redesign. **2009**—More power and passenger room. A 248 hp 4.6L V8 hooked to a 4-speed automatic transmission replaced the 202 hp V6 as the base engine. A 292 hp version of the 4.6L and a 310–320 hp 5.4L V8, both matched to a 6-speed automatic, also came on board that model year.

Safety Summary

All models/years: Tie-rod and front torsion-bar failures send the truck out of control. • Dangerous front-end bounce. • Sudden acceleration and chronic stalling, mostly blamed on the poor design and positioning of the accelerator and brake pedals. • Sticking accelerator pedal. • Frequent automatic transmission failures; transmission slippage. • Airbag malfunctions. • Brake failure as pedal goes to the floor. • Wheel lug nut failures. • Firestone and Goodrich tire-tread separation. • Gas and brake pedals are mounted too close together. **All models: 2000–01**—Truck parked with emergency brake set rolls down an incline. **2000–02**—Windows suddenly shatter while vehicle is underway. **2001–02**—High seats positioned so that driver stares into the tinted top part of the windshield, and inside rear-view mirror blocks forward visibility. **2001–03**—Driver's seat belt buckle won't fasten. **2002**—Fire ignites under the power-adjusted seat mechanism. • Headlights and dash lights fail intermittently. • Small wheel hubs cause vehicle to vibrate excessively. **2003**—Faulty EGR valve causes throttle to stick wide open and brakes to fail. • Rear axle failure; wheel comes off. • One truck's left front wheel separated, and the truck ran into a wall. • Harley Truck Owners Club (*www.nhtoc.com*) reports that rubber strips on stainless steel gas pedals peel off, making the pedal too slippery. • Fuel-tank leakage. **2004**—Driving with rear window open makes the cabin vibrate violently. • Painful, high-pitched noise comes from the dash area. • Tire chains cannot be used. • Wiper leaves a 15 cm blind spot near the driver's side pillar. **2004–05**—Tailgate falls off. • Excessive vibration and rear-end shudder at highway speeds.

2005—Many complaints of sudden, unintended acceleration with complete loss of braking capability. • When parked, vehicle slips out of gear and goes into Reverse. • Tire jack won't raise truck high enough to allow the mounting of a fully inflated spare. • Faulty ignition keys. 2006—Many complaints of 5.4L V8 engine hesitating or stalling when accelerating. • Reports of faulty fuel pumps leaking fuel onto the exhaust system. • Poorly designed suspension causes the vehicle to jump and shake wildly when passing over a small bump in the road. • Rack-and-pinion steering falls apart. • Sudden brake loss. • Ice accumulates in the wheels. • Many complaints relative to prematurely worn Hankook DynaPro original-equipment tires. 2006–07—Unintended acceleration when braking, or when the cruise control is enabled. 2007—Steering failure in rainy conditions. • Fuel gauge shows empty when the tank is full. • Vision hampered by dash reflection (glare) onto front windshield. • Tire valve stem cracking. 2008—Two separate fires: one ignited under the hood; the other was sourced to the passenger-side dash area. • Fuel poured out of the gas tank from a faulty plastic connection to the fuel pump. • Many reports of sudden, unintended acceleration:

> I own a 2008 Ford F-150 XLT Supercrew ID#1FTPW14578FB09248/ I have been having acceleration problems. Once sitting at an intersection. Luckily I was the first one at the light. This vehicle just started racing and took off on me. Luckily my light just turned green. I put both feet on the brakes and it didn't do a thing as the TAC was buried and engine revving as fast as it would go by then I was in the middle of the intersection and still out of control. I put the truck into neutral. The truck stopped but the engine was racing so fast I thought it was going to blow up. I then put it in park and shut the truck off.

• The accelerator pedal is too large and can be applied when one is braking. • Starter gear shaft self-destructed. • The Special 60th Edition Ford F-150's driveline vibrates excessively. • AC blows hot air only. • Cracked front upper door hinges. • Hankook P235 75R17 tires aren't very durable and Dill tire valve stems on all tires are prone to cracking. • Vehicle side steps aren't sturdy. • Ford's stated towing capability for the F-150 maybe dangerously inaccurate:

> I think it a crime that Ford's put towing weights on their web sites and in booklets and it is false. We bought Ford 150 in March so that we could tow our 32' travel trailer that weighs 7,000 lbs. All documentation states it can pull 9,000 lbs. We have pulled our unit 3 times and every time we pray that we make it to our destination and home safely. I would like to know who rates these vehicles' towing capacity. Our new truck struggles and sways so bad. We have a sway bar too. I am going to go as far as I can to prevent any other poor soul from experiencing what we are experiencing.

2009—Sudden, unintended acceleration. • 6-speed automatic transmission allows the truck to roll backwards when stopped on a grade. • Automatic transmission slips, chatters, surges, and slams into gear. • Water accumulation in the right side kickplate. • Deep grooves in brake rotors. • Smart junction box failure caused the headlights to go out. • Loss of brakes. • Seat belt tightened up and would not release a child.

F-250: **2005**—Faulty diesel engine fuel injectors and exhaust system cause sickening exhaust fumes to enter the cabin. • When the diesel engine is turned off for fuelling, it cannot be restarted. • Engine blows because of a faulty camshaft fuse. • Frequent fuel-pump failures. • Truck will not shift down automatically when carrying a load. • On the highway, the truck vibrates excessively and sways uncontrollably. **2006**—Automatic transmission gear slippage and stalling. • Transmission suddenly downshifts abruptly slowing the truck down. • Recessed gauges and windshield glare impair visibility. • Vehicle stalls just as the accelerator pedal is released. **2007**—Truck is easily stolen:

> All it took for a thief to break into my Ford F-250 was, what the police officer determined, a flat-head screwdriver. It is extremely disturbing to think that all a person has to do is jam a screwdriver under the plate, for the door handle/lock plate, pry down and the door pops open.

• Engine goes to idle with no response to the accelerator. • Violent shaking when passing over a bumpy highway. • Severe dash glare onto the front windshield. *F-350:* **2008**—Diesel exhaust fumes enter into the cabin. • Long delay when accelerating. • Converter/transmission snap ring and solenoid failures. • Multiple brake failures. • When towing a trailer, the brakes don't work at low speeds (10–15 km/h). • Defective brake booster and engine oil pump. • Weak coil springs won't support a plow. **2009**—Sudden loss of power.

Secret Warranties/Internal Bulletins/Service Tips

All models: 1999–2002—High idle speeds; throttle sticks in cold weather. **1999–2005**—Ford will install a special axle kit to stop rear axle noise. Ford's bulletin admission of this defect is actionable in small claims court if the company won't pay for the six-hour repair. • Water leaking from the roof flange area accumulates in the headliner. The leak may also occur at the cab floor pan area. • Drivetrain drive-away shudder or vibration. **1999–2006**—A driveline clunk may signal that the slip yoke needs lubrication. Check this out before spending money on more-involved tests or repairs. • Tips for correcting a rough idle. • Paint delamination, peeling, or fading. • Troubleshooting broken intake manifold studs. **2000–05**—Seat belts slow to retract. Engine power loss in hot weather. • Vacuum or air leaks in the intake manifold and engine. • Faulty ignition switch lock cylinder. **2003–06**—Inoperative AC; compressor leakage. **2004**—Faulty handle cables could make it impossible to open the doors from the inside. **2004–05**—Remedy for warm engine knocking or ticking. • Correction of axle chatter, shudder, or vibration during low-speed turning. • Remedies for steering-wheel and body vibrations. • Upgraded brake rotors will be installed to stop brake shudder and vibration. • Cooling fan noise on trucks equipped with 4.6L and 5.4L engines. • Butyl bed pad removal to prevent corrosion. **2004–07**—Aluminum body panel corrosion. **2004–08**—Power-steering-line fluid seepage in cold weather. • Excessive steering-wheel vibration (80–105 km/h). • High-speed driveline vibration. • Intermittent brake vibration, shudder. • Side cowl panel may pop up. • Power steering fluid leakage in cold weather. • Tailgate rattle. • Erratic fuel gauge readings:

2004–08 F-150; 2006–08 Mark LT

ISSUE: Some 2004–08 F-150 and 2006–08 Mark LT vehicles, built before 12/3/2007, may exhibit erratic fuel gauge operation or illuminated malfunction indicator lamp (MIL) with diagnostic trouble codes (DTCs) P0460 or P0463, and/or Instrument Cluster Module DTC B1201. This may be caused by sulfur contamination in the fuel causing an open or high resistance in the fuel level sender.

ACTION: Install a new fuel level sender following the service procedure instruction sheet provided in the fuel sender kit.

WARRANTY STATUS: Eligible Under Provisions Of New Vehicle Limited Warranty Coverage and Emissions Warranty Coverage.

Is that clear? This is a warrantable item. Don't pay a cent for this fuel gauge repair (estimated non-warranty cost: $300).

2005—Engine stalls when shifting into Drive or Reverse, or when coming to a stop. • Hard starts; rough running; engine won't crank. • Excessive steering-wheel shimmy after passing over bumps. **2005–07**—Power rear sliding window may need a new motor. • Power windows are slow to roll up. **2005–08**—Sunroof water leaks. • Troubleshooting steering wheel nibble, vibration. • Cannot control AC output temperature. • Grinding noise heard when the AC changes modes. • Banging, clunking front suspension noise when driving in cold temperatures (install new front springs under warranty). **2005–10**—Inadvertent transmission lock-up during 1–2 shifts. **2006–08**—Shudder on acceleration and deceleration; binding in turns. **2007–08**—Engine RPM flare during 3–4 upshift; runs rough, hesitates after a cold start; misfires while cruising; idler pulley noise after a cold start. • Free tire valve stem inspection or replacement. **2009**—Engine, shift hesitation. • Erratic operation of the automatic transmission. • Steering assist varies. **2009–10**—Low frequency hot idle engine knocking noise. • Right driveshaft slip, bump condition. • Shudder, vibration upon acceleration. Water leak near right-hand assist handle. *Diesels:* **2003–04**—Remedies for 6.0L diesel engines that lose power, have fuel in oil, or run roughly are covered in TSB #03-14-6. **2003–05**—Troubleshooting tips for misfire, lack of power, excessive smoke, and excessive cranking to start. Keep in mind that Ford *must* pay for this troubleshooting and repair under the little-publicized, though much-longer, emissions warranty. Don't take no for an answer. **2003–06**—TSB #06-9-7, issued May 15, 2006, gives more diagnostic and repair tips for poorly performing diesel engines. **2003–07**—Erratic automatic transmission shifting over 90 km/h. **2008–09**—Customer Satisfaction Campaign #09B08 will replace the 6.4L diesel engine injectors for free, plus give you a free oil filter and oil change, no matter the mileage or number of previous owners. **2008–09**—Cold weather automatic transmission failures on vans and trucks equipped with a 6.4L diesel engine and a 5R110W transmission. • One-way clutch failure is common. Ford will cover the failure under its warranty.

F-SERIES PROFILE

	2001	2002	2003	2004	2005	2006	2007	2008	2009
Cost Price ($)									
XL	22,710	23,310	23,380	22,850	23,840	22,499	22,499	22,199	24,199
Fireside STX	—	—	—	—	—	—	27,099	26,699	—
Used Values ($)									
XL ▲	3,500	4,000	5,000	6,000	7,000	8,000	10,000	11,500	16,500
XL ▼	3,000	3,500	4,000	5,000	6,000	7,000	8,500	10,000	15,000
Fireside STX ▲	—	—	—	—	—	—	11,500	14,000	—
Fireside STX ▼	—	—	—	—	—	—	10,000	12,500	—
Reliability	2	2	2	2	3	3	4	4	4
Crash Safety (F)	5	5	—	5	5	5	5	5	5
Side	5	5	5	—	—	—	—	—	5
Ext. cab	4	4	4	—	—	—	—	—	5
Side (IIHS)	5	5	5	—	—	—	—	—	5
SuperCrew	—	5	5	—	—	—	—	—	5
Offset	1	1	1	5	5	5	5	5	5
Head Restraints (F)	—	—	—	1	1	1	1	1	5
Rollover Resistance	—	—	3	4	4	4	4	4	4
4×4	—	—	2	4	4	4	4	4	4

Ford/Mazda

RANGER/B-SERIES ★★★★

RATING: Above Average (2008–09); Average (1999–2007). Mazda pickups are generally the least expensive of the "gang of three" small Japanese pickups (Mazda, Nissan, and Toyota). From the 1994 model onward, your Mazda is really a Ford Ranger. Overall, both the Ford and Mazda are acceptable buys, but their highway performance is mediocre. Powertrain defects are worrisome for their frequency and their high repair cost. **Ideal model year:** Get a 2008 XL front-drive Ranger that for about $7,000. It originally cost $15,400. Earlier, cheaper Rangers have too many powertrain, suspension, and brake failures. **"Real" city/highway fuel economy:** 4×2 and 2.5: 11.7/8.8 L/100 km. 4×2 and 3.0: 14.0/9.4 L/100 km. 4×2 and 4.0: 13.9/9.7 L/100 km. 4×4 and 3.0: 14.8/10.6 L/100 km. 4×4 and 4.0: 14.7/10.9 L/100 km. Owners report fuel consumption is often way higher than these averages. **Maintenance/Repair costs:** Below average; the wide availability of cheaper, independent garages keeps costs down. **Parts:** Parts are easy to find and relatively inexpensive when bought from independent suppliers. **Extended warranty:** A toss-up. Most components are fairly durable, except for some powertrain, brake, and electrical glitches. **Best alternatives:** A Dodge Ram, equipped with manual transmission and a Cummins diesel, a Honda Ridgeline, or a Nissan Frontier V6. **Helpful websites:** *www.carcomplaints.com/Ford/Ranger*; *www.therangerstation.com/forums/forumdisplay.php?f=86*; and *http://forums. mazdaworld.org/109-b-series-truck*.

 ## Strengths and Weaknesses

Good engine performance (4.0L V6), well-designed interior, comfortable seating, user-friendly control layout, four-door extended cab, good off-road handling, and good resale value. On the minus side: a weak 4-cylinder engine (carried over into early 2001), a fuel-thirsty 3.0L V6, a harsh ride, excessive braking distance, the 4×4's extra height hinders easy entry and exit, rear doors are hinged at the back and won't open independent of the front doors, the spare tire can be difficult to remove, and many safety-related complaints reported to NHTSA. Assembly and component quality are average. Reliability isn't impressive. Owners note some engine problems (poor idle, surge, and stalling), erratic transmission performance and failure, and brake and fuel system problems. Other negatives: wind noise from the windshield cowl, top-of-door glass seal, or the weather stripping moulding area; water leaks through the rear window; mediocre AC performance; and premature paint peeling and delamination.

VEHICLE HISTORY: 2001—Models got the Explorer's 207 hp 4.0L SOHC V6; the flexible-fuel feature on the 3.0L V6 is dropped; and a new base 2.3L 4-cylinder replaced the 2.5L. ABS is a standard feature. **2002**—Models joined by an XLT FX4 off-road 4×4 model, which comes equipped with heavy-duty suspension, 31-inch tires, a heftier skid plate, and tow hooks. **2003**—3.0L V6 engine gets eight more horses. All model add thicker glass and more insulation. **2006**—A slightly restyled exterior. **2009**—No more 3.0L V6. Model lineup is reduced to a 143 hp 2.3L 4-cylinder or a 207 hp 4.0L V6.

Safety Summary

All models/years: Ford Ranger and Mazda B-series passengers slam their heads into the back glass during sudden stops or in rear-end collisions. • Steering-wheel lock-up. • Excessive shaking when cruising. • Malfunctioning airbags; burns caused by airbag deployment. • Defective tie-rod. • When parked on an incline with shifter lever in Park, vehicle jumps into Neutral and rolls away. • Transmission failures:

> Ford tech consultants revealed that this is happening to many Ford Rangers, but no recall has been issued. Apparently, the torque on the transmission was increased without redesigning the transmission or seals to be able to withstand the higher torque.

• Driveshaft sheared off while driving at high speed. • Fuel leaks (tank and fuel lines). • Sudden acceleration, often when braking. • A faulty idle air control valve may be responsible for the vehicle not decelerating properly. • Stalling. • Complete loss of ABS. • Gas and brake pedals are too close together. • Brakes don't work properly, with stuck brake calipers, overheating, and excessive pad and rotor wear. • Windshield wiper comes on by itself, or won't come on at all. • Tire-tread separation. *Ranger:* **2001**—Excessive wander on the highway, especially when passing over uneven terrain or after hitting potholes. • Inaccurate fuel-tank level indicator and fuel gauge. • Fuel tank overflows when refuelling. • Brake line abraded by rubbing against leaf spring. • Excessive vibration. • Passenger-side seat belt unbuckles at random. **2002**—A large number of serious safety-related incidents have been reported. • Sudden acceleration after vehicle jumps from Park into gear. • Premature replacement of clutch slave cylinder. • Complete brake failure because of a defective idle control, among other causes. • Rear shock absorbers quickly wear out. • Front tire falls off because of defective carter pin. • Interior and exterior lights go out intermittently. **2003**—Throttle sticks as pedal sinks to the floor. • Misaligned driver-side door allows wind and water entry. **2004**—Chronic stalling, loss of power. • Stuck accelerator. • Airbags failed to deploy. • Vehicle left in Park with the engine idling shifted into Reverse. • Transmission slippage; slams into gear. • Frequent brake lock-up when brakes are applied. • When the front seat was pushed rearward, a window popped out. • High rear head restraints block side and rear visibility. • Odometer can't be seen in daylight. **2005**—Vehicle stalls on the highway repeatedly because of a defective inertia switch. • Ford assembly-line worker says the Ranger rear axle sway bar is mounted incorrectly and designed poorly. **2006**—Many more reports that a faulty inertia switch causes the truck to stall randomly:

> This switch is designed to cut electric to fuel pump in crash but most often fails during normal driving operation. This is not a unique complaint to 2006, but by other years reported on the Internet. This problem has existed for many years and is probably responsible for more deaths due to errant operation than it saved lives in a crash. Another example of what seems like a good idea gone bad.

• Leaking drivetrain seals cause the pinion bearing to fail ($1,000 U.S. to repair). • Front wheel bearing failures. • Rapid wearout of Goodyear Wrangler tires. • Wipers come on when they shouldn't and won't engage when they should. • Steering wheel cap has a gap that catches driver's clothing, cuffs, buttons, when the wheel is turned. **2007**—Fire ignites in the passenger-side dash airbag housing. • Airbag failed to deploy. • Sudden failure of the front control arm. • Side doors shake and rattle at highway speeds. • Excessive shimmy and shake at 70 km/h. • Exterior mirrors are too small. • Ice and snow build up in the grooves of the wheels. • Many complaints of cracked tire valve stems that cause tires to rapidly lose air on the road:

> They indicate that if my vehicle is still under warranty they can be replaced free of charge. Well I drive a lot and have 50K on my truck. Ford has poor warranties and it is not my fault they did not properly test these valve stems prior to deploying them. I only had my truck for 1 1/2 years before the first failure. This kind of stuff needs to be fixed.

2008—Fire ignited from fuel leaking from the gas tank. • Chronic stalling on the highway forces driver to "stand" on the brakes to avoid hitting other vehicles. • When the vehicle is underway, the front passenger-side door moves as if it were not properly latched. • The non-tilting steering wheel hampers tall drivers from lifting their foot from the gas pedal to apply the brakes. • The brake and gas pedals are too close together and placed at the same height. • Goodyear Wrangler tires are suitable only for passenger cars, not light pickups; the tires hydroplane too easily. 2009—Truck won't slow down after the gas pedal is released. • Rotors need to be turned after a year's use. • Excessive steering shake. • In cold weather, doors freeze shut. • Continental Conti-Trac tire sidewall blows out.

Secret Warranties/Internal Bulletins/Service Tips

All models: Keep in mind that Ford service bulletins will likely also apply to Mazda, and Mazda's to Ford. *Ranger:* **1993–2008**—Paint delamination, peeling, or fading. **1995–2002**—Automatic transmission slips or has a delayed engagement. **1997–2003**—Front-drive axle vent tube leaks. *B-series:* **All years:** TSB #006/94 outlines all the possible causes and remedies for brake vibration or pulsation. **1997–2005**—Front axle leaks. **1998–2003**—Wind noise around doors. • Seat track rattling. **1998–2005**—Driveline clunk remedy. **2001**—Unable to reach wide open throttle, lack of power. • 3.0L engine leaks oil at the oil filter mounting surface. • Vacuum or air leaks in the intake manifold. • 4.0L engine may lose power or have a low idle when first started. • Clutch may be hard to disengage. • Delayed Reverse engagement. • Faulty speedometer. • 2.3L engine may idle poorly and surge or hesitate when accelerating. • Automatic transmission fluid leaks. • Manual transmission–equipped vehicles may lose power when decelerating. • Damaged fuel-return line. • Fluid leaks from the front axle vent tube. • Heater core leaks. • Air leaks or vacuum in the intake manifold or engine. • Faulty ignition switch lock cylinder. **2001–10**—4.0L engine buzzing. **2002–03**—Noisy manual transfer-case shifter. **2002–09**—Rear brake "grabbing." **2003–06**—Inoperative AC; compressor. **2004–05**—No Third gear. **2004–08**—Clutch slave cylinder noise when shifting. **2004–09**—Squeaking clutch pedal. **2005–08**—Steering wheel vibration, nibble. **2007–09**—On vehicles equipped with a 4.0L engine: starter motor screeching; delayed engagement from Park or Neutral to Drive or Reverse. **2007–10**—Delayed automatic transmission engagement. **2008–09**—Window chatter/shudder when it is operated. **2008**—Coolant leak from the block heater. *Mazda 2300:* **2002–09**—Rear drum brakes grabbing. **2007–09**—Engine drone, moan at idle. **2007–10**—Cold starts produce a high idle speed.

RANGER/B-SERIES PROFILE

	2001	2002	2003	2004	2005	2006	2007	2008	2009
Cost Price ($)									
Ranger/XL	16,995	18,595	17,395	16,775	17,810	18,299	18,299	15,399	15,899
B2300/3000	16,680	16,680	16,995	17,395	17,595	17,995	17,995	14,995	15,250
B4000 4×4	27,495	27,495	28,840	28,495	28,695	27,295	27,496	22,375	18,995

Used Values ($)								
Ranger/XL ▲	2,000	2,500	3,000	3,500	4,500	5,000	6,000	7,500	9,500
Ranger/XL ▼	1,500	2,000	2,500	3,000	4,000	4,500	5,000	6,000	8,000
B2300/3000 ▲	1,500	1,500	2,000	2,500	3,000	3,500	5,500	7,000	9,000
B2300/3000 ▼	1,000	1,000	1,500	2,000	2,500	3,000	4,000	6,000	7,500
B4000 4×4 ▲	3,500	4,000	4,500	5,000	6,000	7,500	10,000	11,000	12,500
B4000 4×4 ▼	3,000	3,500	4,000	4,500	5,000	6,000	8,500	10,000	11,000

Reliability	3	3	3	3	3	3	3	4	4
Crash Safety (F)	4	4	4	4	4	4	5	5	5
Side	4	5	5	5	5	5	5	5	5
Offset	—	—	—	—	—	—	—	3	3
Head Restraints (F)	—	—	—	5	5	1	1	1	1
Rollover Resistance	3	3	3	—	3	3	3	3	3

Note: Although a new Mazda B4000 4×4 once cost almost $10,000 more than the Ford Ranger, this difference is now just a few thousand dollars.

General Motors

C/K, SIERRA, SILVERADO ★★★

RATING: Average (2006–09); Below Average (1999–2005). **Ideal model year:** Get a mediocre 2007 front-drive Silverado for about $8,000, instead of the $25,000 it cost new. Yes, it is improved, but only when compared with earlier Silverado models. At least you keep your buy-in low, may have some original warranty left, and can sell it a few years down the road for $5,000. For diesel towing, I'd save my pennies and get a new 2011 diesel-equipped model. **"Real" city/highway fuel economy:** *4.3 V6 manual: 14.1/9.5 L/100 km. 4.3 V6 automatic: 14.6/10.6 L/100 km. 4.8 V8 automatic: 14.6/10.5 L/100 km. 5.3 V8 automatic: 16.2/12.0 L/100 km. 5.3 V8 automatic hybrid: 10.4/13.2 L/100 km. 6.0 V8 automatic: 16.6/11.7 L/100 km.* **Maintenance/Repair costs:** Upkeep costs for these trucks are high; use independent garages to keep costs down. **Parts:** Mechanical parts are widely available and reasonably priced due to the proliferation of independent suppliers. The 2007 model's body parts may be costly and in short supply due to that year's changes and the reluctance of most dealers to invest in large parts inventory. **Extended warranty:** A good idea for the powertrain, judging by consumer complaints and the high incidence of diesel engine deficiencies. **Best alternatives:** A used Dodge Ram with a manual transmission and a Cummins diesel, Ford's Ranger or F-Series, Honda's Ridgeline, a Mazda B-Series, or a Nissan Frontier V6. **Helpful websites:** *www.gmtruckclub. com/forum/forum.php*; *www.carcomplaints.com/Chevrolet/Silverado*; and *www. carcomplaints.com/Chevrolet/1500_Pickup.*

Strengths and Weaknesses

Similar to Detroit's other pickups, these models are classed as 1500 half-ton, 2500 three-quarter-ton, and 3500 one-ton models. They come with a wide range of engine options, body styles, and bed sizes. The "C" designation refers to 4×2, and the "K" designation to 4×4. The 3500 series offers a four-door cab with a full rear seat. The variety of cab and cargo bed combinations, along with a choice of suspensions, makes these pickups adaptable to just about any use. Standard features include one of the biggest cabs among pickups, a fourth door, a three-piece modular truck frame, rack-and-pinion steering, and four-wheel disc brakes with larger pads and rotors.

An AutoTrac AWD drivetrain allows the driver to select an automatic mode that delivers full-time 4×4 (particularly useful if you live in a snowbelt area), while a 4-speed automatic features an innovative tow/haul mode that stretches out the upshifts to tap the engine's power at its maximum. GM also offers a potent family of four Vortec V8s in addition to a 6.6L turbodiesel (360 hp), 16-inch tires and wheels, and the highest minimum ground clearance among the Detroit pickups.

Chevy and GMC full-sized pickups are good domestic workhorses—when they're running. Of course, that's the problem: They're not dependable. On the one hand, they have a large, quiet cabin and give relatively easy access to the interior. On the other hand, their size and heft make for lousy fuel economy, a mediocre ride, and subpar handling and braking. Resale value? Don't ask.

For over a decade, Sierras and Silverados have been plagued with severe vibrations that GM has routinely ignored. Owners have nicknamed their trucks "Shakerados," and they say that the new frame braces added to the 2001s to stop the shakes haven't worked (see *agmlemon.freeservers.com/index.html*).

Never-ending powertrain and brake repairs and complaints of excessive vibration often sideline the vehicle for days at a time, and dealer repair suggestions often don't make any sense. GM plant workers claim that the porous frame used on both Sierras and Silverados cracks behind the cabin and near the tow hook. Original-equipment springs are also failing en masse:

> The front springs on 2003 Chevrolet 1500 [Silverado] Quad Cab trucks are collapsing and GMC/Chevrolet knows about problem and says…the owners [are] responsible to fix their mistake in designing and engineering the truck. They sent out a technical service bulletin to all dealers about [the] problem and [it] says…the owners need to pay $18.00…for rubber bushing to push up spring and $380.00 in labor.

The 1999–2006 models got many new features that make them more powerful, versatile, and accommodating, and they're safer than previous models. However, these changes also make them less reliable than the pickups they replaced. Major powertrain, brake, suspension, electrical system, and body deficiencies have turned these "dream machines" into motoring nightmares.

The 6.0L Duramax diesel has always had serious reliability and performance problems. The base 4.3L V6 needs more grunt, the transmission hunts for the right gear and produces an incessant whine, the base suspension provides a too-compliant ride, and there's insufficient room for the driver to reach between the door panel and seat to access the seat-adjusting mechanism. And an incredibly high number of performance- and safety-related complaints regarding 2006 and earlier models have been reported to NHTSA and confirmed through confidential bulletins, whistle-blowers, and disappointed owners.

2007–09 Sierra and Silverado

This redesign for 2007 produced mediocre trucks with only marginally improved performance and reliability. The new diesel engines are expected to have serious performance and quality failings during their first few years on the market, judging by the Duramax's prior performance. Nevertheless, these models do have a number of improvements that include a larger cabin, high ground clearance, good noise insulation, and a rattle-resistant body. You will also find a more-stylish interior; user-friendly instruments and controls; large, supportive seats; lots of leg clearance; and wide-opening doors with useful pull-lever handles.

On the other hand, there are many minuses with the newer models: Hybrid systems and cylinder deactivation haven't produced promised fuel savings. You still get a mediocre ride, problems with brakes and steering are omnipresent, and handling continues to be compromised by lots of body roll and under-steer when cornering, and by serious chassis shake when going over potholed roads. Quality control is only slightly better than with previous models.

VEHICLE HISTORY: 2001—Debut of three-quarter-ton and one-ton versions of the Silverado. They offer two engines: the 6.6L Isuzu-built Duramax V8 diesel and GM's homegrown 8.1L Vortec V8. A traction-assist feature is introduced on rear-drive V8 automatics. The Sierra C3 luxury truck offers a number of new features, including a 325 hp 6.0L Vortec V8, full-time all-wheel drive (no 2-speed transfer case for serious off-roading, though), upgraded four-wheel disc anti-lock brakes, an increased-capacity suspension system, and a luxuriously appointed interior. The Sierra HD truck lineup comes with stronger frames; beefed-up suspensions, axles, brakes, and cooling systems; new sheet metal; bigger interiors; and three new V8s: a 6.6L Duramax turbodiesel and two gas engines, a hefty 8.1L and an improved 6.0L. **2003**—Quadrasteer expands to other models; improved electrical system and passenger-side airbag sensor; a new centre console; and dual-zone temperature and steering-wheel controls. **2004**—Standard cruise control, power door locks, and a CD player. **2006**—A new 360 hp 6.6L V8 turbodiesel engine late in the model year; Quadrasteer option dropped. **2007**—Active Fuel Management cylinder deactivation with the 5.3L V8; more-powerful engines (the 4.8L V8 gets 10 more horses, the 5.3L gets five more, and the 6.0L gets 22 more); a 980 kg (2,160 lb.) payload rating; and towing capability boosted to 4,763 kg (10,500 lb.). Also, a reinforced chassis, upgraded suspension and steering systems, a larger cabin and bed, and new exterior and interior styling. Standard stability control on

Crew Cabs. **2008**—A minor instrument panel revision. **2009**—A hybrid model for the 1500; a new 403 hp 6.2L V8; and a 6-speed automatic transmission.

Safety Summary

All models/years: Sudden, unintended acceleration. • Airbag fails to deploy. • Intermittent loss of power steering. • Brake failures (pedal goes to the metal with no braking effect) with ABS light constantly lit. • Brake pad failure and warped rotor. • Parking brake doesn't hold. • ABS doesn't engage; results in extended stopping distances and wheel lock-up. • Chronic stalling. **All models: 2000–01**—Fuel line leakage; allows fuel to spray out rear. **2001**—Loose lug nuts cause left rear wheel to fall off. • Spongy brakes lead to extended stopping distances. • After driving in snow and parking vehicle, brakes won't work. • When accelerating from a stop, vehicle momentarily goes into Neutral. • Transmission suddenly shifts from Fifth down to Third or Second gear while cruising on the highway. • Defective transmission valve body results in transmission jumping out of gear. • Drifting all over the highway. • Driver's seat belt causes pain in the shoulder. • Upper ball joint and right sway bar ends may be missing nuts and cotter keys. **2002**—Fire ignites in the dash. • Throttle sticks. • Chronic engine surging when braking. • Automatic transmission suddenly downshifts when accelerating, as engine surges then clunks into gear. • Passenger-side front end suddenly collapses (replace outer tie-rod end). • Steel wheel collects water that freezes and throws wheel out of balance. • Steering-column bolt comes apart. • Interior rear-view mirror distortion. • Dimmer switch overheats. • Driver's seatback will suddenly fall backwards. • Head restraint blocks vision to right side of vehicle. **2002–04**—Steering wheel locks up while driving. **2003**—Fire ignites in the engine compartment. • Cracked transmission transfer case. • Automatic transmission slips when shifting from First to Second gear. • 4×4 shifts erratically, causing serious highway instability. • Seat belts lock up. • Tailgate pops open. **2004**—Front axle assembly collapses. • Sway bar mounting bracket breaks, causing the frame and mounting bar to come off. • Brakes are too soft and set too close to the accelerator pedal. • Cruise control surges when going downhill. • Transmission suddenly jumps from Second gear to Reverse. • Tailgate falls apart. • Doors won't unlock in cold weather. • Driver's door window shatters for no reason. • Hood coil spring fails. • Jack slips off the vehicle. • Side mirrors constantly vibrate and are easily scratched when wiped clean. **2005**—Airbag warning light comes on, even when seat is occupied by an adult. • Sudden acceleration and chronic stalling:

> Diesel system has a problem transferring fuel into the truck for use. It runs out while the front fuel tank is still full of fuel. The fuel tank never reads over half full.

• Transmission slips when accelerating, making the truck an easy target when turning into an intersection. • Sudden driveshaft failure:

> GMC Sierra 1500 Crew Cab; while driving at interstate speed, the drive shaft fell off the vehicle and shattered. There was substantial damage to the underside of the vehicle, including muffler, yoke, heat shield, and drive shaft.

• The 4.3L engine and 4-speed automatic transmission work poorly together, constantly downshifting and gear hunting when going up an incline. • On diesels, fuel gauge and transfer pump fail repeatedly. • Rear diesel tank sprays fuel on the highway. • Vehicle is hard to move from a stopped position; feels like the rear brakes are locked up (change master cylinder). • Front brakes seem to stick, then overheat and catch fire. • Leaf springs aren't very durable. • Wheel hubcap nuts overheat, and the hubcaps fly off. • Interior door handles easily snag clothes or purse straps when opening the door. • Front doors won't close properly. • Outside rear-view mirrors don't show the rear bumper area when backing up and are useless when hauling a trailer. • Jack bends under weight of vehicle and collapses. **2006**—Erratic cruise-control performance:

> When you are driving using the cruise control and start up a hill the truck slows down at least 10 miles an hour [16 km/h] then suddenly without warning the cruise control system jolts the truck forward trying to compensate for the loss of speed.... It has happened to us going up hills and around hilly curves. If I did not keep both hands on the wheel I very well could have lost control and crashed.

• Rear drum brakes perform poorly. • Loose steering:

> The intermediate shaft on the steering wheel column is loose. The dealer and manu-facturer have told me that they are aware of this problem, but there is no fix for it. The front end on the vehicle will feel loose and bounce while driving over uneven pavement and bumps and more so while driving on freeways.

• Out-of-round General tires; Goodyear Wrangler tire-tread separation. • Front tires rub against the suspension when the steering wheel is turned. • Automatic door lock cannot be overridden. • Headliner falls down. **2006–07**—Hard-shifting manual transmission. **2007**—Passenger-side airbag is disabled even though an adult is seated. • The 5.3L V8 with Active Fuel Management will not idle properly or slow down in a timely manner. • Steering, brake lock-up. • Dash gauges are hard to read in daylight (especially the speedometer). • Truck bounces all over the road. • Failed welds under the front seat. • Windshield distortion. • Windshield wiper and washer fluid come on for no reason. • Prematurely worn Bridgestone Dueler tires. • Inoperative tire-pressure monitor system. • Cracked tow hitch receiver. **2008–09**—Failure of doorlock actuators, accompanied by a shock to whomever touched the inside door handle to exit the truck. **2008**—Vehicle will suddenly stall while underway. • Erratic AC performance. • Fire ignites near the transmission. • Premature wearout of the brake pads and rotors. • Spare tire is different than the others. • Windshield cracking under the driver-side moulding. • Rear driver-side tire/wheel fell off. **2009**—Vehicle caught fire due to a defective under-hood wiring harness. • In another fire, the fire's origin was determined to be the electronic control module in the front dash area. • A third fire reportedly started in the passenger-side dashboard area, also while parked. • Sudden, unintended acceleration. • Airbag fails to deploy. • Both curtain side airbags deployed when truck went over a pothole • Poorly designed head restraints. Short drivers will have their head pushed too far forward. • Engine suddenly shuts down. Driver must wait five minutes, then re-start. • Cruise control doesn't slow down the vehicle on grades or small slopes. • Overheated door wiring can burn a hole in the interior door panel. • Child can open the doors while truck is in motion. • Doors shake and rattle when driving, despite recall to change the striker plate (hinges, latches, and seals were all replaced. • Weak brake pedal back pressure causes the brakes to feel spongy as they go all the way to the floor. Driver has to continually pump the brake to stop:

> Really bad in an emergency stop or when you have a light trailer on that doesn't require separate brakes on trailer. I had it both on 1500 4×4 2008 GMC and on the same 2009 Chevy I have now.

• Premature brake rotor (warped) replacement. • Headlights flicker constantly. They flash on and off whenever the brakes are applied. • Sun visors don't block the sun's rays sufficiently. • Passenger's rear window shattered while the pickup was parked. • General AmeriTrac tires have premature wear on the sides and flat spots on the tread. • Spare tire is 17 inches; all four original equipment tires are 18. • Spare tire fell from underneath the 2500 Silverado. It was determined the tire was too heavy for the supporting brackets.

Secret Warranties/Internal Bulletins/Service Tips

All models: 1999–2004—Prematurely worn and noisy brake rotors and pads may be replaced with higher-quality aftermarket parts for about half the price. • GM says in TSB #00-05-23-005B that owners should invest in a GM mud flap kit (Part #15765007) to make their rear brakes last longer. Again, save money by shopping at independent retailers. • Inoperative power windows. • Remedy for steering-wheel clunk. • Suspension clunk, slap. **1999–2005**—Install an exhaust system flex pipe kit to stop an exhaust moan, vibration. **1999–2007**—Engine misfire may be due to an ECM ground terminal that has corroded with rust. Inspect the main engine wiring harness ground terminal (G103) for this condition. **1999–2009**—Silencing rear leaf spring noise. **2000–04**—Troubleshooting delayed gear engagement. **2000–05**—Rattle, squeak from front of vehicle. **2001**—Loose engine connecting-rod bolts may cause engine knock and complete engine failure. • No-starts or hard starts. • Harsh shift remedies. • When in 4×4 and in Reverse gear, engine won't go over 1000–1300 rpm. • Transmission slips when placed in 4×4. • Automatic transmission 2–4 band or 3–4 clutch damage. • Inoperative wiper motor; fuse blows repeatedly. • Windows are slow to defrost. • Steering-column lock shaft doesn't lock. **2001–02**—Troubleshooting tips to correct no-starts, a blank PRNDL, or slow or no automatic transmission engagement. **2001–03**—The torque converter relief spring and lube regulator spring may need to be changed to correct automatic transmission delayed shifts or loss of power. • TSB #01-07-30-043 and 03-07-30-031 explain why the automatic transmission may slip or leak. **2001–05**—Fuel gauge reads empty on trucks with a spare tank. **2002**—1–2 shift shudder. • Clunk noise from under the hood. • Clunk, bump, or squawk heard when accelerating or coming to a stop. • Shudder or vibration when accelerating from a stop. • Driveline growl or prop shaft ring noise. • Steering shaft clunk. • Noisy brakes. • Water leak at the roof centre clearance light. • Inability to control temperature setting. • Intermittent failing of the tail lights, backup lights, or trailer harness. **2002–09**—Front axle whine or click. **2003**—Harsh automatic transmission 1–2 shifting; slipping caused by a faulty pressure control solenoid (TSB #03-07-30-020, May 2003). **2003–04**—Inoperative front power window. **2004**—Cold engine rattling. **2004–10**—Underbody pop, clunk when turning. **2005** Troubleshooting tips for poor automatic transmission performance. • Free replacement of the powertrain/engine control module; courtesy transportation available. **2004–07**—Noisy engine drivebelt. **2005–11**—Reduced engine power (repair instrument panel to body harness connector. **2006–07**—V8 engine oil leaks. • AC doesn't cool; noisy compressor. **2007**—No-starts; loss of power. • Power-steering leaks. • Water leaks into the rear footwell area. • Exhaust system noise. **2007–08**—Sunroof water leak onto headliner. • Front fender buzz, rattle. • Compressor, serpentine belt noise. • AC defaults to full Hot or full Cold. **2007–09**—Flare and/or harsh 2–3 shifts. • Oil leak at oil cooler hose/pipe assembly. • Clunk noise when stopping or starting out. • Buzzing, snapping, or popping exhaust system. • Door wind noise and water leaks. **2007–10**—Rear suspension clunking noise. • Excessive interior wind noise. • Engine valve lifter tick noise at startup. • Inoperative heated seats. • Warped fender liners. • Troubleshooting sunroof leaks. • Sun visor fails to stay in place **2007–11**—Engine oil leak at engine oil cooler hose/pipe adapter to engine. • Inoperative low-beam headlights. • Front end suspension noises. • Exhaust heat shield buzz. • Squeak noise from rear of vehicle. **2008**—Campaign for tire bead inspection and free tire replacement if needed. **2008–09**—Poor AC performance; not cold enough. • Side door window problems. • Water leaks onto driver's side floor. **2008–11**—Steering fluid leaks. **2009–11**—Front brake pulsation, vibration (install upgraded brake pads). • Exhaust system leak, rattle, or rumble. *Diesel engines:* **1999–2002**—Special policy covers fuel injection pump failure up to 11 years/193,000 km:

SPECIAL POLICY ADJUSTMENT (REPLACE INJECTOR)

BULLETIN NO.: 04039   DATE: JUNE 2004

2001–02 Silverado/Sierra (6.6l Duramax Diesel)

CONDITION: Some customers of 2001–02 model year Chevrolet Silverado and GMC Sierra vehicles, equipped with a 6.6L Duramax Diesel (RPO LB7—VIN Code 1) engine, may experience vehicle service engine soon (SES) light illumination, low engine power, hard start, and/or fuel in crankcase, requiring injector replacement, as a result of high fuel return rates due to fuel injector body cracks or ball seat erosion.

SPECIAL POLICY ADJUSTMENT: This special policy covers the condition described above for a period of 7 years or 200,000 miles (320,000 km), whichever occurs first, from the date the vehicle was originally placed in service, regardless of ownership. The repairs will be made at no charge to the customer.

2001–04—Free O-ring replacement:

2001–06—Troubleshooting a turbocharger failure. **2004–10**—Oil leak at charge air cooler/air inlet adapter. **2007–09**—GM say 6.6L Duramax diesel ticking is acceptable. **2008**—Free replacement of the turbocharger vane position sensor on the 6.6L diesel.

C/K, SIERRA, SILVERADO PROFILE

	2001	2002	2003	2004	2005	2006	2007	2008	2009
Cost Price ($)									
Sierra, Silverado	21,960	22,410	23,330	24,070	24,925	22,650	28,245	28,395	23,990
Hybrid	—	—	—	—	35,140	42,040	33,025	—	46,725
Used Values ($)									
Sierra, Silverado ▲	3,500	4,000	4,500	5,000	6,500	8,000	12,000	14,000	16,500
Sierra, Silverado ▼	3,000	3,500	4,000	4,500	5,000	7,000	10,500	13,000	15,000
Hybrid ▲	—	—	—	—	8,000	9,500	12,500	—	29,000
Hybrid ▼	—	—	—	—	7,000	8,500	11,500	—	27,000
Reliability	2	2	2	3	3	3	3	3	3
Hybrid	—	—	—	—	2	3	3	3	3
Crash Safety (F)	—	—	—	4	4	4	5	5	—
Ext. cab	3	3	4	4	4	—	5	5	—
Side	—	—	—	—	—	—	1	1	1
Side (NHTSA)	—	—	—	—	—	—	5	5	—
Offset	2	2	2	2	2	2	5	5	5
Head Restraints	1	1	1	1	1	1	3	3	3
Rollover Resistance	—	—	—	4	4	4	4	4	—
Ext. cab	3	3	4	4	4	4	4	4	—
Ext. cab 4×4	3	3	3	4	4	4	4	4	—

Note: Hybrid prices are all over the board. Drive a hard bargain.

All ratings on a numbered scale where ⬜ is good and **1** is bad. See page 132 for a more detailed description.

Honda

RIDGELINE   ★ ★ ★ ★ ★

RATING: Recommended (2007–09); Above Average (2006). Almost a perfect pickup, except for its high initial buy-in price, which can be easily avoided buying used. A big plus is that Honda's first-year vehicles and redesigns haven't been as glitch-prone as Detroit's new products, Toyota's redesigned Sienna, or Nissan's revamped Quest. **Ideal model year:** A 2007 EX-L front-drive for $18,500 is the best buy; the truck will have depreciated about $22,000 and Honda will have corrected most of the first-year production mistakes. **"Real" city/highway fuel economy:** 14.4/10.1 L/100 km. **Maintenance/Repair costs:** Very low due to good quality control and the availability of servicing at any Honda dealership or independent garage. **Parts:** Mechanical parts are widely available and reasonably priced due to the proliferation of independent suppliers. Body parts may be costly and in short supply due to Honda's quasi-monopoly of body panels. **Extended warranty:** A waste of money. These pickups are too well made to need any extra warranty help. Also, if a vehicle failure falls outside of the warranty period, Honda has been quite generous in granting "goodwill" coverage to pay for the repairs. **Best alternatives:** The Dodge Ram with a manual transmission and a Cummins diesel, Ford's Ranger or F-Series, a Mazda B-Series, or a Nissan Frontier V6. **Helpful websites:** *www.carcomplaints.com/Honda/Ridgeline* and *www. ridgelineownersclub.com/forums.*

Strengths and Weaknesses

The Ridgeline, built in Alliston, Ontario, is Honda's first truck—a crew cab cloned from the company's Pilot sport-utility. It's about as long as the Explorer Sport Trac and comes with lots of standard features like all-wheel drive, a 5-speed automatic, Vehicle Stability Assist (electronic stability control) with traction control, ABS, front side airbags and full-length side curtain airbags with rollover sensor, and power locks, windows, and mirrors. 2006–10 models haven't changed much, except for a minor exterior and interior restyling of the 2009s.

This pickup has quite a lot going for it, beginning with soft prices due to slumping truck sales throughout the industry. Very smooth engine performance with exceptionally quick, carlike throttle response; agile handling and enhanced ride comfort, thanks to front and rear independent suspension; and good braking. The truck uses a smooth and reliable 5-speed automatic transmission borrowed from the Pilot and extra traction can be obtained by using a dash-mounted button to lock in power to the rear wheels. The vehicle is well appointed, with plenty of innovative and easily accessed cabin storage compartments; large, user-friendly cabin instruments and controls; plenty of rear legroom; and rear seats that can be stowed vertically, creating extra storage space. The versatile box has a trunk built into the floor, accessed through a tailgate that swings out as well as down; the bed surface has a strong plastic protective layer with tie-down hooks and tire indents to carry motorcycles or an ATV; and there's no rear wheelwell intrusion into the bed area. Excellent fit and finish; and the unibody construction reduces body flexing and creaking, keeping road noise to a minimum. Good quality control.

Some of the Ridgeline's minuses: It's overpriced for a compact truck; acceleration is a bit slower than with competitive V6-equipped pickups; no powertrain options; lacks low-range gearing; low-speed steering is a bit slow; not built for heavy-duty hauling, towing, or serious off-roading; and there's excessive body lean when cornering. Rear visibility is hampered by the sloping sides and small rear window, rear-seat padding is thin, the seatback is too upright, door openings are a bit narrow, and there's no long-bed option

Owner complaints include hesitation when accelerating and fuel pump, tie-rod, and suspension strut failures. There are some complaints of water leaking into the cabin, windshield stress cracks, and wipers overwhelmed by heavy snow. The truck bed is easily scratched, and early Ridgelines don't support trailers with surge brakes. When pulling a trailer, make sure you are within the recommended towing range: some owners report that their rear axle collapsed. Cracked wheel rims are common and some drivers' power seats "rock" back and forth; it costs $1,200 to replace the seat and mechanism.

Safety Summary

2006—Fire originating in the AC. • Airbags fail to deploy, and seat belts malfunction in a collision. • Some child safety seats cannot be installed. • Accelerator surging. • Engine shuts down suddenly; must be replaced. • Fuel tank is easily punctured by road debris. • Parking lights will not stay lit. • Tire jack will not raise vehicle high enough to change a tire. **2007**—Complete separation of side wall tread from Michelin tires. • Child safety seat tether strap fails to lock. • Gas and brake pedals mounted too close together. **2008**—Engine surging. • Rear side window implodes. • Many reports that the AC wiring harness melts. • Wipers work well until they pack the snow on the bottom part of the windshield and then they quit. Tailgate cables loosen. • The car jack can barely lift the car and bends at its maximum height (see *www.ridgelineownersclub.com/forums/showthread.php*). **2009**—Overheated automatic transmission. • Vehicle constantly pulls to the right.

Secret Warranties/Internal Bulletins/Service Tips

2006–07—Automatic transmission is hard to shift into Fourth gear. • Vehicle pulls, drifts to one side. • Drivetrain ping, squeal, or rattle upon light acceleration. • Rear differential noise, judder on turns. • Steering wheel, interior squeaking noise. **2006–08**—Timing belt chirping. **2006–09**—Parking brake won't release in cold weather because of water infiltration. • Noise and judder when turning. **2006–10**—Steering column clicking when turning. **2006–11**—Rear seat leg doesn't fold flat. **2009–10**—Headliner vibrates or rattles. • Whistling from the front door windows. • Gap between the front bumper and the fender/headlamp. **2009–11**—Tailgate won't open in swing mode; handle is stiff.

RIDGELINE PROFILE

	2006	2007	2008	2009
Cost Price ($)				
LX/DX	35,200	35,600	35,820	34,490
EX-L	39,700	40,300	40,520	40,790
Used Values ($)				
LX/DX ▲	12,500	17,000	20,500	24,000
LX/DX ▼	11,000	15,500	19,000	22,500
EX-L ▲	14,500	18,500	23,000,	28,000
EX-L ▼	13,000	17,000	22,500	26,500
Reliability	4	5	5	5
Crash Safety (F)	5	5	5	5
Side	5	5	5	5
Side (IIHS)	5	5	5	5
Offset	5	5	5	5
Head Restraints	2	2	2	5
Rollover Resistance	4	4	4	4

Nissan

FRONTIER　　　　　★★★★★

RATING: Recommended (2005–09); Above Average (1999–2004). Nissan has hit a home run with its Frontier. Year after year, this "Baby Titan" pickup performs well without any major complications, bypassing the serious design glitches found with Nissan's earlier Titans. It's as good as the Mazda and Honda competition, and is more frugal and better performing than GM's puny, Isuzu-bred Canyon/Colorado munchkins. Sure, the pre-2005s are mediocre performers; nevertheless, they are reliable, relatively inexpensive, competent for light chores, easy to maintain, and fun to drive. Plus, they won't "run away" from you like Toyota's Tacoma and Tundra pickups. **Ideal model year:** A 2006 V6 equipped King Cab SE for $8,000 is the best choice as far as cost and features are concerned. **"Real" city/highway fuel economy:** *2.5 4 cylinder:* 10.7/8.7 L/100 km. *2.5 4 cylinder automatic:* 12.6/9.2 L/100 km. *4.0 V6:* 13.5/10.1 L/100 km. *4.0 V6 automatic:* 14.4/10.2 L/100 km. *4.0 V6 4×4:* 14.8/10.6 L/100 km. **Maintenance/Repair costs:** Upkeep costs for these pickups are relatively low. **Parts:** Mechanical parts are widely available and reasonably priced due to the generic nature of most Frontier parts and the proliferation of independent suppliers. **Extended warranty:** Not needed. **Best**

alternatives: A Honda Ridgeline, or a Mazda B-Series pickup. Chrysler's Ram is also an acceptable choice as long as you choose the Cummins diesel and manual transmission. **Helpful websites:** *www.carcomplaints.com/Honda/CR-V* and *www.crvownersclub.com/forums*.

Strengths and Weaknesses

Introduced in 1985, these pickups perform better, are more comfortable, and aren't as rust-prone as their Datsun predecessors. The different 4-cylinder engines offered through the years have all provided adequate power and reasonable reliability. Although the powerful 6-cylinder is more fuel-thirsty, it's the engine of choice for maximum hauling and off-roading versatility.

You won't have to look far to find a reasonably priced Nissan pickup. These small pickups, like Mazda's trucks, didn't cost much when they were new, and their used prices have drifted downward accordingly. On newer models, though, you'll find prices have firmed up considerably because of the general popularity of 2- and 3-year-old crew-cab pickups and downsized sport-utilities. Depending on the year, you'll find a standard 4- or 5-speed manual or an optional 3- , 4-, or 5-speed automatic. Later 4-speed automatics have a fuel-saving lock-up torque converter, but a manual transmission will get the most power and economy out of these motors. The 4×4 option is available with either manual or automatic hubs. The manual version is a pain because you have to stop and turn the hubs. Furthermore, manual transmissions have poorly designed clutches that result in slave cylinder, disc, and pressure plate failures:

> Inherent design flaw. Brake master cylinder and clutch system share same fluid reservoir. Poss brake failure may result. I am a retired GM master mechanic, I possess more skills on car and trucks than most. This system really requires redesign possible conversion to linkage clutch throw-out bearing system and a more heavy-duty flywheel (not dual mass) and more like a stage 2 or stage 3 competition clutch configuration.

The automatic isn't much better because it can't be engaged above 50 km/h, and to disengage it you have to stop and back up a metre or two. These pickups handle impressively well, though, and they provide a firm but reasonably comfortable ride, although some owners say the bucket seats fit only bucket bottoms and rear-seat comfort is an oxymoron. The King Cab is a must for tall drivers.

2005–09 models

These newer Frontiers are significantly improved pickups that are larger, more powerful, easier to handle, and safer than previous models. The entry-level King Cab carries a 152 hp 2.5L 4-cylinder engine, while most other Frontiers use a 265 hp 4.0L V6. A 5- and 6-speed automatic replaced the 4-speed. A new dual-range 4×4 set-up with shift-on-the-fly electronic control, rack-and-pinion steering, and a slew of handling improvements was also carried over this year. Overall, these models carry better-performing, more powerful engines (especially with the V6 and vehicles equipped with a manual transmission); the new 5-speed automatic transmission shifts more smoothly than the previous 4-speed, and it conserves fuel. They boast nice handling; a very comfortable ride up front; are fairly reliable; and have a high resale value.

2004 and earlier models

Okay choices, but not the best vintage for performance and value. Standard four-wheel ABS on some models; a user-friendly interior layout; fairly reliable; an acceptable ride over smooth roads; and reasonably good handling.

The negative side? The 4.0L will run on regular fuel (wink, wink; nudge, nudge), but 91-octane is recommended. Test-drive your choice for engine performance—Nissan has been notorious for overrating their engines. You will also find poor steering feedback, a cheap-looking interior, and limited rear seating on base models. Look for engine exhaust intake manifold failures; drive shaft and ball joint defects that cause excessive vibration; premature front brake wear; electrical short circuits; and minor trim and accessory defects.

Expect poor acceleration (4-cylinder); lots of body lean when cornering; mediocre braking; a small cargo bed on the Crew Cab; and few standard features. Some reports of drive shaft carrier bearing failures on earlier models and lots of engine, wind, and tire noise. The automatic transmission shifter obstructs the view of the climate controls and blocks access to the wiper switch. A choppy ride over uneven terrain ("rear-end hop") is accentuated with an empty load and slow, vague steering offers little feedback.

Difficult rear entry and exit (King Cab); limited rear legroom on the hard rear bench seat; low seats make the height-adjustment feature essential for many drivers; and the King Cab's rear jump seat is laughably small. The cabin looks like plastic central, and many gauges are too recessed to be easily read. Expect mediocre fuel economy on 2001–05 models. There have been some safety complaints relative to sudden acceleration and brake failures.

VEHICLE HISTORY: 2001—A supercharged 210 hp V6 on SE King Cabs and Crew Cabs along with a slight restyling and standard 17-inch wheels. Other additions: a new instrument cluster, interior upgrades, and a security system. **2002**—The regular-cab model is dropped, Crew Cabs are offered with a long bed, and all pickups get a restyled interior. **2003**—6-cylinder engines for the 4×4s, Crew Cabs get 10 more horses, and more options are added, like a tire-pressure monitor and anti-skid/traction control. **2006**—Redesigned.

Frontier pickups have always been reliable and versatile haulers. Most models initially used a lethargic 143 hp 2.4L 4-cylinder, supplemented by a better-performing 180 hp 3.3L V6 and a barely-worth-the-trouble, premium-fuelled, temperamental supercharged 210 hp V6 variant. The King Cab V6 addition gave these pickups the power boost they lacked in the past. ABS is standard on the rear wheels and optional on all four wheels. It's standard, however, on all recent 4×4s and Crew Cabs and on the Desert Runner.

Safety Summary

2001—High idle at low speeds with clutch depressed. • Fuel overflows from filler neck. • Brakes lack sufficient hydraulic pressure to stop vehicle. • Blocked cowl vent restricts fresh air flow. **2001–02**—Airbags fail to deploy. **2002**—Automatic transmission jumps out of Park into Reverse. • Leaking fuel tank. • Brake failure. • Sudden loss of power caused by defective oxygen sensor or Nissan speed limiter kicking in. • Controller fuse blows repeatedly, shutting down vehicle. • Gas and brake pedal set too close together. • Tail light fills with water. **2003**—Sudden, unintended acceleration when brakes are applied. • Engine has to be shut down to turn off AC if defroster is engaged. **2004**—Truck slips out of Park and rolls downhill. • Excessive vibration caused by corroded upper and lower ball joints. **2005**—Truck won't start because of a corroded fuel-sending unit. • Power-assisted driver-side mirror can't be adjusted to eliminate a blind spot. • Tailgate falls off due to its poor design. • Tailgate gap allows sand or other fine material to spew out. • Water leaking into the tail light can cause the truck to shut down. **2006**—Rollover airbags deploy for no reason. • Powertrain transfer case sticks in 4×4. • Gas and brake pedals are mounted too close together. • Right front wheel falls off due to the shearing of the wheel lug nuts. • Rear brake assembly bolts fall out, and the disc caliper flies off. • Transmission doesn't hold a vehicle stopped on an incline. • Many complaints of loss of steering due to defective steering-column bearing. **2007**—Engine surges when brakes are applied. • Poor braking causes excessive stopping distance. • Steering pulls suddenly to the right; steering doesn't return to centre. • Electronic computer module failure causes the vehicle to suddenly shut down. **2008**—Inadvertent airbag deployment. • Airbag is disabled when the passenger seat is occupied. • Brake master cylinder failure. • Cruise control may not stay on. • Loose rear brake caliper nut. • Excessive wind buffeting. **2009**—Brake and gas pedal are mounted too close together. • Brake pedal falls to floor when fully pressed. • Notoriously weak manual transmission clutch. • Incorrect fuel readings. • Driver-side sun visor doesn't stay in place. • Tire jack won't raise the vehicle high enough to change the tire. • Tailgate falls off when opened; may affect Frontiers going back to the 2005 models.

Secret Warranties/Internal Bulletins/Service Tips

1999–2002—Troubleshooting tips for noisy, hard transfer-case shifting. • Loss of supercharged engine power. • Surging, no automatic transmission upshifts. • Steering pull during braking. • Silencing bearing noise from the transfer-case area. • Knocking noise above idle. **2000–03**—ABS warning light stays lit. **2001**—Warm air from fresh air vents. • Speedometer may not work. **2003**—Remedy for AC that won't turn off. **2003–04**—Cold engine start-up rattle. **2004–05**—Troubleshooting spray-in bed liner defects. **2005**—More engine rattles. • Free body control module sub-harness to improve electrical connection for trailering. **2005–06**—Rear leaf spring squeaks • Right front seatback rattles and moves sideways. **2005–07**—Buzzing, whining engine timing chain. • Engine chirping, squealing. • Jump seats won't stay up while driving. **2005–08**—Drivebelt noise on startup. • Low airflow from front AC air vents. • Sunroof doesn't seal correctly. • Erratic fuel gauge readings. **2005–09**—Rear driveshaft support bearing noise. **2005–10**—Rear differential axle seal leaks. • Inoperative AC blower motor. • Engine buzz, whine from timing chain area. • Front suspension popping, squeaking, and clunking. • Driveshaft U-joint noise, vibration. • Heat shield rattling. **2007–08**—Sunroof malfunctions. • Inoperative "auto up" power window. • Right front seat back vibration at highway speeds. • Front end squeaking while driving. **2007–09**—Sunroof inoperative or operates erratically. **2008**— Engine bump, thump felt on light acceleration. • AC refrigerant leaks from connections. • Troubleshooting brake judder, "feel," and noise. • Front door window rattles, creaks when windows are partially open. • Left turn signal won't cancel after turning. **2009**—Nissan will re-weld the torsion tube (it was welded out of specification and can become heavily corroded) free of charge under Voluntary Service Campaign #PC007.

FRONTIER PROFILE

	2001	2002	2003	2004	2005	2006	2007	2008	2009
Cost Price ($)									
4×2	20,998	22,890	23,498	23,450	22,998	24,298	24,448	24,448	22,598
4×4	26,498	27,553	27,398	27,400	28,998	29,598	29,748	29,748	28,148
Used Values ($)									
4×2 ▲	3,000	3,500	4,500	5,000	6,000	8,000	10,500	13,000	15,000
4×2 ▼	2,500	3,000	3,500	4,500	5,000	7,000	9,500	11,500	13,500
4×4 ▲	3,500	4,500	6,000	7,000	7,500	10,000	13,500	16,500	19,500
4×4 ▼	3,000	4,000	5,000	6,000	7,000	9,000	12,500	15,000	18,000
Reliability	5	5	5	5	5	5	5	5	5
Crash Safety (F)	—	4	4	4	4	4	4	4	4
Ext.	—	—	—	—	—	3	3	4	4
Side	4	5	5	4	5	5	5	5	5
Side (IIHS)	—	—	—	—	5	5	5	5	5
Offset	—	—	—	—	2	2	2	2	2
Head Restraints	—	—	—	—	1	1	1	1	1
Roof Strength	—	—	—	—	5	5	5	5	5
Rollover	3	3	3	—	—	3	3	3	3

Toyota

TACOMA ★

RATING: Not Recommended (2002–09); Below Average (1987–2001). Originally a low-tech, unadorned pickup, it was more reliable during its early years. Recent models are more refined and more failure-prone. They have been downgraded due to their propensity for serious sudden, unintended acceleration and for the presence of other life-threatening safety-related design defects. "Oh! What a feeling: Scared." **"Real" city/highway fuel economy:** *4×2, 2.4, and automatic:* 11.1/8.8 L100 km. *4×4 and 2.7:* 13.1/10.4 L/100 km. *4×4 and 3.4:* 13.6/10.9 L/100 km. *4×2 and 4.0:* 13.5/10.1 L/100 km. *4×4 and 4.0:* 15.0/10.9 L/100 km. **Maintenance/Repair costs:** Upkeep costs for these trucks are high; use independent garages to keep costs down. **Parts:** Mechanical parts are widely available and reasonably priced due to the proliferation of independent suppliers. **Extended warranty:** A good idea for the powertrain, judging by consumer complaints and the high incidence of engine deficiencies. **Best alternatives:** A Dodge Ram, equipped with a Cummins diesel hooked to a manual transmission, Honda's Ridgeline, the Mazda B-Series, or a Nissan Frontier V6. **Helpful websites:** *www.carcomplaints.com/Toyota/Tacoma* and *www.toyotanation.com/forum/forumdisplay.php?f=164.*

Strengths and Weaknesses

Toyota has been building good cars for quite a while, but its pickups have always missed the quality and performance mark because they were undersized, underpowered, and glitch-prone. Their mechanical reliability is no longer any better than that of American pickups, which is shameful. Tacomas don't offer a lot of razzle-dazzle or carlike handling, and their powertrain deficiencies can be dangerous to life, limb, and your pocketbook.

2004 and earlier models

Competent V6 engine performance; rugged, impressive off-road capability; good braking, when the brakes work as they should; roomy interior; and relatively good build quality. The Tacoma's traditionally high resale value and reasonable fuel economy has kept operating costs down in the past. However, Toyota's quality decline and sudden, unintended acceleration turmoil have cut Toyota's truck values about 10 percent since December of 2009.

These earlier versions are more primitive models best known for their mediocre ride, poor wet-weather handling, and lots of engine and road noise. They have less towing capability than domestic competitors, and may not meet the stated towing capacity (be very wary). Bereft of many standard features offered by competitors; the front seat is set too low and far back; cushions are too small in the rear seat, where legroom is limited; climate controls are obstructed by the cupholders;

difficult entry and exit require a higher step-up than with other 4×4 pickups. They come with a smaller bed than what's offered by other automakers and the StepSide bed is quite narrow.

There have been many reports of powertrain, brake (especially 2000–03 models), and AC failures; electrical shorts; premature front brake wear; and subpar fit and finish (excessive paint chipping, wind noise, and water leaks). Some report that the engine seizes after ingesting water when the vehicle passes through a puddle, the truck is hard to start, and the inadequate lumbar support with the driver's seat is painful on long drives

2005–08 models

More powerful 4- and 6-cylinder engines give smoother performance without guzzling much fuel; ride and handling are improved with firmer, shorter springs, gas shocks, a limited slip differential, and larger tires; towing capability increased by 680 kg (1,500 lb.); additional interior room makes back seats acceptable for adult passengers. Upgraded interior and a new composite cargo bed with extra storage compartments and adjustable tie-down anchors. Additional safety features like side curtain airbags.

While adding features to make these trucks safer, Toyota neglected other areas that present serious safety risks. For example, handling can be extremely dangerous, due to hazardous cruise control malfunctions and engine surging when braking. Overall performance is still somewhat truck-like; the 6-speed manual transmission is a bit clunky at times; rear drum brakes are not as efficient as disc; and the bed is still quite small.

Redesigned for the first time in 10 years, the 2005 Tacoma targeted the Dodge Dakota crowd with a powerful V6 and a 6-speed manual/5-speed automatic transmission to counter Dodge's at-the-time less sophisticated powertrain set-up. Set on the same platform as the 4Runner and Lexus GX 470, recent Tacomas are about 15 cm (6 in.) longer, 10 cm (4 in.) wider, and 5 cm (2 in.) taller than 2004 and earlier versions.

This compact pickup is available as a Regular Cab, Xtracab, or Double Cab (a four-door crew cab) in 4×2 or 4×4. There's no denying the added convenience of four doors, but the Double Cab also provides a 60/40 folding rear bench seat for more versatility. The 236 hp V6 beats Dodge's 215 hp 3.7L V6, Ford's 202 hp 4.2L V6, and GM's 200 hp 4.3L V6. Available engines on 2004 and earlier models are a 2.4L and 2.7L 4-cylinder and a 3.4L V6. A dealer-installed supercharger package gives the V6 59 additional horses. The shift-on-the-fly 4×4 system is optional on 4×4 trucks and standard on the 4×4 SR5 V6.

VEHICLE HISTORY: 2001—Debut of the Double Cab and a new StepSide version, revised front styling and new alloy wheels, a differential locking system, 31-inch tires on alloy wheels, and a tachometer. **2003**—Standard ABS and upgraded child restraint anchors. **2005**—Larger, more powerful, and equipped for the first time with side curtain airbags.

The 2005's changes brought their own set of problems to subsequent model years, including chronic cruise control and transmission breakdowns; oil leaks between the transmission and crankshaft; assorted short circuits; water leaks onto the floorboard from the A-pillar; easily chipped paint (rocker panels, lower doors, and front of the bed sides); tailgates that fail while vehicles are underway; and acid sprayed around the engine compartment by the Delphi battery. Cabin mount bolts and bushings contract and loosen in cold weather, resulting in a loud banging noise in the cabin area.

Reliability has been compromised during the past several decades by lapses in quality control, leading to expensive V6 engine head gasket failures through 2004. Automatic transmission and brake problems have carried over to the latest models.

 Safety Summary

All years: The Tacoma is Toyota's poster-child for incidences of sudden, unintended acceleration:

> Over a period of several months after purchasing a new 2007 Toyota Tacoma, I experienced five incidents of brake/acceleration problems finally resulting in a crash. First incident: Stopped at a traffic light with my foot on the brake, the truck lunged forward a few feet. The dealership told me they could not find any problem. A month later, stopped in a gas station drive with my foot on the brake waiting to exit, the rear wheels began spinning out of control. I pressed on the brake as hard as I possibly could to keep from entering traffic. Three weeks later, approaching the bottom of a hilly sharp turn, I tapped the brakes to slow down. Again the rear wheels accelerated to a high rate of speed. I could not stop the truck to keep from striking a van in front of me so I crossed over a double yellow line to avoid a collision. It took about a thousand yards to gain control.

• Airbag malfunctions. • Brake failures, overheating, extended stopping distance, and prematurely worn calipers and rotors. • Vehicle wanders all over the road after hitting a bump. • Firestone, Goodyear, and Dunlop tire-tread separation. • Loose or poorly fitted trip panels. **2001**—Incorrectly installed ABS sensor leads to brake failure. • Vehicle is prone to hydroplaning over wet roads at relatively slow speeds. • Intermittently, alarm system fails to unlock vehicle. • Loose front drive shaft bolts. • Rear wheel falls off. **2002**—Brake and gas pedal mounted too closely together. • Brake master cylinder leaks. • Automatic transmission shudders, clunks, surges, shifts erratically, and jumps from gear to gear. • Transmission line blows out. • Defective front and rear shock absorbers. • Water enters the cabin through the driver-side support handle. • Defective wheel rims and tires. • Poorly designed jack handle makes for risky tire-changing. **2003**—Sudden rollover. • Sudden engine surging caused by a defective throttle actuator control. • Loss of power caused by a faulty throttle body sensor (maybe the second defect could "cure" the first?):

You can only open the throttle body butterfly the first 25% with the pedal, then the computer opens it the rest of the way. These throttle by wire [or highly-responsive accelerators] are crapping out left and right. [Toyota claims they are covered under the less-generous 3 year/60,000 km bumper-to-bumper warranty and not the 5 year/100,000 km powertrain warranty].

• Truck sways and pitches excessively. • Shifter can be accidentally bumped and will shift into Neutral. • Front seats rock back and forth. • Water leaks through the passenger door onto the driver-side floor. • Doors don't close fully or lock. • Broken wheel lug nuts:

While the inspector was placing the tires back onto the truck, two of the wheel studs broke on the front hub. He stated that this happens on almost every 2000–2003 Toyota pickup they work on. He even showed me that the stud wasn't cross-threaded and removed the stud from the lug nut using a pair of pliers. The stud came right out with little pressure.

2004—Several incidents of fires igniting while vehicles are being driven. • Front airbags don't deploy as required. • Transmission jerks when going into gear. • Both rear springs fail when cornering. • Side mirrors fog up badly. • Loss of braking ability in inclement weather. • Parking brake hits driver's knee. • Seat lumbar supports cause lower back pain. 2005—6-speed manual transmission has serious judder and shifts only with considerable difficulty. • Skid plate catches air and causes the vehicle to shake violently at highway speeds. • Exhaust crossover pipe hangs below the transfer-case mount and can be easily crushed when off-roading. This would allow carbon monoxide to enter into the cabin. • Left-turn signal quits intermittently. • Right side mirror vibrates excessively (especially on windy days) and also creates a large blind spot in the right front quarter of the vehicle. • Tailgate is dangerously weak, unable to support normal weight without bending out of shape. 2006—Surging when braking, particularly on vehicles equipped with cruise control. • Throttle sticks. • Erratic cruise control/transmission operation causing violent gear shifts into the wrong gear. • Transmission pressure plate failure. • Sun visor drops down when pushed forward. • Water leaks through the firewall. 2007—More than the average number of safety-related complaints for Toyota vehicles, including many hair-raising incidents where the vehicle suddenly accelerates during braking. • Many complaints that the cruise control suddenly goes into Overdrive. • Extremely fast idle and engine surge after a cold start. 2008—Airbags failed to deploy. • Sudden rear differential lockup. • More cases of sudden, unexpected acceleration. One theory:

It is my belief that my BlackBerry's electromagnetic frequencies interfere with my Tacoma's electrical system when the phone is either too near the dash or plugged into the car charger.

Toyota's answer: "The vehicle is performing as designed." • Loss of brakes after passing over a pothole or a speed bump. • Excessive steering, suspension vibration. • Suspension bottoms out with a light load. • A child's booster seat will not fit in the rear seat. • Rainwater/drops accumulate on door window and mirror. • Contrary to claims, plastic bed cannot tie down motorcycles. **2009**—Sudden, unintended acceleration caused by a "demented" Tacoma:

> My 2009 Toyota Tacoma has a demented mind of its own when it comes to unexpected acceleration. I will describe what it has done at least 10 times in the year and a half since I (unfortunately) purchased it. As I take my foot off the accelerator and apply it to the brake, the engine speeds up to more than 7,000 rpm. I continue pressing on the brake which starts to slip. To avoid a crash I must quickly shift the transmission into neutral. As the engine reaches maximum rpm's, it then dies back to an idle. It is not the floor mat or the acceleration pedal causing this.

• Owners complain that the driver has to "put the pedal to the metal" for acceptable braking; others report complete loss of braking capability.

Secret Warranties/Internal Bulletins/Service Tips

All years: If there is a delay when shifting from Park or Neutral to Reverse, Toyota will install an upgraded B3 return spring, B3 Brake piston O-rings, and a low-coast modulator spring to correct the problem. Toyota doesn't say if the repair will be covered by its base warranty or "goodwill"; however, a good rule of thumb is that any transmission malfunction, like a delay in this case, would be the automaker's responsibility for at least the first 7 years/160,000 km. • Musty odours emanating from the AC may be caused by a blocked evaporator-housing drain pipe. • TSB #BR95-003 says Toyota has a new brake pad kit that reduces brake noise and increases brake durability. • Consult TSB #BR94-002 and #BR95-001, where the company outlines all the possible ways brake pulsation/vibration can be further reduced. Incidentally, this problem has affected almost all of Toyota's cars and trucks over the past decade. **1997–2004**—Tips on plugging body water leaks. **1999–2002**—Tube step knocking, squeaking, and rattling fix. • Loose fender flare pad. • Tearing of the seat material on Double Cabs. **2001–03**—Special Service Campaign relative to the fuel inlet protector. **2001–04**—Front door window pane improvement. • Dash pad rattle repair tips. **2002**—Off-centre steering wheel. • MIL stays lit. **2002–06**—Correction for vehicles that pull to the side. **2003–04**—Intermittent hard cranking. • Extended engine cranks can be corrected by installing an improved fuel section-tube sub-assembly. **2004–10**—Front seat squeaks. **2003–11**—Tips for silencing an upper or lower windshield ticking noise. **2005**—No-start in cold temperatures. • Front cowl water leaks. • Suspension slap, squeak noise. **2005–06**—Deformed window runs. **2005–07**—Intermittent no-starts. • Front brake noise when brakes applied while backing up. • Harsh rear spring ride. • Windshield wind noise. **2005–08**—Oil leaks from the engine timing cover. • Rear differential howl, whine. • Driveline vibration. • Bent rear tailgate. **2005–09**—Suspension squeaks. **2005–10**—Manual transmission clutch slippage. • Harsh rear suspension ride with heavy loads. • Rattling on rough roads. • Water leaks onto rear carpet. • AC blower ticking, clicking. **2007–10**—AC defrosts poorly; insufficient output. • Blower motor squealing when cold.

	2001	2002	2003	2004	2005	2006	2007	2008	2009
Cost Price ($)									
Base	21,630	21,920	22,370	22,570	22,125	22,535	22,635	22,760	20,215
4×4	27,045	27,335	28,065	29,400	29,240	29,560	29,660	29,785	24,855
Used Values ($)									
Base ▲	3,000	3,500	4,000	4,500	6,000	7,500	9,000	12,000	14,000
Base ▼	2,500	3,000	3,500	4,000	5,000	6,500	7,500	10,500	12,500
4×4 ▲	4,000	4,500	5,000	6,500	8,000	10,000	14,000	16,500	16,000
4×4 ▼	3,500	4,000	4,500	5,500	7,000	8,500	12,500	15,500	14,500
Reliability	3	3	3	2	2	2	2	2	2
Crash Safety (F)									
4×2	—	4	—	—	5	5	5	5	5
Ext. Cab	3	3	3	3	5	5	5	5	5
Double	—	—	4	4	—	—	—	—	—
Side									
4×2	—	5	—	—	5	5	5	5	5
Ext. Cab	3	3	3	3	5	5	5	5	5
Double	—	—	5	5	—	—	—	—	—
Side (IIHS)	—	—	—	—	5	5	5	5	5
Offset	3	3	3	3	5	5	5	5	5
Head Restraints	—	—	—	—	—	—	—	—	5
Roof Strength	—	—	—	—	2	2	2	2	2
Rollover	2	2	4	4	—	4	4	4	4
Ext. Cab	—		2	—	—	4	4	4	4

TUNDRA ★

RATING: Not Recommended (2000–09). The rating has been downgraded because the competition has safer, better-performing models, better quality control, and cheaper prices. The many instances of sudden, unintended acceleration, brake and transmission failure complaints, and severe "bed bounce" are other negative factors. **"Real" city/highway fuel economy:** *4×2, 3.4, and manual: 14.3/11.1 L/100 km. 4×2, 3.4, and automatic: 14.1/10.9 L/100 km. 4×4, 3.4, and manual: 15.4/12.1 L/100 km. 4×4, 3.4, and automatic: 14.4/12.3 L/100 km. 4×2, 4.0, and automatic: 12.7/9.7 L/100 km. 4×2, 4.7, and automatic: 15.6/11.9 L/100 km. 4×4, 4.7, and automatic: 15.4/12.6 L/100 km. 5.7 V8, and automatic: 15.6/11.9 L/100 km. 4×4, 5.7 V8, and automatic: 15.4/12.6 L/100 km.* **Maintenance/Repair costs:** Upkeep costs for the Tundra are outrageously high (imagine, a complete paint job every couple of years); use independent garages to keep repair costs down. **Parts:** Mechanical parts aren't widely available, and prices are what the market will bear. Tundras aren't widely supported by independent parts suppliers. **Extended**

warranty: A good idea for the powertrain, judging by consumer complaints and the high incidence of diesel engine deficiencies. **Best alternatives:** A Dodge Ram equipped with a Cummins diesel hooked to a manual transmission, Honda's Ridgeline, the Mazda B-Series, or a Nissan Frontier V6. **Helpful websites:** *www. carcomplaints.com/Toyota/Tundra* and *www.tundratalk.net/forums*.

Strengths and Weaknesses

Larger, stronger, safer, and roomier than its T100 predecessor, the 2001 Tundra was Toyota's first serious foray into the lucrative, though crowded, full-sized pickup market. Unfortunately, Toyota's new truck wasn't quite full-sized and sales suffered.

Toyota corrected that shortcoming with its 2004 models by stretching the Dana-built frame to make the Tundra more competitive with Detroit's Big Three pickups. Unfortunately, this increase in size was accompanied by a continuing decline in overall quality, which was never seriously addressed in subsequent years. Two engines, a 190 hp 3.4L V6 and a 240 hp 4.7L V8, are offered up to the 2005 model year, when the 4.0L came on board.

More power, performance, convenience, and value were added by twin-cam V8 acceleration; low-range gearing for off-roading; a smoother, quieter ride; a roomier Double Cab (2004); easier front access; better fit and finish; standard transmission and upgraded engine oil coolers; and the passenger-side airbag that can be switched off with a key.

Yet the Tundra couldn't shake its early image as a poorly designed, low-quality, glitch-prone pickup. Owners point out that the steering and suspension design is so bad that the truck can easily go out of control when passing over slightly irregular roadways. Electronics and brakes continue to be seriously weak areas, and fit and finish is deplorable:

> I have the blue streak color and it has many scratches. The white undercoat shows through. I showed it to the dealer. He saw the scratches and chipping paint but did not acknowledge that there was a problem. He did nothing to rectify it.

2006 and earlier models

Less engine torque than the competition; difficult rear exit and entry; 4×4 can't be used on dry pavement (unlike the GM Silverado and Sierra); excessive body sway, and tends to be a quite bouncy; poorly performing rear brake drums; rear-hinged back doors on the Access Cab don't open independently of the front doors; no four-door Crew Cab model available; and the V8 requires premium fuel. The 2003 and earlier models aren't as roomy in the rear half of the extended cab as other extended full-sized trucks—you feel like you're entering a Dodge Dakota or Ford Ranger. Paint is not up to Toyota standards. Dash LCDs are unreadable with sunglasses. Weak door indents; bland styling; and an incredibly high rate of safety-related defects involving sudden, unintended acceleration, and brake, airbag, and seat belt failures.

VEHICLE HISTORY: 2002—The Limited gets a standard in-dash CD changer, anti-lock braking, and keyless remote entry. **2003**—A new V8-equipped Access Cab StepSide model. New features include ABS, a redesigned grille and bumper, power-sliding rear window (Limited), 17-inch wheels (optional on the SR5), and a revamped centre console. **2004**—A more powerful, brawnier Double Cab that gains 30 cm (12 in.) in wheelbase and length and 7 cm (3 in.) in width. **2005**—More power, new transmissions, and optional side curtain airbags; a 245 hp 4.0L V6 replaces the 190 hp 3.4L; a 6-speed manual transmission replaces the 5-speed, and a 5-speed automatic replaces the 4-speed; the 4.7L V8 gets 42 more horses. **2007**—A redesigned Tundra. It's larger, more powerful (now equipped with an optional 381 hp 5.7L V8), and better appointed. **2008**—More variations with the Double Cab and CrewMax models, standard power front bucket seats, heated mirrors and mudguards. Limited version gets standard front and rear parking assistance.

The Tundra's safety-related defects, low quality, and poor reliability got worse with this last redesign. Owners report chronic stalling and surging, frequent brake failures, excessive brake caliper and rotor wear, premature transmission replacements, engine manifold rust-outs, paint peeling, and poor-quality original-equipment tires. The 2007 and 2008 models have mostly been plagued by the above-mentioned problems, plus faulty camshafts and torque converters, cracking tailgates, and even more cases of paint scratches and peeling:

> Paint is very thin (one coat). Paint cannot even be washed without scratching. Truck has scratches on it from leaning over the bed, also around all the door handles from just opening the doors, not to mention all the marks around the door and tailgate from just our hands.

Other deficiencies include excessive front-brake vibration or pulsation that makes the truck almost uncontrollable and causes it to shake violently when brakes are applied. Brake drums and rotors warp within 7,000 km; steel wheels rust prematurely; the automatic transmission binds; and overall transmission performance is poor. The ABS make a loud banging sound upon engagement; the 4×4 system grinds and pops out of gear; there's chronic rear axle noise and suspension knocking; V8 engine knocking when started in cold weather; and excessive drivetrain vibration at 100 km/h.

With many of the above deficiencies, owners say that Toyota often dismisses the problems as "normal," or blames customers for its own manufacturing errors while stonewalling legitimate claims.

 **Safety Summary**

All years: Sudden, unintended acceleration. • "Lag and lurch" acceleration. • Airbags fail to deploy. • Seat belt/retractor failures. • Vehicle rolls away after it is put in Park and the emergency brake is applied. • An incredibly high number of brake complaints relative to brake failures, rotor and drum warping, and excessive vibration/shudder. • Brakes overheat and fade after successive application; extended braking distance. • Ball joint failure causes wheel to separate. **2001**— Exhaust manifold cracking. • With a full fuel tank and when riding uphill, gas fumes enter the cabin. • Gear selector fails to engage the proper gear. • When applying lube to the drive shaft bearings, the grease just squirts around the fitting, not in. • Broken weld in tow hitch. **2002**—Cab separates from chassis. • Automatic transmission goes into the wrong gear or slams into gear. • Sudden brake lock-up. • Lug nuts are easily broken when tightened. • Bent wheel rims. **2003**—Vehicle stalls out. • Engine oil leaks. • Sudden tie-rod failure can cause Tundra to flip. • Transfer-case malfunction leads to reduced power and excessive vibration. • Faulty transmission Overdrive causes engine surge. **2004**—Many reports of the ball joint or lower control arm suddenly failing on vehicles not included in the recall to fix the problem. • Broken wheel lug nuts. • Defroster draws carbon monoxide into the cab. • Rear window pops out, sunroof explodes. **2005**—Automatic transmission failure (won't go into gear, or jumps out of Drive into Neutral). • Cruise control downshifts two gears on slight upgrades. • Extreme pulling to the left and right. • Driver's captain chair rocks back and forth. • Faulty tire-pressure monitoring system. **2006**—Vehicle suddenly shuts down. • Malfunctioning cruise control. • Sudden brake loss. • Excessive Bridgestone tire wear. • When fuelling, the filler nozzle will eject from the vehicle. **2007**— Instruments cannot be seen in daylight. • Headlights are difficult to aim properly. • Heat duct falls and blocks access to the brake pedal. • Bad Bridgestone Dueler tires. • Truck is bouncy on the highway; described by one owner as producing excessive cab shake, wobble, and jerkiness. **2008**—Driver severely injured after a sudden acceleration crash:

> I approached a turn, and removed my foot from the accelerator and applied the brake, but the accelerator remained stuck down, the vehicle's speed exponentially increased and as a direct result I lost control of the truck and it slammed into a tree going 65 miles + per hour. The result is that the truck is "totaled". I will live with permanent injuries, including broken neck, ribs, hip and partial paralysis.

• Many complaints of "lag and lurch" acceleration. • "Piston slap" caused by the 5.7L V8 engine piston hitting against the cylinder wall. • Vehicle was in Park with the engine running and the parking brake engaged when the truck rolled backwards down a hill and crashed into a building. • Transmission and transfer case failures. • Tundra bounces all over the highway and shakes violently when approaching 100 km/h:

> Anyone familiar with "shaken baby" syndrome will recognize this defect. On certain sections of pavement and at certain speeds, this vehicle sets up a harmonic vibration

and shakes so violently that infants are at risk. The events are easily repeated and are known to the manufacturer.

•

A Google search of Tundra rumble strip vibration will yield information on the issue. Los Angeles Toyota motor sales officials have nicknamed the problem "the rumble strip" because the slippage causes vibration similar to the sensation of driving over the wake-up strips at the side of highways. The rumbling usually lasts several seconds. But the problem sometimes worsens to the point that some owners can't shift into certain gears. The problem has been reported only in six-speed transmissions, which are linked to the popular 5.7-liter V-8 engine. Since the 2007 Tundra's February launch, the 5.7-liter engine has been installed in 70 percent of about 135,000 Tundras sold. That means the problem could affect nearly 100,000 vehicles.

• Premature wheel bearing failure. • Ventilation system allows rodents to enter the ductwork from the engine compartment. Consequently, the cabin air is laced with rodent feces, which may sicken or kill occupants who breathe the air. **2009**—Sudden, unintended acceleration. • Toyota asked owner to pay for recall repair:

Contacted Toyota dealership as part of pedal/floor mat recall. Told that I would have to purchase separate retainer to secure floor mat. Does not make sense to have a recall and then insist that customers pay for Toyota's failures and defects. The safety retainer should have come with the vehicle. It does in other vehicles.

• Automatic transmission "hunts" for the right gear and slips when in gear. • Early driveshaft replacement. • On 2007–2010 models, Tundra headlights can blind approaching drivers.

Secret Warranties/Internal Bulletins/Service Tips

2000–02—Hard starts/no-starts. **2000–04**—If the AC doesn't sufficiently cool the cabin, TSB #AC004-04 says the water control valve is the likely culprit. **2000–05**—Troubleshooting front and rear brake vibrations. • Engine squealing noise on cold start. • Front-door window rattles. **2001**—New parking struts developed to reduce rear brake vibration. • Inaccurate temperature gauge. • Inadequate application of seam sealer in driver's footwell area. **2001–03**—Oil pressure gauge reads abnormally low. • Front brake repair tips. **2002–06**—Remedy for vehicle pulling hard to the left or right. **2003–11**—Tips for silencing an upper or lower windshield ticking noise. **2004**—Extended engine cranks can be corrected by installing an improved fuel section-tube sub-assembly. **2004–05**—Rear shock squeaking. • No-start in cold temperatures. • AC blower noise. **2004–06**—Ticking noise from lower A-pillar when passing over rough terrain. **2004–10**—Front seat ticking. **2005–09**—Front power seat, grinding, and groaning. **2007**—Automatic transmission shifter slide binding. • Rear brake squeak. • Tailgate latch won't open. **2007–08**—Troubleshooting a no start condition. • Transfer case not shifting in cold temperatures. • Drivetrain clunk or thunk. • Front differential howl or growl. • Rattle from under the rear seat. • Instrument panel rattles. • Keyless entry no-start. • Condensation drips from dome lamp headliner. • Loose driver-side air vents. **2007–09**—Gap between A-pillar and instrument panel. • Rust on steel step boards. **2007–10**—Tube step pad cracking, lifting. • Front driveshaft ticking. • Snow ingestion into air cleaner box. • Front end grinding noise when in four-wheel drive. • Rear differential growl, whine:

REAR DIFFERENTIAL GROWL/WHINE WHILE DRIVING

BULLETIN NO.: T-SB-0297-10   DATE: NOVEMBER 2, 2010

INTRODUCTION: Some vehicles may exhibit a growl or whine noise from the rear when the vehicle is in motion. Production changes have been made to prevent this noise. Follow the procedure in the bulletin to address this noise condition.

• A choppy ride that can be severe at times with the extended cab version. Don't pay for this modification; Toyota made the mistake:

CHOPPY RIDE

BULLETIN NO.: T-SB-0270-10   DATE: SEPTEMBER 13, 2010

INTRODUCTION: Some 2007–10 Tundra vehicles may exhibit a body vibration when driving under certain road conditions. A newly designed cab mount has been developed to improve this condition. **NOTE:** The Tundra performs similarly to other long wheelbase trucks on choppy, broken concrete surfaces. The enhanced cab mounts of this TSB reduce the amplitude of body vibrations caused by uneven road surfaces, but they do NOT eliminate the sensation entirely. Also, reducing speed by as little as 5 mph has a considerable positive effect in reducing body vibration.

TUNDRA PROFILE

	2001	2002	2003	2004	2005	2006	2007	2008	2009
Cost Price ($)									
Base	23,110	23,520	23,520	24,565	25,580	26,100	25,255	23,475	23,855
4×4 V6/V8	28,600	29,270	29,270	30,320	30,650	31,080	29,320	27,540	27,400
Used Values ($)									
Base ▲	3,000	3,500	4,000	5,000	6,500	8,000	9,500	11,500	13,500
Base ▼	2,500	3,000	3,500	4,500	5,000	6,500	8,000	10,000	12,000
4×4 V6/V8 ▲	4,500	5,500	6,500	7,000	8,000	9,500	11,000	13,000	15,000
4×4 V6/V8 ▼	4,000	5,000	6,000	6,500	7,000	8,500	9,500	12,000	13,500

All ratings on a numbered scale where   is good and **1** is bad. See page 132 for a more detailed description.

Reliability	2	2	1	1	1	1	1	1	2
Crash Safety (F)	3	4	4	4	4	4	4	4	4
Side	—	—	—	—	5	5	—	—	—
Extended	—	5	5	5	5	5	—	—	—
Side (IIHS)	—	—	—	—	—	—	3	3	3
Offset	5	5	5	5	5	5	5	5	5
Head Restraints	—	—	—	—	3	3	3	3	3
Rollover	—	—	—	—	—	3	3	3	3
Extended	3	3	3	—	—	3	3	3	3

INGLORIOUS BEATERS

The more I see the newer auto offerings, the more thankful I am for "beaters"—cheap, older cars that may not be all that pretty or refined, but they are mostly reliable and easy to find.

As the automobile industry shakes off the Great Recession and its bankruptcies, I am concerned that cars are getting so complicated that the average driver no longer has freedom of choice and has to frequent the dealership where the vehicle was purchased. This is a scary thought and certainly works against dealers building up their customer base through honest and competent service. Beaters break automaker/dealer monopolies and allow motorists to go where service is the best and cheapest.

Here, we include thumbnail sketches of some of the vehicles we passed over in Part Three. "Beginners" are recent models that were discontinued after only a few model years or sell only in small numbers in Canada, so they haven't generated enough owner feedback or manufacturer service bulletins to be reviewed thoroughly. "Beaters," a uniquely Canadian expression, describes used vehicles that may have been passed down through families for 20 years or more. They are usually vehicles that are no longer built—inexpensive wheels that will hopefully tide you over until you can get that more-expensive dream machine you've always wanted.

In my years of writing *Lemon-Aid*, I have seen an interesting vein of regret from Baby Boomers who say their first "beater" was the best car they ever owned, and they wish they had never given it up.

Phil's Beginners

Cars

The mid-sized 2003 **Acura CL** is an Above Average buy; the 1997–2002s are Average, due to serious first-year factory glitches and powertrain problems. 1998 saw the debut of the 2.3L engine; 2003 CLs have plenty of power from the quiet, smooth-running 3.2L V6. And handling is better than average, thanks to an upgraded suspension, variable assisted steering, and 16-inch wheels.

A 2003 CL is now worth about $8,000 (new models sold for $37,800); 1997–2003 prices vary from $3,000 to $6,500. Good alternative vehicles are the BMW 318 and Honda Accord.

Owners have reported that the 2003 models have troublesome gearboxes. Sudden, unintended acceleration and hesitation problems are thought to be transmission-related also. Premature brake pad and caliper wear and warped brake rotors continue to be serious problems.

Based on the Honda Civic, the Acura **Integra** evolved into more of a sports car than an econocar. Dramatically redesigned for 1994, the 1994 through 2001 models provide a smoother ride than previous versions, and crash protection was augmented by the use of front airbags (1996 frontal collision protection was rated four stars by NHTSA). The powerful VTEC engine, however, requires lots of shifting, and interior room is problematic. Nevertheless, these are the benchmark cars for optimum savings, performance, and quality. Expect to pay $2,500 to $4,500 for one of the above model years.

What Integras give you in mechanical reliability and performance, they take away in poor quality control on body components and accessories. Water leaks, excessive wind noise, low-quality trim items, and plastic panels that deform easily are all commonplace. Owners also report severe steering shimmy, excessive brake noise, and premature front brake-pad wearout. Squeaks and rattles frequently crop up in the door panels and hatches, and the sedan's frameless windows often have sealing problems.

The 2002–06 Acura **RSX** is built on the Civic platform, and is powered by a base 160 hp 2.0L twin-cam iVTEC 4-banger or a torquier 210 hp variant used by the high-performance Type S. Three transmissions are available: the first two, a 5-speed manual and a 4-speed automatic, are offered with base models, while a 6-speed manual is found on the Type S. Both engines are torquier than the powerplants they replaced; however, the base engine has more useful commuting low-end torque than the so-called sportier Type S engine. Your best buy would be a much-improved 2005 model that sells for $8,500–$9,500

The RSX appeals to drivers who want to shift fast and often, and who don't mind a firm ride. The car is well appointed; has good acceleration and handling above 3000 rpm; provides user-friendly gauges and controls; brakes well, especially with the Type S; gives good fuel economy; depreciates slowly; has garnered a five-star frontal crash rating for both the driver and front-seat passenger, and a four-star front side-impact rating; and has head restraints that IIHS rates Good up front and Average in the rear. The car has high-quality construction, except for brakes, electronics, and transmission components.

On the downside, the car exhibits so-so acceleration in lower gears; overall acceleration that's compromised by the automatic transmission; heavy steering that's a bit vague; limited front and rear passenger space; excessive road and engine noise; and rear visibility that's obstructed by small side windows, thick roof pillars, and a tall rear deck. Peruse transmission complaints at *forums.clubrsx.com*.

Chrysler's 2004–07 **Crossfire** is an expensive, low-volume luxury sports coupe that gets a Below Average rating. It offers a cramped interior, high windowsills, and a low roofline that combine to create a claustrophobic cabin. Crashworthiness scores for the 2004–05s are quite good, with five stars given for frontal occupant protection, side protection, and rollover resistance; 2007s got similar marks.

Crossfire owners reported numerous safety defects to NHTSA, though. Some, like the one below, are particularly frightening:

> Lack of power when at a stop, even though you might be mashing in the gas pedal (pedal to the metal) So if you fear for your life when you're in the middle of an intersection and your car won't move, don't worry because it's normal.

Other problems include sudden acceleration when the brakes are applied; high-performance tires and a low-slung body that impair safe handling in inclement weather; airbags that fail to deploy; chronic stalling; transmission breakdowns; a manual transmission that abruptly slips out of First gear into Neutral; defective wheel bolts that lead to the wheel separating from the car; a short circuit in the dash wiring harness that poses a fire risk; $400 wheel rims that are easily bent in normal driving; front and rear strut failures; headlights that don't adequately illuminate the road; lights that dim at stoplights and at idle; and erratic voltage (possibly due to a faulty voltage regulator) that fries powertrain computer modules and other electronic components. Yikes!

Depreciation has also been brutal: A 2005 base coupe, which cost $40,100 new, is now worth only $8,000–$9,000—a good price for a bad car.

The 1981–2000 **Ford Escort/Lynx/Tracer** is a front-drive small car that is cheap to buy and economical to operate, if you get the right vintage. It provides a comfortable, though jittery, ride and adequate front seating for two adults. Escorts have been off the market for almost a decade, but there are many units still sold due to the car's popularity. *Lemon-Aid* gives it both a Not Recommended and a Below Average rating, because this is a Dr. Jekyl and Mr. Hyde car. The 1981–90 models were lemons with their chronic brake, powertrain, and electrical system failures in addition to Ford's lack of parts and servicing support in Canada. In 1991, though, the car was upgraded with quality Mazda 323 and Protegé components, available from Ford or Mazda dealers. Almost instantly, the frog turned into a prince and Escorts were hopping off dealer lots. So spend the additional loonies and get the more reliable, better performing year 2000 ZX2 for about $1,000. Incidentally, the slightly cheaper base Escort has three-star (average) front, side, and rollover crash protection; the ZX2 has only a one-star side crashworthiness score.

Bland but solid-looking, the spacious 2005–07 Ford **Five Hundred** and **Freestyle** (an SUV wagon clone) front-drive and AWD family sedans failed to capture buyers' hearts at first, due to a combination of high gas prices, mediocre highway performance, and early reports of poor-quality powertrain and other components affecting the 2005 and 2006 models. Now that fuel prices are lower, used prices are still depressed, but quality has improved markedly with the 2007 and 2008 versions. Consequently, the 2007–08 models represent Average buys, while the two earlier years are rated Below Average. Used 2005 versions are selling for only $5,500; 2006 models are worth barely $7,000; and 2007s go for $9,000–$10,500. Tack on another $1,000 for an AWD variant. A 2008 Taurus goes for $14,000; AWD will cost $1,500 more.

The Ford Five Hundred.

The 2008 **Taurus** and **Taurus X** are the Five Hundred and Freestyle's renamed, restyled carryover models that have a more-powerful 260 hp 3.5L V6 hooked to a 6-speed automatic transmission and are equipped with a retuned suspension. Both cars are rated Average and are priced within a few thousand dollars of each other. A 2008 Taurus goes for $12,000; AWD will cost $1,500 more. A Taurus X is $13,500; again, add another $1,500 for AWD.

The 2008 Ford Taurus X is the new name for Ford's Freestyle crossover. Along with the name change, this SUV gets freshened styling and more power. Taurus X is essentially a wagon version of the Ford Taurus (formerly Five Hundred) sedan. Front-wheel-drive and all-wheel-drive models are available in SEL, Eddie Bauer, and Limited trims. The sole powertrain teams a 260 hp 3.5L V6 engine with a 6-speed automatic transmission.

These cars use a modified Volvo XC90 SUV and S80 wagon/sedan platform, which give some SUV advantages such as higher seating, increased interior space, and optional four-wheel or all-wheel drive. Additionally, crash test scores are impressive: Front and side crash protection are rated at five stars, and rollover resistance scored four stars. 2007s come with side airbags.

There are also plenty of performance shortcomings with these large cars. For example, the 203 hp V6 isn't powerful enough for a 1,860 kg vehicle; it has a very limited towing capability of approximately 907 kg (2,000 lb.); the self-levelling shocks are unproven; the optional all-wheel-drive system is part Volvo, part Ford (not the best combination for trouble-free performance, or servicing); front occupants will want more legroom; and the 18-inch tires make for a stiff, choppy ride.

Owners are most unhappy about a number of serious factory-related defects, primarily affecting the engine, automatic transmission, fuel supply, and ignition (unintended acceleration, hard starts, stalling, and dieseling):

They report that the transmission jumps out of Park into Reverse, has no intermediate or Second gear for descending mountains, and often hesitates as it hunts for the right gear. Also, the engine surges and lurches when accelerating; brake and suspension components require early replacement; the fuel gauge gives incorrect readings; rear seat belts cross at children's necks; doors leak water into the interior; Continental tires may fail prematurely; and the dash is insufficiently lit and reflects onto the windshield.

The Ford **Cougar** and **Thunderbird** are Not Recommended from both a reliability and performance perspective. The early rear-drives (1985–97) were plagued by powertrain, electrical, suspension, and brake defects; the 1999–2002 front-drive iterations carry over these same deficiencies and add more problems common to Ford's front-drives, namely, gear "hunting" and drivetrain failures. As for the resurrected 2003–05 Thunderbird's low rating, its lackluster highway performance and quality shortcomings clearly signalled that Ford would not improve the model and was simply pimping a warmed-over, less reliable version of what was once a classic car. Owners report that repairs are costly and take forever to complete because few garages have the parts and experience to repair these complicated long-gone beasties.

1999–2002 **Cougars** are Not Recommended despite their attractive styling, easy handling, and low $1,500–$2.500 price. For these low prices, owners have to put up with mediocre acceleration in the base models; problematic transmission performance; a narrow, claustrophobic interior for a four-seater; limited rear seat room; obstructed rear visibility; an ugly and superfluous trunk-lid spoiler; and excessive interior noise.

2002–05 **Thunderbirds** are Not Recommended buys that sell for $8,000 to $15,000. They are just as badly built as the Cougar, but charge a premium-car price.

After a brief hiatus, the Thunderbird name returned for the 2002 model year, affixed to a $51,550 retro-styled two-seater rear-drive convertible that looks nothing like its 1955–57 namesake or the $25,095 '97 model it replaced (now worth $3,000–$3,500). This T-Bird shares variations of the engine and chassis used by the Lincoln LS and Jaguar S-Type as well as their 5-speed automatic transmission. Power is supplied by a retuned 280 hp 3.9L V8.

This is one dull-looking luxury roadster with few features that distinguish it from half a dozen cheaper imports in the same genre. Other minuses: a tiny, shallow trunk; a cheap-looking, boring instrument panel; limited headroom; an unwieldy folding top cover; and excessive air turbulence when driven with the top down. NHTSA rated frontal occupant protection and rollover resistance Above Average for both vehicles, while the Cougar's side crashworthiness was judged Average. Head restraints were rated Poor by IIHS.

Ford's 2000–08 **Jaguar S-Type** is Not Recommended, primarily because of its persistent factory-related and design deficiencies, small dealer network, chaotic Ford mismanagement, and its acquisition (along with Land Rover) by Tata, an Indian conglomerate. The S-Type is an attractively styled small rear-drive luxury sedan that shares its platform with the Lincoln LS. Resale prices reflect a stunningly high depreciation rate. A 2003 model originally selling for $59,950 is now worth barely $9,500; the $62,795 2005 version is now worth $11,000; and the $62,000 2007 is now $17,500.

The S-Type's V8 engine provides plenty of power, and the car handles well. Nevertheless, it's a terrible buy due to its clunky, failure-prone automatic transmission; limited cargo room; unreliable engine, electronics, and fuel delivery system; and frequently needed brake repairs.

The 1999–2005 **GM Alero** and **Grand Am** are rated Below Average buys due to their mediocre road performance and chronic engine, transmission, brake, and electrical system failures. If there is a bright side, it is that these cars can be repaired anywhere since they use relatively cheap and easily found generic parts. Also, these cars cost almost nothing to own: A 1999 version goes for about $1,500, while a 2005 Grand Am sells for $6,000. Nevertheless, keep aside a few thousand dollars for powertrain and brake repairs and also consider these less risky alternatives: the Acura Integra; Honda Accord; Hyundai Elantra wagon, Sonata, or Tiburon; and the Mazsa3 and Mazda6.

Redesigned in 1999, these cars aren't very impressive. The best engine choice for power, a smooth ride, and value retention is the 207 hp 3.4L V6; it gives you much-needed power and is quite fuel-efficient. The 2.2L engine is quieter, but its lack of power is noticeable, particularly when coupled with an automatic transmission. Stay away from the Computer Command Ride option; true, it allows you to choose your own suspension settings, but the settings aren't quite what they pretend to be and the feature is hellacious to fix.

Grand Ams and Aleros from 1999 to 2005 are well-appointed with many more standard features, like traction control, than offered with previous versions. They have a competent V6, good steering and handling, and average quality control. Some of their disadvantages include a mediocre ride over rough terrain, excessive 4-cylinder noise, and a noisy interior. Also expect difficult rear-seat access (coupe), awkward radio controls, rear visibility that's obstructed by the spoiler, problematic trunk access, annoying body creaks and rattles, and doubtful long-term powertrain reliability.

Overall quality control is poor and crashworthiness is inconsistent. Owners report expensive engine and automatic transmission failures and premature brake pad and rotor wear. Also mentioned are electrical problems; suspension squeaks; and substandard body assembly that produces more squeaks and rattles, water leaks, and poor paint adhesion. NHTSA says the Grand Am merits an Above Average score for frontal collision occupant protection and rollover resistance, but frontal offset, side protection, and head restraint effectiveness vary between Poor and Average.

The 1999–2003 GM **Aurora** and **Riviera** are orphaned cars that haven't been built for almost a decade. They are rated Not Recommended buys because they are unreliable, expensive-to-service gas guzzlers. Resale values have nosedived, making these cars attractive buys to gullible shoppers who can't pass up a 2003 Buick Riviera for $4,000. Be prepared to pay higher than average repair costs; if you can find a mechanic willing to tackle a repair job, this will solve only half your problem. The remaining worry will be finding parts. Most of the complicated electronic and emissions hardware is hard to find and junkyards have almost been picked clean. NHTSA and IIHS give both cars Above Average crashworthiness scores. Consider downsizing to an Acura Integra, TL, or RL; a rear-drive Cadillac DeVille, Fleetwood, or Brougham; a Ford Crown Victoria or Mercury Grand Marquis; or a Lincoln Town Car.

There are still many generic deficiencies affecting the automatic transmission (torque converter constantly engages and disengages); engine, fuel, and electrical systems; computer modules; AC compressor; brakes (rotor warpage and premature pad replacement); steering; suspension; and fit and finish (surface rust and poor paint quality are the most common body complaints for all model years). Because of their problematic brakes, these cars usually have a pronounced low-speed shudder/vibration and severe pull that intensifies when passing over uneven terrain or when braking.

The Aurora is a front-drive Olds luxury sedan that uses the same basic design as the Riviera but doesn't share the same major mechanical features or popular styling. A 2003 model will cost about $5,000. The Aurora's main advantages are its sporty handling and unusual aero styling. In contrast to the Riviera, the Aurora seats only five and offers a 4.0L V8 derived from the failure-prone, hard-to-repair Cadillac 4.6L V8 Northstar engine. Acceleration is underwhelming (this is a heavy car) but adequate for highway touring. Road and wind noise are omnipresent, and the trunk's small opening compromises its ability to handle odd-sized objects.

1995–2000 Auroras have similar quality failings to those of the Riviera, but they're not as extensive and generally become less common with the 2001–03 models. Nevertheless, owners of recent models complain of engine coolant leaks, chronic electrical and fuel supply glitches, harsh shifting, drivetrain vibrations, brake failures, water leaks through the front corner moulding, and overall high maintenance costs.

The 1999–2002 GM **Camaro** and **Firebird** are Above Average buys that were dropped for the 2003 model year. Fun to drive and easily repaired, these early cars are more reliable than the Mustang, despite having elicited similar safety-related complaints such as airbag deployment injuries, sudden acceleration, brake failures, and steering loss. Be especially wary of brake rotor warpage, which requires rotor replacement every two years (about $300 each time). Bargain-hunter alert: Although these cars originally sold for $23,000–$40,000, today you can pick up a used V8-equipped Camaro convertible for about $7,500 (the best choice for retained value a

The Camaro and Firebird (*above*) are relatively reliable and fun to drive.

few years down the road). But you can also do quite well with the cheaper base coupe equipped with a high-performance handling package. Other money-saving advantages: repairs can be done by any independent garage, parts are plentiful, and the cars always draw buyers. Other cars worth considering are a thoroughly checked-out Ford Mustang, a Mazda Miata or Mazda3, and the Toyota Celica.

Camaros and Firebirds remain reasonably priced rear-drive muscle cars that perform reasonably well, have steady resale values, and produce Above Average crash protection scores (except for head restraints, which were rated Poor by IIHS). Overall performance, however, varies a great deal depending on the engine, transmission, and suspension combination. Base models equipped with the V6 powerplant accelerate reasonably well, but high-performance enthusiasts will find them slow for sporty cars. Like all rear-drive Detroit iron, handling is compromised by poor traction on wet roads, minimal comfort, and a suspension that's too soft for high-speed cornering and too bone-jarring for smooth cruising. The Z28, IROC-Z, and Trans Am provide smart acceleration and handling but at the expense of fuel economy—a small drawback, however, when you save thousands buying used. How many thousands? For example, a potent, head-turning 2002 Firebird Trans Am can be had for less than $10,000. A same-year Camaro will cost a few thousand less, and a 2002 convertible won't cost much over $12,000.

Stick with the 1996–2002 models for the best performance and price. Overall, they are much better performers than previous models, and additional standard safety features are a plus. These sporty convertibles and coupes are almost identical in their pricing and in the features they offer (the Firebird has pop-up headlights, a more-pointed front end, a narrower middle, and a rear spoiler). All models got a complete makeover in 1995, making them more powerful and aerodynamic with less spine-jarring performance, but with the disadvantage of numerous first-year redesign problems.

Owners report premature automatic transmission failures, a noisy base engine, and excessive oil consumption with the larger engine. Fuel economy is unimpressive, the AC malfunctions, the front brakes (rotors and pads, mostly) and MacPherson struts wear out quickly, servicing the fuel-injection system is an exercise in frustration, electrical problems are common, and gauges operate erratically. Body problems are frequent. These include door rattles, misaligned doors and hatches, T-roof water and air leaks, a sticking hatch power release, and poor fit and finish. Owners also complain that the steering wheel is positioned too close to the driver's chest and the low seats create a feeling of claustrophobia. Visibility is limited by wide side pillars, and trunk space is sparse with a high liftover. (See *www.autosafety.org/autodefects.html* and *www.sportscarforums.com.*)

GM's 2005–07 **G6** is rated Below Average. The G6 is a mid-sized replacement for the Grand Am and is built on GM's 2004 Chevy Malibu platform. It comes with a weak, fuel-thirsty 2.4L 4-cylinder engine and a barely competent 219 hp 3.5L V6— much less power than what's offered with most of the family-sedan competition. A 2005 sold for $24,670 new, but now sells for about $6,000 used, while a 2006 is now worth $7,000. Crash test scores vary considerably; 2005–06 frontal and side crash protection are scored five and three stars, respectively, and rollover resistance scored between four and five stars. The 2007 and 2008 models, however, garnered five stars in all three categories.

These cars have major reliability problems that may put both your life and your wallet in danger. The most frightening of these is the problem with the steering system, which can suddenly lock up, throwing your car out of control.

The 1999–2005 **Park Avenue** is given a Below Average rating. Originally sold for $47,545, a 2005 model is now worth $7,500–$8,500. A 1999 version can be picked up for $2,500. Crash ratings are very good, with four-star scores for front, side, and rollover crash protection.

These front-drive cars provide lots of room (but not for six), as well as luxury, style, and—I'm going to regret saying this—performance. Granted, plenty of power is available with the 205 hp 3.8L V6 engine and the 240 hp supercharged version of the same powerplant. On the other hand, owners decry the car's ponderous handling; over-assisted steering; obstructed rear visibility; hard braking accompanied by a severe nosedive; interior gauges and controls that aren't easily deciphered or accessed; and surprisingly high fuel consumption.

Although the Park Avenue models improved over the years, they have compiled one of the worst repair histories among large cars. Main problem areas are the starter, engine, brakes, steering, alternator, automatic transmission, fuel system, and electrical system (including defective PROM and MEMCAL modules), plus the badly assembled, poor-quality body hardware. The 3.0L V6 engine is inadequate for a car this heavy, and the 3.8L has been a big quality disappointment.

Maintenance costs are higher than average, but thankfully, repairs aren't dealer-dependent. Some good alternatives are the Cadillac DeVille, Ford Five Hundred/Freestyle (2007 or later), and Nissan Maxima.

Pontiac's 1976–94 **Sunbird** (renamed the **Sunfire** in 1995) was GM's smallest American-built car, along with its twin, the Chevrolet **Cavalier**. Discontinued in 2005, these models are rated Below Average due to parts shortages and powertrain failures. The 2004 models received above-average crashworthiness scores, except for side protection, which IIHS rated Poor. The 2003–05 models carried the better-performing 2.2L Ecotec 140 hp 4-cylinder engine. Expect to pay $3,000 for a recent model, and half as much for a 2002 or earlier version.

The **Saturn Astra** (2007–08) and **Aura** (2008) are two Not Recommended cars. Both models are recent arrivals that are relatively fuel frugal and not as failure prone as the VUE, but now that Saturn has left the marketplace, servicing for the low-volume Astra and Aura is more problematic, and resale values are dropping. The compact Astra is a warmed-over Belgian-built Opel that carries a 1.8L 138 hp 4-cylinder engine coupled to a 5-speed manual or 4-speed automatic transmission. The 2008 Aura is a mid-sized car that may be powered by a 219 hp 3.5L V6 (down from 224 horses in the 2007 model) or a 252 hp 3.6L V6 hooked to a 6-speed automatic transmission. The 2008 hybrid variant uses a 164 hp 2.4L 4-cylinder engine that has six fewer horses than the previous year's Green Line (hybrid) model. Auras have been afflicted by some brake, suspension, and body glitches; Astras appear to be slightly better built. Although the base price for the Astra was given as $17,910, many dealers discounted them to less than $12,000. Today, a 2008 Astra sells for about $7,000. Auras suffer from a similarly high rate of depreciation: A 2008 that originally sold for $24,240 can now be found for $9,000. The Astra hasn't been tested by NHTSA; the Aura got the agency's top five-star rating for frontal and side protection and four stars for rollover protection.

The Saturn **Sky** and Pontiac **Solstice** convertibles (2007–08) went through only three model years before the Saturn and Pontiac divisions began closing down. Both vehicles are rated Below Average following owner reports of powertrain, fuel, electrical, and brake system problems, plus very poor fit and finish. The Sky and Solstice received four stars for front and side crashworthiness and five stars for rollover protection. A 2008 Sky convertible that originally sold for $33,125 is now worth about $14,500; the high-performance Red Line version sells for about $3,000 more.

Hyundai's 1997–2008 Above Average **Tiburon** is a steal for buyers who want some high-performance features without spending much money. Essentially a sportier variant of the Elantra, this is a fun-to-drive budget sport coupe with a good overall reliability record. Since dealer maintenance and repair costs can be a bit higher than average, owners usually go to independent garages to get cheaper inspections and repairs. Used prices vary from $2,500–$10,000 for 1997–2008 models. On early models, the base 16-valve 1.8L 4-cylinder engine is smooth, efficient, and adequate when mated to the 5-speed manual transmission. If you put in an automatic transmission, performance suffers somewhat and engine noise increases proportionally. Overall handling is crisp and predictable. The 1998 versions use a stronger 145 hp 2.0L engine, and the $5,000 2003 GT is powered by a sizzling 2.7L V6.

Crashworthiness and rollover resistance as tested on the 2004 model have been outstanding: five stars for frontal and side occupant protection and four stars for rollover resistance. 2007 models did almost as well, with five-star frontal protection and four-star side and rollover protection ratings. The 2008s got four stars for side and rollover protection. Head restraints were judged Poor up to the 2003 models, but Good thereafter. Brakes are adequate, though sometimes difficult to modulate. As with most sporty cars, interior room is cramped for average-sized occupants. Although no serious defects have been reported, be on the lookout for oil leaks, body deficiencies (fit, finish, and assembly), harsh shifting, clutch failures, slipping between gears (with the automatic), and brake glitches (premature front brake wear and excessive brake noise).

Mitsubishi sold the following 2005–08 models in Canada: the compact **Lancer** ES ($15,998); the mid-sized **Galant** DE ($23,998); and the **Eclipse** GS ($25,498), GT ($32,998), and **Spyder** ($35,148 for the 2005). A convertible Spyder GS version returned as a $31,998 2007 model, and is now worth about $13,500. Earlier 2005 Spyder GS versions can be found for $8,000–$10,000, while a 2008, which originally cost $32,298, is now only $17,500. As for the Lancer and Galant versions, the 2007 Galant ES (there wasn't a Lancer for that model year) sells for about $9,500. 2005 and 2006 Galants are worth $7,000 and $8,500, while the cheaper 2005 and 2006 Lancers go for $3,500 and $5,000.

These entry-level front-drive econocars offer an incredible choice of vehicles that run the gamut from the cheap and mundane ES to the high-performance street racer called the OZ Rally. Yes, Mitsus depreciate faster than most Japanese vehicles, but if you're shopping for used models, that's an important advantage. And don't forget: Mitsubishis are just as reliable as other Asian makes, and can be serviced practically anywhere. There's not much to dislike with the **Lancer**, and that's why we've given it an Above Average rating. You get spirited acceleration with the OZ Rally's turbocharged engine, excellent frontal and offset crashworthiness scores, and good overall quality. The only drawbacks: The base engine is a bit horsepower-challenged (especially with the automatic transmission), you can expect some parts delays, and side crashworthiness is below average.

The **Galant** is another Above Average Mitsubishi. It's reasonably priced, carries competent 4- and 6-cylinder powerplants, handles very well, enjoys good crashworthiness scores, and is fairly reliable, as was its Colt predecessor over a decade ago. On the downside, some model years don't have a manual transmission to make full use of the car's spirited engine, and rear-seat entry and exit can take some acrobatics. Technical service bulletins cover rear suspension rattling, seat adjustments, window glass freezing to the moulding, and tips for reducing brake noise.

The **Eclipse** is an Above Average, beautifully styled, reasonably priced sporty coupe; however, its on-road performance lags behind its looks. As with other Mitsubishis, early models quickly lose their value, making the car a bargain if bought used. A $23,857 2003 model sells for $4,000; a $23,998 2004 is now worth $5,500; and a $35,148 2005 Spyder (if you get the cheapest model available) is now worth $7,500–$10,000.

There are two engine choices available: a 162 hp 2.4L 4-banger and a 263 hp V6. A manual 5-speed is standard, but the optional automatic 5-speed and the 6-speed manual are better performers. Both engines have plenty of grunt throughout their power range when mated to a manual gearbox, but much less when hooked to an automatic transmission. Handling is exceptionally good on all models, but the sportier GT and Spyder are better than the rest (a 2007 version runs about $18,000). Some of the Eclipse's deficiencies include an automatic transmission that isn't quick enough for confident highway merging; frequent shifting with the manual transmission; and, with the automatic tranny, real-world fuel economy that's much less than promised.

Porsche's 1999–2008 **911 Carrera coupe** and **turbo** are rated Average. The 911 was redesigned in 1999, and gaining additional length, width, and 8 cm to the wheelbase. The 3.4L engine switched from air-cooling to water-cooling and produces 296 hp—more than the previous 3.6L powerplant. A 6-speed manual transmission, side airbags, and ABS are standard. 2007 models saw the return of the glass-roof Targa coupes. Although originally sold for $100,400, a 2004 911 Carrera is now worth barely one-third of that amount, or about $32,000. A 2005 now sells for $30,000, and a 2007 model will run you $53,000. The 2000 models got four more horses; 2001 models came with a 415 hp 3.6L twin-turbo engine; and 2002 models adopted the 320 hp 3.6L engine and upgraded the 5-speed automatic transmission.

These cars are famous for high-performance acceleration and handling and impressive braking. As with most sports cars, you can expect lots of engine and road noise, acrobatic entry and exit, cramped rear seating, and limited storage space. *Consumer Reports* and internal service bulletins confirm that all model years have a higher-than-average number of factory-related problems, highlighted by engine, transmission, fuel system, and fit and finish deficiencies. If you've got "Porsche fever" but don't want to spend all of your money at once, consider investing in a 1999–2008 rear-drive **Boxster**. It competes with the Mercedes-Benz SLK, the BMW Z3, and the Mazda Miata.

Volkswagen's **Phaeton** full-sized luxury sedan was greeted by underwhelming sales and restrained dealer enthusiasm when it was launched in Canada as a 2004 model. After all, who in their right mind would buy a $96,500 V8 VW sedan that is now worth barely $17,000? 2006 was the car's last year in Canada, and those models vary in value between $20,000 for the entry-level model and $23,000 for the top-of-the-line W12 four-passenger version that originally sold for $144,000. The Phaeton's platform is shared with the Bentley Continental GT, and some powertrain components are also used in the Audi A8. No crashworthiness scores are available. Owner feedback has been insufficient to offer a reading on the long-term reliability of these vehicles.

Sport-Utilities

Rated Above Average, the **Acura RDX** is marketed as the SUV version of Acura's sporty TSX. This luxury crossover combines an innovative powertrain (turbocharger, etc.), lots of safety gear, high-tech standard features, a sporty platform, and a versatile, plush interior. It was launched as a 2007 model, and returned in 2008 relatively unchanged, except for an engine upgrade. A 2007 version can be found for $18,000, or about $23,000 less than its original selling price.

Some complaints: Road noise is omnipresent, and the ride is stiff. You get the impression that the RDX is trying too hard to target the BMW "sporty" SUV market, especially since the 42 buttons and knobs mounted in the centre console area copy BMW's earlier confusing iDrive cockpit controls.

The Acura **MDX** gets an Above Average rating for the 2007–08 models, but just an Average score for the 2001–06 versions. The 2007 improvements made a world of difference to the car's road performance and comfort. Still, why spend $23,500 (2007) for a warmed-over Odyssey when you can do better with the cheaper 2007 Honda Pilot ($16,500)?

On the plus side, the MDX accelerates well, with plenty of low-end power. It's nicely appointed, has a roomy interior with a standard third-row seat, and employs a gas-saving engine cylinder deactivation system. 2007 and later models have successfully tackled most of the negatives found with 2006 and earlier models, and the 2007's extra horsepower is a critical improvement. The MDX's real-world fuel economy is mediocre, and premium fuel is required. The steering wheel can't be adjusted for reach, forcing small drivers to sit perilously close to the airbag housing. Reliability shouldn't be a problem, unless you actually believe this vehicle can go off-road. If so, make sure you get an extended warranty and find a friendly garage. Buying the second-series model in March 2007 or later will save you from some of the first-year glitches commonly found with most reworked makes. 2007 and later models have registered only a few complaints, concerning premature brake wear, minor electrical shorts, AC compressor failures, and some fit and finish concerns.

Chrysler's **Aspen** is a Not Recommended model that's essentially a $49,995 Dodge Durango with a different front grille. A 2007 Aspen will cost about $17,000, or $5,000 less than a 2008. The identical Durango was rated five stars for frontal collision occupant protection and three stars for rollover protection.

The 2007 **Ford Edge** and **Lincoln MKX** are Not Recommended models that sold new for $32,999 and $42,399, respectively. A 2007 Edge is now worth $15,500; an MKX goes for $20,500. These practically identical small car-based SUVs use the Mazda6 platform, share Volvo CX-7 parts, and take their styling cues from the Ford Fusion. In the past, an infusion of Mazda parts has always helped bring up the quality of Ford's cars and trucks, including the Escort/Tracer, Probe/

MX6, and Escape/Tribute. However, mixing in Volvo components when Ford has Volvo on the auction block presents added risks. The 3.5L V6 (265 hp) mated to a 6-speed automatic transmission makes both vehicles better-than-average performers. Big minuses are mediocre fit and finish and the absence of third-row seating. Crash test scores are excellent, though. Competitors worth considering: the Honda CR-V, Hyundai Tucson or Santa Fe, the Nissan Murano, and the Toyota RAV4.

The 2007 and 2008 **GM Acadia**, **Enclave**, and **Outlook** are practically identical mid-sized models that are rated Above Average. The trio sold new for $36,495 (2007), $40,895 (2008), and $33,990 (2007), respectively. Today, they're worth $18,000 (2007), $26,500 (2008), and $14,500 (2007). They all offer front-drive/all-wheel-drive powertrains and use a car-based platform that incorporates a third-row seat, allowing for a maximum of eight passengers. Power is provided by a 3.6L V6 mated to 6-speed automatic transmission. Standard safety features abound. A wide stance and low centre of gravity reduce the threat of a rollover. NHTSA crashworthiness scores are quite good: five stars for front- and side-impact occupant protection and four stars for rollover resistance.

Some of the minuses inherent in GM's new crossover trio: third-row seating is a bit cramped, the new 6-speed tranny has yet to prove itself, and the V6 powerplant is a mixed-breed design from Australia, Germany, Sweden, and North America that was first introduced on Cadillac's CTS sedan and SRX SUV crossover. CTS and SRX complaints logged by NHTSA and others frequently mention engine and transmission/differential failures, and early 2010 *Consumer Reports* member survey results show some automatic transmission problems with the 2007 models.

The Not Recommended **Saturn VUE** (2002–08), the company's oldest model since the L-Series was dropped in 2005, is no longer sold since the Saturn division shut down in October 2010. Stay away from the problem-plagued GM-bred 4- and 6-cylinder powerplants and opt instead for the more durable Honda V6 first used in 2004. The CVT (continuously variable transmission) is another failure-prone component to avoid.

The **Cadillac SRX**, Not Recommended, is a failure-prone mid-sized rear-drive or all-wheel-drive luxury crossover. It has been on the Canadian market since 2004, then selling for $52,250 as a front-drive SUV, $54,875 with AWD, and $63,965 for a V8 AWD. Today, the same vehicles are worth $11,000, $12,000, and $13,000, respectively. SRX owners report frequent transmission and differential breakdowns, in addition to brake and electrical failures and fit and finish deficiencies. The 2004–07 models earned four stars for front crashworthiness and five stars for side-impact protection. The 2008s got similar ratings, but they also scored three stars for front-drive rollover resistance and four stars for AWD rollover protection.

The 2003–08 **GM Hummer H2** SUV and SUT (the SUT being a pickup version launched in 2005) are Not Recommended due to their overall poor reliability, mediocre highway performance, and head-spinning depreciation. Furthermore, since GM shut down its Hummer division, warranties and servicing aren't worth much. A 2004 H2 SUV that originally sold for $73,500 is now barely worth $14,000; a 2008 SUV or SUT that sold for $67,700 new has already lost half its original value. Outward visibility is severely compromised by the small windshield and wide roof pillars, and NHTSA hasn't crash tested the H2 yet. Still, the H2 is a good off-road performer (it uses the Tahoe's previous generation platform), and it appeals to those who like ultra-macho styling.

The more-moderately priced 2006–08 Hummer **H3** is also Not Recommended, mainly because its mechanicals are derived from the poor-quality GM Canyon/Colorado and it has been on the market for only a few years. Depreciation is unusually rapid: a $40,000 2008 H3 now fetches less than $12,000. Like its big brother, the H3 is a good off-roader, but for this attribute you must sacrifice reliability, access, visibility, a quiet interior, and a comfortable ride. The base engine is noisy, has little grunt, and is a gas-guzzler. It was replaced by a 3.7L engine in late 2007. A 300 hp 5.3L V8 powers the 2008 H3 Alpha variant. NHTSA has given the H3 its top, five-star rating for frontal and side crashworthiness, beginning with the 2006 model, although passenger protection is rated only four stars for side impacts.

Jeeps (Wrangler excepted) are Not Recommended. To be fair, the Jeep's tendency to roll over isn't as high as that of other small sport-utilities; parts aren't yet hard to find; and servicing, if not given with a smile, at least isn't accompanied by a snarl or head-scratching from Helmut or Akido. Nevertheless, Chrysler's recent bankruptcy makes the Jeep division a prime candidate for the auction block if the Chrysler-Fiat Fandango doesn't play out. And if the company is sold, there will be fewer dealers, warranties will be worthless, parts will be hard to find, and resale values will plummet even more. Early Cherokees, CJs, and Wagoneers have been known for their rattle-prone bodies, air and water leaks, electrical glitches, and high-cost brake maintenance. Expect to spend $1,500–$2,500 (tops) for a decade-old entry-level CJ or Wrangler. A 2007 Grand Cherokee Laredo sells for about $13,500, much less than its $40,285 original sales price.

Land Rover and Jaguar models are also Not Recommended. Sold to Tata Motors in March 26, 2008, both models are destined to be hits in China and some European enclaves, but duds in North and South America. Why such a negative prediction? Simple. Build quality is early Jurassic; reliability is about as sure as the U.K.'s Tory–Lib Dem coalition, and servicing is rationed by service managers trained by the Marquis de Sade. Parts availability also suffers from an inefficient U.K./Ford/Tata alliance and parts costs reflect the added commission of each member of that alliance.

Mazda's **CX-7** and **CX-9** 2007 and 2008 models, rated Above Average, were sold in Canada for $32,095 and $36,795 (2007), respectively, with an AWD version costing about $2,000 more; they are now worth $12,500 and $16,000. The sporty five-passenger CX-7 is a promising unibody, four-door crossover SUV based on the

Mazda5 and Mazda6. It isn't suitable for off-roading, even though it looks like it could go anywhere. The turbocharged 4-cylinder engine is taken from the MazdaSpeed6 and hasn't accumulated enough road time to determine its long-term durability. Nevertheless, CX-7 owners report some problems with the fuel and climate control system, as well as minor engine glitches. The CX-9 has had fewer complaints, though fit and finish remains disappointing. Electronic stability control is a standard feature. A longer version, the CX-9, is equipped with a V6 and a third-row seat. Both models have earned high crashworthiness rankings for the 2007–08 models: five stars for occupant protection in front and side impacts, and four stars for rollover resistance.

Next, we come to **Mercedes-Benz** and its problem-racked foray into luxury sport-utilities, first launched in 1997. Known collectively as the **M-Class**, these SUVs are Not Recommended from 1998 to 2007. ML320, ML350, ML430, and ML500 models are a far cry from being cheap wheels, even though they depreciate about 50 percent after five years (a $48,600 2001 ML320 is now worth about $7,000). The ML350 was launched as a 2003 model and sold for $50,600; it's now worth about $11,500. A 2005 ML500 that originally sold for $68,690 is now worth approximately $17,000. The main drawbacks of these luxury lemons are poor quality control; unreliable, limited servicing; and so-so parts availability. Owners report automatic transmission failures, frequent engine oil leaks and engine oil sludge, and electrical system shorts. Other problems afflict brake pads, rotors, master cylinders, fuel pumps, oxygen sensors, mass airflow sensors, and fit and finish.

Porsche's **Cayenne** is Below Average, mainly due to its limited servicing network, mediocre performance, and outrageously high retail price—reserved for Canadians who are too naive to know they're being scammed. In fact, we're paying a retail price that is still way too high, even after having been cut by more than $10,000 following *Lemon-Aid*'s criticism of Porsche's greed in late 2007. For example, Canadian dealers sold the 2006 V6, V8, and AWD V8 Turbo Cayennes for $60,100; $80,100; and $126,900, respectively. Meanwhile, these luxury SUVs sell for $43,400; $57,900; and $93,700 in the States. Incidentally, used 2006 Canadian versions of the above models cost $21,000; $26,500; and $42,000.

First launched as a 2003 model, the Cayenne skipped the 2007 model year and returned as a 2008 model. A mid-sized unibody SUV, the Cayenne shares many of the VW Touareg's parts (remember, VW, Audi, and Porsche are all under the same corporate umbrella); hence, reliability has been subpar. Cayenne does have some limited off-road capability, thanks to its low gearing, sophisticated electronics, and Touareg-sourced V6 engine, as well as Porsche V8 and twin-turbo variants—a 247 hp 3.2L V6, a 340 hp 4.5L V8, a 450 hp 4.5L Twin-Turbo V8, and another, more-powerful 520 hp 4.5L Twin-Turbo V8. Transmissions consist of a 6-speed manual and a 6-speed automatic. On-road capability is a big disappointment, however, since the vehicle lacks Porsche's usual handling prowess. Furthermore, many of the cabin controls are needlessly complex and confusing. Crashworthiness has not yet been rated.

The 2003–06 **Subaru Baja** is a Below Average all-wheel-drive crossover. It provides the handling and passenger-carrying characteristics of a car, with the open-bed versatility and, to a lesser degree, the load capacity of a pickup truck (think of a small 1959–60 Chevrolet El Camino, or a mini GM Avalanche). Baja's unibody platform borrows heavily from Subaru's Legacy and Outback.

The car is too small to offer much that is useful or fun. Still, poor sales mean deeply discounted used prices. For example, a 2006 version that sold new for almost $30,000 is now available for about $10,500. Some of the Baja's minuses: uncomfortably upright rear seating; the bed is too short to carry a bike without extending the tailgate as part of the bed; there's no 5-speed automatic transmission; and the absence of a folding midgate means the flip and fold versatility isn't as practical as Subaru pretends.

The **Toyota FJ Cruiser** takes its inspiration from the Toyota FJ40 Land Cruiser, built between 1956 and 1983. First model year 2007s sold for $30,000 and are now worth $13,500; 2008 used prices are only a couple of thousand dollars more. The Cruiser is an Above Average buy that competes especially well off-road against the Ford Escape, Honda Element, Jeep Liberty or Wrangler, and Nissan Xterra. It is powered by a competent 239 hp 4.0L V6 that can be used for either two- or four-wheel drive. A 5-speed automatic transmission comes with both versions, and a 6-speed manual gearbox is available with the all-wheel drive. Although the FJ's turning circle is about 1.5 m larger than those of similar-sized SUVs, off-roading should be a breeze if done carefully, thanks to standard electronic stability control, short overhangs, and better-than-average ground clearance.

Of course, if you don't mind driving a really old Toyota, there's nothing wrong with a 1987–89 Toyota **Land Cruiser**, which sells for about $2,000. Just be sure to pull the wheels off to examine the brakes, check for undercarriage corrosion, and make sure the engine head gasket is okay.

VW's **Touareg** is a Not Recommended model that is living on borrowed time due to poor sales and quality-control deficiencies. Restyled in 2007, it's now cleaner-burning and more fuel-efficient. But the Touareg has been earning a bad reputation for poor reliability and expensive servicing ever since it was first launched as a 2005 luxury SUV listed at $55,010 (now worth $14,000); a new 2006 sold for almost 10 percent less at $50,790. The 2004 is now worth about $12,000.

Minivans and Vans

GM's 1999–2005 **Astro** and **Safari** run-of-the-mill, squarish "bread box" minivans are Average buys. Still, when compared with GM's failure-prone front-drive minivans, these rear-drives don't look too bad. They have fewer safety-related problems, are easy to repair, and cost only about $4,000 for a 2005 version. Stay away from the unreliable all-wheel-drive models, though: they're expensive to repair, parts are always on back order, and repairs don't last long.

More a utility truck than a comfortable minivan, the Astro and Safari are built on a reworked S-10 pickup chassis. As such, they offer uninspiring handling, average-quality mechanical and body components, and relatively high fuel consumption. Best alternatives depend upon how much interior room and power you need. For example, Honda minivans have better handling and are more-reliable and economical people-movers, but they are way overpriced and lack the Astro's considerable grunt, essential for cargo hauling and trailer towing. On the other hand, a full-sized, rear-drive GM van

The GM Safari.

like the Savana or Express can give you both the pulling power and interior space for camping or running a small business.

2000–05 models are a bit more reliable and better performing than previous models, inasmuch as they underwent considerable upgrading by GM. Nevertheless, buyers should pay extra attention to the following areas: automatic transmission clunk; electrical system shorts; excessive vibration transmitted through the AWD; sliding-door misalignment and broken hinges; heating and AC performance hampered by poor air distribution; electronic computer module and fuel-system glitches that cause the Check Engine light to remain lit; hard starts, no-starts, or chronic stalling, especially when going downhill; and poor braking performance (brake pedal hardens, and brakes don't work after going over bumps or rough roads) and expensive brake maintenance. NHTSA rates frontal crashworthiness and rollover protection as Average and side occupant protection as Above Average. On the other hand, IIHS rates the head restraints and offset collision protection as Poor.

A $5,500–$7,500 Not Recommended buy, the 2002–06 **Mazda MPV** is a particularly risky purchase because it's an orphaned low-volume model serviced by a dealership network that is reluctant to service or supply parts for a vehicle it would prefer to think never existed. Mazda threw in the towel and dropped the MPV after the 2006 model year.

Mazda's only minivan quickly became a bestseller when it first came on the market in 1989, but its popularity fell just as quickly when larger, more-powerful competitors arrived. Early MPVs embodied many of the mistakes made by Honda's first Odyssey: Its 170 horses weren't adequate for people-hauling, and it was expensive for what was essentially a smaller van than buyers expected. Crashworthiness scores are mixed: NHTSA gives the MPV an Above Average rating for frontal and side crash protection and an Average score for rollover resistance. IIHS rates head restraints and side protection as Poor. Offset crash protection received an Average score.

Pickups

All of the small Japanese pickups are good performers. **Mazda**'s **B-Series** trucks, though, are the weakest brand for reliability and durability when compared with Nissan and Toyota. Mazdas are particularly vulnerable to powertrain, suspension, brake, and fuel system failures. But interestingly, fit and finish is better with Mazda than with other Asian automakers.

Nissan's small trucks are the most reliable, although body fit and finish and accessories (AC, sound system, and electrical systems) are problem-prone.

Toyota's small pickups have the second-worst reliability record, but come nowhere near Mazda's dismal reputation. Most of Toyota's glitches mirror Nissan's, except for one major rusting problem: Toyota will repair or buy back 1995–2000 **Tacoma** pickups affected by rust-damaged structural frames. An estimated 813,000 Tacomas from this era are still on North American roads and may be affected, especially if driven in areas with snow where road salt is used. The excessive rusting is caused by inadequate anti-corrosion undercoating applied at the factory.

As for larger trucks, the Toyota **Tundra** beats out Nissan's **Titan**. Although Toyota has had a number of powertrain, brake, suspension, and fuel delivery problems, the scope of these deficiencies doesn't come close to the Nissan Titan's deficiencies, which comprise all of the above, plus accessories and body fit and finish.

Although information on this is still hazy, service bulletins and a small number of owner complaints show that the **Honda Ridgeline** has far fewer performance and reliability/durability complaints than do either Mazda or Toyota trucks.

Cheaper Beaters

There are plenty of cheaper, still-reliable used cars, vans, and trucks out there that will suit your driving needs and budget. In the 1970s, the average car was junked after approximately seven years or 160,000 km; almost four decades later, the average car was driven for almost eight years or 240,000 km. Industry experts now say that most new models should last 12 years or 350,000 km before they need major repairs. This means you can get good high-mileage vehicles for less than one-quarter to of their original price, and expect to drive them for up to 10 years or more.

But having said that, it can be tough to find a 10-year-old vehicle that's safe and reliable. Personally, I'd be reluctant to buy any decade-old vehicle from someone I don't know, or one that has been brought in from another province. All of that accumulated salt is a real body killer, and it's just too easy to fall prey to scam artists who cover up major mechanical or body problems resulting from accidents or environmental damage.

Nevertheless, if you know the seller and an independent mechanic gives you the green light, you might seriously consider a 10-year-old, beat-up-looking car, pickup, or van (but heed my advice about old SUVs, following). Look for one of those listed in this appendix, or, if you have a bit more money to spend and want to take less of a risk, look up the Recommended or Above Average models found in Part Three.

Old Sport-Utilities

Anyone buying a sport-utility that's a decade old or older is asking for trouble, because many SUVs are worked hard off-road. The danger of rollovers for vehicles not equipped with electronic stability control is also quite high. Safety features are rudimentary, dangerous, and unreliable (especially ABS); overall quality control is very poor; and performance and handling cannot match today's models.

Depreciation Quirks

Depreciation varies considerably among different vehicle types and models. For example, minivans depreciate a bit more slowly than cars, and diesel cars and trucks hold their value better than gas-powered vehicles do.

Gas-electric hybrids, which have been on the market since 1999, apparently lose their values at about the same rate as conventional cars. Undoubtedly, this is because used-car buyers are afraid to replace the costly high-tech components (imagine paying $6,000 for a replacement battery once the eight-year warranty has expired).

10 Beater Rules

1. Try to buy a vehicle that's presently being used by one of your family members. Although you may risk a family squabble somewhere down the road, you'll likely get a good buy for next to nothing, you'll have a good idea of how it was driven and maintained, and you'll be able to use the same repair facilities that have been repairing your family's vehicles for years. Don't worry if a vehicle is almost 10 years old—that's becoming the norm for Canadian ownership, particularly the farther west you go.
2. Buy from a private seller—prices are usually much cheaper, and sales scams are less frequent.
3. Cut insurance and fuel costs. Use the Internet (*www.insurancehotline.com*) to compile a list of models that are the cheapest to insure. Be wary of diesel-equipped or hybrid cars that may require more-expensive dealer servicing and thus wipe out any fuel-consumption savings. Also, pay attention to the quality and performance of your fuel-efficient choice: A 2001–03 fuel-sipping Ford Focus will likely have higher repair bills than gas bills, and a 4-cylinder minivan, though cheap to run, can make highway merging a nightmare.
4. Find out the vehicle's history through a franchised dealer, CarProof, or provincial licensing authorities. Then, have an independent garage (preferably CAA-affiliated) check out the body and mechanical components.

5. Look for high-mileage vehicles sold by rental agencies like Budget Rent A Car—a company that offers money-back guarantees and reasonably priced extended warranties.

6. Refuse all preparation or "administration" fees, as well as 50/50 warranties where the repair charges are submitted by the seller.

7. Stay away from vehicles or components known for having high failure rates. American front-drives, for example, have more-frequent failures and costlier repairs than rear-drives. "Orphaned" American models like the Ford Taurus/Sable and Windstar or GM front-drive minivans are also poor choices because of low-quality components and inadequate servicing support from dealers who wish these cars were never made. Other sinkholes: any vehicle equipped with a turbocharger or supercharger or with multiple computers (BMW's 7 Series, for example); Cadillacs with 4.1L engines and/or front-drive; and Chryslers with sludge-prone 2.7L engines or 4-speed automatic transmissions. If the engine has a timing chain instead of a belt, you will save a fortune. Timing chains frequently survive the lifespan of the engine, whereas timing belts must be replaced every 70,000–100,000 km.

8. Steer clear of European models. They are often money pits. Parts and competent, reasonably priced servicing will likely be hard to find, and quality control has declined considerably over the past decade.

9. Buy three-year-old Hyundais, but stay away from Excels or early Sonatas. Also try to avoid early Kias or Daewoos. Instead, look for five- to 10-year-old single-owner Japanese models.

10. Shop for used rear-drive full-sized wagons or vans instead of front-drive American minivans.